THE CAMBRIDGE HISTORY OF
THE EUROPEAN UNION
*
VOLUME II
European Integration Inside-Out

Volume II examines the history of the European Union from an inside-out perspective, focusing on the internal developments that shaped the European integration process. Split into three parts, Part I covers the principles that have defined European integration, exploring the treaties and their changes through time, with Brexit being a core milestone. Part II considers the different instruments within the architecture of European integration, with special focus on the development of policies, the euro and enlargement. Part III concentrates on the various narratives surrounding European integration, in particular the concepts, goals and ideas that both spoke and failed to speak to the hearts and minds of Europeans. This includes the 'longue durée' concept, peace, European culture, (the absence of) religion, prosperity and (a lack of) solidarity and democracy.

MATHIEU SEGERS is Professor of Contemporary European History at Maastricht University. His book on the Netherlands and European Integration was awarded the Dutch prize for best political book in 2013. He is a member of The Netherlands Scientific Council for Government Policy (WRR) and the SSH Board of the Dutch Research Council (NWO).

STEVEN VAN HECKE is Professor in Comparative and EU Politics at the Public Governance Institute of the University of Leuven. His research focuses on EU institutions, political parties and the history of European integration.

THE CAMBRIDGE HISTORY OF
THE EUROPEAN UNION

Split into two volumes, *The Cambridge History of the European Union* focuses on European integration from a diachronic, multidisciplinary and multi-institutional angle to provide the most comprehensive and contemporary history of the European Union to date. The volumes do not present a strict timeline of historical events; instead they look at the various themes and changes over time in order to shed light both on the more well-known and on the lesser-known moments in European history. Ranging from the first steps of European integration to the latest developments, the fifty essays from experts across the field provide a wholly unique perspective that changes the way we look at European integration history. This is a much-needed addition to the history of the European Union.

VOLUME I

European Integration Outside-In

EDITED BY MATHIEU SEGERS AND STEVEN VAN HECKE

VOLUME II

European Integration Inside-Out

EDITED BY MATHIEU SEGERS AND STEVEN VAN HECKE

THE CAMBRIDGE
HISTORY OF
THE EUROPEAN UNION

*

VOLUME II
European Integration Inside-Out

*

Edited by
MATHIEU SEGERS
Maastricht University
and
STEVEN VAN HECKE
University of Leuven

 CAMBRIDGE
UNIVERSITY PRESS

Shaftesbury Road, Cambridge CB2 8EA, United Kingdom

One Liberty Plaza, 20th Floor, New York, NY 10006, USA

477 Williamstown Road, Port Melbourne, VIC 3207, Australia

314–321, 3rd Floor, Plot 3, Splendor Forum, Jasola District Centre,
New Delhi – 110025, India

103 Penang Road, #05–06/07, Visioncrest Commercial, Singapore 238467

Cambridge University Press is part of Cambridge University Press & Assessment,
a department of the University of Cambridge.

We share the University's mission to contribute to society through the pursuit of
education, learning and research at the highest international levels of excellence.

www.cambridge.org
Information on this title: www.cambridge.org/9781108478939

DOI: 10.1017/9781108781480

© Cambridge University Press & Assessment 2024

First published 2024

Printed in the United Kingdom by TJ Books Limited, Padstow, Cornwall

A catalogue record for this publication is available from the British Library

A Cataloging-in-Publication data record for this book is available from the Library of Congress

Two-Volume Set ISBN 978-1-009-28437-0 Hardback
Volume I ISBN 978-1-108-49040-5 Hardback
Volume II ISBN 978-1-108-47893-9 Hardback

Contents

Contents

Contents

Figures

Tables

Contributors to Volume II

CARLO EDOARDO ALTAMURA is Swiss National Science Foundation Ambizione Research Fellow, Department of International History and Politics, Graduate Institute of International and Development Studies, Geneva

PHILIP BAJON is Researcher, Max Planck Institute for Legal History and Legal Theory, Frankfurt am Main

IVAN T. BEREND is Distinguished Research Professor, History Department, University of California Los Angeles

GÉRARD BOSSUAT is Professor Emeritus (2010–16), University of Cergy-Pontoise, Jean Monnet ad Personam Chair, History of European Unity, UMR SIRICE Paris-1

EMMANUEL COMTE is Senior Research Fellow, Hellenic Foundation for European and Foreign Policy (ELIAMEP) and Professorial Lecturer, Vienna School of International Studies

AMANDINE CRESPY is Professor, Faculty of Philosophy and Social Sciences, Vrije Universiteit Brussel

DESMOND DINAN is Professor, Schar School of Policy and Government, George Mason University, Virginia

MICHAEL GEHLER is Professor and Head of the Institute of History at the University of Hildesheim, Jean Monnet Chair for History of Europe and European Integration History

CARINE GERMOND is Professor of European Studies, Department of Historical and Classical Studies, Norwegian University of Science and Technology (NTNU)

CLAUDIA HIEPEL[†] was Adjunct Professor, Faculty of Humanities, History Department, University of Duisburg–Essen

ANDRÁS JAKAB is Professor of Constitutional and Administrative Law, University of Salzburg

LANDO KIRCHMAIR is Deputy Professor for National and International Public Law with a Focus on the Protection of Cultural Heritage, Department of Social Sciences and Public Affairs, Bundeswehr University Munich

N. PIERS LUDLOW is Professor of International History, London School of Economics

MARC MARESCEAU is Jean Monnet Chair ad personam Ghent University and Visiting Professor, College of Europe (Bruges and Natolin)

JÖRG MONAR is Honorary Professor, College of Europe (Bruges and Natolin)

ANNE-ISABELLE RICHARD is University Lecturer, Institute for History, Leiden University

MALCOLM ROSS is Emeritus Professor of European Law, University of Sussex

MATHIEU SEGERS is Professor of Contemporary European History and European Integration at Maastricht University

JORRIT STEEHOUDER is Assistant Professor in History of International Relations and European Integration, University of Utrecht

CLAUDIA STERNBERG is Principal Research Fellow, UCL European Institute, University College London

STEVEN VAN HECKE is Professor in Comparative and EU Politics at the Public Governance Institute of the University of Leuven

SOPHIE VANHOONACKER is Professor, Politics Department, Faculty of Arts and Social Sciences, Maastricht University

AMY VERDUN is Professor, Department of Political Science, University of Victoria and Visiting Professor at the Institute of Political Science, Leiden University

NICOLAS VERSCHUEREN is Professor, Cevipol/Institute of European Studies, Université libre de Bruxelles

LAURENT WARLOUZET is Professor, Department of History, Sorbonne University, Paris

WOUTER WOLFS is Lecturer and Senior Researcher, Public Governance Institute, University of Leuven

HUBERT ZIMMERMANN is Professor, Institute for Political Science, Philipps University, Marburg

Acknowledgements

Editing a study like this is a team effort. *The Cambridge History of the European Union* (CHEU) aims to be a comprehensive, multidisciplinary, diachronic and transnational history of the process of European integration based on original archival and primary source research. The outline of the two books was first conceived in 2017. Since then, the project has developed into a major international, multidisciplinary, *and* inter-generational project that resulted in two volumes that reflect the richness of the state-of-the-art research in the broad field of 'European Studies' with a focus on the topical and often even feverish urge to better understand what the Europe of European integration was, is and represents. Therefore, we hope that this scholarly project will serve not only as a source of reference, insights, analysis, inspiration and stimulation for our fellow scholars, students, policy-makers and other experts, but also as an accessible introduction to the history, present and future of the EU for a wider public.

We thank all of the contributors for the spirit of cooperation and the concentration on content and the willingness to revise their contributions and work together on overlapping and inter-linked topics. And this all took place despite the pandemic, which made our work on the project even more challenging in unforeseen ways. Nonetheless, we managed to keep up with the original planning, although, regretfully, we had to cancel all our plans for working conferences.

We, the editors, are grateful for the uniquely cross-disciplinary and inspiring cooperation with all the contributors in this project. We remain indebted to all of them for their commitment to the CHEU. Next to that, a limited but crucial number of others deserve a huge thank you for all their efforts to pull off the CHEU. Our editorial assistants in different stages of the project, Annelies van Rijen, Toine Paulissen, Kate Rudd and Lucas Robbroeckx, have been indispensable in realising our ambitions – within this reliable team of young colleagues Angus Foster deserves our special gratitude for his year-long, consistent and professional role as the anchor in coordinating the editorial process. Michael Watson, Liz Hanlon, Emily Sharp, Lisa Carter, Steven Holt and Victoria Inci Philips, our editorial team at Cambridge University Press, formed a rock-solid basis throughout the whole process right from the inception of the project. We feel both lucky and grateful for the unique opportunity the CHEU has offered us to intensely collaborate on the subject that keeps us working, thinking and reflecting and stirs our passions in so many ways. It has brought, and still brings, us so much more than what we hoped for.

Abbreviations

ACP	African, Caribbean and Pacific
ACUSE	Action Committee for a United States of Europe
AFSJ	Area of Freedom, Security and Justice
AI	Atlantic Institute
ATR	Avions de Transport Régional
BIS	Bank for International Settlements
CAP	Common Agricultural Policy
CDU	Christlich Demokratische Union
CEA	Commissariat à l'énergie atomique
CEECs	Central and eastern European countries
CEPES	Comité européen pour le Progrès économique et social
CET	Common External Tariff
CFLN	Comité français de Libération nationale
CFSP	Common Foreign and Security Policy
CJEU	Court of Justice of the European Union
CM	Common Market
CMEA	Council for Mutual Economic Assistance
CoG	Committee of Governors
Comecon	Council for Mutual Economical Assistance
COREPER	Comité des représentants permanents
CSCE	Conference on Security and Co-operation in Europe
CSDP	Common Security and Defence Policy
CSO	Civil society organisation
CTCE	Conseil tripartite de coopération économique
CVCE	Centre Virtuel de la Connaissance sur l'Europe
DG	Directorate General
DM	Deutsche Mark
DNE	Detached national expert

EAC	European Advisory Committee
EAGGF	European Agricultural Guidance and Guarantee Fund
EC	European Community
ECA	Economic Commission for Africa
ECA	Economic Cooperation Administration
ECB	European Central Bank
ECC	European Citizens' Consultation
ECE	Economic Commission for Europe
ECHR	European Court of Human Rights
ECI	European Citizens' Initiative
ECJ	European Court of Justice
ECOFIN	Economic and Financial Affairs Council
ECSC	European Coal and Steel Community
ECU	European Currency Unit
EDC	European Defence Community
EEA	European Economic Area
EEC	European Economic Community
EFSF	European Financial Stability Facility
EFTA	European Free Trade Association
EIB	European Investment Bank
ELEC	European League for Economic Cooperation
EM	European Movement
EMCF	European Monetary Cooperation Fund
EMF	European Monetary Fund
EMS	European Monetary System
EMU	Economic and Monetary Union
EP	European Parliament
EPA	European Political Authority
EPA	Economic Partnership Agreement
EPC	European Political Community
EPC	European Political Cooperation
EPP	European People's Party
EPU	European Payments Union
ERDF	European Regional and Development Fund
ERP	European Recovery Programme
ERT	European Round Table of Industrialists
ESA	European Space Agency
ESCB	European System of Central Banks
ESM	European Stability Mechanism

ESPRIT	European Strategic Programme for Research and Development
ETS	Emissions Trading System
ETUC	European Trade Union Confederation
EU	European Union
EU-27	European Union, the remaining twenty-seven members after Brexit
Euratom	European Atomic Energy Community
EWS	Early Warning System
FDI	Foreign direct investment
FINEX	External Finance (France)
FRG	Federal Republic of Germany
FSU	Financial Services Union
FTA	Free trade area
GATT	General Agreement on Tariffs and Trade
GDP	Gross domestic product
GDR	German Democratic Republic
GNP	Gross national product
GPRF	Gouvernement provisoire de la République française
G7	Group of Seven
HA	High Authority
HAEU	Historical Archives of the European Union
HDI	Human Development Index
HEH	House of European History
HR	High Representative
IEPS	Intra-European Payments Scheme
IGC	Intergovernmental conference
IIA	Inter-institutional agreement
ILO	International Labour Organization
IM	Internal Market
IMF	International Monetary Fund
IR	International relations
IRA	International Ruhr Authority
IRI	Istituto per la Ricostruzione Industriale
JHA	Justice and Home Affairs
MEP	Member of the European Parliament
MRP	Mouvement républicain populaire
NATO	North Atlantic Treaty Organization
NEI	Nouvelles Équipes Internationales
NGO	Non-governmental organisation

OCA	Optimal/optimum currency area
OECD	Organisation for Economic Co-operation and Development
OEEC	Organisation for European Economic Co-operation
PCF	Parti communiste français
PES	Party of European Socialists
PHARE	Poland–Hungary Action for Reform
PPI	Partito Populare Italiano
PSPP	Public Sector Purchase Programme
PU	Political Union
QMV	Qualified majority voting
R&D	Research and development
REH	Reconciliation of European Histories
RRF	Recovery and Resilience Facility
SEA	Single European Act
SED	Sozialistische Einheitspartei Deutschlands
SFIO	Section française de l'Internationale Ouvrière
SGCI	Secretariat General of the Interministerial Committee
SGP	Stability and Growth Pact
SMEs	Small and medium-sized enterprises
SMP	Single Market Programme
SPD	Sozialdemokratische Partei Deutschlands
STABEX	System for the Stabilisation of Export Earnings
SURE	Support to Mitigate Unemployment Risks in an Emergency
TECE	Treaty Establishing a Constitution for Europe
TEN	Trans-European Networks
TESS	Transnational European Solidarity Survey
TEU	Treaty on the European Union
TFEU	Treaty on the Functioning of the European Union
UC	Units of account
UEF	Union Européenne des Fédéralistes
UK	United Kingdom
UKIP	United Kingdom Independence Party
UN	United Nations
UNECE	United Nations Economic Commission for Europe
USSR	Union of Soviet Socialist Republics
VP	Vice President
WEU	Western European Union
WTO	World Trade Organization

Reflections on the History
and Historiography of European
Integration

MATHIEU SEGERS AND STEVEN VAN HECKE

Introduction

European integration is not the result of a preconceived plan. It rather consists of messy procedures and heated discussions. Ad hoc decision-making, crises and even utter chaos have been constants in the history of the European Union (EU). This complex reality has induced scholars to zoom in on its infamous 'muddling through' to better understand what is going on in European integration. Consequently, the primary focus of research has been on ways, means and outcomes: inter-state bargaining, and the resulting treaties and European institutions. However, this focus on institutional ways and means, and on the outcomes of inter-state bargaining has implied that ideas about Europe's future mostly have been treated as proxies of specific, rather one-dimensional, state, or institutional, interests. This leads to distorted images of history. If the recent crisis years made one thing very clear, it is this: that it proves quite complex to adequately analyse the multilevel, multipolicy and *demoi-cracy* muddling through that characterises the EU's laborious management of crises and day-to-day politics and policies, let alone that a mere focus on institutional interests would be sufficient. Putting it even more strongly, existing theories to understand European integration, which were developed mostly during the heyday of integration, turn out to be insufficient to fathom the evolution of European integration, especially since the Treaty of Maastricht (1992).

Indeed, the Treaty of Maastricht redefined European integration afresh in terms of 'deepening' and 'widening' in the totally new, and largely unforeseen, situation of a post-Cold-War world order. Stylised images of conflicting national interests, archetypical antitheses between federalist Europhiles and patriotic Eurosceptics, or one-dimensional alternatives in terms of supranational versus intergovernmental integration proved insufficient to grasp the essence either of this plot of history or of its narrative, let alone to understand why and how European integration engaged itself in the highly risky undertakings of a single currency and an unprecedented enlargement process on 'shaky foundations', as the former German minister of Foreign Affairs, Joschka Fischer, characterised the state of play in the EU in terms of institutional groundwork in 2011.

To get an answer to (revived traditional) grand questions like whether the Treaty of Maastricht was a crucial moment of metamorphoses of European integration or an episode of continuation, or what the 'nature' of the historical process of European integration in essence entails, research ought to delve into the history underneath the surface of European integration's day-to-day institutional development. On that deeper level, we find that European integration is drawn from an ongoing 'battle of ideas' concerning what Europe may or should become in the future. Indeed, European integration is the product of never-ending battles among such plans, which have sprung from ideas (both causal and principled) as well as from ideals. In addition, these ideas and ideals often have been working across national frontiers, crosscutting member states, as well as political parties and conventional political camps within them.[1] Rival designs and grand designs for Europe continuously usher in rivalling concrete proposals in various policy fields, which then become the subject of European negotiations on different levels. However, the continuous competition of concepts and plans this induces has often been hidden from public and scholarly view, also because 'loser grand designs' disappear in the *ex post facto* depictions that dominate the historiography.

European Integration: What It Is and What It Is about

After they had actively engaged themselves in integration through the establishment of the European Coal and Steel Community (ECSC) in 1951, the governments of the six founding members (Belgium, France, the Federal Republic of Germany, Italy, Luxembourg, and the Netherlands) were able neither to escape the ongoing battles of ideas over the future of European integration, nor to control what sprang from the widely popular idea of European unification. Instead, the new phenomenon of European integration penetrated domestic politics and caused deep splits within cabinets and

---

1 C. Parsons, *A Certain Idea of Europe* (Ithaca, NY, Cornell University Press, 2003); J. Vanke, *Europeanism and European Union* (Palo Alto, CA, Academica Press, 2010).

parliaments, crosscutting conventional political camps, and stirring up national versions of heated debate between federalists, con-federalists, Euro-sceptics and others. At the same time, however, behind the scenes, the lack of national control of this process encouraged unorthodox coalition formation across national frontiers, bureaucracies and transnational lobbies and networks – as recent archival research and fresh investigations within the neo-functionalist approach underscore. Moreover, European negotiations encapsulated both state- and non-state actors right from the start – including transnational lobbies such as Jean Monnet's Action Committee and the Roundtable of Industrialists, but certainly also less well-known lobbies such as those organised in the world of churches and international banking, allowing for coalition formation across national frontiers and state and European institutions, such as the European Commission and the European Parliament (then still in the making). Influencing the integration process thus presupposed a certain 'transnationali-sation' of European policies right from its earliest days.

This all has been underrated in the historiography. And there is an empirical reason: the governments' convincing but false claim to control the integration process. However, the idea of a striking match between the emerging integration and clear-cut national economic and/or geopolitical rationales essentially was an *ex post facto* depiction of largely unforeseen developments, in which ad hoc issue-linkages and path-dependencies have been shaping forces. The situation was continually characterised by contested actor positions and unclear coalitions. This is the 'normal condition' in the unprecedented process of European integration. In such instances, ideas can facilitate institutional reform and/or radical policy change, for instance, through redefinition of actors' interests as a result of 'inter-elite persuasion'.[2]

So far, research has had serious difficulties in the attempt to master these national *ex post facto* rationalisations. Moreover, state-centric, and issue-specific subdivisions still hinder the design of projects concerned with 'European' path dependences and issue linkages from a more diachronic perspective. In the exceptional cases in which these phenomena have been studied over a longer period, the scope has been limited to either path dependence or issue linkage. This is a serious shortcoming in the historiography, for instance because long-term institutional consequences may well have

---

2 M. M. Blyth, '"Any More Bright Ideas?" The Ideational Turn of Comparative Political Economy', *Comparative Politics* 29, no. 2 (1997): 229–50; M. Blyth, *Great Transformations: The Rise and Decline of Embedded Liberalism* (Cambridge, Cambridge University Press, 2002).

been 'by-products' of actions taken for short-term reasons inherent in specific issue linkages in earlier episodes.

During the 1940s the Western quest for more international stability and coordination resulted in an institutional 'system' that the American political scientist John Ruggie famously described as the 'regime of embedded liberalism'.[3] Although the scholars of embedded liberalism never really engaged with it,[4] European integration may have formed an integral and inspirational – yet subdued – part of this primary financial-economic dimension of the *pax Americana*. After all, if they were to stand a chance, plans of European integration had to be nested within the transatlantic institutional structures that were already in the making. Pre-1950 Western multilateralism built a 'laboratory' in which different initiatives for European integration were developed and tested, long before the process of European integration took root. The evolution of ideas for a new order in Europe within this transatlantic world was shaped by ongoing – and still highly topical – debates about the 'dialectics' of free world capitalism, such as those between domestic and international stability and social cohesion and competitiveness. To a certain extent institutions like Land-Lease, Bretton Woods, the International Monetary Fund (IMF), the International Trade Organization (ITO, later General Agreement on Tariffs and Trade, GATT), the Marshall Plan, the Organisation for European Economic Co-operation (OEEC, later Organisation for Economic Co-operation and Development, OECD), the European Payments Union (EPU), the ECSC and the European Common Market were all part of the same quest for welfare and stability via resilient capitalism and democracy, with a special focus on Europe and/or western Europe. Regarding the latter, the fact that early common market grand designs were often inspired by Cold War and/or colonial geography has long been omitted in the existing literature. It is telling in this regard that the inter-linkage of the process of European integration with the history of decolonisation has scarcely been researched as an integral part of European integration.[5]

3 J. G. Ruggie, 'International Regimes, Transactions, and Change: Embedded Liberalism in the Postwar Economic Order', *International Organization* 36 (1982): 379–415.
4 G. J. Ikenberry, 'The Liberal International Order and Its Discontents', *Millennium: Journal of International Studies* 38, no. 3 (2010): 509–21.
5 Important exceptions are M.-T. Bitsch and G. Bossuat (eds.), *L'Europe unie et l'Afrique: De l'idée d'Eurafrique à la Convention de Lomé I* (Brussels, Bruylant, 2005); P. Hansen and S. Jonsson, *Eurafrica: The Untold History of European Integration and Colonialism* (London, Bloomsbury, 2014); N. P. Ludlow, 'European Integration and the Cold War', in M. P. Leffler and O. A. Westad (eds.), *The Cambridge History of the Cold War* (Cambridge, Cambridge University Press, 2010), vol. II, pp. 179–97.

In more general historical terms, the evolution of the Common Market can be considered illustrative for the dynamics sketched out above. Europe's market project has been offered detailed counter plans and nuanced alternatives ever since its inception. Starting from the treaty negotiations over the European Economic Community (EEC) during the mid 1950s, premature EEC concepts clashed with other plans, among others, plans for a European free trade area (which later became the European Free Trade Association, EFTA), a plan for an institutionalised Atlantic market, and schemes for a (non-American) continental market. This can be considered a striking example of an ongoing battle of ideas, in the form of clashing grand designs for a future Europe of cooperation. Moreover, the above-mentioned EFTA and Atlantic market plan implied the membership of the United Kingdom (UK), whereas the EEC concepts were very sceptical about this, and continental schemes argued in favour of widening towards eastern Europe, instead of in Atlantic directions. Moreover, traditional historiography paid little attention to the neo-colonial undertones that were very present in the first plans and practices concerning the European common market, and connected this project to a history that stretched back far beyond the Second World War and the twentieth century – it is only very recently that historians of European integration have begun to take this dimension and its imperial and racial features more seriously as an integral part of the history of European integration (see below).

The crucial point here is that the existing historiography merely deals with the EEC extensively. The EFTA appears only at the margins. There is a simple reason for this. Plans and projects like the EEC and EFTA can be attributed to the conflicting 'national interests' of France and the UK, respectively. History has been bent accordingly, and a biased image of the history of the making of Europe's common market may have been the result. The consequences thereof still resonate in (mis)understandings of what is going on in the Europe of integration until today, while European integration, in essence, is a history of many plans and ideas, not just one, as is so often claimed and believed. Indeed, no idea, ideal, plan, design or grand design has ever been strong enough to continuously subordinate the alternatives to its institutional logic, despite the fact that post-war European integration did channel Europe's (classic) drifts towards unification within an unprecedented institutional framework of 'community method integration' and its self-reinforcing boundaries of integration–expansion (see, for example, Articles 38, 39 and 237 of the EEC Treaty).

If we want to better understand why things went how they did in European integration, we must do more work on the reconstruction of this unique episode in contemporary history that continues until today, by both broadening the conceptual scope (in multidisciplinary and interdisciplinary ways) and deepening the historical perspective (by stretching European integration history, harking back to histories before 1950 and the Second World War). This is exactly what this *Cambridge History of the European Union* (CHEU) aims to do.

The Genealogy of Post-war (Western) Europe[6]

The unprecedented stability and prosperity realised in (western) Europe in the second half of the twentieth century was neither 'evident in 1945' nor 'an automatic consequence' of the horrors of the Second World War. While the western Europe that was to emerge in the first post-war decades started to take shape in the mid 1940s, this 'new Europe' was not created during or after the Second World War. Instead, crucial pieces amongst the wreckage of the first decades of the twentieth century formed its central building blocks. The post-war developments in western Europe were strongly linked to the inter-war years, when, on the one hand, the juxtaposed processes of 'de-globalisation' and 'nationalisation', accompanied by a transnational 'turn to private corporatism', shook up the societal and political order, while, on the other hand, possibilities for 'one-worldism' and lofty pacifism were being explored in international politics.[7]

After the unmatched horrors of the First World War, American President Woodrow Wilson's call for a 'worldwide settlement' gained traction at the Paris Peace Conference. Hopes were high that, as the British commentator and writer H. G. Wells had put it during the first year of the Great War, this war would be 'the war that will end war'.[8] At Versailles in 1919, the 'Big Four' powers – the United States, the UK, France and Italy – knew all too well 'that

---

6 This section is based on M. Segers, *The Origins of European Integration: The Pre-history of Today's European Union, 1937–1951* (Cambridge, Cambridge University Press, 2023), Chapter 1.

7 A. Preston and D. Rossinow (eds.), *Outside In: The Transnational Circuitry of US History* (New York, NY, Oxford University Press, 2017), pp. 1–2; M. Hewitson and M. D'Auria (eds.), *Europe in Crisis: Intellectuals and the European Idea, 1917–1957* (New York, NY and Oxford, Berghahn, 2012), p. 13; Poul F. Kjær, 'The Transnational Constitution of Europe's Social Market Economies: A Question of Constitutional Imbalances?', *Journal of Common Market Studies* 57, no. 1 (2019): 143–58; D. W. Ellwood, *The Shock of America: Europe and the Challenge of the Century* (Oxford, Oxford University Press, 2016), p. 182.

8 H. G. Wells, *The War That Will End War* (London, Frank & Cecil Palmer, 1914).

there had never been an attempt at a worldwide settlement'; indeed, as the historian Margaret McMillan wrote in 2013, 'there has never been one since'. While the post-Great War period was unique in that the populations of the warring states were ready and keen to embrace universalism and world peace, McMillan noted that, if anything, the Treaty of Versailles made the Great War into 'the war that ended peace'.[9] In other words, the peace settlement of 1919 failed to 'make the world safe for democracy' (this is the phrase Wilson used on 2 April 1917 in a speech before Congress to obtain permission to declare war against Germany, which he obtained 4 days later) – quite the contrary. Moreover, this was the moment the United States became definitively involved in European and world politics. By the time Wilson was bypassed as presidential candidate for the 1920 elections, his 'Fourteen Points' outlining his principles of peace had already been dead in the water for quite some time. Wilson's proactive and idealistic vision for world cooperation became buried under the essentially reactive and opportunistic cost–benefit reasoning enshrined in the agreements of the Versailles Peace Treaty. This was also 'an illustration of how ill-defined Wilson's ideas were as practical politics'.[10]

The brute reality on the ground in Europe tore down the American-inspired aspirations for a better world and relegated them to naïve utopianism, ultimately symbolised by the fate of the League of Nations, which proved to be tragically dysfunctional in the inter-war years. Europeans turned a deaf ear to the politics of reconciliation touted by politicians such as Gustav Stresemann and Aristide Briand.[11] What re-emerged was a Europe of conflict, violence, uncertainty and poverty. It was a Europe that was plunging into even greater darkness than before, transfixed by a feverish search for an escape. This was the Europe of the Spanish Civil War and of Pablo Picasso's *Guernica* (1937), the mural-sized painting portraying the suffering of people and animals during the bombing of the eponymous city by German and Italian aircraft. This was the Europe of rampant poverty and gloom, which the young American journalist Walter Lippmann had implicitly warned about in his coverage of the Paris Peace Conference. This was the Europe that was captured by the German-Swiss painter Paul Klee in his painting *Europa* (1933): a goddess still, but one of wild despair and expressionism.

---

9 M. McMillan, *The War That Ended Peace: The Road to 1914* (London, Profile Books, 2014).
10 A. Williams, *Failed Imagination? The Anglo-American New World Order from Wilson to Bush*, 2nd ed. (Manchester, Manchester University Press, 2007), pp. 19–21, 38–44.
11 H. Kissinger, *Diplomacy* (New York, NY, Simon & Schuster, 1994), pp. 266–88.

A new generation of American descendants of well-to-do East Coast families came to know Europe while living there during the inter-war years as part of the twentieth-century American variant of the Grand Tour, often travelling together with the intellectual American *avant-garde* in Paris. It was this generation of Americans that fell in love with the struggling old continent, and it was this emotional attachment that partly explains why key figures among these Americans – who were to take up influential positions in government and business during the 1940s – pushed passionately for a brighter European future after the Second World War. Indeed, the outlook of their generation would carry the 'American century' along with an emerging, 'altogether new, emblematic, Atlantic world, bound together in mind and deed'.[12] Politically, their activism often had its origins in the direct involvement of the United States in the post-First World War peace negotiations, then also labelled 'America's geopolitical coming-out party',[13] where many of them had been present as diplomatic youngsters or journalists.

Indeed, the American point of view on the Second World War was that it was the Great Depression and the devastating inequality, nationalism, and racism it had unleashed that was at the root of the extraordinary violence that ravaged Europe during Hitler's war. This meant that the work of the many American diplomats, policy-makers, journalists, businessmen and politicians involved in the American mission of 'building Europe' entailed a dual battle against both poverty and the collapse in international coordination. This mission eventually culminated in the Marshall Plan in 1947 – the programme Wilson didn't have.

It was crucial, however, that the Europeans themselves promote and defend the new transnational policies of international organisation, mobilising the commitment of their fellow Europeans to embrace a radically different post-war experience than the one 25 years earlier. To American analysts, it was immediately obvious that making this work would be no walk in the park, to say the least.[14] Or to put it in more cynical terms: to be acceptable, and paradoxically enough, real unity was not allowed to exist.[15] This was the

12 K. Weisbrode, *The Atlantic Century: Four Generations of Extraordinary Diplomats Who Forged America's Vital Alliance with Europe* (Cambridge, Da Capo, 2009), p. 10.

13 N. D. Lankford, *The Last American Aristocrat: The Biography of Ambassador David K. E. Bruce* (New York, NY, Little, Brown, 1996), pp. 42–3.

14 Nationaal Archief, Dutch National Archives (DNA), The Hague, 2.21.408 (Nalatenschap Beyen), B.2.2.2.1, 71; 'Anglo-American Relations in the Post-war World', Yale Institute of International Studies, May 1943, pp. 5f. See also Weisbrode, *The Atlantic Century*, p. 104.

15 P. Mélandri, *Les États-Unis face à l'unification de l'Europe, 1945–1954* (Paris, Éditions A. Pedone, 1980), p. 26.

harsh dictum on a continent of warring nation-states. It also was one of the key lessons of the failure of Wilsonian idealism in 1919. Any new Europe must also remain an old Europe. In practice, this meant that post-war Europe was still to be based on its nation-states (no matter how worn out and discredited they may have been) and their traditions (no matter how dark these may have been). Moreover, the 'new Old World' of post-war Europe would remain an ongoing experiment in new and more just forms of capitalism and democracy, oscillating between the past and the future, the national and the supranational.[16]

Planning a New Europe

But whatever the ideas of politicians and intellectuals, one constant remained dominant in Europe's realities: the ordinary people of Europe were not really interested in the grandiose plans of the elites. Matters of individual security, food, housing and clothing simply took precedence. Indeed, this was the most evident continuity in the lives of many Europeans.[17] It made European societies fundamentally insecure, uncertain and desperate for stability and security. That was the case after the Second World War, just as it had been before that war had started.

The uncertainty that accompanied these parallel developments – the increasingly nationalist focus of governments in parallel with talk of a world government – did not arise in a historical vacuum. According to the Romanian-British policy expert and scholar David Mitrany – the father of functionalism and champion of post-war functionalist planning – it was during the nineteenth century that two political trends emerged that 'moved on two and opposite lines'. The first line enhanced 'the enfranchisement of the individual, the person becoming a citizen' (anchored in the Renaissance, humanism and anti-totalitarianism). The second line led to 'the enfranchisement of national groups through states of their own' – a process that would radically intensify during the first five decades of the twentieth century, when Europe's nation-states became more ethnically homogeneous, often as a result of very violent politics.[18]

---

16 P. Anderson, *The New Old World* (London, Verso, 2011).

17 Preston and Rossinow (eds.), *Outside In*, pp. 1–2; Hewitson and D'Auria (eds.), *Europe in Crisis*, p. 13; P. F. Kjaer, 'The Transnational Constitution of Europe's Social Market Economies', 146; A. Shennan, *Rethinking France: Plans for Renewal 1940–1946* (Oxford, Clarendon Press, 1989), p. 13.

18 T. Judt, *Postwar: A History of Europe since 1945* (London, Pimlico, 2007), pp. 27–8; I. de Haan, 'The Western European Welfare State beyond Christian and Social Democratic Ideology', in D. Stone (ed.), *The Oxford Handbook of Postwar European History* (Oxford, Oxford University Press, 2012), pp. 299–318, 305, 312.

Mitrany stressed that it was the task of post-war Europe 'to reconcile these two trends'.[19] Indeed, this may have been the key challenge of the post-war era in western Europe, given that the uncertainty mentioned above persisted into the first post-war years.

This confronted the planners of the post-war West, and European integration in particular, with the dilemma endemic to the multilateral management of interdependence. The 'two trends' identified by Mitrany continued unabated in a geopolitical and geo-cultural context marked by unremitting ambiguity. On the one hand, this context was characterised by nation-states that were increasingly becoming culturally homogeneous. On the other hand, it was coloured by the phenomenon of economic, political and cultural 'Americanisation', especially in western Europe,[20] where societies increasingly became spellbound by the United States and its films, its music, its automobiles, its stimulation of the senses, its money.[21]

This cultural–commercial trend was mirrored in new political visions. The backdrop of Americanisation allowed the idea of an 'Atlantic Community' to win relevance in western Europe. But it had been the outbreak of the war against Hitler's Germany that allowed this idea to truly catch the mood of the time, as the concept of the Atlantic Community could be easily linked to Allied cooperation, in particular to the politics and policies that sprang from the strongly intensified Anglo-American partnership but also to the drafting of plans for post-war Europe by the European exile governments in wartime London.[22] Nonetheless, the translation of this 'easy link' into a concrete and coherent grand design ultimately failed. As a result, the visionary concept of an Atlantic Community was put on the back burner and turned into a transatlantic politico-economic incubator space facilitating the international cooperation of open societies and promoting 'liberalism as a pan-Western exercise' but remaining 'unguided by overall strategy'.[23]

19 D. Mitrany, *A Working Peace System: An Argument for the Functional Development of International Organization* (London, Royal Institute of International Affairs, 1943), pp. 26–7.

20 B. L. Blower, *Becoming Americans in Paris: Transatlantic Politics and Culture between the World Wars* (Oxford, Oxford University Press, 2011).

21 P. Gassert, 'The Spectre of Americanization: Western Europe in the American Century', in D. Stone (ed.), *The Oxford Handbook of Postwar European History* (Oxford, Oxford University Press, 2012), pp. 180–200, 184.

22 M. Conway, 'Legacies of Exile: The Exile Governments in London during the Second World War and the Politics of Post-war Europe', in M. Conway and J. Gotovitch (eds.), *Europe in Exile: European Exile Communities in Britain 1940–45* (New York, NY, Berghahn, 2001), pp. 255–74.

23 V. R. Berghahn, *Europe in the Era of Two World Wars: From Militarism and Genocide to Civil Society, 1900–1945* (Princeton, NJ, Princeton University Press, 2009), p. 6; Gassert, 'The Spectre of Americanization', p. 196; J. Gillingham, 'From Morgenthau to Schuman

Be that as it may, the 'better world' envisaged during the inter-war decades and the war years did build the foundation for stability, prosperity and well-being in post-war western Europe. Moreover, despite the global aspirations often simmering below the surface in post-war planning, this new reality of free societies, progress and international cooperation remained a strictly Western affair for more than four decades, crafted from ideas of an 'Atlantic civilisation' and a distinct and coherent Western unity – or even union – and identity. In the 1966 republication of his influential pamphlet *A Working Peace System* (first published in 1943), David Mitrany starts the reworked introduction as follows: 'When this short study was first published in the summer of 1943, there was great confidence in the unity which had grown up during the war, and [we] were thinking mainly of how to consolidate that unity and expand it.'[24] However, when the time was ripe to put such ideas into practice in post-war western Europe, this 'Atlantic imagination' of a 'better world'[25] had already lost much of its power. In its place, a messier western European variant emerged, morally indebted to its American precursors, yet focused in practical terms on devising a European method of American-inspired socio-economic and financial-economic planning, a European style of state intervention, inter-state coordination and supranational organisation.

If there was a clean historical break with the post-First World War past after 1945, it was reflected in the modern phenomenon of economically legitimised state intervention elaborated in projects of planning and the policies of the welfare state. The credibility of planning and policy offered a fresh solution to the political problems that had torn Europe apart in the first decades of the twentieth century. During the 1940s, planning and policy even evolved into something much bigger than a set of instruments to organise society. It became a belief, a movement, a kind of pseudo-religion. It became the binding mission that drove the Western quest for a resilient, free world: 'if a democracy was to work, if it was to recover its appeal, it would have to be *planned*';[26] and primarily economically planned, focused on the battle against unemployment and on providing 'welfare for all'.[27]

Plan: The Allies and the Ruhr, 1944–1950', in J. Gillingham, *Coal, Steel, and the Rebirth of Europe, 1945–1955: The Germans and French from Ruhr Conflict to Economic Community* (Cambridge, Cambridge University Press, 1991), pp. 97–117, 111.

24 D. Mitrany, 'Author's Foreword, 1966', in D. Mitrany, *A Working Peace System* (Chicago, IL, Quadrangle Books, 1966 [1943]), p. 25.

25 A. S. Milward, *The Reconstruction of Western Europe 1945–51* (London, Methuen, 1984), p. 55.

26 Judt, *Postwar*.

27 D. de Bellefroid, 'La Commission belge pour l'Étude des Problèmes d'Après-Guerre (CEPAG), 1941–1944' (degree thesis, University College London, 1987), pp. 124–9.

In taking on this mission, the leading planners designed a society that was more organised than the inter-war societies had been when Europeans had experimented with a mix of wild capitalism and even wilder politics. These experiments had only led the continent into economic depression and societal unrest. Given this dark historical backdrop, it was felt that the adventures of the inter-war years had to be avoided at all costs. Planners now took the lead, presenting themselves as unsullied by political ideology. And there was a reason. They were not only able to learn from their own sobering experiences of the 1920s and 1930s, but also had recourse to the preparatory work carried out by the bureaus of the League of Nations and its academic and non-governmental partners. The moribund committees and bureaus of the League – which had found themselves increasingly orphaned in a Europe under the spell of fascism, nationalism, and Nazism – had formed a breeding ground for what would turn out to be an 'epistemic community in the making'.[28] With the benefit of hindsight, the broad, loose and diverse community of internationally oriented and universalistic inspired people, scattered over and around the League's committees and secretariats, can be seen to have been a kind of 'training centre' for the post-war years of reconstruction. It was here that thinking was focused on practical and implementable plans.

These planners and designers helped politicians build their promised 'better world' of prosperity and multilateralism by drawing up a programme of practical politics that the Western world had lacked. This earned them political trust, and it made their claim that rational policies of international cooperation could prevent disaster even more convincing and thus appealing. The most prominent of the planners even presented themselves as 'statesmen of inter-dependence' – as apolitical experts operating within an emerging international order based on the cooperation of free and open societies, social justice and the practical and material benefits of functionalism and market expansion, cheap production and mass consumption.[29] Initially, this conversion of American ideas into Atlantic and western European practices of international cooperation and organisation was achieved mainly by promoting and managing economic interdependence in the fields of monetary policy, trade and financial-economic affairs.

28 K. K. Patel, *The New Deal: A Global History* (Princeton, NJ, Princeton University Press, 2016), p. 292; P. Clavin, *Securing the World Economy: The Reinvention of the League of Nations, 1920–1947* (Oxford, Oxford University Press, 2013).

29 F. Duchêne, *Jean Monnet: The First Statesman of Interdependence* (New York, NY, W. W. Norton, 1994); compare John Foster Dulles quoted in Berghahn, *Europe in the Era of Two World Wars*, p. 136.

Renewing the Historiography of European Integration

The work undertaken by the planners of a new (western) Europe was soon given a powerful boost by the success story – unparalleled in history – of economic growth, prosperity, and general progress. As Alan Milward has noted, 'nothing in the history of western Europe resembles its experience between 1945 and 1968 ... the material standard of living for most people improved uninterruptedly and often very rapidly'.[30] In combination with the geopolitical and ideological black-and-white logic of the Cold War, this makes it seem – *ex post facto* – as though the early post-war rationalist planners had triumphed. This influential perception, however, is fundamentally incomplete because it obfuscates the non-economic origins of European integration and falsely portrays European integration as a purely rational affair.

This notion forms the starting point for the historical research that underpins the CHEU and mirrors a relatively recent development in the historiography of European integration.[31] The CHEU aims to make an important contribution to the existing historiography by integrating three relatively new insights from the emerging revisionist literature into a new comprehensive approach.

The first new insight derived from the revisionist literature is that the governments involved in initiating European integration were unable to control what emerged out of the widely popular idea of European unification. Once the genie was let out of the bottle, European integration took on a life of its own, penetrating domestic politics and causing deep splits within cabinets and parliaments, cutting across conventional political camps and stirring up heated debates between federalists, confederalists, isolationists, nationalists and so on. The lack of national control over this process of integration also led to the formation of unorthodox transnational coalitions, lobbies and networks. Moreover, the transatlantic and European negotiations that prepared the ground for the revolutionary first steps of European integration involved both state and non-state actors from the very beginning, which meant that the drafting of plans and the formation of coalitions occurred across national frontiers and that state and non-state institutions

---

30 Milward, *The European Rescue of the Nation-State*, p. 21.
31 For a useful and complete overview of the historiography concerning European integration, see K. K. Patel, 'Widening and Deepening? Recent Advances in European Integration History', *Neue Politische Literatur* 64 (2019): 327–57.

worked together. This was, in essence, its own 'polity' in the making.[32] Influencing the integration process presupposed access to this polity. In addition, there was a certain degree of 'transnationalisation' of European politics and policies from its earliest days. This has not been given sufficient attention in the historiography, and the CHEU strives to correct this.

The second new insight is the need to delve deeper into the past to understand the origins of European integration. The state-centric and issue-specific historiography mentioned above impedes efforts to understand transatlantic path dependences and issue linkages from a more diachronic perspective. In the rare cases in which these phenomena have been studied over a longer period, the scope has been limited either to intellectual history or to institutional path dependence or issue linkage within and between certain policy domains – of which the latter two typically remain limited to the traditional timeframe of European integration, meaning post-1950 or even post-1990.[33] Obviously, this is a major shortcoming in the literature, for instance, because long-term institutional consequences may well have been 'by-products' of decisions taken for short-term reasons inherent in specific issue linkages (of earlier episodes). It is essential for historians to go back beyond 1950, beyond 1945, and even beyond the Second World War to the inter-war period and the First World War in order to widen their diachronic scope of research.[34] The 'new Europe' of cooperation and integration was not created from scratch after the Second World War; instead, post-war develop-ments were deeply rooted in the inter-war years, if only because it was ultimately the Great War that plunged Europe into a period of 75 years of war, unrest and division – 'the longest of its civil wars'[35] – that ended only in

---

32 W. Kaiser, B. Leucht and M. Rasmussen (eds.), *The History of the European Union: Origins of a Trans- and Supranational Polity 1950–72* (London, Routledge, 2008). The importance of factoring in the transnational and polity dimensions has been underscored by relatively recent studies of diplomatic history, as well as research within the neo-functionalist tradition in political science research, for instance, Weisbrode, *The Atlantic Century*; M. Segers, 'Preparing Europe for the Unforeseen, 1958–63: De Gaulle, Monnet and European Integration beyond the Cold War: From Cooperation to Discord in the Matter of the Future of the EEC', *International History Review* 34 (2012): 347–70; A. Niemann, *Explaining Decisions in the European Union* (Cambridge, Cambridge University Press, 2006).

33 See, for example, Hewitson and D'Auria (eds.), *Europe in Crisis*; P. Pierson, 'The Path to European Integration: A Historical Institutionalist Analysis', *Comparative Political Studies* 29, no. 2 (1996): 123–63; W. Sandholtz and A. Stone Sweet (eds.), *European Integration and Supranational Governance* (Oxford, Oxford University Press, 1998); L. Friis, '"The End of the Beginning" of Eastern Enlargement – Luxemburg Summit and Agenda-Setting', *European Integration Online Papers* 2, no. 7 (1998), 16 pp.

34 Hewitson and D'Auria (eds.), *Europe in Crisis*.

35 N. Davies, *Europe: A History* (London, Bodley Head, 2014), p. 14.

1990 with the Treaty on the Final Settlement with Respect to Germany allowing the two German states to reunite. It was this treaty that laid the foundations for the end of the Cold War and the reunification of Europe, facilitated by the process of European integration and re-enshrined in the Treaty on European Union in 2007. Together, these treaties explicitly built on the multilateral order of the post-war West and its ideals of international cooperation and human rights. The CHEU also entails an effort to reconstruct this fragmented history of the Western world in the twentieth century in which post-war (western) Europe was – and still is – so firmly embedded.

The third new insight that has emerged from recent historiography is the conviction that to understand how European integration developed the way it did, historians must delve beneath the surface of day-to-day politics, diplomacy, and the development of institutions. On that deeper level, it becomes apparent that European integration was drawn from a relentless 'battle of ideas' over Europe's future. It was not the result of a preconceived plan but the product of never-ending battles over such plans – battles that were fuelled by ideas and ideals that crossed national frontiers as well as political parties. Grand designs for a new European, regional and world order inevitably ushered in a competition of proposals from very general and political ones to ones that were extremely technical and focused on very specific policy fields. This ceaseless competition between different concepts and plans is key to understanding what happened and why. And yet the unsuccessful grand designs are largely neglected in the *ex post facto* depictions that dominate the historiography. The CHEU hopes to paint a more complete picture of these ideational dynamics and struggles than is usually presented in scholarly works on European integration.

Other ways in which the CHEU aims to enrich the existing literature on European integration are the addition of innovative conceptual elements (from disciplines other than contemporary history) and the highlighting of key dimensions in the history of European integration that often have been overlooked, such as the above-mentioned neo-colonial dimension, which was very present in the initial phases of European market integration. Another example of such an overlooked dimension is the (very) active role of the churches and leading ecclesiastics, often made possible through the trans-European and transatlantic networks of Christian Democracy, especially in the first phases of European integration. This represented a vital political force in all free societies of post-war Europe, where political, technocratic and clerical networks often overlapped in an emerging world of transatlantic cooperation that fostered partnerships that were pivotal in the post-war West. The interconnectedness of the world of the churches and the process of (re)building Europe has been largely ignored in the historiography.[36]

Theorising European Integration: A Brief History

Generally speaking, European integration theories, fuelled by various strands of political science, have taken these insights – like the role of ideas or non-state actors and the power of path dependence or transnational networks – into account. Historically, these theories – borrowed from international relations, comparative politics and public management and applied to a unique case often labelled as sui generis – followed clear trends in trying to explain the range, degree and speed of European integration, or the lack thereof. The big questions of how and why followed certain waves, clearly corresponding to the ups and downs of the process of (political) integration itself.

Neo-functionalism was the first theory trying to explain this unique phenomenon in international politics.[37] Neo-functionalism explained the coming about of the ECSC and the Rome Treaties (EEC and Euratom) by noting the internal logic and dynamics of the integration process, with special emphasis on processes of socialisation. Its failure to provide explanations for certain shortcomings or even stagnation in the process of European integration – such as the failure of the European Defence Community (EDC) or the Empty Chair Crisis – triggered a renewed attention towards actors' self-interests and preferences, first and foremost driven by national interests of the member states. This theory of intergovernmentalism became dominant when neofunctionalist (and rather linear) explanations and predictions had been disavowed by events like the failure of the EDC.[38] Intergovernmentalism assumes that integration proceeds only when states envisage more benefits than costs in cooperating with each other. Consequently, intergovernmentalists consider European integration to be the reflection of the national interests of the most powerful states and

---

36 Recent attempts to fill this gap in the historiography include W. Kaiser, *Christian Democracy and the Origins of the European Union* (Cambridge, Cambridge University Press, 2007); S. Shortall, *Soldiers of God in a Secular World: Catholic Theology and Twentieth-Century French Politics* (Cambridge, MA, Harvard University Press, 2021); G. Chamedes, *A Twentieth-Century Crusade: The Vatican's Battle to Remake Christian Europe* (Cambridge, MA, Harvard University Press, 2019).

37 E. B. Haas, *The Uniting of Europe: Political, Social and Economical Forces, 1950–1957* (Notre Dame, IN, University of Notre Dame Press, 1958).

38 S. Hoffmann, 'Obstinate or Obsolete? The Fate of the Nation-State and the Case of Western Europe', *Dædalus* 95, no. 3 (1966): 862–915.

corresponding policy choices, be they 'geopolitical', 'socio-economic' or 'commercial'; the latter under the banner of 'liberal intergovernmentalism'.[39]

These long-dominant 'varieties of intergovernmentalism', however, share comparable problems in their efforts to capture the institutional dynamics of the Community system, as this system clearly contains normative features, transnational dynamics, fragmented national governments, caprices of public support for European integration, and non-state actors – and also in the accurate and/or balanced use of sources.[40]

From this perspective it may not be a surprise that the quest for a grand theory – shaping much of the infant historiography in the early decades of integration – that can explain the overall European integration process has been increasingly abandoned by scholars in the past two decades.[41] Instead, so-called meso-theories (such as social constructivism, multilevel governance and 'Europe as an empire') tried to analyse specific elements or phenomena within European integration, which seem located at the heart of the process – for instance the variation inherent in it.[42] Most of the time, however, this has been done by borrowing frameworks and concepts from existing academic disciplines and subdisciplines, mainly in the social sciences, which were not focused on European integration per se.[43] Even the efforts to theoretically explain 'the

39 H.-J. Küsters, 'West Germany's Foreign Policy in Western Europe 1949–1958', in C. Wurm (ed.), *Western Europe and Germany* (Oxford and Washington, DC, Berg, 1995), pp. 55–85; Milward, *The European Rescue of the Nation-State*; A. Moravcsik, 'Liberal Intergovernmentalism and Integration: A Rejoinder', *Journal of Common Market Studies* 33, no. 4 (1995): 611–28; A. Moravcsik, *The Choice for Europe: Social Purpose and State Power from Messina to Maastricht* (London, UCL Press, 1998); A. Moravcsik, 'De Gaulle between Grain and *Grandeur*' (Parts 1 and 2), *Journal of Cold War Studies* 2, no. 2 (2000): 3–43 and 2, no. 3 (2000): 4–68; A. Moravcsik, 'Preference, Power and Institutions in 21st-Century Europe', *Journal of Common Market Studies* 56, no. 7 (2018): 1648–74.

40 M. Kleine and M. Pollack (eds.), 'Special Issue: Liberal Intergovernmentalism and Its Critics', *Journal of Common Market Studies* 56, no. 7 (2018); L. Hooghe and G. Marks, 'Is Liberal Intergovernmentalism Regressive? A Comment on Moravcsik (2018)', *Journal of European Public Policy* 27, no. 4 (2019): 501–8; Niemann, *Explaining Decisions in the European Union*; Kaiser et al. (eds.), *The History of the European Union*; R. H. Lieshout, M. L. L. Segers and A. M. van der Vleuten, 'De Gaulle, Moravcsik, and the Choice for Europe: Soft Sources, Weak Evidence', *Journal of Cold War Studies* 6, no. 4 (2004): 89–139.

41 S. Hix and B. Høyland, *The Political System of the European Union* (New York, NY, Red Globe Press, 2011).

42 F. Schimmelfennig and B. Rittberger, 'The EU as a System of Differentiated Integration. A Challenge for Theories of European Integration?', in J. Richardson and S. Mazey (eds.), *European Union: Power and Policy-Making*, 4th ed. (London, Routledge, 2015), Chapter 2; E. Hirsch Ballin, E. Ćerimović, H. Dijstelbloem and M. Segers, *European Variations as a Key to Cooperation in the European Union* (Cham, Springer, 2020).

43 S. Hix, 'The Study of the European Community: The Challenge to Comparative Politics', *West European Politics* 17, no. 1 (1994): 1–30.

age of crisis' (the euro and Schengen/migration, 'the two flagship integration projects of the 1990s'),[44] as well as forms of 'differentiated integration' and disintegration,[45] particularly Brexit, did not preclude the appearance of a new grand theory. What did happen, was the adaption and nuancing of the 'old grand theories', so as to include new insights and relate them to a decade of crises. This led to theories such as postfunctionalism (which assesses the causes and effects of the increasing 'politicisation' of European integration) and new varieties of 'liberal intergovernmentalism'.[46] The communis opinio more and more seems to be that the relevance of European integration theories lies in 'elucidating the EU's polycrisis or its distinctive features', also given that 'one theory might not be apt for explaining all the crises the EU has faced since 2009, different theories explain distinct empirical realities'.[47]

Interestingly, by giving up the ambition to understand what is going on in Europe in a more general sense, the 'new theories' do generally indicate that the Treaty of Maastricht has been a turning point in the history of European integration. In other words, 'Maastricht' may have changed the nature of the integration process as such. For some 'Maastricht', for instance, finally proved that the ultimate nature of European integration is in building a common political future and for the EU to become a more political player, both internally and externally, in one way or another.[48] And there is an obvious, albeit still not much mentioned, direct reason for this turn to *Realpolitik*: The post-Maastricht era was also characterised by geographical 'widening' of integration, next to nation-state penetrating 'deepening'; the latter especially via the Economic and Monetary Union (EMU).

Indeed, what the last 30 years of European integration do force us to confront is the far-reaching significance of a Europe of the euro, namely the money and the banks. That Europe has actually been achieved. The deep grooves that the euro crisis has gouged across the EU and its member states have pushed the history of that same EU towards other, new perspectives. It is difficult as yet to see what they are, but we can already conclude that the

---

44 F. Schimmelfennig, 'European Integration (Theory) in Times of Crisis. A Comparison of the Euro and Schengen Crises', *Journal of European Public Policy* 25, no. 7 (2018): 969–89.

45 H. Vollaard, *European Disintegration: A Search for Explanations* (London, Palgrave Macmillan, 2018).

46 Hooghe and Marks, 'Is Liberal Intergovernmentalism Regressive?'

47 S. Gürkan and N. Brack, 'Understanding and Explaining the European Union in a Crisis Context: Concluding Reflections', in N. Brack and S. Gürkan (eds.), *Theorising the Crises of the European Union* (London, Routledge, 2020), p. 247.

48 L. van Middelaar, *De nieuwe politiek van Europa* (Groningen, Historische Uitgeverij, 2019).

origins of the monetary dimension of European integration will perhaps prove even more important for the history of integration than was long asserted, believed or estimated. That is one reason why the CHEU devotes considerable attention to the origins and developments of the EMU, and the 'order of Maastricht' (replacing the 'order of Rome'), within which the EMU became a reality. Moreover, the pre-history of the EMU explains much of the how and why of the Europe of European integration and its endemic internal and external struggles. All in all, the state of the art of the historical research on the EMU, as presented in the CHEU, provides new insights into the tangled state of crisis in which the *enlarged* Europe of European integration of today finds itself.

It is, however, only since the EU launched its overwhelming enlargement policy towards the central and eastern European countries that enlargement has become a serious topic of scholarly debate.[49] Until now, studies have either presented insightful, yet single, case studies focusing on specific key dimensions and/or actors,[50] or remain preoccupied by post-Cold War eastern enlargement as the ultimate falsification of rational choice theories.[51] These shifts in scholarly efforts to elucidate what European integration is have implications for the study of the general phenomenon itself.

Moreover, these shifts suggest that new ways of thinking and other disciplines (next to the usual suspects and their 'European studies' sub-branches: history, political science, law, and economics) ought to be encapsulated in the study concerning the 'why and how' of European integration, to rejuvenate the research and anticipate new perspectives the transformation of 'Maastricht' may require. At the same time, however, the traditional 'big questions' of European integration history, about the role of ideas, interests and institutions, have neither been answered sufficiently nor lost their relevance. One of the most prominent of these concerns the position of reunified Germany, 'the German Question' in the reality of post-Cold War history. Since 'Maastricht', and even more so since the euro crisis, the migration crisis, the Covid-19 crisis and the Russian war in Ukraine, this old European question has again become

---

49 N. Nugent (ed.), *European Union Enlargement* (New York, NY, Red Globe Press, 2004).

50 F. Kaiser and J. Elvert (eds.), *European Union Enlargement: A Comparative History* (London, Routledge, 2004); H. Sjursen (ed.), *Questioning EU Enlargement: Europe in Search of Identity* (London, Routledge, 2006).

51 F. Schimmelfennig, 'The Community Trap: Liberal Norms, Rhetorical Action, and the Eastern Enlargement of the European Union', *International Organization* 55, no. 1 (2001): 47–80; F. Schimmelfennig and U. Sedelmeier, 'Theorizing EU Enlargement: Research Focus, Hypotheses, and the State of Research', *Journal of European Public Policy* 9, no. 4 (2002): 500–28; U. Sedelmeier, *Constructing the Path to Eastern Enlargement: The Uneven Impact of EU Identity* (Manchester, Manchester University Press, 2005).

very topical and is hotly debated. The same holds true for that other traditional European question: the British relationship with the continent. The latter is more topical than ever in the present context of Brexit – a feverish search to understand why and how the British struggle with post-Maastricht Europe culminated in the Brexit vote. Or, more generally, the geopolitical questions: what role is left for the EU, next to its Anglo-Saxon allies, in the immediate neighbourhood of the western Balkans, along its unstable borders in the east and the south, vis-à-vis openly revisionist powers like Russia and China?

Aim and Organisation of the CHEU

The CHEU offers a unique opportunity to open up a truly diachronic research scope on the history of European integration. Next to that, it also offers a rare opportunity – on the basis of this research scope – to re-conceptualise the history of European integration, taking on board the latest insights from sub-branches of the study of European integration and inter-disciplinary research on the theme. In other words, the CHEU entails a re-visiting of the big questions of the why and how of this European integration process. Indeed, the CHEU offers the opportunity to take on this challenge from an interdisciplinary and empirically, historically, informed angle, which fits the essentially sui generis aspects of the process. The key questions are as follows: why did we do it, and how does it work? How does the interplay between contingency, clashing ideas and inherent urge for endurance and expansion of the integration process function? What are the outcomes of this interplay?

In order to find answers to these questions, the present book studies European integration history from a (1) diachronic, (2) multidisciplinary and (3) multi-actor angle in order to present an innovative, comprehensive and up-to-date CHEU. Therefore, and unlike many textbooks as well as edited volumes on this topic, we do not organise the two volumes along a strict and classical timeline, starting with the first steps of European integration and finishing with the latest developments. Instead, time and change over time are integrated within the various chapters. Moreover, we invited historians as well as political scientists (and other social scientists and colleagues from other disciplines) to shed light both on traditional topics (such as foreign policy or economic and monetary cooperation and integration) and on non-traditional topics of European integration (like the role of narratives). Such a multidisciplinary approach is guaranteed between but also often within the different chapters. Finally, we neither analyse the European integration process from a state-centric perspective (with chapters on Germany, France, the UK, etc.), nor with a primary focus on European institutions (the European Commission, European Parliament, etc.). Instead, we introduce a thematic approach in which countries and institutions will be discussed from a variety of angles.

In the first volume of the CHEU the outside-in approach is dominant: what does the EU look like from the outside, and which outside forces shaped and co-designed the process of European integration? External events have played a major role in the tempo and direction of European integration. Moreover, research on European integration was nourished by a fairly long tradition of deep interest from US scholars – the influence of their 'eye of the beholder' perspective on European integration has been profound, both in the reality of the making of European integration and in the historiography concerning the why and how of the take-off of European integration and its development. This volume builds on these insights, yet also on recent developments in history and political science that have laid more emphasis on the limits of a Western or western European perspective. In addition, this volume of the CHEU also benefits from how European integration is understood outside the typical European Studies disciplines.

- Part I (Critical Junctures) pays attention to the main external events that have steered the European integration process. Instead of treaties, the emphasis is on 'critical junctures', defining moments in post-Second World War world history, as well as in international geopolitical arenas, in which (western) Europe evolved, found its form and transformed into the EU; this includes the division and reunification of Germany, the history of the Cold War and its legacy, decolonisation and the EU's eastern enlargement.
- Part II (Multilateralism and Geopolitics) considers various international trends that are not unique to the European integration process, but have been strong shaping forces in European integration, such as globalisation and (the return of) geopolitics (to post-war Europe). The analyses in this second part of the first volume specifically focus on causes and effects of these trends on the market, in society and with regard to global challenges adopted by the Europe of European integration. This 'outside-focus' mirrors the 'inside-focus' on instruments of the Europe of integration discussed in the second part of the second volume (see below).
- While the first two parts have institutions, countries and international organisations as the main actors, Part III (Perspectives and Ideas) focuses

on the role of ideas, people, networks, public opinion, culture, religion and memory in the development of what is today the EU. Non-exclusive to the EU but increasingly salient within contemporary academic research, the analyses of these phenomena by scholars from various disciplines certainly contribute to an innovative take on the history of European integration.

The second volume takes an opposite perspective by looking at European integration from an inside-out perspective, an 'inside the black box' approach with a keen eye for the outside effects of internal dynamics in the process of European integration. This means that the authors first of all focus on the internal developments that have shaped the European integration process. The aim of the volume is to shed light on the most important aspects of this process by looking at this process from an inside-out perspective. With the benefit of hindsight and with the typical academic distance, we cover the main events, instruments of European integration and narratives that have shaped the internal development of European integration.

- The scope of Part I (Milestones) concerns the basic rules that have defined European integration. In other words, in this part of the CHEU the treaties and their many changes are (chronologically) analysed by referring to the partly event-driven internal dynamics that have led to the establishment of a legal and political architecture of European integration. Brexit is considered here as a milestone in the history of European integration.
- Part II (Instruments of Integration) zooms in on the different instruments within the architecture of European integration, and elucidates how policies are developed, with a special focus on the (pre-)history of the EMU and the euro, so central to today's European integration. To a certain extent similar to political entities at lower levels, the Europe of European integration has rules, money and coordinated management of economic and monetary policies at its disposal to steer the behaviour of public and private organisations, as well as that of its citizens. To make the system work, it also produces specific internal and external policies. In other words, by studying these instruments this part will make clear how European integration developed (in terms of politics and policy-making) within an expanding range of competences (policies). Special attention is paid to enlargement and the wider challenges of expansion of European integration, because, amongst other reasons, the (unforeseen) swift accession of new countries to the EU has had a profound impact on the internal development of European integration.

- In Part III (Narratives and Outcomes) the focus is on the many narratives the Europe of European integration is historically linked to and/or produced itself for internal use. More *'longue durée'* concepts, goals and ideas such as peace, (the promise of) prosperity, (the lack of) solidarity and democracy over time have all played a crucial mobilising role in the making of European integration (both in material terms and in mental and (collective) psychological terms). These concepts and ideas, as well as their evolutions and impact, deserve a critical and innovative analysis, since they constitute an essential force in the history of European integration, and determine how the process both spoke and failed to speak to the hearts and minds of the Europeans.

The choice of this particular organisation of the two volumes, especially the outside-in and the inside-out perspectives (in that order) is a deliberate choice by us, the editors. We believe it offers the best chances for an adequate, up-to-date, and innovative approach to the history of the Europe of European integration and enables us to present the wide variety of relevant insights and perspectives in the making of the history *and* historiography in a comprehensive way.

Outlook

History is never finished, and neither is historiography. This also applies for the EU, and its still fairly recent history and pre-histories. Nonetheless, its past determines to a great extent its present and prefigures its future in ways we do not know yet.

Knowing and understanding integration history helps us to distinguish between what is acquired – like peace (or the absence of war) in (the western part of) the European continent – and what is not, and what is at stake. This is an urgent matter, not only of the research agenda of European integration history. The achievements of more than seven decades of European integration – economic prosperity, solidarity and democracy – are increasingly under pressure. On the one hand this is happening from within: think about the rise of illiberalism in a number of member states and the difficulties in coping with that for the EU institutions. But certainly the pressure is coming also from outside, with the volatility of the United States, the aggression of Russia and the so-called new Cold War with China. It puts the very idea of European integration under stress. This *project* is criticised because of its ambitions and goals ('why European integration?') that are never really reached, or tend to satisfy too few. Also its competences, institutions, modes of decision-making and geographical scope trigger multiple unanswered questions. Evidently, the complexity of the EU is more of a certainty than its results. Given the fact that there is no consensus on what the project is and where it should lead, it is easier (but also elucidatory) to focus on the *process*. This means that European integration might be defined not by its destiny (like the United States of America) but rather as a permanent series of actions, in reaction to but also anticipating events. From this perspective, EU history often seems a flux of conflicts, crises and compromises.

The latter view is certainly true for the way in which the EU handled the Covid-19 pandemic and the war Russia started in Ukraine on 24 February 2022. After a decade in which European integration was almost identified with crisis management, these extraordinary new challenges shook the foundations of the EU anew. The jury is still out as the long-term consequences of the Covid-19 crisis are still unclear at the time of writing, and the horrific war in Ukraine is radically changing Europe's post-war history and the history of the EU while the two volumes of the present Cambridge History are being copy-edited and produced. The complete manuscript of the CHEU was handed in on 1 February 2022. This means that these two volumes cover the history of European integration until the Russian war in Ukraine.

In relation to the Covid-19 pandemic, three things are already clear. First of all, like many previous crises, it did not in the end lead to a quantum leap in European integration. Secondly, it did trigger some change within the EU, but without entirely changing the EU itself.[52] Here too, resilience is a characteristic of (the empirical) reality in the first place, although many would like to attribute it even more to the EU itself. Thirdly, the crisis management of the pandemic reaffirmed that European integration is about messy procedures and heated discussions. Ad hoc decision-making, crises and even utter chaos have been constants in the recent history of the EU, as the EU's reaction to the war in Ukraine reconfirms once more. And yet, at the same time, the history of European integration also remains a history of persistent ideas about some sort of European unity and purpose in world history – these ideas represent a deeper and older Europe, an undercurrent to the history of treaties of European integration, a history regarding which we feel that it must not be neglected in analysing the latest

---

52 S. Van Hecke, H. Fuhr and W. Wolfs, 'The Politics of Crisis Management by Regional and International Organizations in Fighting against a Global Pandemic: The Member States at a Crossroads', *International Review of Administrative Sciences* 87, no. 3 (2021): 672–90.

trends and modes, if only because it represents a certain resilience of European civilisation and its promises, an urge – despite everything – to look forward, to define a purpose, to imagine a better world.

Note on Archival and Primary Sources

Given the 30-year rule of archival release (that mostly applies for key archives), most relevant archival sources are accessible to researchers of the history of European integration only after that period of 30 years. Consequently, broad international archival research into the history of European integration did not really start until the beginning of the 1980s (and now extends up to the end of the 1980s). Since then, time and time again, one conclusion has proved inescapable: none of the parties involved – the governments of the member states, European institutions and their predecessors, the business community, lobbies, political parties, individuals and so on – have ever been able to control the integration process, let alone dominate it, not even for a short time. The process has been uncontrollable from the very beginning, even for the United States.

This general insight into the history of European integration has consequences for the research agenda. From an operational and methodological perspective any research approach that sets itself the task of attempting to fathom what has been going on in the history of European integration must build also on multinational and/or transnational archival research. Every chapter in the CHEU is based on original multinational archival research, or (regarding the chapters dealing with the more recent history) on new primary sources (as for instance those made available through the EU institutions), new combinations of primary sources or new original empirical research. All of the chapters encapsulate the ambition to stretch the research across the boundaries of 'silo studies' (on, for example, the Marshall Plan, Bretton Woods, the European Payments Union, the ECSC) and try to approach their subject matter from a richer and more comprehensive perspective, including a keen eye for the inter-linkages between the silos.

Vast collections of governmental and European documents are accessible for the period from 1950 up to the early 1990s, including the key episodes around the coming about and first crystallisations of the Treaty of Maastricht. Moreover, for the more recent history, a significant number of published sources, EU sources and private paper collections/ego-documents are available and accessible already, also in the form of interviews with key figures and numerous ego-documents, and – most notably – in other, and in a way enriching, forms, such as films and interactive datasets. Indeed, the list of relevant archives is extensive, and includes, next to the national archives, among many others 'European archives' such as the Historical Archives of the EU (HAEU) in Florence, the Jean Monnet Foundation in Lausanne, the Archives of European Integration (AEI) at the University of Pittsburgh, the Centre Virtuel de la Connaissance sur l'Europe (CVCE) in Luxembourg and national, European and trans-European political party archival collections.

Thanks to its initial focus on archival and primary source research, the CHEU unearthed a true wealth of archival and empirical sources. This obviously includes the archives from numerous EU member states and key countries outside the EU, including the United States, the UK and Switzerland, but, in addition, many of the CHEU's chapters also build upon in-depth research in private paper collections and non-governmental archival collections all over the world, many of them less well known. References to the archival and primary sources used are available in detail in the footnotes to each chapter. We, the editors, believe that this makes these sources checkable and accessible for follow-up research in the most adequate way.

PART I

MILESTONES: TREATIES AND TREATY CHANGES

I

Early Forms of European Unity

GÉRARD BOSSUAT

When did the first institutional forms of contemporary European unity emerge? There are essentially two approaches to answering this question. The first is to take the perspective of poets, writers and intellectuals. The second is to consider the projects and achievements of politicians. If we take the first approach, we must refer to all thinkers of European consciousness who imagined European unity, from the Abbé de Saint-Pierre and Victor Hugo to Émile Mayrisch and, more recently, Stefan Zweig. If we take the second, we must focus instead on institutional forms of unity, the ways in which citizens participate in it, and then assess its effects. We must present the most effective agents of unity, and explain their reasons for taking action.

In the 10 years following the end of the Second World War, societal changes were initiated by democratic structures. Historical research sought to establish links between projects for European unity and the future of Europe following the Nazi catastrophe. It was decided that unity on the Old Continent would provide a satisfactory response to the misfortunes of the war. But it soon became apparent that, at the same time, nation-states were recovering and generating much-needed growth. Was the American intervention in Europe about building unity, or rather about responding to the Soviet threat? Was European unity American in its origin and form, or a European product *sui generis*? Did the European identity exist in harmony or in dissonance with national identities? It was soon necessary to decide whether the governance of European unity would be federal, intergovernmental or mixed. The creation of the Council of Europe on 5 May 1949 oriented the institutions towards intergovernmentalism, yet the Schuman Plan of 9 May 1950 created a federal organisation. Thus, both paths remained open.[1] Would European unity remain an act of cooperation, subject to the goodwill of national sovereignties? What was meant by supranationality, and

1 S. Saurugger, *Théories et concepts de l'intégration européenne* (Paris, Presses de Sciences Po, 2010).

how far could states and citizens tolerate the surrender of sovereignty? Would that which was deemed acceptable in 1945, in the wake of the Second World War, still be acceptable 10 years later, once the old Europe had entered into double-digit growth? Another question then arose: was European unity still needed as the nation-states managed to recover? How could the search for unity be justified? Although by 1954 the argument in favour of unity as a means of maintaining peace was still valid, it was undoubtedly less effective than it had been in 1945: citizens rejected a European defence community under American leadership, as well as a European federal government in the light of the failure of the European Defence Community (EDC) and the European Political Authority (EPA).

Historians are still debating whether the European unity movement was caused by the cataclysm of two world wars and tend to conclude that it was. But there is also an alternative narrative which suggests that unity was a defensive reaction to Atlantic capitalism. Indeed, the creation of a large customs union or common market in Europe has been beneficial for business. Some still wonder whether unity was in fact the result of determined action by providential men such as Monnet, Schuman, De Gasperi, Adenauer and Spaak. Perhaps it was a consequence of the Cold War, hence born of a specific, dramatic moment in contemporary international relations? But we know that a complex event does not stem from a single cause. Thus, the appetite for unity can be explained by invoking two coexisting factors: on the one hand, the idealism of certain agents in society and, on the other hand, the benefits of having a large liberal, capitalist, Euro-Atlantic market. Two periods of the Cold War – its development (in the 1950s and 1960s) and its end (1989–2004) – curiously facilitated this unity. The first saw the birth of the European Coal and Steel Community (ECSC), the Common Market and the European Atomic Energy Community (Euratom), whereas the second gave rise to the European Union's eastward enlargement and its advancement under the Maastricht Treaty. The Cold War and the legacy of uneven European development that preceded it split Europe in two. Yet, the seemingly self-explanatory enlargement process has created some serious challenges for European unity, and its very purpose has been called into question by new members, including Hungary and Poland.

The Europe of Free Nations

In occupied Europe, the resistance movements and exiled governments set about fighting against propaganda promoting a German Europe, instead desiring a different Europe, founded on freedom and democracy. Without consultation amongst each other, they unknowingly shared a common plan for a 'Europe of Free Nations'. Was this the basis of today's European unity?

In France, the aspiration to European federal unity manifested itself relatively early – yet to a lesser extent – within the resistance movements. The German issue haunted the resistance fighters, all of whom wanted Germany to be broken up. But reason prevailed; as Léon Blum stated: 'You cannot destroy a people, a language, a tradition, a legend.'[2] Nonetheless, many political players daydreamed about the 'international nationalisation' of the Ruhr's industrial resources, for example. Belgium, Denmark and Norway showed particularly favourable reactions to European unity. A European federation, to which a democratic Germany could accede, was called for by anti-Hitler conspirators Helmuth James von Moltke and Adam von Trott zu Solz (of the Kreisau Circle) and Hans and Sophie Scholl (of the White Rose group) prior to their beheading. In Ventotene, Italy, in June 1941, Altiero Spinelli and Ernesto Rossi wrote a manifesto for a European federation. The spirit of Ventotene influenced the progressive parties. In Switzerland, in May 1944, European federalists drafted a declaration of the European resistance movement at the home of Pastor Visser 't Hooft, and in July of that year, at the initiative of Rossi and Spinelli, as well as Frenay and others, the Declaration of the European Resistance Movements affirmed the need for a federal union to safeguard peace and freedom.

However, behind this facade of unanimity, the debate brought to the fore the real issues at stake. How big should a European union be? What place should Britain occupy in relation to the continent? Should European states join an Atlantic community or a European community? Would a union be liberal or socialist, federal or confederal? All of these fundamental questions, which were posed between 1944 and 1945, are still very relevant to this day. But, in July 1944, there was hope that the European resistance movement would disprove Thomas Mann's claim that 'This generation only wants to take leave of its own self forever. What it wants, what it loves, is intoxication.'[3] The aftermath of war had allowed Europeans to recover their soul, their freedom and democracy. However, in 1945 the European ideal was not the main focus of the Allies' struggle, as demonstrated by the major conferences of the Allied powers in Teheran, Yalta and Potsdam. Alternative ideals to Europeanism emerged: freedom of peoples, social

2 L. Blum, *À l'échelle humaine* (Paris, Gallimard, 1945).
3 T. Mann, *Avertissement à l'Europe* (with preface by A. Gide. *Esprit*, 6, no. 63 (1937): 460–2.

welfare, economic modernisation and, above all, the organisation of world peace.

British Prime Minister Winston Churchill alone seemed capable of focusing on the desire for unity, but, although his calls from as early as 1942 for a 'United States of Europe' were sincere, he did envisage Britain as occupying a position outside the European unity that was reserved for continental Europe. In Zurich in 1946, Churchill called for the creation of a Council of Europe. The post-war years were described and experienced by contemporaries as the 'springtime of Europe'. Now let us take a closer look at their hopes.

The Failure of French Solutions for Europe,
1945–1947

During these years, European governments developed their own European policy objectives. With the eastern European states succumbing to Soviet imperialism and Germany out of the picture, Britain, France and the three Benelux states (or some combination thereof) were capable of taking the initiative for unity. By 1945, France held the key to European unity and stated three demands: a breaking up of Germany, access to the coal from the Ruhr and, ultimately, for economic reasons, the unification of western continental Europe under French leadership.

The Failure of the European Coal Community in 1945

An initial attempt at a European coal community, in the form of a little-known proposal by Jean Monnet while on a mission to the United States for the Gouvernement provisoire de la République française (Provisional Government of the French Republic, GPRF, 3 June 1944 to 1946), failed in the summer of 1945. (Monnet (1888–1979) was at the time Commissioner General of the French Modernisation and Equipment Plan (1946–51). He had previously been working as commissioner in charge of supplies in General de Gaulle's Comité français de la libération nationale (French Committee for National Liberation, CFLN) in Algiers (1943–4), which became the GPRF.) His solution, which he put to US Assistant Secretary of State William Clayton in June 1945, was to appoint a 'coal dictator' to draw up a coordinated plan to increase production in Germany.[4] This 'dictator' would chair an

---

4 FJME (Lausanne), AME 57/1/177 and AMF 4/3/6, 24 September 1945, from Monnet to Clayton.

intergovernmental committee with real autonomy over Rhine coal and the ability to influence the development of Ruhr-dependent economies. Monnet hoped to promote French access to Ruhr coal through a transnational European organisation of the type he had invented in 1920 – the famous Upper Silesian Arbitration Tribunal. His 'concern for Europe' was linked to economic necessity, but President Dwight D. Eisenhower opposed it.

The French Commissariat Général du Plan de Modernisation (General Planning Commission for the Modernisation and Re-equipment Plan), headed by Monnet at the beginning of 1946, was also behind a project for an autonomous international organisation responsible for the Rhine, Elbe, Danube and Oder valleys. The powers of this New Deal-type organisation would have been immense, presenting both an alternative to the plan to break up Germany and supranational institutional innovation at a higher level than the states.[5] Monnet was far removed from the ideologues of federalism; his functionalist method meant that he was looking for concrete solutions that could be easily transformed into federal solutions. However, he was not able to win the support of European governments.

The British Isolate Themselves (1945–1946)

The French government wanted to reach an agreement with the British to aid the recovery of Europe and France. The Franco-British financial agreement of 27 March 1945, for a commercial overdraft of £100 million, opened an era of trust. But was Britain ready to commit itself further? In September 1945, Britain had obtained a $3.5 billion loan from the Americans to accelerate the convertibility of the pound, but it soon became clear that the British were more interested in the recovery of their own international financial prowess than in that of the French economy. The departure of General de Gaulle in January 1946 and the fear of the communists in Paris caused the British to distance themselves from the continent, despite the proximity of Labour Party values to those of the Section française de l'Internationale Ouvrière (French Section of the Workers' International, SFIO), as the French socialist party was then named. Labour, under Clement Attlee, felt that concerning itself with European unity would reduce Britain's global sway (a point that was raised again 70 years later with regard to Brexit). The Labour Party also feared for their welfare state, as they believed that their political system was superior to any other.

5 AMF 4/3/93, 15 February 1946, preliminary draft concerning the negotiations to be undertaken by France on the subject of Germany. See paragraph (c) Strengthening of German Regional Feeling, 4 pages, illegible signature.

The 'Greater Benelux' Option

The so-called Benelux option – a Franco-Benelux agreement for a small economic union – was, at first, a less appealing strategy than one involving Britain, due to the Benelux countries' weaker economic clout. Yet it did have economic and political advantages. Belgian Minister of Foreign Affairs Paul-Henri Spaak (a socialist who was the Belgian prime minister from March 1947 to March 1949) expressed his concern about the Soviet threat to liberated Europe in March 1944. He saw France as a good example of how to organise western Europe. In 1945, General de Gaulle's Minister for the Economy, Pierre Mendès France, approved a collaboration with the Benelux countries. The idea was to create 'a Western bloc', as imagined by de Gaulle on 18 March 1944, in a speech to the Assemblée Consultative d'Alger (Algiers Consultative Assembly). But the French approach was thwarted by British action, Russian defiance and American silence. Having failed to create a Western bloc, an economic cooperation agreement was signed by France with the Benelux countries on 20 March 1945. The French newspaper *Le Monde* reported that a Conseil Tripartite de Coopération Économique (Tripartite Council for Economic Cooperation, CTCE) would facilitate trade, define a common policy on Germany and 'pave the way for the conclusion of a customs union between the four countries'. The French turned the CTCE into a para-political structure in order to get the Benelux countries to accept France's policy on Germany, which provoked negative reactions in the Netherlands. The Benelux Union approved the reduction of German steel capacity, but the British rejected a so-called 'Greater Benelux'. The French proposed the specialisation of the signatories' economies and a customs union,[6] which would have resurrected the pre-war cartels. But, after Bretton Woods, the General Agreement on Tariffs and Trade (GATT) imposed anti-cartel clauses. The French succeeded only to the extent of persuading the four countries to adopt a common position on the GATT in order to prevent the immediate compulsory liberalisation of trade for war-torn countries. The failure of a continental customs union was due to the pusillanimity of the Belgians, Luxembourgers and Dutch concerning Great Britain, from where they sought their inspiration. According to the Ministère des Affaires Étrangères (French Ministry of Foreign Affairs), 'This

---

6 AMAE, Z Europe 1944–1949, Belgium, 34, 21 February 1945, note from the *Département des Affaires Étrangères* (French Department of Foreign Affairs, DAE), Franco-Belgian economic and financial negotiations. F 60 898, DAE, 29 December 1944, note from the *Ministère des Affaires Étrangères* (French Ministry of Foreign Affairs, MAE), customs union project between France, Belgium, Luxembourg and the Netherlands.

circumstance was more or less the death of all French initiatives.'[7] But what did the British want instead? By 1947, France could not deny that it had failed to achieve its objective of an anti-German European economic union. The vision of Europe imagined by the French in 1943 was collapsing, and Britain refused to take the lead in a Franco-British Europe backed by the French.

So, what should be done with the British, wondered the French? In fact, despite their official friendship, Britain did not trust France. During the negotiation of the Franco-British Treaty of Dunkirk (4 March 1947), Paris had unsuccessfully pleaded for the coordination of the two countries' production plans and for a customs union in western Europe. The French were victims of Britain's elusive manoeuvres. In the months that followed, the French-invented European customs union rivalled the globalisation envisaged by the Bretton Woods agreements and the strategic rivalries of the major powers. But never again would France be so willing to accept a Franco-British co-leadership of western Europe. In 1947–8, the idea of an Atlantic community became more popular, following the failed solution of a continental European union. Perhaps this was the end of European independence in foreign policy. The British were completely oblivious.

Uncertain Dreams of European Unity (1946–1947)

The interest in European unity was due to war. The failure of European nation states had, since 1919, prompted intellectuals, writers and even political idealists to seek the security of the people in international or European institutions. But was the creation of a European customs union or the return to global liberalism necessary? And should this union be limited to western Europe? Moreover, what did the Americans want? The institutional forms of European unity were far from clearly defined.

The popularity of the idea of a European union manifested itself in the proliferation of European federalist movements, the influence and limits of which deserve further examination. Two political figures were capable of making the aspiration to unity a reality: Churchill and de Gaulle, neither of whom was a Europeanist idealist. Former Prime Minister Winston Churchill's speech in Zurich on 19 September 1946 was a legendary moment. Before a crowd of overexcited Europeanist activists, and to the surprise of his listeners, the former prime minister called for a Franco-German reconciliation to enable the construction of 'a kind of

---

7 AMAE, Z Europe 1944–1949, Belgium, 48.

United States of Europe' or a 'Commonwealth of Nations'. With Germany participating in the new system, smaller nations, he said, would count as much as larger ones, and would gain their honour by contributing to the common cause. 'Let Europe arise,' he concluded to rapturous applause.[8] Churchill, who was no longer in power, chose to rely on the United European Movement, the unionist movement of his son-in-law, Duncan Sandys. (Sandys (1908–87) was several times a minister, chairman of the European Movement and leader of the Confederalist Unionists.) The project, which had become fiercely anti-Soviet since Churchill's March 1946 speech on the Iron Curtain in Fulton, Missouri, carried a Cold War overtone and played on the ambiguity of the term 'European Commonwealth' to gain popularity.

De Gaulle, for his part, had affirmed in September 1945 that he was in favour of European unity, without specifying exactly what kind of Europe he had in mind. As the Algiers Consultative Assembly saw emerging talks of a federation of free people, de Gaulle commissioned several studies, while the French Constitution of 11 April 1946 consented to the surrender of sovereignty in return for reciprocity. But the German question was crucial, and the success of European unity would be determined by the solution chosen for this issue. On 5 October 1945, in Baden-Baden, de Gaulle promised an 'economic and moral union' with Germany, but still no union for Europe.

Did European public opinion support European unity? The many pro-European, federalist or unionist movements failed to succeed in creating a unitary dynamic. A united, anti-communist Europe could not be a geographical Europe, and there was reason to hesitate. The Catholic and Protestant churches were working towards a Franco-German reconciliation, following the example of the Pax Christi movement or the Jesuits of Father Jean du Rivau. Meetings were organised between French, English and German academics. The Alpbach Forum in the Tyrol, founded in 1945 by former resistance fighter Otto Molden, brought together eminent personalities, including Louis Aragon and Hans Urs von Balthasar. The Geneva International Meetings, founded in September 1946, in turn assembled intellectuals, such as Denis de Rougemont, Julien Benda, Georges Bernanos and Jean Guéhenno, in addition to the German Karl Jaspers. Christian Democracy gave rise to the Nouvelles Équipes Internationales (New International Teams, NEI),

---

8 *The Times*, 20 September 1946; W. Churchill, 'Address Given by Winston Churchill (Zurich, 19 September 1946)', www.cvce.eu/en/obj/address_given_by_winston_ch urchill_zurich_19_september_1946-en-7dc5a4cc-4453-4c2a-b130-b534b7d76ebd.html.

founded in June 1947. In France, the left-wing SFIO, led by Marceau Pivert, Henri Frenay and Claude Bourdet's review *Socialisme et Liberté* and European socialist activists organised a Comité d'études et d'action pour les États-Unis socialistes d'Europe (Committee for Studies and Action for the Socialist United States of Europe), which became the Mouvement pour les États-Unis socialistes d'Europe (Movement for the Socialist United States of Europe) and then the Mouvement démocratique pour les Etats-Unis d'Europe (Democratic Movement for the United States of Europe). Its first congress, held in June 1947 in Montrouge, rallied representatives from fourteen European countries. The committee was opposed to the Union of Soviet Socialist Republics (USSR), which it viewed as the land of coercion, and to economic liberalism in general. However, its lofty dreams of becoming the 'third major power' did not come to fruition.

The wide range of Europeanist movements called for closer ties. In May 1946, Hans Bauer with the Europa-Union, Léo Van Vassenhove in Bern and Umberto Campagnolo, the secretary general of the Movimento Federalista Europeo (Federalist European Movement), decided to create a large federalist movement. The twelve points of the final declaration of Hertenstein (Switzerland, 21 September 1946) proclaimed the supranational nature of the project for Europe. It was intended to be a step towards a world government, which could become this coveted third global power. Federal Union, a pro-European British group launched in November 1938, advocating a federal Europe, and one of the key driving forces in the international federalist movement, remained dissatisfied and convened another meeting a month later in Luxembourg. A fierce debate raged between European federalists and globalists. Eventually, a rapprochement took place, and the European Union of Federalists (UEF) was born in Paris in December 1946. Chaired by the Dutch socialist Henri Brugmans, it united more than 100,000 members and some 50 movements. It developed a decentralist and popular federalism, but ultimately failed to succeed in imposing federalist ideas on all Europeanists.

Despite the rapprochements of 1946, the UEF was unable to obtain significant commitments from European governments. Two visions for the future of a united Europe coexisted: the UEF's federal vision, oriented towards a non-aligned Europe, and the Churchillian vision of a union of western European states. An attempt to integrate these visions was made in The Hague in May 1948 at the Congress of Europe, a major congress of pro-European unionist and federalist movements.

The Marshall Plan as a Factor of European Unity in the West

With the announcement of the Marshall Plan on 5 June 1947, followed by the agreement between the European communist parties at a conference hosted from 22 to 27 September 1947 in Szklarska Poręba, a small mountain town in western Poland (Lower Silesia), to create the Communist Information Bureau, the official information agency of the world communist movement, in October 1947 and the 'Prague Coup' of February 1948, it became impossible to unite the great historical Europe.

European Unity in the Cold War

In the east, the Soviet government rejected plans for a Danube federation and a Polish–Czechoslovak confederation. It also rejected any idea of a European Federation, calling Europeanists 'Wall Street Banksters', but was more amenable to the creation of the UN's European regional organisation, the United Nations Economic Commission for Europe (UNECE). Intellectuals, Marxists and fellow travellers of the Parti Communiste Français (French Communist Party, PCF) professed virulent anti-Europeanism, based on the pacifism of the Mouvement Mondial des Partisans de la Paix (World Movement of Supporters of Peace) associated with Jean-Paul Sartre and on the Stockholm Appeal calling for an absolute ban on nuclear weapons (March 1950).[9] A Congress for the Freedom of Culture, founded in West Berlin in 1950, responded in opposition to totalitarianism. World-famous writers participated, including Arthur Koestler, Nicolas Nabokov, Denis de Rougemont, Benedetto Croce and Bertrand Russell. In Paris, the anti-totalitarian journal *Preuves*, among others, quickly rallied French liberal and left-wing Europeanist circles, along with dissident intellectuals from eastern Europe (Czesław Miłosz, Konstanty Jeleński, Mircea Eliade, etc.) and those who had broken away from authoritarian communism (Edgar Morin, Ignazio Silone). They opened the debate on European unity and on the 'kidnapped West' (Milan Kundera) that had become eastern Europe. A debate on European cultural unity was organised by the magazine *Comprendre*, produced by the Société Européenne de la Culture (European Society of Culture), which was founded in Venice in 1950.

9 O. Le Cour Grandmaison, 'Le Mouvement de la paix pendant la guerre froide: Le cas français (1948–1952)', *Revue Communisme* no. 18–19 (1988): 120–38.

The OEEC, Negotiated and Adaptable Unity

After George C. Marshall's speech of 5 June 1947, diplomats shifted the focus from forms of unity to a new Euro-Atlantic axis. European governments were forced to show support for western European unity in order to gain the support of the US Congress. The Three-Power Conference, which brought Great Britain, the USSR and France together in Paris at the end of June 1947 in response to Marshall's offer, placed the creation of a common pan-European organisation on the agenda. Although the Europeanist movements wanted a general, political union, this union would be solely economic. And the break – of the Soviets' own making – with the USSR meant that it would be a Western economic organisation, much to Léon Blum's amazement and dismay. The outcome was the founding of the Organisation for European Economic Co-operation (OEEC) by the Marshall Plan countries.

But what about the Americans? It soon became clear that they wanted a Western European Union that included the Germans. Clayton, who was displeased at the procrastination of the sixteen European Marshall Plan countries, demanded the creation of a European customs union at the very least and reiterated the demands of Congress for the removal of barriers and the creation of a permanent European organisation. In response, the French diplomat Hervé Alphand called for the creation of a customs union, to which only Italy responded favourably. (Alphand (1907–94) was the Director of Economic Affairs of the CFLN and, in 1944, Director General at the Ministère des Affaires Étrangères (Ministry of Foreign Affairs). He was appointed ambassador in Washington in 1950, then Secretary General of the Ministère des Affaires Étrangères (1965–72).) Jean Monnet was well aware that Germany would have to be included in the European Recovery Programme (ERP) prepared by the Europeans.

The false goodwill of the sixteen nations severely indisposed Washington, and fresh Euro-American negotiations took place in Washington in October 1948. According to US Secretary of Commerce Averell Harriman, Vyacheslav Molotov's departure from the Franco-Anglo-Soviet conference in Paris in early July and the Zhdanov Declaration in September had opened 'a new phase in world history'. (Molotov (1890–1986) was the USSR's Foreign Minister from 1939 to 1949. He signed the German–Soviet non-aggression pact and directed the great Stalinist purges. Harriman (1891–1986) was a businessman, US Ambassador to the USSR (1943–6), coordinator of the Marshall Plan and Secretary of Commerce between 1948 and 1953 under President Harry S. Truman. He then became an advisor to President

Eisenhower and Governor of New York State between 1955 and 1958.) The
Cold War had definitely begun. According to the French ambassador to the
United States, Henri Bonnet, the Marshall Plan was intended to serve not
only in the economic reconstruction of Europe, but also in the defence of 'a
certain form of civilisation that we all share'. In the absence of a sixteen-
nation customs union, France, the Benelux countries and Italy signed a small
agreement on multilateral payment clearing. The prominent Labour Party
politician Ernest Bevin raised spirits by announcing a Western Union at the
Brussels Pact negotiations in January 1948, describing a 'kind of Federation' or
'spiritual union' of the West against Russia. (Bevin (1881–1951) was Minister of
Labour and National Service in the coalition government during the Second
World War, then Foreign Secretary in the post-war Labour government
(1945–51).) The British plan was vague but anti-Soviet. The French would
have preferred a customs union with Benelux and Italy, rather than an anti-
Soviet Western Union with Germany. But, in the end, Bevin's Western
Union project took the form of a 'regional economic and political security
pact' *erga omnes*, in the spirit of the United Nations (UN). It became the
Brussels Pact, which was signed by Britain, France and the three Benelux
states on 17 March 1948. Nonetheless, it was impossible for the Brussels Pact
to replace the large operation involving the sixteen Marshall Plan countries,
and the diplomat René Massigli wisely asked whether France's priority was
the sixteen nations or the five. (Massigli (1888–1988) joined de Gaulle in
London in early 1943, becoming Commissaire aux Affaires Étrangères
(Commissioner for Foreign Affairs) in the Comité national français (French
National Committee), CFLN and GPRF (from 3 June 1944 to
10 September 1944), French Ambassador to the United Kingdom and
Secrétaire Général du Ministère des Affaires Étrangères (Secretary General
of the French Ministry of Foreign Affairs) (1955–6). He was opposed to the
Europe of Jean Monnet.) In any case, a sixteen-country solution was
undoubtedly necessary to satisfy the American Congress.

For the European organisation of the Marshall Plan, the French and
Italians envisaged a strong executive which could take initiatives and assume
responsibilities within the general framework of the sixteen countries. But
the British preferred an intergovernmental organisation operating by unanimity. The French wanted a secretary general who would answer to an
executive committee of five or six members, with the economist and politician Robert Marjolin, who had been approached for this role, even speaking
of 'supranationality'. (Marjolin (1911–86) joined Monnet in London in 1943. He
was the Director of External Economic Relations in 1945, and became the first

Secretary General of the OEEC. As a diplomat he was involved in the formation of the European Economic Community (EEC) and in the Euratom Treaties of Rome. In March 1957, he was appointed Vice-President of the EEC Commission.) He had prepared a text predicting the gradual integration of the participants' economies 'into a true European economy', with decisions taken by a majority vote.[10] However, due to the outright refusal of the British, the conference founded the OEEC, led by a Council of Member States deciding unanimously through an executive committee of five members. The Secretariat General was international in nature and derived its authority from the Council. It was headed by Marjolin and based in Paris at the Château de la Muette. Its vertical and horizontal technical committees formed the backbone of the OEEC. The treaty was signed in Paris on 16 April 1948 by sixteen member states, plus the British, French and US Allied occupation zones in Germany.

But what was the federating power of the OEEC beyond that of words? Monnet defined it very bluntly as a system of intergovernmental cooperation, which was congenitally weak, far from being a federation of western Europe. Blum, Aron and Marjolin believed that the OEEC was the birth of a European Federation, but they were completely mistaken. The Americans felt the failure to achieve a western European federation keenly, and raised their demands on the conditions for aid. Thus, in June–July 1948 they punished the sixteen nations by forcing them to sign a particularly demanding bilateral treaty in order to receive aid. The OEEC drew up an initial 1-year ERP, but there was to be no 'economic government of Western Europe'.

But was the OEEC capable of harmonising the reconstruction and development plans of the member countries – a feat which the French had attempted in vain with Britain and the Benelux countries? The Plan à Long Terme (Long-Term Plan) was a very Gallocentric clone of the Plan de Modernisation. Indeed, in a letter to the head of the French government in July 1948, Monnet said: 'cooperation is certainly necessary, but it will come later, building on the national efforts preceding and preparing for it'. The French also felt that the British Long-Term Plan was protectionist and that the British were unwilling to work towards European economic unity. Specifically, they were unwilling to offer the continentals a large sterling area deficit with respect to European countries. The French wanted to buy more from the sterling area than they sold, in order to favour their reconstruction and modernisation. The European Recovery Programme was

---

10 R. Marjolin, *Le travail d'une vie: Mémoires 1911–1986* (Paris, Éditions Robert Laffont, 1986).

supposed to harmonise national long-term plans, but to arbitrate between interests would have required a centralised European organisation, which was not in place since decisions were taken unanimously.

Another solution would have been for the French and the British to reach an agreement to specialise their economies and solve payment problems. The French wanted to grant this power of intervention or regulation to a European Investment Bank (EIB), a sort of equivalent of the International Bank for Reconstruction and Development for Europe. A meeting took place between the French Minister of Finance, Maurice Petsche, and the British Chancellor of the Exchequer, Stafford Cripps, in February 1949. The French suggested economic specialisation, but failed to convince the British, whose doubts persisted and who were clearly reluctant to consider industrial specialisation. According to the Secrétariat Général du Comité Interministériel (Secretariat General of the Interministerial Committee, SGCI) for European Economic Cooperation Issues, the term offended the British, who therefore denied the OEEC the right to harmonise investments, making specialisation impossible. (The SGCI for European Economic Cooperation Issues was created in 1948 as the contact of the European Cooperation Administration (ECA) for administration of the Marshall Plan.) All in all, a European economic and monetary union was equally unattainable, as the sixteen countries failed to put together a long-term plan for the reconstruction of Europe.

The Marshall Plan prompted some ministries to show great fervour for European unity in order to obtain aid. France, like other countries, was virtuous by necessity. But in 1948 the British were primarily to blame for derailing European unity. Their inertia on the customs union and their objections to the concerted organisation of European economies blocked the organic process of union in Europe. The lack of reaction from the United States was, however, surprising. The clue to its behaviour lay in the Soviet counter-model. Despite the clamour of enthusiasm at the Congress of Europe in The Hague in May 1948 and the activism of Europeanist movements, European unity was not an historical imperative in April–May 1948. Thus, inertia took hold.

The Market over Unity? The European Payments Union

The Americans did not give up on trying to obtain economic unity from the sixteen Marshall Plan nations, despite the failure of the OEEC and the Council of Europe. On 31 October 1949, at the OEEC, the ECA's administrator, Paul Hoffman, disparaged the Europeans' weakness and threatened to cut off aid if they failed to increase their cooperation. He called on them to liberalise trade among themselves and to open a general common market. The French felt encouraged to create a 'payments union' with Italy and the Benelux countries – 'the Finebel' – and even to envisage an economic union with a single market, a common currency, a common external tariff and specialisations. The British once again rejected these plans, but the French continued to demand the creation of an EIB at the behest of the governments. The EIB would have had a regulatory role for economies, a remit to coordinate production and manage a common European market for liberalised products. In response, the OEEC limited itself to freeing up 50 per cent of private trade. At the end of 1949, the OEEC was faced with two opposing logics: the concerted organisation of markets associated with the liberalisation of trade under the direction of an EIB, or the liberalisation of trade without a governing institution, but based instead on intergovernmental decisions.

To free up trade, currencies had to be made convertible. Exchange controls prevented trade liberalisation so, to overcome this obstacle, a European Payments Union (EPU) was created at the OEEC in September 1950. An initial payments system based on Marshall Aid in dollars had been invented in 1948 by the Directeur Général des Finances Extérieures (Director General of French External Finance, FINEX), Guillaume Guindey, which operated for a year and was then replaced by the EPU in 1950. (Guindey (1909–89) was a senior civil servant in the Ministry of Finance, Director of FINEX (1946–53).) The system, which originated in America, was intended to make payments within the OEEC automatic and to restore liberalism. The general principle was to partially finance inter-European clearing deficits with credits from the EPU and the Marshall Plan, up to a certain level, and to reimburse the creditor countries with EPU credits or gold. Creditors were rewarded, and debtors were encouraged by the OEEC to balance their accounts. The EPU was very warmly received in the United States, thanks to its multilateral aspect. The agreement was a success for those who believed that international relations could be organised, rather than left to 'automatic market equilibria'. It became impossible to justify inter-European trade quotas because of difficulties with balancing payments, thus ushering in the collapse of protectionism. The creation of the EPU was also a victory for those who could not conceive of Europe without Britain. However, the EPU was clearly not the way in which European unity was expected to be organised, as it was set up provisionally, without the intention of extending it to other areas of European interest. Its remit was neither to serve as a customs union or an organised common market, nor to bring about trade liberalisation or a European political union.

The EPU was an adequate technical agreement which, although not central to the project of unity, did facilitate the liberal unity of European markets. In fact, the British accepted the EPU in order to protect themselves from the continental European construction desired by the Americans and recently invented by the French: the Schuman Plan of 9 May 1950.

The OEEC lost the opportunity to build a European economic union on the heels of the EPU due to continental nationalism, the carefully calculated isolation of Britain and the events in Korea, which undermined inter-European cooperation. The French were unable to make the OEEC the framework for a European economic government.

The Dream of a European Political Assembly

While the search for European economic unity was developing in concrete terms as a result of the Marshall Plan, other avenues were opening up for the inventors of unity. The private Europeanist meeting in The Hague in May 1948 ushered in the period of the European People's Spring.

The Debates

On Friday 7 May 1948, at 2.30 p.m., Winston Churchill and his wife led a solemn procession into the Knights' Hall, the Ridderzaal, which was decorated with flowers and flags marked with a red 'E' on a white background. (The red 'E' was replaced by a green 'E' in September 1948 in Strasbourg at the European Movement Congress.) About 1,000 people were gathered in the hall: 775 delegates from 24 European states, American and Canadian observers, and journalists. They were joined by politicians, clergymen, industrialists, trade unionists, economists, academics, writers, scholars and artists, including the English philosopher Bertrand Russell and the political scientist Raymond Aron. Nobel Prize winners were also present. The French delegation was the largest, with 130 members, including political leaders. There were also a large number of British delegates, despite Labour's defection. The Belgians, Dutch, Italians, Swiss and Danes also had several dozen delegates. The German delegation, led by Konrad Adenauer and Walter Hallstein, was large, yet discreet and of little influence. (Hallstein (1901–82) was a lawyer, academic and diplomat, negotiator of the ECSC and Rome Treaties, and President of the EEC Commission (1957–67).) A few exiled Spanish Republicans and eastern European personalities were seen. This crowd attended the Congress of Europe for 4 days, eagerly awaiting the miracle of unity.

Churchill opened the meeting with a cautious – yet anticlimactic – speech on content and form. Three committees were set up: a political committee chaired by Paul Ramadier, an economic committee chaired by Paul Van Zeeland and a cultural committee chaired by Salvador de Madariaga. A 'Message to the Europeans' was drafted and read out by the great Swiss writer and federalist Denis de Rougemont. But Sandys removed the call for a common defence at the last minute as a result of an extremely heated battle between the Unionists (Churchill, Sandys) and the Federalists (Brugmans), liberals and interventionists.

The Hague Congress essentially recommended reconsidering national sovereignty. It wanted Germany's integration into Europe, the creation of a deliberative European Assembly, the drafting of a Charter of Human Rights and the establishment of a Supreme Court. In the mind of the Congress, the creation of a European Union would be a step towards a world union. However, the British did not want federal institutions, but desired agreements that respected states' sovereignty. The French, for their part, were more federalist. The Congress approved the end of economic nationalism in Europe, but took for granted the privileged links between the metropoles and their colonies. It called for the abolition of inter-European quotas and the free convertibility of currencies. The message centred around a common programme for the development of economic resources and the coordination of policies for full employment. The creation of a European Centre for Culture and a European Children's Institute was discussed. The most ardent enthusiasm was expressed in the aforementioned 'Message to the Europeans', which closed the Congress with a federal, liberal tone.

However, the states were not ready to fulfil the wishes of the participants at the Hague Congress. Three months later, after much reflection, Georges Bidault and the French government proposed the creation of a European Assembly to the Brussels Pact countries (19 July 1948). (Bidault (1899–1983) was a history teacher, a journalist and a resistance fighter who fought alongside Frenay. He became President of the CNR in September 1943 following the arrest of Jean Moulin. He was several times French Minister of Foreign Affairs, in 1946 President of the GPRF and President of the Council (1949–50).) In doing so, Bidault was pandering to the pro-European sentiment of his party, the Christian democratic Mouvement Républicain Populaire (Popular Republican Movement, MRP), and responding to the wishes of the United States. He created the conditions for Germany's integration into Europe. A debate on the powers of the future organisation divided the French and the British. The latter would have been satisfied with a simple five-way consultation on European issues, without an assembly, but the Brussels Pact Five set up an eighteen-person-strong committee to study and develop the European Federation on 25 October 1948. It was composed of five Frenchmen, including Édouard Herriot and Léon Blum, five Britons, including Hugh Dalton, three Belgians, three Dutchmen and two Luxembourgers. (Herriot (1872–1957) was a politician of the Third Republic, several times in government and mayor of Lyon. He was a radical Europeanist, but anti-EDC. Dalton (1887–1962) was Labour's Chancellor of the Exchequer (1945–7) and managed the return to a peacetime economy.) On 19 January 1949, Herriot called for the creation of an assembly, with sovereign powers to be ceded by the states. Ernest Bevin accepted the future institutions under the condition that the assembly was to be purely consultative and the Committee of Ministers was to decide unanimously. The federalists had failed. The European Movement, which brought together various federalist and unionist movements, was simultaneously working on a Charter of Human Rights, a Social Charter and European economic unity.

A European Economic Conference was held in Westminster during 20–25 April 1949. It was convened by the European Movement to refine The Hague's economic proposals and in the end the liberals prevailed, although the notion of European-controlled cartels was accepted. There was a trend towards the coordination of core European industries in four sectors (coal, steel, electricity and transport) through European public institutions and the organisation of agricultural markets. The French and Belgians succeeded in mobilising the Brussels Pact Council to create a European political union: the Council of Europe.

Despite the remarkable work of the pro-European movements and the enthusiasm of the 1948 activists, the European idea – whether federal, unionist or functionalist in nature – had not triumphed, either in the OEEC or in the Council of Europe. The Europeanist movements had held a wide-ranging public debate, the outcome of which did not live up to their expectations. Moreover, not all of the European intelligentsia were in favour of unity. Some elites believed that Europe represented imperialism, colonialism and racism. Sartre, Morin, Frantz Fanon and Aragon even expressed their disgust for Europe. The necessities of time, the Cold War and financial aid held more sway in the debate on Europe than the ideas of the Europeanists. The idea of undermining national sovereignty, which had been very powerful in 1945, had lost ground. According to the historian Alan Milward (1935–2010), the nation-state had saved itself.[11] The original framework of western

11 A. Milward, *The European Rescue of the Nation-State* (London, Routledge, 1992).

European unity, in its institutional forms, was established in a way far removed from the utopias of Europeanist 'fanatics'. The nation-states defended their national interests, while accepting European unity when it reinforced their national recovery projects. The French pursued their own objective, which dictated their position on unity: access to German coal. They wanted the ownership of the Ruhr coal mines to be internationalised and proposed setting up an International Authority for the Ruhr (IAR) to control the use of its coal. However, the Americans, who, whether out of provocation, naïvety or sincerity, were unwilling to support the French project, went so far as to propose a common authority for the entire European steel industry, which, according to the American ambassador to the United Kingdom, Lewis Douglas,[12] would have military control over not only the Ruhr but also 'the industrial activity of France and the Benelux countries'. This came as a harsh shock for the French, who felt they were being punished, and the proposal was withdrawn. The French did not succeed in obtaining international management of the mines, but instead obtained only control over coal distribution. They were thus clearly motivated more by the achievement of vital economic goals than by the prospect of European unity.

The Failure of a Franco-British Europe in the Council of Europe

The French and the British clashed once again in the preparation of the new European organisation, the Council of Europe. Faced with a Labour government which was determined not to cede an ounce of sovereignty, Bidault and Spaak were able only to obtain the creation of a consultative assembly made up of delegates from national parliaments. In the Committee of Ministers, decisions on the fate of the assembly's deliberations were taken unanimously. The Council of Europe was just a 'forum', notes the historian Pierre Gerbet.[13] Ten countries signed the treaty on 5 May 1949 in London: the Brussels Pact Five, along with Ireland, Italy, Denmark, Norway and Sweden. In September 1949, the Consultative Assembly gathered together staunch

---

12 'The Ambassador in the United Kingdom (Douglas) to the Secretary of State', in W. Slany and C. S. Sampson (eds.), *Foreign Relations of the United States, 1948, Germany and Austria*, vol. II (Washington, DC, US Government Printing Office, 1973), p. 98, Delsec 1587, 28 February 1948, 11 a.m., https://history.state.gov/historicaldocuments/frus1948v02/d66; P. Mélandri, *Les États-Unis face à l'unification de l'Europe*, vol. I: *L'Ère des frustrations 1945–mai 1952* (Lille, Atelier des thèses, 1977), pp. 282–3.

13 See G. Bossuat, P. Gerbet and T. Grosbois, *Dictionnaire historique de l'Europe unie* (Brussels, André Versaille, 2009), pp. 445–9.

Europeanists and major political players, including Winston Churchill from Britain, Georges Bidault and Guy Mollet from France, Pieter Kerstens from the Netherlands, Éamon de Valera from Ireland and the Belgian Paul-Henri Spaak, who presided over the Consultative Assembly until his resignation in December 1951. Despite a brilliant first session of the Consultative Assembly and the launch of the OEEC a year and a half earlier, the defence of national interests prevailed. The failure of Franco-British Europe, both in the OEEC and in the Council of Europe, marked the end of a period of innocence for the builders of unity. The OEEC was in disarray, as was the Consultative Assembly, due to the states' refusal to give them a super-sovereignty which could be imposed on each of the states. The objective of unity was replaced by trade liberalisation, which was easier to achieve.

The State of the Union at the End of 1949

Would unity progress further? What conclusions could be drawn in the autumn of 1949? In Italy, Alcide De Gasperi and Carlo Sforza were in favour of integration with the American–English bloc. European unity could only mean the unity of western Europe in America's shadow. In Belgium, the parties rejected neutrality; they oscillated between aligning with the United States (liberals, Paul-Henri Spaak in the Belgian Socialist Party) and seeking the unity of Europe as a whole (Victor Larock). In the Netherlands, the Dutch placed their faith in the UN and open trade, as the Catholic party was very fearful after the Prague Coup of February 1948. It was therefore possible to justify the construction of a western Europe. The British Labour Party was interested only in regional agreements between countries of the same culture. In Ireland, the Republican Seán MacBride, who was Minister for Foreign Affairs of the Republic of Ireland, the founder in 1946 of Clann na Poblachta (a republican party which participated in John Costello's government and disappeared in 1965) and a Europeanist, launched a federalist campaign in the hope of solving the problem of Northern Ireland. In the western occupation zones of Germany, Kurt Schumacher's Sozialdemokratische Partei Deutschlands (SPD) proposed the integration of a unified Germany into a federated Europe on an equal footing, in keeping with its internationalist tradition exemplified by the 1925 Heidelberg Programme, 'For the United States of Europe'. (Schumacher (1895–1952), who was mutilated during the First World War and had been interned by the Nazis, was the SPD's chairman (1945–52) and an opponent of Adenauer.) In the Christlich Demokratische Union, Adenauer advocated a western European federation on the basis of an economic union. The hope of building European unity 'legitimised' the creation of West Germany on 23 May 1949. But should Adenauer, 'Chancellor of the Allies', create Europe prior to Germany's reunification? In 1945, the Danes believed primarily in the UN and attempted to keep an even balance between the Americans and the Soviets until 1947. Sweden sought to create a Nordic Defence Community, while Norway rejected neutrality. In short, the Scandinavian sister countries could not agree on how to build a regional union. In the summer of 1947, the head of Swiss diplomacy, Max Petitpierre, participated in the Paris conference on US aid to Europe, without ruling out the possibility of becoming a member of a European organisation for cooperation or integration. (Petitpierre (1899–1994) represented Switzerland in the OEEC without joining the Marshall Plan. He supported the creation of the European Free Trade Association.)

In the United States, Truman wanted the commercial unification of Europe as a whole, linking the breadbaskets of central Europe with the industrial regions of northwestern Europe. The waterways of central Europe would be internationalised, which Stalin refused outright at Potsdam. Despite Churchill's Iron Curtain speech, in 1946 there was still hope in the United States for Europe-wide unity. However, this did not last beyond the 1947 Marshall Plan conference.

The Schuman Plan – an Enigma

To the amazement of many, the Schuman Plan for a High Authority for Coal and Steel of 9 May 1950 was a success. Robert Schuman, French Minister of Foreign Affairs in the Bidault government, read out the preamble to the plan on Tuesday 9 May 1950 in the Salon de l'Horloge at the Quai d'Orsay (the French Ministry of Foreign Affairs):

> It is no longer a question of vain words but of a bold act, a constructive act. France has acted and the consequences of its action can be immense. We hope they will be. France has acted primarily for peace and to give peace a real chance. For this it is necessary that Europe should exist. Five years, almost to the day, after the unconditional surrender of Germany, France is accomplishing the first decisive act for European construction and is associating Germany with this.[14]

This founding text, which remains highly relevant, ushered in a new period in the history of European unity, at a time when the action of the OEEC and

---

14 'Schuman Declaration May 1950', https://european-union.europa.eu/principles-countries-history/history-eu/1945-59/schuman-declaration-may-1950_en.

the Council of Europe had reached an impasse. The policy of reaching out to Germany and thus creating supranational unity was a surprising success.

Innovation and Heritage

Jean Monnet and his team at the Commissariat Général du Plan (General Planning Commission) had spent several weeks preparing the Schuman Declaration. The French government proposed placing all European coal and steel production under a supranational 'common High Authority', which would be the cornerstone of a European Federation essential for the preservation of peace. It was unexpected, to say the least.

But in what way was the Schuman Plan so surprising and different from its predecessors? About ten projects for European cooperation in the field of coal and steel had been presented since 1945 and there had been talk of 'inter-European companies', so cooperation was far from a conceptual revelation. The surprise was twofold. First, it created a supranational, federal authority, whereas the policy of French governments had until that point been built on intergovernmental cooperation. The second surprise came in the form of the unequivocal offer to build a common steel industry with Germany.

The supranational High Authority solution stemmed from the resurgence of the constraints of the time. Despite the creation of the IRA, access to German coal was not secure. (The London Agreements of 28 April 1949, signed by Great Britain, the Benelux countries, France and the United States, created the IAR in charge of coordinating Ruhr production activities with the decisions of the OEEC. It was responsible for allocating Ruhr products between German consumption and export, and for combating any discrimination in the transport and pricing of Ruhr products. It was dissolved on 27 May 1952.) The US Congress was impatient, fearing a German–Soviet entente: war loomed. The Western Conference, scheduled in London for 10 May 1950, was going to allow the immediate rearmament of Germany. Robert Schuman's success in this project was ultimately the fruit of his personal commitment, to a greater extent than his condition as a German citizen. The new idea for a supranational High Authority signalled the restoration of equal rights between France and Germany, providing the main surprise of 9 May and immediately restoring France's prestige. The Schuman Plan was an act against the Cold War, conceived by Monnet as a condition for German reunification and marking the beginning of a new organisation of Europe and international relations. This Franco-German entente, regulated by a supranational organisation, guaranteed France's security.

The Schuman–Monnet offer nevertheless had its limits. Although it was addressed to all Europeans, it was accepted by only six countries, and was formally rejected by Britain. It risked weakening the intergovernmental cooperation policy in the OEEC and threatened to put an end to the possibility of an EIB. The Schuman offer also seriously disturbed some government departments and certain ministers in France. Thus, a political battle took hold between those who wanted to continue intergovernmental cooperation in the OEEC and those who considered the organisation outdated. Guy Mollet, a socialist and French representative to the Council of Europe, was surprised by the special appeal to Germany; he regretted Britain's refusal. Yet, federalism appealed to him, and he persuaded Jean Monnet to create an assembly to accompany the new ECSC. But Monnet refused to allow an organic relationship to develop between the Schuman Plan and the Consultative Assembly of the Council of Europe. Many political players wanted a larger Europe and so did not unconditionally support the Schuman Plan, although Paul Reynaud was highly enthusiastic about it. The new French government, led by René Pleven (from 12 July 1950 until February 1951) found itself in an awkward position, and claimed that the creation of the EPU in the OEEC, the European transport unification project prepared by the UNECE in Geneva and the Schuman Plan were all in line with the Council of Europe. Historians have demonstrated that those supporting this claim were fundamentally mistaken. But Guy Mollet, a socialist attached to the Council of Europe, had to be kept on to ensure the smooth negotiation of the ECSC Treaty.

The scene was set for a four-speed Europe, comprising the OEEC, sectoral supranational organisations (the Schuman Plan, ECSC and Green Pool, and soon after the EDC and EPA), the Council of Europe, and the UN Commission for Europe in Geneva. Each of these organisations represented an incomplete form of European unity.

The Scope of the Schuman Plan

But would the Schuman Plan spell the dawn of a United States of Europe? According to Pierre Uri, a member of the Schuman Plan's Monnet team, the ECSC option was determined 'by political and economic necessity'. Europe needed peace and French industry needed coal. The negotiation of the ECSC Treaty, between June 1950 and March 1951, was not an idyllic path towards a European federation. In fact, the Schuman Plan even represented a short-term failure for the federation of Europe. Why did it fail? Because France refused to accept shared sovereignty affecting very symbolic aspects of people's lives and because the United States of Europe did not include Britain or central and eastern Europe. Consequently, the ECSC was not a definitive model of European unity. The technocrat Monnet was obliged by Guy Mollet to reduce the powers of the High Authority. The ECSC, alongside the Council of Europe and the OEEC, thus became a heretical structure and the democrats protested against the dictatorship of the experts. Schuman, who refused to 'allow the essence of the independent authority to be distorted', decided to continue without Britain. It was a daring, almost unthinkable choice.

In economic terms, Germany won in the long run because the Schuman Plan freed up German industrial forces. In 1950, France was producing 32 per cent of the steel in the ECSC, but by 1955 it was producing only 24 per cent. Germany peacefully regained equal economic rights, despite its defeat. French policy in the Saarland was dismantled, as the Saar's collieries came under the jurisdiction of the High Authority. The Schuman Plan posed an enormous challenge to the generalist, political conception of the Consultative Assembly of the Council of Europe, since unity seemed to be being advanced through sectoral unions. But was it the ideal model of unity? Despite its success, the Schuman Plan did not have an immediate impact. French Minister of Agriculture Pierre Pflimlin's Green Pool plan foundered in the OEEC. Some of America's reactions proved that the United States was wary of any European integration that reinforced commercial or monetary specificities. Thus, the Schuman Plan was not an easy phase in the long march towards European integration, as some authors claim – whether knowingly or not. It was not even an expression of French politicians' dominant thinking on unity. Of course, no one debated the merits of European unity, but the battle raged on over its nature: should it be a European economic union, negotiated with difficulty in the OEEC, or a specialised, supranational European union comprising a small number of countries?

In terms of international power relations, the Schuman Plan could be considered the dawn of lasting peace, as it established Franco-German equality. However, questions remained over the much-celebrated reconciliation. Coinciding with attempts to restrain Germany through the Schuman Plan, France continued to seek a special place within the North Atlantic Treaty Organization (NATO). The Schuman Plan and the EPU saved the Marshall Plan. The armistice promised peace, and was accepted more for the sake of Franco-German cooperation than for its supranational institutions. The Schuman Plan came too late for a Europe that in 1948 refused a binding organisational formula for European economies. The founders' mistake was to make people believe that 'the dawn of the United States of Europe' had arrived for the people of Europe.[15] While the Schuman Plan was fortuitous in France's European policy, it was very much in the spirit of the economic contractualisation that marked France's objectives in the OEEC. It demonstrated that there were several approaches to contractualisation, involving cooperation and federation.

The Return to the Nation State?

The success of the Schuman Plan led Schuman and Monnet to use the ECSC formula to attempt other forms of unity, including the EDC and the EPA or EPC project.[16]

Monnet and the Council President, Pleven, invented the European army to prevent the unilateral rearmament of Germany. Given the international context of the Korean War, it was expected that the United States would press for West Germany's rearmament. In contrast to the Schuman Plan, this project was carried out in an atmosphere of urgency and fear. The term 'European army' had already been used by Churchill, de Gaulle and the Council of Europe. The Pleven government was Atlanticist and opposed to German rearmament. On 3 September 1950, Monnet handed Pleven an impressive note suggesting that he should launch 'general political action that would orient public opinion and national forces towards the construction of a community of free peoples, the organisation of defence and peace'. Unlike everyone else, Monnet did not envisage German rearmament outside French control, instead believing it was possible to organise the free world with the United States, the British Empire and 'continental western Europe federated around an expanded Schuman Plan'. The idea of a European army was thus a component of Euro-Atlantic diplomatic machinery.

Monnet prepared a plan for Schuman, who was leaving for the Atlantic Conference in New York on 9 September 1950, outlining a federal organisation for the rearmament of western Europe, in which Germany would participate. But in New York, Schuman told the Atlantic Council on 15 September that Germany was convalescing but not yet cured, and that a German army was undesirable in the short term. Dean Acheson, however, was calling for German participation in an Atlantic army.

---

15 J. Van Helmont, *Options européennes 1945–1985* (Luxembourg, Office des Publications officielles des Communautés européennes, 1986).
16 G. Bossuat and A. Wilkens, *Jean Monnet, l'Europe et les chemins de la paix* (Paris, Publications de la Sorbonne, 1999).

Pleven continued to be troubled by the demand for German rearmament due to the burden of Indochina. Before 'integrating German military units into an army for the defence of Europe', he said, it was first necessary to create a Europe. On 20 September, the Council of Ministers opposed the revival of a German army and declared itself in favour of West Germany's participation in the collective security effort. Monnet, for his part, insisted on French leadership in Europe, outlining a large European union which merged markets and production and organised its defence with the integration of German resources. Monnet went beyond the scope of a European army to address the issue of total federal unity under French leadership. He came up with the notion of a 'High Authority of the European army' or a 'Single Supranational Authority'. The fierce Franco-American clashes on German rearmament, which took place in New York with both Schuman and the French Minister of Defence, Jules Moch, pushed Pleven into action. Resistance to German rearmament remained strong, while the Americans threatened to negotiate directly with the German generals. To counter the revival of a German army, Monnet called for the construction of an enlarged EDC with a political vocation, capable of federating western Europe to make it one of the strongholds of the West, while at the same time controlling the threat posed by Germany.

Nonetheless, René Pleven launched the European army project on 24 October 1950 in the National Assembly. The introduction to his declaration was taken from a note written by Monnet on 21 October. The French government 'proposed the creation of a European army for common defence, attached to the political institutions of a united Europe'. This European army project was indeed born of circumstance, being the result of the Korean War and widespread Western panic. Monnet accepted German rearmament, but invented a political structure to control Germany, which would have had to be set up prior to the creation of a European army. The project was therefore no longer a functionalist union, and its reception by the Atlantic world was cold. At the Atlantic Council, Pleven gave reassurances that the French government wanted a unified Atlantic force which would include the European army. The appointment of Eisenhower as Supreme Commander of the Supreme Headquarters Allied Powers Europe eased tensions, following repeated interventions by Monnet in July 1951. The success of the ECSC negotiations made a new European community possible.

The Atlantic Council of 18 December 1950 agreed to the creation of German combat units, either in a European army or in an integrated

Atlantic army. Two conferences were opened: the Petersberg Conference on German rearmament in Bonn, with the participation of West Germany, the United Kingdom, France and the United States; and the Paris Conference on the European army. Robert Schuman opened the Paris conference on 15 February 1951. Five countries took part: France, West Germany, Belgium, Italy and Luxembourg. American, Canadian, British, Danish, Dutch, Norwegian and Portuguese observers were present. In the preamble of the memorandum for the opening session of the Paris Conference, the French Minister of Defence and negotiator, Jules Moch, warned that a European army should not be expected in the near future, since it was an 'unattainable ideal'.[17] Although he correctly highlighted the difficulty of the task at hand, his choice of words was unfortunate – the negotiations, which had barely taken shape, were already in crisis. France's desire for European unity was non-existent in comparison with its desire to control Germany. The stakes were raised by the Germans, who appeared to be indispensable. The Paris Conference resulted in a draft European army comprising 43 divisions, each of 12,000 men, including 12 German divisions. The draft EDC treaty of February 1952 established the principle of merging armed forces under supranational institutions, a common budget and the standard-isation of weapons. States that were militarily engaged abroad would retain national forces for their overseas territories or sovereignty missions in Berlin, Austria and Korea. The use of the European army would depend on NATO. In a thirty-seven-page report, Alphand reiterated that the EDC offered France security guarantees, since Germany, which was locked into the ECSC, would also be locked into the EDC. On 26 May 1952 in Bonn, France, Britain and the United States signed contractual agreements with West Germany that ended the occupation of West Germany. On 27 May 1952 in Paris, the six participating countries signed the treaty creating the EDC. Its ratification was none-theless delicate, as few guarantees were given by Britain and the United States.

The debate in France developed into sharp criticism of Britain's non-participation and the limited geographical extent of the Community. According to Michel Debré, it posed a threat to French unity, while others, such as Herriot, Édouard Daladier, de Gaulle, Reynaud and Alphonse Juin, thought they could discern a revival of German arrogance. (Debré (1912–96) was a jurist, resistance fighter, senator of Indre-et-Loire, prime minister

17 Archives nationales 560 AP 45, 'Mémorandum au sujet des aspects militaires de l'organisation de l'armée européenne, Paris le 7 février 1951', n° 93 EMCFA-11.

under General de Gaulle (1958–62), Minister of Economy and Finance, Foreign Affairs and National Defence, senator of Réunion Island, mayor of Amboise.) The French obtained additional, interpretative Protocols on 24 March 1953. Although 45 per cent of those polled were in favour of a European army including Germans in 1952 (compared with 26 per cent against), the feeling that Germany posed a threat persisted, with 56 per cent of those polled believing that German rearmament was risky.

At the initiative of De Gasperi, Article 38 of the EDC Treaty provided for the creation of a federal European political authority, which was approved by the French. Reservations were expressed about delegating sovereignty. On 13 September 1952, the Six decided to have an Ad Hoc Assembly, composed of members of the ECSC Common Assembly, study a project for general European unity. Monnet encouraged the drafting of a constitution for Europe but, as expected, the British opposed this, proposing instead the Eden Plan, which would allow the existing specialised authorities to be headed by the Council of Europe, doing away with supranationality.

The Ad Hoc Assembly set to work with zeal, notwithstanding the hostile reactions of several of its members, including the nationalist Gaullist Michel Debré. The initial conclusions led to the idea that the EPC, as it was now called, would take over the remit of the ECSC and the EDC. Maximalist logic triumphed, with the EPC receiving 'practically unlimited' foreign and financial policy powers. The constituents were gripped by hysteria. Telegrams from the French ambassador in Rome, Jacques Fouques-Duparc, warned of an EPC that would see France deprived of its role in the world after seceding overseas territories, left with zero power in NATO and inundated with German products – in short, a nightmare.

For Monnet, the EPC represented the achievement of his plans, to a greater extent than the Schuman Plan or the Pleven Plan. It was to be the real European federal political union, capable of building new sectoral unions. Monnet rejected any subordination of the EPC's executive to the states. The European one-upmanship was accentuated at the end of 1952 when the Dutch Foreign Minister, Johan Willem Beyen, together with Joseph Luns, launched a project for a common market. The EPC would have been responsible for the EDC, the ECSC, a common market and the foreign policy of the member states.

In January 1953, the new French Minister of Foreign Affairs, Georges Bidault, began negotiations on the EPC. But French government departments sounded the alarm, in the name of eternal France. According to the French Foreign Ministry's legal advisor, Professor André Gros: 'If the notion of the extension of powers were adopted, one wonders whether, at a later date, historians would not be amazed at how France itself raised the problem of its own succession.' (Gros (1908–2004) was a legal advisor of the French Ministry of Foreign Affairs, an advisor to the French National Committee in London in 1943, participated in the organisation of the Nuremberg Tribunal and was a judge at the International Court of Justice.) Michel Debré imagined Jean Monnet appointing 'European residents in Morocco or European governors-general in Madagascar.'[18] The anti-federalist resistance of certain government departments and personalities found its arguments in the United States' objections to French policy in NATO and in France's overseas territories.

The Limit of French Openness to Europe: The Vote of 30 August 1954

The new Mayer government (January–May 1953) wanted the EDC to be ratified so as to avoid any direct Franco-German confrontation. The policy of European integration was seen as a must for security. Unlike the Schuman Plan, the EDC and the EPC had only immediate disadvantages for France. The Constitutional Committee of the Ad Hoc Assembly unveiled the draft Constitution of the EPC in February 1953. Article 68, which was strongly disputed in France, stipulated that 'The European Executive Council shall negotiate and conclude treaties or international agreements on behalf of the Community,'[19] meaning that French foreign policy would no longer be independent. The draft created federal institutions. Bidault emphatically saluted the 'adventurers', adding: 'Germany, Belgium, Holland, Italy, Luxembourg, or France is my motherland, but Europe is my destiny!' Yet Bidault did not really support the EPC's draft constitution, as it would leave national sovereignty too greatly diminished. With regard to Monnet and Alphand, French President Vincent Auriol confided to Massigli: 'This is the reign of the technocrats.' French military society was split on the issue of the EDC. The Joseph Laniel government disavowed the anti-EDC position of Marshal Juin. On the other hand, the Chief of Staff of the French Armed Forces, General Ely, associated the EDC with strengthening Europe against the Eastern bloc.

Worried by the seriousness of the issues at stake and disturbed by the dispute over the EDC, Bidault concluded that it was necessary to create the

18 Archives nationales, 363 AP 23, 'M. Debré, Conseil de la République, 22 janvier 1953 à R. Mayer'.
19 SGCI, F 60 classement provisoire, carton 4, boîte 10, 'Projet de pacte pour une Union d'États européens, présenté par M. Debré, janvier 1953 à l'Assemblée Ad Hoc'.

EPC, to make a European union without dismantling the French Union.[20] France, which was weaker in 1953 than it had been in 1950, no longer controlled the process of unity. Reactions to the two major projects of the EDC and the EPC led to the 'French EDC crisis', which was resolved by the negative vote of French deputies on 30 August 1954. The debate on European unity had escaped from the secrecy of institutional corridors and spread throughout society at large. But Monnet had lost his fight for a united, supranational Europe long before the August 1954 vote, upon Bidault's implicit rejection of the EPC in February 1953. The EDC was officially scrapped in the National Assembly on 30 August 1954, under the government of Pierre Mendès France. A preliminary motion for the adjournment of the debate, launched by *cédistes* (advocates of the EDC), was opposed by anti-*cédistes* (opponents of the EDC), whose victory put an end to the ratification of the EDC Treaty. The anti-EDC motion won by 319 votes to 264, finally putting an end to the EDC.

When did the French government abandon the policy for a 'federal' Europe, which it had inaugurated on 9 May 1950? According to all the evidence, even on 9 May 1950, the French government and political elites were against the idea of sharing the country's sovereignty. The steps towards a federation were contrived for reasons of circumstance or political expediency. The failure of the EPC and the EDC demonstrated Monnet's loss of influence over the French state apparatus, following Schuman's departure from the Quai d'Orsay in January 1953. But the rejection of the EPC and the EDC essentially stemmed from France's inability to control unity for its own benefit. France was still afraid of Germany and, having been weakened by its failures in the OEEC, decolonisation in Indochina and in the north African protectorates, it was unable to invent new forms of relations with its neighbours. It retreated into a fantasy world and clung to its ambition to be recognised as the third major power in the Western world. France became delusional about its global power and its European federal consciousness.

For the Europeanists, working with young minds remained a militant objective which took the form of the Mouvement Européen's Campagne Européenne de la Jeunesse (European Youth Campaign), between 1951 and 1958. This initiative was intended to inform and train the youth of Council of Europe countries on the construction of European unity. Paul-Henri Spaak

---

20 Speech by Georges Bidault, 9 March 1953, www.epgencms.europarl.europa.eu/cmsd ata/upload/cf20f90d-3d50-4efe-bda1-a21a4b171fc3/10068952_Speech_Bidault_EN.PDF.

was Chair of the Steering Committee, and Jean-Charles Moreau and Philippe Deshormes were General Secretaries for Youth.

Major endeavours were pursued in western Europe between 1945 and 1954, some of which were successful: the OEEC, the Council of Europe, the EPU, the Schuman Plan, the EDC (failed) and the EPC (failed). A small federal Europe was rejected as a method of building European unity. The Schuman Plan – through which Europeanists hoped to extend the union to other functional areas of public life – was not a model for unity. Although the Common Market and Euratom emerged from it in 1957, there was no supranational European High Authority in the Treaties of Rome, nor has there been since. The overriding objective of French governments of the Fourth Republic, namely to maintain France's position as a great power, seriously hampered their attempts to construct a federal Europe from 1953 to 1954. For those who were not in favour of an EDC or an EPC, René Mayer had this message: 'But I ask you, if France is not yet strong enough for European politics, is it strong enough for the politics of isolation?' (19 November 1953).[21] The goal of the British, who thwarted European federal unity, was to reclaim their global power. In both countries, the representation of power by the elites and the awareness of their nation's role in world history seriously impeded the construction of an innovative, federal European political community.

Recommended Reading

Bossuat, G., P. Gerbet and T. Grosbois. *Dictionnaire historique de l'Europe unie* (Brussels, André Versaille, 2009).

Bossuat, G. and A. Wilkens. *Jean Monnet, l'Europe et les chemins de la paix* (Paris, Publications de la Sorbonne, 1999).

Marjolin, R. *Le travail d'une vie: Mémoires 1911–1986* (Paris, Éditions Robert Laffont, 1986).

Milward, A. *The European Rescue of the Nation-State* (London, Routledge, 1992).

Saurugger, S. *Théories et concepts de l'intégration européenne* (Paris, Presses de Sciences Po, 2010).

---

21 See G. Bossuat, 'Conversion à l'Europe et contraintes (OECE, plan Schuman, CED)', in G. Bossuat, *La France et la Construction de l'unité européenne: De 1919 à nos jours* (Paris, Armand Colin, 2012), pp. 79–108.

2

From Messina and Rome to the Single European Act

MICHAEL GEHLER

Introduction

This chapter presents the relevant integration policy decisions from the European Coal and Steel Community (ECSC) Conference in Messina (1955) to the Single European Act (SEA) (1987). It will trace the genesis of the Rome Treaties (1955–7), the foundation of the European Free Trade Association (EFTA) (1958–60), de Gaulle's policies (1958–65), the development from the Merger Treaty to the Hague Summit (1965–9), the Common Agricultural Policy (CAP) and the 'northern enlargement' (1973). The question of whether the 1970s were times of 'Eurosclerosis' is answered. The path to 'southern enlargement', the settlement of the British budget dispute and the departure for reforms follow as further topics, whereby the Exchange Rate Mechanism (ERM) and the European Monetary System (EMS) as well as the SEA are dealt with.[1]

This chapter identifies the resistances built up against integration, attempts to overcome it and corresponding political compromises. It will discuss relevant actors, together with their motives and positions regarding integration policy. It will also reflect the international background and wider global contexts (the Cold War as an ideological and regulatory systemic competition, the process of political détente, the economic slowdown in the second half of the 1960s, the oil-price shocks and the recession of the 1970s, the internationalisation of politics and the globalisation of the world economy since the 1980s and forms of a new Cold War during 1980–5). It will concretise the question of intergovernmental and supranational dimensions of methods and procedures as well as effects and consequences of integration policy and also offer a periodisation of Europe's integration from 1955 to 1987.

1 For a good overview, see G. Bossuat, 'L'avenir de l'unité européenne et les experiences communautaires 1957–1987', in G. Grin, F. Nicod and B. Altermatt (eds.), Formes d'Europe: Union européenne et autres organisations (Paris, Éditions Economica, 2018), pp. 17–47.

For that period, the archive-based state of research can be described as very good. The Historians' Liaison Group at the Commission has published numerous anthologies for the entire period,[2] and there is also a wealth of specialised literature in various journals on the most diverse facets of Europe's unification.

The Fast Track to the Treaties of Rome as the Communities' 'Basic Law' (1955–1957)

Following the political failure of the European Defence Community (EDC) on 30 August 1954, the ECSC[3] foreign ministers decided in Messina on 2 June 1955 to make a fresh effort 'to build Europe first in the economic sphere' and to instruct a committee chaired by the Belgian socialist Paul-Henri Spaak to report 'on the possibilities of a general economic union and a union in the field of nuclear energy'. As chairman of the Brussels Intergovernmental Conference (IGC), which opened on 26 June 1955 and began its work only in autumn, Spaak coordinated various committees and subcommittees that prepared specific parts of the definitive proposal. France and the Federal Republic of Germany (FRG) were the main actors, but the role played by the Benelux countries should not be neglected, and neither should Italy with its own claims. Whereas Paris wanted to push ahead with the nuclear community (as preferred by Jean Monnet[4]), Bonn was more in favour of a 'common market' (as preferred by Konrad Adenauer[5]), although

---

2 K. Schwabe (ed.), *Die Anfänge des Schuman-Plans 1950/51: Beiträge des Kolloquiums in Aachen, 28.–30. Mai 1986* (Baden-Baden, Nomos, 1988); E. Serra (ed.), *Il rilancio dell'Europa e i Trattati di Roma/La relance européenne et les Traités de Rome/The Relaunching of Europe and the Treaties of Rome, Actes du colloque de Rome 25–28 mars 1987* (Brussels, Milan, Paris and Baden-Baden, Bruylant and Nomos, 1989); A. Deighton and A. S. Milward (eds.), *Widening, Deepening and Acceleration: The European Economic Community 1957–1963* (Baden-Baden and Brussels, Nomos and Bruylant, 1999); W. Loth (ed.), *Crises and Compromises: The European Project 1963–69* (Baden-Baden, Nomos, 2001); J. van der Harst (ed.), *Beyond the Customs Union: The European Community's Quest for Deepening, Widening and Completion, 1969–1975* (Brussels, Paris and Baden-Baden, Bruylant and Nomos, 2007); J. Laursen (ed.), *The Institutions and Dynamics of the European Community, 1973–83* (Baden-Baden, Nomos, 2014); M. Gehler and W. Loth (eds.), *Reshaping Europe: Towards a Political, Economic and Monetary Union, 1984–1989* (Baden-Baden, Nomos, 2020).
3 J. Gillingham, *Coal, Steel, and the Rebirth of Europe, 1945–1955* (Cambridge, Cambridge University Press, 1991).
4 K. Schwabe, *Jean Monnet: Frankreich, die Deutschen und die Einigung Europas* (Baden-Baden, Nomos, 2016), pp. 325–44.
5 H. J. Küsters, *Die Gründung der Europäischen Wirtschaftsgemeinschaft* (Baden-Baden, Nomos, 1983), pp. 79–88, related to Adenauer: 39–42, 225–7, 319–25, 422–4; H. J. Küsters, 'The Origins of the EEC Treaty', in Serra (ed.), *Il Rilancio dell'Europa*, pp. 211–38.

this view was not without controversy internally (being opposed by Minister of Economic Affairs Ludwig Erhard[6]). It was finally possible for Spaak to link the two concerns of sectoral integration (atomic energy) and broader economic integration (the 'common market') in separate organisations with separate treaties. On 19 May 1956 in Venice, the ECSC Foreign Ministers approved the 'Spaak Report' with the decision to open IGC negotiations. These led to the establishment of the European Economic Community (EEC) and the Atomic Energy Community (Euratom)[7] aiming at horizontal integration, which was expressed in the Treaties of Rome, which were signed on 25 March 1957 and came into force on 1 January 1958.[8] The EEC Treaty has been amended several times, most notably by the SEA (1987), the Treaty of Maastricht (1992) and the Treaty of Amsterdam (1997). Its preamble, unlike the ECSC Treaty, expressed the intention to 'lay the foundations of a closer union among the peoples of Europe'. The EEC Treaty provided for the free movement of goods, persons, services and capital, as well as a customs union and common external tariffs and various Community policies in the fields of agriculture and transport. The EEC's institutional structure was modelled on the ECSC, but had a stronger Council of Ministers and a weaker Commission in comparison with the High Authority. The idea of supranationality was already on the defensive after the failure of the EDC in 1954. The Common Assembly was to be the future European Parliament (EP)[9] jointly for the

6 U. Lappenküper, '"Europa aus der Lethargie herausreißen": Ludwig Erhards Europapolitik 1949–1966', in M. König and M. Schulz (eds.), *Die Bundesrepublik Deutschland und die europäische Einigung 1949–2000: Politische Akteure, gesellschaftliche Kräfte und internationale Erfahrungen. Festschrift für Wolf D. Gruner zum 60. Geburtstag* (Stuttgart, Franz Steiner, 2004), pp. 105–27.

7 P. Weilemann, *Die Anfänge der Europäischen Atomgemeinschaft: Zur Gründungsgeschichte von Euratom 1955–1957* (Baden-Baden, Nomos, 1982).

8 L. Herbst, W. Bührer and H. Sowade (eds.), *Vom Marshallplan zur EWG: Die Eingliederung der Bundesrepublik Deutschland in die westliche Welt* (Munich, Oldenbourg, 1990); E. Bussière, M. Dumoulin, S. Schirmann et al., *L'expérience européenne: 50 ans de construction de l'Europe 1957–2007/Experiencing Europe: 50 Years of European Construction* (Brussels, Communauté européenne, 2006), CD ROM; M. Grazia Melchionni and R. Ducci, *La genèse des traités de Rome: Entretiens inédits avec 18 acteurs et témoins de la négociation* (Paris, Éditions Economica, 2007); M. Gehler (ed. in collaboration with A. Pudlat), *Vom gemeinsamen Markt zur europäischen Unionsbildung: 50 Jahre Römische Verträge 1957–2007/From Common Market to European Union Building: 50 Years of the Rome Treaties 1957–2007* (Vienna, Cologne and Weimar, Böhlau, 2009); M. Gehler, *Europa: Ideen – Institutionen – Vereinigung – Zusammenhalt*, expanded new ed. (Reinbek, Lau, 2018), pp. 242–64, 270–80; W. Loth, '60 Years Ago: The Foundation of EEC and EAEC as Crisis Management', *Journal of European Integration History* 23, no. 1 (2017): 9–28; M. Gehler, *The Signing of the Rome Treaties 65 Years Ago: Origins, Provisions and Effects* (Bonn, ZEI, 2022), pp. 38–41.

9 S. Guerrieri, *Un Parlamento oltre le nazioni: L'Assemblea Comune della CECA e le sfide dell'integrazione europea (1952–1958)* (Bologna, Il Mulino, 2016), pp. 55–92.

EEC, ECSC and Euratom. The ratification of the treaties in Paris had become questionable after the fall of the Guy Mollet government in France in May 1957. Jean Monnet's 'Action Committee for the United States of Europe' helped to overcome the obstacles through its network. It pushed for early ratification in the German Bundestag by succeeding in winning over trade unions and the Sozialdemokratische Partei Deutschlands (SPD), which had previously been opposed both to the ECSC and to the EDC. With the green light from Bonn, Monnet concentrated his lobby work on the Assemblée Nationale, where the treaty received a respectable majority on 9 July 1957.[10]

The common market project was controversial in France, with its tradition of protectionism and subsidisation. Concessions on guaranteed support for French overseas territories (the Lomé Convention) and the inclusion of agriculture led to approval. The broad outlines of the CAP were laid down shortly after the EEC Treaty came into force at the conference in Stresa in July 1958, which provided, inter alia, for a common agricultural price system and higher productivity. The Commission then drew up proposals for a common organisation of the agricultural market. At the end of the first phase of the transitional period, the Council of Ministers adopted a 'package of measures' in January 1962 that was based on a compromise on the prices of cereals, one of the most important Community goods.[11]

Along with the CAP, competition policy was one of the important policy areas of the EEC, where initial progress was achieved, thanks in part to Commissioner Hans von der Groeben. Regulation 17/62 successfully established a European anti-trust law, whereas the legislation for a 'Societas Europaea', with which the legal form for a company law was connected, failed.[12]

The European Investment Bank (EIB) was developed during the negotiation of the Treaties of Rome. Its purpose was to provide capital for structurally weak regions in the member states and to support weaker sectors of the economy. Despite consensus on its objective, controversial debates started about the structure and function of the EIB due to differences among the economies. The need for the EIB to raise money on international financial markets forced the governments of the member states to grant the

10 F. Duchêne, *Jean Monnet: The First Statesman of Interdependence* (New York, NY, Norton, 1994); Schwabe, *Jean Monnet*, pp. 293–344.
11 G. Thiemeyer, *Vom 'Pool Vert' zur Europäischen Wirtschaftsgemeinschaft: Europäische Integration, Kalter Krieg und die Anfänge der Gemeinsamen Europäischen Agrarpolitik 1950–1957* (Munich, Oldenbourg, 1999).
12 S. Hambloch, 'EEC Competition Policy in the Early Phase of European Integration', *Journal of European Integration History* 17, no. 2 (2011): 237–52.

credit institution also its own funds and its own statute as a legal entity and to introduce the principle of majority voting. The EIB thus became a recognised partner of the international financial community as a supranational EEC institution.[13]

EFTA as the EEC's Stepsister and Charles de Gaulle's Ambivalent Veto Policy (1958–1965)

During the Messina Conference, the United Kingdom (UK) had proposed a large intergovernmental free trade area (FTA) within the Organisation for European Economic Co-operation instead of a 'protectionist' common market, in order to enjoy the benefits of free trade without a common agricultural policy and external tariffs. However, the negotiations, which had been going on since the second half of 1956, were halted by French President Charles de Gaulle in November 1958. In a real sense, the general saved the EEC.[14]

As a further result of the predictable FTA defeat, the UK initiated EFTA.[15] It was the result of an initiative by a group of Whitehall officials in the spring of 1958, the core of which was the so-called Uniscan group, made up of industrialists and Scandinavians, to form a small FTA as an alternative to the EEC for lack of anything better.[16] The Stockholm Convention was initialled on 20 November 1959, creating a second economic area in western Europe, encompassing Denmark, the UK, Norway, Austria, Portugal, Sweden and Switzerland (Finland was associated), which entered into force on 3 May 1960 after being signed on 4 January. With a small secretariat in Geneva and occasional ministerial meetings to at least promote free trade between its member states, EFTA *faute de mieux* was only a substitute for the exclusive EEC, which neutral and other states could not or did not want to join.[17]

13 L. Coppolaro, 'Setting Up the Financing Institution of the European Economic Community: The Creation of the European Investment Bank (1955–1957)', *Journal of European Integration History* 15, no. 2 (2009): 87–104.

14 L. Warlouzet, 'De Gaulle as a Father of Europe: The Unpredictability of the FTA's Failure and the EEC's Success (1956–1958)', *Contemporary European History* 20, no. 4 (2011): 419–34.

15 M. Gehler, 'Das Scheitern der Großen Freihandelszone 1958 und die Gründung der EFTA 1959/60', in M. Gehler (ed.), *Vom gemeinsamen Markt zur europäischen Unionsbildung*, pp. 243–82.

16 R. Maurhofer, 'Revisiting the Creation of EFTA: The British and the Swiss Case', *Journal of European Integration History* 7, no. 2 (2001): 65–82; R. T. Griffiths, 'The Origins of EFTA', in K. Byrn and G. Einarsson (eds.), *EFTA 1960–2010: Elements of 50 Years of European History* (Reykjavík, University of Iceland Press, 2010), pp. 43–60.

17 L. Rye, 'The European Free Trade Association. Formation, Completion and Expansion', in Grin et al. (eds.), *Formes d'Europe*, pp. 341–61.

Following the French rejection of the British proposal for a large FTA in 1958, EFTA was an intergovernmental organisation, retaining the various national external tariffs and the sovereignty of the member states, whereas the EEC states were striving for an 'ever closer political union of the peoples of Europe'.[18] Already in the late 1950s, British Prime Minister Harold Macmillan started to realise that only EEC membership would provide a chance to avert the dwindling of Britain's political influence and economic position in the world. The great supporter of EFTA was suddenly the first to want to leave it, and in 1961 applied for EEC membership, quickly followed by Denmark and Ireland, which were dependent on Britain for their foreign trade.[19]

However, de Gaulle vetoed Britain's entry negotiations into the EEC on 14 January 1963, after negotiations on a trilateral nuclear force with the Anglo-Americans had previously failed due to British resistance.[20] This was shortly followed by the conclusion of the Franco-German Elysée Treaty on 22 January 1963, which amounted to an exclusive bilateral partnership and irritated the other EEC members. Therefore, at the insistence of the majority of the government in the Bundestag, a new preamble had to be inserted into the treaty in May 1963, which reaffirmed Germany's primary commitment to existing alliance obligations and subordinated the Franco-German entente to Germany's multilateral obligations in the Atlantic Alliance, the EEC and even

18 M. af Malmborg and T. B. Olesen, 'The Creation of EFTA', in T. B. Olesen (ed.), *Interdependence versus Integration: Denmark, Scandinavia and Western Europe, 1945–1960* (Odense, Odense University Press, 1995), pp. 197–212; W. Kaiser, 'Challenge to the Community: The Creation, Crisis and Consolidation of the European Free Trade Association 1958–72', *Journal of European Integration History* 3, no. 1 (1997): 7–33; W. Kaiser, 'A Better Europe? EFTA, the EFTA Secretariat, and the European Identities of the "Outer Seven", 1958–72', in M.-T. Bitsch, W. Loth and R. Poidevin (eds.), *Les institutions européennes et l'identités européennes* (Brussels, Bruylant, 1998), pp. 165–84; V. Curzon Price, 'The European Free Trade Association', in A. M. El-Agraa (eds.), *Economic Integration Worldwide* (London, Macmillan, 1997), pp. 175–202.

19 C. Lord, *Absent at the Creation: Britain and the Formation of the European Community, 1950–52* (Aldershot, Dartmouth Publishing, 1996); W. Kaiser, *Using Europe, Abusing the Europeans: Britain and European Integration, 1945–63* (London, Palgrave Macmillan, 1996); J. Tratt, *The Macmillan Government and Europe* (Basingstoke and London, Palgrave Macmillan, 1996); N. P. Ludlow, *Dealing with Britain: The Six and the First UK Application to the EEC* (Cambridge, Cambridge University Press, 1997); H. Young, *This Blessed Plot: Britain and Europe from Churchill to Blair* (London, Macmillan, 1999); J. Ellison, *Threatening Europe: Britain and the Creation of the European Community, 1955–1958* (Basingstoke and London, Palgrave Macmillan, 2000); J. W. Young, *Britain and European Unity 1945–1999*, 2nd edition (New York, NY, St Martin's Press, 2000); A. S. Milward, *The Rise and Fall of a National Strategy: The UK and the European Community*, vol. 1 (London, Frank Cass, 2012 [2002]); A. S. Milward, 'The United Kingdom and the European Union', *Journal of European Integration History* 20, no. 1 (2014): 73–80.

20 W. Kaiser, 'The Bomb and Europe. Britain, France and the EEC Entry Negotiations (1961–1963)', *Journal of European Integration History* 1, no. 1 (1995): 65–85.

the GATT.[21] Then it was not until the early 1970s that the EC negotiated separate trade agreements with all of the EFTA countries to bridge the trade gap in western Europe.

The emergence of the CAP in the first half of the 1960s was marked by Franco-German conflicts that often led to community crises.[22] The Commission's proposals, presented by Walter Hallstein,[23] to combine a financial envelope for the CAP with more powers for itself and the EP did not meet with the approval of de Gaulle, who was also opposed to the introduction of majority voting in the Council of Ministers, which, according to the EEC Treaty, should have come into force in January 1966.[24] He withdrew the French representative from the Council in July 1965 and announced that he would not send him back until the member states agreed to postpone majority voting, which they refused. The crisis continued until de Gaulle suffered losses at the hands of strongly pro-EEC rival François Mitterrand in the December 1965 presidential elections, whereupon France returned to the negotiating table. Although the FRG was unable to prevent the EEC's biggest constitutional crisis to date, German Foreign Minister Gerhard Schröder (of the Christlich Demokratische Union), who determined West Germany's European policy, became de Gaulle's vehement opponent. Schröder was able to secure a leading role within the coalition of French partners and, with a policy of extreme risk, to force France to return to the negotiating table.[25] Belgium served as mediator, with Spaak and the Belgian ambassador to Paris, Marcel-Henri Jaspar,[26] but the FRG was much more important because it acted as a pressure generator that played the central role

21 R. Steininger, 'Großbritannien und De Gaulle. Das Scheitern des britischen EWG-Beitritts im Januar 1963', Vierteljahrshefte für Zeitgeschichte 44, no. 1 (1996): 87–118; R. Davis, 'The "Problem of de Gaulle": British Reactions to General de Gaulle's Veto of the UK Application to Join the Common Market', Journal of European Integration History 32, no. 4 (1997): 453–64; I. Clark, Nuclear Diplomacy and the Special Relationship: Britain's Deterrent and America, 1957–62 (Oxford, Oxford University Press, 1994).

22 C. Germond, 'The Agricultural Bone of Contention: The Franco-German Tandem and the Making of the CAP, 1963–1966', Journal of European Integration History 16, no. 2 (2010): 25–44.

23 See W. Hallstein, United Europe: Challenge and Opportunity (Cambridge, MA, Harvard University Press, 1962).

24 M. Schönwald, 'Walter Hallstein and the "Empty Chair" Crisis 1965/66', in Loth (ed.), Crises and Compromises, pp. 157–71.

25 P. Bajon, 'De Gaulle Finds His "Master". Gerhard Schröder's "Fairly Audacious Politics" in the European Crisis of 1965–66', Journal of European Integration History 17, no. 2 (2011): 253–69; N. P. Ludlow, 'The Eclipse of Extremes. Demythologising the Luxembourg Compromise', in Loth (ed.), Crises and Compromises, pp. 247–65.

26 V. Genin, 'La politique étrangère de la Belgique face à la France lors de la crise de la chaise vide (1965–1966). Rôle d'un "petit pays", poids d'une relation bilatérale', Journal of European Integration History 19, no. 2 (2013): 259–76.

in managing the crisis, while the Benelux countries did not always harmonise their actions in the course of the 1950s and 1960s.[27]

The crisis ended at the Luxembourg EEC Foreign Ministers' Conference on 28–29 January 1966, which agreed on a provisional financial regulation for the CAP, deferring the question of additional powers for the Commission. A terse statement reaffirmed the principle of majority voting, but acknowledged that 'on very important issues, discussions must continue until unanimous agreement is reached'. The result was seemingly a draw, practically a victory for de Gaulle. The Council did approve temporary funding for the CAP in May 1966, but in the meantime the Commission's ambitious proposals had been rejected. The so-called Luxembourg Compromise prevented effective decision-making in the Council for almost 20 years, because the insistence on unanimity strengthened the awareness of particular interests and fostered a reluctance to call a vote in the Council even when no vital interests were at stake. It was not until the political and economic changes in the mid 1980s that members of the European Communities (EC) were forced to reform decision-making in the Council.

Fusion and Departure for New Shores: From the Merger Treaty to the Hague Summit (1965–1969)

On 1 July 1967, the 'Merger Treaty' of 8 April 1965 came into force, which provided for the creation of a common single Council and a common Commission. The ECSC, EEC and Euratom henceforth formed the EC on the basis of the existing treaties. The new Commission took up its work on 6 July 1967; at the same time, the term of office of the members of the ECSC High Authority and the EEC and Euratom Commissions ended. Owing to de Gaulle's opposition, Hallstein, the outgoing President of the EEC Commission, who later on compared integration to a bicycle that would stop and fall over if one didn't pedal all the time ('Integration is like a bicycle [. . .] You either move on or you fall off'),[28] was not appointed president of the new, single Commission and instead the less ambitious Belgian Jean Rey became its first president.[29]

---

27 S. Nasra and M. Segers, 'Between Charlemagne ande [sic] Atlantis: Belgium and the Netherlands during the First Stages of European Integration (1950–1966)', *Journal of European Integration History* 18, no. 2 (2012): 183–206.

28 Cited in 'Western Europe: Pulling Apart', *Time Magazine* 93, no. 7 (1969): 38, http://content.time.com/time/subscriber/article/0,33009,900621,00.html.

29 V. Dujardin and M. Scheid, 'Jean Rey (1967–1970): Europe Whenever Possible', in J. van der Harst and G. Voerman (eds.), *An Impossible Job? The Presidents of the European Commission, 1958–2014* (London, John Harper, 2015), pp. 51–71.

On 1 July 1968, 18 months earlier than provided for in the EEC Treaty, the customs union came into force, abolishing internal customs duties and introducing a common external tariff for trade with third countries. However, the regulation of agricultural policy remained a problem: it swallowed up over half of the common budget. The EEC of the 1960s moved in the political shadow of de Gaulle,[30] who is always said to have had a 'Europe of fatherlands' in mind, which is not really proven, but was a supporter of stronger political cooperation among the states of Europe. He used it to perpetuate French hegemony over the western part of the continent and the exclusion of the UK from the EC (1963–9), vetoing British accession a second time in 1967. From the Treaties of Rome in 1958 to de Gaulle's resignation in France in 1969, it was a decade of progress in trade and customs integration, but also a period of supranational stagnation.

Unstable currency situations became apparent as early as 1968 and already heralded the end of the brittle Bretton Woods system. The weakness of the dollar, pound and franc contrasted with a strong D-Mark. In November, the crisis was heading for a climax. Speculations pushed into the German foreign exchange market. The FRG resisted the EC partners' demand for a D-Mark revaluation, which was seen as a form of 'political revenge'. Against the background of this experience, the idea of establishing an economic and monetary union was born, with the aim of combining economic convergence and monetary solidarity.[31]

After this mixed period (1958–68), the Hague Summit of 1 and 2 December 1969 marked a turning point, combined with a new departure in integration policy. This event symbolised the EC's emergence from the political shadow of de Gaulle, who had blocked enlargement and supranationalism. Against the background of the D-Mark gaining in purchasing power and the FRG's increasing economic power, France felt compelled after de Gaulle to call in a second controlling power for Germany.[32] Faced with the feared consequences of Germany's new Ostpolitik, with rapprochement to the USSR and domestic political pressure for a French initiative in the EC, France's new President Georges Pompidou, who found common ground with the FRG's Chancellor Willy Brandt,[33] called a special summit, which took place in the Netherlands,

30 L. Warlouzet, 'Charles de Gaulle's Idea of Europe. The Lasting Legacy', *Kontur. Tidsskrift for Kulturstudier* no. 19 (2010): 21–31.
31 A. Wilkens, 'L'Europe et sa première crise monetaire', *Journal of European Integration History* 18, no. 2 (2012): 221–44.
32 For this period, see also K.-H. Narjes, *Europäische Integration aus historischer Erfahrung: Ein Zeitzeugengespräch mit Michael Gehler* (Bonn, ZEI, 2004), pp. 45–6.
33 C. Hiepel, *Willy Brandt et Georges Pompidou: La politique européenne de la France et de l'Allemagne entre crise et renouveau* (Lille, Presses universitaires du Septentrion, 2016);

which held the rotating EC presidency at the time. In addition to Brandt and Pompidou, the Dutch, Belgian, Italian and Luxembourgish prime ministers – respectively Piet de Jong, Gaston Eyskens, Mariano Rumor and Pierre Werner – made a far-reaching new start possible after the difficult de Gaulle period. It was the first meeting of EC heads of state and government since the celebration of the tenth anniversary of the Treaties of Rome (1967). With the summit came 'the spirit of The Hague'. Its importance cannot be overstated, because important decisions for the advancement of integration were taken during the period 1958–68. Especially the year 1968 was important in that the complete dismantling of EEC internal tariffs, the introduction of a common external tariff and the acceptance of a CAP were achieved. On the one hand, the summit at The Hague was a failure because no consensus was reached on a concrete date for enlargement, nor was any real impetus given to political and monetary cooperation. On the other hand, it was a success because the Brussels Council at the end of December 1969 succeeded in breaking the financial deadlock that was partly responsible for the empty chair crisis and endangered the Communities. The transfer of budgetary powers to the EP was a breakthrough after years of dithering. The Hague was also a success because a settlement of CAP financing was welcomed, but it was also a potential time bomb. Raising their own resources and determining financial outlays, prepared at The Hague and decided in Brussels, were costly solutions that placed a heavy burden on donor countries, especially the UK when it joined in 1973.[34]

The EEC had no competences in foreign, security and defence policy, but its founding fathers had wished to speak with one European voice in world politics. After the failure of the EDC with its plan for a political community in 1954, the Fouchet plans of 1961–2, named after the French diplomat Christian Fouchet, also remained unsuccessful. The EC foreign ministers, mandated by the decisions taken at the 1969 summit at The Hague, reported in November 1970 that progress could be made through exchange of information, consultation and coordination of international action among the members. It was settled by a committee chaired by the Belgian diplomat (and later Commissioner) Étienne Davignon that led to the European Political Cooperation (EPC). It consisted of twice-yearly meetings of foreign ministers prepared by a Political Committee composed of the heads of the political

C. Hiepel, 'Willy Brandt, la France et l'Europe au temps de la grande coalition, 1966–1969', in A. Wilkens (ed.), *Willy Brandt et l'unité de l'Europe: De l'objectif de la paix aux solidarités nécessaires* (Brussels, Peter Lang, 2011), pp. 213–30.

34 J. van der Harst, 'The 1969 Hague Summit: A New Start for Europe?', *Journal of European Integration History* 9, no. 2 (2003): 5–9.

departments of the foreign ministries, which should meet four times a year. However, the EPC remained informal, without a treaty basis, and was to be detached from the EC. Because of the intensity of consultations due to increasing international crises, a telex liaison system called COREU was established. The intergovernmental pragmatics of the EPC were accompanied by rhetorical flourishes. The Arab–Israeli war of October 1973 had shown that, although member states were able to agree to consult, they were still guided by their self-interests in major international conflicts. What became relevant was the 1974 Paris Summit decision to create the European Council, with regular meetings of heads of state and government, which strengthened the EPC and gave it a platform at the highest level. However, there remained an overall unfulfilled desire for a common European foreign and security policy.[35]

The Disastrous CAP and 'Northern Enlargement', Bridging Western Europe's Trade Gap and the UK as a Recalcitrant 'Opting Outer' (1969–1975)

At the summit at The Hague, consensus was also reached on the financing of the CAP and the strengthening of the EP's competences. In order to achieve the objectives of the CAP's market organisation, the Council of Ministers had set up the European Agricultural Guidance and Guarantee Fund (EAGGF) in April 1962 to gradually take over CAP expenditure. This fund covered expenditure on the guaranteed minimum price and export refunds, and expenditure on agricultural structural policy. Originally, the CAP was financed jointly by the EEC and its members. Under an agreement of April 1970, the EAGGF was fully integrated into the EC budget, as a result of the 'empty chair' crisis disputes that were largely fought over the financing of the CAP. The EAGGF was based on the 'common market' with a system of uniform prices, Community preference by guaranteeing import prices and levies, and financial solidarity. Although the CAP fulfilled the treaty's objectives ('ensuring supply' and 'increasing agricultural productivity by promoting technical progress'), its overall performance was disastrous. The price guarantee was above the world market level and led to massive overproduction, burdening the EC budget while farmers' incomes paradoxically fell.

35 R. Ginsberg, *Foreign Policy Activity of the European Community* (Boulder, CO, Lynne Rienner, 1989); M. Holland (ed.), *The Future of European Political Cooperation: Essays on Theory and Practice* (London, Macmillan, 1991); S. J. Nuttall, *European Political Co-operation* (Oxford, Clarendon Press, 1992).

In addition to public criticism, the CAP became also a bone of contention in the EC's external economic relations. Most industrialised countries pursued a policy of agricultural export promotion, whereby the United States too subsidised its agricultural product exports. To end the destruction of agricultural surpluses, reduce costs and facilitate multilateral trade agreements, the EC embarked on a lengthy process of CAP reform, beginning in 1984 with the introduction of a quota system for dairy production. As part of a comprehensive restructuring of the EC's budget (the Delors I package), adopted in February 1988 after a year of negotiations, the EC's agricultural expenditure was strictly controlled as part of a tightened 'budget discipline'.[36]

On the question of admitting new member states, the Commission took a very cautious position in 1961–3. Then, in 1967–72, there was a significant shift from defensiveness to a more open-minded position, even if this was not expressed very openly.[37]

Insofar as 'northen enlargement' was concerned, accession negotiations with Denmark, Ireland, the UK and Norway began in 1970. The Acts of Accession were signed on 22 January 1972 and implemented with the exception of Norway, in which a referendum gave a negative result (53 per cent against accession). On 1 January 1973, the accessions took legal effect.[38] The EC thus became a community of nine and was increasingly perceived as an international player. It concluded bilateral free trade agreements with neutral European states (Austria, Sweden, Switzerland and later Finland) and other EFTA states (Portugal, Iceland and Norway), creating a free trade area

---

36 C. D'Aloya and M. Mezzadri, 'Common Agricultural Policy (CAP)', in D. Dinan (ed.), *Encyclopedia of the European Union* (Houndmills, Basingstoke and New York, NY, Palgrave Macmillan, 2000), pp. 71–6, 72–3; J. Marshand and B. Green (eds.), *The Changing Role of the Common Agricultural Policy: The Future of Farming in Europe* (London, Belhaven, 1991); M. Petit, M. De Benedictis, D. Britton, M. de Groot, W. Henrichsmeyer and F. Lechi, *Agricultural Policy Formation in the European Community* (Amsterdam, Elsevier, 1995); A.-C. L. Knudsen, *Farmers on Welfare: The Making of Europe's Common Agricultural Policy* (Ithaca, NY, Cornell University Press, 2009); K. K. Patel (ed.), *Fertile Ground for Europe? The History of European Integration and the Common Agricultural Policy since 1945* (Baden-Baden, Nomos, 2009).

37 N. P. Ludlow, 'A Welcome Change: The European Commission and the Challenge of Enlargement, 1958–1973', *Journal of European Integration History* 11, no. 2 (2005): 31–46.

38 C. Preston, *Enlargement and Integration in the European Union* (London and New York, NY, Routledge, 1997), pp. 23–45; W. Kaiser, '"What Alternative Is Open to Us?": Britain', in W. Kaiser and J. Elvert (eds.), *European Union Enlargement: A Comparative History* (London and New York, NY, Routledge, 2004), pp. 10–33; J. Laursen, 'A Kingdom Divided: Denmark', in Kaiser and Elvert (eds.), *European Union Enlargement*, pp. 34–56; E. Moxon-Browne, 'From Isolation to Involvement: Ireland', in Kaiser and Elvert (eds.), *European Union Enlargement*, pp. 57–74.

including all of western Europe.[39] As a result, the common EC external tariff for commercial and industrial products was no longer applied to these countries, and a free trade zone for these groups of goods became possible. The western European trade division thus came to an end. Now, after the UK's joining, the new EC also saw itself as playing a role in world politics, which was expressed by the legally non-binding 'Declaration on European Identity' at the Copenhagen summit on 14–15 December 1973. On this occasion the heads of state and government of the Nine reaffirmed their will to incorporate the concept of 'European identity' into their common external relations.[40]

The UK had joined the EC at a time of economic slump and recession. Furthermore, London began its membership as a reluctant outsider. It remained a difficult partner and behaved like a 'stranger' in the Community.[41] Increasingly, there were problems with the British contribution to the EC budget. A provisional solution was reached at the European Council in Dublin on 10–11 March 1975. However, the intra-community burden of this question came to an end only on 5 June when the islanders voted by a large majority (67 per cent) in a referendum to remain in the EC. Downplaying the political importance of the EC, the insertion of a corrective formula in the EC budget system and import concessions for New Zealand butter helped to overcome the domestic political hurdles.[42]

'Eurosclerosis' in the 1970s?

In the mid 1970s, the situation in Europe was characterised by increasing unemployment, slowing growth and crises in various sectors, such as in the textile industry, but especially in the iron and steel industry, developments that followed the 'oil-price shock' of 1973, which did not make governing in

---

39 B. Rabaeus, 'A Turning Point for EFTA and for the Trading Arrangements of Western Europe', in Council of Europe (ed.), *European Yearbook 1973* (The Hague, Martinus Nijhoff, 1975), pp. 54–66, 54.

40 'Declaration on European Identity (Copenhagen, 14 December 1973)', www.cvce.eu/en/obj/declaration_on_european_identity_copenhagen_14_december_1973-en-02798dc9-9c69-4b7d-b2c9-f03a8db7da32.html.

41 S. Wall, *A Stranger in Europe: Britain and the EU from Thatcher to Blair* (Oxford, Oxford University Press, 2008), p. 48; J. Gillingham, *European Integration 1950–2003: Superstate or New Market Economy?* (Cambridge, Cambridge University Press, 2003), pp. 164–79.

42 J. Smith, 'The 1975 Referendum', *Journal of European Integration History* 5, no. 1 (1999): 41–56; S. Hug, *Citizens, Referendums, and European Integration* (Lanham, MD, Boulder, CO, New York, NY and Oxford, Rowman & Littlefield, 2002), pp. 23–45, 115–20. For the outcomes of all of the referendums, see S. Binzer Hobolt, *Europe in Question: Referendums on European Integration* (Oxford, Oxford University Press, 2009), p. 9.

Europe any easier, but the challenge could be taken up with 'Bonn at the center of the European stage'.[43] The price of oil quadrupled as a result of the embargo imposed by Arab oil producers and the cartelisation that followed the Middle East war.[44]

The need to develop social policies in the Community became apparent at the beginning of the 1970s, when the problems of unemployment and economic crisis seriously preoccupied European governments. As a result, trade unions began to promote a social dialogue with the European institutions. For example, Italian Minister of Labour Carlo Donat-Cattin pursued a strategy aimed at mitigating the negative consequences of the completion of the CAP and the possible formation of an economic and monetary union, and intended also to address poverty and unemployment, which were particularly high in the underdeveloped Mezzogiorno.[45]

The prevailing feeling of 'stagnation' in the EC in the 1970s due to energy, currency and economic crises is referred to in simplistic terms as 'Eurosclerosis', which, however, is not an accurate description of that decade in terms of integration policy initiatives and community law. The term refers to a stagnation in terms of integration until the early 1980s, with little or no progress in achieving integration. This constituted a negative myth and a retrospectively constructed assessment to legitimise new steps towards integration. The much-quoted word 'Eurosclerosis' is a tactically motivated exaggeration. Were the 1970s a 'departure for new shores' on the continent,[46] or a 'departure for second-generation Europe'?[47] The answer is probably the latter, as the 1970s were not that bad.

Luxembourg"'s Prime Minister Pierre Werner was tasked with preparing a report on an Economic and Monetary Union (EMU) in order to deepen the state of integration before the forthcoming 'northern enlargement'. The Werner Committee developed the plan, which had to be taken up again 10 years later and implemented a further decade later. In October 1970, Werner presented a seven-step plan to implement the project through institutional

---

43 L. Warlouzet, *Governing Europe in a Globalizing World: Neoliberalism and Its Alternatives Following the 1973 Oil Crisis* (Abingdon, Routledge, 2018), pp. 214–24, 220–4.

44 G. Müller, 'Folgen der Ölkrise für den europäischen Einigungsprozeß nach 1973', in F. Knipping and M. Schönwald (eds.), *Aufbruch zum Europa der zweiten Generation* (Trier, WVT Verlag, 2004), pp. 73–93.

45 M. E. Guasconi, 'Paving the Way for a European Social Dialogue. Italy, the Trade Unions and the Shaping of a European Social Policy after the Hague Conference of 1969', *Journal of European Integration History* 9, no. 1 (2003): 87–110.

46 G. Brunn, *Die Europäische Einigung von 1945 bis heute* (Stuttgart, Reclam, 2002), pp. 179–227.

47 F. Knipping, *Rom, 25. März 1957: Die Einigung Europas* (Munich, dtv, 2004), pp. 156–217.

reforms and closer political cooperation over the next 10 years. The plan proposed a parallel approach through economic policy coordination and monetary policy measures, with differences arising between Paris and Bonn over the pace and scope. Pompidou was a strong supporter of monetary policy coordination, but did not want measures that promoted a supranational community. In the medium term, Brandt pursued the project of an EMU. From 1971 onwards, the international currency crisis that had now come about brought to light the differing German and French interests and ideas and led to a premature termination of the exchange. The subsequent efforts to reach a Franco-German understanding on the currency issue were limited to more modest goals, but on the whole represented an important learning process on the difficult path to developing European monetary solidarity.[48]

Brandt and other Community leaders saw the Werner Plan as an ideal opportunity to accelerate and deepen integration. Accordingly, at the Paris summit on 19–20 October 1972, they called for the formation of an EMU by 1980. However, the Werner Plan soon fell victim not to 'Eurosclerosis' but to the changed global economic conditions of the 1970s: high inflation and increasing economic divergence made the goal unrealistic. Only at the end of the 1980s was EMU coupled with the Single Market Programme (SMP) under far more favourable conditions.

At the Paris summit on 9–10 December 1974, heads of state and government commissioned the Belgian Christian Democrat, prime minister and federalist Leo Tindemans to draw up proposals for the further development of the Community into a 'European Union'. Tindemans interviewed officials in Brussels and in the capitals of the nine EC countries the following year, and presented his findings in January 1976. The report focused less on the question of a European federal state than on EC institutional reform, including reducing the number of commissioners, replacing the unanimity principle with qualified majority voting (QMV), extending the 6-month Council presidency, and expanding the EC's foreign and security policy responsibilities. The part of the report concerning a 'two-speed Europe', with different speeds depending on willingness and ability, was controversial. Smaller EC states feared the creation of an EC with first- and second-class member states; larger ones – with the exception of the FRG and Italy – rejected any new loss of sovereignty. France's President Valéry Giscard d'Estaing arrogated to himself the monopoly of decision-making, handled the project dilatorily through his

---

48 A. Wilkens, 'Westpolitik, Ostpolitik and the Project of the Economic and Monetary Union. Germany's European Policy in the Brandt Era (1969–1974)', Journal of European Integration History 5, no. 1 (1999): 73–102.

officials and ultimately, to Tindemans' disappointment, rejected the report. The heads of state and government asked their foreign ministers to consider the report, and these ministers delegated this task to senior officials. A report on the report was delivered to the European Council in The Hague on 29–30 November 1976, whereupon the Council dropped the whole project.[49]

In the most turbulent post-war phase, with the collapse of the international monetary system (due to the end of fixed exchange rates as a major blow to the Bretton Woods system arising from US President Richard Nixon's decision to give up the gold–dollar parity), the escalating Vietnam War and the greater virulence of international terrorism, the signing of the Final Act of the Conference on Security and Co-operation in Europe (CSCE) on 1 August 1975 by the heads of state and government of thirty-five participating countries (all European countries except Albania, plus the USSR, United States and Canada)[50] initiated a process of détente between East and West in Europe and allowed the EC states to demonstrate their cohesion. In three 'baskets', or categories of commitments, the accord covered political, economic, cultural, humanitarian, information and military confidence-building issues.[51]

Thanks to the European policy of détente, Brussels was able to become more active internationally. The EC established diplomatic relations with the People's Republic of China (PRC) on 16 September 1975, and concluded a trade agreement with the PRC on 3 April 1978. Sir Christopher Soames, Vice-President and Commissioner for External Relations, was largely responsible for these initiatives, although individual EC institutions were also able to distinguish themselves in the inter-institutional quest for new competences. On the one hand, the EC defined specifically for itself what détente meant to it; on the other, its enlargement further promoted détente in Europe as well.[52] This self-confident position was remarkable because at the same time the 1970s represented a decade of crisis for the North Atlantic Treaty Organization (NATO). Especially the Mediterranean region on the southern flank could be

---

49 J. Nielsen-Sikora, 'Europe in Transition: The Tindemans Report of 1975', *Historische Mitteilungen* 19 (2006): 277–96.

50 J. J. Maresca, *The Conference on Security and Cooperation in Europe, 1973–1975* (Durham, NC, Duke University Press, 1987); M. Cotey Morgan, *The Final Act: The Helsinki Accords and the Transformation of the Cold War* (Princeton, NJ and Oxford, Princeton University Press, 2018).

51 D. C. Thomas, *The Helsinki Effect: International Norms, Human Rights, and the Demise of Communism* (Princeton, NJ, Princeton University Press, 2001); M. Peter and H. Wentker (eds.), *Die KSZE im Ost–West-Konflikt: Internationale Politik und gesellschaftliche Transformation 1975–1990* (Munich, Oldenbourg, 2012).

52 M. J. Chenard, 'Seeking Détente and Driving Integration: The European Community's Opening towards the People's Republic of China, 1975–1978', *Journal of European Integration History* 18, no. 1 (2009): 25–38.

perceived as a threatened region, which seemed to be confirmed by the electoral successes of Eurocommunist parties in Italy, France and Spain, and also gave rise to exaggerated concerns in the Western states about a 'trojan horse' of the Soviet Union.[53] At the same time, the EC increasingly presented itself as a promoter of human rights in Africa and Latin America.[54]

The EPC became more important because of an increase in international and European conflicts, such as the war waged in Afghanistan by the Soviet Union, NATO's Double-Track Decision in 1979 and the 1981 imposition of martial law in Poland against the trade union movement Solidarność. Until then, the EC and EPC had worked either side by side or even against each other. Thereafter the aim pursued was, therefore, to achieve closer team-work between them. The question which thus arises is whether the EPC led to a Europeanisation of the foreign policy of the EC members or whether national interests continued to dominate.[55]

Through the foreign policy coordinating mechanism of the EPC, the EC member states played a prominent part in the negotiations leading to the CSCE's Final Act, in numerous follow-up meetings (Belgrade, 1977–9; Madrid, 1980–3; Vienna, 1986–9; and Helsinki, 1992) and in occasional special conferences. During the renewal of Cold War tensions in the late 1970s and early 1980s, the CSCE proved invaluable in at least keeping the protagonists together at the negotiating table.[56]

53 A. Varsori, 'Crisis and Stabilization in Southern Europe during the 1970s: Western Strategy, European Instruments', *Journal of European Integration History* 15, no. 1 (2009): 5–14; N. Dörr, 'NATO and Eurocommunism. The Fear of a Weakening of the Southern Flank from the Mid 1970s to Mid 1980s', *Journal of European Integration History* 20, no. 2 (2014): 245–58. See also A. Romano, 'Re-designing Military Security in Europe: Cooperation and Competition between European Community and NATO during the Early 1980s', *European Review of History/Revue européenne d'histoire* 24, no. 3 (2017): 445–71; J. Raflik, 'OTAN–Europe. Aux sources d'une ambiguïté', in Grin et al. (eds.), *Formes d'Europe*, pp. 327–40.

54 L. Ferrari, 'The European Community as a Promoter of Human Rights in Africa and Latin America, 1970–80', *Journal of European Integration History* 21, no. 2 (2015): 217–30; K. Christiaens, 'Europe at the Crossroads of Three Worlds: Alternative Histories and Connections of European Solidarity with the Third World, 1950s–80s', *European Review of History/Revue européenne d'histoire* 24, no. 6 (2017): 932–54.

55 G. Clemens, A. Reinfeldt and T. Rüter (eds.), *Europäisierung von Außenpolitik? Die Europäische Politische Zusammenarbeit (EPZ) in den 1970er Jahren* (Baden-Baden, Nomos, 2019), pp. 372–88; M. E. Guasconi, *Prove di politica estera: La Cooperazione politica europea, l'Atto Unico Europeo e la fine della guerra fredda* (Milan, Mondadori, 2020), pp. 208–14; M. E. Guasconi, 'European Political Cooperation and the Single European Act', in Gehler and Loth (eds.), *Reshaping Europe*, pp. 131–48.

56 A. Brait and M. Gehler, 'The CSCE Vienna Follow-up Meeting and Alois Mock, 1986–1989', in M. Gehler, P. H. Kosicki and H. Wohnout (eds.), *Christian Democracy and the Fall of Communism* (Leuven, Leuven University Press, 2019), pp. 75–91; H. Wentker, 'Die KSZE als Ordnungsfaktor. Höhenflug und Bedeutungsverlust einer Idealvorstellung

On 1 December 1975, the European Council, which met informally two or three times a year, 'above' the EC, and which consisted of the heads of state and government, decided in Rome to implement immediately direct election of the members of the EP (MEPs). Now the Community struggled to take the decision already envisaged in the EEC Treaty, which marked the beginning of partial and indirect democratisation. From 7 to 10 June 1979, the citizens of the nine EC member states elected MEPs by universal and direct suffrage for the first time. The configuration of socialist parties in the Communities – that in 1992 became the Party of European Socialists – and the Christian democratic European People's Party were the main winners.[57]

European parliamentarism developed in five stages.[58] A difficult period of formation and acclimatisation in 1952–8 was followed by a period of familiarisation, experience and preparation of new group formations and faction building before the first direct elections in 1979. Thereafter a generally directly and freely elected EP existed, but still with hardly any competences. The modest powers were initially reflected in its limited ability to influence key EC decision-making areas (such as agricultural and trade policy). 'If you have a grandpa, send him to Europe' was an irreverent verdict on the first generation of directly elected parliamentarians. However, the mandatories did not shy away from disputes with the Council on budgetary issues and the legislative procedure and referred their concerns to the European Court of Justice. Powers and function within the EC system developed gradually. In 1970 and 1975, new budgetary powers were conferred on the EP. In 1987, the SEA introduced a new legislative cooperation procedure and gave the EP the right of assent to accession treaties and association agreements. After a phase of emancipation, self-discovery and understanding in 1980–9 came the negotiation of the Maastricht Treaty on the EU, which gave the EP considerable co-decision rights. This was followed by a phase of politicisation and profiling in 1991–9, which reached a first climax with the indirectly forced resignation of the Santer Commission because of irregularities.[59]

europäischer Politik (1989–1991)', in T. Geiger, J. Lillteicher and H. Wentker (eds.), *Zwei plus Vier: Die internationale Gründungsgeschichte der Berliner Republik* (Berlin and Boston, MA, De Gruyter, 2021), pp. 125–41.

57 Gehler, *Europa*, pp. 318–19; W. Kaiser, 'Shaping Institutions and Policies: The EPP Group in the European Communities', in L. Bardi, W. Gagatek, C. Germond, K. M. Johansson, W. Kaiser and S. Sassano (eds.), *The European Ambition: The Group of European People's Party and European Integration* (Baden-Baden, Nomos, 2020), pp. 23–88.

58 Gehler, *Europa*, 661–2.

59 M. Gehler, 'Jacques Santer (1995–1999): President of the Commission in Times of Transition', in van der Harst and Voerman (eds.), *An Impossible Job?*, pp. 197–222, 215–21.

The era of 'Eurosclerosis' can be summarised as follows: the 1970s were a decade of trial and error and of concentrating forces for a new start in integration policy. In this process, important starting positions for the further development of the institutional preconditions for integration were created, and substantial progress was also achieved.[60]

The Arduous Journey to the 'Southern Enlargement', Resolution of the British Budget Dispute and Departure for New Reforms (1975–1986)

When Greece (in 1975) and Portugal and Spain (both in 1977) applied for full membership, the EC was confronted with new wishes for enlargement while intentions to deepen had not been realised. The political structures of all three countries had only recently become compatible with democratic conditions. Because of their differences in economic development compared with the Community, they were expected to confront the EC with a number of problems, not only of financial nature, but also with regard to the smooth functioning of all EC institutions. There was also a need for more democracy within the Community, as has been shown above.[61]

Greece had been associated with the EEC since 1962. Its path to EC membership was blocked in 1967 when a military junta overthrew the democratic government in Athens. After democracy was restored in 1974, the Greek state again received economic aid and technical assistance from the EC and became a candidate country. The application for accession succeeded due to the diplomacy of conservative Prime Minister Konstantinos Karamanlis (1955–63, 1974–80) and the support of Giscard d'Estaing, with whom he maintained a close relationship. The EC Commission rejected the application from Athens on the grounds that the economic conditions were not in place for full membership, but, for political reasons, the Council of Ministers ignored the Commission's objections and approved the Greek application in order to prevent the restoration of an authoritarian dictatorship by the military. This was also supported by the Council of Europe with its human rights aspirations.[62]

---

60 D. Dialer, A. Maurer and M. Richter (eds.), *Handbuch zum Europäischen Parlament* (Baden-Baden, Nomos, 2015).
61 Preston, *Enlargement and Integration*; Kaiser and Elvert (eds.), *European Union Enlargement*.
62 Preston, *Enlargement and Integration*, pp. 46–61; V. F. Soriano, 'Facing the Greek Junta: The European Community, the Council of Europe and the Rise of Human-Rights Politics in Europe', *European Review of History/Revue européenne d'histoire* 24, no. 6

This political priority set a precedent for later accessions for late democracies. After negotiations had officially begun in July 1976, Greece and the EC were able to sign the Accession Treaty in Athens on 28 May 1979, which provided for a 5-year transitional period during which the Greek economy was to be gradually brought into line with that of the other EC members. The EC pledged considerable financial resources for this purpose. The treaty entered into force on 1 January 1981.[63]

Hopes that the Greek economy would benefit from better EC market access were unfounded. The high-performing northern European industries made it difficult for the less competitive industries of Greece to adapt. A year before accession, the gross domestic product (GDP) per capita of Greece was 58 per cent of the EC average; 10 years later it had fallen to 52 per cent of the EC average. However, Greek democracy was further stabilised by EC membership.[64]

Right from the beginning of Spain's negotiations with the Commission in 1967, be it through an association or trade agreement during the previous decades,[65] the West German government had complied with Spanish requests for support and stood up for Spanish interests.[66] Spain submitted its EC membership application in July 1977, 2 years after the end of Francisco Franco's dictatorship (1936–75) and just after the first democratic elections. The request was unanimously supported by all of the Spanish parliamentary parties, public opinion, employers' organisations and trade unions, in order to secure democracy and put an end to foreign policy isolation. The negotiations, which began on 5 February 1979, proved to be long and complicated. The main obstacles were the reluctance of France, which feared competition from Spanish agricultural products from the Mediterranean, and the demand for Madrid to join NATO, which took effect on 30 May 1982. Negotiations were finalised in March 1985, and the accession treaty was signed on 12 June, so that accession could take place on 1 January 1986 under General Secretary

(2017): 358–76; B. Wassenberg, 'The Council of Europe's Role in the History of European Integration. An Intergovernmental Organisation in the Shadow of the European Union?', in Grin et al. (eds.), *Formes d'Europe*, pp. 267–99.

63 Preston, *Enlargement and Integration*, 46–61; K. Ifantis, 'State Interests, External Dependancy Trajectories and "Europe": Greece', in Kaiser and Elvert (eds.), *European Union Enlargement*, pp. 70–92.

64 P. Kazakos and P. C. Ioakimidis, *Greece and EC Membership Evaluated* (New York, NY, St Martin's Press, 1994).

65 F. Guirao, 'Association or Trade Agreement? Spain and the EEC, 1947–1964', *Journal of European Integration History* 3, no. 1 (1997): 103–20.

66 B. Aschmann, 'The Reliable Ally: Germany Supports Spain's European Integration Efforts, 1957–67', *Journal of European Integration History* 7, no. 1 (2001): 37–51.

of the Socialist Workers' Party (1974–97) and Presidente del Gobierno (Prime Minister) Félipe Gonzales Márquez (1982–96), who got on well with German Chancellor Helmut Kohl (1982–98), leading to the development of a strong orientation of Spanish politics towards Brussels. German business, in particular, had strong investment interests in the Iberian Peninsula. Spain's negative trade balance was gradually reduced from 1986 onwards by the profitable export business due to its EC membership.[67] Spanish industry received preferential treatment. With the exception of tariffs in certain sensitive sectors, such as motor vehicles and iron and steel products, tariffs on Spanish industrial exports were to be eliminated within 7 years, while tariffs on EC exports to Spain were reduced over a longer period. In return, Spain had to make concessions in agriculture and fisheries, sectors in which the country had a competitive advantage over other EC countries. Thus accession had a positive effect on Spain's foreign trade balance and foreign investment, as well as on the criteria for participation in the EMU.[68]

For Portugal, an EFTA member since 1960, the authoritarian system under the rule of António de Oliveira Salazar (1932–68) and Portugal's colonial wars made a closer relationship with the EC impossible. This changed only after the Carnation Revolution in 1974, with the introduction of a democratic system in 1976. The Socialist minority government that emerged from the parliamentary elections of 25 April 1976, under the then Prime Minister Mário Alberto Soares (1976–7, 1978, 1983–5), gave absolute priority to EC membership. The application was submitted on 28 March 1977 and was approved by the EC Council of Ministers. The Commission also reacted positively, but pointed out structural deficits in the Portuguese economy. Negotiations officially started in Luxembourg on 17 October 1978, but were not practically launched until 1980, with several difficulties. The delays were caused by the coupling with Spain's application for membership, since Spain, as a larger country, had more negotiating material and a bigger need to adopt European law. Many EC Council presidencies, several governments, various ambassadorial and ministerial meetings and dozens of months of negotiations were needed. It was in fact the longest negotiation in the history of enlargement of

67 Preston, *Enlargement and Integration*, 62–86; R. Martin de la Guardia, 'In Search of Lost Europe: Spain', in Kaiser and Elvert (eds.), *European Union Enlargement*, pp. 93–111; M. Alorda, 'The European Community's Struggle with the Agro-budgetary Problem: Its Impact on the Spanish Accession Negotiations, 1979–1985', in Gehler and Loth (eds.), *Reshaping Europe*, pp. 349–72.
68 R. Bassols, *España en Europa: Historia de la adhésion a la CE, 1957–85* (Madrid, Cámara de Comercio, 1995).

the EC up to that time.[69] In the meantime, Portugal had to be granted two standby credits from the International Monetary Fund and pre-accession financial aid from the EC to keep the economy from turbulence. The accession treaty could be signed only on 12 June 1985, so that the entry took place on the same date as that of Spain.

The EC membership had positive effects. Structural funds promoted economic transformation. Portugal received about 1.2 billion European Currency Units (ECU) from the European Regional Development Fund alone between 1986 and 1988 and about ECU 2.6 billion in EIB loans between 1986 and 1990. Following the reform of the Structural Funds in 1988, the first Common Support Framework amounted to some ECU 7.4 billion for the period between 1989 and 1993. These funds were used to build up and modernise economic infrastructure, develop human resources, agriculture and rural areas, promote industrial recovery and regional development and, last but not least, stabilise democracy. Ultimately, over the long period of struggle for Portuguese membership, the negotiation process also led to the Europeanisation of the country on the westernmost part of the Iberian Peninsula.[70]

On 14 April 1987, Turgut Özal submitted an EC accession application for Turkey, which already had an association agreement with the EEC through the Treaty of Ankara of 12 September 1963. The EC Commission's President Walter Hallstein had called Turkey 'Europe' at that time. However, a fundamental dilemma for Brussels from the outset was whether Turkey should be considered a natural 'insider' or a significant 'outsider'. Turkey's domestic politics posed an obstacle, with repeated military coups. It was also not easy for Ankara to comprehend the ever-changing nature of the communities and the need for deeper integration.[71]

The Community of Twelve created new challenges for the EC institutions and older member states. Even though the feared internal migration

---

69 A. Costa Pinto, 'From Atlantic Past to European Destiny: Portugal', in Kaiser and Elvert (eds.), *European Union Enlargement*, pp. 112–30; A. Cunha, 'The Least Loved Policy: EEC's Enlargement to Portugal', in Gehler and Loth (eds.), *Reshaping Europe*, pp. 373–92.

70 J. da Silva Lopes (ed.), *Portugal and EC Membership Evaluated* (London, Pinter, 1993); J. M. Magone, *The Changing Architecture of Iberian Politics (1974–92): An Investigation on the Democratic Structuring of Democratic Political Systemic Culture in Semiperipheral Southern European Societies* (Lewiston, NY, Edwin Mellen Press, 1996); J. M. Magone, *European Portugal: The Difficult Road to Sustainable Democracy* (Basingstoke, Macmillan, 1996).

71 Z. Öniş, 'An Awkward Partnership: Turkey's Relations with the European Union in Comparative-Historical Perspective', *Journal of European Integration History* 7, no. 1 (2001): 105–19.

of 'cheap' southern European workers to the core regions of Europe did not materialise, the feared structural differences in the economy and the enormous prosperity gap between the founding members and the laggards could not be quickly compensated for. These issues caused a systemic problem in the long run because the competitiveness of the economies of Greece and Portugal remained limited. The political motives for contributing to the consolidation and stabilisation of the southern European democracies were decisive, although there were concerns about the economic backwardness of these countries. The financing requirements were enormous, but the democratic and regulatory policy argument not only gained the upper hand, but also proved to be correct for the 1980s and 1990s.

On 19 November 1981, the foreign ministers of the FRG and Italy, Hans-Dietrich Genscher and Emilio Colombo, presented proposals for a European Act to the EP, arguing for reform of EC decision-making processes, an extension of the EPC to security and defence, and its merger with the EC's external economic relations. The proposals elicited only a mixed response from EC member states. The United States distrusted the notion of a separate European security and defence identity ('Genscherism'). The European Council, meeting in London on 26–27 November 1981, asked foreign ministers to consider and report on the Genscher–Colombo initiative, whereupon, divided on how to proceed, they did not agree to the relatively modest proposals. Their report led only to an insubstantial, vague and non-binding 'Solemn Declaration on European Union' by the Stuttgart European Council of 17–19 June 1983, which reaffirmed the EC's international identity.[72]

The most ambitious initiative at this time was the EP's 'Draft Treaty Establishing the European Union', which was based on ideas by the Italian federalist Altiero Spinelli. This was adopted on 14 February 1984, after more than 3 years of deliberation, by 232 votes to 31, with 43 abstentions. This draft constitution was a treaty requiring ratification. It equated the Union with a federal or federation-like structure. The reactions of the member states, however, showed that the realisation of such a far-reaching concept was still far from being conceivable.[73]

More decisively, however, the EC summit in Fontainebleau on 24–25 June 1984 led to a breakthrough after a 5-year dispute over the British

---

72 D. Cuccia, 'The Genscher–Colombo Plan: A Forgotten Page in the European Integration History', *Journal of European Integration History* 24, no. 1 (2018): 59–78.

73 D. Preda, 'Spinelli's Initiative and the European Parliament's Union Project', in Gehler and Loth (eds.), *Reshaping Europe*, pp. 99–118.

budget contribution. The long, arduous and tenacious path to resolving the dispute over the British membership fees for the EC (1979–84) demonstrates the tension existing between half-hearted integration and partial disintegration.[74] Prime Minister Margaret Thatcher had argued very aggressively that Britain was paying too much and receiving too little. After tough negotiations, she secured a rebate equal to 66 per cent of Britain's net annual contribution. French President François Mitterrand, who held the EC presidency, helped to compromise. Member states agreed to cut CAP spending and increase revenues for the EC, which made agricultural and budget reform possible, reaching an agreement on the issue of agricultural overproduction and environmental protection (air pollution). Fontainebleau also led to the establishment of an ad hoc committee on institutional reforms under the Irishman James Dooge, which formed the basis for the SEA and led to the revival of the EC in the second half of the 1980s.

From ERM and EMS to the SEA and Internal Market Programme (1978–1987)

The economic policy objectives of the early 1970s remained on the agenda. German Chancellor Helmut Schmidt (1974–82) of the SPD and French President Valéry Giscard d'Estaing (1974–81) presented a proposal drawn up in bilateral secret agreements at the Copenhagen Summit in April 1978. In essence, it was about an ERM in which the currency value of the member states could fluctuate only within predefined bands of ±2.25 per cent. The project was initiated by Commission President Roy Jenkins,[75] who saw the potential for new integration momentum in an EMS. Schmidt was particularly concerned about the appreciation of the D-Mark against the US dollar, which would make German exports uncompetitive, reduce profits and increase unemployment. He and Giscard d'Estaing saw the devaluation of the dollar as a sign of weakness in US leadership under President Jimmy Carter (1977–81).[76]

---

74 P. N. Ludlow, 'A Double-Edged Victory: Fontainebleau and the Resolution of the British Budget Problem, 1983–84', in Gehler and Loth (eds.), *Reshaping Europe*, pp. 45–71.

75 M. Yeager, 'Roy Jenkins (1977–1981): "My Fear Always Is That We Shall Go Too Slow"', in Van der Harst and Voermans (eds.), *An Impossible Job?*, pp. 133–49; N. P. Ludlow, *Roy Jenkins and the European Commission, 1976–1980: At the Heart of Europe* (Basingstoke, Palgrave Macmillan, 2016), pp. 231–51.

76 M. Calingaert, *European Integration Revisited: Progress, Prospects and U.S. Interests* (Boulder, CO, Westview, 1996).

Their contention was that Europe should react to this with political unity and economic cooperation. The two of them convinced the other EC heads of state and government to commission a study with policy coordination, a commitment to intervene in foreign exchange and to establish a new institution, a European Monetary Fund (EMF), to manage foreign exchange reserves and provide balance-of-payments assistance. Controversial details were dealt with at the summit in Bremen in July 1978.[77]

The stronger currency members, led by the FRG with the Deutsche Bundesbank, insisted that the fight against inflation should not be jeopardised, while weaker currency members, especially France and Italy, relied on a more flexible system to secure their participation. At issue was the extent to which a weaker currency member would be obliged to stabilise its exchange rate through fiscal or monetary policy changes or through currency intervention and other stronger members would guarantee ERM stability in partnership. Member states were largely responsible for adjusting their own policies in order to remain in the EMS. Although the ECU provided a formal point of reference, the D-Mark remained the de facto pivot, so that those with currency weaknesses had to adjust to low inflation standards. The EMF with its own ECU pool to alleviate dependence on the D-Mark and help weaker countries adjust was tacitly abandoned.[78]

From 9–10 March 1979, the European Council met in Paris and put into force the EMS, which had already been planned in Bremen the previous year. It was based on four basic elements: an artificial currency, namely the ECU, an exchange rate, intervention and credit and transfer mechanisms. The EMS was a result of the Bonn–Paris axis after the abandonment of the gold standard to cover the dollar and the international monetary system dominated by the collapse of the US reserve currency. The ERM started on 13 March. Its predecessor, the so-called 'snake in the tunnel', had previously failed to stabilise nominal exchange rates. The ERM was therefore met with scepticism, but exchange rate fluctuations declined and the number of members increased, leading to the revival of ideas on monetary integration and a single currency. With the exception of the UK, which remained in the EMS, all of the EC member states (Belgium, Denmark, France, Germany, Ireland, Italy, Luxembourg and the Netherlands) participated in the ERM. Its results exceeded expectations, as severe shocks were survived in the wake of

---

77 F. Giavazzi and A. Giovannini, *Limiting Exchange Rate Flexibility* (Cambridge, MA, MIT Press, 1989).

78 P. Ludlow, *The Making of the European Monetary System* (London, Butterworth Scientific, 1982).

the second oil-price crisis of 1979 and the recession of the early 1980s, with an awareness of collective responsibility and multilateral communication in the Committee of Central Bank Governors and the Council of Economic and Finance Ministers, both of which controlled the functioning of the EMS. Membership was maintained despite an initial period of large currency fluctuations and frequent exchange rate adjustments (1979–83), through a transition period of smaller fluctuations and adjustments (1983–7) to a period of exceptionally stable exchange rates (1987–92). Capital controls were reduced in 1979–92 due to the envisaged SMP and preparations for EMU. With three more members joining – Spain in 1989, the UK in 1990 and Portugal in 1992, despite wider fluctuation bands – the EMS was a success of integration. A series of ERM crises in September 1992, devaluations, the exit of the British pound and the Italian lira from the EMS, and the decision to widen the permitted fluctuation bands from 2.25 per cent to 15 per cent cast doubt on its future.[79] Nevertheless in 1994–5, currency values were to stabilise again and provide a basis for the introduction of the euro.

During the first half of the 1980s, a new concerted Franco-German integration policy began to take shape, which was based on the previous decisions of Giscard d'Estaing and Schmidt. The main players were now French President François Mitterrand, President of the European Commission Jacques Delors and Federal Chancellor Helmut Kohl. It started with the decision to dismantle border controls, the finalisation of the EEC Treaty by launching the SEM and the preparation of a monetary union.

Since the end of the 1950s, initiatives to reduce border obstacles have been established at the EEC's internal borders. The EUREGIO Rhine–Ems–IJssel in the German–Dutch border region was one of the first cross-border cooperations, which serves as an example of how an 'euregional' identity developed precisely in peripheral locations on the edges of the respective countries and promoted the growing together of Europe on a small scale. The idea of a 'Europe of the regions', as it emerged in the context of Maastricht at the beginning of the 1990s, had thus already been anticipated, which is also to be added to the history of integration.[80]

On 14 June 1985, an agreement was negotiated in the Luxembourg town of Schengen, near the German and French borders, between Belgium, the FRG,

---

79 B. Eichengreen and C. Wyplosz, 'The Unstable EMS' (1993), www.brookings.edu/bp ea-articles/the-unstable-ems.

80 C. Hiepel, '"Borders are the Scars of History"? Cross-Border Co-operation in Europe – the Example of the EUREGIO', *Journal of European Integration History* 22, no. 2 (2016): 263–78.

France, Luxembourg and the Netherlands, leading to the abolition of border controls, the facilitation of the movement of persons, the reduction of restrictions on trade to a minimum, common principles for visa and asylum policies, and cooperation on issues such as drugs, migration, tax fraud, terrorism and the right of police hot pursuit across national borders.[81]

Cooperating interest groups, but also the cross-border and export-oriented economy, played a significant role in this process. Two parallel tendencies of Europeanisation can be observed: Europeanisation through the dismantling of border controls on the one hand, and, on the other, Europeanisation through Benelux cooperation, with Luxembourg, the Netherlands and Belgium paving the way.[82] Owing to the German–German developments in 1989–90 and the opening of the east, at Bonn's request the implementation of Schengen had to be postponed to a later date.

Despite the formation of the customs union in 1968, the EC encountered difficulties in developing a SEM without barriers in the 1970s and 1980s because non-tariff barriers to trade remained, leading to high unemployment, increased competition from outside Europe and indifferent growth. In the early 1980s, these shortcomings of the incomplete 'common market' increased private sector pressure. Various companies such as large European firms and international corporations influenced, for instance through the European Roundtable of Industrialists,[83] Europe's integration process in getting the SEM off the ground; among them were Fiat, Mercedes Daimler Benz, Nestlé, Philips and Siemens. A complementarity between the various interest groups played a role. They all regarded the SEM as a meaningful objective, precisely due to the challenge of an increasingly globalised economy. However, this process had begun before 1985. Max Kohnstamm[84] as

---

81 A. Pudlat, 'Perceptibility and Experience of Inner-European Borders by Institutionalised Border Protection', *Quaestiones Geographicae* 29, no. 4 (2010): 7–13; A. Pudlat, 'Der lange Weg zum Schengen-Raum: Ein Prozess im Vier-Phasen-Modell', *Journal of European Integration History* 17, no. 2 (2011): 303–26; S. Paoli, 'Migration in European Integration: Themes and Debates', *Journal of European Integration History* 22, no. 2 (2016): 279–96; A. Siebold, 'Open Borders as an Act of Solidarity among Peoples, between States or with Migrants: Changing Applications of Solidarity within the Schengen Process', *European Review of History/Revue européenne d'histoire* 24, no. 6 (2017): 991–1006, 991–3.

82 S. Paoli, 'The Relaunch of the Benelux and the Origins of the Schengen Agreement: The Interplay of Two Sub-regional Experiences', in Gehler and Loth (eds.), *Reshaping Europe*, pp. 73–97.

83 S. Schirmann, 'Der Europäische Roundtable of Industrials (ERT) und der europäische Integrationsprozess', in M. Gehler, A. Brait and P. Strobl (eds.), *Geschichte schreiben – Geschichte vermitteln: Inner- und interdisziplinäre Perspektiven auf die Europaforschung* (Hildesheim, Georg W. Olms, 2020), pp. 453–61.

84 A. G. Harryvan and J. van der Harst, *Max Kohnstamm: A European's Life and Work* (Baden-Baden, Nomos, 2011).

Secretary General of the High Authority of the ECSC, the above-mentioned activities of the ERT of industrialists and Jean Monnet's Action Committee for the United States of Europe,[85] as well as the Kangaroo Group,[86] which was established in 1979 as an informal group in the EP with free movement and security as its motto, were active as networks in the background. Not only European companies, but also transnational business corporations and globalised companies, because of their involvement in the world economy, were particularly interested in the SEM project.[87] This is how the European economy was Europeanised by transnational globalised companies. The project also favoured a politicisation of the EC, which in turn Europeanised a new governance.[88]

A favorable factor was the fact that Jacques Delors, the new Commission President in office since January 1985, set himself the goal of accelerating integration. The realisation of the internal market programme was his most important instrument. His congenial partner in achieving this goal was Francis Arthur Lord Cockfield, a former British minister and successor to the German Commissioner Karl-Heinz Narjes with responsibility for the 'common market', taxation and the customs union. This partnership was crucial. Delors provided the intellectual, communications and political leadership; Cockfield worked obsessively on the details and drove the programme vigorously. The strategy for the SMP was set out in a 'White Paper' issued by the Commission. It explained the background to the project and listed the obstacles to the four freedoms within the EC (free movement of goods, services, capital and persons). It listed the types of measures needed to overcome these obstacles. The legislative programme to achieve these objectives included about 300 measures, some of which were already under consideration and others yet to be developed. The three main obstacles consisted of physical (movement of goods and people across borders), technical (lack of uniformity of standards across member states, restrictive practices in public procurement, restrictions on the free movement of workers and liberal professions) and fiscal obstacles (differences in value-added and excise taxes). The key to success was a comprehensive package of measures and a concrete timetable. For each of these issues, a deadline was set for each

---

85 Schwabe, *Jean Monnet*, pp. 293–303.   86 See www.kangaroogroup.de.

87 A. Harryvan, 'The Single Market Project as Response to Globalization: The Role of the Round Table of European Industrialists and Other Non-state Actors in Launching the European Union's Internal Market (1983–1992)', in Gehler and Loth (eds.), *Reshaping Europe*, pp. 211–25.

88 E. Bussière, 'Le Livre Blanc sur le marché intérieur: Objectif et instrument de la relance Delors', in Gehler and Loth (eds.), *Reshaping Europe*, pp. 227–45.

stage of the legislative process, culminating in a final measure either by virtue of a regulation by the Council or by implementation of a directive by the member states no later than the end of 1992. The main obstacle to the project, however, was still the need to obtain widespread unanimity in the Council of Ministers.[89]

The Milan summit of 28–29 June 1985 marked a turning point in the history of integration because the heads of state and government approved the Commission's White Paper on the SEM. However, the Dooge Committee's recommendations on institutional and decision-making reform and on extending the EC's powers were controversial. Three prime ministers were against: Thatcher, the Danish Poul Schlüter and the Greek Andreas Papandreou resisted amending the EEC Treaty and wanted only informal agreements to improve legislative decision-making. Italy's prime minister, Bettino Craxi, advocated an intergovernmental conference to negotiate treaty reform, as allowed by Article 236 of the EEC Treaty. Once it had turned out that Thatcher, Schlüter and Papandreou continued to resist, Craxi called for a vote in the European Council, paving the way for the IGC that led to the SEA 6 months later. The Milan summit was neither a failure nor a breakthrough, but it ultimately helped prepare the ground for reform that strengthened majority voting, and thus transformed the EC. It ended in a split vote with a majority of seven to three in favor of an IGC on powers of the institutions, new competences of the EC and the creation of a SEM with the aim of an additional treaty to supplement the EEC Treaty and a contractual basis for the EPC. On 17 February 1986, this amending treaty was signed in Luxembourg by a total of nine of the twelve members (Belgium, France, Germany, Ireland, Luxembourg, the Netherlands, Portugal, Spain and the UK). Denmark, Greece and Italy followed on 28 February, after a referendum on the treaty had been held in Denmark. The SEA amended and supplemented the EC Treaties. Political union was not adopted, but remained a declared goal. The SEA formulated the goal of creating a SEM by 31 December 1992. To this end, the SEA reformed the legislative process by introducing the cooperation procedure and extending QMV to new areas. The qualified majority in the Council was a decisive factor in implementing the EC's internal market programme in 1992. Furthermore, it was agreed for the first time that the European Council would meet at least twice a year.

89 For a general overview, see G. Grin, *The Battle of the Single European Market: Achievements and Economics 1945–2000* (London, New York, NY and Bahrain, Routledge, 2003), pp. 111–66.

The SEA entered into force on 1 July 1987, after Ireland ratified it on 25 June 1987, the last of the twelve members to do so.

An important means of propagating the wisdom and desirability of the SEM was the so-called Cecchini Report, named after Paolo Cecchini, an Italian banker and economist who, in 1986–7, worked with a group of researchers in a major Commission-funded project to quantify the 'costs of non-Europe' that the EC would incur by maintaining an incomplete market. Using data from the four largest member states, Cecchini's team of independent consultants assessed the disadvantages and advantages of the status quo by analysing the effects of market barriers and comparing EC and US markets. It looked at the financial costs to business of administrative procedures and delays associated with complying with customs formalities, opportunity costs of lost trade and costs to national governments that would result from customs controls.

The study, published on 29 March 1988, followed the European Council meeting in Brussels on 11–13 February 1988, at which the tug of war over the shape and timing of the SEM had ended with the adoption of the Delors I package. The study held out the prospect of strong additional growth and increased stability for the Europe of the Twelve if, according to the SEA, it succeeded in creating an area 'without internal frontiers in which the free movement of goods, persons, services and capital . . . is ensured' (Article 8a). The main thesis of the voluminous sixteen-volume publication was that existing physical, technical and fiscal barriers to trade would cost the EC 3–6 per cent of GDP annually. Although its methodology was criticised and its conclusions proved to be exaggerated, the Cecchini Report was an important communicative, propagandistic and psychological prop for conveying and enforcing the '1992' programme.

The Hanover European Council of 27–28 June 1988 decided to establish a committee, chaired by Delors, to study the EMU mentioned in the SEA. This included the central bank governors of EC member states, another Commissioner and three independent experts. It produced a report, officially titled 'Report of the Committee for the Study of Economic and Monetary Union', which was completed in April 1989. The so-called Delors Report outlined three stages for the realisation of EMU. Stage 1 involved the introduction of free movement of capital in the EC and closer monetary and macroeconomic cooperation among member states and their central banks. Stage 2 provided for a new European system of central banks to oversee and coordinate national monetary policies. Stage 3 envisaged 'irrevocably fixed' exchange rate parities, with full responsibility for economic and monetary policy devolved to EC institutions. The European Council discussed the Delors Report at the

Madrid Summit in June 1989 and decided to launch stage 1 on 1 July 1990. Six months later, at the Strasbourg Summit in December 1989, the European Council decided, despite British objections, to convene an IGC to determine the treaty changes necessary for the transition to stages 2 and 3. The IGC opened in Rome in December 1990 and concluded at the Maastricht Summit in December 1991. The provisions of the Treaty on EU for EMU largely followed the contours outlined in the Delors Report. The 'Delors Package' (which provided for a reform of the financing system), the CAP and the increase in the EC Structural Funds, and the 'three-stage Delors Plan' to create the EMU all demonstrated the new rationality of the drive towards integration.

In the meantime, Europe was still in the middle of the Cold War. While Paris rejected the Strategic Defense Initiative programme of US President Ronald Reagan, Bonn found itself in a dilemma. France worked hard to reach a security policy consensus with the FRG. In 1985–6, a satisfactory agreement was achieved between Kohl and Mitterrand. A certain desire for 'strategic independence' arose between the two partners on either side of the Rhine.[90] The background to these German–French security policy agreements was the 'Reykjavík effect' (named after the meeting place) of the 1986 disarmament agreements between Mikhail S. Gorbachev and Ronald Reagan, who negotiated the Intermediate-Range Nuclear Forces Treaty over the heads of the Europeans, which was to be signed in 1987.

The agenda of the Maastricht Treaty negotiations owes much to the tendencies of the European integration process in the 1980s: the use of amendments to the Treaties of Rome, the desire for renewal even outside the formal Community context and an increasingly strong belief in institutional change as a means of coping with the EC's ever-growing tasks and new challenges, not to mention integration policy synergy effects.[91]

Conclusion

Western European integration from 1955 to 1987 meant the continuation of a unique historical process. Progress and setbacks[92] alternated. Starting with the ECSC, which laid the institutional foundations for the further course of

90 F. Schotters, 'European Emancipation within the Atlantic Alliance? Franco-German Initiatives in European Defense', in Gehler and Loth (eds.), *Reshaping Europe*, pp. 461–76.
91 N. P. Ludlow, 'European Integration in the 1980s: On the Way to Maastricht?', *Journal of European Integration History* 19, no. 1 (2013): 11–22.
92 D. Dinan, *Europe Recast: A History of European Union* (Basingstoke, Palgrave Macmillan, 2014), pp. 123–59.

integration, the Treaties of Rome formed a basic law of gradual progress up to the Maastricht Treaty with its first pillar. From Messina to the SEA there were several turning points. The formation of two other communities (the EEC and Euratom, 1957–8), de Gaulle's double veto of British membership (in 1963 and 1967) and his closing of ranks with Adenauer (1963) strengthened the Franco-German axis as a basis for further bilateral cooperation. The alternative British option of a large FTA as counterpart to the EEC Treaty was prevented thanks to de Gaulle, who thus became the 'saviour' of the EEC. The Hague Summit (1969) was another turning point because it set the course for the 'northern enlargement' after de Gaulle's resignation. However, the problem of the costly and budget-burdening CAP remained unsolved. The trade divide between EC and EFTA states was overcome through customs and trade agreements for industrial products (1973), and the UK was integrated as an increasingly recalcitrant partner. While the deepening of the Communities was held up by de Gaulle's internal veto policy and delayed, with all its consequences, by two decades from the mid 1960s to the mid 1980s, the 1970s cannot be described as a break or discontinuity with the previous development of integration. In contrast to the prejudiced catchword of 'Eurosclerosis', there were also trend-setting impulses and decisions in this phase, with the ERM and EMS and the first direct elections to the EP. There was continuity in the sense of the enlargements from six, to nine and finally twelve members. On the one hand, the resolution of the dispute over the British membership fees weighed heavily on the Community (1975–84); on the other hand, the UK was firmly committed to the SMP. The SEA (1985–7) then represented another turning point, because it laid the decision-making basis for the creation of the Single Market. The development from the mid 1950s to the mid 1980s was, on the whole, more one of integration than of disintegration and created the conditions for further opportunities for deepening. There were various crises that generated different needs for solutions. The crisis surrounding the failure of the EDC (1954) was quickly overcome with the Treaties of Rome (1957); de Gaulle's empty chair policy was a blow to the community method. The EC did not recover from this until two decades later. The accession of the UK (1973) created more community problems than progress in integration.

European reconstruction is understood as a 'revolution of a continent'.[93] With Messina (1955), Venice (1956) and Rome (1957), initially only western

---

93 G. Grin, *Construction Européenne: La Révolution d'un continent* (Lausanne, Fondation Jean Monnet pour l'Europe, 2021).

Europe regained a kind of partial sovereignty. With The Hague (1969) and 'northern enlargement', a global external perspective opened up with British membership (1973). With the 'southern enlargement', the maritime dimension of the Communities was completed by the Mediterranean as a European sea. The SEA (1987) paved the way for further deepening towards a single market, which strengthened the internal partial sovereignty of western Europe, but the question of the *finalité politique* (political end destination) remained open. The community method was too weak to bring the question of confederation or federation with more supranationality to a decisive solution. Despite all setbacks in the light of Europe's history, the phase from 1955 to 1987 can be understood as a story of progress.

Recommended Reading

Bussière, E., V. Dujardin, M. Dumoulin, P. N. Ludlow, J. W. Brouwer and E. Palmero (eds.). *The European Commission 1973–86: History and Memories of an Institution* (Luxembourg, Publications Office of the European Union, 2014).

Deighton, A. and A. S. Milward (eds.). *Widening, Deepening and Acceleration: The European Economic Community 1957–1963* (Baden-Baden and Brussels, Nomos and Bruylant 1999).

Dumoulin, M. (ed.). *The European Commission 1957–72: History and Memories* (Luxembourg, Publications Office of the European Union, 2007).

Gehler, M. (ed., in collaboration with A. Pudlat). *Vom gemeinsamen Markt zur europäischen Unionsbildung: 50 Jahre Römische Verträge 1957–2007/From Common Market to European Union Building: 50 Years of the Rome Treaties 1957–2007* (Vienna, Cologne and Weimar, Böhlau, 2009).

Gehler, M. *The Signing of the Rome Treaties 65 Years Ago: Origins, Provisions and Effects* (Bonn, ZEI, 2022).

Gehler, M. and W. Loth (eds.). *Reshaping Europe: Towards a Political, Economic and Monetary Union, 1984–1989* (Baden-Baden, Nomos, 2020).

Kaiser, W. 'Shaping European Union: The European Parliament and Institutional Reform, 1979–1989' (2018), www.europarl.europa.eu/RegData/etudes/STUD/2018/630271/EP RS_STU(2018)630271_EN.pdf.

Laursen, J. (ed.). *The Institutions and Dynamics of the European Community, 1973–83* (Baden-Baden, Nomos, 2014).

Loth, W. (ed.). *Crises and Compromises: The European Project 1963–69* (Baden-Baden, Nomos, 2001).

Van der Harst, J. (ed.). *Beyond the Customs Union: The European Community's Quest for Deepening, Widening and Completion, 1969–1975* (Brussels, Paris and Baden-Baden, Bruylant and Nomos, 2007).

Van der Harst, J. and G. Voerman (eds.). *An Impossible Job? The Presidents of the European Commission 1958–2014* (London, Harper, 2015).

L. Warlouzet, *Governing Europe in a Globalizing World: Neoliberalism and Its Alternatives Following the 1973 Oil Crisis* (London, Routledge, 2017).

3

The Making of the European Union

SOPHIE VANHOONACKER

Introduction

Coinciding with radical regional and global changes, the period 1986–93 is a fascinating time in the history of European integration. The fall of the Berlin Wall (November 1989) opened the prospect of ending the division of the European continent and the bipolar world order, raising fundamental questions for both international and intra-European relations.

The momentous events coincided with a renewed dynamism in European integration.[1] In June 1985, the member states of the European Communities (EC) had adopted a Commission White Paper with almost 300 measures required to complete the internal market of goods, services, persons and capital by the end of 1992.[2] The Single European Act (SEA), a series of treaty amendments aimed at more democratic and effective policy-making, laid the constitutional groundwork for the realisation of this ambitious plan. The decision on the completion of the internal market also relaunched the debate about the creation of an Economic and Monetary Union (EMU), and, at the European Council of Madrid (June 1989), the political leaders of the twelve EC member states agreed to organise an intergovernmental conference (IGC) on how to gradually realise such a union. Following the fall of the Iron Curtain, the debate was successively broadened to a Political Union (PU).

Under the leadership of the successive Luxembourg and Dutch presidencies, the IGCs on EMU and PU led to the adoption of the Maastricht Treaty in December 1991. With provisions on the creation of an EMU,

---

1 P. Ludlow, 'From Deadlock to Dynamism. The European Community in the 1980s', in D. Dinan (ed.), *Origins and Evolution of the European Union*, 2nd ed. (Oxford, Oxford University Press, 2014), pp. 217–32.
2 Commission of the European Communities, 'Completing the Internal Market: White Paper from the Commission to the European Council (Milan, 28–29 June 1985)', https://op.europa.eu/en/publication-detail/-/publication/4ff490f3-dbb6-4331-a2ea-a3ca59f974a8/language-en.

a Common Foreign and Security Policy (CFSP), cooperation in Justice and Home Affairs (JHA) and important institutional and policy reforms, it is undoubtedly one of the most important treaty revisions in the history of European integration.

Subsequent to this debate on strengthening the Union's integration, the revolutionary European developments also put the question of an eastern expansion on the agenda. While many in the EC felt that welcoming the countries of central and eastern Europe was their moral and political duty, there were also concerns about the resilience of these young democracies and emerging market economies.[3] In that light, the European Council of Copenhagen made accession conditional on stable political institutions, a well-functioning market economy and the capacity to take on the obligations of membership.[4]

In summary, the period from 1986–93 comprises at least three important milestones in the history of European integration: the SEA (June 1987); the IGCs on PU and EMU leading to the Maastricht Treaty; and the historical decision to welcome the countries of central and eastern Europe under the condition that they would fulfil the Copenhagen criteria.

This chapter starts by giving an overview of the state of the art of the relevant academic literature. Secondly, it describes the main developments and, finally, it provides an in-depth discussion of key issues which continue to be of high relevance to this day, such as democratic legitimacy and the deepening as well as widening of European integration. The chapter concludes with a reflection on the relevance of this period for the broader process of European integration.

The State of the Art

As a result of the renewed boost in European integration, the period 1986–93 has received ample attention in the academic literature.[5] Broadly speaking, the literature can be grouped into three bodies of scholarship. The first group primarily describes and analyses the *substance* of the numerous policy and

3 A. Michalski, 'The Enlarging European Union', in Dinan (ed.), *Origins and Evolution of the European Union*, pp. 274–301.
4 European Council, 'European Council in Copenhagen, 21–22 June 1993. Conclusions of the Presidency', www.consilium.europa.eu/media/21225/72921.pdf.
5 This section partly builds on F. Laursen and S. Vanhoonacker, 'The Maastricht Treaty', in *Encyclopedia of European Union Politics* (Oxford, Oxford University Press, 2019), https://oxfordre.com/politics/oso/viewentry/10.1093$oo2facrefore$oo2f9780190228637.001.0001$oo2facrefore-9780190228637-e-1067.

institutional changes taking place in the European polity. Not surprisingly, legal scholars are especially well represented here. A second cluster, strongly dominated by political scientists, is more interested in questions about *process and agency*. A third group uses the new impetus in European integration as a moment to reflect on the broader theoretical puzzle of why states cooperate and pool sovereignty.

The substantial policy changes introduced by the SEA and the Maastricht Treaty triggered several publications describing and analysing these changes. A good example of this is a series of articles in the *Common Market Law Review*, one of the most prominent journals of EC law at the time. Contributors examine questions such as the SEA's implications for various areas, including the Internal Market (IM), European democracy and decision-making, foreign policy cooperation and environmental policy.[6] Journals that are more geared towards an audience of political scientists, such as the *Journal of Common Market Studies* and the *Journal of European Integration*, also pay attention to the subject, although to a lesser extent than the EC legal journals.[7] Economists focus on diverse aspects of the IM, delving into questions such as firms' strategies to exploit the new opportunities, the impact on foreign direct investment, questions of regulatory competition and the IM's impact on developing countries.[8]

The stream of publications on the Maastricht Treaty is even larger. Owing to the importance of the treaty and the high number of amendments in

---

6 See, for instance, R. Bieber, J. Pantalis and J. Schoo, 'Implications of the Single Act for the European Parliament', *Common Market Law Review* 23, no. 4 (1986): 767–92; S. Davidson and D. Freestone, 'Community Competence and Part III of the Single European Act', *Common Market Law Review* 23, no. 4 (1986): 793–801; A. G. Toth, 'The Legal Status of the Declarations Annexed to the Single European Act', *Common Market Law Review* 23, no. 4 (1986): 803–12; D. Edward, 'The Impact of the Single Act on the Institutions', *Common Market Law Review* 24, no. 1 (1987): 19–30; C. D. Ehlermann, 'The Internal Market Following the Single European Act', *Common Market Law Review* 24, no. 3 (1987): 361–409; L. Kramer, 'Single European Act and Environmental Protection: Reflections on Several New Provisions in Community Law', *Common Market Law Review* 24, no. 4 (1987): 659–88.

7 J. Lodge, 'The Single European Act: Towards a New Euro-dynamism', *Journal of Common Market Studies* 24, no. 3 (1986): 203–23; J. Lodge, 'The Single European Act and the New Legislative Cooperation Procedure: A Critical Analysis', *Journal of European Integration* 11, no. 1 (1987): 5–28.

8 P. Buigues and A. Jacquemin, 'Strategies of Forms and Structural Environments in the Large Internal Market', *Journal of Common Market Studies* 28, no. 1 (1989): 53–67; A. Koekkoek, A. Kuyvenhoven and W. Molle, 'Europe 1992 and the Developing Countries: An Overview', *Journal of Common Market Studies* 29, no. 2 (1990): 111–31; B. Heitger and J. Stehn, 'Japanese Direct Investments in the EC – Response to the Internal Market 1993?', *Journal of Common Market Studies* 29, no. 1 (1990): 1–15; J. Pelkmans, 'The New Approaches to Technical Harmonization and Standardization', *Journal of Common Market Studies* 25, no. 3 (1987): 249–69; J. Sun and J. Pelkmans, 'Regulatory Competition in the Single Market', *Journal of Common Market Studies* 33, no. 1 (1995): 67–89.

a wide range of fields, this is not surprising.[9] While some articles deal with the treaty in its entirety, others focus on particular policy fields.[10]

A second body of literature is more interested in the constitutionalisation process, from agenda-setting to ratification, and the position and power struggles among the different protagonists. It concerns both accounts by actors who themselves were involved in negotiations[11] and theory-informed contributions by academics with attention both to the domestic- and to the European-level debates and struggles.[12] While the majority of studies concentrate on the bigger member states, a study conducted by the European Institute of Public Administration under the lead of Laursen and Vanhoonacker analyses the position of all twelve member states in the IGC on PU and also includes some of the key policy proposals submitted by the member states.[13] In the case of the Maastricht Treaty, the academic literature also pays specific attention to

9 See, for example, V. Constantinesco, R. Kovar and D. Simon, *Traité sur l'Union européenne (signé à Maastricht le 7 février 1992): Commentaire article par article* (Paris, Éditions Economica, 1995); R. Corbett, *The Treaty of Maastricht: From Conception to Ratification: A Comprehensive Reference Guide* (Harlow, Longman Current Affairs, 1993); F. Descheemaekere, *Mieux comprendre le Traité de Maastricht* (Paris, Les Éditions d'Organisation, 1992); E. Noël, 'Reflections on the Maastricht Treaty', *Government and Opposition* 27, no. 2 (1992): 148–57; A. Raoux and A. Terrenoire, *L'Europe et Maastricht: Le pour et le contre* (Paris, Chercher midi, 1992).

10 J. Monar, 'Justice and Home Affairs: The Treaty of Maastricht as a Decisive Intergovernmental Gate Opener', *Journal of European Integration* 34, no. 7 (2012): 717–34.

11 J. De Ruyt, *L'acte unique européen: Commentaire* (Brussels, Éditions de l'Université de Bruxelles, 1987); P. S. Christoffersen, *Traktaten om den Europæiske Union: Baggrund – Forhandling – Resultat* (Copenhagen, Jurist- og Økonomforbundets Forlag, 1992); J. Cloos, G. Reinesch, D. Vignes and J. Weyland, *Le traité de Maastricht: Genèse, analyse, commentaires* (Brussels, Bruylant, 1993); R. Corbett, 'The Intergovernmental Conference on Political Union', *Journal of Common Market Studies* 30, no. 3 (1992): 271–98; Y. Doutriaux, *Le Traité sur l'Union européenne* (Paris, Armand Colin, 1992); T. Padoa-Schioppa, *The Road to Monetary Union in Europe: The Emperor, the Kings, and the Genies* (Oxford, Clarendon Press, 1994).

12 D. B. Cameron, 'The 1992 Initiative: Causes and Consequences', in A. Sbragia (ed.), *Euro-politics: Institutions and Policymaking in the 'New' European Community* (Washington, DC, The Brookings Institution, 1992), pp. 23–74; M. J. Baun, 'The Maastricht Treaty as High Politics: Germany, France, and European Integration', *Political Science Quarterly* 110, no. 4 (1995–6): 605–24; K. Dyson and K. Featherstone, *The Road to Maastricht: Negotiating Economic and Monetary Union* (Oxford, Oxford University Press, 1999); G. Garrett, 'The Politics of Maastricht', *Economics and Politics* 5 (1993): 105–23; C. Mazzucelli, *France and Germany at Maastricht: Politics and Negotiations to Create the European Union* (New York, NY and London, Garland, 1997); R. B. Pedersen, *Danmark under traktaterne: Et case studium af regerings- og parlamentsrelationerne under forhandlingerne om Fælles Akten og Maastricht-traktaten* (Aarhus, Politica, 2009); T. Christiansen, S. Duke and E. Kirchner, 'Understanding and Assessing the Maastricht Treaty', *Journal of European Integration* 34, no. 7 (2012): 685–98.

13 F. Laursen and S. Vanhoonacker (eds.), *The Intergovernmental Conference on Political Union: Institutional Reforms, New Policies and International Identity of the European Community* (Maastricht, European Institute of Public Administration; Dordrecht, Martinus Nijhoff, 1992).

the ratification process, which, in contrast to the SEA, was rather problematic in some of the member states.[14] In Denmark, which organised a national referendum (as did France and Ireland), the amended treaty was first rejected, and was approved only after further concessions had been made.[15]

The third body of literature tries to understand the decisions made in Maastricht in the light of the broader theoretical debate on how to make sense of processes of regional integration. Different theoretical schools advance competing explanations for what happened. Important points of discussion include the relative weight of supranational actors versus the member states and (geo)political versus economic factors. One of the most prominent voices in the debate is Andrew Moravcsik, the principal representative of the liberal intergovernmentalist school. In *The Choice for Europe* (1998), he argues that it is the combination of converging economic interests, the relative (economic) power of member states and concerns for credible commitment that can best account for the form, outcome and timing both of the SEA and of the Maastricht negotiations.[16] In the case of the SEA, for example, he argues that the outcome can best be explained as an inter-state bargain between France, Germany and the United Kingdom (UK), at a time when the economic policies in these most important European economies were converging towards increased support of liberalisation. The extended use of qualified majority voting (QMV) is seen as an important instrument for realising credible commitment and to avoid deadlock in the decision-making process.

While Moravcsik, like classical intergovernmentalists, puts the nation state and its relative power at the centre of his analysis, neo-functionalists emphasise the key role of supranational actors.[17] While distancing themselves from the neo-functionalist idea of spillover from one policy field to the other,

14 F. Laursen and S. Vanhoonacker (eds.), *The Ratification of the Maastricht Treaty: Issues, Debates and Future Implications* (Maastricht, European Institute of Public Administration; Dordrecht, Martinus Nijhoff, 1994).

15 F. Laursen, 'Denmark and the Ratification of the Maastricht Treaty', in Laursen and Vanhoonacker (eds.), *The Ratification of the Maastricht Treaty*, pp. 61–86; P. Svensson, 'The Danish Yes to Maastricht and Edinburgh. The EC Referendum of May 1993', *Scandinavian Political Studies* 17, no. 1 (1994): 69–82; T. Worre, 'First No, Then Yes: The Danish Referendums on the Maastricht Treaty 1992 and 1993', *Journal of Common Market Studies* 33, no. 2 (1993): 235–57.

16 A. Moravcsik, 'Negotiating the Single European Act: National Interests and Conventional State Craft in the European Community', *International Organization* 45, no. 1 (1991): 19–56. See also A. Moravcsik, *The Choice for Europe: Social Purpose and State Power from Messina to Maastricht* (Ithaca, NY, Cornell University Press, 1998), pp. 314–378 (on the SEA), 379–471 (on Maastricht).

17 E. B. Haas, *The Uniting of Europe: Political, Social, and Economic Forces, 1950–1957* (Stanford, CA, Stanford University Press, 2004 [1958]); L. Lindberg and S. Scheingold, *Europe's*

Sandholtz and Zysman, for instance, argue that, in the case of the SEA, the European Commission led by President Jacques Delors in cooperation with a transnational industrial elite has been fundamental for the new dynamism in European integration in the late 1980s.[18] In a well-researched study on EMU, Dyson and Featherstone opt for an actor-centred approach with the aim of getting a better understanding of the role of individual negotiators such as political leaders and transnational experts.[19] Their key argument is that negotiations are always multidimensional and that the EMU negoti-ations can best be understood as a process where both cognitive and strategic processes have played a crucial role.

For (neo-)realists, who generally are better at explaining the reluctance of states to delegate sovereignty, the revitalised EU raised challenges, as it defied their assumptions about states and international institutes. For Kenneth Waltz, the father of neo-realism, the willingness of the EC member states to cooperate with the United States could best be explained by invoking the Cold War bipolar system, and scholars such as Mearsheimer argued that, after the unification of both Germany and the European continent, the period of stability and peace would soon come to an end.[20] Trying to come to grips with the empirical anomaly of intensified European cooperation after the end of the Cold War, Joseph Grieco proposes revisiting the neo-realist assumptions about international organisations and comes up with the amended proposition that, when states share a common interest, they may cooperate under the condition that the rules of the game give them sufficient space to voice their concerns and interests.[21]

Historians are currently still under-represented in this overview. Owing to the 30-year rule, according to which government documents are not released until three decades after their creation, they have been deprived of indispens-able access to archival resources. First steps to historicise the SEA and the Maastricht treaty include a volume edited by Gehler and Loth and a special issue of the *Journal of European Integration History*, edited by Geary, Germond

Would-Be Polity: Patterns of Change in the European Community (Englewood Cliffs, NJ, Prentice-Hall, 1970).

18 W. Sandholtz and J. Zysman, '1992: Recasting the European Bargain', *World Politics* 42, no. 1 (1989): 95–128.

19 Dyson and Featherstone, *The Road to Maastricht*.

20 J. Mearsheimer, 'Back to the Future. Instability in Europe after the Cold War', *International Security* 15, no. 1 (1990): 5–56.

21 J. M. Grieco, 'The Maastricht Treaty, Economic and Monetary Union and the Neo-realist Research Programme', *Review of International Studies* 21, no. 1 (1995): 21–40.

and Patel.[22] It is to be expected that, with the gradual disclosure of archives, the period 1986–93 will receive increased attention from historical scholars.

From the SEA to Copenhagen

With the benefit of hindsight, one may get the impression that the steps taken in the period 1986–93 were the result of a linear process, with one move more or less automatically leading to the next. In reality, however, every phase was the result of long discussions and hard-fought compromises. The decision on the 1986 IGC, for instance, was not taken by unanimous agreement, as both Denmark and Greece, as well as the UK, opposed the treaty change.[23] In addition, it is crucial to recognise that important decisions such as the completion of the IM and the creation of an EMU were the culmination of a long process that had already started well before the mid 1980s. As will be discussed below, the break with the 1970s and early 1980s was therefore less drastic than is often suggested in the literature. At the same time, it cannot be denied that the collapse of communism in central and eastern Europe was truly revolutionary and placed some of the earlier discussions on European integration in a radically altered context.

Completing the IM

The revival of European integration did not come out of the blue but was the result of a variety of both external and internal factors. Important external challenges included the fierce economic competition with Japan and the United States, as well as tensions in transatlantic relations about how to best deal with the increased Cold War rivalry. Internal factors included the member states' high dependence on exports to other EC countries, the coming to power of centre and centre-right governments in most of the member states and the economic volte-face in France moving away from Keynesian economic policies, as well as the 1984 settlement at Fontainebleau on the protracted British budgetary question.[24] Following a German–Italian initiative for a draft

---

22 M. Gehler and W. Loth (eds.), *Reshaping Europe: Towards a Political, Economic and Monetary Union, 1984–1989* (Baden-Baden, Nomos Verlag, 2020); M. Geary, C. Germond and K. Patel, 'The Maastricht Treaty Negotiations and Consequences in a Historical Perspective. Introduction', *Journal of European Integration History* 19, no. 1 (2003): 5–9.

23 D. Dinan, 'The Single European Act: Revitalising European Integration', in F. Laursen (ed.), *Designing the European Union: From Paris to Lisbon* (London, Palgrave Macmillan, 2012), pp. 124–46, 130.

24 Cameron, 'The 1992 Initiative', pp. 35–45; N. P. Ludlow, 'A Double-Edged Victory: Fontainebleau and the Resolution of the British Budget Problem, 1983–84', in Gehler and Loth, *Reshaping Europe*, pp. 43–72.

European Act on further European integration, also known as the Genscher–Colombo Plan, the European leaders, meeting in Stuttgart in June 1983, had adopted the 'Solemn Declaration on European Union'. They called for 'deepening and broadening the scope of European activities, so that they coherently cover, albeit on a variety of legal bases, a growing proportion of the member states' mutual relations and of their external relations'.[25]

A first important step in realising these objectives was made during the Milan European Council of June 1985 by deciding to endorse the Commission White Paper on completing the IM, which was developed under the leadership of Commission President Delors.[26] In addition, the national leaders also discussed a report on institutional reform by the so-called Dooge committee, an ad hoc forum named after its chair, the Irish senator Jim Dooge.[27] The most important decision, however, was to convene an IGC to work out the required treaty amendments necessary to realise these ambitions.[28]

The IGC text – an amending treaty called the SEA – was adopted by the European Council of Luxembourg (December 1986) and entered into force in July 1987, after ratification by the national parliaments and – in the case of Ireland – a referendum. In contrast to the Commission, the European Parliament (EP) was not part of the IGC negotiations, but it had expressed its views through a Draft Treaty Establishing the European Union (1984) prepared under the leadership of Altiero Spinelli, a Member of the EP (MEP) and European federalist.[29] This draft treaty was an interesting illustration of how the directly elected EP tried to position itself in regard to the inter-institutional dynamics.[30]

Beyond the commitment to complete the IM by 1992, the amended treaty included provisions on the environment, research and development and economic cohesion. Greece, Portugal and Spain, all of which feared that the IM initiative would widen regional disparities, demanded compensation

25 'Solemn Declaration on European Union. European Council, Stuttgart, 19 June 1983', *Bulletin of the European Communities* no. 6 (1983): 24–9, http://aei.pitt.edu/1788/1/stut tgart_declaration_1983.pdf.
26 European Council, 'Conclusions, Milan, 28–29 June 1985', www.consilium.europa.eu/ media/20646/1985_june_-_milan__eng_.pdf.
27 Dinan, 'The Single European Act', pp. 126–7.
28 G. Grin, 'The Negotiations on the Single European Act', in Gehler and Loth, *Reshaping Europe*, pp. 149–66.
29 European Parliament, 'Draft Treaty Establishing the European Union' (1984), https:// op.europa.eu/en/publication-detail/-/publication/52f9545f-202d-40c6-96a6-5a896a46ad70.
30 D. Preda, 'Spinelli's Initiative and the European Parliament's Union', in Gehler and Loth, *Reshaping Europe*, pp. 99–118.

through structural funds.[31] Monetary integration was also discussed, but, although the preamble repeated the 1972 commitment to 'the progressive realisation of Economic and Monetary Union', the British demanded that any further cooperation in economic and monetary policy involving institutional changes would require an IGC. This gave them a de facto veto.[32]

The most important measures in terms of efficiency and democratic decision-making involved the extension of QMV and the introduction of the cooperation procedure, a new legislative procedure applicable to most IM decisions. Although it fell short of making the EP a full co-legislator on equal footing with the Council, the latter was an important step beyond the mere consultation of the EP.[33]

Last but not least, the SEA also codified European Political Cooperation (EPC), the foreign policy cooperation among the member states that took place outside the treaty framework.[34] With growing tensions in East–West relations and irritation because the United States and the Soviet Union were discussing European security over the member states' heads, the member states decided to integrate the EPC provisions into the revised Treaty of Rome in a new Title III. By setting up a small secretariat in Brussels under the authority of the rotating presidency, they also made a further step in the 'Brusselisation' of EPC. Foreign policy cooperation kept its intergovernmental character. The 'High Contracting Parties' continued to make decisions by consensus while the Commission was only associated with EPC and the EP was merely informed of these decisions post factum. As before, the decisions of EPC were not subject to the jurisdiction of the European Court of Justice.

The political leaders also agreed to work more closely on the political and economic aspects of security, but strengthened military cooperation remained a taboo. Discussions in the early 1980s had made clear that this was not acceptable either for neutral Ireland or for Denmark and Greece. In 1984, the other EC member states had therefore turned to the Western European Union (WEU) as a forum for closer security cooperation. In 1987, the WEU member states adopted a Platform on European Security Interests[35] in which they

31 D. Dinan, 'The Single European Act'.
32 M. Thatcher, *The Downing Street Years* (London, Harper Collins, 1993), p. 355.
33 Dinan, 'The Single European Act', pp. 137–8.
34 M. E. Guasconi, 'European Political Cooperation and the Single European Act', in Gehler and Loth, *Reshaping Europe*, pp. 129–48; G. Clemens, A. Reinfeldt and M. A. Telse Rüter, *Europäisierung von Aussenpolitik? Die Europäische Politische Zusammenarbeit (EPZ) in den 1970er Jahren* (Baden-Baden, Nomos Verlag, 2019).
35 Western European Union, 'Platform on European Security Interests' (1987), http://aei.pitt.edu/43384/1/WEU.Platform.pdf.

expressed their commitment to develop the European pillar of the North Atlantic Treaty Organization (NATO) and create a European defence identity.[36]

Maastricht

British Prime Minister Margaret Thatcher's hope that the SEA (Table 3.1) would lead the EC to concentrate primarily 'on its role as a huge market' was not realised.[37] On the contrary, the decision to complete the IM gave new impetus to an EMU, the idea of which had been around since the 1969 Hague summit. In March 1979, the member states set up the European Monetary System (EMS), which, after a difficult start, evolved into a system of relatively stable exchange rates.[38] While the EMS was generally seen as a success, the French were heavily frustrated by their limited say in

Table 3.1 Key dates for the SEA

Time	Event
European Council, Luxembourg 29–30 June 1981	The EC heads of state or government express concern about the poor state of the IM
Solemn Declaration on European Union 19 June 1983	The EC heads of state or government call for a deepening and widening of EC activities
European Council, Fontainebleau 25–26 June 1984	Agreement on British rebate
European Council, Milan 28–29 June 1985	Decision to endorse the Commission White paper on completing the IM and on convening an IGC
European Council, Luxembourg 2–4 December 1986	Agreement on the SEA
17 and 28 February 1986	Signature of the SEA
26 May 1987	Irish referendum on the SEA
1 July 1987	The SEA comes into force

---

36 P. Tsakaloyannis, *Western European Security in a Changing World: From the Reactivation of the WEU to the Single European Act* (Maastricht, European Institute of Public Administration, 1988).

37 Thatcher, *The Downing Street Years*, p. 356.

38 R. Griffith, 'Under the Shadow of Stagflation. Europe's Integration in the 1970s', in Dinan (ed.), *Origins and Evolution of the European Union*, pp. 165–88; P. Ludlow, *The Making of the European Monetary System: A Case Study of the Politics of the European Community* (London, Butterworth, 1982).

monetary policy-making, resulting from the position of the Deutsche Mark as the system's de facto anchor currency. Following several French proposals, Germany put the question of a monetary union on the agenda of their Council Presidency, and at the European Council of Hannover (June 1988) the European leaders appointed Commission President Delors as the chair of a committee tasked to propose concrete stages leading to an EMU.[39] Following a discussion of the Delors report[40] on the development of an EMU in three stages, the European Council of Madrid (June 1989) agreed to convene an IGC on an EMU once the first stage, expected in July 1990, had started.[41]

Barely 5 months after the Madrid decision, the revolutionary events in central and eastern Europe placed the EMU debate in a new geostrategic context, raising questions about the position and role of a united Germany in Europe and the future shape of transatlantic relations, as well as Europe's relations with the Soviet Union/Russia. In April 1990, French President François Mitterrand and German Chancellor Helmut Kohl therefore proposed to launch an IGC on PU to further strengthen the EC's institutional architecture and democratic legitimation and develop a common foreign and security policy.[42] The proposal for a second and parallel IGC was agreed on at the Dublin European Council in June 1990.[43] This late decision implied that the IGC on PU was much less well prepared than the one for EMU, where many of the institutional issues such as the statutory independence of the European Central Bank (ECB) had already been settled before the start of the IGC.[44]

The IGCs on EMU and PU, launched in December 1990 and chaired by the Luxembourg (first half of 1991) and Dutch (second half) presidencies, were concluded after 1 year of negotiations during the European Council in Maastricht (9–10 December 1991). The Maastricht Treaty amended the earlier

39 'European Council in Hannover, 27–28 June 1988. Conclusions of the Presidency', www.europarl.europa.eu/summits/hannover/ha_en.pdf.

40 Committee for the Study of the Economic and Monetary Union, 'Report on Economic and Monetary Union in the European Community' (1989), http://aei.pitt.edu/1007/1/monetary_delors.pdf.

41 European Council, 'Presidency Conclusions European Council, Madrid, 26 and 27 June 1989', www.consilium.europa.eu/media/20589/1989_june_-_madrid__eng_.pdf. See also Cameron, 'The 1992 Initiative', pp. 26–7.

42 'Kohl–Mitterrand Letter to the Irish Presidency, 19 April 1990', in Laursen and Vanhoonacker (eds.), The Intergovernmental Conference on Political Union, p. 276.

43 European Council, 'Presidency Conclusions, Dublin, 25 and 26 June 1990', www.consilium.europa.eu/media/20562/1990_june_-_dublin__eng_.pdf.

44 D. Heisenberg, 'From Single Market to Single Currency', in Dinan (ed.), Origins and Evolution of the European Union, pp. 233–54.

Treaties of Rome and Paris. The European Economic Community was rebaptised as the EC and became the first pillar of the new European Union (EU), with a second pillar on CFSP and a third pillar on JHA. The upgrade from a Community to a Union was an important step, as it reflected the European leaders' ambition to move beyond a common market towards integration in core areas such as monetary policy and internal and external security.

The most important achievement in Maastricht was undoubtedly the agreement on the creation of an EMU. As proposed by the Delors report of 1989,[45] it was decided to gradually move towards an EMU via a three-step process. The final stage in this process was the creation of a single European currency – at that time still called 'Ecu' – and the ECB. Membership was dependent on fulfilling convergence criteria involving sustainable public finances (public debt and deficit), price stability, exchange rate stability and interest rate stability. If the date of the third stage was not set by the end of 1997, it would begin in January 1999.[46]

The IGC on PU enhanced democratic legitimacy and institutional efficiency by making the EP a co-legislator on equal footing with the Commission in several policy areas, including the IM, and by further extending QMV. In addition, the member states tried to counterbalance the EC's strong economic bias by strengthening social policy and introduced shared competences in a wide range of areas, including education, culture, public health, consumer protection, trans-European networks, industrial policy and development cooperation. Two further important innovations were the introduction of the principles of subsidiarity and European citizenship.[47] Subsidiarity (a key priority for the German *Länder*, which feared that the new treaty would impinge upon their core competences) stipulated that in the area of non-exclusive EC competences, decisions would be left to lower levels of governance unless EU action was more effective.[48] At the instigation of Spain, the treaty also established the principle of European citizenship

45 Committee for the Study of the Economic and Monetary Union, 'Report on Economic and Monetary Union in the European Community' (1989), https://ec.europa.eu/econ omy_finance/publications/pages/publication6161_en.pdf.
46 K. Dyson, *Elusive Union: The Process of Economic and Monetary Union in Europe* (London, Longman, 1994).
47 F. Laursen and S. Vanhoonacker, 'The Maastricht Treaty: Creating the European Union', in *Encyclopedia of European Union Politics* (Oxford, Oxford University Press, 2019), https://oxfordre.com/politics/oso/viewentry/10.1093$002facrefore $002f9780190228637.001.0001$002facrefore-9780190228637-e-1067.
48 C. van Wijnbergen, 'Germany and European Political Union', in Laursen and Vanhoonacker (eds.), *The Intergovernmental Conference on Political Union*, pp. 49–78.

whereby every citizen holding the nationality of one of the member states was automatically also a citizen of the Union.[49] It included the right to vote and stand as a candidate in local and European elections (not national elections), free movement and residence within EU territory and consular protection by the embassy or consulate of any other member state, as well as the right to petition the EP and apply to the European Ombudsman.

A dimension which is sometimes overlooked is that the treaty was also an important milestone for the public debate concerning Europe. Now that Europe was no longer just a matter of technical rules and standards but also touched upon core issues of sovereignty such as money and foreign affairs, European integration became much more of a topic of public discussion and controversy. The Danish *'nej '*, the French *'petit oui '* and the heavy British parliamentary debates about Maastricht made it clear that the long period of 'permissive consensus' whereby the general public had been quiescent on European affairs was over. Public opinion started to increasingly impact both the content of EU decisions and the EU decision-making process. In contrast to the past, political parties now had an interest in politicising the EU.[50] The majority of Danes approved the treaty in a second referendum only after the European Council of Edinburgh (December 1992) had allowed them to opt out of participation in an eventual European defence policy (alongside the earlier opt-out on EMU) as well as making a further clarification that European citizenship would not replace national citizenship.[51] The new treaty finally entered into force on 1 November 1993.

Central and Eastern Europe

The Europe in which the Maastricht Treaty (Table 3.2) was implemented was radically different from that of the mid 1980s when the relaunching of European integration had started. The collapse of communism catapulted the relationship with the central and eastern European countries (CEECs) to the top of the EU's agenda. Liberated from the Soviet Union, the CEECs were keen to join the West (NATO and the EU), hoping that doing so would

---

49 A. J. Gil Ibáñez, 'Spain and European Political Union', in Laursen and Vanhoonacker (eds.), *The Intergovernmental Conference on Political Union*, pp. 99–114.

50 L. Hooghe and G. Marks, 'A Post-functionalist Theory of European Integration: From Permissive Consensus to Constraining Dissensus', *British Journal of Political Science* 39 (2008): 1–23; F. Laursen, 'The Not-So-Permissive Consensus: Thoughts on the Maastricht Treaty and the Future of European Integration', in Laursen and Vanhoonacker (eds.), *The Ratification of the Maastricht Treaty*, pp. 295–314.

51 F. Laursen, 'Denmark and the Ratification of the Maastricht Treaty', in Laursen and Vanhoonacker (eds.), *The Ratification of the Maastricht Treaty*, pp. 70–3.

Table 3.2 Key dates for the Maastricht Treaty

Time/place	Event
European Council, Hannover, 27–28 June 1988	Appointment of committee to work out the stages for an EMU, under the lead of Commission President Delors
European Council, Madrid, 26–27 June 1989	Decision on IGC on EMU
9 November 1989	Fall of the Berlin Wall
European Council, Dublin, 26–27 June 1990	Decision to organise an IGC on PU
European Council, Rome, 14–15 December 1990	Launch of IGCs on EMU and PU
European Council, Maastricht, 9–10 December 1991	Conclusion of IGCs on EMU and PU
Maastricht, 7 February 1992	Signing of Maastricht Treaty
2 June 1992	First Danish referendum
18 May 1993	Second Danish referendum
1 November 1993	The Maastricht Treaty comes into force

bring economic prosperity as well as political stability in a region suffering from a security vacuum after the collapse of the Warsaw Pact and the Soviet Union. The EU member states felt a moral obligation to support their eastern neighbours suffering from the aftermath of communist rule, but were also concerned about the CEECs' capacity for a successful transition to a free market economy and parliamentary democracy.

At the European Council of Copenhagen in December 1993, the member states agreed that 'the countries in Central and Eastern Europe that so desire shall become members of the Union', but they made becoming a member conditional upon the countries' ability 'to assume the obligations of membership by satisfying the economic and political conditions'.[52] Beyond the traditional requirement of adopting the EU's political and economic *acquis*, CEECs also had to fulfil criteria with regard to stable political institutions, a well-functioning market economy and the capacity to take on the obligations of membership.

The five East German *Länder* of the former German Democratic Republic (GDR) were a separate case. The 17 million GDR citizens were integrated into

52 European Council, 'European Council in Copenhagen, 21–22 June 1993'.

the EU with neither the normal accession negotiations (which required a unanimous vote by the Council and assent by the EP) nor the usual revision of the treaties.[53] When it became clear that nothing would stop Chancellor Kohl from moving ahead with German unification, the European Council of April 1990 agreed that, as soon as it was a reality, a series of transitional arrangements would enter into force that realised the full integration of the GDR into the EC as soon as possible.[54] When, on 3 October 1990, the East German *Länder* joined the Federal Republic of Germany (FRG), the FRG became by far the largest EU member state. The unified Germany did not ask for more votes in the Council, nor did it require an additional Commissioner, but the number of German MEPs was increased from eighty-one to ninety-nine.[55]

Key Themes

In this final section, we will – in line with this volume's ambition to give a bird's eye perspective – consider in more depth the key debates and changes in the period 1986–93, which are also of broader relevance for our understanding of the long-term process of European integration. These include the themes of the democratic legitimation of the EU, deepening and widening.

Increasing the EU's Democratic Legitimation

The institutional structures of the EC were set up in the 1950s for a club of six member states. The scope of the competences was initially relatively limited, and European integration happened largely outside the view of the broader public. By 1986, the EC's membership had grown to twelve, and, with the SEA and the Maastricht Treaty, integration moved well beyond questions of regulatory standards and touched increasingly on issues directly affecting the daily life of EU citizens. As a result, questions of democratic legitimacy grew in importance. Both the 1986 and the 1991 IGC explored how to increase

---

53 M. Gehler and A. Jacob, 'East Germany, the European Commission and German Reunification', in V. Dujardin, E. Bussière, P. Ludlow, F. Romero, D. Schenkler and A. Varsori (eds.), *The European Commission 1986–2000: History and Memories of an Institution* (Luxembourg, Publications Office of the European Union, 2019), pp. 503–14.
54 'Special Meeting of the European Council. Dublin, 28 April 1990', www .consilium.europa.eu/media/20571/1990_april__-_dublin__eng_.pdf.
55 D. Spence, 'The European Community and German Unification', *German Politics* 1, no. 3 (1992): 136–63; M. Birchen, 'The European Parliament and German Unification' (2009), https://op.europa.eu/nl/publication-detail/-/publication/0c4ff25f-0e3f-43d4-bca7-f0a5278e0745.

citizens' participation (input legitimacy) and enhance the quality of the governance process (throughput legitimacy).[56]

The challenge of strengthening the participation of European citizens was mainly addressed by extending the decision-making powers of the directly elected EP. As a first step, the SEA involved the EP more closely in the legislative process through the so-called cooperation procedure of two readings, particularly in the area of the single market. Also, the consultation procedure, whereby the EP is merely consulted, was further extended to new policy areas, and the EP received the right of assent for accession and association agreements.[57] Although the SEA did not go as far as suggested by the previously mentioned EP Draft Treaty Establishing the European Union, it was nevertheless an important step forwards that paved the way for a further strengthening of the EP's powers in Maastricht.

Under the new Article 189b of the Maastricht Treaty, the EP finally received full legislative powers in the key area of the IM, placing it on equal footing with the Council. If the Council and EP could not come to an agreement through a specially established conciliation committee, the EP always had the possibility of vetoing the law.[58] In order for its powers to be extended to the important area of agriculture, the EP would still have to wait until the Lisbon Treaty came into force (December 2009). The Maastricht Treaty also codified the practice of consulting the EP on the nomination of the Commission and made the college of Commissioners subject to a vote of approval by the EP. Furthermore, the parliament also received the right to set up committees of enquiry on maladministration or contraventions.

Both in Maastricht and during the IGC that led to the SEA, the strongest advocates for enhanced parliamentary powers were Germany and Italy.[59] For France, these enhanced powers were not a priority at all, and the UK was strongly opposed to them. Early on during the IGC on PU, the German and Italian ministers of foreign affairs, Hans-Dietrich Genscher and Gianni De Michelis, had submitted a joint declaration in which they requested making the EP a co-legislator for all legislative proposals, which would give the EP an enhanced role in the appointment of the Commission and increased

---

56 V. Schmidt, 'Democracy and Legitimacy in the European Union Revisited: Input, Output and "Throughput"', *Political Studies* 61, no. 1 (2013): 2–22.

57 Dinan, 'The Single European Act', pp. 128, 138.

58 For a full list, see F. Laursen, 'Explaining the Intergovernmental Conference on Political Union', in Laursen and Vanhoonacker (eds.), *The Intergovernmental Conference on Political Union*, pp. 229–65, 250.

59 F. Laursen, S. Vanhoonacker and R. Wester, 'Overview of the Negotiations', in Laursen and Vanhoonacker (eds.), *The Intergovernmental Conference on Political Union*, pp. 3–33, 14.

monitoring powers. Italian Prime Minister Giulio Andreotti had on several occasions proclaimed that his country would ratify the treaty only after agreement by the EP, and for German Chancellor Kohl addressing the democratic deficit was a condition for approving the EMU.[60]

In the discussion on improving the quality of the governance process, the question of the efficacy of institutional rules and processes played an important role. Both in the SEA and in the Maastricht Treaty, it was primarily addressed by expanding QMV in the Council. Since the Luxembourg compromise of 1966,[61] member states could always invoke unanimity in the case of vital national interests. This gave every single player around the table a de facto veto. With the SEA, QMV would become the norm for about two-thirds of the decisions necessary to complete the single market,[62] and, in Maastricht, the list was further expanded to policy fields such as EMU, visas, trans-European networks, health, development aid, consumer protection and transport.[63] In the area of the CFSP, however, decisions continued to be taken by unanimity.

The subsequent doubling in number of member states as a result of the eastern expansion and the fact that the EU was increasingly having an impact on the daily lives of its citizens meant that the questions of institutional reform and a more legitimate Union would stay with the Union for the coming decades and consequently be high on the agenda of the IGCs that led to the Amsterdam, Nice and Lisbon Treaties.

Deepening

The years of the SEA and the Maastricht Treaty are undeniably a period of major deepening in the European integration process. Beyond the completion of the IM, which was primarily of a regulatory nature, European citizens were also experiencing a major transfer of sovereignty in monetary affairs and foreign policy, which were traditionally core functions of the state. While the move towards EMU received an important boost as a result of the IM initiative, the development of a CFSP was the result of the determination to have an independent European voice in the superpower-dominated world of international affairs. While both the debate on the development of an EMU and that on a stronger European foreign policy role had begun well before

60 E. Martial, 'Italy and European Political Union', in Laursen and Vanhoonacker (eds.), *The Intergovernmental Conference on Political Union*, pp. 139–53, 146; van Wijnbergen, 'Germany and European Political Union', p. 58.
61 See Chapter 2 by M. Gehler in this volume.
62 Dinan, 'The Single European Act', p. 136.
63 Laursen, Vanhoonacker and Wester, 'Overview of the Negotiations', p. 22.

the 1991 IGC, the fall of the Berlin Wall brought the German question back to the heart of European politics and further increased the urgency of these debates.

While many associate EMU with the period of the Maastricht Treaty, the development of a single European currency could never have been realised without the prior steps in monetary cooperation that occurred from the 1970s onwards.[64] While the Werner plan (October 1970) proposing a gradual development of a single currency through a three-stage process was never realised, it was nevertheless indispensable for the setting up of the EMS, which itself was an important stepping stone for EMU.[65] By the mid 1980s, the EMS had developed into a relatively stable exchange rate system in which the Deutsche Mark was fulfilling the role of anchor currency.[66]

As previously explained, the preparations for an IGC on EMU were already well under way before the revolutionary developments took place in the GDR and central and eastern Europe. Notwithstanding, the unexpected fall of the Berlin Wall on 9 November 1989 changed the dynamics of these preparations. The fall led Chancellor Kohl to start the IGC in December 1990 instead of 1991 and reduced the German pressure on France to make equally important progress in the negotiations on PU.[67]

While the Franco-German couple was committed to the idea of an EMU, Bonn and Paris did not necessarily agree on how to give it shape. For France, along with the European Commission and such countries as Belgium, Italy and Spain, it was important to move quickly and agree on a firm timetable. For Germany, and players like Denmark and the Netherlands, it was important to first create economic convergence. The compromise was that, in exchange for an agreement on stringent economic convergence criteria, the irreversible character of the EU's move to the third stage of a single European currency was set in stone and a concrete date for the start of EMU was arranged. If a majority of member states had fulfilled the criteria in 1996, EMU would start in January 1997. If not, those that met the criteria by 1998 would join EMU in January 1999.

The UK, which had joined the Exchange Rate Mechanism of the EMS in 1990 (only to leave it again in 1992), was highly sceptical of the idea of an

---

64 See also Chapter 2 by M. Gehler in this volume.
65 E. Mourlon-Druol, *A Europe Made of Money: The Emergence of the European Monetary System* (Ithaca, NY, Cornell University Press, 2012); P. Ludlow, *The Making of the European Monetary System: A Case Study of the Politics of the European Community* (London, Butterworth Scientific, 1982); Dyson and Featherstone, *The Road to Maastricht*.
66 Cameron, 'The 1992 Initiative', pp. 46–7.
67 Heisenberg, 'From Single Market to Single Currency'.

EMU, also after Margaret Thatcher (1979–90) was succeeded by John Major (1990–7). The only way to come to an agreement was to create an opt-out mechanism, whereby the UK would not be obliged to move to the third stage 'without a separate decision to do so by its government and Parliament'.[68] After this concession to the UK, the also reticent Denmark received an exemption from automatically moving to the third stage when Denmark met the convergence criteria.[69] These opt-out mechanisms illustrate how, in an increasingly large and diverse Union, it was not always possible to move forward as a bloc. Although the opt-out principle was only reluctantly agreed upon, it was seen as preferable to Denmark and the UK preventing the rest of the countries from moving forward.

A second major example of deepening was that of foreign policy. The end of the Cold War and the uncertainties about the future of US engagement in Europe gave an important boost to the question of whether Europe should take on an independent international role. For more than 40 years, the EC member states had entrusted their security to the United States through NATO. While this arrangement allowed the EC to concentrate on its economic recovery and integration, it meant that the political weight of the Communities was considerably more limited than its economic clout. The EC's poor performance in addressing the Yugoslav crisis, the first post-Cold War conflict within European territory, showed the limits of a 'civilian power' Europe and resuscitated the old dividing lines between the Atlanticists and the Europeanists. While countries such as the UK, the Netherlands and Portugal advocated the strengthening of the European pillar of NATO, the Europeanists, with France in the lead, argued for an autonomous European role in security and defence. The carefully formulated provision in Title v of the Maastricht Treaty stipulating that the CFSP included 'all questions related to the security of the Union, including the eventual framing of a common defence policy, which might in time lead to a common defence' (Article J.4, paragraph 1) well reflects the delicate balance between the conflicting positions as well as the lack of political will to deal with this matter as a short-term priority. The compromise included that the

---

68 'Protocol on Certain Provisions Relating to the United Kingdom of Great Britain and Northern Ireland', annex to the Treaty Establishing the European Union (Luxembourg, Office for Official Publications of the European Communities, 1992), pp. 191–3. See also Dyson and Featherstone, *The Road to Maastricht*, pp. 534–690.
69 'Protocol on Certain Provisions Relating to Denmark', annex to the Treaty Establishing the European Union (Luxembourg, Office for Official Publications of the European Communities, 1992), p. 194.

implementation of EU decisions with defence implications would be entrusted to the WEU (Article J.4, paragraph 1).[70]

A further important point of discussion related to the institutional architecture of the CFSP. Despite the single institutional framework for both the EC and the intergovernmental pillars of the CFSP and JHA, the competences and the decision-making procedures continued to differ. Unanimity in the Council remained the rule. The European Commission shared its right of initiative with the member states, and the role of the EP was merely consultative.

Despite their many limitations, the new provisions on the CFSP were nevertheless a breakthrough, as they equipped the EU for its role as a crisis manager agreed upon under the Amsterdam Treaty (May 1999). The decision on a single institutional framework for the EC, CFSP and JHA prepared the way for a further Brusselisation of the decision-making structures. The EU's foreign policy ambitions also implied that it needed to start reflecting on its strategic direction and the values and norms it would project through its policies. The first substantial attempt to do so would come with the European Security Strategy of 2003.[71]

Widening

The renewed dynamism not only impacted the EU's internal dynamics, but also increased the Union's attractiveness to outside countries. Following the EU's expansion to Spain and Portugal in 1986,[72] Turkey and Morocco applied for membership in 1987, followed by Malta and Cyprus in 1990. Furthermore, several European Free Trade Association (EFTA) countries expressed their interest. In the period 1989–92, the European Commission successively received applications from Austria, Sweden, Finland, Switzerland and Norway. Last but not least, the Copenhagen summit of 1993 opened up the possibility for a 'Big Bang' of expansion to the east.

In contrast to Malta, a small and well-developed country, and Morocco, which did not fulfil the treaty's condition of being a European state, the candidacies of Cyprus and Turkey were rather complex. The Cypriot application was made by the Republic of Cyprus, which controlled only the Greek zone of the island and thus risked importing a protracted territorial dispute

---

70 *Treaty on European Union* (Luxembourg, Office for Official Publications of the European Communities, 1992).

71 European Council, 'A Secure Europe in a Better World: European Security Strategy' (2003), https://data.consilium.europa.eu/doc/document/ST-15895-2003-INIT/en/pdf.

72 See Chapter 2 by M. Gehler in this volume.

within the Union and raising tensions with Turkey.[73] Although the Commission opinion had identified the so-called 'Cyprus problem' as a major obstacle for accession, the European Council of Corfu (June 1994) did not link the opening of the negotiations to a solution of the Cyprus problem, leaving open the question of whether a divided Cyprus could ultimately join. In the end, the Republic of Cyprus would join in 2004, without a solution for the conflict with the Turkish Cypriots. The biggest challenge, however, was Turkey, a country with at the time a population of 65 million. It was economically much less developed and still had important steps to make in terms of human rights and the rule of law. After the establishment of a customs union in December 1995, Turkey would be accepted as a candidate for full membership in December 1999.[74]

The second wave of membership applications concerned several of the EFTA countries. In the first instance, the renewed dynamism as a result of the 1992 programme had led the countries to seek closer relations with the EU without the full obligations of membership. Through the European Economic Area (EEA), they were offered full access to the EU's internal market and some of its flanking policies. The deal was less satisfactory than expected, and the changed geopolitical context opened new possibilities for neutral countries to align with the West. As a result, Austria, Sweden, Finland and Switzerland all submitted their applications for full membership. Also, NATO member Norway, which had rejected accession after a negative referendum result in 1972, decided to apply again.[75] All in all, the negotiations took a little more than a year. Economically and culturally, all four countries were close to the existing members. It also helped that all of those applicants, with the exception of Finland, would become net contributors.[76] As members of the EEA, they were already part of the internal market and had integrated the EC *acquis*. After referendum campaigns that were lively but resulted in positive results, Austria, Sweden and Finland joined in January 1995. The Norwegian citizens rejected membership for a second time, with the result that Norway simply remained part of the EEA agreement which had been signed earlier. Switzerland decided

---

73 N. Nugent, 'EU Enlargement and the Cyprus Problem', *Journal of Common Market Studies* 38, no. 1 (2000): 31–50.

74 L. M. McLaren, 'Turkey's Eventual Membership of the EU: Turkish Elite Perceptions on the Issue', *Journal of Common Market Studies* 38, no. 1 (2000): 117–29.

75 N. Nugent, 'The Deepening and the Widening of the European Community: Recent Evolution, Maastricht, and Beyond', *Journal of Common Market Studies* 30, no. 3 (1992): 311–27; Michalski, 'The Enlarging European Union', p. 286.

76 F. Granell, 'The European Union's Enlargement Negotiations with Austria, Finland, Norway and Sweden', *Journal of Common Market Studies* 33, no. 1 (1995): 117–41, 131.

to no longer pursue EU membership after Swiss citizens rejected the EEA agreement in a referendum in December 1992.

The biggest challenge, however, was that of a potential expansion to the east. Once the first euphoria about the revolutionary developments had calmed down, the aspirations of CEECs to become part of the EC received mixed reactions. Germany, the UK and Denmark favoured an early and firm commitment to eastern expansion, but most other countries wanted to postpone the decision or even opposed the idea. British Prime Minster Thatcher, a strong proponent of quick expansion to the east put it as follows: 'the emergence of free, independent and anti-socialist governments in the region would provide me with potential allies in my crusade for a wider, looser Europe'.[77] Such countries as France, Italy and Belgium that favoured more integration feared that the widening would come at the expense of further deepening.[78] Strong beneficiaries of the Common Agricultural Policy or the structural funds saw the CEECs as competitors for scarce means and markets. In addition, there were doubts as to whether the CEECs' radical transition towards a liberal democracy and a market economy would be successful. France, one of the strongest opponents of widening the EC to the east, came up with alternatives such as President Mitterrand's idea for a European Confederation (1989) and Prime Minister Balladur's proposal for a Stability Pact for Europe (1994).[79]

As a first step, the member states invested in concluding association agreements, the first of which were finished in December 1991. While not making a formal commitment to the eastern expansion, the European Council of Lisbon of June 1992 agreed to assist CEECs 'to prepare the accession to the Union which they seek'.[80] One year later, at the European Council of Copenhagen (23–24 June 1993), the member states gave in to the increasing pressure and agreed that 'the associated countries in Central and Eastern Europe that so desire shall become members of the European Union'.[81] As

77 See Thatcher, *The Downing Street Years*, p. 759.
78 S. Van Hecke, 'Less Europe in a Larger Union: Belgium and Its Old and New Eastern Neighbours', in M. Gehler and M. Graf (eds.), *Europa und die deutsche Einheit: Beobachtungen, Entscheidungen und Folgen* (Göttingen, Vandenhoeck & Ruprecht, 2017), pp. 505–20; F. Schimmelfennig, 'The Community Trap: Liberal Norms, Rhetorical Action, and the Eastern Enlargement of the European Union, *International Organization* 55, no. 1 (2001): 47–80.
79 Schimmelfennig, 'The Community Trap', 56.
80 European Council, 'European Council in Lisbon, 26/27 June 1992: Conclusions of the Presidency', www.consilium.europa.eu/media/20510/1992_june_-_lisbon__eng_.pdf, p. 13.
81 European Council, 'European Council in Copenhagen, 21–22 June 1993'.

has been argued convincingly by Schimmelfennig, an important factor in this gradual move towards support for membership was the CEECs' successful framing of the membership question in normative rather than material terms. As advocates of the liberal Western order, it was hard for the EU member states to deprive the newly 'liberated' countries of the values that the member states had been promoting for decades.[82] At the same time, accession was made conditional on the predefined criteria of member countries being stable institutions that guaranteed democracy, the rule of law, human rights and respect for minorities; and had a functioning market economy and the capacity to cope with competition and market forces, as well as the ability to take on the obligations of membership.[83] Five years later, in March 1998, the EU opened accession negotiations with the Czech Republic, Estonia, Hungary, Poland and Slovenia (as well as with Cyprus). At the Helsinki European Council of December 1991, the group was extended with the addition of Bulgaria, Latvia, Lithuania, Slovakia and Romania (as well as Malta).[84]

The enlargement pressures, which ultimately led to a doubling of the number of member states, made the strengthening of the EU's institutional architecture more urgent than ever. The conclusions of the 1993 Copenhagen summit had already made the point that, during enlargement, it was in the general interest both of the EU and of the candidate countries to take into account the Union's so-called absorption capacity.[85] At the European Council of Corfu (June 1994), European leaders agreed to establish a Reflection Group consisting of representatives of the ministers of foreign affairs and the European Commission that would pay particular attention to the institutional questions resulting from expansion.[86] From Amsterdam to Nice, to the constitutional treaty and Lisbon, institutional reform would remain high on the agenda during every single IGC.

Conclusion

After the crisis-ridden 1970s and early 1980s, European integration received an important new boost in the period 1986–93. The completion of the internal market, the creation of a single currency and the potential opening up of

82 Schimmelfennig, 'The Community Trap', p. 55.
83 European Council, 'European Council in Copenhagen, 21–22 June 1993'.
84 European Council, 'Helsinki European Council, 10 and 11 December 1999: Presidency Conclusions', www.europarl.europa.eu/summits/helr_en.htm.
85 European Council, 'European Council in Copenhagen, 21–22 June 1993'.
86 European Council, 'European Council at Corfu, 24–25 June 1994', www.europarl.eur opa.eu/summits/corr_en.htm. See also Chapter 4 by D. Dinan in this volume.

membership to central and eastern Europe were landmark decisions that impacted the further development both of the EU and of the European continent for years to come.

Zooming out from the detailed analysis provided in this chapter, this conclusion addresses two questions. First, it asks what this period teaches us about the dynamics of European integration. Secondly, it reflects on the relevance of this period for the broader history of European integration.

When it comes to the first question, we identify at least three important lessons that can be drawn. First, it is clear from this chapter that the achievements during the period 1986–93 were very much built upon earlier developments in European integration. The debates on completing the IM and creating an EMU go back to the Hague Summit of 1969, and a single monetary policy would have been highly unlikely without the prior experience built up in the EMS. The co-decision for the EP would have been unthinkable if, at the Paris Summit, the European leaders had not decided on direct European elections 'in or after 1978'.[87] In other words, for many of the steps that were taken, the seeds had already been planted well before 1986.

Secondly, the second half of the 1980s and the early 1990s also teach us something about the question of agency in European integration. While Commission President Delors was part of the game, it was primarily the member states, and more particularly the heads of state or government who met in the European Council, that were in the lead. They were the ones adopting the treaty amendments required in order to realise the momentous changes and agreeing on concrete deadlines both for the IM and for EMU. As in earlier years, the Franco-German 'motor' continued to be of central importance, while the UK was often the one putting its foot on the brake. At the same time, the initial Danish rejection of the treaty was a strong reminder of the importance of a public debate about the European project, especially when it comes to crucial questions such as security and money.

Thirdly, the events of the late 1980s also remind us of the importance of an outward-looking perspective and the need to recognise the impact of the broader international context. The IM project, for instance, was partly also a response to the fierce competition of Japan, and the tensions over transatlantic security were an incentive for closer European foreign policy cooperation. Without the collapse of the bipolar world system, an opening up of EU

---

87 'Final Communiqué of the Paris Summit (9 and 10 December 1974)', www.cvce.eu/content/publication/1999/1/1/2acd8532-b271-49ed-bf63-bd8131180d6b/publishable_en.pdf.

membership to the countries of central and eastern Europe would simply have been unthinkable.

The second question relates to the bearing of the decisions taken in the years 1986–93 on the broader history of European integration. While the findings of this chapter do not support a 'radical break with the past' narrative and show that key achievements like EMU were built on earlier realisations, there are two major developments which meant that European integration received an important new twist after 1993. First, with a single currency and cooperation in the field of foreign policy and JHA, the European project became more than merely a common market. The transfer of sovereignty in these core areas boosted the public debate and the politicisation of European integration, putting the legitimacy question centre stage.[88] The earlier narrative of Europe as the harbinger of the post-1945 peace and stability would no longer suffice, leading to a new debate on Europe's identity and its collective purpose.

A second key difference from earlier periods was that European integration was no longer confined to western Europe. The importance of the decision at the European Council of Copenhagen in 1993 to open membership up to the east can hardly be overstated, as it would radically change the internal dynamics and further increase the political, socio-economic and cultural diversity of the EU.

In summary, while building to a large extent on discussions and preparations realised during the previous decade, the period 1986–93 was an important turning point for Europe in the sense that it brought new transfers of sovereignty in major new areas and opened the European integration project to the eastern part of the European continent.

Recommended Reading

Dinan, D. (ed.). *Origins and Evolution of the European Union*, 2nd ed. (Oxford, Oxford University Press, 2014).

Gehler, M. and W. Loth (eds.). *Reshaping Europe: Towards a Political, Economic and Monetary Union, 1984–1989* (Baden-Baden, Nomos Verlag, 2020).

Laursen, F. (ed.). *Designing the European Union: From Paris to* Lisbon (London, Palgrave Macmillan, 2012).

Moravcsik, A. *The Choice for Europe: Social Purpose and State Power from Messina to Maastricht* (Ithaca, NY, Cornell University Press, 1998).

88 P. de Wilde, A. Leupold and H. Schmidtke, 'Introduction: The Differentiated Politicisation of European Governance', *West European Politics* 39, no. 1 (2016): 3–22.

4

From Maastricht and Copenhagen
to Amsterdam and Nice

DESMOND DINAN

Introduction

The cities in the title of this contribution were the locations of summits at which European Community (EC)/European Union (EU) leaders made historic decisions that shaped the future of the European project. At three of those summits – Maastricht in December 1991, Amsterdam in June 1997 and Nice in December 2000 – leaders agreed on changes to the founding treaties on which the EC and the EU are based. Of the three treaty changes, which subsequently bore the names of the cities themselves, Maastricht was by far the most consequential, not only because it ushered in the EU but also because of its provisions for Economic and Monetary Union (EMU), the Common Foreign and Security Policy (CFSP) and cooperation on Justice and Home Affairs. In Copenhagen, in June 1993, leaders agreed not on a treaty change, but on the criteria for EU membership with a view to the likely accession in the near future of up to ten newly independent countries in central and eastern Europe, plus Cyprus and Malta.

As the significance of the summits suggests, fundamental changes to the nature, policy scope and institutional arrangements of the EU characterised the development of European integration that began in the late 1980s. The momentum generated by the single market programme, fallout from the end of the Cold War and the need to strengthen the EU's legitimacy while at the same time improving its institutional efficiency drove those changes, which were facilitated by what Bruno De Witte has called the 'golden age (1985–2000) [. . . of] European treaty revision [. . .] when amendments were successfully made and implemented in accordance with the traditional method of intergovernmental conferences followed by national ratifications'.[1]

1 B. De Witte, 'Treaty Revision in the European Union: Constitutional Change through International Law', *Netherlands Yearbook of International Law* 35 (2004): 51–84.

Scholarship on the EU was revived alongside the revival of the EC and emergence of the EU. Not surprisingly, this included efforts to explain and understand the grand bargains that made possible the acceleration of European integration, thanks notably to the Single European Act and the Maastricht Treaty; in other words, 'how [Intergovernmental Conference (IGC)] bargaining works by examining which member states get what they want in negotiations with their fellow member states and why'.[2] Liberal intergovernmentalism, developed by Andrew Moravcsik, became the dominant theory of inter-state bargaining and deal-making concerning EU institutional and policy arrangements that characterised the conduct and shaped the outcomes of major IGCs. Liberal-intergovernmentalism holds that national preferences are formed on the basis of domestic economic interests and that bargaining power depends largely on a country's size and economic weight. Given that an IGC is an intergovernmental process, it privileges national governments at the expense of supranational actors, although the ensuing agreement may strengthen supranational institutions as a means of securing credible commitments among member states.[3]

Yet the supposed 'golden age' of treaty reform was marred by ratification difficulties and delays, notably with respect to the Maastricht and Nice Treaties. This was a stark reminder to EU leaders that public opinion was becoming increasingly sceptical towards 'Brussels', which had become a synonym for an unfamiliar system of supranational governance. The unexpected difficulty of ratifying the Maastricht Treaty, in particular, epitomised growing dissatisfaction in many member states with deeper European integration.

This chapter begins with the Maastricht ratification crisis, as it came to be called. Ratification is the penultimate stage in the process of treaty change,

---

2 J. B. Slapin, 'Bargaining Power at Europe's Intergovernmental Conferences: Testing Institutional and Intergovernmental Theories', *International Organization* 62, no. 1 (2008): 131–62, 132.

3 A. Moravcsik, *The Choice for Europe: Social Purpose and State Power from Messina to Maastricht* (Ithaca, NY, Cornell University Press, 1998); A. Moravcsik and F. Schimmelfennig, 'Liberal Intergovernmentalism', in A. Wiener, T. A. Borzel and T. Risse (eds.), *European Integration Theory*, 3rd ed. (Oxford, Oxford University Press, 2019), pp. 68–87. For contending views, see W. Sandholtz and A. Stone Sweet (eds.), *European Integration and Supranational Governance* (Oxford, Oxford University Press, 1998); J. B. Slapin, 'Bargaining Power at Europe's Intergovernmental Conferences: Testing Institutional and Intergovernmental Theories', *International Organization* 62, no. 1 (2008): 131–62; G. Falkner, 'How Intergovernmental Are Intergovernmental Conferences? An Example from the Maastricht Treaty Reform', *Journal of European Public Policy* 9, no. 1 (2002): 98–119.

allowing the new treaty to come into effect (ensuing implementation is the final stage). The process starts when national governments decide to embark on treaty change. This is followed by a preparatory stage, and then by the launch of an IGC, the formal setting in which national governments negotiate a draft treaty incorporating changes to the existing treaties. National ministers, in the General Affairs Council, are responsible for the IGC, in which the Commission and observers from the European Parliament (EP) are also involved. An IGC operates at three levels: the working level of national representatives – normally the member states' Permanent Representatives (a country's most senior Brussels-based national officials); meetings of national ministers in the General Affairs Council; and meetings of national leaders in the European Council, where key decisions are taken. Although more than one meeting of the European Council may take place during an IGC, an IGC invariably concludes at either a regular or a special meeting of the European Council, where national leaders often haggle over the final, politically most-sensitive details of the draft treaty. The draft treaty is then tidied up by linguist-jurists, before being signed by national ministers on behalf of their member states, usually in the city where the definitive European Council took place several weeks previously.

This chapter moves chronologically from the ratification of the Maastricht Treaty to cover the Copenhagen criteria, the Amsterdam Treaty and the Nice Treaty. The EU's leaders approved the Copenhagen criteria without much preparatory work or political disagreement, in June 1993. In contrast, preparing and negotiating the Amsterdam Treaty required considerable time and effort. No sooner was the Amsterdam Treaty ratified than national governments embarked on another treaty change, culminating in the Nice summit and resulting in the Nice Treaty.

Whereas the Maastricht Treaty was hugely important for the EU, the Amsterdam Treaty, although constitutionally significant and wide-ranging in many respects, lacked a 'big project' of the kind associated with the Maastricht Treaty or the Single European Act. Indeed, the Amsterdam Treaty became associated with the failure of EU leaders to resolve a number of institutional problems that supposedly had been the main reason for convening an IGC in the first place. The Nice Treaty was far narrower in scope. In the event, it failed to deal satisfactorily with the institutional issues left over from the Amsterdam Treaty. As a result, 10 years after the celebrated Maastricht summit, the utility and effectiveness of treaty change by means of the traditional IGC method seemed highly questionable. As De Witte acknowledged, increasing criticism of the IGC method relating to 'the exceedingly diplomatic (and therefore opaque) character of treaty negoti-ations, and to the excessive rigidity caused by the "double lock" of overall consensus by all governments at the intergovernmental conference, followed by universal ratification in all the member states' led to calls for a new approach to treaty change in the form of the convention method.[4] The EU's leaders appreciated that the next round of reform would have to be more ambitious in scope and more inclusive in preparation, going beyond the usual set of officials and politicians representing national governments. This was the genesis of the Convention on the Future of Europe.

Following a discussion of the significance of each of the summits men-tioned in the title, this chapter concludes with some observations about the institutional actors involved in the outcome, including the paramount importance of the European Council, the increasing involvement of the Commission and the EP, and the contribution of the rotating Council presidency.

From Maastricht

On 7 February 1992, government ministers of the then twelve member states signed the Treaty on European Union (TEU) at a ceremony in Maastricht.[5] The event took place in the same building where, 6 weeks previously, national leaders had reached a political agreement on the treaty, thereby concluding a year-long round of often difficult intergovernmental negoti-ations. Following the December 1991 Maastricht summit, legal and linguistic experts tidied up the draft treaty for national ministers to sign on behalf of their member states.

The next step, before the treaty could come into effect, required ratifica-tion by each member state. Moving from Maastricht, in the metaphorical sense of completing the ratification process, became unexpectedly trouble-some, notably with respect to national referendums on the subject.[6] Parliamentary ratification was not as difficult.[7] Overall, ratification turned

---

4 De Witte, 'Treaty Revision in the European Union', 51.
5 'Treaty on European Union (TEU), 7 February 1992', *Official Journal of the European Communities* C 224/1 (1992).
6 F. Laursen and S. Vanhoonacker (eds.), *Ratification of the Maastricht Treaty: Issues, Debate and Future Implications* (Dordrecht, Martinus Nijhoff, 1994); R. Corbett, *The Treaty of Maastricht: From Conception to Ratification: A Comprehensive Reference Guide* (Harlow, Longman, 1993).
7 See S. Hug and T. König, 'Ratifying Maastricht: Parliamentary Votes on International Treaties and Theoretical Solution Concepts', *European Union Politics* 1, no. 1 (2000): 93–124.

into a long and arduous process that presaged serious political problems for the nascent EU in the years ahead.

Denmark and Ireland were the only countries constitutionally obliged to hold a referendum on ratification. The Danes voted first on 2 June 1992. To almost everyone's surprise, a narrow majority – 50.7 to 49.3 per cent – chose to reject the treaty. There were many reasons for the result: some were specific to the treaty or the EC generally, others pertained more to national politics; some were rational, others not. Many Danes rightly complained about the incomprehensibility of the treaty, even if relatively few had attempted to read it.[8]

Regardless of the reasons for the referendum result, EC leaders were well aware that Denmark's rejection of the treaty was symptomatic of widespread public dissatisfaction with the institutions and processes of European integration. Their immediate challenge was nonetheless to save the treaty – unless ratified in all member states, it could not come into effect. Ireland's resounding endorsement of the treaty in a referendum only 2 weeks later was somewhat reassuring, but did not resolve the Danish dilemma.[9] The only solution appeared to be for Denmark to vote again, on the basis of minor treaty changes specifically addressing Danish concerns, in the form of opt-outs and other concessions. The real purpose of those changes was to try to reassure a sufficient number of voters in order to secure a positive result in a second referendum.

In the meantime, hoping to stage a dramatic show of support for the European project, French President François Mitterrand called for a referendum on the treaty, although the French parliament had already ratified it. Mitterrand, who had domestic political motives as well as broader European ambitions, miscalculated badly. General disgruntlement with the president and with the EC, stoked by misinformation about the nature and purpose of the TEU, almost caused a disaster. Instead, the result of the referendum, held on 20 September 1992, was an embarrassingly small

8 On the Danish referendums, see S. B. Hobolt, 'From No to Yes: The Danish and Irish Referendums on the Maastricht and Nice Treaties Europe in Question', in S. B. Hobolt (ed.), *Europe in Question: Referendums on European Integration* (Oxford, Oxford University Press, 2009), pp. 161–203; F. Laursen, 'Denmark and the Ratification of the Maastricht Treaty', in Laursen and Vanhoonacker (eds.), *Ratification of the Maastricht Treaty*, pp. 61–86; H. Rasmussen, 'Denmark's Maastricht Ratification Case: Some Serious Questions about Constitutionality', *Journal of European Integration* 21, no. 1 (1998): 1–35; P. Giortler, 'Denmark. Ratifying the Treaty on European Union: An Interim Report', *European Law Review* 18 (1993): 356–60.
9 See M. Holmes, 'The Maastricht Treaty Referendum of June 1992', *Irish Political Studies* 8, no. 1 (1993): 105–10.

majority in favour of ratification: 51.05 to 48.95 per cent.[10] This brought the Maastricht Treaty into further disrepute. There could be no doubt now about the extent of public unease with the EC throughout the member states.

The Danish and French results emboldened Eurosceptics in the United Kingdom (UK). Faced with a virulent Eurosceptical wing in his Conservative Party, and a rabidly anti-EU popular press, Prime Minister John Major procrastinated. The currency crisis of September 1992, which prompted the government to pull sterling out of the exchange rate mechanism of the European Monetary System, added greatly to Major's woes. Instead of bringing the treaty up for ratification in parliament before the stipulated deadline of December 1992, Major decided to wait until after the second Danish referendum, scheduled for May 1993.

Following the first referendum, the Danish government had produced a White Paper outlining various options for a possible solution to the ratification problem. Those formed the basis for a number of opt-outs for Denmark from the TEU, which the European Council approved at a meeting in Edinburgh, in December 1992.[11] Chief among them were Danish non-participation in the third stage of EMU and in foreign policy decisions that had defence implications.[12]

Buoyed by the European Council conclusions, a new Danish government managed to convince a majority of voters to ratify the TEU in the May 1993 referendum. The result was a comfortable majority of 56.8 per cent in favour. Encouraged by this outcome, but still dogged by conservative Eurosceptics, Major brought the treaty up for a vote in the House of Commons soon afterwards. On 20 May 1993, the Commons approved ratification, with most of the Labour Members of Parliament abstaining.[13] By that time, ratification had proceeded successfully in most of the other member states. Germany was an exception. There, despite large majorities in parliament in favour of the treaty, a legal challenge to its constitutionality held up ratification until the outcome of a case before the country's constitutional court.[14]

---

10 A. Stone, 'Ratifying "Maastricht": France Debates European Union', *French Politics and Society* 11, no. 1 (1993): 70–88.

11 'European Council in Edinburgh, 11–12 December 1992: Conclusions of the Presidency', www.consilium.europa.eu/media/20492/1992_december_-_edinburgh__eng_.pdf.

12 H. Krunke, 'From Maastricht to Edinburgh: The Danish Solution', *European Constitutional Law Review* 1, no. 3 (2005): 339–56.

13 E. Szyszczak, 'United Kingdom. Ratifying the Treaty on European Union: A Final Report', *European Law Review* 18 (1993): 541–4; E. Best, 'The United Kingdom and the Ratification of the Maastricht Treaty', in Laursen and Vanhoonacker (eds.), *Ratification of the Maastricht Treaty*, pp. 245–78.

14 R. Beuter, 'Germany and the Ratification of the Maastricht Treaty', in Laursen and Vanhoonacker (eds.), *Ratification of the Maastricht Treaty*, pp. 87–112; U. Everling, 'The *Maastricht* Judgment of the German Federal Constitutional Court and Its Significance

Eventual approval in the UK and a favourable ruling in the German court, in October 1993, removed the last hurdles delaying ratification of the TEU, which finally came into effect in November 1993. Governments, EU institutions and other actors quickly came to terms with the treaty's provisions. The EMU was already on track; and member states had begun to cooperate more closely on foreign and security policy, as well as in the policy field of justice and home affairs. Nevertheless, the drawn-out ratification process had spoiled the celebration of the TEU's implementation and signalled serious political problems ahead for the fledgling Union. Indeed, according to Joseph Weiler, it was 'the public reaction, frequently and deliciously hostile', that made the Maastricht Treaty 'the most important constitutional moment in the history of the European construct'.[15]

Copenhagen

At the Copenhagen summit of 21–22 June 1993, the EU's leaders did not discuss further treaty reform, but took an important decision concerning EU accession, which undoubtedly was constitutionally significant. The background to what became known as the 'Copenhagen Criteria' for accession was the desire of the newly independent countries of central and eastern Europe to seek EU membership. The EC was no stranger to enlargement, but the expansion of the original six member states to twelve, by 1986, was a gradual and relatively easily manageable process. Similarly, the anticipated accession of Austria, Finland, Norway and Sweden was not a cause of concern (Austria, Finland and Sweden joined in 1995; Norway did not join).[16] In contrast, the prospect of ten central and eastern European countries seeking EU membership at the same time – countries that were unfamiliar with European integration, had limited administrative capacity and were in the process of transitioning to democratic governance and market economics – concentrated the minds of EU leaders on the accession criteria, something to which they had never previously given much thought.

Although the 1993 Copenhagen summit is now synonymous with the Copenhagen criteria, the term was not used in the summit conclusions. Indeed, the Copenhagen criteria covered only one paragraph in a set of

for the Development of the European Union', *Yearbook of European Law* 14, no. 1 (1994): 1–19.
15 J. H. H. Weiler, *The Constitution of Europe*, (Cambridge, Cambridge University Press, 1997), p. 4.
16 J. Redmond, *The 1995 Enlargement of the European Union* (Aldershot, Dartmouth, 1997).

conclusions that extended to more than fifteen pages, including several annexes. Not only that, but the edition of the *Bulletin of the European Communities* in which the conclusions were published noted, in the introduction, that 'Unemployment and the economic recession eclipsed all other issues at Copenhagen, with the European Council demonstrating its resolve to tackle the problems at Community level through a series of short- and long-term measures.'[17] Enlargement, which became, in retrospect, the defining issue of the Copenhagen summit, was not seen in that light at the time.

This is what the paragraph on enlargement said, and what the Copenhagen Criteria came to mean:

> The European Council today agreed that the associated countries in Central and Eastern Europe that so desire shall become members of the European Union. Accession will take place as soon as an associated country is able to assume the obligations of membership by satisfying the economic and political conditions required. Membership requires that the candidate country has achieved stability of institutions guaranteeing democracy, the rule of law, human rights and respect for and protection of minorities, the existence of a functioning market economy as well as the capacity to cope with competitive pressure and market forces within the Union. Membership presupposes the candidate's ability to take on the obligations of membership including adherence to the aims of political economic and monetary union. The Union's capacity to absorb new members, while maintaining the momentum of European integration is also an important consideration in the general interest of both the Union and the candidate countries.[18]

Specifying the criteria for EU membership was one step on the long road to the accession of eight central and eastern European countries in May 2004 and of two more in January 2007. Indeed, the Commission's opinion on a candidate country's suitability for EU membership – regardless of the location in Europe of that country – is an essential part of the enlargement process that draws primarily on the Copenhagen Criteria. Given the impact of enlargement on the EU's composition and character, the decision of the European Council regarding accession, taken at the Copenhagen summit in June 1993, was undeniably important, although academic assessments of the implementation and overall significance of the Copenhagen criteria have been harsh.[19]

---

17 'Copenhagen European Council', *Bulletin of the European Communities* 26, no. 6 (1993): 7–23.
18 Ibid., 13.
19 See, in particular, D. Kochenov, *EU Enlargement and the Failure of Conditionality: Pre-accession Conditionality in the Fields of Democracy and the Rule of Law* (Amsterdam, Kluwer Law International, 2008). For a kinder assessment of the Copenhagen criteria,

Amsterdam

National leaders concluded the first post-Maastricht IGC on treaty change at a meeting of the European Council in Amsterdam, on 16–17 June 1997.[20] The ensuing Amsterdam Treaty, which came into effect on 1 May 1999, amended the TEU and the Treaties Establishing the European Communities in a number of noteworthy respects.[21] In general, however, the Amsterdam Treaty was disappointing, largely because it failed to resolve institutional problems that the leaders themselves had identified as being one of the main reasons for convening the IGC.

Regardless of the perceived need for institutional reform, the TEU mandated that an IGC begin in 1996, with a view to reviewing and possibly improving the functioning of the CFSP, which was one of the treaty's signature innovations. By the time that the IGC was due to take place, the likely institutional implications of the next round of enlargement, involving up to ten central and eastern European countries, were becoming apparent, plus the small Mediterranean countries of Cyprus and Malta. An EU substantially larger than its existing fifteen member states (as of 1995) seemed unworkable without major institutional reform. Although it had not originally been intended for that purpose, the forthcoming IGC gave national governments an ideal opportunity to tackle this problem.

In an effort to facilitate a smooth and relatively swift IGC, EU leaders established a high-level committee – the Reflection Group – to prepare the ground for the new round of treaty change. The group's remit was to draw up the agenda for the conference, possibly going beyond the CFSP and institutional reform, and identify areas of likely agreement. The Reflection Group met for the first time in Messina, Sicily, in June 1995. This was a nod to the original Messina conference, 40 years earlier, that had paved the way for the Treaty of Rome, which established the European Economic Community.

Different national preferences on a range of issues were evident from the start of the Reflection Group's deliberations, with the more integration-minded countries, such as Belgium, Germany, Italy, Luxembourg and the Netherlands, ranged against those less inclined towards supranational

see R. Janse, 'Is the European Commission a Credible Guardian of the Values? A Revisionist Account of the Copenhagen Political Criteria during the Big Bang Enlargement', *International Journal of Constitutional Law* 17, no. 1 (2019): 43–65.

20 'European Council in Amsterdam, 16–17 June 1997: Conclusions of the Presidency', www.consilium.europa.eu/uedocs/cms_data/docs/pressdata/en/ec/032a0006.htm.

21 'Treaty of Amsterdam, 2 October 1997', *Official Journal of the European Communities* C 340/1 (1997).

solutions, especially the UK. Indeed, growing Euroscepticism within the UK's governing Conservative Party overshadowed the Reflection Group's work, just as it would overshadow all but the final stage of the ensuing IGC.

The controversial question of differentiated integration or flexibility (deeper integration in selected policy areas among like-minded member states) emerged during the Reflection Group's deliberations as a subject likely to dominate the intergovernmental negotiations.[22] Concern about Italy's inability to meet the convergence criteria for EMU and about the UK's exceptionalism within the EU, as well as impending enlargement on an unprecedented scale, triggered speculation about the usefulness and possibly even the inevitability of differentiated integration. Italy was deeply concerned, as were some other member states which feared that differentiated integration could result in a Franco-German decision to pursue closer integration in a number of policy areas outside the EU system. Prime Minister Major responded with offhand remarks about the desirability, in his view, of an à la carte, pick-and-choose EU.[23]

In its report to the European Council, the Reflection Group reviewed the debate and outlined the different national positions on differentiated integration, without making a specific recommendation. Otherwise, the report identified three general areas for further treaty reform: making the EU more relevant to its citizens; improving the EU's institutional efficiency and democratic accountability; and improving the EU's ability to act internationally. In all cases, the report emphasised the likely impact of enlargement.[24]

The IGC began at a special meeting of the European Council in Turin, on 29 March 1996.[25] The conference lasted longer than expected, largely because of the timing of the next UK general election, which was due to happen by May 1997 at the latest. Other leaders hoped that Major, whose government was holding up progress on a range of issues, would be replaced by Tony Blair, the Labour Party leader. Although relatively unknown outside the UK, Blair seemed refreshingly pro-EU for a prominent UK politician. Much to the relief of many other EU leaders, Labour swept the Conservatives from office

22 See G. Edwards and A. Pijpers (eds.), *The Politics of European Treaty Reform: The 1996 Intergovernmental Conference and Beyond* (London, Pinter, 1997).

23 J. Major, 'Europe: A Future That Works', William and Mary Lecture, Leiden University (1994), https://johnmajorarchive.org.uk/1994/09/07/mr-majors-speech-in-leiden-7-september-1994-2.

24 'Report by the Reflection Group: A Strategy for Europe (Brussels, 5 December 1995)', www.cvce.eu/en/obj/report_by_the_reflection_group_a_strategy_for_europe_brussels_5_december_1995-en-307c412a-9be0-4137-a0e9-1fc8c86c8aa3.html.

25 'European Council in Turin, 29 June 1996: Conclusions of the Presidency', www.consilium.europa.eu/media/21169/turin-european-council.pdf.

in the May 1997 election. The change of government in London facilitated the swift conclusion of the IGC.[26]

The most obvious impact of the political upheaval in London was Blair's agreement to scrap the Social Protocol of the TEU, an artefact of Major's resistance during the Maastricht summit to strengthening social policy in the EU, and bring social policy squarely into the body of the TEU, via the Amsterdam Treaty. Instead of the other member states conducting social policy independently of the UK, using a protocol attached to the treaty, the UK would join the other member states in conducting social policy within the framework of the TEU proper.

With a much more pro-EU government in the UK, the question of differentiated integration lost some of its sting. If anything, the subject generated more academic interest than political passion during the IGC.[27] Although some countries remained wary, a consensus emerged that, in

26 On the conduct and outcome of the ICG, see F. Dehousse, *Amsterdam: The Making of a Treaty* (London, Kogan Page, 1999); Y. Devuyst, 'Treaty Reform in the European Union: The Amsterdam Process', *Journal of European Public Policy* 5, no. 4 (1998): 615–31; S. Langrish, 'The Treaty of Amsterdam: Selected Highlights', *European Law Review* 23 (1998): 3–19; J. Lodge, 'Intergovernmental Conferences and European Integration: Negotiating the Amsterdam Treaty', *International Negotiation* 3, no. 3 (1998): 345–62; A. Moravcsik and N. Kalypso, 'Explaining the Treaty of Amsterdam: Interests, Influence, Institutions', *Journal of Common Market Studies* 37, no. 1 (1999): 59–85; M. Petite, 'The Treaty of Amsterdam', The Jean Monnet Center for International and Regional Economic Law and Justice, NYU School of Law, Jean Monnet Working Papers, 2/98 (1998), https://jeanmonnetprogram.org/archive/papers/98/98-2-.html; U. Sverdrup, 'An Institutional Perspective on Treaty Reform: Contextualizing the Amsterdam and Nice Treaties', *Journal of European Public Policy* 9, no. 1 (2002): 120–40; P. W. Thurner, F. U. Pappi and M. Stoiber, 'EU Intergovernmental Conferences: A Quantitative Analytical Reconstruction and Data-Handbook of Domestic Preference Formation, Transnational Networks, and Dynamics of Compromise during the Amsterdam Treaty Negotiations' (2002), Mannheimer Zentrum für Europäische Sozialforschung, https://core.ac.uk/download/71741575.pdf.
27 See especially G. de Búrca and J. Scott, 'Introduction', in G. de Búrca and J. Scott (eds.), *Constitutional Change in the EU: From Uniformity to Flexibility? Essays on the New 'Flexible' Nature of the Constitutional Arrangements of the European Union* (Oxford, Hart, 2000), pp. 1–7; D. Curtin, 'The Shaping of a European Constitution and the 1996 IGC: 'Flexibility' as a Key Paradigm?', *Aussenwirtschaft* 50, no. 1 (1995): 237–52; C. D. Ehlermann, 'Differentiation, Flexibility, Closer Co-operation: The New Provisions of the Treaty of Amsterdam', *European Law Journal* 4, no. 3 (1998): 246–70; D. Hanf, 'Flexibility Clauses in the Founding Treaties, From Rome to Nice', in B. De Witte, D. Hanf and E. Vos (eds.), *The Many Faces of Differentiation in EU Law* (Antwerp, Intersentia, 2001), pp. 3–26; A. Kölliker, *Flexibility and European Unification: The Logic of Differentiated Integration* (Lanham, Rowman and Littlefield, 2006); E. Philippart and G. Edwards, 'The Provisions on Closer Co-operation in the Treaty of Amsterdam: The Politics of Flexibility in the European Union', *Journal of Common Market Studies* 37, no. 1 (1999): 87–108; J. Shaw, 'The Treaty of Amsterdam: Challenges of Flexibility and Legitimacy', *European Law Journal* 4, no. 1 (1998): 63–86; A. Stubb, *Negotiating Flexibility in the European Union: Amsterdam, Nice and Beyond* (Basingstoke, Palgrave Macmillan, 2002).

principle, differentiated integration should be included in the TEU as long as it was limited, in practice, to precisely defined conditions that would not endanger the existing body of EU laws, rules and regulations. Negotiators eventually agreed to a formula that included both general enabling clauses, for member states wishing to cooperate more closely, and particular provisions governing the use of differentiated integration in certain policy areas. Hedged with qualifications and safeguards, it turned out that differentiated integration would be difficult to put into practice.

As expected, institutional affairs became the most contentious subject in the IGC. Questions relating to the EP – its size, its legislative power and the location of its plenary sessions – were relatively easy to resolve. Negotiators accepted the EP's own proposal to set a ceiling of 700 members and agreed to include in the TEU an earlier political agreement among national leaders to hold most of the EP's plenary sessions in Strasbourg (a persistent French demand). Thanks in large part to the change of government in the UK, the conference was able to agree to strengthen the procedure for legislative decision-making that gave the EP a role approximately equal to that of the Council (co-decision), which had been introduced in the Maastricht Treaty. Separately, the conference agreed to extend the use of co-decision to additional policy fields.

As for the Council, most national government also favoured extending the use of qualified majority voting to additional policy fields. This became bound up with the technical but highly sensitive question of the reweighting of Council votes, which would dominate debates about institutional reform during the next 10 years. The big member states advocated either an increase in the number of their votes or the introduction of a new system, based on a double majority, combining the traditional requirement for a qualified majority with a new demographic criterion. Without such a change, they argued, a qualified majority could be formed, following central and eastern European enlargement, by a group of countries that together would not represent a majority of the EU's population.

Negotiations about the reweighting of votes inevitably touched on another highly controversial issue: the size and composition of the Commission. Nearly every government conceded that the Commission was too large to be optimally efficient, but few would countenance a Commission with fewer members than the number of EU member states. With the big member states pushing to increase their relative voting weight in the Council, the other member states adamantly opposed the idea of radically reducing the size of the Commission, possibly resulting in the loss of 'their' Commissioner. With varying degrees of enthusiasm, the big member states expressed a willingness to give up at least their second Commissioner (France, Germany, Italy, Spain and the UK then had two Commissioners each), but only in return for a reweighting of votes in the Council.

Meeting in Amsterdam, on 16–17 June 1993, to conclude the IGC, the European Council negotiated at length to reach a final agreement, but failed to reach a breakthrough on institutional reform. Instead, EU leaders settled on a temporary solution: a protocol attached to the TEU stipulating that the Commission would comprise one member per member state as soon as the next enlargement took place, providing that Council votes were reweighted in order to compensate the big member states for the loss of a second Commissioner. The protocol also stipulated that the EU would hold another IGC as a prelude to further treaty change before the next round of enlargement, in order to settle the outstanding institutional issues.

From the perspective of institutional reform, the Amsterdam Treaty was far from satisfactory. Giving more legislative and other power to the EP and extending the reach of qualified majority voting were not insignificant achievements, but were unlikely by themselves to enhance the EU's efficiency, credibility or legitimacy. Nevertheless, the Amsterdam Treaty was striking for a number of changes to the TEU of a constitutional kind, which became increasingly important as the EU enlarged and matured in the years ahead.[28] Those included imbuing the EU with core political values and making it possible for the EU to sanction a member state that deviated from them, even if such a sanction would be difficult to approve because of a requirement for unanimity in the European Council.

Given the original purpose of the conference, as specified in the Maastricht Treaty, and the fact that the negotiations took place in the shadow of the Yugoslav wars, the Amsterdam Treaty included a number of changes that would prove highly significant for the development of the CFSP. Apart from several procedural improvements, those included establishing a Policy Planning and Early Warning Unit in the Council Secretariat and creating

---

28 See M. Nentwich, 'The EU Intergovernmental Conference 1996/97: The Moment of Constitutional Choice for a Democratic Europe?', in A. Føllesdal and P. Koslowski (eds.), *Democracy and the European Union: Studies in Economic Ethics and Philosophy* (Berlin, Springer, 1998), pp. 81–107; K. Neunreither and A. Wiener (eds.), *European Integration after Amsterdam: Institutional Dynamics and Prospects for Democracy* (Oxford, Oxford University Press, 2000).

the position of High Representative for the CFSP, in part to strengthen the EU's external image and effectiveness.

At the same time, rising public concern about the risks of transnational criminal activity within the Schengen Area, together with the internal security implications of growing external insecurity, led national governments to strengthen considerably the TEU's provisions relating to justice and home affairs. Governments agreed, therefore, to move all but police and judicial cooperation out of the TEU's intergovernmental pillar on justice and home affairs and into the supranational first pillar. They also agreed to bring the Schengen regime – the body of legislation and regulation that made possible unfettered cross-border travel among participating countries – into the EU's legal framework. A protocol attached to the Amsterdam Treaty provided for the incorporation of Schengen into EU law, with special provisions for non-Schengen EU members (Denmark, Ireland and the UK).

Despite those undoubted improvements, a treaty change that was intended to make the EU more intelligible to its citizens was almost unintelligible even to experts. As part of a supposed simplification exercise, the Amsterdam Treaty renumbered the articles of the Rome Treaties in the consolidated version of the Treaty Establishing the European Community, and renumbered the articles of the TEU in the consolidated version of the TEU. Although useful and eventually widely accepted, initially these changes merely added to the post-Amsterdam fog of treaty reform. All-in-all, the Amsterdam Treaty was a fitting testimonial to the challenge of reconciling the complexity of EU governance with the desirability of making the EU easier for people to understand, a challenge that would become far more acute in the years ahead.

Acting on behalf of their member states, foreign ministers signed the new treaty, in Amsterdam, on 2 October 1997. In contrast to the fate of the Maastricht Treaty, ratification of the Amsterdam Treaty proceeded without difficulty or drama, slowly but surely, throughout the EU.[29] Only Denmark and Ireland held referendums, with large majorities in each country endorsing the treaty at the first attempt. The revised TEU finally came into effect on 1 May 1999.

---

29 On the ratification of the Amsterdam Treaty, see S. Hug and T. König, 'In View of Ratification: Governmental Preferences and Domestic Constraints at the Amsterdam Intergovernmental Conference', *International Organization* 56, no. 2 (2002): 447–76; S. Hug and T. König, 'Divided Government and the Ratification of the Maastricht Treaty', in R. Pahre (ed.), *Democratic Foreign Policy Making: Problems of Divided Government and International Cooperation* (Basingstoke, Palgrave Macmillan, 2006), pp. 133–50.

Nice

Frustration with the Amsterdam Treaty begat the Nice Treaty.[30] The Amsterdam Treaty had barely come into effect when member states embarked on another IGC, in February 2000, to try to sort out the so-called Amsterdam leftovers (the weighting of Council votes and the size and composition of the Commission). As part of a broader institutional reshuffle, governments also addressed the number of EP seats and the weighting of Council votes for the prospective new member states. Ordinarily, the institutional aspects of accession would have been dealt with in each candidate country's entry negotiations. Given the large number of countries soon about to join, however, EU leaders decided to include those institutional aspects of the accession negotiations in the IGC on treaty reform.

The narrowness of the agenda set this IGC apart from previous ones, and was inherently unsatisfactory.[31] It left little room for side-bargains or trade-offs among participants. As expected, the negotiations on voting weights in the Council and on the Commission's size – issues that were all about the ability of governments to make EU decisions and shape EU policies – opened a can of worms. A split soon emerged along familiar lines, with the big countries wanting to increase their share of Council votes and reduce the size of the Commission to fewer than the number of EU members, and most of the small countries wanting to keep their share of Council votes and maintain national representation in the Commission.

A spectacular row erupted among EU leaders at an informal summit in October 2000, their first discussion of institutional reform since the rancorous Amsterdam summit in June 1997. French President Jacques Chirac irritated many of his fellow leaders by proposing a radical reduction in the size of the Commission, while suggesting a system for the selection of a smaller Commission that would aim for equality among member states. Leaders of the small member states were unconvinced, distrusting France and fearing that the big member states would skew a new arrangement against them. Chirac claimed that the sharp exchange among EU leaders cleared the air in

---

30 The Treaty of Nice, 26 February 2001, *Official Journal of the European Communities C* 80/ 10 (2001).

31 On the negotiation of the Nice Treaty, see E. Best, M. Gray and A. Stubb, *Rethinking the European Union 2000: IGC 2000 and Beyond* (Maastricht, European Institute of Public Administration, 2000); M. Bond and K. Feus (eds.), *Intergovernmental Conferences and Treaty Reform: The Nice Experience* (London, Federal Trust for Education and Research, 2001); M. Gray and A. Stubb, 'The Treaty of Nice – Negotiating a Poisoned Chalice', *Journal of Common Market Studies* 39, no. S1 (2001): 5–23.

the IGC. In fact, it led many leaders of small member states to dig in their heels, and set the stage for a bruising battle at the Nice summit in December 2000, where the European Council concluded the IGC.

The discussion of voting weights had been equally acrimonious. France was determined to keep the same number of Council votes as Germany, a far more populous country, even more so following unification in 1990. Chirac, a Gaullist, even quoted Jean Monnet, a founding father of the European project and an avowed anti-Gaullist, to bolster his alleged claim that institutional equality between France and Germany was an inviolable part of the original Franco-German bargain.[32] German Chancellor Gerhard Schröder, participating in his first IGC, was willing to maintain parity in the number of votes for France and Germany in return for the addition of a demographic criterion for qualified majority voting, which would give Germany an advantage over France. At the same time, the Netherlands offended Belgium, its less populous neighbour, by demanding more Council votes, thereby ending the traditional parity between those two Benelux countries.

When they convened in Nice, on 7 December 2000, EU leaders were so far apart and out of sorts with each other that it looked to two officials involved in the IGC 'as if eighteen months of preparation had been thrown out the window and the negotiations [were restarting] from scratch'.[33] After spending 2 days discussing other business, EU leaders spent another 2 days concluding the IGC, making the Nice summit the longest thus far in the history of the European Council. They haggled until the final minutes of the summit over the reallocation of Council votes. Belgium, still refusing to accept fewer votes than the Netherlands, eventually acquiesced in return for the promise of hosting all meetings of the European Council in Brussels. France managed to keep nominal parity with Germany, but the decision to add a demographic criterion to the calculation of a qualified majority gave Germany extra voting weight. In the end, the treaty increased the number of votes allocated to each member state, but the increase was higher for the most populous member states. As a result, the five biggest member states among the fifteen EU member states would have 60 per cent of votes, compared with 55 per cent before implementation of the Nice Treaty.

Efforts to reach agreement on the threshold for a qualified majority in an EU of twenty-seven member states (a number based on the existing fifteen

32 See M. Segers, 'Preparing Europe for the Unforeseen, 1958–63. De Gaulle, Monnet, and European Integration beyond the Cold War: From Co-operation to Discord in the Matter of the Future of the EEC', *The International History Review* 34, no. 2 (2012): 347–70.
33 Gray and Stubb, 'The Treaty of Nice', p. 13

plus the twelve candidate countries) were equally vexing. A declaration on qualified majority voting, included in the treaty, stated that the threshold for a qualified majority in an EU of twenty-seven member states would rise to 73.4 per cent of the total votes.

By the end of the summit, the EU's leaders had agreed that, as of 1 November 2004, the attainment of a qualified majority in decision-making would be determined by three elements: the threshold of votes cast; the number of countries contributing to that threshold, which must be a majority of the member states; and a demographic criterion, whereby a qualified majority represented at least 62 per cent of the total population of the EU (this would apply only if a member state requested verification).

Apart from the modalities of qualified majority voting, the Nice Treaty extended the scope of Council decision-making by qualified majority, and also extended the scope of the co-decision procedure. Thus, following implementation of the Nice Treaty, most legislative measures for which the Council was allowed to act by qualified majority vote would ultimately be decided by the Council and the EP by means of the co-decision procedure.[34]

Insofar as the size and composition of the Commission were concerned, the Nice Treaty called for the big member states to give up their second Commissioner when the next Commission took office, and for the number of Commissioners to be reduced to fewer than the number of member states, when the EU consisted of twenty-seven member states. Under the new arrangement, member states would rotate Commission appointments according to a system yet to be worked out. This generated a Nice leftover, following the precedent of the Amsterdam leftovers.

The Nice Treaty changed the procedure for nominating the Commission President: the European Council would nominate the President, acting by qualified majority, and the EP would then approve the nominee. The treaty also gave the President the power to decide the internal organisation of the Commission; to allocate portfolios to the new Commissioners and, if necessary, to reassign responsibilities during the term of the Commission's mandate. Moreover, the Commission President could appoint the vice-presidents, whose number was no longer specified in the treaty, and could demand a Commissioner's resignation, subject to the Commission's approval.

The Nice Treaty included a new distribution of seats in the EP, in the light of imminent enlargement, and increased the size of the Parliament to

34 D. S. Felsenthal and M. Machover, 'The Treaty of Nice and Qualified Majority Voting', *Social Choice and Welfare* 18 (2001): 431–64.

a maximum of 732 members, as of the next elections, in May 2004. As well as strengthening the legislative power of the EP by expanding the scope of the co-decision procedure, the treaty gave the Parliament new responsibilities with respect to the possible use of enhanced cooperation, in areas covered by the co-decision procedure, and the procedure introduced in the Amsterdam Treaty for declaring that there existed a clear danger of a serious breach of fundamental rights.

The treaty also included reforms to the EU's legal system, with a view to tackling a big backlog of cases before the Court of Justice. For instance, the treaty made it possible to set up internal chambers to deal at first instance with certain proceedings. Arguably the treaty's most significant innovation, or so it appeared at the time, was to ease the criteria under which differentiated integration could come into effect, with governments having agreed to remove the national veto on its possible use and reduce the number of member states necessary to initiate the procedure.

The time that EU leaders spent working out the final details of the treaty seemed not to justify the effort. Aware of the treaty's shortcomings, EU leaders agreed at their December 2001 summit, in Laeken, to a declaration on the future of Europe, which set out four main areas of reform that would be tackled in the next IGC, to be launched in 2004: the allocation of competences between the EU and the member states; the status of the Charter of Fundamental Rights, which the European Council had approved at the Nice summit; simplification of the treaties (yet again); and the role of national parliaments in the EU system (a specific request of the UK).

Given widespread dissatisfaction with the Nice Treaty, it was not surprising that foreign ministers signed the final document without much fanfare, on 26 February 2001. Even as the ratification process began, the Swedish Presidency launched an EU-wide consultation process to solicit opinion from governments and the private sector, academia, civil society and the general public about the next round of treaty change. Soon afterwards, Irish voters rejected the treaty in a referendum, on 8 June 2001.[35] The Irish government had not campaigned actively for the treaty, thinking that it would easily pass. Opponents included those who were concerned about aspects of the treaty, such as its call for an eventual diminution in the size of the Commission, and those who had concerns about the modernisation of Irish politics and society,

---

35 See B. Laffan, 'The Nice Treaty: The Irish Vote', *Notre Europe*, 6 July 2001; E. Murphy, 'The Nice Treaty and the Irish Referendum: What Values Are at Stake?', in *Studies: An Irish Quarterly Review* 91, no. 362 (2002): 114–24; House of Commons, 'The Irish Referendum on the Treaty of Nice', Research Paper 01/57, 21 June 2001.

developments that were unrelated to the treaty but associated with the process of European integration.

The European Council announced only a week later that the EU would enlarge regardless of the referendum result, whether the Nice Treaty was implemented or not.[36] In February 2002, the Convention on the Future of Europe, intended to prepare for a more far-reaching round of treaty reform, held its inaugural session in Brussels. As the purpose of the Convention and ensuing treaty change was to strengthen the EU in anticipation of enlargement, it was hard to understand why the EU put such emphasis on ratifying the Nice Treaty. Clearly, EU leaders felt strongly that having put so much effort into the IGC, the treaty would have to be ratified and implemented. Pressed by other governments and eager to prove its commitment to the European project, the Irish government organised a second referendum, on the basis of some small changes to the original treaty intended to appease Irish voters.[37] This time around, the government campaigned actively and more people turned out to vote. To the relief of the Irish and other national governments, a majority voted to approve the Nice Treaty in the referendum of 19 October 2002. Ratification proceeded smoothly elsewhere in the EU, and the treaty came into effect on 1 February 2003.

The political legacy of the Nice Treaty negotiations was more enduring than the treaty's institutional and other provisions. The conduct and disappointing outcome of the IGC turned political and public opinion against the negotiation of treaty reform using the traditional method. The Convention on the Future of Europe offered a more inclusive method for the preparation of treaty change, although treaty change itself would still require the convening of an IGC. This was the dilemma that the EU would have to resolve as it sought to end the situation of diminishing returns from the negotiations that had produced not only the Nice Treaty, but also the earlier Amsterdam Treaty.

Conclusion

As the title of this chapter suggests, several summit meetings in the years between 1991 and 2000 were decisive for the development of European integration, specifically with regard to treaty change and the elaboration of criteria for EU accession. Those summits took the form of meetings of the

---

36 'Presidency Conclusions: Göteborg European Council, 15 and 16 June 2001', www .consilium.europa.eu/media/20983/00200-r1en1.pdf.
37 See Hobolt, 'From No to Yes'.

European Council, the most politically powerful body in the EU's institutional architecture. Though a relative newcomer, and not yet a formal EU institution, the European Council was at the apex of the EU's organisational structure. Only the national leaders, meeting in the European Council, had the authority to take decisions on a range of issues of high political salience in their home countries, such as on contentious aspects of treaty change.

European Council conclusions, which tended to be much longer in the 1990s than in the decades ahead, were generally prepared well in advance by the foreign ministers, meeting in the General Affairs Council. National leaders debated and decided among themselves only a few, outstanding issues to finalise the meeting's conclusions. In the case of the Maastricht, Amsterdam and Nice summits, those details pertained to tricky and often highly complicated components of the draft treaties.

The leaders of the big member states have an inherent advantage in IGC negotiations, not because they necessarily have a better grasp of the issues, but because their countries' oversized influence confers on them additional sway in the European Council. Much depends, of course, on the perceived importance of the issue under discussion for each member state. Those dynamics were at play during the Maastricht, Amsterdam and Nice negotiations. Unlike in Maastricht, however, where the French and German leaders worked closely together and were perceptibly powerful in shaping the ensuing treaty, the leaders of France and Germany did not work well together at the Amsterdam and Nice summits. As has often been the case in Franco-German relations throughout the course of European integration, the reasons for this had to do with personal as well as policy considerations.

The rotating Council presidency played a key role in the Maastricht, Amsterdam and Nice negotiations. As well as chairing meetings of the national officials engaged in the IGC and of foreign ministers in the General Affairs Council, the country in the rotating presidency chaired meetings of the European Council. Only later, following implementation of the Lisbon Treaty, did the European Council acquire its own, standing President. The informal names of the treaty changes derived from the location of the concluding European Council in the IGC, and the choice of those locations was at the discretion of the country in the rotating presidency. The Netherlands, in the presidency in the second half of 1991, chose the city of Maastricht, in the far south of the country, for the December summit. In the presidency again in the first half of 1997, the Netherlands decided to hold the December summit in the country's nominal capital of Amsterdam.

France, in the presidency in the second half of 2000, hosted the December summit in the coastal Mediterranean city of Nice.

Although difficult to evaluate, the quality of each country's performance in the presidential rotation differs considerably from that of other countries. Some countries have a reputation for exceptional performance, others are known for making less of an effort. The small member states tend to exert themselves more in the Council presidency than the big member states, perhaps because it offers a welcome opportunity to shine on the international stage. The Netherlands, a small, original member state with considerable experience of being in the Council presidency, had mishandled the ICG in 1991, before the negotiations reached their dénouement at the Maastricht summit. Perhaps because of that experience, the Dutch government resolved to conduct an efficient and uncontroversial IGC in the first half of 1997, in the run up to the Amsterdam summit. The unsatisfactory outcome of the IGC, with respect to institutional affairs, was not the fault of the Dutch Council presidency.

The French presidency in 2000 was an entirely different affair.[38] President Chirac did not attempt to play the role of 'honest broker' during two meetings of the European Council, in October and December 2000, but openly pushed his own positions on contentious IGC issues, notably on the reweighting of Council votes. Chirac alienated many other national leaders, especially those from the small member states. Chirac's behaviour may have reflected his personal approach to international negotiations, and may also have owed something to a difficult domestic political situation, with France experiencing a spell of 'cohabitation', whereby the President belonged to one political party, on the centre-right, and the Prime Minister to another, on the left.

The UK, a big member state, was in the Council presidency in the second half of 1992, at a crucial time in the Maastricht Treaty ratification process. Although Prime Minister Major had set the UK apart from the other member states in the negotiations for the Maastricht Treaty, he was determined to run a successful and highly creditable Council presidency. In particular, he sought to help Denmark, and the EU as a whole, resolve the problem of treaty ratification caused by the result of the first Danish referendum, in June 1992. Thanks in part to Major's handling of the negotiations, the European Council reached agreement in Edinburgh, in December 1992, on a number of

---

38 See C. Lequesne, 'The French Presidency: The Half Success of Nice', *Journal of Common Market Studies* 39, no. S1 (2001): 47–50.

concessions to Denmark that made possible the second referendum, in May 1993, and helped bring about a successful result.

As it happened, Denmark followed the UK in the Council presidency rotation, in the first half of 1993. Like most countries in the Council presidency, Denmark wanted to put a distinctive stamp on its presidential semester. At the same time, the Danish government was eager to burnish its EU credentials both at home and abroad, especially in the light of the ongoing ratification drama. Accordingly, Denmark focused during its presidency on doing everything possible to facilitate enlargement into central and eastern Europe, which, although unlikely to happen until the end of the decade, at the earliest, already posed a major challenge for the EU (the accession of possibly four new member states – Austria, Finland, Norway and Sweden – was already in train).

Although the EU had enlarged a number of times by the early 1990s, it had never specified in any detail the criteria for a country's accession. Doing so seemed essential, given the likely accession of up to ten central and eastern European countries, whose recent history was so different from that of the existing member states. Drawing up the accession criteria was not an especially arduous or controversial task, but required attention and leadership, which the Danish presidency ably provided. Although it was not at all theatrical, compared with the Maastricht, Amsterdam and Nice summits, the Copenhagen summit was nonetheless consequential for the development of European integration, specifically with respect to enlargement, one of the most significant ways in which the EU took shape and form after 2004 and 2007.

IGCs on treaty change, including negotiations in the European Council, are exactly that: interactions among national representatives and, in the case of the European Council, among national leaders. Their prevalence and importance since the Maastricht summit have bolstered academic arguments in favour of 'new intergovernmentalism', the idea that integration since the early 1990s has proceeded without supranationalism, thanks in large part to the primacy of the European Council.[39] Regardless, the Commission has been a player, albeit not a central one, in the developments under review in this chapter. For instance, the Commission was represented in the IGCs, and the Commission President, as a member of the European Council,

---

39 C. J. Bickerton, D. Hodson and U. Puetter, 'The New Intergovernmentalism: European Integration in the Post-Maastricht Era', *Journal of Common Market Studies* 53, no. 4 (2015): 703–22.

participated in the Maastricht, Amsterdam and Nice summits (and in the Copenhagen summit).

The extent of the Commission's impact is debatable. The Commission seemed to be influential in the pre-Maastricht IGC, and President Jacques Delors was a leading protagonist in the Maastricht summit, but the Commission's influence – including that of Delors' successors – appeared to have waned considerably thereafter (Jacques Santer was not prominent in the Amsterdam summit; Mario Monti was not prominent in the Nice summit). The Commission played a part in drawing up what became known as the Copenhagen criteria, although, at the time of the Copenhagen summit, Delors' influence as Commission President was clearly in decline. Moreover, as mentioned previously, the Copenhagen criteria owed more to the Danish Council presidency than to any other national or EU-level institutional actor.

If the Commission's role was constrained in a setting that is primarily intergovernmental, the same was true – even more so – for the EP. The EP was consulted before national governments called for an IGC, and was peripherally involved in the IGCs of 1996–7 and 2000, in ad hoc ways. Parliament was more actively involved in preparations for the pre-Nice IGC. The EP passed a resolution on 7 April 1992 in support of the Maastricht Treaty, while drawing attention to what it saw as the treaty's many drawbacks, such as the pillar structure and the inadequacy of the new co-decision procedure.[40] In a resolution on 19 November 1997, the EP recommended that member states ratify the Amsterdam Treaty, but regretted the IGC's failure to bring about the institutional reforms that it considered necessary for the effective and democratic functioning of an EU likely to include more than twenty-five countries in the near future.[41] In a resolution adopted on 31 May 2001, the EP grudgingly welcomed the Nice Treaty, while regretting that it 'provided a half-hearted and in some cases inadequate response to the matters encompassed within the already modest Intergovernmental Conference agenda'. Accordingly, the EP hoped that 'the deficits and shortcomings with regard to the establishment of an effective and democratic European Union can be dealt with in the course of the post-Nice process'.[42]

---

40 European Parliament, 'Resolution on the Results of the Intergovernmental Conference', 7 April 1992, *Official Journal of the European Communities*, no. C 125/81.

41 European Parliament, 'Resolution on the Amsterdam Treaty' (CONF 4007/97-C4-0538/97) A4-0437/97, 19 November 1997.

42 European Parliament, 'Resolution on the Treaty of Nice and the Future of the European Union' (2001, 2002(INI)), Brussels, 31 May 2001.

The treaty changes of the 1990s and early 2000s were major events in the development of European integration, but were far from unalloyed successes for the EU. They came at a cost of growing public dissatisfaction with the EU and deep disillusionment with the existing method of treaty reform, because of a widespread perception of diminishing returns from IGCs. The EU's image in the 1990s suffered also from the violent fragmentation of Yugoslavia. The first war of Yugoslav secession broke out in Slovenia in June 1991, as the EC's leaders, meeting in Luxembourg, were negotiating what would become the Maastricht Treaty. The last war of Yugoslav secession, in Kosovo, ended in June 1999, at a time when the EU's leaders were preparing to embark on another IGC, focusing on a narrow range of institutional issues. The EU's CFSP, a major component of the Maastricht Treaty, proved inadequate to meet the challenges of Yugoslavia, even after the changes that were made to it in the Amsterdam Treaty. Like the wars in Slovenia, Croatia and Bosnia before then, the war in Kosovo revealed both political and practical obstacles to the EU becoming an effective international peacemaker and peacekeeper.

At the same time, the launch of the euro, in January 1999, was a major achievement for the EU. The launch of the European Security and Defence Policy – an effort by the EU to tackle the obvious inadequacies of the CFSP – at a summit in Cologne in June 1999 was another positive development. Both suggested a considerable deepening of European integration, as did the imminent accession of up to ten central and eastern European countries, plus Cyprus and Malta, despite the attendant challenges that enlargement would bring. Notwithstanding progress on monetary union, foreign, security and defence policy, and enlargement, the unsatisfactory outcome of the Nice summit, coming as it did soon after the Commission's resignation due to allegations of corruption and mismanagement, seemed a fitting end to a particularly demanding decade in the history of European integration.

Recommended Reading

Best, E., M. Gray and A. Stubb. *Rethinking the European Union: IGC 2000 and Beyond* (Maastricht, European Institute of Public Administration, 2000).

Dinan, D. *Europe Recast: A History of European Union*, 2nd ed. (London, Palgrave Macmillan, 2014).

Edwards, G. and A. Pijpers (eds.). *The Politics of European Treaty Reform: The 1996 Intergovernmental Conference and Beyond* (London, Pinter, 1997).

Gilbert, M. *European Integration: A Political History*, 2nd ed. (Lanham, MD, Rowman and Littlefield, 2021).

Kochenov, D. *EU Enlargement and the Failure of Conditionality: Pre-accession Conditionality in the Fields of Democracy and the Rule of Law* (Amsterdam, Kluwer Law International, 2008).

Neunreither, K. and A. Wiener (eds.). *European Integration after Amsterdam: Institutional Dynamics and Prospects for Democracy* (Oxford, Oxford University Press, 2000).

Redmond, J. *The 1995 Enlargement of the European Union* (Aldershot, Dartmouth, 1997).

5

The Constitution Project, Lisbon and Beyond

JÖRG MONAR

Introduction

In 2000 the European Union (EU) entered the new millennium after two substantial treaty reforms, those of Maastricht and of Amsterdam, that had significantly expanded its mission and objectives, capacity for internal and external action and democratic credentials. Two fundamental treaty objectives, Economic and Monetary Union and the Area of Freedom Security and Justice (AFSJ), had been added, with the first resulting in the successful introduction of the euro on 1 January 2001 and the second equipping it in time with possibilities for action in a common European response to the new challenges of global terrorism in the wake of the 9/11 attacks that was unprecedented in terms of the range of instruments used. Treaty reforms were seen as a vital enabling factor in these and other recent progressive developments of the European construction, and there was significant support both in the EU institutions and in many capitals for a continuation of the treaty reform dynamic: on the one hand, because it was felt that still more changes were needed to prepare the EU adequately for the incorporation of up to thirteen new potential member states, with which the Union was at the time negotiating; and, on the other hand, because there was support, though more diffuse, for a further 'qualitative' leap forward of the European construction before or coinciding with the rapidly approaching 'quantitative' leap of enlargement. It was the combination of these two reform motives, the first more functional and the second more aspirational, which accounted for arguably the most ambitious European treaty-making effort – after the initially sobering experience of the 2000 Nice Treaty negotiations – since the founding European Community (EC) Treaties of the 1950s.

The eventual construction of this reform effort around the concept of a 'constitution for Europe' became at least in symbolic terms the high-water mark of European integration treaty-making since the founding treaties.

The use of the term 'constitution' was not without its ambiguities: on the one hand, because it was applied to a 'Union'/'Community' based on an international treaty concluded by its member states, with those states being its constituent members and not its citizens; and, on the other hand, because the term became a receptacle for a wide array of different treaty-reform propositions ranging from the truly radical, aiming at no less than steps towards a supranational transformation of the existing European construction into something like a federal state, to various treaty changes oriented at making the Union 'merely' more effective and democratic under a 'constitutional' label suggesting further consolidation rather than fundamental system change.

In any case, embarking on establishing a 'constitution' for the existing Union/Community carried its risks as such a venture would inevitably generate different connotations and emotions, with the very concept of a European 'constitution' likely to be more understandable and less prone to raise fears about some sort of a European super-state in countries that already had a federal constitutional order, such as Belgium and Germany, than in those with no such experience and, in addition, a strong sense of national sovereignty. The United Kingdom (UK), which had neither a federal order nor a written constitution, was probably the foremost example of the latter, but far from alone, with also some of the newly acceding countries not being keen on seeing their newly regained sovereignty glide partially out of their hands in a European 'constitution'. But the risk was taken – and perhaps it had to be taken at some stage to test how far the member states as 'masters of the treaties' were willing to go with their common construction, which remains unique in the world.

This chapter will focus first on the genesis and content of the EU's 'constitution' project as it emerged from the combination of a 'Convention' with an Intergovermental Conference (IGC). It will then look at the ratification disaster which engulfed the project, its not altogether smooth partial rescue by the Treaty of Lisbon and the long aftermath of Lisbon, concluding with a consideration of the role of member states as 'masters of the treaties' in the ending of the EU's longest era of consecutive major treaty reforms so far.

The 'Nice Leftover'

As was shown in the previous chapter, the IGC leading to the 2001 Treaty of Nice had been convened essentially to deal with a number of institutional issues which the Treaty of Amsterdam had left unresolved. These 'Amsterdam leftovers' – primarily concerning the size and composition of the European

Commission, the extension of and redefinition of member states' weighting under qualified majority voting (QMV) as well as the future size of the European Parliament (EP) – were indeed addressed, in spite of many criticisms, by the hard-won compromises at the Nice European Council in December 2000. Yet the new treaty came with its own sort of a 'leftover' which was at the same time broader in scope and less clear in its content.

The 'Nice leftover' consisted of no less than the very large unanswered question of the further orientation of the whole European project in a post-enlargement perspective. This went far beyond securing its institutional functioning and the resolution of balance-of-powers issues between the member states. The EP had already criticised the IGC on 3 February 2000 for its 'excessively narrow agenda', which 'might well jeopardise the process of European integration'.[1] This partly corresponded to – and responded to – a warning from the Commission published a few days before that the EU would be 'profoundly changed' by the upcoming major enlargement and that it 'must not be weakened by it'.[2] There was indeed an increasingly prevalent perception that the Union needed to fundamentally reconsider and reinforce its purpose, with some urgency since a widening without parallel (or even prior) deepening might well carry risks of disintegration because of the much increased diversity after enlargement. While member states were haggling inside the IGC – with few indications of more strategic visions – over the aforementioned institutional issues, outside the IGC not only activists and academic experts but also many politicians felt that a fundamental reconsideration of the future shape and orientation of the Union was urgently needed. In some member states these views found public expression at the highest political level.

On 12 May 2000, German Foreign Minister Joschka Fischer, speaking in a private capacity, presented at the Humboldt University in Berlin some thoughts on the 'finality of European integration' in which he advocated the development of the Union into a 'European Federation' with 'nothing less than a European Parliament and a European government which really do exercise legislative and executive power within the Federation' on the basis of a 'constituent treaty'.[3] To this forceful appeal for a further deepening of the European project, French President Jacques Chirac responded on

1 Resolution of the European Parliament on the convening of the Intergovernmental Conference, OJ C 309, 27 October 2000, p. 85.
2 Commission of the European Communities, 'Adapting the Institutions to Make a Success of Enlargement' (2000), https://op.europa.eu/en/publication-detail/-/publication/f8427b8c-f6ba-447d-ab61-f1083db578c1, p. 3.
3 J. Fischer, 'Vom Staatenverbund zur Föderation – Gedanken über die Finalität der europäischen Integration' (2000), English translation J. Fischer, 'From Confederacy to

27 June 2000 in a speech before the German Federal Diet with a less federalist vision, but still pronouncing himself in favour of an 'institutional refoundation' leading to a 'European constitution'.[4] On 21 September 2000, Belgian Prime Minister Guy Verhofstadt followed with 'A Vision of Europe' presented at the European Policy Centre in Brussels which – while avoiding the term 'constitution' – called for a clarification of the Union's 'ultimate goals' and warned about 'slipping further' towards an intergovernmental approach.[5] In the face of mounting federalist and constitutional ambitions, British Prime Minister Tony Blair felt prompted, in a speech given to the Polish Stock Exchange on 10 October 2000, to pronounce himself in favour of the Union becoming a 'superpower' via further efficiency-oriented reforms, but not a 'super-state', and advocated a 'statement of principles' rather than a legally binding 'constitution' as part of the objectives of the ongoing reform process.[6]

It was, of course, a deliberate choice by Blair to give his October 2000 speech on the future of the EU in Poland as there were increasing concerns amongst the candidate countries that they were being sidelined in the debate on the future of the construction they were aspiring to join. Blair's hint in his Warsaw speech that 'nations like Poland, who struggled so hard to achieve statehood [. . .] are not going to give it up lightly' as well as his reference to 'a Europe of free, independent sovereign nations' could hardly have gone further in trying to enlist support from the candidate countries against more ambitious federalist designs. There were indeed mounting concerns amongst some current EU member states that the recently independent and sovereignty-conscious central and eastern European applicants would favour the preservation of the EU's intergovernmental features.[7] To those states, various forms of differentiated integration

---

Federation – Thoughts on the Finality of European Integration' (2000), https://ec
.europa.eu/dorie/fileDownload.do?docId=192161&cardId=192161.

4 J. Chirac, 'Déclaration de M. Jacques Chirac, Président de la République, sur l'importance de la relation franco-allemande pour la construction européenne, la réforme des institutions communautaires avec notamment la notion de constitution européenne ainsi que le renforcement de l'intégration européenne et de la coopération franco-allemande, Berlin le 27 juin 2000', www.vie-publique.fr/discours/208829-declaration-de-m-jacques-chirac-president-de-la-republique-sur-limpo.

5 G. Verhofstadt, 'A Vision of Europe (21 September 2000)', www.cvce.eu/content/pub lication/2005/7/22/e1570f15-55ae-4b60-b9e7-861ccc6876ad/publishable_en.pdf.

6 T. Blair, 'Address Given by Tony Blair to the Polish Stock Exchange (Warsaw, 6 October 2000)', www.cvce.eu/de/obj/address_given_by_tony_blair_to_the_polish_ stock_exchange_warsaw_6_october_2000-en-f8c765d9-ad33-4ce3-bfbe-7dd6d0114id7.html.

7 On the positioning of the applicant countries at that time, see M. J. Baun and D. Marek, 'The Candidate-States and the IGC', Journal of International Relations and Development 4 (2001): 13–37.

appeared as potential safeguards against the risk of a standstill of the integration process after the approaching major enlargement. In their aforementioned speeches both Joschka Fischer – with a reference to a 'centre of gravity' – and Jacques Chirac – with a reference to a 'pioneering group' – had actually more than hinted at potential differentiation in the post-enlargement Union.

The full extent of the 'Nice leftover' was in the end recognised by the EU heads of state and government through their adoption on the occasion of the signing of the Treaty of Nice on 26 February 2001 of a Declaration on the Future of the European Union.[8] It called for a 'deeper and wider debate' about the future of the EU, with all stake-holders, including the candidate countries, addressing, inter alia, the questions of the division of powers between the Union and its member states, the status of the Charter of Fundamental Rights, the simplification of the treaties, the role of national parliaments and ways to improve democratic legitimacy and transparency, all in view of the convocation of a new treaty-revision IGC in 2004. Never before in the history of the European construction had a new treaty been accompanied by a more extensive immediate political mandate for it to be followed and surpassed by another.

The Laeken Declaration

What became known as the 'future of Europe debate' rapidly gained political momentum during 2001. The main driving factors were the widespread dissatisfaction, not the least on the side of the EP and the Commission, with the limited reforms brought by the Nice Treaty and the undignified intergovernmental horse-trading which had marked the IGC, the (later overturned) rejection on 7 June of the Nice Treaty by a first referendum in Ireland (showing the difficulty of communicating treaty reforms to EU citizens) and other indications of public disenchantment with the Union.[9] The 'significant breakthroughs' in the accession negotiations announced by the Göteborg European Council on 16 June[10] added to the pressure as this development made an early enlargement more likely and, at least for those advocating 'no widening without deepening', agreement on further

8 Declaration 23 adopted by the Intergovernmental Conference, OJ 80, 10 March 2001, pp. 85–6.
9 See C. Barbier, 'The Future of the Union and the Laeken Declaration', in C. Degryse and P. Pochet (eds.), *Social Developments in the European Union 2001* (Brussels, ETUI, 2002), pp. 119–22.
10 Presidency Conclusions, Göteborg European Council, 15–16 June 2001, Council document SN 200/1/01 REV 1, p. 1.

substantial EU reform in time for the pending expansion more necessary. It was in this context that the idea of some sort of 'constitution' as an objective for the next treaty reform round, which had already been scheduled, was steadily gaining ground, strongly advocated by some and contested by others. Prior to the 'future of Europe debate' the question of whether the EU needed a constitution or perhaps already had one without the name because of the existing treaty framework had been a subject of discussion for legal scholars and those with federalist aspirations rather than mainstream EU politics.[11] The increasing 'constitutional' component of the debate can be largely explained by invoking a sustained and relatively effective effort of the EU institutions, the governments of several member states and countless supporters of further European integration to seize what was perceived as an almost 'now or never' chance of a fundamental supranational breakthrough ahead of or just in time for the rapidly approaching 'big' enlargement.

When the heads of state or government met for the European Council in Laeken on 14–15 December 2001 political pressure to widen the mandate, the legitimacy base and the transparency of the next treaty reform round had become very strong, resulting in their adoption of the Laeken Declaration on the Future of the European Union.[12] This provided an unusually detailed list of about sixty fairly specific questions the upcoming treaty reform should address in order to achieve a better definition of the EU's competences, simplification of its instruments and enhanced democracy, transparency and efficiency, including at the end the politically most charged question of whether the envisaged simplification and reorganisation might not lead in the long run to 'the adoption of a constitutional text' and what the basic features of such a constitution 'might be'. The language for this final programmatic part was clearly rather tentative, reflecting the unease of some member states regarding the declared constitutional ambitions of others. But if the European Council had clearly not been able to achieve consensus on the desired outcome of the now-programmed new treaty reform round, it decided definitively on an alternative method for preparing it.

In order to render the next IGC 'as broadly and openly as possible', the Laeken Declaration announced the convening of a 'Convention' to 'consider

11 On the surge of constitutional projections in the debate at the time, see J.-C. Piris, 'Does the European Union Have a Constitution? Does It Need One?', Jean Monnet Centre Paper, NYU School of Law (2000), https://jeanmonnetprogram.org/archive/papers/00/000501.html; B. de Witte, 'The Nice Declaration: Time for a Constitutional Treaty of the European Union?', *The International Spectator* 36 (2001): 21–30.
12 *Bulletin of the European Union* no. 12 (Luxembourg, Office for Official Publications of the European Communities, 2001), pp. 19–23.

the key issues arising for the Union's future development and try to identify the various possible responses' and to 'draw up a final document' – the term constitution was carefully avoided here – 'which may comprise either different options, indicating the degree of support which they received, or recommendations if consensus is achieved'.[13] Aware that with this course of action they were to some extent entering uncharted territory, the EU heads of state or government took care to clarify that the final document would merely provide 'a starting point for discussions' in the subsequent IGC, to which the ultimate decisions would be left.

With the appointment of former French President Valéry Giscard d'Estaing as chairman of the Convention and of former Prime Ministers Giuliano Amato (Italy) and Jean-Luc Dehaene (Belgium) as vice-chairmen, personalities of considerable political standing were put in charge of the Convention process. In the Convention overall the fifteen representatives of the heads of state or government would be in a minority vis-à-vis thirty members of national parliaments (two from each member state), sixteen members of the EP and two Commission representatives. Particularly innovative was the inclusion of 39 representatives of the 13 candidate countries (1 government representative and 2 members of the national parliament from each country) among the total of 105 members, although the Laeken Declaration stipulated that the candidate countries' representatives would not be able to prevent any consensus which might emerge among the member states. While the composition of the Convention on the Future of Europe was largely modelled on that of the European Convention which had elaborated the Charter of Fundamental Rights of the European Union in 1999–2000, both the much wider and politically more charged mandate and the participation of the candidate countries' representatives made this Convention right from the start a rather different exercise from the previous one.

However, impressively wide-ranging and at least in part remarkably innovative as the Laeken mandate was, the large number of detailed questions formulated provided a sort of dense veil hiding a gaping void at the core of the new reform round. There was in fact hardly anything in the mandate indicating any common vision amongst the member states about the ways in which the Union should become more than it already was, and there was not even much in terms of what additional fundamental tasks it should be entrusted with. This lack of a common vision was both a huge opportunity for the new Convention, as it could try to fill that largely empty space of the Union's future shape and mission through its treaty reform proposals, and

13 Ibid., p. 23.

a considerable risk, as in trying to do so it might endanger the whole new reform process by not being able to secure sufficient support for its proposals in the subsequent IGC.

The Convention Process

The decision to put Valéry Giscard d'Estaing at the helm of the Convention process had attracted many critical comments, mainly on grounds of his advanced age of seventy-six. Some governments may possibly have thought him to be a 'safe' choice on account of his being someone lacking much current political weight (he was politically largely marginalised in France) and also very much aware of the constraints of intergovernmental consensus-building in the EU (he had been present at the origin of the creation of the European Council together with Helmut Schmidt in the 1970s). But already at the inaugural session of the Convention in Brussels on 26 February 2002, the chairman, right from the start referred to as the 'President', left no doubt about his view that the Convention would be neither some sort of IGC nor a 'place for expressing diverging opinions' but 'a group of men and women meeting for the sole purpose of preparing a joint proposal' with a unique mission and the potential to 'write a new chapter in the history of Europe'.[14] Having thus ruled out the possibility of the Convention serving merely as a pre-negotiation forum for the subsequent IGC, Giscard d'Estaing also declared that its aim should be 'to achieve a broad consensus on a single proposal' which thus 'would open the way towards a Constitution for Europe',[15] thereby sidelining the other Laeken Declaration option of the Convention merely identifying 'various possible responses' for the IGC's subsequent consideration.

The potential risk of the Convention's proceedings being rendered unmanageable by a disorderly inflow and circulation of proposals from the wide range of different stakeholders was largely contained by the adoption of the Rules of Procedure which gave the President and his colleagues in the praesidium extensive procedural management powers. Articles 3 and 4,[16] providing that all documents and contributions submitted to members would first have to go through the praesidium, proved to be particularly important in this respect. Although Giscard d'Estaing's leadership in the

14 Introductory Speech by President V. Giscard d'Estaing to the Convention on the Future of Europe, 28 February 2002, Council Document SN 1565/02, pp. 3, 12–13.
15 Ibid., p. 11.
16 European Convention, Draft Rules of Procedure, CONV 3/02, 27 February 2002, pp. 2–3.

Convention proceedings – at times operating on the borderline between the authoritative and the authoritarian – was not uncontroversial, it provided a sense of mission around which most Convention members could regroup. The President's tight agenda and timetable management, the praesidium's efforts to focus the plenary debates on key issues and choices and also the effective support provided by the negotiating and drafting skills of British diplomat Sir John Kerr and his collaborators in the Convention's Secretariat[17] contributed much to making a final single draft treaty proposal possible.

The Convention went successively through a 'listening phase', aimed at identifying the expectations and needs of all major stakeholders from governments to citizens, a 'deliberating phase', focused on the comparison and assessment of the various inputs received, and a final 'proposing phase' dedicated to the drafting of recommendations for the IGC. Eleven themed working groups explored key subjects such as subsidiarity, competences, simplification of instruments and procedures and external action in greater depth, with numerous expert hearings, and presented their reports to the plenary from September 2002 to February 2003. The first months of the Convention proceedings were marked by a much more transparent and fluid deliberation of central issues than had been usual for previous IGC-based treaty reforms. This was so not only because of the public nature of the proceedings, but also because of the hundreds of contributions submitted both from within the Convention and from outside. While national government representatives, especially those of the larger member states, inevitably brought considerable weight to bear in the proceedings, there were other highly influential actors who would surely have been marginalised or even totally excluded in a traditional IGC context, such as the very active delegation of the EP headed by the Spanish Member of the EP (MEP) Íñigo Méndez de Vigo. However, the Convention's formal interaction with civil society was limited to only two sessions, later qualified by Giscard d'Estaing in an interview with H. Bribosia as 'more talk than anything', and a 'Youth Convention' bringing together representatives of youth organisations held in July 2002 also failed to make much of an impact, being, according to the President, absorbed by 'squabbles about posts' rather than questions of substance.[18]

17 On the Secretariat's often underestimated role, see F. Deloche-Gaudez, 'Le secrétariat de la convention européenne: Un acteur influent', *Politique européenne* no. 13 (2004): 43–67.
18 'Transcription of the Interview with V. Giscard d'Estaing (Paris, 17 November 2008), www.cvce.eu/content/publication/2011/3/3/b3e39520-70b9-4bda-9ad2-02d83be29649/publishable_en.pdf, p. 8.

The final months of the Convention, when it engaged in the actual drawing up of what was to become the Draft Treaty Establishing a Constitution for Europe (TECE), were increasingly overcast by the shadow of the impending IGC. Declared positions of governments, such as the more integrationist Franco-German proposals and the more intergovernmental British–Spanish position,[19] started to bear heavily on the proceedings. The Convention's already tenuous outreach to European citizens was at the same time further weakened by the shifting of political compromise bargaining between the main stakeholders (i.e., primarily government representatives and national and European parliamentarians in various often issue-specific coalitions) to meetings and exchanges that were largely outside the plenary sessions and not open to public scrutiny.[20] Institutional reforms proved, as in previous IGC contexts, extremely contentious, with changes to QMV, to the appointment and composition of the European Commission and to the rotating presidency system being amongst the issues which nearly made the Convention miss its already extended June 2003 deadline. (In the Laeken Declaration it had been foreseen that the Convention would complete its work 'after a year', which would have meant by March 2003.) In the end, its President was able to present Part I (Principles and Institutions, 59 articles) and Part II (Charter of Fundamental Rights, 54 articles) of the new Draft Treaty to the Thessaloniki European Council on 20 June 2003, and – after a further slight extension of the deadline – Part III (Policies and Functioning, 342 articles) and Part IV (Final Provisions, 10 articles) to the Italian Presidency on 18 July 2003.[21]

From Draft to Treaty: The 2003–4 IGC

In his final report to the European Council Valéry Giscard d'Estaing stressed the 'broad consensus' which the Convention had reached on the Draft TECE, with only 4 members out of 105 formally dissenting.[22] This and the fact that

---

19 Most prominently reflected – with regards to the Union's institutional set-up – in the joint contributions by Ministers J. Fischer and D. de Villepin of 16 January 2003 (CONV 489/03), on the one hand, and Ministers P. Hain and A. de Palacio (CONV 591/03), on the other.

20 P. Magnette and K. Nicolaïdes, 'The European Convention: Bargaining in the Shadow of Rhetoric', West European Politics 27 (2004): 381–404.

21 The European Convention, Draft Treaty Establishing a Constitution for Europe, CONV 850/03, 18 July 2003; OJ C 169, 18 July 2003, pp. 1–105.

22 The European Convention, Report from the Presidency of the Convention to the President of the European Council, CONV 851/03, 18 July 2003, pp. 4–5. For a fairly comprehensive multidisciplinary coverage of the transformation of the Convention's draft into the 'constitutional' treaty and its subsequent fate, see F. Laursen (ed.), The Rise and Fall of the EU's Constitutional Treaty (Leiden, Martinus Nijhoff, 2008); N. Barber, M. Cahill and R. Ekins (eds.), The Rise and Fall of the European Constitution (London, Hart, 2019).

this 'consensus' included the representatives of both current and future member states – several of whom were serving government ministers – put considerable pressure on the subsequent IGC, which was opened in Rome on 4 October 2003. Never before had the EU heads of state or government had a complete draft treaty as the point of departure for their reform negotiations, which was based, in addition, on a wide-ranging representation of obvious stakeholders. The Draft Treaty provided for a wide range of legal framework reforms, institutional reforms and policy-area-related changes which went much further than those of the Nice Treaty and were in some respects even more substantial than those which had been introduced by the Treaties of Maastricht and Amsterdam.

Of particular significance amongst the *legal framework reforms* foreseen by the Draft Treaty was the placing of the new treaty edifice under the politically heavily charged term 'constitution', whose symbolic weight was reinforced by the formal provision in Article IV-I (here and in the following, article numbers are based on the numbering of the Convention Draft, see note 23), for a flag, anthem and motto of the Union as well as the celebration of 9 May as Europe Day. In line with the Laeken simplification mandate, the treaty architecture was to be consolidated in a single treaty merging the provisions of the EC and EU Treaties, with a clearer structural separation between fundamental and functional provisions. The Union was to succeed the EC, to obtain a legal personality (Article 6) and to be vested with three categories of competence, namely exclusive, shared and complementary competences (Article II), replacing existing less transparent division-of-powers arrangements. A step towards simplification was also taken with the reduction of the legal instruments to mainly two, 'European laws' and 'European framework laws', although these were new in name rather than substance, taking the place of the existing EC regulations and directives. The Charter of Fundamental Rights was to be upgraded from a political document to an integral and binding part of the new Treaty (Part II), corresponding to a stronger emphasis on the Union's values both in the (slightly flowery) Preamble and in Articles 1 and 2. The potential challenge of one or more member states fundamentally deviating from the Union's objectives was addressed for the first time ever by provisions allowing the voluntary withdrawal of a state from the Union (Article 59). Further treaty reforms were to be made easier by a choice for the European Council between a Convention-based ordinary revision procedure and a non-Convention-based simplified revision procedure (Article IV-7).

Amongst the proposed *institutional reforms*, the most innovative were the introduction of a new semi-permanent President of the European Council – elected for two-and-a-half years, renewable once (Article 21) – and of a Union Minister for Foreign Affairs, who would be at the same time also a Vice-President of the European Commission (Article 27) and in charge of a new European External Action Service (Article III-197). In its Draft Treaty the Convention had also made a brave attempt to address the thorny issues of a reduction of the members of the Commission by foreseeing only thirteen Commissioners selected on the basis of a system of 'equal rotation' (details of which remained to be specified) between the member states (Article 25) and of the replacement of the existing complicated QMV weighting by a simpler 'double majority' requiring a threshold of a majority of member states representing at least three-fifths of the EU's population (Article 24). Both the simplification and the enhanced-democracy components of the Laeken mandate were served by the Draft Treaty replacing the diversity of legislative procedures that had historically arisen by a standard 'ordinary legislative procedure' (Article III-302) with QMV in the Council and co-decision by the EP – extended to twenty-two additional legal bases,[23] including the sensitive domains of the EU's own resources and criminal law – with only a relatively small number of Council unanimity-based 'special procedures' for particularly sensitive matters such as taxation issues. The EP's position was also strengthened with regard to the appointment of the President of the Commission – whom it was now to 'elect' on the basis of a QMV-based proposal by the European Council which should 'take into account' the EP elections (Article 26) – and to the EU's budgetary procedure – whose compulsory expenditure category on which the Council and not the EP had the final say was to be abolished (Article III-310). The Union's democratic legitimacy base was to be widened by a new article on 'participatory democracy' making, inter alia, provision for a new legislative 'citizens' initiative' (Article 46) and a strengthening of the information rights of and control over subsidiarity of national parliaments.

Amongst the draft *policy area reforms*, those concerning the Union's AFSJ and Common Foreign and Security Policy (CFSP) were the most substantial. The intergovernmental 'third pillar' (Article v of the Treaty on the European Union (TEU)) part of the AFSJ – police and judicial cooperation in criminal matters – was to be communitarised both in terms of legal instruments and in

---

23 The European Convention, 'List of Legal Bases for Which the Draft Constitution Changes the Adoption Procedure in Comparison with the Present Treaties', CONV 727/03, 27 May 2003, pp. 116–21.

terms of legislative procedures, although with a few fields still subject to a requirement for unanimity. The EU's competences were slightly extended, in particular to harmonisation in criminal procedural law (Article III-171) and the potential establishment of a European Public Prosecutor's Office (Article III-175), with a new emphasis on solidarity in what were to become 'common policies' on asylum and immigration as well as with regard to border management (Article III-167). The CFSP and its Common Security and Defence Policy (CSDP) component, although retaining their essentially intergovernmental basis, were to be strengthened not only by a new European Union Foreign Minister (an upgrading of the existing High Representative) but also by an extension of so-called 'Petersberg' CSDP mission tasks (Article III-210), the introduction of the possibility of a 'permanent structured cooperation' amongst member states with higher military capabilities for the 'most demanding missions' (Article 40(6)), clauses for mutual defence (Article 40(7)) and solidarity (Article 42), and the creation of a legal basis for a European Armaments, Research and Military Capabilities Agency (Article III-212). A further noteworthy reinforcement of the EU's external action capabilities was the proposed extension of the EU's exclusive Common Commercial Policy (CCP) competences to tariff and trade agreements relating to services and the commercial aspects of intellectual property (Article III-217). A new legal base was also introduced for a 'special relationship' with the EU's neighbouring countries (Article 56) to strengthen the EU's capacity to respond to challenges posed by its post-enlargement geostrategic environment.

While the range of the proposed reforms was large and not lacking in substance, it was also clear that the Convention – well aware that the Draft Treaty would have to pass the subsequent IGC – had shied away from any radical federal-state-like transformation of the Union. The Draft Treaty retained the member states as the basis of the EU's fundamental legitimacy, the member states' supreme *Kompetenz-Kompetenz*, their control over the Union's own resources and the international treaty status of the envisaged 'Constitution'. It also did not provide for any significant transfers of new exclusive powers from the national to the Union level and strengthened the position of the Union's most intergovernmental institution, the European Council. The use of the term 'constitution' – together with the other symbols linked to it – suggested nonetheless a much more fundamental change of the Union's status and nature than warranted by the Draft Treaty's content. More far-reaching, system transforming ambitions for the future of the Union had manifestly foundered during the Convention process, leaving the Draft

Treaty in a sense with larger and more resplendent clothes than its body could fill.

An unravelling by the IGC of the entire package of the draft 'constitutional treaty' – as it was widely called – would have meant not only a disavowal to a considerable extent of the contributions many governments had made to the Convention proposals through their representatives but also reneging on the Laeken commitment to a more inclusive and democratic treaty reform process. Anything looking like a rejection by the IGC was also likely to face serious difficulties in the EP and also some national parliaments which had made important contributions to the Convention process. At the time, it was already clear before the start of the IGC that, because Poland and Spain were concerned about their respective 'weights' in the decision-making process, they would not accept the proposed 'double majority' QMV solution – which made an opening of the package inevitable – and practically all other governments, though less forcefully, had also indicated that they wished to see a number of changes, mostly on institutional and competence issues.

The Italian Presidency, wishing to achieve a breakthrough before the end of its period in office, tried to deal with the most difficult issues – such as the QMV question – early on,[24] which proved a tactical mistake as the failure to make much progress on these issues also blocked progress on the others. An (ultimately unsuccessful) effort by Italy, Poland and Slovakia to add a reference to Europe's Christian values, nicknamed the 'God question', and protracted haggling over the function titles to be given to the new 'Foreign Minister' and 'President' of the European Council provided further unhelpful distractions. In the end, the Brussels European Council of 12–13 December 2003 had to announce that it had not been possible for the IGC 'to reach overall agreement on a draft constitutional treaty at this stage'.[25] Although the European Council's reference to a 'constitutional treaty' indicated a common commitment of the member states to such an outcome of the IGC, the absence of an agreement during the Italian Presidency – and in time for the EU enlargement on 1 January 2004 – was widely seen as an at least partial failure of the Convention's Draft Treaty. In one of its harshest resolutions ever on the work of an ongoing IGC, on 18 December 2003 the EP 'deeply deplore[d] the failure of the European

24 See European Commission, 'Schedule for the 2003–2004 Intergovernmental Conference (IGC)' (2004), www.cvce.eu/obj/schedule_for_the_2003_2004_intergovernmental_conference_igc-en-516eacfd-927c-427b-ade5-729d1db7494f.html.
25 Council of the European Union, Brussels European Council 12 and 13 December 2003. Presidency Conclusions, Council Document 5381/04, 5 February 2004, p. 2.

Council to reach an overall agreement', 'note[d] once again the failure of the Intergovernmental Conference method' and 'deplore[d] the evident lack of focus at the IGC on the common European interest', reaffirming its commitment to the Convention Draft.[26]

It was left to the following Irish Presidency to refloat the IGC by a combination of a different approach – with more emphasis on preparatory 'listening' and bilateral meetings – with more favourable political circumstances – in particular a change of government in Spain in April 2004 and a slight softening of the Polish position on the QMV issue.[27] In at times very difficult negotiations, the Convention's 'double majority' was redefined and raised to now consist of at least 55 per cent of the members of the Council, comprising at least fifteen of them and representing member states comprising at least 65 per cent of the population, with an added provision for a blocking minority requiring at least four Council members (Article 1-25). (Here and in the following, article numbers are based on the numbering of the signed (but not ratified) TECE.[28]) While this complex formula was hardly in line with the Laeken aim of simplification, it safeguarded the interests both of smaller and of medium-sized member states, including most of the new member states, against those of France and Germany, which had wanted to maintain the Convention formula. With most of the small member states wishing to retain their permanent seat on the Commission, the Convention's proposed radical reduction of the Commission's size on a rotational basis was watered down, also with additional complexity, to maintaining one Commission seat per member state for the first Commission under the Constitution and thereafter changing to a number of members corresponding to representatives from two-thirds of the member states selected on the basis of equal rotation (Article 1-26). Nice Treaty-type intergovernmental bargaining – which the Convention method had been intended to relegate to the past – also re-emerged with regard to the composition of the EP, for which the small(est) member states insisted on their minimum representation threshold being raised from the four proposed by the Convention to six, with Germany having to accept a reduction of its delegation to 96 instead of 99 and the overall size of the EP being increased from 736 (the Convention proposal) to 750 MEPs (Article 1-20).

26 European Parliament, Resolution on the Outcome of the Intergovernmental Conference, OJ C 91E, 14 April 2004, p. 647.
27 An insightful comparison of the IGC roles of the Italian and Irish presidencies is provided by L. Quaglia and E. Moxon-Browne, 'What Makes a Good EU Presidency? Italy and Ireland Compared', *Journal of Common Market Studies* 44 (2006): 349–68.
28 'Treaty Establishing a Constitution for Europe', OJ C 310, 16 December 2004, pp. 1–47.

Even if these institutional issues absorbed (again) much of the time and energy of the IGC delegations, the prevention of a loss of national controlling power over the exercise of key EU competences was also high on the agenda of several member states, and in particular that of the UK, which left right from the start little doubt about a number of 'red lines' that it would defend, armed with credible veto threats. The British position, partially backed by Ireland, largely accounted for a return from the Convention proposed QMV to decision-making by unanimity on the EU's own resources (Article 1-54(3)) and Multi-annual Financial Framework (Article 1-55) as well to the introduction of so-called 'emergency brakes' providing for a referral of controversial legislation to the European Council as a safeguard with regard to the use of QMV on social security for migrant workers (Article III-136) as well as procedural and substantive criminal law (Articles III-270 and III-271) foreseen by the Convention. An informal coalition of the UK, Ireland, Cyprus, Estonia and Malta also secured the removal of QMV-based provisions on combating tax fraud and company taxation that had been proposed in the Convention. Other member states also successfully insisted on issue-specific returns to unanimity in the Council, such as Finland and Sweden with regard to commercial policy aspects of foreign direct investment and social educational and health services (Article III-315). Inevitably, the IGC had also to cater to a number of interests of specific individual member states, such as those of Denmark in protecting its existing opt-outs, which resulted in a corresponding protocol. The ten new member states, for the first time at an EU IGC table, showed little enthusiasm for an expansion of the EU's powers and at least as much concern for their respective weights in the decision-making process – in the case of Poland even more – than the average of the old member states.

These and other, more minor, changes to the Convention draft negotiated at the IGC resulted primarily in a slight alteration of the balance of power in favour of smaller and medium-sized member states and a reinstatement of national veto powers in policy-making fields that were considered particularly sensitive. In a few cases the IGC improved on a number of rather vague provisions of the Convention's Draft Treaty, such as in the case of a clearer specification of the 'simplified' treaty revision procedure – not requiring an IGC – concerning internal Union policies and action not increasing the EU's competence (Article IV-445). However, when, on 18 June 2004, the Irish Presidency was able to announce a final agreement on the new TECE, around 90 per cent of the original Convention draft, with most of the aforementioned substantive changes, had survived the IGC unchanged, a more than respectable record for the new treaty reform process initiated at Laeken. But, as a satisfied EP President Pat Cox announced at the Irish

Presidency's press conference on that day, it was now time 'to explain it to the public, to sell it and to ratify it'.[29]

The Ratification Disaster

When the heads of state or government of the EU and their foreign ministers signed the TECE in Rome on 29 October 2004 – an obvious effort was made to connect the solemn occasion with the signing of the founding Rome Treaties in March 1957 – it was already clear that the 'selling' of the new treaty in view of its ratification would have its challenges. Whereas in the past only Denmark and Ireland had regularly ratified a new EC/EU Treaty by way of a referendum, this time no fewer than eight more member states – starting with British Prime Minister Tony Blair's in the House of Commons on 20 April 2004 – announced their intention do so. The reasons for the proliferating recourse to referendums ranged from obvious constitutional (Ireland) and/or political constraints (Denmark – because of the now firmly established referendum tradition, and the Czech Republic – because of the opposition of Czech President Václav Klaus to the treaty), via intentions to seek and politically capitalise on a popular vote approval of current governments' European policy (Luxembourg, Poland, Portugal and Spain) to more specific political reasons, such as the British government's desire to defuse divisive domestic Eurosceptic positioning, French President Jacques Chirac's seeking to reaffirm his popular legitimacy base and divide the opposition, and an almost accidental result of Dutch coalition manoeuvring. Although all of these governments emphasised in their justification of the referendum the 'constitutional' nature of this new treaty, thereby making it look like a more fundamental departure from the basis of the existing treaty than it actually was, the decision to engage in what the failed 1992 Danish referendum on the Maastricht Treaty and the failed 2001 Irish referendum on the Amsterdam Treaty had shown to be a rather risk-prone way of ratification had more to do with domestic political considerations than with the actual content of the treaty. Even Tony Blair, who otherwise tried to downplay the changes brought by the new treaty, referred in his justifying statement before the House of Commons on 20 April 2004 to the intention of letting 'the Eurosceptics, whose true agenda we will expose, make their case' for the people then to 'have the final say'.[30]

---

29 Government of Ireland, 'Press Release by the Irish Council Presidency (18 June 2004)', www.cvce.eu/content/publication/2005/1/20/0a549613-af3f-4965-a59a-b8367544bd23/publishable_en.pdf.
30 *Hansard*, House of Commons, 20 April 2004, Oral Answers to Questions (vol. 420, col. 157).

Although the parliamentary ratification procedures started well enough with huge majority votes in favour of the treaty in the Lithuanian (11 November 2004), Hungarian (20 December 2004), Italian (25 January 2005) and Slovenian (1 February 2005) chambers, it soon became clear that the treaty was entering turbulent waters where it needed citizens' approval. Although the first referendum, in Spain on 20 February 2005, resulted in a large majority (76.73 per cent in favour to 17.24 per cent against, with 6.03 per cent blank or invalid votes),[31] in spite of the Spanish government's huge efforts – it engaged celebrities to read excerpts from the treaty in daily television broadcasts and had 5 million copies distributed with Sunday newspapers – participation was rather low (42.32 per cent). At the same time opinion polling in the Czech Republic, France, the Netherlands and the UK showed increasing risks of the treaty being rejected. In France the almost frantic efforts of the 'yes' campaign during spring 2005 and the personal engagement of President Chirac did not manage to turn a tide which on 29 May resulted in a 54.68 to 45.32 per cent victory of the 'no' campaign, with a (quite respectable) participation rate of 69.34 per cent. The French vote, shocking as it appeared to many as coming from one of the large founding members of the European construction, was followed only 2 days later, on 1 June, by an even clearer negative result in the Dutch referendum – in another founding member state – with 61.54 to 38.46 per cent against and 63.30 per cent participation. Although in the meantime four other parliamentary ratifications (in Lithuania, Hungary, Slovenia and Italy) had been completed, the negative French and Dutch referendum results were rapidly seen as having sealed the fate of the treaty. The unexpectedly narrow win of the 'yes' campaign in the Luxembourg referendum on 10 July (with only 56.52 to 43.48 per cent in favour and a participation rate of 90.44 per cent) in spite of Prime Minister Jean-Claude Juncker having announced that he would resign in the event of a 'no' vote and the temporary freezing of the German ratification process because a case against the treaty had been brought before the German Constitutional Court did nothing to mitigate the impression of a major political disaster for the EU. All further planned referendums were cancelled, with opinion polls both in the Czech Republic and in the UK indicating a high probability that the treaty would have been rejected by considerable majorities in both countries.[32]

31 These and all subsequent figures on the referenda held are taken from the useful table in C. Church and D. Phinnemore, 'The Rise and Fall of the Constitutional Treaty', in M. Cini (ed.), *European Union Politics* (Oxford, Oxford University Press, 2007), p. 57.
32 On the Czech Republic, see L. Rovná, 'Constitutionalizing the European Union: The Lisbon Treaty and the Czech Republic', *L'Europe en Formation* no. 362 (2011): 101–23, 114.

The responsibility for the EU's 'constitutional' disaster was subsequently conveniently assigned by many to French and Dutch domestic politics. But even if Chirac's almost frivolous resort to the risky instrument of a referendum primarily for tactical political gains and the Dutch coalition government's inept handling of the ratification issue could be faulted, the problem with the constitutional treaty was both wider and more fundamental. While the French and Dutch 'no' votes expressed in part dissatisfaction with current governments' policies and specific domestic concerns (mainly of a socio-economic nature in France; mainly about a multicultural dilution of national identity in the Netherlands), EU-related issues too had played a critical role in the referendum campaigns, such as concerns about the liberal economic orientation of the EU in France and the economic consequences of the euro in the Netherlands, and – less prominently – about EU enlargement in both countries.[33]

None of these concerns was addressed by the proposed new treaty, which rather seemed to 'constitutionalise' an evolution of the EU that was considered far from satisfactory by many voters. This could, perhaps, have been compensated for, if the new treaty had been associated with a new vision, major new projects and/or clearly identifiable new benefits for citizens, but instead what was offered to voters was a revamped version of the existing framework, sold as a 'Constitution' (which legally it was not), with a number of real improvements, but improvements which were far removed from citizens' daily concerns and not easy to explain to the non-expert. Eurobarometer opinion poll data suggest that the more EU citizens heard about their new 'Constitution' during 2004–5, the less enthusiastic they became, and the low turnout in the Spanish referendum indicates that, even in a country with strong general support for the European construction, many citizens felt that the EU's new 'Constitution' was not worth turning out to vote on. Support for the very idea of a European Constitution dropped from autumn to spring (i.e., exactly during the period in which governments tried to 'sell' the treaty to their citizens), from 68 to 61 per cent.[34] In other countries with somewhat more Eurosceptic leanings – such as the Czech Republic and the UK – even the on the whole rather moderate reforms

On the UK, see UKPollingreport, http://web.archive.org/web/20120512232236/http://ukpollingreport.co.uk/issues/europe.

33 As brought out in the thorough analysis of S. Hobolt and S. Brouard, 'Contesting the European Union? Why the Dutch and the French Rejected the European Constitution', *Political Research Quarterly* 64 (2011): 309–22.

34 European Commission, 'Eurobarometer 63 – First Results, Brussels, July 2005', https://europa.eu/eurobarometer/surveys/detail/505, p. 23.

suggested in conjunction with the attributes of an EU 'constitution', 'flag', 'anthem' and 'motto' some sort of sinister move towards a European superstate, so that some degree of real hostility on one side of the political spectrum was in a sense met by a lack of enthusiasm on the other. While the Convention's failure to reach out more effectively to civil society during the 2002–3 drafting process may partly account for the treaty's failure to connect with the EU's citizenry, the main responsibility must rest with the member states' governments, which could neither construct the 'Constitution' around a renewed common vision for the future of the now enlarged EU nor adequately explain its rationale and content to their own citizens.

From Crisis to Rescue

Although parliamentary procedures for ratification of the constitutional treaty continued until well into 2006 – with Estonia as the sixteenth and last member state ratifying it by parliamentary vote on 5 December 2006 – the Dutch and French governments rapidly made clear that they would not try to get the TECE approved in a second referendum as the Danish government had done in 1993 and the Irish in 2002. Bulgaria and Romania, which joined the EU on 1 January 2007, did not need to ratify the TECE as they had accepted it as part of their accession treaties, so that the total number of member states which eventually approved the treaty was eighteen out of twenty-five. However, to declare the TECE dead, which many 'no' voters surely had hoped, was not really an option for the EU heads of state or government as this would have meant having to publicly declare the bankruptcy of a joint 'future of Europe' reform process that by then had lasted for more than 4 years and to forgo a number of treaty changes considered useful or even necessary. It would have reduced the successful ratification efforts of a sizeable number of other member states to naught and heightened the general mood of crisis, which could only weaken the EU's standing both internally and internationally. The media, as usual in the case of major difficulties relating to the EU, had in fact left their normal lethargy of reporting on European affairs behind, in order to now do their best to fan the flames of the undeniable ratification disaster into a headline-worthy potentially terminal crisis of the Union.[35] Given all that, the heads of state

---

35 On the unhelpful blowing-up of the EU's 'constitutional crisis' by the media, see the thorough analysis in M. D. Cross, *The Politics of Crisis in Europe* (Cambridge, Cambridge University Press, 2017), pp. 108–59.

or government could agree on little more at their first meeting after the French and Dutch referenda, at the Brussels European Council of 16–17 June 2005, than damage limitation and giving themselves more time. In a formal declaration on 'the ratification of the Treaty' they reaffirmed, on the one hand, their continuing commitment to treaty reform 'to ensure that an enlarged European Union functions more democratically, more transparently and more effectively' and, on the other, recognised that citizens had 'expressed concerns and worries which need to be taken into account', that a 'period of reflection' enabling a 'broad debate' was now needed for an assessment of how to proceed further during the first half of 2006.[36]

Although think tanks, scholars and political activists were very busy over the next few months discussing various ways of saving the TECE, ranging from adopting only part of it (there was a proliferation of 'mini-treaty' projects), via its adoption by only a core group of countries to a complete renegotiation, there was actually so little happening at the EU political level that in May 2006 Quentin Peel quipped in the *Financial Times* that the 'pause for reflection' had turned into 'all pause and no reflection'.[37] The British Presidency of the EU of the second half of 2005 and the Austrian one of the first half of 2006 showed considerable risk aversion as regards any revival of the pending treaty issue. The new German Chancellor Angela Merkel's initial unwillingness to invest much political capital in the treaty's fate and the lame-duck situation affecting French President Chirac after the negative referendum did not help, either. Equally, neither the European Commission's October 2005 'Plan D for Democracy, Dialogue and Debate'[38] fostering citizens' debate and participation nor high-level public events such as the Austrian Presidency's 'Sound of Europe' conference in Mozart-connected Salzburg in January 2006 celebrating European identity(ies) and values[39] contributed much to resolving the treaty deadlock. The Brussels European Council of 15–16 June 2006 had little option but to give itself even more time, although it now agreed that a report 'based on extensive consultations with

---

36 European Council, 'Declaration by the Heads of State or Government of the Member States of the European Union on the Ratification of the Treaty Establishing a Constitution for Europe', Council Document SN 117/05, Brussels, 16–17 June 2005.

37 Q. Peel, 'EU Must Revise Rules on Enlargement', *Financial Times*, 23 May 2006, www .ft.com/content/8e3e8ca4-ea77-11da-9566-000077ge2340.

38 European Commission, 'Plan D for Democracy, Dialogue and Debate' (2007), https:// eur-lex.europa.eu/EN/legal-content/summary/plan-d-for-democracy-dialogue-and-debate.html.

39 Austria Presse Agentur, 'Konferenz "The Sound of Europe" vom 26. bis 28.1.2006 in Salzburg' (2006), www.ots.at/presseaussendung/OTS_20060112_OTS0091/konferenz-the-sound-of-europe-vom-26-bis-2812006-in-salzburg.

the Member States' would be presented 'with regard to the Constitutional Treaty and explore possible future developments' during the first half of 2007.[40] Perhaps, after all, taking more time had its merits, as the doom and gloom commentaries about the treaty's failure signalling the end of the EU had started to subside by then. The EU visibly continued to function without paralysis on the basis of the existing treaties, even though in some domains, especially in those of the AFSJ and CFSP, there was evidence that the postponement of treaty reforms was hampering the EU's ability to take necessary action.

The Finnish Presidency of the second half of 2006, which had indicated its commitment to the treaty reform process by keeping its national process of ratification of the treaty on track for completion on 5 December, duly engaged in bilateral consultations which indicated sufficient support in the EU capitals for preserving many of the treaty's reforms, albeit without there being any consensus about the form this should take. This, however, provided a sufficient basis for the succeeding German Presidency to put the resolution of the EU's constitutional imbroglio high on its agenda. On 17 January 2007, Angela Merkel staked her first major claim to a leadership role in the European domain by declaring in a speech before the EP in Strasbourg that the 'reflection period is behind us' and that 'we now have to come up with new decisions by June'. The German Chancellor established in her speech a link between the current treaty reform process and the upcoming fiftieth anniversary of the Rome Treaties, to be celebrated in Berlin in March, and also emphasised the need to complete the process before the next EP elections in 2009.[41]

With the stakes thus raised for a relaunch of the reform process, the German Presidency started to engage in intensive bilateral consultations, seeking compromise lines between the three main diverging positions: that of those member states which had already ratified the treaty and were at most willing to consider minor amendments, with in particular Belgian Prime Minister Verhofstadt, who had just reinforced his federalist credentials with a prize-winning book on the 'United States of Europe',[42] forcefully arguing against any substantive 'roll-back'; that of those member states which wanted

40 European Council, 'Brussels European Council 15/16 June 2006, Presidency Conclusion', Council Document 11177/1/07 REV 1, Brussels, 17 July 2006, pp. 2 and 24–9.
41 Bundesregierung, 'Rede von Bundeskanzlerin Dr. Angela Merkel vor dem Europäischen Parlament am 17. Januar 2007 in Straßburg' (2007), www.bundesregierung.de/breg-de/service/bulletin/rede-von-bundeskanzlerin-dr-angela-merkel-797836.
42 G. Verhofstadt, Les États-Unis d'Europe (Waterloo, La Renaissance du Livre, 2006).

to give up altogether on the treaty and proceed at most with a few reforms of existing treaty provisions (the UK, the Czech Republic, Poland and – unsurprisingly – France and the Netherlands); and finally the position of those who wanted to save at least the institutional and procedural reforms by way of a politically downgraded 'mini-treaty' resulting from a short IGC.[43] The Blair government, keen on downgrading the TECE to escape from its referendum promise, complicated the situation by establishing new 'red lines' regarding the application of the Charter of Fundamental Rights, the implications of the CFSP reforms for the autonomy of British foreign policy and national control over judicial and police matters.[44] The chances for a breakthrough reform process looked rather slim until newly elected French President Nicolas Sarkozy, who had already advocated a new reduced treaty when still a minister, came out forcefully in favour of a rapidly to be agreed 'mini-treaty' – contrary to the position of his predecessor Chirac – immediately after having taken up office on 16 May 2007. While this brought a new dynamic into the search for a solution, one major obstacle remained.

As the first major indication that enlargement, which had been extended to twelve new member states after the joining of Bulgaria and Romania on 1 January 2007, could indeed, as feared by some, complicate EU treaty reforms, Poland raised (again) the issue of its weight under QMV rules, this time indicating its fundamental opposition to the 'double majority' requirement proposed by the Convention and redefined by the 2003–4 IGC. The German Presidency was forcefully reminded that enlarging the Union always also meant bringing some potentially heavy historical baggage into the common venture when Polish Prime Minister Jarosław Kaczyński justified Polish insistence on its QMV weight not being based on its current population size by the curious radio-broadcast argument that if 'Poland had not had to live through the years 1939 to 1945, Poland would be today looking at the demographics of a country of 66 million'[45] instead of its current 38 million. In one of her not so many failures of patience, an exasperated Angela Merkel then floated the idea of seeking an agreement without Poland among the remaining twenty-six member states, but such a solution was rejected by the Czech Republic and Lithuania, indicating the risk of an east–west fracturing

---

43 A constellation well described in A. Maurer, 'Managing Expectations and Hidden Demands: Options for the German EU Presidency', *Perspectives* 27 (2007): 100–16, 103–4.

44 M. Tempest, 'Blair Sets Out Red Lines on EU Constitution', *The Guardian*, 18 June 2007, www.theguardian.com/world/2007/jun/18/eu.politics.

45 I. Melander, 'Poland Told Not to Mention the War', Reuters, 21 June 2007, www.reuters.com/article/uk-eu-treaty-poland/poland-told-not-to-mention-the-war-idUK L218030642007062I?edition-redirect=uk.

of the EU reform process. Almost at the last hour, a compromise was worked out with the help of Blair, Juncker and Sarkozy, according to which the 'double majority' system would be postponed by 5 years, with additional safeguards protecting the Polish position on QMV for the time thereafter.[46]

It was mainly the earlier French change of position, coming with indications of considerable flexibility regarding the content of a 'mini-treaty', and the QMV compromise with Poland which then enabled the German Presidency to achieve a breakthrough at the Brussels European Council of 21–22 June 2007. The heads of state and government not only agreed on the launching of a new IGC 'to resolve the issue' with completion at the end of the year but also approved an unusually detailed mandate with sixteen pages of instructions and pre-formulated treaty amendments which was aimed at preserving much of the substance of the 'Constitution', but with major changes to its form.[47] Previously floated ideas of a reconvening of the Convention to work on the new treaty had already been unceremoniously buried. This time the heads of state and government wanted to keep a tight rein on the process.

The 2007 IGC and the Treaty of Lisbon

If the Convention process had to some extent been an exercise in 'dressing-up' as a 'constitution' what had in fact been in many respects a 'normal' treaty reform, the 2007 IGC was to a considerable extent a 'dressing-down' exercise in making much of what had been presented as the 'constitution' appear as a limited – though necessary – treaty revision.[48] This was already reflected in the initial title for the new treaty – the 'Reform Treaty' – and also in the speed of proceedings. Rather unusually for an IGC, the incoming Portuguese Presidency presented a complete draft of the new treaty[49] as soon as at the formal start of the IGC on 23 July 2007. This draft was entirely based on the detailed June 2007 IGC mandate, making no reference either to the

---

46 S. Kurpas and H. Riecke, 'Is Europe Back on Track? Impetus from the German EU Presidency', CEPS Working Document no. 273 (2007), https://papers.ssrn.com/sol3/papers.cfm?abstract_id=1337981, p. 13.

47 European Council, 'Brussels European Council 21/22 June 2007, Presidency Conclusions', Brussels, 20 July 2007, Council Document 10633/1/06 REV 1, pp. 1 and 16–17.

48 The most insightful and primary-source-based monograph on the genesis of the Treaty of Lisbon remains D. Phinnemore, *The Treaty of Lisbon: Origins and Negotiation* (Basingstoke, Palgrave Macmillan, 2013).

49 Council of the European Union, CIG 1/07 (treaty) and CIG 2/07 (protocols), CIG 3/07 (declarations) and CIG 4/07 (preamble), 23 July 2007.

Commission's (largely concurring) formal Opinion of 10 July[50] or to the EP's (partially critical) Resolution[51] of 11 July. This draft was first checked by legal experts, chaired by the very effective Jean-Claude Piris from the Council's Legal Service, essentially on its compatibility with the IGC mandate, and then subjected to political-level negotiations amongst the member states' foreign ministers at an informal 'Gymnich'-type meeting on 7–8 September. A revised complete draft[52] was submitted by the Presidency to an informal European Council in Lisbon on 18–19 October, at which full agreement was reached on the final text. This brought the IGC 2007, which was the shortest in the EU's history to result in a full new treaty, to a close, with the signing of the new Treaty of Lisbon following at a solemn occasion in the Jerónimos Monastery near Lisbon on 13 December 2007.

If one leaves the mere structural changes aside, the Lisbon Treaty changed no more than about 5 per cent of the substantive provisions of the TECE, meaning that it provided even fewer changes than the TECE had brought with regard to the Convention's original Draft Treaty. The most visible changes concerned the form and the symbols. The single-treaty format was abandoned in favour of retaining two treaties, the TEU, now enriched by a large part of the revised institutional and CFSP provisions of the TECE, and the EC Treaty, renamed as the Treaty on the Functioning of the European Union (TFEU), now absorbing the until then TEU-based 'third' (AFSJ) pillar. The use of the term 'functioning' was part of the dressing-down effort, with its emphasis on the merely 'functional' as opposed to the 'constitutional' nature of the abandoned TECE being potentially helpful to weaken cases for further referendums. The term 'constitution' was entirely removed, as were the provisions for the Union's flag, anthem and motto and the celebration of 9 May as Europe Day, changes with regard to the TECE which had all been regretted by the EP in its Resolution of 11 July. In the same vein the position of the 'European Union Foreign Minister' was down-titled – without changes to its TECE-foreseen functions – to High Representative of the Union for Foreign Affairs and Security Policy. The incorporation of the EU Charter of Fundamental Rights, which had been one of the pillars of the TECE architecture – and a too prominent one for some governments – was also given up on. However, Article 6 of the TEU now established the Charter as having the

---

50 European Commission, COM(2007)412, 10 July 2007.
51 European Parliament, 'Resolution of 11 July 2007 on the Convening of the Intergovernmental Conference (IGC)', OJ C 175 E, 10 July 2008, 347.
52 Council of the European Union, CIG 1/1/07 REV 1 (treaty), CIG 2/1/07 (protocols), CIG 3/1/07 REV 1 (declarations), 5 October 2007.

same legal value as the treaties, so that in legal terms the taking out of the Charter was just another act of political cosmetics. The same applied to a new more strongly worded protection of national competences in Article 4 of the TEU which provided that 'competences not conferred upon the Union in the Treaties remain with the Member States' (Article 4(1) TEU) and that 'in particular, national security remains the sole responsibility of each Member State' (Article 4(2) TEU). As the TECE had already provided for the principle of conferral (Article I-11 TECE) and also the 'safeguarding of national security' as an essential state function the Union had to 'respect' (Article I-5 TECE), this meant less a substantive change than a reinforced emphasis, though the second of these clauses increased a latent tension in the treaties between protected national security competences and the ambitious EU security objectives in the context both of the CSDP and of the AFSJ.

The Treaty of Lisbon bore the marks – one could also say the scars – of a range of specific staunchly defended national interests going beyond the merely symbolic. In some respects, the largest package of concessions had been secured by Poland, which obtained not only the aforementioned postponement of 'double majority' voting to 1 November 2014,[53] with the possibility of a member state still being able to request the application of the 'old' QMV rules until 31 March 2017,[54] but also the codification in a declaration attached to the treaty of a Ioannina-type clause[55] enabling a reduced blocking minority of countries to oppose the vote for an act by QMV from 2014 onwards,[56] a specific solidarity provision regarding energy supply[57] indicative of concerns about Poland's dependence on Russian supplies, an opt-out – shared with the UK – from the justiciability of rights under the Charter of Fundamental Rights[58] reflecting the Polish government's concerns about being potentially forced to grant homosexual couples the same benefits as heterosexual couples and – for good measure – a permanent advocate-general position at the European Court of Justice (which required an increase of the total number of advocates-general

---

53 Article 16(4) TEU and 238(3) TFEU. Initially 2012, but then 2014 because of the treaty's later entry into force.

54 Article 3(2) of the Protocol on Transitional Provisions. Initially 2012, but then 2014 because of the treaty's later entry into force.

55 See 'Ioannina Compromise', https://eur-lex.europa.eu/EN/legal-content/glossary/ioannina-compromise.html.

56 'Declaration (7) on Article 16(4) of the Treaty on European Union and Article 238(2) of the Treaty on the Functioning of the European Union', OJ C 326, 26 October 2012, pp. 340–1. Applicable initially 2012, but then 2014 because of the treaty's later entry into force.

57 Article 122 TFEU.

58 'Protocol (30) on the Application of the Charter of Fundamental Rights of the European Union to Poland and to the United Kingdom', OJ C 326, 26 October 2012, pp. 313–4.

from eight to eleven).[59] The British government, finding itself under relentless domestic pressure to hold a referendum, had not only played a key role in the elimination of all of the TECE 'constitutional' symbols, but also obtained the extension of its existing opt-out arrangements from the AFSJ to the formerly 'Third-pillar' fields of police and judicial cooperation in criminal matters (which was promptly claimed also by Ireland), an opt-out from the justiciability of rights under the Charter of Fundamental Rights (shared with Poland,[60] but in the British case the opt-out was sought because of concerns about the Charter's implications for British labour law), a declaration in relation to the delimitation of the EU's competences[61] providing explicitly for the options of repealing EU legislative acts and reducing – through treaty revisions – the EU's competences and finally two declarations concerning the CFSP explicitly protecting the autonomy of member states' foreign policies and international representation as well as ruling out any increase of the Commission's right of initiative and of the EP's role in this domain.[62] Neither did the French government leave the IGC empty-handed, having secured – mindful of French voters' apparent disquiet about the EU's liberal economic orientation – the elimination of the Article 1-3(2) TECE reference to 'an internal market where competition is free and undistorted' and, together with the Dutch government, the inclusion of 'conditions of eligibility' for future applicant countries to be defined by the European Council (Article 49 TEU). The latter was clearly motivated by concerns about EU enlargement which had come to the fore in the referendum campaigns in both of those member states. Amongst the minor distractions settled were Italy's concerns about losing parity with France and the UK in terms of its number of MEPs – resolved by increasing the size of the EP to 751 MEPs – and newly acceded Bulgaria's successful insistence on the euro notes bearing the currency denomination also in Cyrillic script.

Amongst these and other essentially 'negative' changes – negative in the sense of marking steps back with regard to the TECE and/or restrictive protections of national interests – the 2007 IGC managed to agree only two new 'positive' elements. The first was a further reinforcement, partially

---

59 'Declaration (38) on Article 252 of the Treaty on the Functioning of the European Union Regarding the Number of Advocates-General in the Court of Justice', OJ C 326, 26 October 2012, p. 352.
60 'Protocol (30)'.
61 'Declaration (18) in Relation to the Delimitation of Competences', OJ C 326, 26 October 2012, p. 346.
62 'Declarations 13 and 14 Concerning the Common Foreign and Security Policy', OJ C 326, 26 October 2012, p. 345.

motivated by the critical voices heard in several national parliaments during the uncompleted ratification process of the TECE, of the role of national parliaments, which were now enabled to oppose – under what became known as the 'orange-card' procedure – a draft legislative act within 8 weeks of its introduction on the grounds of non-compatibility with the principle of subsidiarity. The Commission would then have to re-examine the draft, with the possibility that a majority of 55 per cent of the members of the Council or a majority of the votes cast in the EP could definitively reject the Commission's proposal if it were judged not compatible with the principle of subsidiarity.[63] The second 'positive' innovation was a new 'particular' emphasis on 'combating climate change' in the context of the EU's international action on environmental problems (Article 191(1) TFEU). All of the other substantive reforms brought by the Treaty of Lisbon – from the legal framework via the institutional reforms to the policy-area reforms – were still those contained in the original Draft Treaty proposed by the Convention with the limited amendments made by the TECE (see above), although now they were presented not in a coherent text but as a long series of amendments to the existing treaties. Given the TECE's ratification disaster and the in many respects diverging positions of the member states, the 'treaty rescue' operation by the German and Portuguese Presidencies of 2007 had been remarkably successful. Former Convention President Giscard d'Estaing noted with some satisfaction in an article in the British *Independent* newspaper that in the Lisbon Treaty 'proposals in the original constitutional treaty are practically unchanged', but added that the few changes made 'sound a significant retreat from European political ambition'. He also warned that, with the original single draft constitution text 'blown apart into separate elements' merely attached to the existing treaties, the Lisbon Treaty would be 'unpenetrable for the public'.[64]

A Second Ratification Disaster – Averted

As much of the renegotiation had focused on avoiding the need for referendums, the German Presidency aimed at an entry into force of the new treaty on 1 January 2009, well in time for the June 2009 EP elections. The ratification

---

63 'Article 7 of the Protocol (2) on the Application of the Principles of Subsidiarity and Proportionality', OJ C 326, 26 October 2012, p. 208.
64 V. Giscard d'Estaing, 'The EU Treaty Is the Same as the Constitution', *The Independent*, 30 October 2007, www.independent.co.uk/voices/commentators/val-eacute-ry-giscard-d-estaing-the-eu-treaty-is-the-same-as-the-constitution-398286.html.

process started well enough, with the Hungarian parliament approving the Lisbon Treaty already on 17 December 2007. Both in France and in the Netherlands, governments brought parliamentary ratification under way rapidly, doing their best to present the new treaty as a fundamental departure from the rejected TECE. The British government, under vitriolic attacks for not wishing to hold a referendum, was able to defeat a pro-referendum motion in the House of Commons on 5 March 2008 by 311 votes to 248. But it had always been clear that a referendum could not be avoided in Ireland, and when it came, on 12 June 2008, the result was another 'no', by a margin of 53.4 to 46.6 per cent, with a turnout of 53.13 per cent. This new blow to the treaty reform process was rendered even heavier when Polish President Lech Kaczyński, an outspoken opponent of the treaty in spite of the Polish concession package, announced on 1 July 2008 that he would not sign the treaty, its fate now being in the balance, although it had already been ratified by the Polish parliament.[65]

While the Irish 'no' votes were to a considerable extent motivated by concerns about the treaty threatening various aspects of Irish identity (including its Catholic values) and sovereignty (including neutrality) as well as Ireland losing its 'own' Commissioner as a result of the reduction in size of the Commission foreseen in the Lisbon Treaty, subsequent analysis revealed that a lack of knowledge about the treaty had been a key factor explaining both the proliferation of mostly ill-substantiated threat perceptions and the lack of enthusiasm for turning out to vote for the treaty.[66] It had also not helped that Irish Prime Minister Brian Cowen had admitted that he had not 'read cover to cover' the treaty[67] and that Irish Commissioner Charley McCreevy added shortly before the referendum that 'no sane, sensible person' would read it either,[68] suggesting that the Lisbon Treaty was 'unpenetrable' not only for the public – as Giscard d'Estaing had predicted – but also for some of the politicians who would be responsible for its implementation.

A lot of pressure was almost immediately put on Ireland to find a solution, with French President Sarkozy rather undiplomatically suggesting early on

65 BBC News, 'Poland in New Blow to EU Treaty', 1 July 2008, http://news.bbc.co.uk/2/hi/europe/7482660.stm.
66 See J. O'Brennan, 'Ireland Says No (Again): The 12 June 2008 Referendum on the Lisbon Treaty', *Parliamentary Affairs* 62 (2009): 258–77.
67 RTE news, 'Lisbon Treaty "Not Impenetrable": Cowen', 12 May 2008, www.rte.ie/news/2008/0512/103157-eulisbon.
68 *The Irish Times*, 'No "Sane" Person Would Read Full Treaty – McCreevy", 24 May 2008, www.irishtimes.com/news/no-sane-person-would-read-full-treaty-mccreevy-1.1214799.

that the Irish would simply have to vote again.[69] Other EU leaders were less outspoken, but a second Irish referendum – as in the case of the Nice Treaty – was clearly the preferred option to avoid another protracted treaty reform crisis. This, of course, meant treating some member states as more equal than others, as no leader had seriously suggested making the French and Dutch vote a second time in the 2005 referendums disaster – which did not help with the internal Irish debate. Concessions clearly had to be made, and at the Brussels European Council of 11–12 December 2008 the heads of state or government decided to return to the formula of one Commissioner per member state – reversing one of the key institutional reforms originally proposed by the Convention – and to give Ireland legal guarantees against any extension of EU powers in the field of taxation, any implications for its traditional policy of neutrality and any impact on the provisions of the Irish Constitution in relation to the right to life, education and the family. These concessions were further refined and formalised in a 'Decision' adopted by the European Council in Brussels on 18–19 June 2009.[70] On this basis, the Irish government engaged in a second referendum, which this time, on 2 October 2009, endorsed the Lisbon Treaty by a resounding 67.1 to 32.9 per cent, though with a not overwhelming turnout of 59 per cent. While a more sustained supply of government information about the treaty and a more coherent 'yes' campaign clearly helped to achieve the positive outcome, there was also ample evidence that the severe recession Ireland had entered since the end of 2008 in the wake of the global financial crisis made many Irish voters appreciate membership of the EU and its solidarity dimension more than before.[71]

It was not only in Ireland, though, that the Lisbon Treaty met with difficulties. In Germany the treaty was challenged before the Federal Constitutional Court on its compatibility with the German Grundgesetz (Basic Law). In its judgment rendered on 30 June 2009, the Bundesverfassungsgericht (Federal Constitutional Court) ruled that the Lisbon Treaty was compatible with the Basic Law, but imposed a revision of German national implementing

69 *Le Figaro*, 'Sarkozy: "Les Irlandais devront revoter" le traité', 15 July 2008, www.lefigaro.fr/politique/2008/07/15/01002-20080715ARTFIG00409-sarkozy-les-irlandais-devront-revoter-le-traite-.php.
70 Council of the European Union, 'Brussels European Council 18/19 June 2009. Presidency Conclusions', Council Document 11225/2/09 REV 2, 10 July 2009, pp. 2–3 and 17–19.
71 France24, 'Crisis Sees Ireland Warm to Lisbon Treaty', 30 January 2009, https://web.archive.org/web/20121022031441/http://www.france24.com/en/20090130-crisis-poll-ireland-favour-lisbon-treaty-europe.

legislation to reinforce the controlling rights of the two German parliamentary chambers with regard to possible increases of EU competences and changes to decision-making rules under the new treaty and engaged in an unusually far-reaching consideration of the limits which the Basic Law would impose on further treaty reforms. Most notably, the Constitutional Court stated that, if 'the threshold were crossed to a federal state and to the giving up of national sovereignty, this would require a free decision of the people in Germany beyond the present applicability of the Basic Law' and that 'a structural democratic deficit' incompatible with the Basic Law would exist 'if the extent of competences, the political freedom of action and the degree of independent opinion-formation on the part of the institutions of the Union reached a level corresponding to the federal level in a federal state', which 'in the worst case' would require the Federal Republic of Germany 'even to refuse further participation in the European Union'.[72] The judgment was widely seen, especially in Germany, as a shot across the bows of any further ambitions to deepen European integration and an unprecedented judicial reaffirmation of sovereign statehood in Germany's participation in the European construction.[73]

In the Czech Republic, the Lisbon Treaty was even challenged twice before the Ústavní soud (Constitutional Court). In its judgements of 26 November 2008 and 3 November 2009, the Constitutional Court ruled that the Lisbon Treaty was compatible with the Ústava České republiky (Constitution of the Czech Republic). It explicitly rejected the restrictive doctrine of national sovereignty defended by Czech President Klaus with a remarkable consideration of sovereignty as a 'means for fulfilling the fundamental values on which the construction of a democratic state governed by the rule of law stands' rather than an 'aim in itself'. However, it reserved its right to review in the future 'whether any act by Union bodies exceeded the powers that the Czech Republic transferred to the European Union'.[74]

---

72 Bundesverfassungsgericht, 'Judgment of the Second Senate of 30 June 2009' – 2 BvE 2/08, paras. 263–4 (official translation), www.bundesverfassungsgericht.de/SharedDocs/Entscheidungen/EN/2009/06/es20090630_2bve000208en.html.

73 See, for instance, D. Thym, 'In the Name of Sovereign Statehood: A Critical Introduction to the Lisbon Judgment of the German Constitutional Court', *Common Market Law Review* 46 (2009): 1795–1822; C. Tomuschat, 'Lisbon – Terminal of the European Integration Process?', *Zeitschrift für ausländisches öffentliches Recht und Völkerrecht* 70 (2010): 251–82.

74 Ústavní soud, 'Decision 2009/11/03 – Pl. ÚS 29/09: Treaty of Lisbon II' (official translation), paras. 145–62 (with reference to the judgement of 26 November 2008).

Just before the November 2009 Czech Constitutional Court ruling, President Klaus had been successful in wringing from the European Council on 29–30 October 2009 as a final Lisbon Treaty concession to national interests (and the European past) a 'Declaration' including the Czech Republic in the British and Polish opt-out from the Charter of Fundamental Rights.[75] This was to guarantee that the Charter could not be invoked against the confiscation of the property of ethnic Germans and Hungarians after the Second World War under the Beneš Decrees. Deprived of any means to further delay the signing of the act of ratification, President Klaus did so on 3 November 2009. With President Kaczyński having finally completed the Polish ratification with his signature on 10 October, this removed the last obstacle, so that the Treaty of Lisbon could finally enter into force on 1 December 2009.

The completion of the Lisbon ratification process with its final inter-governmental manoeuvring around another opt-out also showed that the 'big' EU enlargement of the decade to include a total of twelve new member states was in a sense the major anticlimax of the protracted treaty-revision process. While it was a forceful initial driving factor for launching the process, it had hardly any major impact on the substance of the negotiations beyond the haggling over QMV weightings, EP seats and Commissioner numbers, resulting in adaptations of the treaty rather than a fundamental overhaul. The new member states also had lost little time to behave in IGCs like ordinary 'masters of the Treaties', having learned quickly from the 'older' member states how to squeeze out of EU treaty-revision negotiations the maximum possible amount of concessions in terms of institutional adjustments, opt-outs and cosmetic changes to satisfy perceived national interests, just short of bringing the whole process to a halt.

The Aftermath of the Lisbon Treaty

Compared with the Lisbon Treaty's signing ceremony in 2007, its entry into force 2 years later was a low-key affair, with the only relatively bold statement coming from Commission President Manuel Barroso, who, after the protracted efforts to avoid any further consultations of EU citizens in refer-endums, bravely asserted that the new treaty would be putting 'citizens at the

---

75 European Council, 'Brussels European Council 29/30 October 2009, Presidency Conclusions', Brussels, 1 December 2009, Council Document 15265/1/09 REV 1, p. 14.

centre of the European project'.[76] After nearly 9 years of efforts – starting with the February 2001 Declaration on the Future of Europe – the failed referendums, the renounced 'constitutional' ambitions and the numerous national interest buy-offs, the prevailing mood both in the capitals and in the EU institutions was relief rather than any triumphalism. Unlike after the Amsterdam and Nice Treaties, no government showed any intention to reopen in the foreseeable future what the EU's first post-Lisbon President of the European Council, Herman Van Rompuy, later called the 'Pandora's box' of a further major EU treaty reform.[77] The first decade after the Lisbon Treaty reforms – 2010–20 – became in fact the first since the 1970s without any new amending treaty reform of the European construction, reflecting both the absence of any major new political project for the Union on the side of the member states and a considerable degree of risk aversion regarding treaty change after the experiences with the TECE and the Lisbon Treaty. Debates and demands for further fundamental treaty reforms have occasionally flared up, but never to the extent of generating a critical mass of support amongst member states to launch for a fundamental revision. But this has not meant a complete standstill.

There were, again, 'left-overs' which had to be dealt with. As a result of the later than planned entry into force of the Treaty of Lisbon, the June 2009 elections of the EP were still held on the basis of the Nice Treaty, which had provided for a lower number of seats. With the Lisbon Treaty allocating 18 additional seats to 12 member states and Germany losing 3 seats due to the new quotas, a compromise was arrived at between the EP and the European Council, allowing the 18 additional MEPs to take their seats without waiting for the 2014 elections and the 3 'extra' German MEPs (elected in 2009) to maintain their seats until 2014 – which temporarily increased the size of the EP to 754 MEPs. This solution was enacted via a very short IGC, not requiring the convocation of a Convention, launched by the June 2010 Brussels European Council and organised at Comité des représentants permanents (COREPER) II level on 23 June 2010. This resulted in a protocol to that effect, which was attached to the Lisbon Treaty and subsequently ratified by all of the member states.[78] Another Lisbon left-over was the need to codify in the

---

76 European Commission, 'European Commission Welcomes the Entry into Force of the Treaty of Lisbon', Press Release IP/09/1855, 1 December 2009, https://ec.europa.eu/commission/presscorner/detail/en/IP_09_1855.

77 H. Van Rompuy, 'Do We Need a New Pact for Europe?' (2015), www.socialeurope.eu/do-we-need-a-new-pact-for-europe.

78 'Protocol Amending the Protocol on Transitional Provisions', OJ C 263, 29 September 2010, p. 1.

treaties the European Council 'Decision' of June 2009 regarding the additional Lisbon Treaty-related guarantees given to Ireland. This was done in the form of an additional protocol,[79] which was adopted, again by a COREPER II-level short IGC, on 13 June 2012. Because of lengthy national parliamentary ratification procedures, it did not enter into force until 1 December 2014.

In the case of the two Lisbon left-over issues, the newly defined 'simplified' treaty revision procedure under Article 48(6) of the TEU had worked perfectly smoothly. Its biggest test so far arose in conjunction with the sovereign debt crisis which had increasingly engulfed the EU since 2010. Because of the so-called 'no-bailout' clause of Article 125(1) of the TFEU prohibiting the EU and its member states from assuming the commitments of another member state, the unprecedented financial lending and guarantee capabilities created under the European Financial Stability Facility and the European Financial Stability Mechanism to support Greece and other member states in budgetary and financial difficulty rested on not altogether solid legal foundations. This was of major concern to the German government, which had to defend German participation in the assistance mechanisms before the Federal Constitutional Court. Chancellor Merkel's preferred option, namely to resolve the issue by a corresponding EU treaty change, had to overcome considerable reluctance on the side of the other governments, which were wary about engaging in another treaty revision procedure. After Merkel had secured the support of French President Sarkozy in October 2010, the European Council agreed to start consultations in view of only a 'limited treaty change', at the same time making it clear that it expected the member states of the Eurozone – and not the EU – to address the wider issue of a 'permanent crisis mechanism to safeguard the financial stability of the euro area as a whole'.[80] The 'limited treaty change' then took the form, agreed at the December 2010 European Council, of adding to Article 136 of the TFEU a new paragraph 3, according to which member states were authorised to 'establish a stability mechanism to be activated if indispensable to safeguard the stability of the euro area', with financial assistance 'to be made subject to strict conditionality'. As this minimalist solution avoided any extension of EU competences, the simplified treaty revision procedure under Article 48(6) of the TEU could again be applied, leading, after the mandatory

---

79 'Protocol on the Concerns of the Irish People on the Treaty of Lisbon', OJ L 60, 2 March 2013, p. 131.
80 European Council, 'Brussels European Council 28/29 October 2010, Presidency Conclusions', Brussels, 30 November 2010, Council Document EUCO 25/1/10 REV 1, p. 2.

consultations of the EP, the Commission and the European Central Bank, to a European Council Decision adopted on 11 March 2011 amending the TFEU accordingly.[81] It entered into force on 1 January 2013, after having been ratified by parliamentary ratification in all of the member states. For the time being, this was the last substantive change of the EU Treaties.

The Article 136 TFEU amendment surely avoided the opening of the 'Pandora's box' of another major Convention-based treaty revision round, but at the price of relegating the more far-reaching Eurozone issues arising from the sovereign debt crisis to a solution outside the framework of the EU Treaties through the signing in March 2012 of the intergovernmental Treaty on Stability, Coordination and Governance in the Economic and Monetary Union by twenty-five of the twenty-seven member states (the UK and the Czech Republic did not participate). Given that member states were even willing to accept solutions outside the EU Treaties for issues of such obvious relevance to the EU rather than 'risk' another major treaty reform, it cannot be surprising that ever since then even occasional high-level initiatives envisaging more comprehensive treaty reforms – such as French President Emmanuel Macron's 4 March 2019 letter to the 'Citizens of Europe' advocating a 'European Renaissance'[82] – have at best been met with a lukewarm response. The Council's June 2020 position on the Conference on the Future of Europe, which was launched at the initiative of the Commission, the Council and the EP, not only excelled in presenting broad objectives but also explicitly stated that the 'conference does not fall within the scope of Article 48 TEU'. The Council thereby excluded any direct link with a potential treaty revision, providing only for a report to be submitted to the European Council in 2022.[83] In their 'Joint Declaration' on 10 March 2021, the Presidents of the Commission, the Council and the EP went no further than to invite the conference, which has a membership more than three times as large as the 2002–3 Convention and will rely heavily on a multilingual digital platform and 'European Citizens' Panels' to find out what citizens 'expect' from the EU, to 'provide guidance on the future of Europe'.[84] On the occasion of the launch of the conference on

---

81 'European Council Decision of 25 March 2011 Amending Article 136 of the Treaty on the Functioning of the European Union with Regard to a Stability Mechanism for Member States Whose Currency Is the Euro', OJ L 91, 6 April 2011, p. 1.
82 E. Macron, 'Pour une Renaissance européenne' (2019), www.elysee.fr/emmanuel-macron/2019/03/04/pour-une-renaissance-europeenne.
83 Council of the European Union, 'Conference on the Future of Europe Council Position', Council Document 9102/20, 24 June 2020, p. 7.
84 Conference on the Future of Europe, 'Joint Declaration on the Conference on the Future of Europe', 10 March 2021, https://futureu.europa.eu/uploads/decidim/attach

9 May 2021 in Strasbourg, President Macron expressed the wish that it would 'ring the hour of the return of the great projects, great ambitions and great dreams' and that its results should serve in 2022 to 'reform Europe'.[85] Yet the conference's first plenary session on 19 June 2021 – perhaps unsurprisingly, given its large and diverse membership, ambitious civil-society outreach agenda and vaguely defined mandate – was largely absorbed by an enormous variety of statements of objectives and organisational and procedural debates.[86] In terms of potential treaty reform proposals, this conference, although also coming under the heading of the 'future of Europe', had neither the benefit of a Laeken-type reform agenda nor that of a Valéry Giscard d'Estaing driving proceedings – which may well be exactly what most EU governments preferred.

Next to the risks (and frustrations) perceived to be connected with another major reform round, there may also be an increased scepticism about treaty reforms actually being that what the EU needs most to address its problems. A 2019 study produced by the EP's Research Service indicated no less than thirty-four legal bases in the TEU and TFEU which, in spite of the need for action by the EU in the respective fields, remain unused or under-used.[87] If invoking under-used treaty reforms is one way to weaken the case for further ones, the restrictive interpretation of reformed provisions is another. EU citizens, when next called to vote on an EU Treaty reform, may be forgiven for having certain doubts, given the European Council's deviation in 2019 from the EP elections-based *Spitzenkandidaten* process applied after the 2014 elections to appoint the President of the European Commission on the basis of Lisbon Treaty-amended Article 17(6) of the TEU. In spite of the trumpeted placing of the citizens at the heart of the European project after Lisbon, the European Council managed to impose a candidate largely unknown outside Germany, German Defence Minister Ursula von der Leyen, as a sort of last minute 'rabbit out of the hat', who had not even been a candidate for the position when EU citizens voted in the June 2019 EP elections. There are

ment/file/6/EN_-_JOINT_DECLARATION_ON_THE_CONFERENCE_ON_TH E_FUTURE_OF_EUROPE.pdf.

85 Présidence de la République, 'Lancement de la Conférence sur l'avenir de l'Europe' (2021), www.elysee.fr/emmanuel-macron/2021/05/09/lancement-de-la-conference-sur-lavenir-de-leurope.

86 Conference on the Future of Europe, Agenda of the Inaugural Plenary of 19 June 2021 and video extracts, https://futureu.europa.eu/en/pages/plenary? format=html&locale=en.

87 European Parliamentary Research Service, *Unlocking the Potential of the EU Treaties* (Luxembourg, European Parliament, 2019). See also É. Bassot (ed.), 'Unlocking the Potential of the EU Treaties: An Article-by-Article Analysis of the Scope for Action' (2020), www.europarl.europa.eu/RegData/etudes/STUD/2020/651934/EPRS_STU (2020)651934_EN.pdf.

also quite simply limits to what treaty reforms can achieve. When it came to the EU's major 2015–16 migration crisis, the treaties, not least because of the Lisbon reforms, had provided tools for a more effective response – notably QMV under Articles 78 and 79 of the TFEU and the solidarity principle of Article 80 of the TFEU – but to a large extent member states were unable to agree on using them effectively. Similarly, the member states have failed to react more forcefully to the mounting evidence, since 2016, of serious challenges to the rule of law posed both by the Hungarian government and by the Polish government, although the treaties offer mechanisms and instruments – Article 7 of the TEU and beyond – to do so. No treaty reform can possibly remedy or compensate for the lack of a common political will of treaty signatories to address fundamental challenges and issues.

Conclusions

Looking at the first two decades of EU treaty-reforms in the twenty-first century, one can think of the image of a wave of 'constitutional' ambition first surging on the momentum generated by the treaty reforms of the 1990s and the need for reforms generated by the upcoming EU enlargements to the east and southeast, reaching its peak, but already starting to break, in the Convention on the Future of Europe, and fully breaking in the ratification disaster of the 'constitutional' treaty, but still having enough force to ensure substantial reforms to the existing EU Treaties. In symbolic terms, at least, the crest of the wave overturned for breaking in February 2003 when no fewer than thirty-four members of the Convention, no doubt encouraged by British official insistence on the offending 'F-word' being eliminated,[88] strongly objected to the reference in Article 1 of the first draft for the new treaty to the Union exercising its competences 'on a federal basis'.[89] The Praesidium, which had proposed the formulation, retreated; and the term 'federal' never re-entered subsequent drafts of what eventually became the TECE.

At the end of these two decades it appears perhaps clearer than ever before in the history of European integration that the member states as 'masters of the Treaties' represented by their governments are, at least collectively and for now, not prepared to engage in any treaty reform which would transform the European construction into some sort of federal state-like entity having

88 Ian Black, 'UK Rails at F-Word in Draft EU Document', *The Guardian*, 7 February 2003, www.theguardian.com/world/2003/feb/07/politics.eu.
89 The European Convention, 'Reactions to Draft Articles 1 to 16 of the Constitutional Treaty – Analysis', 26 February 2003, CONV 574/1/03 REV 1, p. 2.

not only states but also citizens as its constituent basis. The underlying logic of not engaging in any such more fundamental transformation of the European construction which some of them, rather innovatively and courageously, launched 70 years ago is more pragmatic and less based on an obsession with national sovereignty than it may seem. As Alan Milward brilliantly argued,[90] there was a strongly instrumental approach in the member states' engagement in the European construction right from the start, with European cooperation and integration being seen by governments as an effective, even necessary, response to rapidly evolving economic and international challenges to ensure that nation-state settings could continue to fulfil their citizens' expectations regarding public policy delivery. Moving towards some sort of federal European state went right from the start far beyond this primarily instrumental approach.

When the EU started two decades ago with what turned into a 'constitutional' treaty-revision process, Joschka Fischer and others brought the federal transformation question to the fore, but, in spite of divergent positions, the collective answer of the member states' governments, as given during the Convention and in the two subsequent IGCs, was clear: the EU Treaties were to be reformed to make the post-enlargement EU better 'fit' both its larger membership and the greater need for common action on which the member states could agree, including as a corollary the strengthening of its legitimacy base through the Charter rights and reinforced parliamentary control. But at no stage of the process were the national governments prepared to develop their common creation into a federal state-like polity becoming an end in itself and replacing, at least in some respects, the member states as primary providers of public policy. The 'masters of the Treaties' were willing to concede at most the symbols – the 'constitutional' label, a flag, an anthem and a Europe Day – but not the substance of such a qualitative leap. Even though the backing of any form of federal integration leap by European citizens, at least in a number of member states, was always more than doubtful, those governments which in 2005 voluntarily put the TECE to their citizens for approval by referendum embarked upon what looks, with hindsight, like a daring gamble. In essence it meant trying to sell EU citizens a 'constitution', which was no such thing, with reforms of the already-complex existing EU system that were inevitably difficult to communicate made even more bewildering to the 'innocent' citizen by intergovernmental

---

90 A. Milward, *The European Rescue of the Nation-State*, revised ed. (London, Routledge, 1994).

compromises on competences, QMV weights and opt-outs, and all of this without adding any new vision or redefining the mission of the Union.

The 'rise and fall' of the EU's 'constitutional' treaty has occasionally been presented, and to some extent rightly, as a dramatic and defining moment of its history. But, as has been shown in this chapter, the TECE never 'rose' as high as a system-transforming treaty reform as this formulation suggests, but neither did it 'fall' as low, because much of its substance was saved by the Lisbon Treaty rescue. The latter also means that, in a *functional* sense, it can be regarded as fairly successful insofar as a number of its legal framework, institutional and policy-area reforms clearly equipped the enlarged EU with improved instruments for the major post-Lisbon challenges, such as the Eurozone sovereign debt crisis, the 2015–16 migration crisis and even – with the provision for an 'orderly' exit procedure under Article 50 of the TEU – the first departure ever of a member state. Arguably the post-Lisbon Treaty framework, with its many still under-used action potentials, constitutes a solid enough plateau for the Union to continue to deliver its objectives as currently defined.

But on the *aspirational* side, the recasting of the 'constitutional' treaty as the mere 'reform' Treaty of Lisbon marked a clear retreat of political ambition. This, together with the serious difficulties both treaties had to face in several member states during ratification and the reluctance of the 'masters of the Treaties' after Lisbon to open the perceived 'Pandora's box' again, would suggest that the process of European integration will not return soon, if ever, to a new era of major evolution through almost continuous treaty reforms as was the case from the Single European Act to the Lisbon Treaty. The stern *Ecclesiastes 3* dictum that 'to everything there is a season' appears thus also perfectly applicable to the evolution of the Union's treaties.

Recommended Reading

Barber, N., M. Cahill and R. Ekins (eds.). *The Rise and Fall of the European Constitution* (London, Hart, 2019).

Hodson, D. and I. Maher. *The Transformation of EU Treaty Making: The Rise of Parliaments, Referendums and Courts since 1950* (Cambridge, Cambridge University Press, 2018).

Laursen, F. (ed.). *The Rise and Fall of the EU's Constitutional Treaty* (Leiden, Martinus Nijhoff, 2008).

Phinnemore, D. *The Treaty of Lisbon: Origins and Negotiation* (Basingstoke, Palgrave Macmillan, 2013).

Piris, J. C. *The Lisbon Treaty: A Legal and Political Analysis* (Cambridge, Cambridge University Press, 2010).

6

Moving beyond British Exceptionalism

N. PIERS LUDLOW

Introduction

It is tempting to interpret the convoluted narrative that led to Brexit as a story of British exceptionalism. The fit between European integration and the United Kingdom (UK) had never been easy – much less natural, it would appear, than for any other country in Europe. It was for this reason that the British initially stood aside from the process, spurning repeated chances to join the institutional precursors to the European Union (EU). When they did belatedly change their mind and join the European Economic Community (EEC), moreover, they did so amid sustained domestic controversy. The deep-seated mismatch between Britain and its European partners was to become a leitmotiv of the country's forty-six years as an EC/EU member state. The UK was never at ease within the EC/EU, but instead at odds with important aspects of the process, divided internally on the necessity of membership and liable to see itself as an 'awkward partner', the malcontent within. The 2016 decision to leave could thus be interpreted as the logical, maybe even inevitable, outcome of this profoundly difficult link-up, the end of a long aberration rather than a surprising and contingent development.

This chapter will acknowledge that there is some substance to this case. Britain's road to Community membership and its path throughout its four decades of membership have indeed been bumpy, and there have been many aspects of the interaction between the UK and its continental partners that have made Britain stand out as a particularly problematic participant. Some space will hence be devoted to exploring the fragilities of Britain's European membership. But the chapter will also caution against too easy an assumption that the UK and the EC/EU were never really compatible and that a break between them was foreordained. To argue this risks overlooking the significant ways in which Britain has been able to influence, and in turn be influenced by, the European integration process. There has been a tale of positive engagement and mutual benefit to stand alongside the narrative of discomfort and confrontation. Too forceful an emphasis on British exceptionalism and the underlying difficulties of the match also risks devaluing the shorter-term contingencies that led to the 2016 referendum and to its narrow but decisive outcome. Perhaps most seriously of all, the emphasis on Britain as the misfit, the perpetual outsider, wrongly implies a degree of effortless fit between most other EU member states and the integration process. All participating states have struggled at times with the implications of close cooperation and tight interdependence, and all have rebelled against certain aspects. And yet, most other European countries have overcome such hesitations and repeatedly reaffirmed their commitment to working together. Britain's failure to do the same is therefore a reflection not of structural inevitability, but of deliberate policy choices. Brexit may have been, to some extent at least, an accident waiting to happen. But this does not mean that the country's leaders had no agency. Instead, Britain's departure from the EU reflected the failure by the country's political elite to explain the realities of tight cooperation to its wider population.

A Contested Literature

Given the huge topical interest in the subject matter, it should come as no surprise that a sizeable academic literature has emerged on the relationship between Britain and the process of European integration. The full bibliography is too extensive to be properly analysed in a few paragraphs, but in setting the scene for a piece on Brexit, it is worth pointing to four broad categories of writings.

The first is constituted by books that seek to contextualise the UK's troubled dealings with the process of European integration through the much longer history of interaction between the British Isles and continental Europe. Some of these emerged in the 1990s or in the early years of this century;[1] the run-up to and aftermath of the Brexit vote of 2016 produced a second such wave.[2] Each author reached somewhat different conclusions from their overview, but all underline that controversy over whether and

---

1 J. Black, *Convergence or Divergence?: Britain and the Continent* (Basingstoke and London, Macmillan, 1994); K. Robbins, *British Isles and Europe, 1789–2005* (London, Hodder Arnold, 2005).

2 B. Simms, *Britain's Europe: A Thousand Years of Conflict and Cooperation* (London, Penguin, 2017); D. Reynolds, *Island Stories: Britain and Its History in the Age of Brexit* (London, William Collins, 2019).

how Britain should interact closely with its geographical neighbours is an enduring theme in British history.

A second, rather larger category, is formed by the numerous works which focus on Britain's role in the post-1945 history of European integration. A handful sketch out long chronological portions of the story, starting with the widespread assumption in the immediate aftermath of the Second World War that the UK would lead any attempt to unify Europe. These then continue tracing the tale through the disappearance of such hopes, the break between Britain and the six countries which would go on to found the forerunners of today's EU, Britain's hesitant decision to re-engage with the process and the country's uneven track record within the EC/EU.[3] Rather more works zero-in on particular sub-periods. Amongst the most extensively studied are the 'parting of the ways' between Britain and the Six in 1950, and the UK's first application to the EEC in 1961–3.[4] A recent flurry of publications means that we are also well-provided with studies of the 1975 referendum on Community membership.[5] Additionally, there is a significant amount written about Britain's 1978 decision to opt out of full participation in the European Monetary System (EMS).[6] Other crucial moments, by contrast, still await detailed, archivally based historical treatment: the best investigation of the 1970–2 membership negotiations is still unpublished; we have little on

---

3 H. Young, *This Blessed Plot: Britain and Europe from Churchill to Blair* (Basingstoke, Macmillan, 1998); J. W. Young, *Britain and European Unity, 1945–1999* (Basingstoke, Macmillan, 2000); D. A. Gowland and A. Turner, *Reluctant Europeans: Britain and European Integration, 1945–1998* (London, Longman, 2000); B. J. Grob-Fitzgibbon, *Continental Drift: Britain and Europe from the End of Empire to the Rise of Euroscepticism* (Cambridge, Cambridge University Press, 2016).

4 E. Dell, *The Schuman Plan and the British Abdication of Leadership in Europe* (Oxford, Oxford University Press, 1995); C. Lord, *Absent at the Creation: Britain and the Formation of the European Community, 1950–2* (Aldershot, Dartmouth, 1996); A. S. Milward, *The UK and the European Community*, vol. 1: *The Rise and Fall of a National Strategy, 1945–1963* (London, Frank Cass, 2002), pp. 48–77, 310–483; W. Kaiser, *Using Europe, Abusing the Europeans: Britain and European Integration, 1945–63* (London, Palgrave Macmillan, 1996); J. Tratt, *The Macmillan Government and Europe: A Study in the Process of Policy Development* (Basingstoke, Macmillan, 1996); A. Deighton and A. S. Milward (eds.), *Widening, Deepening and Acceleration: The European Economic Community 1957–1963* (Baden-Baden, Nomos, 1999); N. P. Ludlow, *Dealing with Britain: The Six and the First UK Application to the EEC* (Cambridge, Cambridge University Press, 1997).

5 R. Saunders, *Yes to Europe!: The 1975 Referendum and Seventies Britain* (Cambridge, Cambridge University Press, 2018); L. Aqui, *The First Referendum: Reassessing Britain's Entry to Europe, 1973–75* (Manchester, Manchester University Press, 2020).

6 E. Mourlon-Druol, *A Europe Made of Money: The Emergence of the European Monetary System* (Ithaca, NY, Cornell University Press, 2012). For the British 'no', see E. Dell, 'Britain and the Origins of the European Monetary System', *Contemporary European History* 3, no. 1 (1994): 1–60; K. Hirowatari, *Britain and European Monetary Cooperation, 1964–1979* (Basingstoke, Palgrave Macmillan, 2015).

Margaret Thatcher's early engagement with the integration process, and even less on the Conservative in-fighting over Europe that first contributed to her fall from power and then bedevilled the premiership of her successor, John Major.[7] The timetable for the release of official papers from the British National Archives means, furthermore, that the frontier of detailed historical research is likely to move only slowly into the final decade of the twentieth century, let alone into the 2000–16 period. The planned appearance of a third 'official' history volume by Stephen Wall, who is given earlier than normal access to government documents, will begin to fill the gap.[8] But archival studies of the European policies of Tony Blair or David Cameron are unlikely to appear any time soon.

A third category of writing on Britain and Europe is constituted by books, often by journalists, practitioners or political scientists, that were written shortly after the events analysed and were intended as contributions to the debate about contemporary affairs, but which can now be re-visited as important first drafts of history. These have a long pedigree: Anthony Nutting's *Europe Will Not Wait*, published in 1960, helped trigger the debate about whether the UK had made a disastrous mistake in allowing others, notably France, to assume the leadership of the integration process.[9] But Nutting's analysis of recent developments was followed by equally important studies by Miriam Camps, Uwe Kitzinger, David Butler, Peter Ludlow, Stephen Wall and Philip Stephens.[10] Furthermore, many works on Britain

7 D. Furby, 'The Revival and Success of Britain's Second Application for Membership of the European Community, 1968–71' (Ph.D. thesis, Queen Mary University of London, 2009). On Thatcher, partial exceptions are M. Haeussler, *Helmut Schmidt and British–German Relations: A European Misunderstanding* (Cambridge, Cambridge University Press, 2019); N. P. Ludlow, 'Solidarity, Sanctions and Misunderstanding: The European Dimension of the Falklands Crisis', *The International History Review* 43, no. 3 (2020): 1–17; N. P. Ludlow, 'A Double-Edged Victory: Fontainebleau and the Resolution of the British Budgetary Problem, 1983–1984', in M. Gehler and W. Loth (eds.), *Reshaping Europe towards a Political, Economic and Monetary Union, 1984–1989* (Baden-Baden, Nomos, 2020), pp. 45–71. On Conservative in-fighting, see N. J. Crowson, *The Conservative Party and European Integration since 1945: At the Heart of Europe?* (London and New York, NY, Routledge, 2007).

8 See also S. Wall, *The Official History of Britain and the European Community*, vol. II: *From Rejection to Referendum, 1963–1975* (Abingdon, Routledge, 2012); S. Wall, *The Official History of Britain and the European Community*, vol. III: *The Tiger Unleashed, 1975–1985* (Abingdon, Routledge, 2019).

9 A. Nutting, *Europe Will Not Wait: A Warning and a Way Out* (London, Hollis & Carter, 1960). For context, see O. J. Daddow, *Britain and Europe since 1945: Historiographical Perspectives on Integration* (Manchester, Manchester University Press, 2004).

10 M. Camps, *Britain and the European Community, 1955–1963* (Princeton, NJ, Princeton University Press, 1964); U. W. Kitzinger, *Diplomacy and Persuasion: How Britain Joined the Common Market* (London, Thames and Hudson, 1973); D. Butler and U. Kitzinger,

and Europe have been produced by political analysts, lawyers or economists throughout the period of UK membership.[11] The methodology of such studies is often very different from that normally employed by historians, with a far greater reliance on interviews or questionnaires, or on various datasets. But they can provide vital insights, especially into the substantial period for which governmental papers remain inaccessible. Also useful – although to be used with caution – are the memoirs of many of the protagonists, civil servants as well as ministers, and the biographies of some of the key characters in the story of Britain and Europe.[12]

Finally, there is the small but fast-growing literature on Brexit itself, a category which includes a mixture of journalistic 'instant history', the testimonies of some of those involved and detailed analysis of the trends and tendencies that led to the 2016 vote and its messy aftermath. The most vivid of the journalistic accounts are Tim Shipman's two volumes, *All Out War* and *Fall Out*; one of the better insider stories is *Unleashing Demons* by

The 1975 Referendum (London, Macmillan, 1976); P. Ludlow, *The Making of the European Monetary System: A Case Study of the Politics of the European Community* (London, Butterworths, 1982); S. Wall, *A Stranger in Europe: Britain and the EU from Thatcher to Blair* (Oxford, Oxford University Press, 2008); P. Stephens, *Politics and the Pound: The Tories, the Economy and Europe* (London, Macmillan, 1997).

11 Good examples include D. Baker and D. Seawright (eds.), *Britain for and against Europe: British Politics and the Question of European Integration* (Oxford, Oxford University Press, 1998); S. Bulmer, S. George and A. Scott (eds.), *The United Kingdom and EC Membership Evaluated* (London, Pinter, 1992); O. J. Daddow, *New Labour and the European Union: Blair and Brown's Logic of History* (Manchester and New York, NY, Manchester University Press, 2013); O. Daddow, 'The UK Media and "Europe": From Permissive Consensus to Destructive Dissent', *International Affairs* 88, no. 6 (2012): 1219–36; A. Menon and J.-P. Salter, 'Britain's Influence in the EU', *National Institute Economic Review* no. 236 (2016): 7–13; S. Bulmer and M. Burch, *The Europeanisation of Whitehall: UK Central Government and the European Union* (Manchester, Manchester University Press, 2009).

12 M. Thatcher, *The Downing Street Years* (London, HarperCollins, 2012); J. R. Major, *John Major: The Autobiography* (London, HarperCollins, 2000); T. Blair, *A Journey: My Political Life* (London, Hutchinson, 2010); D. Cameron, *For the Record* (London, HarperCollins, 2019); G. Howe, *Conflict of Loyalty* (London, Macmillan, 1994). Amongst civil servants, see M. Butler, *Europe: More Than a Continent* (London, Heinemann, 1986); D. Hannay, *Britain's Quest for a Role: A Diplomatic Memoir from Europe to the UN* (London, I. B. Tauris, 2013); R. Denman, *The Mandarin's Tale* (London, Politico's, 2002). Biographies include J. Campbell, *Margaret Thatcher: Grocer's Daughter to Iron Lady* (London, Random House, 2009); J. Campbell, *Margaret Thatcher*, vol. 11: *The Iron Lady* (London, Jonathan Cape, 2003); C. Moore, *Margaret Thatcher: The Authorized Biography*, vol. 1: *Not for Turning* (London, Allen Lane, 2013); C. Moore, *Margaret Thatcher: The Authorized Biography*, vol. 11: *Everything She Wants* (London, Penguin, 2015); C. Moore, *Margaret Thatcher: The Authorized Biography*, vol. 111: *Herself Alone* (London, Allen Lane, 2019); J. Campbell, *Roy Jenkins: A Well-Rounded Life* (London, Jonathan Cape, 2014); N. P. Ludlow, *Roy Jenkins and the European Commission Presidency 1976–1980: At the Heart of Europe* (Basingstoke, Palgrave Macmillan, 2016); C. Lee, *Carrington: An Honourable Man* (London, Viking, 2018).

Craig Oliver, Cameron's former head of communications; and the economic historian Kevin O'Rourke has attempted a *Short History of Brexit*.[13] We also now have the diaries of Michel Barnier, as chief negotiator on the EU side, and Philip Stephens' assessment of how Brexit has affected Britain's place in the world.[14] Such books are flanked by an array of shorter pieces ranging from lectures to blogs, via multiple chapters in edited volumes, journal articles and a range of longer newspaper and magazine exposés.[15] Few political events have so quickly spawned so extensive a literature as the 2016 referendum and its consequences.

Britain's European Discomforts

The UK's ambivalence when confronted with the idea of tight European cooperation quickly became apparent in the years following the Second World War. Most British leaders had concluded from their wartime experiences that the country could not stand aloof from what was happening on the other side of the Channel. The UK had to be deeply involved with the reconstruction of Europe and the prevention of any future conflict. But Britain's political elite were also wary of entering into too tight a pattern of cooperation with their neighbours. This reflected a preference for closer links to the British Empire/Commonwealth and/or the United States, rather than with continental Europe. It also sprang from a fear that most European countries were too weak to constitute reliable partners.[16]

The way out of this dilemma proved to be to bring in the Americans. Ernest Bevin, the Foreign Secretary of the post-war Labour government, deserves huge credit for his role in persuading the United States to commit

---

13 T. Shipman, *All Out War: The Full Story of How Brexit Sank Britain's Political Class* (London, William Collins, 2016); T. Shipman, *Fall Out: A Year of Political Mayhem.* (London, HarperCollins, 2018); C. Oliver, *Unleashing Demons: The Inside Story of Brexit* (London, Hachette, 2017); K. H. O'Rourke, *A Short History of Brexit: From Brentry to Backstop* (London, Penguin, 2019).

14 M. Barnier, *La grande illusion: Journal secret du Brexit (2016–2020)* (Paris, Gallimard, 2021); P. Stephens, *Britain Alone: The Path from Suez to Brexit* (London, Faber and Faber, 2021).

15 One of the most prolific and well-informed lecturers on the subject has been Sir Ivan Rogers. See, for example, I. Rogers, 'Where Did Brexit Come From and Where Is It Going to Take the UK?' (2019), www.ucl.ac.uk/play/categories/politics-society/sir-ivan-rogers-where-did-brexit-come-and-where-it-going-take-uk. The three best Brexit-centred blogs are UK in a Changing Europe (https://ukandeu.ac.uk), the LSE Brexit Blog (https://blogs.lse.ac.uk/brexit) and Chris Grey's Brexit & Beyond (https://chris greybrexitblog.blogspot.com). For an astute article-length analysis, see R. Saunders, 'Brexit and Empire: "Global Britain" and the Myth of Imperial Nostalgia', *The Journal of Imperial and Commonwealth History* 48, no. 6 (2020): 1140–74.

16 Milward, *The Rise and Fall of a National Strategy, 1945–1963*, pp. 10–47.

itself to European security through the North Atlantic Treaty Organization (NATO).[17] But this very triumph created a situation in which Britain felt able to allow six of its European neighbours to press ahead with supranational integration without UK participation. The 1950 split over the Schuman Plan was then reaffirmed 5 years later with the British decision to stand aloof from the negotiations that would establish the EEC. By the end of the 1950s, an enduring divide had emerged between those European countries prepared to cooperate tightly through supranational structures and those, led by Britain, unwilling to do so.[18]

Within the British government, though, there was mounting unease about this division. In 1950, there had been annoyance at the manner in which the French had precipitated the split, but little real anxiety about what the emergence of European structures might mean for Britain's power. Before the decade was out, however, such complacency was waning, replaced instead by a fear that exclusion from a prospering EC could harm the UK both economically and politically.[19] The unsuccessful Free Trade Area scheme of 1956–8 was an early indication of this changing perspective; the first membership application to the EEC submitted by Harold Macmillan's government in 1961 was an even clearer sign. But the course alteration was hesitant and contested – factors that almost certainly contributed to the failure of the first membership bid.[20] Hesitancy and contestation were to persist throughout the 1960s as Britain's path into the EEC was twice blocked by the French president, General de Gaulle, and on into the 1970s when membership was finally attained. The lingering British uncertainty about the decision to join would be underlined by the 1974 attempt to renegotiate the terms of entry, as well as the 1975 referendum on whether Britain should continue to participate.[21] This last, it is true, appeared decisive, with 66 per cent of the British population voting to remain within the EEC. Yet, most commentators, at the time and since, were struck by the 'unenthusiastic' nature of this rather sizeable endorsement by the British population.[22] A majority of voters preferred staying within the Community rather than

17 J. Baylis, *The Diplomacy of Pragmatism: Britain and the Formation of NATO, 1942–49* (Basingstoke, Macmillan, 1992).

18 Kaiser, *Using Europe, Abusing the Europeans.*

19 J. Ellison, *Threatening Europe: Britain and the Creation of the European Community, 1955–58* (New York, NY, St Martin's Press, 2000).

20 N. P. Ludlow, 'A Mismanaged Application: Britain and the EEC, 1961–1963', in Deighton and Milward (eds.), *Widening, Deepening and Acceleration*, pp. 271–85.

21 Aqui, *The First Referendum.*   22 Butler and Kitzinger, *The 1975 Referendum*, p. 33.

having to face the economic crisis of the 1970s alone, but this did not mean that they were much enamoured with the EEC.

Similar ambivalence characterised the European policies of successive British governments. Membership itself was seldom questioned – the Labour Party suffered a crushing electoral defeat in 1983 when it ran on a platform that included withdrawal from the EEC – but the British made no effort to hide their dislike of key aspects of the Community system. At first, much of this ire was directed at the Common Agricultural Policy, which was criticised (not without justification) as wasteful, protectionist and cripplingly expensive – although the British proved rather less forthcoming when it came to suggesting constructive reform.[23] In 1978, the Labour government of James Callaghan resorted to the first of many opt-outs by deciding not to participate fully in the Community's biggest new policy development since Britain had joined, the launch of the EMS.[24] From 1979 onwards, the UK embarked upon a determined but disruptive campaign to revise the budgetary rules of the Community.[25] And then, in the late 1980s and early 1990s, the British yet again diverged from their partners on another new central priority of the EU, opting out of, and directing constant criticism at, the goal of a single currency.[26] Further 'opt-outs' would follow: on social policy, justice and home affairs, and Schengen.

The UK's reputation as an 'awkward partner' was reinforced by the behaviour of successive British leaders at meetings of the European Council. Here, the pattern was largely set by Thatcher, whose forceful handbag swinging and readiness to hijack collective meetings of Europe's leaders in pursuit of her own narrow aims won admiration at home. It also overshadowed, in the collective British imagination at least, the more constructive line that she would adopt on some key issues, notably the pursuit of the Single Market. The template of Thatcher's approach has influenced most subsequent British Prime Ministers, obliging them to portray their tactics as confrontational even when their instincts and approach were less aggressive. The way in which Major allowed a soundbite about the Maastricht Treaty being 'game, set and match' to Britain to define his view of the treaty, despite the fact that the words were not his and were at odds with the moderate manner in which he had actually negotiated, underlined how keen all British

---

23 See, for example, A. Swinbank, '"Something Significant to Show for Our Efforts?" British Perspectives on the Stocktaking of the Common Agricultural Policy', *Agricultural History Review* 68, no. 1 (2020): 63–85.

24 Dell, 'Britain and the Origins of the European Monetary System'.

25 Ludlow, 'A Double-Edged Victory'.   26 Stephens, *Politics and the Pound*.

leaders were to be seen as fighting Britain's corner as forcefully as Thatcher had done.[27] Press coverage of the UK's interaction with its European partners, focused as it overwhelmingly was on European Council meetings, thus confirmed Britain's status as the defiant odd one out amongst EC/EU member states. Cameron's abrasive approach to European diplomacy, best exemplified by his December 2011 blocking of the EU treaty designed to resolve the euro crisis, was simply a reprise of an approach to collective European discussion adopted by most of his predecessors.[28]

Explaining British Awkwardness

Why did the British allow themselves to become caught in this cycle of confrontation? This was not what they had sought to achieve by entering the Community. On the contrary, Edward Heath, the Prime Minister who had overseen Britain's entry into the EEC, had spoken eloquently of how, once a member, the UK would move beyond the antagonistic relations with its neighbours that had characterised its years in the EEC's waiting room, and instead treat them as genuine partners in a common endeavour.[29] Heath, like Macmillan and Wilson before him, also believed that the UK would quickly take its place at the helm of the EEC, replacing the dominant Franco-German partnership with a Paris–Bonn–London triangle. So how were such ambitions replaced by a seeming acceptance of perpetual isolation?

Part of the answer, as will be explained below, is that they were not entirely replaced and that a constructive layer of British engagement, even leadership, persisted despite the rows highlighted by the awkward partner narrative. But the latter, while not the whole truth, had a strong grounding in reality. There is therefore a need to explain why the British were so often drawn to the role of European trouble-maker or critic, rather than convinced participant.

One factor was undoubtedly the ongoing existence of strong veins of Euroscepticism within both of the UK's main governing parties, the Conservatives and Labour. For neither was hostility to European integration necessarily the majority viewpoint, although this was the case within the Labour Party during much of the 1970s and eventually in the Conservative

---

27 On the origins of the phrase, see Major, *John Major*, p. 288.
28 'David Cameron Blocks EU Treaty with Veto, Casting Britain Adrift in Europe', *The Guardian*, 9 December 2011, www.theguardian.com/world/2011/dec/09/david-cameron-blocks-eu-treaty.
29 *Hansard*, 28 October 1971, column 2209.

Party from the mid 1990s onwards as well.[30] But even when it was a minority stance, Euroscepticism was sufficiently strong to ensure that few British governments have been able to formulate their European policy without constant backward glances at their own party members or anxious looks at the Opposition benches. This had a number of knock-on effects. For a start, it helped ensure that all British ministers have had to approach negotiations in Brussels with caution, aware that making concessions in order to secure agreement would be liable to attract substantial criticism at home. Such defensiveness has been hard to combine with the type of leadership role to which UK leaders had initially aspired, since leadership in a multilateral body like the EC/EU requires the ability to build consensus even at the expense of one's own national starting point. Furthermore, it has played into a pre-existing British tendency to portray all European negotiations as brutal battles, with each country fighting hard for its own interests and little sense of shared goals or common aspirations. As a result, British ministers have had to portray the outcome of each round of negotiation either as a UK triumph – 'game, set and match' to reprise the Major soundbite – or, in circumstances where such claims were less credible, as an instance where heroic British representatives had bravely prevented the others from advancing as far as would otherwise have been the case. Defiant obstinacy, in other words, became the principal alternative to boasts of European achievement – and one that in periods of rapid advance of the integration process, such as the later 1980s or the early 1990s, became the default mode of presentation. The rhetoric of shared progress or of mutual achievement was, by contrast, notable by its absence.

There is little indication, moreover, that successive British leaders suffered from this adversarial approach in terms of public opinion. On the contrary, one of Thatcher's ministers believed that her forceful rows with her European counterparts 'were the next best thing to a war' in demonstrating her strength as a leader to the wider British public.[31] Nor was direct public disquiet at her European tactics a major element in her fall. Many of her senior ministers had lost faith in her approach by the late 1980s, hence the role of prominent pro-Europeans like Michael Heseltine and Geoffrey Howe in the party revolt that would lead to her resignation. But, to the extent that the Prime Minister's approval ratings had dropped with the wider public, this seems to have had more to do with domestic-centred controversies, such as

---

30 Crowson, *The Conservative Party and European Integration since 1945*; R. Broad, *Labour's European Dilemmas: From Bevin to Blair* (Basingstoke, Palgrave Macmillan, 2001).
31 I. Gilmour, *Dancing with Dogma: Britain under Thatcherism* (London and New York, NY, Simon & Schuster, 1992), p. 244.

the botched introduction of the poll tax, than with her increasingly strained relations with other European leaders.[32] Fighting foreigners still seemed to go down well with much of the UK public. Similarly, while John Major clearly suffered from the deep internal party divisions over Europe that would characterise his premiership, there is little to suggest that his crushing electoral defeat in 1997 constituted a repudiation by British voters of the increasingly abrasive tactics he had resorted to at European level.[33]

Public acceptance of Britain's spiky rapport with its partners was accompanied by a strong disinclination to take pride in, or feel any loyalty towards, European accomplishments. Common European institutions or policies were overwhelmingly viewed as something that had been devised by others, often in the teeth of UK opposition, rather than agreements to which British representatives had been party. Thus, the British public, press and political elite felt free to criticise and complain about, rather than take responsibility for, those aspects of the EC/EU that were deemed to work less well and to derive little pleasure from that which worked – or, in the latter case, to claim national credit for positive outcomes rather than attributing them to European action. The general air of disbelief in Britain at the Nobel Committee's 2012 decision to award the EU the Nobel Peace Prize illustrated the problem well; the even more serious public failure to realise that there was an EU dimension to the peace process in Northern Ireland, which might therefore be adversely affected by Brexit, underlined it further.[34]

More broadly, Britain's geography, history and culture all combined to obstruct any sense on the part of most of the UK's inhabitants that they were a central part of a wider European collective. As an island off the coast of the European mainland, Britain has often liked to tell itself – accurately or not – that it has a choice of whether or not to involve itself in European politics. Meanwhile, its historical self-imagery glorifies those moments when it has either stood proudly aloof from European affairs – the 'splendid isolation' of the late nineteenth century would be the most obvious example – or those when it has boldly defied the threat from the continent. The defeat of the Spanish Armada or Napoleon, as well as the Second World War and especially 1940, when Britain perceived itself as standing alone in the face of Hitler's challenge, all feature prominently in the second category.[35] As a result, deep involvement in the running of Europe was not necessarily seen as a good thing;

32 Moore, *Margaret Thatcher*, vol. III, pp. 471–726.
33 D. Butler, *The British General Election of 1997* (Basingstoke, Macmillan, 1997).
34 For the Nobel Prize episode, see www.bbc.co.uk/news/world-europe-20677654.
35 Reynolds, *Island Stories*, especially pp. 82–7.

indeed, it was a retreat from a period when Britain's reach was global not regional. At the same time, adversarial relations with Europe's other main players were a normal state of affairs – a throwback to the glories of Elizabeth I, William Pitt or Winston Churchill – rather than an anomaly to be ashamed of. Even the English language played a role, most obviously because of the way that in common usage 'Europe' is employed in a fashion that does not include Britain, but more substantively because its ever-growing standing as a world language reinforced the British population's disinclination to learn foreign languages, thereby obstructing easy identification with other European cultures and reinforcing the extra-European pull of fellow English-speaking cultures, including the United States. The manner in which the Conservative Party's transformation from the 'party of Europe' to a largely Europhobic entity ran parallel to its growing ties and fascination with the US Republicans is just one illustration of how much this factor mattered.

None of these factors led directly to Brexit. But they ensured that, despite decades of membership, the UK's status as a member of the EC/EU was still a contested and controversial notion. A serious outbreak of political infighting, between and within political parties, about the UK's position in Europe thus remained a real possibility. Furthermore, these and many more 'fragilities' in Britain's sense of belonging within the European integration process help explain why so many in the UK seemed to accept, and even take pride in, the way the country had become a perpetual outsider in a system that it had originally intended to lead. Newspaper headlines about British isolation in Brussels became badges of honour, rather than an embarrassment.

A Positive Tale

Too narrow a focus on this pattern of dissent and confrontation can, however, distort the record of Britain's four decades of EC/EU membership as much as it enlightens. For a start, simply focusing on the multiple instances of British discomfort with or in Brussels ignores the very significant ways in which the UK was able to shape, even lead, the integration process during its years as a member, and the fashion in which involvement in the EC/EU contributed to economic, political and cultural change within Britain itself. Each of these aspects of UK membership needs to be looked at a little more closely, and used to temper the awkward partner narrative.[36]

36 For a fuller development of these ideas, see N. P. Ludlow, 'Not Just an Awkward Partner: Britain's Experience of EC/EU Membership since 1973', in M. Steber (ed.),

To some extent, the impact of Britain on the European integration process can be connected to those individuals who have worked within the European institutions. The UK has supplied a string of influential Commissioners, from Christopher Soames in the 1970s through to Chris Patten in the early years of the twenty-first century, and a reasonably successful Commission President in the person of Roy Jenkins. Other Britons have served as the President of the European Parliament, as leaders of the party groups there, or as the head of lesser-known European institutions such as the European Investment Bank. Even more crucial have been the large number of UK nationals who, through their occupation of senior posts throughout the European institutional landscape, have helped to alter patterns of work in all of the Community/Union bodies and thus dilute the initial Franco-German administrative traditions with significant and largely positive habits imported from the British civil service and political culture. Needless to say, the British have not been alone in pushing for change in the way in which the institutions of the Community/Union operate, as numerous other national ideas and habits have also been injected into the mix. Equally, not all of the innovations promoted by *fonctionnaires* of British origin have proved entirely successful. But it should hardly come as a surprise that a member state of long standing, with administrative and political traditions as strong and as distinctive as those of the UK, has managed to transfer some of these traditions to Brussels, Strasbourg or Luxembourg, largely to beneficial effect. Amongst the changes most closely associated with the 'British effect' have been better habits in the preservation of official documents, more extensive minute-taking and the wider circulation of such minutes, a more systematic pattern of briefing senior officials prior to important meetings and a greater degree of informality in interactions between staff.[37] It was, for instance, Jenkins who decided that the incoming Commission should meet for the first time in an informal setting away from Brussels, a practice retained by subsequent Commission presidents.

Alongside the impact of individual Britons and British administrative practices, it is also possible to discern policy areas where the UK has left its mark. The foremost example is the establishment of the Single Market in the late 1980s and early 1990s, a goal championed by Thatcher, and closely associated in its implementation with Arthur Cockfield, the Internal Market

Historicizing Brexit: Britain and Europe in the Twentieth Century (Oxford, Oxford University Press, forthcoming).

37 European Commission, *The European Commission 1973–86: History and Memories of an Institution* (Luxembourg: Publications Office of the European Union, 2014), pp. 157–65.

Commissioner in the first Delors Commission.[38] But other key policy initiatives for which the UK has successfully pressed also significantly affecting the shape and operation of the Community/Union in the process, include enlargement, foreign policy cooperation (especially in the 1980s), the TREVI process, which foreshadowed much of the Justice and Home Affairs agenda of more recent times, and the broadening out and modernisation of the association policy with the EC/EU's African, Caribbean and Pacific partners. Here, British influence once again blended with the ideas, innovations and improvements suggested by other member states and with administrative trends that developed within the Community institutions themselves. In so multilateral a system, it is of course hazardous to attribute too much to the efforts of a single member state, however forceful. But there is more than enough evidence of UK policy priorities having a measurable effect on the overall policy mix of the EC/EU to contradict the notion that the UK has always been a frustrated semi-outsider, compelled to watch as others built a Europe with which it had little sympathy. Instead, the British have actively contributed to the shape and operation of the EC/EU institutions, and to the policies that these institutions have carried out. The awkward partner was also an influential and constructive one.

Participation in the integration process also shaped Britain. Disentangling how much of the change that occurred in the UK between 1973 and 2016 is attributable to EC/EU membership, and how much, by contrast, reflects internal trends, policy decisions or other international entanglements is almost impossible. But a strong case can be made that EC/EU membership was an important factor in the country's ability to cast off its previous reputation as the 'sick man of Europe' in terms of economic performance and instead become one of the more dynamic European economies.[39] Being part of the Community/Union was not the only reason why Britain's economic performance from the 1970s onwards was as good as, if not better than, that of France and Germany, despite having been much worse between 1945 and 1973. However, it was a significant contributing factor to be placed alongside domestic economic reform, North Sea oil and the boom in the financial market sector. Ironically, therefore, the belief that the UK economy was likely to outperform its western European rivals, which was so central to

---

38 A. Cockfield, *The European Union: Creating the Single Market* (London, Wiley, 1994).
39 N. Crafts, 'The Growth Effects of EU Membership for the UK: Review of the Evidence' (2016), www.smf.co.uk/wp-content/uploads/2016/04/SMF-CAGE-The-Growth-Effects-of-EU-Membership-for-the-UK-a-Review-of-the-Evidence-.pdf.

the case of those favouring Brexit, may well have had its roots in a British growth surge that was partly attributable to EC/EU membership itself.

The UK's EC/EU membership also played a part in altering the travel patterns, eating habits and career trajectories of many Britons, and, especially in the early twenty-first century, began to alter the demographic make-up of the UK itself. Between 2008 and 2016, for instance, the number of Poles living in Britain doubled, turning the Poles into the single biggest group of immigrants in the UK.[40] This, in turn, had knock-on effects not just on the UK labour market, but also on more everyday questions such as the range of products stocked by British supermarkets – the appearance of rye bread in our local Lidl was attributed to demand from Poles living in the area – or the challenges confronting local educational authorities. In much the same period, the number of Britons deciding to retire to Spain also doubled.[41] Both the identity and the numbers of those leaving the country and those arriving were thus significantly affected by European rules enabling EU citizens to move freely around the bloc. Furthermore, multiple aspects of daily British life were altered by EC/EU membership. To take just one obvious example, the manner in which football, the UK's most popular sport, was organised, played and watched was transformed, in part by the influx of foreign players and foreign managers facilitated by EU membership, but also by the European Court of Justice's Bosman ruling of 1995, which irrevocably altered the manner in which the transfer system functioned. The extent of change is well illustrated by the fact that, from 1888 until 1997, the managers whose team won the first division or later premiership title were exclusively British; since 1998, by contrast, Alex Ferguson has been the only British title winner (albeit nine times), sharing the honour with rivals from France, Portugal, Italy, Spain, Germany and Chile.[42] EU membership has not been the only factor at play here, with some aspects of the change attributable to a wider globalisation of sport in general and football in particular, but the precise manner in which this transformation occurred in the UK was significantly shaped by the ease with which football professionals from continental Europe could settle and work within Britain.

---

40 www.statista.com/statistics/1061639/polish-population-in-united-kingdom/#:~:tex
   t=As%20of%20June%202020%20there,then%20decreased%20by%20June%202020.
41 A. Travis, 'Number of Britons over 65 Living in Spain More Than Doubles in 10 Years',
   The Guardian, 29 June 2017, www.theguardian.com/politics/2017/jun/29/number-of-
   britons-over-65-living-in-spain-more-than-doubles-in-10-years.
42 'List of English Football Championship-Winning Managers', https://en.wikipedia.org
   /wiki/List_of_English_football_championship-winning_managers.

Even more importantly, EC/EU membership played a crucial role in the Northern Irish peace process, one that is only belatedly being recognised after British EU membership has ended.[43] The successful overcoming of the 'troubles', which had beset Northern Ireland since the early 1970s, was one of the UK's most important political achievements of the 1990s and the first decade of this century. But it was not one that at the time was much associated with EU membership. On the contrary, if the role of any international actor was pointed to, it was much more likely to be that of the United States and figures such as Senator George Mitchell.[44] But, with the benefit of hindsight, the European dimension was much more important than was generally realised. For a start, many of the crucial discussions between John Major and then Tony Blair and the Irish Taoiseachs Albert Reynolds, John Bruton and Bertie Ahern took place in the margins of European Council meetings, something that both averted the need for more pressurised bilateral meetings and underlined the degree to which the British and Irish governments were routinely working together as fellow European member states. Secondly, the process of lessening tension on one of the most militarised borders in Europe was greatly facilitated because it was taking place in a context where all of the countries of western Europe were holding detailed collective discussions about how to lessen, if not remove altogether, border formalities and how to facilitate movement, trade and communication across national boundaries. Thirdly, from the mid 1990s onwards, significant amounts of EU money were specifically targeted at Northern Ireland and the promotion of cross-border initiatives. Furthermore, the effort to lobby for this money involved conspicuous levels of cooperation in Strasbourg and Brussels between Northern Irish MEPs such as Ian Paisley and John Hume, who came from opposing political traditions and had seldom worked together.[45] Finally, and perhaps most fundamentally, the transformation of the Irish Republic from one of the poorest countries in western Europe, lagging economically far behind the British-ruled northern provinces of the island, to a 'Celtic tiger' wealthier and more prosperous than Ulster – a development that was inextricably

43 G. Lagana, *The European Union and the Northern Ireland Peace Process* (Basingstoke, Palgrave, 2021).
44 See, for example, R. Mac Ginty and J. Darby, 'Third Parties: External Influences on the Peace Process', in R. Mac Ginty and J. Darby (eds.), *Guns and Government: The Management of the Northern Ireland Peace Process* (London, Palgrave Macmillan, 2002), pp. 106–22.
45 European Commission, *The European Commission 1986–2000: Histories and Memories of an Institution* (Luxembourg: Publications Office of the European Union, 2019), pp. 426–8.

tied up with the Republic of Ireland's own experience of EC/EU membership – dramatically changed the dynamics of interaction between the two parts of Ireland.[46] The wider European framework thus played a crucial enabling role in the process that would end 30 years of bloodshed in Northern Ireland.

All told, Britain contributed more to the integration process and derived more benefits from it than the standard awkward partner label would imply. The UK's experience of membership was certainly bumpy and involved frequent clashes between London and Brussels, and between British representatives and those of the other member states. Equally, it was accompanied by an ongoing debate within Britain about whether or not EC/EU membership was a good thing and a conspicuous absence of the satisfaction at Europe's achievements that characterised the political debate elsewhere in western Europe. But the sulky partner was also an influential one, and the country that so ostentatiously refused to warm to European membership was at the very same time being transformed by it, much more than most of its own citizens recognised. True such transformation was uneven, with some groups of the population more directly affected than others. A well-educated and well-travelled young professional, shaped by a year abroad funded by the EU's Erasmus scheme and aspiring to a career and an eventual retirement which took full advantage of the European single market, was significantly more likely to view EU membership positively, than someone older and less educated, who had no aspiration to travel extensively and few cultural ties with continental Europe. To the latter, the EU might well seem primarily a menace, a source of 'red tape' and immigrants, both of which threatened longstanding facets of English life. The differentiated nature of the EU's impacts, both positive and negative, helps explain why the European issue was so divisive in British politics long before the 2016 referendum was held, and still more why the polarisation between 'Leave' voters and 'Remainers' after the outcome has proven so deep and enduring. A result that was for some a welcome escape from dangerous outside interference, was for others a threat to a whole way of life. At the same time, the depth of the division only underlined the ways in which EU membership had tangibly altered Britain and British life – and hence the magnitude of the change that would occur now that that membership had been ended.

---

46 For the first part of the story, see J. Bradley, 'The History of Economic Development in Ireland, North and South', *Proceedings of the British Academy* 98 (1999): 35–68.

Shorter-Term Contingencies

A further danger of putting too much emphasis on the bumpiness of Britain's relations with the EU is that it can imply that Brexit was all but inevitable, the predictable end to a loveless partnership, thereby largely disregarding the significance of the shorter-term political trends in the first part of the twenty-first century which led to the 2016 vote. This too would be a mistake, for while there were certainly longer-term fragilities about Britain's position within the EU, Brexit cannot be explained without looking carefully at a number of important developments in the latter stages of Britain's 46 years within the EC/EU. Furthermore, to accept the notion of inevitability is also to absolve from responsibility those politicians who took the fateful decisions that would lead to the vote and helped shape its outcome. It is therefore vital to identify those shorter-term factors that helped determine Britain's path to the 2016 referendum. Four largely party-political developments will be highlighted, as well as a crucial change in the previously rather abstract debate about sovereignty.

The first of the party-political developments that would lead to the 2016 referendum was the gradual transformation of the Conservative Party from the 'party of Europe' of Macmillan and Heath into an overwhelmingly Eurosceptical body by the first decade of the twenty-first century. This trend had already begun in the latter half of the 1980s, with the appearance on the Thatcherite right of the party of a belief not only that Britain was now on an economic trajectory that would see it pull well ahead of other countries in western Europe, but also that EC policies, unless kept in check, might begin to impede the UK's success.[47] It was given a huge boost, especially amongst party grassroots, by the circumstances surrounding Thatcher's fall from power in 1990, with many activists interpreting what had happened as their leader being stabbed in the back by a cabal of senior pro-Europeans. The movement was energised by the large-scale backbench rebellion against the Maastricht Treaty and more generally against the pro-European policies of Major's government,[48] and would become the mainstream of the party during the lengthy period that the Conservatives spent in opposition between 1997 and 2010. Such Euroscepticism did not, admittedly, necessarily equate to support for a total British withdrawal from the EU. Enough Tory pragmatism remained

47 See, for example, www.margaretthatcher.org/document/207703.
48 D. Baker, A. Gamble, S. Ludlam and D. Seawright, 'Backbenchers with Attitude: A Seismic Study of the Conservative Party and Dissent on Europe', in S. Bowler, D. M. Farrell and R. S. Katz (eds.), *Party Discipline and Parliamentary Government* (Columbus, OH, Ohio State University Press, 1999), pp. 72–94.

for many senior Conservatives to baulk at taking this radical step. But it did mean that, by the time Cameron became party leader in 2005, out-and-out pro-Europeans in the party like Heseltine or Kenneth Clark resembled isolated relics of the past, criticism of most European policies and total resistance to any further integration had become the norm, and a vocal and growing minority were calling for the UK to leave the EU. The policies and politics of Cameron's two governments would be deeply shaped by this new reality.

The initial stages of this Conservative swing against European integration were counterbalanced by the movement of the Labour Party in the opposite direction – indeed, the two processes reinforced each other, with Labour able to occupy the pro-European terrain that the Conservatives had vacated and the Conservatives encouraged in their Euroscepticism by the need to attack the governments of Tony Blair and Gordon Brown. But Labour's own commitment to the EU weakened substantially in the years after 2010, in part because many on the centre-left strongly disliked the treatment of countries like Greece in the course of the Eurozone crisis, but still more because of a desire by Ed Milliband and then much more obviously by Jeremy Corbyn to distance themselves from the policies associated with the New Labour years. Corbyn's personal views, furthermore, were a direct throwback to the anti-Europeanism that had been typical of the Labour left during the 1970s and early 1980s. The result was a party that lost its appetite for talking about the issue, and shied away from criticising the ever-more sceptical stance of the Cameron government. Labour was not actually hostile to the EU, still less to British membership of it, but its leadership was highly reluctant to take a strong public position on the question.

Labour's growing silence left the Liberal Democrats as the only strongly pro-European force in English politics, although the Scottish Nationalists filled that space north of the border. At one level, this should not have been a problem. Both halves of the Liberal Democrats' ancestry, the Liberal Party on the one hand and the Social Democratic Party of the 1980s on the other, had been deeply associated with pro-European sentiment and the party's commitment to the cause seemed secure. But the party's own electoral fortunes took a disastrous knock from the 2010 decision to join the Conservatives in Cameron's coalition government – working closely with a right-of-centre party proved especially difficult for the party's much more centre-left-leaning activists and voters – and, more particularly, from the U-turn which entering government compelled the party leadership to make on the issue of university fees. The outcome was a near electoral wipe-out in 2015, from which the party has still not recovered. At precisely the moment when the need for a strong pro-European voice in British politics was becoming most acute, the only unambiguously pro-European grouping in England had thus been decimated and demoralised. The void where pro-Europeanism ought to have been in the UK public debate was striking.

In total contrast, the rise of the UK Independence Party (UKIP) in the first 15 years or so of the twenty-first century ensured that the anti-European voice in British politics had never been stronger. There had been anti-European groupings in UK politics before, notably the Referendum Party in the 1990s, and in terms of securing seats at Westminster, UKIP was scarcely more successful than earlier parties had been, with only two MPs, both of whom had defected from the Conservatives. But UKIP had in Nigel Farage a far more effective campaigner than many of his predecessors, able to speak to many within the UK electorate who were disillusioned with the mainstream parties. Furthermore, UKIP's real importance lay in the pressure that it put on the Conservatives to maintain their Eurosceptic credentials and to avoid sliding back to the more pragmatic position that governing parties have often adopted on the question of EC/EU membership. Any softening of Tory criticism of the EU, many of the party's backbenchers feared, could easily lead to the party losing support to UKIP, thereby endangering many of their seats.

The final contextual change that really mattered in explaining both the decision to hold an in–out referendum on EU membership and the outcome of that vote was the rise of immigration as an issue linked to Europe. Controversy about who was entitled to work and settle in Britain was not new in the early twenty-first century. It had been, for instance, a subject of considerable political debate in the 1970s also.[49] But in the earlier period, discussions had overwhelmingly focused on Commonwealth immigration, rather than migration from continental Europe, since the latter remained at a relatively low level. The high number of central and eastern Europeans who took advantage of free movement provisions to come to, and work in, Britain after 2004 changed matters dramatically, and led to a situation in which immigration and EU membership became tightly linked in the minds of many voters. This linkage, and the backdrop of the wider EU migration crisis, made much more concrete the longstanding Eurosceptic complaint about the loss of sovereignty entailed by European integration. Complaints about Britain losing the ability to control its own affairs go back to the very beginning of the

49 R. Hansen, *Citizenship and Immigration in Post-war Britain: The Institutional Origins of a Multicultural Nation* (Oxford and New York, NY, Oxford University Press, 2000), pp. 179–206.

debate about Common Market membership in the late 1950s and early 1960s, and had been at the heart of the 'No' campaign in the 1975 referendum.[50] But while the loss of sovereignty had always been an issue that some felt passionately about, it also suffered from being too abstract for many voters. What did losing sovereignty actually mean? Compared with the numerous highly concrete problems facing the UK in 1975, it largely failed to cut through in the wider public debate. In the run-up to 2016, by contrast, the inability of Britain within the EU to determine for itself who was entitled to live and work in the country became a highly visible and comprehensible embodiment of this loss of sovereignty. In the circumstances, the urge to 'take back control', as the Leave slogan put it, became irresistible for many.

All of this meant that, when Cameron took the misguided decision to promise a referendum in order to end Conservative Party infighting over Europe and halt UKIP's rise, the forces lining up to contest the referendum campaign were much less favourable to the pro-European side than had been the case in 1975. In 2016, the gap in funding between the two sides had largely disappeared, the press was much more evenly balanced and there were far fewer supposedly apolitical organisations ranging from businesses to the Church of England willing to break cover and express a clear-cut opinion on the issue. Saunders is good on the tilt of both business and the church during the first referendum.[51] Much would thus depend on the ability of the rival politicians to capture the public imagination and to win the trust of voters. And in this regard, the Remain campaign fell down badly, not least because, in the absence of strong pro-European voices like Heath or Jenkins in 1975, the role of leading the argument for EU membership fell to such figures as Cameron and his Chancellor, George Osborne, each of whom had spent significant portions of the previous decade speaking of the EU in highly critical terms. Their failure to carry conviction in a straight fight with Leave campaigners who had a much more consistent record of hostility to the EU was unsurprising. Neither were they able effectively to counter the immigration argument, given that their government had not contained migrant numbers, despite repeatedly promising to do so, and that Cameron had failed in his efforts to secure an exemption from EU provisions on the free movement of people during his 2015 'renegotiation'. The narrowness of the eventual 52 to 48 per cent victory for Leave somewhat masked the reality of a poorly planned and executed Remain campaign.

---

50 Saunders, *Yes to Europe!*, pp. 231–53.　51 Saunders, *Yes to Europe!*, pp. 155–82, 210–30.

Rejecting Exceptionalism

The third reason not to over-emphasise the awkward partner narrative is that it wrongly implies that close cooperation is an easy process for other European countries. This is clearly not the case. Tight integration is never wholly natural or effort-free, involving as it does lengthy multilateral negotiation before obtaining a decision that it might, in theory at least, have been possible to take unilaterally and the acceptance of an outcome that is likely to be different from that which purely national needs would have dictated. Frustration can also arise from the sheer impossibility of securing some hoped-for change and from the inevitable frictions that occur when politicians and officials from different countries with different cultures are obliged to bargain with one another incessantly on questions of political and economic sensitivity. In this light, working together can often be particularly hard for larger countries, as they are better able to imagine different circumstances in which they would have been able to arrive at the hoped-for outcome through independent rather than collective action. All of this has meant that Britain is far from unique in having felt discomfort at the need for cooperation, frustration at the outcome of much European bargaining and annoyance, bordering on outright rebellion, about some of the rules it has been obliged to accept. The long trail of newspaper headlines, stretching back to the 1950s, about 'breakdowns in Brussels', 'late-night crisis negotiations' or 'last-ditch compromises' should serve as a reminder that reaching common European decisions has never been, and is never likely to be, easy. The equally lengthy litany of infringement procedures that the European Commission has been obliged to take out against member states that fail to observe the commitments that they have entered into sends a similar message. British discomforts with the process, while distinctive, have certainly not been unique.

In such circumstances, pressing ahead with integration requires national governments and political elites to constantly explain to themselves and to their voters why this effort is necessary. How this is done will vary from country to country, from culture to culture, and will also evolve somewhat according to the precise circumstances. But constant explanation and justification remain profoundly necessary, given the inevitable frustrations and disappointments that accompany the practice of working closely with other countries. This is where successive British governments have fallen down badly, with little effort made to explain, justify or sell Europe between the two referendums of 1975 and 2016.

This failure was made all the more acute by the fact that the original core narrative about why Britain needed to be part of the integration process became less applicable, in appearance at least, as Britain prospered within the EC/EU. Central to the UK's original turn to Europe was the notion that EC membership constituted the best antidote to Britain's post-war 'decline'.[52] Rediscovering a regional role, to put it differently, would help arrest the seemingly inexorable slide from global power to European laggard that the country had undergone during the 1950s and 1960s. This argument loomed large in discussion about why European membership was needed in both main political parties and throughout the British civil service in the years between Macmillan's first application and the UK's belated entry in 1973. It also assumed a prominent role in the rhetoric used during the first referendum, which confirmed the country's European choice.

In the decades that followed, however, the very notion of decline was banished from the mainstream UK debate. The better economic fortunes of the country from the 1980s onwards, the way in which a series of military triumphs in the Falklands or as part of the First Gulf War coalition replaced the slow retreat from empire of the early postwar decades and the charismatic leadership styles of leaders such as Thatcher and Blair combined to make Britain much less prone to self-doubt and angst as it entered the twenty-first century than it had been for much of the middle of the twentieth. This meant that the need for European membership as an antidote to decline diminished accordingly. Other justifications might, and almost certainly should, have been found. These could, for instance, have acknowledged the very limited capacity of any single country, even one that was no longer in decline, to effect meaningful change in the ever more multipolar world of the early 2000s or to confront challenges, such as climate change, that manifestly transcend national borders. But, by and large, the British political class ignored the need, still locked in the cycle of endless sniping at the EU discussed earlier. As a result, when a referendum needed to be fought and a strong case made as to why EU membership was beneficial, no well-established narrative existed. Instead, the Remain campaign in 2016 was obliged to rely on a narrow, purely economic justification, backed up by improbably precise Treasury calculations about how much non-EU membership would cost each British citizen. Compared with the well-crafted 'take back control' campaign, advanced by politicians passionately convinced of their case, it was little wonder that this lacklustre Remain

52 Aqui, *The First Referendum*, pp. 11–13.

campaigned failed to persuade. The 2016 result, in other words, exposed not just the short-term failings of those who led the effort to keep Britain within the EU, but much more seriously the failure by successive British governments to construct and constantly reinforce a persuasive explanation of why the UK needed to cooperate closely with its European neighbours. The fault was not just limited to David Cameron, but stretched back through the New Labour years to the 1980s at least, and perhaps all the way back to 1975. Britain no longer knew why it was within Europe, and as a result voted to leave.

Conclusions

Brexit was not an inevitable outcome. Britain, it is true, has had a bumpy ride as an EC/EU member. This has in part sprung from its distinctive history and culture, as well as its geographical position. The country has also felt, more strongly than many others, the countervailing pull of extra-European partners, especially the United States. But such fragilities, while not insignificant, neither prevented the integration process from being both shaped by and shaping Britain, nor condemned the UK and the EU to a foreordained divorce. Instead, a full explanation of why the 2016 vote was held and of its outcome needs to concentrate both on the short-term set of political contingencies that had so weakened the pro-European voice in British politics and helped stoke unprecedented levels of Euroscepticism and on the longer-term failure of Britain's political leaders to explain, justify and 'sell' EC/EU membership.

This in turn helps give the Brexit story its full significance in the wider narrative of European integration history. Had Britain's departure from the EU been the predetermined outcome of UK exceptionalism, this would have implied that there was little that the twenty-seven remaining member states could have learned from it. All that could have been concluded was that de Gaulle had been right, and that Britain was too insular, too maritime ever to have properly belonged within a European entity. However, if it is recognised that Brexit was not the inevitable end to an aberration, but instead the product of a longstanding failure by generations of British leaders to convince themselves and their voters of why their country needed to cooperate closely with its neighbours, then it does become something from which useful lessons can be learned. For it should stand as a reminder that integration is bound to be uncomfortable and to produce frustrations aplenty, and can hence continue to enjoy the popular sanction upon which it depends only if the realities of interdependence and virtues of multilateral cooperation over unilateral action are constantly explained and reiterated. Britain has paid the price for forgetting this reality; other European countries would do well to learn from its mistake.

Recommended Reading

Grey, C. *Brexit Unfolded: How No One Got What They Want (and Why They Were Never Going to)* (London, Biteback, 2021).

O'Rourke, K. H. *A Short History of Brexit: From Brentry to Backstop* (London, Penguin, 2019).

Reynolds, D. *Island Stories: Britain and Its History in the Age of Brexit* (London, William Collins, 2019).

Saunders, R. 'Brexit and Empire: "Global Britain" and the Myth of Imperial Nostalgia', *The Journal of Imperial and Commonwealth History* 48, no. 6 (2020): 1140–74.

Shipman, T. *All Out War: The Full Story of How Brexit Sank Britain's Political Class* (London, William Collins, 2016).

Stephens, P. *Britain Alone: The Path from Suez to Brexit* (London, Faber and Faber, 2021).

Wall, S. *Reluctant European: Britain and the European Union from 1945 to Brexit* (Oxford, Oxford University Press, 2020).

PART II

★

INSTRUMENTS
OF INTEGRATION

7

In the Name of Social Stability:
The European Payments Union

JORRIT STEEHOUDER

Introduction

In October 1949, the Belgian-American economist Robert Triffin recalled the signing of the Bretton Woods Agreements of July 1944. From a luxurious hotel in the secluded forests of New Hampshire, the world had aimed to stabilise the international economic system by creating a new rules-based global monetary order. At the time, the financial experts of continental Europe had little to say in bringing about this new order, which was predominantly of Anglo-American design. In a parallel effort to the Anglo-American financial experts, most notably John Maynard Keynes and Harry D. White, Europe's leaders envisioned the post-war monetary system differently. They deliberated 'regional monetary groups' that should tie in with a 'skeleton world council' in the form of the International Monetary Fund (IMF). However, these regional monetary groups – proposed within the circles of the exiled European financial experts in London by men such as Paul van Zeeland and Wim Beyen – were deemed 'too slow, pedestrian and cumbersome' by Keynes and White, as Triffin remembered in 1949.° Ironically, the global Bretton Woods system turned out to be 'trying to do too much', and after 5 years it had 'achieved too little'.[1]

In the meantime, regional schemes for monetary multilateralism had become an important vehicle for European integration, most notably through the creation of the European Payments Union (EPU) in 1950, for which Triffin

The research leading to this chapter was carried out as part of the research project Blueprints of Hope, funded by the Dutch Research Council. I am indebted to my colleagues Beatrice de Graaf, Mathieu Segers, Peter-Ben Smit, Clemens van den Berg and Trineke Palm for their comments and criticisms.
1 R. Triffin, 'Institutional Developments in the Intra-European System', 8 October 1949, Box 19, Triffin Papers, YUL.

himself helped lay the intellectual and practical foundations.[2] Beyen, who witnessed the social and economic chaos of the 1930s, also wrote about the events leading up to the establishment of the EPU in 1949 and noted a favourable shift in 'ideas regarding a regional approach' under the Marshall Plan. In fact, by facilitating increased trade and employment, the Marshall Plan enabled western Europe to 'grow into its Bretton Woods coat'.[3] It revived the regionalism that had been advocated by Europe's continental exiles during the war.

The creation of a new European monetary order through the EPU represented the culmination of a decades-long quest for socio-economic stability that had commenced after the First World War, and which was first pursued through the League of Nations' Economic and Financial Organisation in the 1920s and 1930s.[4] During the Second World War the search continued and '[n]either blackout nor bombs' hindered the European policymakers who were jointly studying their financial and economic problems.[5] The post-war economic order, it was widely believed, should be geared to 'create the wealth necessary to achieve social and political ends'.[6] After the war, these social and economic priorities resonated, most notably in the creation of welfare states, but also internationally. In drawing up the blueprints that eventually led to the creation of the EPU, one international official deemed the new system of multilateral payments 'in the interests not only of full employment at home but also of the interests of the group as a whole'.[7] In that sense, monetary multilateralism highlighted a conviction to share socio-economic responsibilities through an international framework.

This gradual post-war regionalisation of monetary order in a western European framework was driven by a quest for socio-economic stability. Yet, the history of the EPU – as well as the preceding series of payments agreements concluded within the Organisation for European Economic Co-operation (OEEC) – generally falls outside the scope of European integration history, which tends to pick up with the European Coal and Steel Community (ECSC) in 1950. Shedding light on the OEEC and the creation of the EPU, including the longer trajectory of ideas rooted in the 1930s and early 1940s that informed post-war European economic cooperation,

2 I. Maes, *Robert Triffin: A Life* (New York, NY, Oxford University Press, 2021), pp. 79–86.
3 J. W. Beyen, *Money in a Maelstrom* (New York, NY, Macmillan, 1949), pp. 204–5.
4 P. Clavin, *Securing the World Economy: The Reinvention of the League of Nations, 1920–1946* (Oxford, Oxford University Press, 2013).
5 Beyen, *Money in a Maelstrom*, p. 142.
6 J. W. Beyen, 'La reconstruction matérielle de l'Europe après la fin de la guerre', *La France Libre*, 15 November 1940, 56.
7 'Trade and Payments Arrangements', 1 December 1949, OEEC 241, HAEU.

helps correct this imbalance. After all, it was through the OEEC and the EPU that pre-1950 instances of Western financial and economic multilateralism were appropriated to a regional western European framework and that the quest for socio-economic stability transpired in the integration of western Europe.

Within the largely technocratic and bureaucratic OEEC, western European countries together laid the practical foundations for a new monetary order. In doing so, they built upon the financial and economic expertise of men who had experienced the social and economic crises of the 1930s, like Triffin and his contemporaries. Some of them had been actively involved in the League of Nations' economic conferences and the creation of regional trade blocs, through which they had hoped to mitigate the socio-economic effects of shrinking world trade. The OEEC, for that matter, constituted a crucial link between the inter-war, war, and post-war periods because it channelled pre-war ideas for European monetary and economic cooperation, early instances of Western multilateralism, their advocates' emotional driving forces and the new post-war political priorities of European welfare states into a pioneering institutional architecture of European economic cooperation.

This chapter analyses both how the socio-economic quest of the West created instances of European integration and how this quest (which was a constant factor from the 1920s to the late 1940s) gained traction through the realities of the war and the post-war years. First, it proceeds with a brief overview of the literature. Secondly, by adopting a diachronic perspective of European integration, it sets forth the reservoir of experiences, ideas and emotions and some of the blueprints accumulated throughout the 1920s and 1930s which underpinned later European economic cooperation. Thirdly, it shows how Europe's continental exiles in wartime London developed a regional approach to the post-war European economic order. Fourthly, it shows that, in the aftermath of the Second World War, the practices of regionalism hardly developed beyond the drawing table until the American government decided to fund European economic recovery through the Marshall Plan. Finally, it analyses the stages through which western Europe integrated its monetary policies within the OEEC. The predominant aim, in that sense, is to show the continuity in terms of the actors involved and the way in which social priorities constantly underpinned the European plans for international monetary and economic cooperation from the inter-war period onwards.[8]

---

8 See also J. Steehouder, 'Constructing Europe: Blueprints for a New Monetary Order, 1919–1950' (Ph.D. thesis, Utrecht University, 2022).

Beyond 'Core Europe' towards 'Laboratory Europe'

Recent scholarship has increasingly shifted focus beyond the 'core Europe' of the ECSC. A growing body of literature 'de-centers the EU's predecessors' as the exclusive sites for European cooperation.[9] Kiran Patel therefore argued that European integration history should be 'embedded more firmly into a wider array of international structures'. This chapter takes up this suggestion by analysing early integration efforts within the OEEC. The focus on 'core Europe' and the ECSC has devoted too much attention to transfers of sovereignty and supranational integration, by which logic the economic cooperation and integration that took off in the OEEC have been considered a 'failed start'.[10] But, as Beyen remarked as early as in 1954, 'European integration' is flexible and undefined, and may be used for 'all aspects, including non-political aspects of this connection'.[11]

In analysing early European institution-building from the perspective of its wider multilateral context, the extent to which it was driven by a desire to solve complex socio-economic problems becomes visible. According to Mathieu Segers, pre-1950 Western (and indeed transatlantic) multilateralism constituted a 'laboratory' in which different forms of European cooperation and integration were developed and tested. A closer examination of this 'laboratory' sheds new light on the emergence of a regionally oriented social market through the pursuit of European integration. After the war, international financial and economic cooperation was guided by a desire to share 'societal responsibilities internationally'.[12]

These social and economic priorities of post-war Europe indicate a basis of continuity upon which European integration emerged. According to Charles Maier, both of Europe's twentieth century's post-war periods 'formed part of a continuing effort at stabilization'.[13] After the end of the First World War,

---

9 K. K. Patel, 'Widening and Deepening? Recent Advances in European Integration History', *Neue Politische Literatur* 64, no. 2 (2019): 327–57, 329.
10 K. K. Patel, 'Provincialising European Union: Co-operation and Integration in Europe in a Historical Perspective', *Contemporary European History* 22, no. 4 (2013): 649–73, 651; K. K. Patel, *Project Europe: A History* (Cambridge and New York, NY, Cambridge University Press, 2020).
11 J. W. Beyen, 'Weerstanden tegen de Europese integratie', 12 February 1954, NL-HaNA, 2.05.117, inv. no. 16850.
12 M. L. L. Segers, 'Eclipsing Atlantis: Trans-Atlantic Multilateralism in Trade and Monetary Affairs as a Pre-history to the Genesis of Social Market Europe (1942–1950)', *Journal of Common Market Studies* 57, no. 1 (2019): 60–76, 61–2.
13 C. S. Maier, *In Search of Stability: Explorations in Historical Political Economy* (Cambridge, Cambridge University Press, 1987), p. 161.

countries increasingly sought to improve social conditions by raising living standards and safeguarding employment levels. These new social priorities went hand in hand with the search for a new international economic order, for example through the League of Nations, which helped pave the road for Bretton Woods.[14]

In an attempt to illuminate the longer trajectories and continuities of the history of European integration across the twentieth century, scholars have increasingly adopted diachronic perspectives, moving beyond the life and death of institutions, and breaking through the standard periodisation of European integration history.[15] One way of doing this is by following actors and the development of their ideas over longer periods of time, conceptualising them as 'carriers of continuity'.[16] In doing so, it becomes possible to analyse how their accumulated experiences with social and economic chaos and war over the course of the 1930s and 1940s informed new and hopeful visions of future European economic cooperation.

As it turns out, the OEEC then emerges as much more than just an intergovernmental organisation with a 'dull but durable bureaucratic routine'.[17] Rather, it becomes a transformer house and laboratory, where the deeper undercurrent of Europe's past of war and depression was fused with practical monetary instruments designed to safeguard social and economic stability in an international framework. Having been witness to the bloodiest consequences of economic crisis, the post-war policymakers of Europe shared a set of similar emotionally fraught experiences, and harmoniously rejected the social inequities caused by *laissez-faire* capitalism.

Regional Multilateralism in Inter-war Europe

Policymakers who became active in post-1945 Europe shared the 1930s as an emotionally fraught 'space of experience'.[18] For men like Robert Marjolin (the French Secretary-General of the OEEC) and Hans Hirschfeld (who

---

14 L. W. Pauly, 'The League of Nations and the Foreshadowing of the International Monetary Fund', *Essays in International Finance* 201 (1996): 1–47.

15 S. G. Gross, 'Introduction: European Integration across the Twentieth Century', *Contemporary European History* 26, no. 2 (2017): 205–7, 205; M. Conway and K. K. Patel (eds.), *Europeanization in the Twentieth Century: Historical Approaches* (London, Palgrave Macmillan, 2010).

16 K. K. Patel and W. Kaiser, 'Continuity and Change in European Cooperation during the Twentieth Century', *Contemporary European History* 27, no. 2 (2018): 165–82, 172.

17 A. S. Milward, *The Reconstruction of Western Europe, 1945–51* (London, Methuen & Co., 1984), p. 172.

18 See the work of the German historian R. Koselleck, *The Practice of Conceptual History: Timing History, Spacing Concepts* (Stanford, CA, Stanford University Press, 2002), p. 111.

headed the Dutch delegation to the OEEC), the many failures of international financial diplomacy, the instability of international currencies and the vengeful economic nationalism of these years constituted a shared experience. Additionally, the memories of the 1920s were 'close enough and their witnesses numerous enough' to be recalled vividly.[19] This was especially the case for men like Triffin and Marjolin, both of whom were born in 1911 and younger than Van Zeeland (born in 1893) and Hirschfeld (born in 1899).

It was in these years before the Second World War that these men developed a shared quest for socio-economic stability that eventually led to the creation of the EPU more than a decade later. Some ideas and instruments designed to bring about a new stability in international economic relations were very similar to those that underpinned the EPU years later. In general, the 1920s and 1930s gave birth to two path-dependences for post-1945 Europe. First, there emerged new priorities for the functioning of capitalism, which needed to be cured of its free market excesses. Secondly, 'Europe' emerged as an 'economic space' with a desire for international cooperation – a counterintuitive conclusion given the subsequent bloodshed of the Second World War. As it turns out, the financial and economic burden of the First World War not only gave rise to an increased sense of nationalism, but also accelerated calls for international cooperation and European unity.

After the First World War, Keynes warned against burdening Germany with reparations, because it could harm the 'economic rehabilitation of Europe'. Keeping Germany economically underdeveloped would negatively impact the value and stability of currencies in Europe, and invoked the danger of spreading inflation, which would have disastrous socio-economic consequences. Such 'rapid depression of the standard of life', observed Keynes, 'drives other temperaments to the nervous instability of hysteria and to a mad despair'.[20] Yet the reparations of the Versailles settlement set the stage for the 1920s, which were characterised by international financial diplomacy between the great powers.[21] Both France and Britain had incurred large debts with the United States, and France in particular depended on German reparations to repay these debts. In 1924 and 1929 the American

---

19 R. Marjolin, *Architect of European Unity: Memoirs, 1911–1986* (London, Weidenfeld and Nicolson, 1989), p. 145.
20 J. M. Keynes, *The Collected Writings of John Maynard Keynes*, vol. II: *The Economic Consequences of the Peace*, eds. E. Johnson and D. Moggridge (Cambridge and New York, NY, Cambridge University Press, 2013 [1919]), pp. 143–4.
21 P. Clavin, *The Failure of Economic Diplomacy: Britain, Germany, France and the United States, 1931–36* (Basingstoke, Macmillan, 1996).

government funded this vicious debt cycle through the Dawes and Young Plans, effectively commercialising German reparations.[22]

To some, this perpetual 'Wirtschaft- und Währungschaos' highlighted the economic necessity for a united Europe – or *Pan-Europa*, as Austrian-Japanese Count Richard Coudenhove-Kalergi dubbed it in 1923.[23] His movement attracted many followers across the continent, including statesmen such as Aristide Briand, Gustav Stresemann and Edvard Beneš. Another hub for the spread of economic internationalism was the League of Nations, where the French industrialist Louis Loucheur advocated the abolition of protectionist policies, which some thought could lead to the creation of a 'United States of Europe'.[24] Pietro Stoppani, an Italian delegate to the League of Nations, was one of the driving forces behind the World Economic Conference of 1927, where he hoped to restore world free trade.[25] But none of these idealistic plans materialised. When the globally interdependent economic system collapsed after the Wall Street crash of October 1929, it set in motion a global surge of protectionism and economic nationalism.

The failure to stabilise the international economy during the 1920s and the subsequent turn to economic nationalism was one of the most pervasive results of the Great Depression, causing what has been dubbed a 'quantum leap in interventionism' across the globe. The excesses of global capitalism led to a renegotiation of the relations between state, society and the individual, and gave rise to a new understanding of the role of the state and the purpose of the economy. The early 1930s witnessed an increased role for the government in the economy (for example, through government-funded infrastructure plans or large-scale nationalisation of industries), which is often referred to as *planisme*.[26] At the heart of these socialist-inspired economic programmes was the desire to preserve social stability, maintain living standards and secure employment.

The most extraordinary example of this surge in state-led capitalism was Roosevelt's New Deal, launched in 1933. It was right about then, in the run-up to Roosevelt's election in September 1932, that Marjolin arrived in New Haven to study at Yale University. During the 1920s, he had been inspired

22 A. Tooze, *The Deluge: The Great War and the Remaking of Global Order, 1916 – 1931* (London, Allen Lane, 2014), pp. 301–3.
23 R. N. Coudenhove-Kalergi, *Pan-Europa* (Vienna, Pan-Europa-Verlag, 1982 [1923]), p. 17.
24 Clavin, *Securing the World Economy*, p. 41.
25 E. Tollardo, 'International Experts or Fascist Envoys? Alberto Theodoli and Pietro Stoppani at the League of Nations', *New Global Studies* 10, no. 3 (2016): 283–306, 299.
26 K. K. Patel, *The New Deal: A Global History* (Princeton, NJ, Princeton University Press, 2016), pp. 41–3, 93.

by socialism and the writings of Marx, and the Great Depression represented to him the ultimate failure of capitalism. But Marjolin also admired Roosevelt's New Deal for its 'energy and action' and for the great social and economic experiment it represented. Roosevelt's New Deal taught Marjolin that a proclivity towards 'social justice and equality' and an 'efficient and productive society' could go hand in hand.[27] It was in those years that he developed a dual commitment towards social goals as well as the preservation of capitalism.

To preserve capitalism, it had to be reformed so as to deliver social and economic stability (which the free market could not) through a mix of socialism and economic planning. However, these new social priorities and the reform of capitalism were carried by a global turn towards state-planning and a devastating trend towards economic autarky and economic nationalism, and not by an internationally coordinated approach. At the time, Marjolin – who later developed strong internationalist ambitions when he became an 'architect of European unity' – had no ideas on how to preserve social domestic stability through an international framework. It was only during and after the Second World War that he embraced the advantages of economic planning and international financial institutions. Others, like Paul van Zeeland, drew more internationalist lessons from the inter-war period, and sought ways out of the global social and economic crisis by means of international cooperation.

'The year 1932', he wrote, 'has come to an end in a state of utter confusion, both political and economic'. Global economic interdependence had led the people of the world 'one after the other, and one because of the other, into the way of economic nationalism'. To get rid of the 'artificial defenses' the world was in need of a 'general plan and on the condition that each one does its part, and at the same time'.[28] Van Zeeland's optimism for finding such an international solution was remarkable but not entirely unjustified. In preceding years, he had been involved in multiple undertakings aimed at international cooperation in the monetary and economic sphere. For example, the Bank for International Settlements (BIS), where he was a board member, emerged as a network of central bankers committed to preserving international monetary stability on the basis of the gold standard.[29]

---

27 Marjolin, *Architect of European Unity*, p. 41; R. Marjolin, *Les expériences Roosevelt* (Paris, La Libraire Populaire, 1934), pp. 2, 32–3.
28 P. van Zeeland, *A View of Europe, 1932: An Interpretative Essay on Some Workings of Economic Nationalism* (Baltimore, MD, The Johns Hopkins University Press, 1933), pp. 1, 150.
29 G. Toniolo, *Central Bank Cooperation at the Bank for International Settlements, 1930–1973* (Cambridge, Cambridge University Press, 2005), p. 131.

Moreover, several smaller European states had signed regional trade agreements, showing that international cooperation was possible. One of these initiatives was the Oslo Convention of 1930, where Belgium, the Netherlands, Luxembourg, Norway, Denmark and Sweden synchronised their tariff policies. They shielded their domestic markets from unexpected shocks from each other, and insulated themselves from the volatile German market – which was at the heart of the European economic crisis.[30] Another example of such 'regional projects' was the 1932 Ouchy Convention between Belgium, the Netherlands and Luxembourg. Together they called for the gradual reduction of economic barriers and hoped to create the foundations for an agreement between an even larger group of European states.[31] Van Zeeland – who was involved in the negotiations – supported these regional projects. Leading up to the League's World Economic Conference of 1933, he even brought them to the attention of the American government.[32]

Van Zeeland hoped that these developments would culminate in a new 'social peace', with 'sufficient stability of prices, of business, of active purchasing power, and of social relationships'.[33] But, soon after the conference started, Roosevelt announced that the United States would not facilitate a return to the gold standard, which sealed the fate of the monetary side of the conference. After this, even the most ardent advocates of international cooperation, like Van Zeeland, Hirschfeld and Beyen, were forced to prioritise protectionist trade policies.

A final attempt to overcome the increasingly strong 'going it alone' attitude in international economic relations was undertaken by Van Zeeland during the late 1930s. Over the course of 1937, he undertook a mission on behalf of France and the United Kingdom (UK) to see whether a 'general reduction of quotas and of other obstacles to international trade' was possible.[34] In doing so, he drew upon a plan by Italian League of Nations delegate Stoppani, who had proposed in 1936 to abolish trade quotas between France, the UK, the United States, Germany and Italy – all in order to avoid another European war.[35]

30 G. van Roon, *Kleine landen in crisistijd: Van Oslostaten tot Benelux, 1930–1940* (Amsterdam, Elsevier, 1985), pp. 150–2.

31 R. Boyce, *The Great Interwar Crisis and the Collapse of Globalization* (Basingstoke, Palgrave Macmillan, 2014), pp. 365, 372–5; Van Roon, *Kleine landen in crisistijd*, pp. 115–16.

32 B. Henau, *Paul van Zeeland en het monetaire, sociaal-economische en Europese beleid van België, 1920–1960* (Brussels: Koninklijke Academie voor Wetenschappen, Letteren en Schone Kunsten, 1995), p. 114.

33 Van Zeeland, *A View of Europe*, p. 152.

34 *Report Presented by Monsieur Van Zeeland to the Governments of the United Kingdom and France on the Possibility of Obtaining a General Reduction of the Obstacles to International Trade* (London, HMSO, 1938), pp. 27–50.

35 Tollardo, 'International Experts or Fascist Envoys?', 301.

It is worthwhile to devote some consideration to the visionary plans and principles Van Zeeland put forth. Most importantly, his endeavour to revive international trade was underpinned by an appeal for socio-economic stability. The basis of a 'pact of economic collaboration', argued Van Zeeland, should be to 'assist the participants to raise the standard of living of their nationals by improving the general well-being'. Clearly, domestic socio-economic stability could be safeguarded only through a framework of international economic cooperation. One of his more practical suggestions to restore trust in the international economic system was for countries to freeze and gradually reduce their tariffs.[36]

Even more visionary was his plan to reorganise Europe's monetary system. He proposed that the United States government deposit a large stock of gold at the BIS in Basle, which could then serve as a 'basis on which to reorganize the monetary systems of Europe'.[37] It would function as a reserve fund for the settling of intra-European debts and payments. This plan was ahead of its time, as it took another 10 years before US Secretary of State George C. Marshall pleaded for billions of US dollars to assist in Europe's economic recovery. And even then, it took 3 years and additional injections of American capital before the EPU incorporated the basic principle of Van Zeeland's proposal. In 1938, when Van Zeeland presented his report, the international response was limited, as Hirschfeld remembered with regret.[38]

Van Zeeland's mission report was cause for both optimism and pessimism. On the positive side, there seemed to be a widespread desire to reduce trade barriers and overcome protectionism in the countries he visited. But there was also a lack of political willingness to see trade liberalisation through, for 'nobody wanted to commit himself to advance in any direction, before being certain that the path had been taken, or that at any rate it had been mapped out, by several others.'[39] At a Cambridge University lecture in 1938, Van Zeeland bitterly observed that the world was still in 'no man's land', because nothing was done towards reviving world trade.[40] Prospects for multilateral economic cooperation eroded with European nations on a collision course for war. But the ideas for regional European cooperation were not abandoned.

---

36 *Report Presented by Monsieur Van Zeeland*, pp. 33, 48.
37 William C. Bullitt to Cordell Hull, 12 June 1937, *Foreign Relations of the United States* (Washington, DC, US Government Printing Office), 1937, Volume I, pp. 678–9, https://history.state.gov/historicaldocuments/frus1937v01/d695.
38 H. M. Hirschfeld, *Herinneringen uit de jaren 1933–1939* (Amsterdam, Elsevier, 1959), p. 111.
39 *Report Presented by Monsieur Van Zeeland*, pp. 30–1.
40 P. van Zeeland, *Economics or Politics? A Lecture on the Present Problems of International Relations* (Cambridge, Cambridge University Press, 1939), p. 12.

Europe in Exile: The Pre-eminence of Economic Cooperation

Thinking about a multilateral economic framework through which socio-economic stability in Europe could be safeguarded continued and deepened during the Second World War. If anything, the regional and socio-economic aspects of post-war European cooperation were strengthened during this period. In London, the exiled governments of continental Europe found a safe haven, where they formed new connections and developed new ideas. Over the course of 1940 and 1941, as Hitler's *Blitzkrieg* took Europe by surprise, the governments of Poland, Czechoslovakia, Belgium, the Netherlands, Luxembourg, Norway, Greece and Yugoslavia, as well as de Gaulle's Free French, fled to London, where they remained for the duration of the war (except that, in 1943, the French moved their headquarters to Algiers). Included in this 'miniature Europe' (the term was frequently used by British government officials and in the press) were Beyen, Marjolin, Van Zeeland and many others.[41] The proximity of so many European officials in London created a wholly new international context in which peace preparations became a growing concern. Czechoslovakia's President Beneš, for example, did not want to 'face the end and be still unprepared for peace'.[42]

Exiles from the heart of Europe – most notably Poland and Czechoslovakia – were well represented on this 'construction site' for post-war Europe, not least because they had been the first to be forced into exile. From 1939 onwards, Beneš and Polish Prime Minister Władysław Sikorski initiated talks on a post-war federation between their countries – an initiative largely motivated by their inter-war experiences at the geographical heart of the continent, where they were squeezed between the ambitions of Hitler and Stalin. However, as a Polish note indicates, it was equally important to provide an alternative to the 'giant German plans of rebuilding the earth' – most notably the 'Funk plan' to arrange Europe as an economic unit centred around Germany – and provide a 'fair allocation of the social revenue' in post-war Europe.[43] The Polish government hoped that through 'the means of

---

41 See P. Jakubec, 'Together and Alone in Allied London: Czechoslovak, Norwegian and Polish Governments-in-Exile, 1940–1945', *The International History Review* 42, no. 3 (2020): 465–84, 467; F. E. Oppenheimer, 'Governments and Authorities in Exile', *The American Journal of International Law* 36, no. 4 (1942): 568–95, 568.

42 H. R. Madol, *The League of London: A Book of Interviews with Allied Sovereigns and Statesmen* (London, Hutchinson & Company Limited, 1942), p. 7.

43 'Opracowanie: Sprawa odbudowy Europy po wojnie' ['Note: Post-war Rebuilding of Europe'], undated [probably 1940], PRM 34, PISM. I am indebted to Weronika Fay for the translation of Polish documents.

economic cooperation', Europe could be prepared for political cooperation. Economic cooperation within a 'tighter all-European federation' should be the cornerstone of post-war Europe.[44]

By late 1940 and early 1941, Sikorski's close confidant Joseph Retinger had shared these ideas with Marcel-Henri Jaspar, the Belgian ambassador in eastern European affairs. Jaspar was especially interested in the economic aspects of post-war cooperation and less so in the federative political framework within which these were wrapped. He wanted Belgium to join the work for this new economic order, because he was convinced that the problem with the Versailles Treaty had been that it catered too much to the 'political claims of states'.[45] At a subsequent meeting, Retinger acknowledged that 'of all the concepts for post-war Europe', it was 'the economic one, that is by far the most serious one', because a future peace would be 'stable only if all of the economic needs of participating states are met'.[46] The first encounters between the European exiles showed that the path towards post-war cooperation was primarily economic, and that economic cooperation essentially was about creating social stability.

This was confirmed during a conference in Oxford hosted by Federal Union – a London-based think tank that advocated federations as a basis for post-war organisation. Here, the idea of an economic federation was discussed within a larger group of European exiles under the auspices of William Beveridge – who later laid the foundations for the British welfare state with the Beveridge Report (1942). As it turned out, the concept of a federation was contested and considered 'too ambitious'. Jaspar concluded that the basis of Europe's post-war order 'lay in the economic structure'.[47] His boss, Foreign Minister Paul-Henri Spaak, agreed, and added that post-war 'economic arrangements' could only be created between countries that possessed a 'natural affinity' and 'homogeneity' – effectively paving the way for a predominantly western European economic unity.[48] The Dutch

44 'Memoriał Rządu Polskiego dla min. Bevina' ['Memorandum of the Polish Government for Minister Bevin'], undated [probably September 1940], PRM 20, PISM.
45 '"Pro Memoria" 2 egz. – Sprawozdanie z lunchu odbytego dn. 5.XII.40 w Ecu de France z p. H. Jaspar i R. Motz o stosunkach polsko-belgijskich' ['"Pro Memoria" 2 copies – Report from Lunch at Ecu de France with H. Jaspar and R. Motz on Polish–Belgian Relations'], 5 December 1940, PRM 53, PISM.
46 'Memorandum z rozmowy między H. Jasparem i Dr. M. Dogilewskim w sprawie zbliżenia polsko-belgijskiego po wojnie' ['Memorandum of Conversation between H. Jaspar and Dr. M. Dogilewski on Polish–Belgian Rapprochement after the War'], 20 December 1940, PRM 53, PISM.
47 'Federal Union Research Institute. Conference', 18–19 January 1941, ARA, Papiers Jaspar, inv. no. 2110.
48 'Rede van den Heer Spaak', 20 February 1941, NL-HaNA, 2.05.80, inv. no. 2558.

government at the time even considered non-economic forms of post-war European cooperation 'pipe dreams'.[49]

Early encounters between the exiled governments in London point to an emerging split between eastern and western Europe, most notably on the extent to which post-war Europe should become a federation. The entry of both the Soviet Union and the United States into the war in 1941 quickly exacerbated these differences. Western European governments (such as those of Norway, Belgium and the Netherlands) were favourably predisposed to the principles of economic cooperation, free trade and social advancement that were set forth in the Atlantic Charter, while they were reluctant to become entangled in 'Eastern European quarrels' through an all-European federation.[50] Belgian Prime Minister Hubert Pierlot wrote to Spaak that he could not see the post-war fate of Belgium tied to eastern Europe in the same way 'as we can envisage our future relations with purely Western countries'.[51]

The Soviet entry into the war in 1941 dramatically altered the strategic landscape for the British, as well as the dynamics between the European exiles. Sikorski's diplomatic position (and Poland's prospect of post-war independence) deteriorated after the Soviet entry and the ensuing British reluctance to support Polish proposals for post-war bloc formation in eastern Europe. From the American ambassador to the exiled governments, Anthony J. Drexel Biddle, Jr., Sikorski could draw equally little hope. Biddle was in London merely to boost the morale of the exiles, or, as Roosevelt put it, to 'hold their hands, look at their tongues, and take their pulses'.[52]

Therefore, Retinger and Sikorski tried seizing the diplomatic initiative amongst the London-based exiles and organised a Conference of Representatives of the Allied Governments in January 1942. While they aimed at a mere declaration of post-war solidary between the exiles in London, the underlying intention to create a post-war European order based on a regional federation was evident to Jaspar.[53] The endeavour was discouraged by the British and the Americans (as it would upset relations with the Soviet Union), and a survey by the Foreign Office indicated that there was division amongst the European exiles as well.[54]

---

49 Note accompanying 'Post-War Reorganisation of Central Europe' by Dr Hubert Ripka, 26 May 1941, NL-HaNA, 2.05.80, inv. no. 2540.
50 A. P. C. van Karnebeek to Van Kleffens, 16 February 1942, NL-HaNA, 2.05.80, inv. no. 2551.
51 Pierlot to Spaak, 7 February 1941, PHS 66, HAEU.
52 'Memorandum for Tony Biddle', 12 December 1941; Biddle to Roosevelt, 31 December 1941, Box 24, PSF, FDRPL.
53 'Memorandum Confidentiel', 2 February 1942, PHS 90, HAEU.
54 Minutes, 9 February 1942, C 1544/1543/62, FO 371/30871, TNA.

As it turned out, the harder Retinger and Sikorski pushed to bring the exiles together, the more evident the split between eastern and western Europe became. Western European exiles from France, Belgium and the Netherlands did not want a political federation and deliberated a different *sortie de guerre*. The Belgian and Dutch governments grafted their plans for the post-war order upon the Atlantic Charter, which laid out the principles for an open economic order, with economic growth and social advancement.[55]

In the margins of the London International Assembly – another London-based think tank – Hervé Alphand (de Gaulle's economic advisor) and Wim Beyen (who advised the Dutch government-in-exile) prepared papers on the post-war international economic order. They agreed that the future economic order should be focused on preventing 'chronic crises of unemployment' and 'securing the individual's social security'. Alphand particularly feared the return of economic nationalism and the implementation of trade barriers in the immediate post-war situation.[56] Shrinking world trade (like in the 1930s) would have disastrous social repercussions. In March 1942, Alphand discussed this with Van Zeeland, who headed the Belgian think tank on post-war problems. Both agreed that free world trade was desirable, but that it would not work unless there was close monetary cooperation. Such monetary cooperation did not necessarily have to be of a universal character, and could also be implemented on a regional basis between several European countries, as long as it was embedded in a global rules-based order of free trade and monetary relations.[57]

Meanwhile, plans for a global monetary order were in the pipeline. Keynes had drafted a proposal for an International Clearing Union in February 1942, which he did not share with the exiles. Nevertheless, reflecting the 'desire to be taken more closely into the counsels of His Majesty's Government' evident in Sikorski's efforts to organise the exiles, the British Treasury invited the financial experts of the exiled governments to discuss their immediate post-war currency problems. Between July 1942 and February 1943, multiple meetings – which included Beyen, Alphand, Marjolin and Hubert Ansiaux (a Belgian central banker) – took place. Nevertheless, Keynes discussed matters with his 'American friends' first, effectively barring the exiles from what became the negotiations over the new Bretton Woods order.[58]

55 'Observations critiques', 23 February 1942, NL-HaNA, 2.05.80, inv. no. 2551.
56 'Rapport préliminaire sur les questions économiques, financières et sociales d'après-guerre', [January 1942], NL-HaNA, 2.05.80, inv. no. 2598.
57 'Conversation avec Monsieur van Zeeland', 25 March 1942, FD 2, HAEU.
58 'Meeting at Treasury', 24 July 1942, NL-HaNA, 2.21.408, inv. no 45; 'Dispatch', 23 March 1942, C 2230/1543/62, FO 371/30871, TNA; Jaspar to Spaak, 2 July 1942, PHS 90, HAEU.

This spurred the exiles to further develop their own plans for regional monetary order. From December 1942 onwards, Dutch and Belgian financial experts (including Beyen and Ansiaux) worked on a monetary agreement that would introduce a mechanism of payments between the two countries and thus stabilise temporary surpluses or deficits in the balance of payments. The agreement was signed in October 1943 and ultimately led to the creation of the Benelux after the war.[59] Moreover, as part of the continued effort by Sikorski and Retinger to bring Europe together, the exiles created the Comité des Ministres des Affaires Étrangères des Gouvernements Alliés during the autumn of 1942. One of the first things this committee did was to create a subcommittee tasked with studying the post-war economic reconstruction of Europe. It was Van Zeeland who became responsible for this undertaking.

After consulting a 'series of eminent personages of all the United Nations' (including Alphand), Van Zeeland finished his report in late 1942.[60] Most importantly, the report shows that Europe's exiles considered post-war economic reconstruction a world-wide responsibility, in which each country must strive for 'economic equilibrium [...] within the framework of a concerted international policy'. This concerted policy, according to Van Zeeland, was tied up with 'the betterment of the standard of living of all citizens' and the recognition that 'political security is reinforced by economic and social security'. The ultimate objective of this internationally concerted post-war economic policy was 'the suppression of endemic, generalised or permanent unemployment'. Among the exiles, Van Zeeland observed a preference for regional economic groups, rather than creating a global trade and monetary regime.[61] His report, for that matter, highlights a distinct social mission for post-war Europe, as well as a desire to achieve this together through regional entities.

The war highlighted two views on post-war international economic order. One was the fruit of Anglo-American planning and had a global character. The other was the result of exile-based planning in London, owed part of its existence to the Polish endeavours for a European-wide federation and was regional in its approach. It was only in the post-war period that the latter

59 J. W. L. Brouwer, 'Divergences d'intérêts et mauvaises humeurs. La France et les pays du Benelux devant la construction européenne, 1942–1950' (Ph.D. thesis, Leiden University, 1997), pp. 37–43.
60 'La France et les problèmes économiques d'après-guerre. Discours prononcé par M. Alphand à l'Institute Tchécoslovaque', 23 November 1942; Alphand to Jaspar, 30 November 1942, ARA, Papiers Jaspar, inv. no. 2176 and 23.
61 'Preliminary Notes on Certain Important Aspects of the Economic Reconstruction of Europe after the War', December 1942, NL-HaNA, 2.05.86, inv. no 260.

gained traction through the new Cold War realities, which effectively ended the prospects of global cooperation and prompted the American government to invest in the economic recovery of western Europe.

Into the Post-war Period: An 'Intermediate Stage'

In a way, the post-liberation period and return from exile was as chaotic and disruptive as the initial move to London in 1940. Once again European governments had to adjust to a new reality: that of the post-war period. By introducing social security legislation and pursuing policies of full employment, western European governments translated wartime demands for higher living standards into practical policies. International institutions comprised a vital aspect of this post-war social and economic stability. By a stabilisation of international currencies through the IMF, inflation could be kept in check, and international economic shocks affecting domestic social order could be cushioned so that they would not set in motion a retaliatory wave of protectionism. But the Bretton Woods institutions were predominantly unfit to deal with the material devastation of war and Europe was not yet ready for global currency convertibility.

It was in this context of post-war reconstruction that 'regionalism' emerged as a practical 'in between', albeit with limited success. The most compelling example is that of the Benelux countries. Another initiative to put regionalism in practice had been advanced by Alphand late in the war. In 1944, he had reached out to the Benelux governments and proposed a customs union with France. He was convinced that the global scope of Bretton Woods should be 'supplemented on an intermediate stage' and he therefore wanted to create 'one or more regional solutions in Europe'.[62] Eventually, Alphand's initiative led to the establishment of the Tripartite Council near the end of the war in March 1945. Its purpose was to study the possibilities of a customs union between the four countries.

From the outset, such examples of regional multilateralism suggest close cooperation and coordination in post-war European reconstruction. In reality, the different priorities of the countries involved caused grave difficulties. Within the Tripartite Council, the French government advocated a dismantling of German heavy industry, partly to shield its own economy from potential German competition and resurgent militarism.[63] Such

---

62 'Conference de Hervé Alphand au Centre d'Études Internationales École Libre des Hautes Études', 15 January 1944, AME 56/2/4, FJME.
63 Brouwer, 'Divergences d'intérêts', pp. 82–3.

a crippling of the German economy was intolerable for the Dutch, whose economy was closely linked to Germany. When the Dutch government sought compensation for the dismantling of German factories, this put them on a collision course with the French. Moreover, the Dutch government feared that, if the economic ties of the Netherlands with the German hinterland were severed, they would become too dependent on trade with France and Belgium. In the end, the monetary agreement between the Benelux countries, as well as the Tripartite Council, all hinged on bilateral trade and payments agreements.[64]

Despite these difficulties, regional multilateralism was considered a practical way to overcome bilateralism and to safeguard socio-economic stability. Within the Emergency Economic Committee for Europe – which administered aid to western Europe between 1945 and 1947 – one Dutch representative regarded 'regionality [. . .] as a progress beyond bilateralism, which in uncertain relations has proven to lead to economic nationalism and continues to lead to economic, but also political chaos'. Furthermore, regionality, or regionalism, could become a stepping stone to universalism, or the dam that could serve as a 'line of defence' in case the global economic system collapsed as it had in the 1930s.[65] Negative consequences of shrinking world trade could then be cushioned through a regional European framework.

By 1947, however, true monetary multilateralism in western Europe had not been achieved. Reflecting a scarcity of 'hard currency', intra-European trade was resumed on bilateral patterns. There was no automaticity or multilateralism in currency clearing, and countries tried to prevent the outflow of 'hard currency' by resorting to bilateral barter and exchange controls. By 1947, hundreds of bilateral trade treaties were created – turning Europe into a 'spaghetti bowl of [. . .] bilateral arrangements'.[66] These necessarily restricted the growth of both trade and production, as each country sought to protect its balance of payments by limiting its imports or exports. While this bilateralism was not as rigid as in the 1930s, the spectre of social and economic crises loomed in post-war Europe.

With the slow pace of European economic recovery, the general dollar shortages, rising communist influence in countries such as France and Italy, and souring relations between the United States and the Soviet Union over

64 R. T. Griffiths and F. M. B. Lynch, 'L'échec de la "Petite Europe"? Le Conseil Tripartite 1944–1948', Guerres mondiales et conflits contemporains 152 (1988): 39–62, 45–7.
65 A. Th. Lamping to L. J. M. Beel, 16 September 1946, NL-HaNA, 2.03.01, inv. no. 2798.
66 B. Eichengreen, The European Economy since 1945: Coordinated Capitalism and Beyond (Princeton, NJ and Oxford: Princeton University Press, 2007), p. 73.

the future of Germany, it was US Secretary of State George Marshall who ripped open the situation of stasis in June 1947. He offered to aid Europe in its economic recovery, as long as the Europeans promised to work together and come up with a joint programme for recovery. Marshall's offer kickstarted an intense 10-month-long deliberation between representatives of sixteen western European countries and the American government, which led to the creation of the OEEC in April 1948. Essentially, it was through this offer of economic aid that the Americans facilitated the rise of western European regionalism.

Bringing Europe Together in Paris

Between 1947 and 1950, the OEEC emerged as a socio-economic think tank for western Europe. Much of the intellectual groundwork had been done during the inter-war and wartime periods, and the necessity to prevent social chaos was ingrained in the minds of most policy-makers. Within the OEEC, these sentiments and ideas were translated into practical policies. For policy-makers like Alphand and Van Zeeland, the Marshall Plan presented the opportunity to take longstanding ideas about regional economic cooperation to the drawing table and transform them into actionable plans. Its most visible results were the OEEC's integrative monetary frameworks that emerged from 1947 onwards and culminated in the creation of the EPU in 1950.

By then, the OEEC had established an impressive bureaucratic workforce and acquired permanent headquarters at the Château de la Muette in Paris. Robert Marjolin became the OEEC's Secretary-General and was at the nerve centre of the novel European organisation, where financial experts developed an 'independent "European" point of view', enabling them to rise above national delegations and introduce new blueprints geared towards socio-economic stability.[67]

The first practical steps towards the EPU were taken during the summer of 1947, when the Committee for European Economic Cooperation assembled in Paris to create the joint European response to Marshall's policy initiative. The participating countries were Austria, Belgium, Denmark, France, Greece, Iceland, Ireland, Italy, Luxembourg, the Netherlands, Norway, Portugal, Sweden, Switzerland, Turkey and the UK. Hirschfeld, who remembered the failed World Economic Conference of London, believed that the

---

67 Lintott to Marjolin, 2 November 1949, ARM 4/6/1, FJME.

lessons of the 1930s should 'not be forgotten'. Convinced that the new European economic order should prevent 'long-term unemployment' and shocks to the social order, he desired a system of 'multi-lateral exchange of payments'. Should European countries fail to transcend the bilateralism in intra-European payments, they risked 'paving the way for a new European crisis'.[68]

Hirschfeld and his Belgian colleague Hubert Ansiaux presented a proposal for a multilateral payments system in July 1947. By making European currencies 'interchangeable' and enabling 'any country which showed an export surplus in one and an import surplus in another' to 'obtain payment which it would not receive otherwise', they hoped to increase intra-European trade. This system, which resembled the Van Zeeland proposal of 1938, required an American dollar-pool in order for it to work. Regional monetary multilateralism, it was envisioned, would allow western Europe a transition period during which economic life could be restored to normal so that the Bretton Woods institutions 'would be able to play the role they have been created for'.[69] The proposal was further developed by a group of financial experts, which included Ansiaux and Stoppani, as well as Raymond Bertrand and Edward Bernstein – two of Triffin's colleagues at the IMF.[70] Hirschfeld lobbied in Washington for a dollar-pool to back up the scheme, but failed to harness the necessary support, because the European Recovery Plan would be based on commodities instead of direct financial transactions.

Despite this, the committee of financial experts drafted an Agreement on Multilateral Monetary Compensation by October 1947 – a mere 4 months after Marshall's speech. Even though it amounted to no more than a bilateral clearing of intra-European payments through the BIS, to which only five countries subscribed, the scheme was met with optimism by Triffin. He had followed the developments in European payments plans on behalf of the IMF, and thought it could be a stepping stone to a much more ambitious 'European Clearing Union', through which countries could settle their balance-of-payments accounts with other countries by using their own currencies.[71]

---

68 H. M. Hirschfeld, *Actieve economische politiek in Nederland in de jaren 1929–1934* (Amsterdam, Elsevier, 1946), pp. 152–4; 'Memorandum Submitted by the Delegation for the Netherlands', 29 July 1947, NL-HaNA, 2.05.117, inv. no. 10487.
69 'Déclaration faite à la séance du Comité Exécutif par le délègue de la Belgique, au nom de la Belgique, du Luxembourg et des Pays-Bas', 31 July 1947, NL-HaNA, 2.21.183.08, inv. no. 20.
70 Maes, *Robert Triffin*, pp. 74–5, 83.
71 R. Triffin, 'The Unresolved Problem of Financing European Trade', 29 December 1947, Box 19, Triffin Papers, YUL. The memo was written in September 1947.

From April 1948 onwards, the OEEC discussed a follow-up to the Multilateral Compensations scheme in the context of the first division of Marshall Plan aid. To alleviate the impact of the reduced Congressional Marshall Plan appropriation for 1948–9, Europeans had to switch imports from the dollar zone with intra-European trade. For that, they needed a better functioning monetary system, in which the dollar played a less central role. The OEEC's Intra-European Payments Committee, chaired by Ansiaux and Stoppani and which included Triffin, paved the road. Triffin proposed to 'multilateralize the system now in existence' and was supported in this by Dutch financial expert F. A. G. Keesing, who warned his colleagues about the alternative of monetary anarchy and a 'general stoppage of trade' that could disrupt social life.[72]

Eventually, the OEEC agreed to a system of drawing rights, which effectively balanced the interests of both creditor and debtor states in intra-European payments. With the negotiations concerning both the division of aid and the new payments scheme in their final stages by early September 1948, the Belgian Chairman of the Council Jean-Charles Snoy et d'Oppuers noted that a failure to agree might have consequences of 'catastrophic proportions', which could put western Europe on track towards a 'reduction of its standard of living, to a dislocation of its economic structure and consequently to social disorder'.[73] After agreement regarding the Intra-European Payments Scheme (IEPS) and the division of aid was reached on 11 September, Alphand noted that a 'tragic regression in the general standard of living' had been avoided.[74] These utterances and recollections of social chaos are the reminders of what was constantly at the back of the minds of all OEEC policy-makers: preserving the social stability of a continent that had just emerged from a devastating war.

Not long after the signing of the IEPS, the American government asked the OEEC to increase its efforts aimed at trade liberalisation, which immediately raised concerns for Europe's socio-economic stability. After Marjolin and a delegation of the OEEC visited Washington to speak with representatives of the American government, they drafted an action programme to free trade from its bilateral shackles. The Council of the OEEC was adamant that trade liberalisation should follow 'an adequate system of intra-European

---

72 R. Triffin, 'Report on Recent Developments on European Clearing', 28 May 1948, Box 19, Triffin Papers, YUL; F. A. G. Keesing, 'Note on the Multilateralization of Intra-European Payments', Annex B, 18 June 1948, PC(48)7, OEEC, OECD.

73 Council, Minutes, 3 September 1948, C/M(48)38, OEEC, OECD.

74 'Exposé de M. Alphand', 11 September 1948, MAEF 341, HAEU.

payments'.[75] In other words, the OEEC put the cart of trade liberalisation behind the horse of an integrative monetary framework.

A new European monetary order was the only carrier upon which trade liberalisation could be grafted without harming Europe's social stability. Frank Figgures, who headed Marjolin's Trade and Finance Department, warned that the American pace of trade liberalisation was forcing Europe along 'dangerous paths'. Fast liberalisation would invoke intolerable competition from foreign markets. On the other hand, slow liberalisation could mean that Europe would 'never become competitive in world markets', which would have 'incalculable effects on the social stability of Europe'.[76] Marjolin agreed, but maintained that the 'danger to the European economic and social structure involved in letting the existing system persist' was even greater.[77]

Creating a multilateral intra-European payments system became a more urgent matter in 1949, with the half-way mark of the Marshall Plan approaching; all the more so because the OEEC showed signs of disunity and even disintegration – particularly because of British obstruction.[78] In the light of another reduced Congressional appropriation of Marshall Plan aid, and the proposed multilateralisation of intra-European payments, the British dragged their feet and clung to bilateralism because they feared that they would lose hard currency through intra-European trade. The British nearly torpedoed the division of aid for 1949–50 when they demanded a larger share.

This British reluctance to bind the UK to the continent motivated France to seek a third way between what Finance Minister Maurice Petsche dubbed the 'narrow British bilateralism' and the American proposals for multilateralisation and liberalisation.[79] Encouraged by the American administrator of the Economic Cooperation Administration (ECA) Paul Hoffman, who (in the light of the British attitude) called for the creation of multiple regional groupings, Petsche suggested that 'some of us can travel further and faster than others along the road of "European integration"'.[80]

75 'Proposals on the Organisation's Plan of Action for 1949-1950', 8 March 1949, CGM(49)8 (Final), OEEC, OECD.
76 Figgures to Marjolin, 26 April 1949, ARM 4/3/6, FJME.
77 'A Proposal for the Liberalisation of Intra-European Trade', 30 May 1949, ARM 4/3/8, FJME.
78 Council, Minutes, 11–12 August 1949, C/M(49)15(Prov.), Annex A, OEEC, OECD.
79 H. Alphand, L'étonnement d'être: Journal (1939–1973) (Paris, Fayard, 1977), p. 211.
80 'Statement by the French Minister of Finance and Economic Affairs', 29 October 1949, CGM(49)17, OEEC, OECD.

It was somewhat ironic that at the moment when American leaders finally seemed ready to adapt their strategy for global monetary multilateralism to a regional European variant, Europeans themselves thought in terms of even smaller entities. With the British having 'shunned away from the joint venture', Petsche led an initiative that became known as the 'Fritalux' and which amounted to an economic and monetary association between France, Italy and the Benelux countries.[81] Notwithstanding French ulterior motives of creating a favourable trading bloc that excluded West Germany, the crux was to liberalise trade and payments in a controlled fashion, without causing inflation, by keeping a 'maximum level of employment' and thereby also 'without risking [. . .] serious social unrest'.[82]

But the small-scale regionalism of Fritalux was torpedoed in favour of a larger OEEC-wide system for intra-European payments by the international civil servants of the OEEC. In December 1949, Figgures and Marjolin proposed a 'European monetary fund' – essentially a 'pool of European currencies' and American dollars through which (structural) surpluses and deficits on intra-European trade could be cleared.[83] Simultaneously, from the other side of the Atlantic, Richard Bissell, one of Hoffman's most seasoned financial experts, launched a proposal for a European Clearing Union. The proposal, which had come about as a result of deliberations by the ECA's financial experts (among whom Triffin also belonged), aimed to create an 'appropriate set of relations between obligations to provide credits and obligations to make settlements in gold or dollar'.[84] It came to pass as the Bissell Plan. Effectively, as Triffin noted, the regional approach, which had been pursued by France with the Fritalux, was now 'in the doldrums'.[85]

Together with a British counterproposal, the Bissell Plan and the Secretariat's proposal were entrusted to a group of financial experts headed by Ansiaux. By the end of December 1949, they had started referring to their project as 'X', or using 'the pool' as the designated name for creating a durable European payments mechanism that would overcome bilateral practices. They essentially aimed for the creation of a European Bretton Woods, or, as the British expert Hugh Ellis Rees put it, it was 'an attempt to

81 Dispatch by R. Schuman to French embassies, 3 November 1949, MAEF 351, HAEU.
82 'Memorandum', 14 November 1949, NL-HaNA, 2.05.117, inv. no. 24064.
83 'Trade and Payments Arrangements', 1 December 1949, OEEC 241, HAEU.
84 J. Wilson, Robert Triffin – Milieux académiques et cénacles économiques internationaux (1935–1951) (Brussels, Versant Sud, 2015), p. 624; 'Trade and Payments Arrangements', 9 December 1949, OEEC 241, HAEU.
85 Triffin to Tasca, 16 December 1949, Box 19, Triffin Papers, YUL.

provide transferability in the limited area of Europe, because the European countries were not yet ready for world-wide transferability'.[86]

In bringing this new monetary order about, the OEEC's financial experts were motivated by an esprit de corps that incorporated a strong inclination to bring about social stability. One delegate who took part in the discussions noted that the 'essential thing was to avoid the risk of the spread of unemployment from countries in which conditions of high unemployment and deflation exist'. Figgures maintained that 'Europe should be able to pay for its requirements by its earnings without a disastrous reduction in its standard of living'. Pierre Uri – a French professor of economics and intimate aide of Jean Monnet – joined the discussions in January 1950 and emphasised that the new system should permit countries with full employment policies to maintain these policies, while at the same time helping other countries to 'obtain full employment'.[87]

In December 1949 and January 1950, the financial experts created the foundations for the EPU. The most important factor was their recognition of the link between domestic employment policies, liberalisation of trade and multilateral payments. One of the central objectives of the EPU, according to their report of late January, was that it should help 'all members to achieve or maintain a high and stable level of trade and employment'. For the 'bold experiment' to work, all countries should aim at an equilibrium in their 'overall balance of payments', as well as 'internal financial equilibrium' – tolerating no internal deficit spending that could create inflationary tendencies. After all, both inflation and deflation should 'not be allowed to endanger the liberation of trade and the maintenance of a high and stable level of employment' and 'render ineffective' the proposed payments mechanism.[88]

After several months of intense negotiations – especially with the British over the position of sterling – the EPU became a fact of life.[89] The EPU members were Austria, Belgium, Denmark, France, Iceland, Italy, Luxembourg, the Netherlands, Norway, Portugal, Sweden, Switzerland, Turkey and West Germany. By early June, the British were accommodated through an American dollar-guarantee which compensated them for any loss

---

86 Minutes, Working Party No. 3, 28 December 1949, EPU/EMA 2, OECD. Other names that were used were European Currency Union, European Currency Reserve Fund and European Credit Union.

87 Minutes, Working Party No. 3, 28–29 December 1949 and 21 January 1950, EPU/EMA 2, OECD.

88 'Payments Arrangements', 24 January 1950, EPU/EMA 2, OECD.

89 See J. J. Kaplan and G. Schleiminger, *The European Payments Union: Financial Diplomacy in the 1950s* (Oxford, Clarendon Press, 1989).

of hard currency on intra-European payments. There was a great sense of relief among those involved. One of them was Marjolin, who also argued that the EPU should 'not be considered as a final goal but rather as a starting point for further progress'.[90] As such, the EPU was a solution to the 'state of bilateralism' that had hampered European economic relations for so long, and it became a 'starting point for further measures of liberalization and integration'.[91] The American government did not consider the EPU a 'miracle drug' that would 'cure' all of the economic problems Europe was grappling with, but saw it as a beginning for further trade liberalisation and European integration.[92] The door of the past, of bilateralism, economic instability and the looming threat of social instability, could finally be closed.

Conclusion

This chapter has shown how Europe's quest for socio-economic stability gained traction through the inter-war, war and post-war periods, and how it culminated in the creation of the EPU in 1950. The roots of Europe's post-war monetary integration must also be placed firmly against the background of the Bretton Woods institutions and Anglo-American wartime financial cooperation. The fact that the quest for socio-economic stability transpired in the integration of western Europe through monetary multilateralism at the OEEC is consistent with the emerging schism in the Cold War and with the longer thinking about western European regional economic order that emerged before and during the Second World War. In that sense, the Cold War and the American intervention in Europe by way of the Marshall Plan merely provided a window of opportunity for European policy-makers to secure their socio-economic priorities of maintaining high employment and low inflation in a western European framework.

While the EPU would have a rough start due to a German balance-of-payments crisis, it signalled a momentous event in European integration. West Germany, by way of the integrative monetary policies of the OEEC, was brought back into the 'European family', as Marjolin so eloquently put it after the conclusion of the IEPS in October 1948.[93] While it hardly had a voice in bringing it about, as its representatives had only been observers to OEEC

---

90 'Statement by the Secretary General', 2 June 1950, C(50)149, OEEC, OECD.
91 'Proposals for an E.P.U.', 14 June 1950, PC(50)31, OEEC, OECD.
92 Tasca to Bissell, 3 July 1950, Box 50, UD 59, RG 469, NARA.
93 'The Agreement for Intra-European Payments and Compensations', 19 November 1948, ARM 7/5/2, FJME.

matters until October 1949, the EPU eventually became a platform upon which West Germany could resume its economic relations with the rest of the continent. Thus, the EPU was at least as important as the creation of the ECSC for West Germany, also because it amounted to economic integration beyond coal and steel. Moreover, with the smooth functioning of the EPU, the participating countries of the OEEC gradually continued the work on a common market through practices of trade liberalisation. To avoid upsetting Europe's socio-economic stability, this happened in a controlled and gradual fashion – just as Van Zeeland had proposed in 1938. The OEEC provided the monetary multilateral framework upon which further European integration – for example, through the ECSC – could move forward.

Recommended Reading

Beyen, J. W. *Money in a Maelstrom* (New York, NY, Macmillan, 1949).

Clavin, P. *Securing the World Economy: The Reinvention of the League of Nations, 1920–1946* (Oxford, Oxford University Press, 2013).

Maier, C. S. *In Search of Stability: Explorations in Historical Political Economy* (Cambridge, Cambridge University Press, 1987).

Milward, A. S. *The Reconstruction of Western Europe, 1945–51* (London, Methuen & Co., 1984).

Patel, K. K. *Project Europe: A History* (Cambridge and New York, NY, Cambridge University Press, 2020).

Segers, M. L. L. 'Eclipsing Atlantis: Trans-Atlantic Multilateralism in Trade and Monetary Affairs as a Pre-history to the Genesis of Social Market Europe (1942–1950)', *Journal of Common Market Studies* 57, no. 1 (2019): 60–76.

Van Zeeland, P. *A View of Europe, 1932: An Interpretative Essay on Some Workings of Economic Nationalism* (Baltimore, MD, The Johns Hopkins University Press, 1933).

8

Competition versus Planning: A Battle That Shaped European Integration

LAURENT WARLOUZET

The European Union (EU) and its forerunner, the European Economic Community (EEC), have been economically organised around a market-oriented philosophy, which has been fed by a constant debate between two opposite poles: indicative planning and competition. This chapter will revisit the history of internal European economic policies, notably in the monetary, industrial and competition realms, by demonstrating that European institutions have usually carried on thanks to successive compromises between planning and competition and that, despite the latter's rise since the 1990s, the contest is not yet over, especially since the advent of the Covid-19 pandemic.

More generally, the debate between planning and competition echoes the long-term controversy between the promoters of free trade and those who are willing to bend free-market rules. The unity of both of these groups should not be overestimated: the second camp consists on the one hand of neomercantilists, who favour industrial development by protectionist measures, and on the other hand of promoters of socially oriented policies, who focus on the most vulnerable; the first group is composed of classical liberals but also of neoliberals.[1] The latter are those who consider competition to be the overarching principle around which society ought to be organised, and thus aim to reduce welfare state provisions.

More precisely, *planning* has been an influential economic philosophy in Europe since the 1930s. In contrast to the Soviet model of imperative planning, the West implemented a liberal version, usually called 'indicative planning'.[2] It translated into the coordination of economic actors by the state

---

1 On the distinction between market-oriented, socially oriented and neomercantilist policies, see L. Warlouzet, *Governing Europe in a Globalizing World: Neoliberalism and Its Alternatives Following the 1973 Oil Crisis* (London, Routledge, 2018); L. Warlouzet, *Europe contre Europe: Entre liberté, solidarité et puissance* (Paris, CNRS Éditions, 2022).

2 M. Christian, S. Kott and O. Matějka (eds.), *Planning in Cold War Europe: Competition, Cooperation, Circulations (1950s–1970s)* (Berlin, De Gruyter, 2018).

authorities (usually after a process of extensive consultation) around soft and non-binding targets, and also involved the use of various tools of macroeconomic and microeconomic policies designed to steer the economy, to channel free-market forces towards the best possible outcome for the society as a whole. Planning rests on the belief that the centralisation of information by public authorities would allow them to maximise growth and other public interest goals, such as enhancing social care or reducing regional disparities, and therefore that public authorities must make explicit political choices. As a result, planning is often associated with ambitious macroeconomic, industrial, social and regional policies that rest on the principle of positive discrimination: public authorities play an important role in choosing who will benefit from certain economic advantages, such as cheap credit, state aid or tax breaks. Planning was a major economic reference in western Europe from the 1940s to the 1970s,[3] and has remained influential after this period in a different guise, such as various attempts at international macroeconomic coordination or at European regional and industrial policy.

In contrast, promoters of *competition* believe that market mechanisms are the best way to maximise collective well-being. Since pure and perfect competition never exists in reality, public authorities have an important role to play to ensure that the stronger actors are not bending free-market rules by imposing excessively high prices.[4] These public authorities must strive to be neutral, like an umpire, without favouring any particular economic actor. As a result, not only does an economic policy based on the principle of competition shy away from the discriminating public measures mentioned above – cheap credit, state aid and tax breaks – but also it should target private practices detrimental to the free setting of prices – such as cartels, mergers leading to oligopolies and monopolies, and the abuse of a dominant position. Private firms have been targeted by US antitrust policy, and then in western Europe after 1945 under the name of 'competition policy'. The EU and its forerunner represent an interesting case as EEC/EU competition policy has targeted both private and public firms, as well as public market regulations, a unique situation in the world. The EU has managed to push the expansion of free-market rules for many areas that were not affected by such rules in the past. Moreover, the European and Monetary Union (EMU) defined in the 1992 Maastricht Treaty is usually associated with a rule-based order predicated upon free-market rules, rather than on a state-led steering of the economy.

---

3 A. Shonfield, *Modern Capitalism: The Changing Balance of Public and Private Power* (Oxford, Oxford University Press, 1965), p. 121.
4 D. Gerber, *Law and Competition in XXth Century Europe: Protecting Prometheus* (Oxford, Clarendon Press, 1998).

The literature has not tackled this question directly, except for one article published in 2019 that covered a shorter timeframe, and with a stronger focus on German ordoliberalism and on French Colbertism.[5] On the whole, the history of EU internal economic policies is dominated by the history of monetary integration, which has led to extensive coverage in the political science and historical literature, with a heavy emphasis on the 1970s and 1980s; coverage of the history of non-monetary economic policies, however, has been considerably more limited. The literature on the history of EU competition policy is thriving, but is not particularly concerned with planning. Notable authors on the history of EEC/EU competition policy include Pinar Akman, Hubert Buch-Hansen, Tim Büthe, Michelle Cini, David Gerber, Brigitte Leucht, Lee McGowan, Kiran Klaus Patel, Sigfrido Ramírez-Pérez, Heike Schweitzer, Katja Seidel and Angela Wigger. The various explicit projects of European planning represent a hitherto neglected topic, except for a few exceptions.[6]

A first short section will examine the institutional foundation of the EEC/EU between 1948 and 1957, by showing that the Treaty of Rome was quite flexible in terms of economic interpretation. The next two sections will delve into the two rival interpretations of the treaty which were devised in the 1960s – but not fully implemented – of which one was based on competition and the other on planning. The following section will then shift to the 1970s, when a last attempt at comprehensive European planning was launched – but eventually materialised only by a failed attempt at macroeconomic coordination dubbed the 'locomotive'. At this point, the section on the 1980s and 1990s will then zero in on the rise of competition policy. A concluding section will highlight that remnants of planning ideology still characterise current EU policies.

The Treaties' Uncertainties

The first European institutions active in the economic field were created between 1948 and 1957 and were all based on a compromise between planning and competition that reflected the prevailing mood in western Europe in

5 L. Warlouzet, 'The EEC/EU as an Evolving Compromise between French Dirigism and German Ordoliberalism (1957–1995)', *Journal of Common Market Studies* 57 (2019): 77–93.
6 L. Warlouzet, *Le choix de la CEE par la France: L'Europe économique en débat de Mendès France à de Gaulle (1955–1969)* (Paris, Cheff, 2011); K. Seidel, 'Robert Marjolin: Securing the Common Market through Economic and Monetary Union', in K. Dyson and I. Maes (eds.), *Architects of the Euro: Intellectuals in the Making of European Monetary Union* (Oxford, Oxford University Press, 2016), pp. 51–73; H. Canihac, 'Un marché sans économistes? La planification et l'impossible émergence d'une science économique européenne (1957–1967)', *Revue française de science politique* 69 (2019): 95–116.

those days. On the one hand, the impetus of reconstruction, the shortages of basic materials (food rationing was generally in force until the late 1940s at least) and prevalent protectionism empowered the state. Even the Americans envisaged the Marshall Plan as an effort to coordinate the reconstruction efforts of European countries, even though its actual implementation eventually gave more leeway to national governments.[7] Beyond this short-term necessity, the need to give a stronger role to public authorities in steering the economy was also predicated on long-term trends, such as the discredit of *laissez-faire* liberalism, which had been associated with the worsening of the 1929 crisis, and the necessity of rebuilding the nation-state covering a larger social basis with an inclusive welfare state. Hence, the state role in the economy grew in many countries compared with the pre-war period (or the pre-fascist era), with nationalisation, extensive welfare state reforms and regional policy. Planning, an idea associated with the 1930s debate concerning the reforms necessary to tackle the Great Depression (especially in 1930s Belgium),[8] was not implemented, except in France.[9] Building on a longstanding dirigist tradition, Paris established a planning agency in 1946. The Commissariat général au Plan elaborated non-binding targets for the French economy, after a process of consultation, and channelled the sparse funds available (notably Marshall Plan aid) to high-priority sectors.

The other lesson of the 1930s was the necessity to shy away from protectionism, and hence to promote liberal internationalism, both from the political perspective and from the economic point of view. The majority of Western elites and people supported an American-led reconstruction predicated upon the restoration of international free trade, to be combined with an inclusive national welfare state, a compromise later dubbed 'embedded liberalism' or 'Keynes at home and Smith abroad'.[10] Only in Germany was

---

7 A. S. Milward, *The Reconstruction of Western Europe, 1945–1951* (London, Routledge, 1984).

8 T. Milani, 'The Planist Temptation: Belgian Social Democracy and the State During the Great Depression, c. 1929–c. 1936', in M. Fulla and M. Lazar (eds.), *European Socialists and the State in the Twentieth and Twenty-First Centuries* (Basingstoke, Palgrave Macmillan, 2020), pp. 77–96.

9 R. Kuisel, *Capitalism and the State in Modern France: Renovation and Economic Management in the Twentieth Century* (Cambridge, Cambridge University Press, 1983); P. Nord, *France's New Deal: From the Thirties to the Postwar Era* (Princeton, NJ, Princeton University Press, 2010); A. Shennan, *Rethinking France: Plans for Renewal 1940–1946* (Oxford, Oxford University Press, 1989); G. Bossuat (ed.), *Jean Monnet et l'économie* (Brussels, Peter Lang, 2018).

10 R. Claassen, A. Gerbrandy and S. Princen, 'Rethinking the European Social Market Economy: Introduction to the Special Issue', in *Journal of Common Market Studies* 57, no. 1 (2019): 3–12; J. G. Ruggie, 'International Regimes, Transactions, and Change: Embedded Liberalism in the Postwar Economic Order', *International Organization* 36 (1982): 379–415.

the Keynesian influence more limited as liberalism came back to the fore with a local variant, ordoliberalism, which was not hegemonic but still influential.[11] Active state policy aimed at steering the economy bore the stigma of the national socialist past, which had combined totalitarianism, capitalism and economic dirigism.[12] Instead, ordoliberals assigned a limited but crucial role to the state: that of enabling free-market forces to go unimpeded. They considered that the public authorities should not meddle with free-market dynamics through discriminatory policies, but should instead remain as neutral as possible. While other influences were visible in post-1945 Germany (notably corporatism, social democracy and social Christian thought, visible notably in codetermination), ordoliberalism certainly influenced economic leaders such as Ludwig Erhard to some extent,[13] through the establishment of independent authorities which were given extensive powers and a wide autonomy from the national government, such as the central bank (the Bundesbank, in 1957) and the competition authority (the Bundeskartellamt, in 1957). Both of those reforms were quite specific to Germany. In the rest of western Europe, a stronger role for the state in steering the economy was generally considered as a given in the 1940s and 1950s, in combinaiton with the restoration of free-market rules. In eastern Europe, the Soviet Union imposed centralised planning.

The first two European institutions, the Organisation for European Economic Co-Operation (OEEC), set up in 1948, and the European Coal and Steel Community (ECSC) born in 1952 were both quite ambitious with regard to planning, while being at the same time predicated upon the promotion of international free trade. In the minds of its US promoters, the OEEC was meant to serve as a coordinating body for national plans. However, it ended up being just an intergovernmental club, which let nation-states rebuild their countries as they saw fit, provided that they abided by the common rules promoting a progressive restoration of intra-European trade.[14]

---

11 W. Abelshauser, *Deutsche Wirtschaftsgeschichte seit 1945* (Munich, C. H. Beck, 2004); M. Spoerer and J. Streb, *Neue deutsche Wirtschaftsgeschichte des 20. Jahrhunderts* (Munich, Oldenbourg, 2013); J. Hien and C. Joerges, 'Dead Man Walking: Current European Interest in the Ordoliberal Tradition', European University Institute Working Paper (2018), https://cadmus.eui.eu/handle/1814/51226.

12 Gerber, *Law and Competition in XXth Century Europe*.

13 M. Segers, 'Eclipsing Atlantis: Trans-Atlantic Multilateralism in Trade and Monetary Affairs as a Pre-history to the Genesis of Social Market Europe (1942–1950)', *Journal of Common Market Studies* 57 (2019): 60–76; V. Hentschel, *Ludwig Erhard, die "soziale Marktwirtschaft" und das Wirtschaftswunder: Historisches Lehrstück oder Mythos?* (Bonn, Bouvier Verlag, 1998).

14 A. S. Milward, *The Reconstruction of Western Europe, 1945–1951* (London, Routledge, 1984).

Later on, in 1960, the OEEC was replaced by the Organisation for Economic Co-operation and Development (OECD), which played an important role in the circulation of economic ideas in the Western world.[15]

Back in the late 1940s, the idea of coordinating the national policies of reconstruction, in particular in the most important sectors for transnational trade, such as steelmaking, remained important. It was aired by major European politicians during the conference of Westminster, held in 1949 by the European movement as a follow-up to the better known 1948 conference held in The Hague. The ECSC, set up in 1952, followed this approach: it brought together six countries in a tight-knit community, which was for the first time semi-supranational. Major powers were devolved to the ECSC authorities, notably to its supranational body, the High Authority, in terms of industrial policy. Tellingly, the first head of the High Authority was Jean Monnet, the first head of the French planning agency. The US and French promoters of the ECSC were willing to use the Community to prevent any recartellisation of German industry, and any domination of the latter over the European economy, so they entrusted the High Authority with considerable power to control, and even monitor, prices, investments, mergers and so on. In parallel, a common market for coal and steel based on free competition had to be set up. Here again, however, the High Authority did not live up to expectations. Its record in terms of competition and industrial policy was uninspiring.[16]

The reverse was true for the 1957 Treaty of Rome that created the EEC, which went farther than expected, without choosing explicitly between competition and planning. As a framework, the Treaty of Rome was flexible enough to accommodate many different economic approaches[17]. Articles 2 and 3 of the EEC Treaty stating its aims include market-oriented and social aims. Article 3 in particular lists the tasks to be carried out, which included 'the creation of a European Social Fund', but also the 'establishment of a European Investment Bank intended to facilitate the economic expansion of the Community through the creation of new resources' (which, according to most negotiators, meant channelling funds to the poorest region of the Community, namely the Mezzogiorno) and 'the association of overseas

15 M. Leimgruber and M. Schmelzer (eds.), *The OECD and the International Political Economy since 1948* (Cham, Palgrave Macmillan, 2017).

16 T. Witschke and L. Warlouzet, 'The Difficult Path to an Economic Rule of Law: European Competition Policy, 1950–1991', *Contemporary European History* 21 (2012): 437–55.

17 A. S. Milward, *The European Rescue of the Nation-State* (London, Routledge, 1992); A. Moravcsik, *The Choice for Europe: Social Purpose and State Power from Messina to Maastricht* (Ithaca, NY, Cornell University Press, 1998).

countries and territories with the Community with a view to increasing trade and to pursuing jointly their effort towards economic and social development'.

The EEC was predicated upon a market-oriented dynamic as its main objective was the establishment of 'The Common Market'. National planning was not affected by the macroeconomic clauses of the treaties, which were limited. Hence, the national credit policies, which were sometimes very discriminatory (notably in France[18]) could continue unimpeded. An EEC-wide competition policy was established by the Treaty of Rome, but its content remained vague, as its provisions resulted from an unambitious Franco-German compromise, with both governments prioritising their national competition policy over the European ones. Provisions on state aid, which could affect industrial and regional policy, were ambiguous. (In particular Article 90 EEC §2, which stated that: 'Any enterprise charged with the management of services of general economic interest or having the character of a fiscal monopoly shall be subject to the rules contained in this Treaty, in particular to those governing competition, to the extent that the application of such rules does not obstruct the de jure or de facto fulfilment of the specific tasks entrusted to such enterprise.') Article 222 of the EEC Treaty explicitly protected nationalised companies. Therefore, the debate over the interpretation of the Treaty of Rome remained open.

The Failed Competition Offensive in the 1960s

The EEC economic policies logically unfolded following a dominant market-oriented approach in the 1960s: internal trade barriers were progressively lifted and disappeared in 1968, while external trade barriers were periodically diminished after international negotiations, conducted by EEC institutions (the Commission and the Council). Most of the national credit, industrial, regional and social policies were left untouched. The only exception was the Common Agricultural Policy (CAP), which followed a neomercantilist approach: internal production was protected by high tariff barriers and supported by huge subsidies. But there was no element of planning in the CAP because its main lever was prices. Hence, any action on the sector's industrial and social structure was indirect.[19]

---

18 E. Monnet, *Controlling Credit: Central Banking and the Planned Economy in Postwar France, 1948–1973* (Cambridge, Cambridge University Press, 2019).

19 K. K. Patel (ed.), *Fertile Ground for Europe? The History of European Integration and the Common Agricultural Policy since 1945* (Baden-Baden, Nomos Verlag, 2009); K. Seidel,

Some European actors wanted to go further by promoting competition as the overarching principle of European economic policies. German Christian-Democrat actors influenced to some extent by ordoliberalism were especially active, notably Hans von der Groeben, the first commissioner for competition. A shrewd European politician and a staunch supporter of European integration, von der Groeben had taken part in the negotiations of the Rome Treaty and had managed to overcome both internal German reluctance towards the EEC, notably from Erhard, and the vast discrepancies among the Six's positions.[20] As a commissioner for competition, von der Groeben secured another success, with an ambitious regulation of cartels, adopted in 1962 and known as Regulation 17/62. It interpreted the Rome Treaty by giving extensive powers to the Commission, which thereby received a monopoly on information, via the notification procedure, and on decisions regarding whether to authorise a cartel. A committee of member state experts was set up, but it was merely consultative.

The literature on Regulation 17/62 fails to highlight two facts, first that many alternatives had been seriously discussed, and as a consequence von der Groeben thus secured a significant success, including against his German compatriots, and secondly that this provision on cartels was only a first step in a larger offensive to promote the principle of competition.[21] In Bonn, initially, the German Ministry of Economics did not want to develop a supranational EEC competition policy. Its leading priority was to preserve the capability of the newly founded Bundeskartellamt. It chose to support von der Groeben's vision only in order to escape a decidedly worse scenario in which French officials would impose their own vision, based on the promotion of non-competition criteria such as industrial, social and regional considerations. In other words, competition policy would have been submitted to an approach more inspired by planning. In the end, however, Regulation 17/62 created a policy focused on cartels, based exclusively on the competition criteria, and implemented almost exclusively by the European Commission (bar the judicial control of the Court). Even after the regulation was passed, German officials were sometimes critical of von der Groeben's policy. For example, they opposed the Commission's

'Adjusting a Flagship Policy: The Common Agricultural Policy in the 1970s and 1980s', in E. Bussière, V. Dujardin, M. Dumoulin et al. (eds.), *Histoire de la Commission européenne, 1973–86* (Brussels, European Commission, 2014), pp. 313–28.

20 B. Löffler, *Soziale Marktwirtschaft und administrative Praxis* (Stuttgart, Franz Steiner, 2002), p. 548. On von der Groeben and ordoliberalism, see also S. Hambloch, 'EEC Competition Policy in the Early Phase of European Integration', *Journal of European Integration History* 17 (2011): 237–51, 238–9.

21 Warlouzet, *Governing Europe*, pp. 157–9.

initial decision to ban a cartel, the Grundig–Consten case, which concerned a distribution agreement between a German producer (Grundig) and a French distributor (Consten).[22] The German government was against the ban because exclusive dealing agreements were a useful tool to penetrate foreign markets (and thus increase competition within the Common Market) for it. The German government later decided to support Grundig's appeal against the decision before the European Court of Justice. The German officials in the Ministry of Economics took this decision after consulting with the advocate-general of the European Court of Justice, Karl Roemer. In the end, the Court merely annulled part of the Grundig–Consten decision and broadly supported the Commission. Therefore, the European competition offensive was not German, in the sense that it did not originate in the German government in Bonn, even if it was carried out by some officials of German nationality. As a matter of fact, the Director General for Competition, who dutifully implemented von der Groeben's agenda, was the Dutch lawyer Pieter verLoren van Themaat.

Besides, the cartel regulation was only a first step in a broader agenda to promote the competition principle. In 1962, von der Groeben hired Ernst-Joachim Mestmäcker, a disciple of Franz Böhm, who was linked to the ordoliberals.[23] Mestmäcker, an important figure among the neoliberal 'globalists' examined by Quinn Slobodian,[24] was assigned the ambitious task of examining the most detrimental state intervention in the economy from the competition point of view. Many French practices, in particular certain types of public regulation of the oil sector, were examined in work conducted in 1963 and 1964.[25] Then, in a speech delivered in June 1965, von der Groeben asserted that the entire EEC 'economic policy' had to be driven by competition policy norms, and therefore that many public interventions in the economy (including monopolies granted to state-owned companies) that could infringe on intra-European trade had to be kept to a minimum.[26] To some extent, this agenda anticipates the neoliberal streak of the late 1980s.

22 On this German episode, based on German archives, see Warlouzet, *Governing Europe*, p. 158.
23 K. Seidel, *The Process of Politics in Europe: The Rise of European Elites and Supranational Institutions* (London, I. B. Tauris, 2010), pp. 135–9.
24 Q. Slobodian, *Globalists: The End of Empire and the Birth of Neoliberalism* (Cambridge, MA, Harvard University Press, 2018), pp. 204, 214, 250.
25 EU archives, Commission, BAC 31/1984/769, note Mestmäcker, 22 October 1963; notes on meetings with Mestmäcker, 13 December 1963 and 5 March 1964.
26 French archives, Foreign Affairs Ministry, RPUE 615, note on von der Groeben's discourse, 16 June 1965.

In the end, this quest led nowhere, as the European competition commissioners were too weak to promote this task. In the 1960s, the Directorate General (DG) for competition was paralysed by the flow of notifications of cartels it received once Regulation 17/62 was in force. It struggled to implement it effectively, and took only a few decisions on cartels, triggering much criticism from the member states for its inefficiencies. In the 1970s, the competition policy commissioners tried to enlarge their competences to new areas, such as mergers and state aid control, but to no avail as they faced stern opposition from neomercantilist actors both within the Commission and in the Council of Ministers.[27] At the same time, a rival European project based on planning was devised in Brussels.

The Project of French-Inspired European Planning

In the 1960s, planning ideas became fashionable in western Europe, in the context of a growing circulation of economic ideas between the East and the West.[28] The apparent economic success of the Soviet Union, which had been the first country to launch a satellite into space with Sputnik in 1957, seemed to bolster the case for state intervention in the economy. With the continuous enlargement of the welfare state in many Western countries, including in the virulently capitalist United States with Medicare and Medicaid in 1965, and the rising technological challenge that only large-scale institutions seemed able to master, the role of the state in the economy seemed bound to increase. Intellectual speculation over convergence between the East and the West's economic policies abounded.

In France, indicative planning bounced back in the 1960s under President Charles de Gaulle. The first plan, launched in 1946, was rather dirigist as it sought to allocate limited resources to a small number of sectors that were deemed to be essential to the reconstruction of the country. In the 1960s, the French economy was embracing mass consumption and opening to international competition. Planning thus morphed into a voluntary coordination of all actors in economic and social policies, in particular state actors, but also non-state ones such as trade unions and business. The aim was not to set targets in stone, but rather to create a shared consensus on priorities. As Pierre Massé, the head of the French planning agency from 1959 to 1966

27 Warlouzet, *Governing Europe*, pp. 158–9 and 166–8.
28 Christian, Kott and Matějka (eds.), *Planning in Cold War Europe*; J. Bockman, *Markets in the Name of Socialism: The Left-Wing Origins of Neoliberalism* (Stanford, CA, Stanford University Press, 2011).

explained: 'devising a plan counts more than having the plan'.[29] What was important was the process of consultation and of voluntary coordination among all actors under the state's steering, and not the final document. Free-market forces were not rejected. On the contrary, the main overall objective of the Fifth Plan was to improve international competitiveness. This was made explicit by de Gaulle himself.[30] In the end, France's exceptionally high growth rate during the 1960s (higher than that of its neighbours) led Harvard experts to examine French planning.[31]

French planning became a model for many thinkers, such as the British Andrew Shonfield, who noted that agencies similar to the French ones blossomed all over Europe in the early 1960s, notably in all EEC countries except Germany.[32] In the UK, a National Economic Development Council was established in 1962, but its staff, its ambitions and its powers were limited. In 1964, the Labour government created a National Board for Prices and Incomes with the Trades Union Congress. In 1965, a Department of Economic Affairs was created, whose task was to devise a National Plan. In Italy, the intervention of the state in industry had steadily increased under fascist rule, with the creation of the massive public industrial conglomerate Istituto per la Ricostruzione Industriale (IRI) in 1933. In 1950, the Cassa per il Mezzogiorno was created to tackle the south's underdevelopment. From 1962 onwards and through the 1960s, the Italian state developed explicit indicative plans to industrialise and modernise the infrastructure for the whole country, notably through IRI and the Cassa.[33]

Even in the Federal Republic of Germany, the mood shifted perceptively. While the West German leaders remained deeply hostile to the notion of general and comprehensive 'planning', which was associated with the reviled Soviet Union and East Germany, the introduction of some planning methods was discussed by experts and civil servants in the 1960s.[34]

29 P. Massé, 'Introductory Comments', in J. H. McArthur and B. R. Scott, *Industrial Planning in France* (Boston, MA, Graduate School of Business Administration, Harvard University, 1969), pp. xvii–xxii.

30 Letter from President C. de Gaulle to Prime Minister G. Pompidou, 24 July 1965, in C. de Gaulle, *Lettres, notes et carnets*, vol. x: *Janvier 1964–juin 1966* (Paris, Plon, 1987), pp. 181–2.

31 J. H. McArthur and B. R. Scott, *Industrial Planning in France*.

32 Shonfield, *Modern Capitalism*, p. 121.

33 F. Lavista, 'Structural Policies, Regional Development and Industrial Specialization in Italy, 1952–2002', *Jahrbuch für Wirtschaftsgeschichte* 58, no. 1 (2017): 83–105, 90–1; C. Grabas, 'Industrial Policy in Italy between Boom and Crisis, 1950–1975', in C. Grabas and A. Nützenadel (eds.), *Industrial Policies in Europe after 1945* (Basingtsoke, Palgrave Macmillan, 2014), pp. 134–61, 150–1.

34 A. Nützenadel, 'Die BRD, Frankreich und die Debatte über eine europäische Wirtschaftspolitik, 1958–65', *Francia* 30 (2003): 84–6.

The debate revolved around the improvement of statistics and the long-term planning of certain public policies. It did not relate to the orientation of private actors as in France. The perception of planning methods evolved more favourably in West Germany after the recession of 1966–7, which led to a short-lived Keynesian burst under Karl Schiller (Schiller was one of the rare top German politicians convinced that there was a case for Keynesian-inspired economic policy aimed at steering the economy), but the adoption of the centralised and state-driven French model was still out of the question.[35]

Drawing on this favourable context, the first European commissioner for economic affairs, the french socialist Robert Marjolin, launched a project of European planning in 1962. It was called 'European programming' and then 'middle-term economic policy' as the term planning was taboo in Germany.[36] The idea was to establish a voluntary coordination of all economic and social policies at the European level, first by consultations and later by a progressive process of Europeanisation. The European commissioner developed very ambitious aims, close to those heralded in the Fourth French Plan, namely to prioritise collective investments over individual consumption, which was seen as symbolic of the excesses of mass consumer society. He was supported by a European network of planners composed in particular of Belgian and Italian officials, mostly European and national civil servants. In the end, Marjolin succeeded in creating a committee for mid-term policy in 1964, but it was only consultative.

In parallel, Marjolin was considering the development of tools to coordinate macroeconomic policies.[37] In 1959, German Deputy Minister for Economy Alfred Müller-Armack had proposed to set up within the OEEC a 'European board of conjuncture' aimed at coordinating short-term macroeconomic policies. His aim was to promote stability-oriented policies. Marjolin took up the proposal for the EEC and removed its competition-only focus. This led to the creation of the committee for short-term economic policies in 1960, but it was merely a consultative body of national civil servants. Later, Marjolin combined forces with Jean Monnet and the Belgian economist Robert Triffin to advocate for more ambitious institutions, such as a European reserve fund or a compulsory coordination of

---

35 A. Nützenadel, *Stunde der Ökonomen: Wissenschaft, Politik und Expertenkultur in der Bundesrepublik 1949–1974* (Göttingen, Vandenhoeck & Ruprecht, 2005), pp. 303–306.

36 On this project, its devising and its implementation between 1960 and 1967, see Warlouzet, *Le choix de la CEE*, pp. 339–56.

37 The following development is based on Warlouzet, *Le choix de la CEE*, pp. 357–69.

monetary policies, but to no avail.[38] In 1964, Marjolin obtained but two supplementary consultative committees gathering civil servants, the budget-ary committee and the committee of governors of central banks.

His planning offensive triggered a counter-offensive. The German Economic Minister Ludwig Erhard attacked the Marjolin Programme at the European Parliament in November 1962.[39] Interestingly, the German President of the European Commission, the Christian Democrat Walter Hallstein, intervened to defend his colleague's project (which was endorsed by the entire team of commissioners). However, Hallstein did not use the same line of argument as Marjolin or the French planners. He deliberately included the 'Marjolin Programme' in the free-market economy, in particular by quoting Walter Eucken, an economist considered as one of the fathers of ordoliberalism. Within the Commission, Hans von der Groeben was the most vocal critic of Marjolin's projects during the internal meeting of the Commission.[40]

More generally, member states disapproved of this project as it was too ambitious. In 1964, the German government finally agreed to create a committee on mid-term policy only because it was merely consultative and would be chaired by a German junior minister, Wolfram Langer.[41] Langer was close to actors influenced by ordoliberal thinking.[42] The French government was very sceptical, too. The French commissioner had devised his projects with the support of several European experts, but independently from the French government. It did not help that the French socialist and pro-European Marjolin had tense relations with the French President Charles de Gaulle.[43]

European planning was thus stillborn, but its intellectual impact remained large. For example, the European Trade Union Confederation (ETUC) organised a large conference on planning in February 1968.[44] The project bounced back a few years later.

38 D. Howarth and J. Schild, 'France and European Macro-economic Policy Coordination: From the Treaty of Rome to the Euro Area Sovereign Debt Crisis', *Modern & Contemporary France* 25 (2017): 171–90; Warlouzet, *Governing Europe*, pp. 147–9.
39 On Erhard and the economist Wilhelm Röpcke, see Segers, 'Eclipsing Atlantis'.
40 Warlouzet, *Le choix de la CEE*, pp. 374–6.
41 Nützenadel, 'Die BRD, Frankreich und die Debatte', 90–1.
42 Bundesarchiv, Koblenz, B 102/134647, letter from W. Langer to A. Müller-Armack, 8 February 1961.
43 Jean Monnet Foundation, Lausanne, private papers of Robert Marjolin, ARM 25/1, notes on two meetings with de Gaulle, on 18 December 1958 and 7 February 1964.
44 Archives of the ETUC, Amsterdam, 2063, Secrétariat syndical européen, 'Les Expériences nationales et communautaire en matière de programmation économique, conférence de Milan, janvier–février 1968'.

From European Planning to the 'Locomotive' Attempt

In the late 1970s, the idea of planning made a comeback at the European level as a tool to fight the economic crisis which engulfed the continent after the 1973 oil-price shock. Two attempts failed: a large-scale project of European planning and a more targeted attempt at coordinating macroeconomic policies.

In 1976, an influential and often cited document was released, the Maldague Report, with the sub-title 'A New Framework for Planning and Negotiation'.[45] This new planning was embedded in the liberal democratic order as it was based on an extensive process of consultation. Each plan had to set targets by sectors and by regions not only from an economic point of view (in terms of outputs), but also from the social point of view. Free-market rules were respected, but it was envisioned that companies should notify their most important investments to the central authorities. Multinational companies had to be controlled to ensure that their activity did not contradict the states' priorities. Markets governed only by *laissez-faire* were considered inefficient, as the economic crisis of the 1970s had demonstrated. It was believed that private investment left to its own devices generated waste and suboptimal outcomes.

The Maldague Report was the outcome of a working group set up by the European Commission to study the problem of inflation. It was chaired by Robert Maldague, who came from the Belgian planning agency. The group included three authors who later published *Capitalism for Development* in 1978, the French Jacques Delors, a moderate socialist, the Italian Franco Archibugi, a professor and former ECSC civil servant, and Stuart Holland, an influential intellectual who belonged to the left wing of the Labour party.[46] Together, these three authors wrote the part of the report devoted to planning as it chimed well with their priorities in those days. A former head of the social department of the French planning agency in the 1960s, Delors was critical of the decline in French planning under the liberal President Valéry Giscard d'Estaing.[47] Holland was an influential labour intellectual, whose thinking on the EEC was widely commented on by

---

45 European Commission, 'Report of the Study Group "Problems of Inflation"' (1976), http://aei.pitt.edu/32793/1/INFLATION-ANNEX.pdf.

46 F. Archibugi, J. Delors and S. Holland, 'Planning for Development', in S. Holland (ed.), *Beyond Capitalist Planning* (Oxford, Basil Blackwell, 1978), pp. 184–202.

47 J. Delors, 'The Decline of French Planning', in Holland (ed.), *Beyond Capitalist Planning*, pp. 25–7.

Whitehall in 1977.[48] He was more critical of the free-market drift of the
Community than Delors, who insisted on the necessity to take into account
'the international environment and competition' and that 'Both public and
private enterprises are possible means to playing a significant role in the
world economy.'[49] In 1978, Holland edited the book *Beyond Capitalist
Planning*, in which he co-authored a chapter with Delors and Archibuigi.[50]
He insisted on the convergence of thinking on planning within the EEC,
including in West Germany, where the 1975 Mannheim Programme of the
Sozialdemokratische Partei Deutschlands mentioned some planning
elements.[51] Other members included Dirk Dolman, a labour member of
the Dutch Parliament, and Heinz Markman, the head of the Economic
Department of the Deutscher Gewerkschaftsbund (the German Trade
Union Confederation). As a result, transnational networks of intellectuals
engaged with planning emerged again in Europe.

Another report on European planning was written in 1977, by the Belgian
expert Albert Kervyn de Lettenhove, who had played a role in the transnational
network which supported Marjolin's idea in the 1960s. The ETUC did not
openly support the establishment of a European planning framework, but it
defended solutions that were inspired by this approach, in particular the coordination of macroeconomic policies towards common European targets. In 1976,
it promoted the adoption of quantified targets on growth (5 per cent), inflation
(4–5 per cent by 1980) and employment (a return to full employment by 1980).[52]
A 1977 report entitled *Unemployment: Structural Problems and Policy
Implications* went further as it requested a stringent coordination of investment
to increase its economic and social efficiency, invoking 'the waste of scarce
resources, and to situations in which private consumption, often of relatively
unimportant and non-essential goods, is overstimulated by such factors as
advertising at the expense of the production of more essential goods and
services'.[53] This theme of the incapacity of the free market to guide investment

48 British National Archives, T 390/283, doc. RE 961, January 1977, Stuart Holland; note
from Labour Party, NEC/EEC Study group, received at the Treasury on
20 January 1977.
49 Delors, 'The Decline of French Planning', p. 32.
50 Archibugi, Delors and Holland, 'Planning for Development'.
51 S. Holland, 'Introduction', in Holland (ed.), *Beyond Capitalist Planning*, pp. 1–6, 4;
N. Wieczorek, 'Perspectives for Planning', in Holland (ed.), *Beyond Capitalist
Planning*, pp. 106–120, 110–15.
52 British National Archives, PREM 16/850, joint statement by the Tripartite Conference,
24 June 1976, Luxembourg.
53 British National Archives, T 390/98, ETUC, 'Unemployment: Structural Problems and
Policy Implications', note in anticipation of the meeting of the committee on political
economy of 9 February 1977.

in a satisfactory way was already present in Marjolin's project. In the 1960s, it meant putting an emphasis on collective social investment, such as hospitals and education infrastructure. In the 1970s, concern for the environment was added.

Western leaders were not immune to these reflections. Instead of implementing full-scale European planning, they nevertheless made progress in the coordination of their macroeconomic policies. The classical reflex of post-war governments when confronted with an economic crisis was to launch a stimulus package, which would relaunch growth and alleviate the burden of unemployment. However, most stimulus packages launched after the 1973 crisis ended in more inflation and more imports, but barely less unemployment.[54] The only visible solution was to coordinate the stimulus package so that all countries could benefit from larger exports at the same time.

The idea of coordinating the EEC's macroeconomic policies was longstanding, but had not been implemented despite the various committees created in 1960 and in 1964. In 1968 and 1969, the French commissioner for monetary affairs Raymond Barre proposed two plans which linked an increased coordination of economic policies with further monetary solidarity.[55] Those reflections were then taken up and reframed in more ambitious projects in the 1970 Werner Plan. In 1974, the EEC Council of Ministers issued a resolution on the necessity to 'attain a high degree of convergence' among member states' economic policy, and they merged three committees (the short-term and the mid-term economic policy committee, as well as the budgetary policy committee) into one European Policy Committee.[56] However, those institutional decisions did not translate into any concrete coordination of economic policies: the European monetary 'snake' put in place in 1972 was riddled with holes, with many currencies leaving and then re-entering because of divergence in monetary (and ultimately) in economic policies.

The Failed 'Locomotive' Attempt

The turning point came with the 'locomotive' attempt of 1978.[57] It postulated that a coordinated reflationary plan would be successful only if countries with a surplus in their current account balance, such as Germany and Japan, were

---

54 N. Ferguson, C. Maier, E. Manela and D. Sargent (eds.), *The Shock of the Global: The 1970s in Perspective* (Cambridge, MA, Harvard University Press, 2011).

55 On Barre's proposals, see Warlouzet, *Le choix de la CEE*, pp. 402–15.

56 E. Mourlon-Druol, *A Europe Made of Money: The Emergence of the European Monetary System* (Ithaca, NY, Cornell University Press, 2012), pp. 19, 25.

57 Warlouzet, *Governing Europe*, pp. 144–5.

to shoulder larger stimulus programmes than the weakest countries, such as Britain and Italy, where the International Monetary Fund intervened in 1976–7 to solve a balance-of-payments crisis. The German chancellor remained hesitant, but he was convinced by his EEC partners, by the newly elected American President Carter and by the OECD, all of which backed a concerted stimulus over 2 or 3 years, the intensity of which would be defined by each government's financial ability to increase spending.

The formal agreement on a concerted stimulus came at the Group of Seven (G7) Summit held in Bonn on 16–17 July 1978. The German and Japanese governments had to reflate (Bonn had to prepare a stimulus equivalent to 1 per cent of gross domestic product), while the Carter administration agreed to fight against inflation and excessive oil consumption. The French and the Dutch should implement limited programmes of expansion, while the weaker British and Italians should engage in only minimalistic efforts. Schmidt yielded to pressure because he wanted a decisive win at the Bonn G7, and as it was necessary to promote a spirit of international cooperation to abate protectionist tensions. The German chancellor implemented this programme, while at the same time constantly reminding the Americans of their obligations in terms of anti-inflationary policy.

In 1979, the second oil-price shock snuffed this success out. In early 1981, for the first time in years, West Germany even experienced a balance-of-payments deficit. The Bundesbank worried for the Deutsche Mark, which underwent a 'crisis of confidence' (in the German Central Bank's own words), while the French franc hit its European Monetary System ceiling.[58] Traumatised by this short-lived deficit, the Germans have refused any attempt at a further concerted stimulus since then.

The idea remained alive in left-wing circles, particularly in the ETUC 1981 manifesto.[59] Internal divisions crippled the transnational planning network, with Stuart Holland supporting the anti-EEC drift of the Labour Party in the early 1980s, despite his book *Out of Crisis*, published in 1983, which still called for a coordination of the European left.[60] More generally, many supporters of

---

58 Bundesbank archives, B 330/11165, 575. 'Sitzung des Zentralbankrats der Deutschen Bundesbank', 19 February 1981.

59 British National Archives, PREM 19/462, 'ETUC Manifesto for Employment and Economic Recovery', 5 May 1981.

60 S. Holland (ed.), *Out of Crisis: An Alternative European Strategy* (Nottingham, Spokesman Books, 1983); S. Holland, 'Out of Crisis. International Economic Recovery', in J. Curran (ed.), *The Future of the Left* (Cambridge, MA, Polity Press, 1984), pp. 243–64; K. Featherstone, *Socialist Parties and European Integration: A Comparative History* (Manchester, Manchester University Press, 1988), p. 64.

planning were not ready to delegate such broad powers to a supranational authority.

At the same time, planning declined, even in France. The collapse of the Bretton Woods system, the increase in international flows of capital and goods, and the economic crisis made forecasting exercises more uncertain. Moreover, the liberal president Giscard d'Estaing was not enthusiastic about it. Instead of a single growth forecast, several hypotheses were taken into account in the Seventh Plan (1976–81), whereas the Eighth Plan (1981–5) did not contain any numerical growth targets.[61] The new head of the French Planning Commissariat, Michel Albert, consulted foreign economic planning experts such as the Russian-American Wassily Leontief and the British Andrew Shonfield. Planning became more and more an exercise in identifying global trends rather than a guide for economic actors. The belief in a state-led national future was revived one last time in 1981, when the socialist François Mitterrand was elected President of the Republic. This last burst of voluntarism waned between mid 1982 and the spring of 1983 due to financial constraints. Faced with a devaluing currency and the prospect of touring Middle Eastern countries to finance the public deficit, the French government changed its orientation by adopting a stability-oriented policy. Eventually, faced with the challenge of globalisation, the General Planning Commissariat published in 1986 a report calling for the completion of the internal market by the removal of non-tariff barriers – which was realised in the 1986 Single Act Treaty – and by the implementation of a European industrial policy. Planning was now officially abandoned as an overarching exercise of coordinating and steering economic actors. A market-oriented dynamic had to take precedence, but targeted interventions were still encouraged. This new liberal environment fostered the rise of competition policy.

The Rise of Competition Policy in the 1980s and 1990s

From the mid 1980s onwards, the competition principle was upheld more firmly within the EEC/EU's internal economic policies, first thanks to the Single Market programme, but most of all thanks to the new boldness of a more neoliberal EEC/EU competition policy.

---

61 Commissariat général au Plan, *Cinquante ans de planification à la française* (Paris, Commissariat général au Plan, 1996), p. 23.

The 1986 Single Act launched the internal market programme, which lifted all internal borders by the end of 1992, thanks to the harmonisation of hundreds of items of legislation in various domains.[62] This effectively increased intra-European competition. Planning was not completely abandoned in the sense that European governments and institutions played a leading role in choosing how to harmonise legislation. For example, when car emission norms were tightened in the late 1980s, the various governments took into account at the same time market-oriented, social and neomercantilist concerns.[63] From the social and environmental points of view, the case to reduce emissions was clear: lead emission was detrimental to human health and nitrogen oxides were held responsible for the acid rain that was destroying forests in Germany and Scandinavia in the early 1980s. The technical solution employed to diminish those emissions was the fitting of catalytic converters, which necessitated the use of unleaded petrol. The German government was keen to promote it not only out of environmental concerns, but also because German industry had mastered this technology. But French carmakers objected to the adoption of the catalytic converter technology, as it entailed what they considered undue costs and also increased fuel consumption. In other words, their neomercantilist concerns trumped the social and environmental case for more stringent regulation. In the end, a market-oriented European compromise prevailed in 1985 and in 1989: as the overarching aim of the EEC in those days was to avoid any division of the internal market (whose internal frontiers were due to be lifted in 1993), Paris and Bonn reached a compromise on a phased adoption of the catalytic converter technology (leaving more time for the smaller cars, such as the French ones, to be adapted). Hence, even though explicit planning was absent from the single market programme, the harmonisation of many laws led to an explicit coordination of national interventionist policy. In the case of car emissions, for example, the French government had to adopt more stringent legislation that it had initially considered.

All in all, the most significant development in terms of the decline of planning was that competition policy – the very embodiment of the competition principle – became a prominent feature of EEC/EU institutions, thanks

62 K. Armstrong and S. Bulmer, *The Governance of the Single European Market* (Manchester, Manchester University Press, 1998); M. Egan, *Constructing a European Market* (Oxford, Oxford University Press, 2001); G. Grin, *The Battle of the Single European Market: Achievements and Economic Thought, 1985–2000* (London, Paul Kegan, 2003).

63 L. Warlouzet, 'A Social Europe with a Greener Perspective: The Evolution of the Delors Commission around 1989', *Studi Storici* 62, no. 1 (2021): 189–209.

to the activism of two neoliberal commissioners, Peter Sutherland (1985–9) and Leon Brittan (1989–93), who targeted state interventions that undermined market competition to steer the economy, rather than corporate practices that went against open competition as had been the case before.[64]

In 1985, the Irishman Peter Sutherland became competition policy commissioner, and embarked on an ambitious agenda to extend competition rules to the regulation of certain national activities that had previously been ignored: control of state aid became more severe, and the liberalisation of the telecommunications and air transportation sectors began.

In terms of state aid, the Treaty of Rome was vague and the Commission was not able to be effective in this area until the mid 1980s. In the late 1970s, several actors – notably at the OECD and in the German government[65] – strived to promote a more severe control of state aid, involving the diminution of all subsidies except those that were temporary and linked to restructuring. Such aid should represent only a temporary boost for an otherwise competitive company. In other words, industrial, social and regional policy considerations (for example, the necessity to support a company in a region affected by massive unemployment) had to give way to pure competition considerations. On the whole, however, this offensive failed as the Commission remained largely dominated by a mix of neomercantilist and social approaches, and because member states successfully resisted this move. Only in the steel sector did the Commission acquire stringent prerogatives to closely monitor state aid, but this was considered an exception, as it stemmed from a decision taken unanimously by the Council in 1980 under ECSC rules, after much wrangling.[66]

Sutherland relaunched the offensive by targeting a massive subsidy delivered by one of the most powerful member states. In 1985, as soon as he arrived in Brussels, he took over the procedure against the state aid granted to Boussac, the largest textile firm in France. In Paris, French officials argued that, since this enormous company was on the verge of bankruptcy, massive layoffs would follow in regions of northern and eastern France that had already been crippled by the crisis of traditional manufacturing. The only solution was to

64 L. Warlouzet, 'Towards a Fourth Paradigm in European Competition Policy? A Historical Perspective (1957–2022)', in A. Claici, A. Komninos and D. Waelbroeck (eds.), *The Transformation of EU Competition Law – Next Generation Issues* (Alphen, Kluwer, 2023), pp. 33–52, available on the SSRN database: https://papers.ssrn.com.
65 Warlouzet, *Governing Europe*, pp. 164–5.
66 Warlouzet, *Governing Europe*, pp. 106–12; Y. Mény and V. Wright (eds.), *The Politics of Steel: Western Europe and the Steel Industry in the Crisis Years (1974–1984)* (Berlin, De Gruyter, 1986).

grant massive state aid. Sutherland replied that, since Boussac was an exporting firm, and since the subsidies were granted without a matching restructuring plan, the aid was illegal under EEC rules. The Irish commissioner was also motivated by the cockiness of French officials, who blatantly ignored EEC rules on state aid and were unwilling to disclose information. During internal debates within the Commission, he proposed to request a massive repayment of FF999 million by the company. François Lamoureux, a French socialist who was a member of Delors' cabinet, reacted angrily by underlining the 'unprecedented disagreement' within the Commission over this initiative. From the technical point of view, the Commission's service in charge of internal market (DG III) followed a more neomercantilist reasoning and insisted on the need to take into account the intensity of Boussac's restructuring and the problem of international competition. From the political point of view, the Irish commissioner entered uncharted territories when he contested evidence provided by a national government, an accusation which was extremely controversial from an institutional point of view. However, the context has changed since the late 1970s. The second oil-price shock had worsened the macroeconomic situation, and neoliberal ideas were on the rise. Eventually, after a tense debate within the college of commissioners, Sutherland secured the Commission's support to sanction the French government, but he had to negotiate with it. He settled for a compromise of FF338 million. The contest went beyond a duel between Brussels and Paris. In fact, European commissioners were divided over the extent of the competition principle, as many of them (mostly from the centre-left) insisted on the necessity of leaving room to manoeuvre for national industrial, social and regional policies. According to them, competition policy had to be congruous with social and neomercantilist aims that could be associated with planning.

The Extension of the Competition Thrust to New Areas

Sutherland also played a decisive role in the liberalisation of air transportation and of telecommunications, in both cases driven by multiple dynamics, some of them independent from European integration such as a growing influence of free-market ideas, and technical innovation.[67] In air transportation, the cost

---

67 In addition to previous references, see also M. Thatcher, *Internationalisation and Economic Institutions: Comparing the European Experience* (Oxford, Oxford University Press, 2007); H. Kassim and H. Stevens, *Air Transport and the European Union: Europeanization and Its Limits* (Basingstoke, Palgrave Macmillan, 2010).

per passenger fell with the arrival of new planes such as the Boeing 747 in 1969 and thanks to a growing competition with Airbus. In the telecommunications sector, digitisation and convergence with the computer industry brought about the development of new services and of new competitors. Goods that were relatively scarce (communications or air transportation capacity) became more abundant, thus more competition in the market was possible. Nevertheless, what was remarkable was that this liberalisation process was tightly regulated by the EEC, thanks to two landmark pieces of legislation adopted in 1987 (for air transportation) and in 1988 (for telecommunications). Liberalisation could have occurred only at the national level, with coordination with the international technical bodies that already existed.

The neoliberal offensive to uphold the competition principle became even more intense under Leon Brittan, the commissioner for competition who succeeded Sutherland. Brittan was a faithful supporter of the British neoliberal Prime Minister Margaret Thatcher. The first tensions over the extent of the competition principle occurred with regard to mergers, as the Commission had acquired in late 1989 the power to ban mergers.[68] In 1991, Brittan decided that the Commission would for the first time forbid a merger, in this case between Avions de Transport Régional (ATR) and De Havilland, two aircraft companies.[69] However, for many experts, the merger made sense since other competitors existed both inside and outside Europe.[70] This operation was hailed as a symbol for an EEC industrial policy in high technology aimed at creating European champions able to compete with the mightier US firms. Indeed, it was the Franco-Italian firm ATR, itself an example of European industrial cooperation, which bought its Canadian competitor De Havilland. Conversely, Brittan opposed it on competition grounds: he adopted a narrow definition of the relevant market in order to demonstrate that the new merged company would have had a dominant position. Within the Commission, Delors supported the merger, but Brittan mustered support among a large coalition of mostly centre-right commissioners, and thus won the case.[71]

---

68 For a summary of the literature on the 1989 merger regulation, see L. Warlouzet, 'The Centralization of EU Competition Policy: Historical Institutionalist Dynamics from Cartel Monitoring to Merger Control (1956–91)', *Journal of Common Market Studies* 54 (2016): 725–41.

69 M. Pollack, *The Engines of European Integration: Delegation, Agency, and Agenda Setting in the EU* (Oxford, Oxford University Press, 2003), pp. 292–9; M. Cini and L. McGowan, *Competition Policy* (Basingstoke, Palgrave Macmillan, 1998), p. 129.

70 F. Jenny, 'Droit européen de la concurrence et efficience économique', *Revue d'économie industrielle* 63 (1993): 193–206, 202–3; C. Goybet, 'La CEE a-t-elle une politique industrielle?', *Revue du Marché Commun* 352 (1991): 753–5, 753.

71 G. Ross, *Jacques Delors and European Integration* (Cambridge, MA, Polity Press, 1995), p. 178.

Italy was also forced to scale back its industrial policy in the 1980s and early 1990s, mostly for reasons independent from EEC/EU institutions, but sometimes as the result of their direct pressure through state aid control, notably in 1992 under Brittan.[72]

On the whole, those developments hampered not only the development of an EU industrial policy, but also the functioning of national industrial policies, at least in the traditional sense of fostering the development of national companies by direct measures, such as subsidies or legal privileges. In other words, the planning idea applied to industrial development was shattered by this rise of the competition-based order. The demise of the socialist planned economy in central and eastern Europe reinforced this dynamic.

On the whole, the competition principle has arisen constantly since the mid 1980s, both in the old field of cartels and in the new domain of merger control, state aid control and the liberalisation of previous monopolies and oligopolies (which has extended to energy, railways and postal services). But this does not mean that its orientation has always been neoliberal. Recently, under Margrethe Vestager, unfair tax aid was targeted more vigorously. Only during the most severe economic crisis has the Commission accepted the need to be considerably more tolerant towards state aid. This was the case in the 1990s, when Germany had to massively subsidise the modernisation of East German industry, and, most of all, during the crisis of 2008–10 and during the recent Covid-19 crisis. Hence, planning was no longer permitted, except in time of crisis to prevent a massive collapse of the industry.

The Persistence of Planning Ideas up to the Post-Covid-19 EU

While explicit planning ideas are absent within the EU's economic framework, its explicit definition as a 'social market economy' exemplifies its ideological flexibility.[73] Hence, it is possible to observe the persistence of the idea of a political steering of economic structures in several domains.

Cohesion policy is the area where traditional planning concerns have persisted. Reducing regional imbalances has always been a major objective

---

72 B. Curli, 'The "vincolo europeo", Italian Privatization and the European Commission in the 1990s', *Journal of European Integration History* 18 (2012): 285–301, 294–5. On EMU, see also L. Quaglia, *Italy and the Economic Monetary Union: The Politics of Ideas* (Lewiston, NY, Edwin Mellen, 2006).
73 On the EU as a social market economy, see the 2019 special issue *Rethinking the European Social Market Economy*, eds. R. Claassen, A. Gerbrandy, S. Princen and M. Segers, of the *Journal of Common Market Studies*.

of planning, or of planning-like policies, notably in Britain and in Italy, and then in France. It has led to the EEC's regional policy, which was created in 1975, on a relatively modest basis, and then gradually expanded both in terms of scope (it became 'cohesion policy') and in terms of budget to deal with the southern enlargement and then the eastern enlargement. Philipp Ther compared its effect on post-socialist countries to that of the Marshall Plan.[74] Cohesion policy is decentralised, so it can be compared not to the centralised version of planning set up in the 1960s, but rather more to a modest version of the project devised in the 1970s. Like them, it hinges on the idea that political authorities have a duty to address market failures, in this case regional imbalances, by orienting growth.

Paradoxically, the history of the EMU has seen the competition principle being upheld so firmly that it had somewhat merged with some planning tendencies. At the start, planning, understood as the voluntary coordination of macroeconomic policies, was almost absent from the EMU blueprint defined in the Maastricht Treaty. Originally, the 1970 Werner Plan was predicated upon a parallel strengthening of both monetary and economic cooperation.[75] The latter was left to a relatively undefined 'decision center for economic policy', which should have been powerful and would have answered to the European Parliament. Instead, the Maastricht Treaty established a three-way process towards a fully fledged federal monetary union (with a federal European Central Bank), flanked by a purely intergovernmental economic union. Economic coordination was left entirely in the hands of national governments and of market forces, despite numerous attempts by French leaders in 1988–9 to improve macroeconomic policy coordination.[76] The 1997 Growth and Stability Pact was designed to address these imbalances, by fostering an explicit coordination of economic policies merging the principles of both planning ('Growth') and competition ('Stability'), but it was largely ignored by the member states, which followed different paths.

Nevertheless, the Eurozone crisis forced everybody to converge towards a common approach, based both on solidarity and on competition. The first principle was visible in relief packages allowing all countries to stay in the Eurozone and in the creation of institutions aimed at funding deficit countries

74 P. Ther, *Europe since 1989: A History* (Princeton, NJ, Princeton University Press, 2016), p. 146.
75 E. Danescu and S. Muñoz (eds.), *Pierre Werner and Europe: His Approach, Action and Legacy* (Brussels, Peter Lang, 2015).
76 Howarth and Schild, 'France and European Macro-economic Policy Coordination', 20–1.

(the European Financial Stability Facility and then European Stability Mechanism), but it was the second principle which gained the upper hand: draconian conditions were imposed on some of the countries that needed assistance. As a result, planning in the sense of coordination of macroeconomic policies was implemented, but in a competition-only vision. On the one hand, Ireland was assisted in order to cover its economic mistakes (the government carelessly pledged to cover all its oversized banking sector's losses at the beginning of the crisis) with only a few strings attached. It was allowed to continue its neoliberal policy of low taxation. On the other hand, Greece, whose governments had cheated on its statistics in order to enter into the euro, was punished by a late debt relief and by a neoliberal monitoring of its economic policy, which entailed axeing its welfare state. The 2012 Fiscal Compact (the Treaty on Stability, Coordination and Governance in the Economic and Monetary Union) was meant to enshrine in the institutions this planned convergence towards stability-oriented policies. In other words, planning was put at the service of a competition-only vision of European integration. France managed to insert into the Macroeconomic Imbalance Procedure, part of the so-called 'Six Pack' legislation, a surveillance of both surplus and deficits of the current account imbalances, but this symmetry was rather theoretical.[77]

Recently, the Covid-19 crisis seemed to have slightly revived the old idea of planning towards neomercantilist and social aims. Brexit has certainly weakened the proponents of a competition-only vision with the departure of its most vocal supporters since 1979. Regarding EMU, the massive stimulus plan partly delivered in grants (and not only in loans) adopted in July 2020 fits into the planning approach, as the 'green deal', unveiled in early 2020, before the pandemic began, but which might be boosted by it. More generally, the recovery plan put forward by the European Commission has been hailed as a 'new Marshall Plan' by EU President Ursula von der Leyen,[78] in a reference to planning as a tool for modernisation. In industrial policy, the new tolerance for state aid to save competitive companies at risk of disappearance because of the pandemic and the Commission's acceptance of a stricter monitoring of foreign takeovers of EU firms also fit into a more planned approach, aimed at

77 Howarth and Schild, 'France and European Macro-economic Policy Coordination', 25–6.
78 European Commission, 'Coronavirus: President von der Leyen Outlines EU Budget as Marshall Plan for Europe's Recovery' (2020), www.pubaffairsbruxelles.eu/eu-institution-news/coronavirus-president-von-der-leyen-outlines-eu-budget-as-marshall-plan-for-europes-recovery.

correcting market imbalances by maintaining a long-term approach to industrial development. Lastly, France has even revived the term 'planning' by restoring its 'Commissariat général au Plan' in August 2020, albeit with a role mainly confined to long-term economic and social forecasting.

Conclusion

European institutions have always been dominated by a market-oriented thrust, which had accommodated both the competition and the planning orientations. Many debates over the economic orientation of Europe have pitted against each other not only the member states, but also the members of other EEC/EU institutions, in particular commissioners defending rival interpretations of the Maastricht Treaty, and various experts. It was not Germany against France, but rather a coalition of competition-oriented actors in Germany, and later in Ireland and the UK, who opposed another coalition, mainly composed of French, Belgian and Italian actors.

During the 1960s, Commissioner von der Groeben developed an ambitious project of a competition-based Community, which clashed with the comprehensive project of European planning devised by his colleague Marjolin. While planning ideas remained influential in the 1970s, they were not enacted despite the promising attempt at a 'locomotive'. From the late 1980s, the principle of competition became prominent thanks to a neoliberal momentum, which was accelerated with the creation of an unbalanced EMU at Maastricht. It even subverted the planning principle by putting it at the service of a competition-only vision, as was enshrined in some decisions taken during the Eurozone crisis. However, the original planning principle, which was based on neomercantilist and social concerns, remains visible in cohesion policies. Its prospects even look brighter in the post-Covid-19 world, where discussions over increased solidarity within the EMU and over the green deal loom large.

On the whole, this debate about competition and planning demonstrates that the EEC/EU has not been an inward-looking island, but rather an organisation fully immersed within the ideological debates of its time. The peak of planning ideas in the 1960s influenced the EEC debates, while the rise of neoliberal ideas in the 1980s moved it into uncharted territory. The current debate on the reorientation of EU policies following the pandemic demonstrates that, despite the institutional momentum and the legal jurisprudence that constrain decision-makers, the European treaties remain relatively flexible, provided that a political willingness exists.

Recommended Reading

Gerber, D. *Law and Competition in XXth Century Europe: Protecting Prometheus* (Oxford, Clarendon Press, 1998).

Leucht, B., K. Seidel and L. Warlouzet (eds.). *Reinventing Europe: The History of the European Union since 1945* (London, Bloomsbury, 2022).

Milward, A. S. *The European Rescue of the Nation-State* (London, Routledge, 1992).

Moravcsik, A. *The Choice for Europe: Social Purpose and State Power from Messina to Maastricht* (Ithaca, NY, Cornell University Press, 1998).

Shonfield, A. *Modern Capitalism: The Changing Balance of Public and Private Power* (Oxford, Oxford University Press, 1965).

Slobodian, Q. *Globalists: The End of Empire and the Birth of Neoliberalism* (Cambridge, MA, Harvard University Press, 2018).

Warlouzet, L. *Europe contre Europe: Entre liberté, solidarité et puissance* (Paris, CNRS Éditions, 2022).

Warlouzet, L. *Governing Europe in a Globalizing World: Neoliberalism and Its Alternatives Following the 1973 Oil Crisis* (London, Routledge, 2018).

Warlouzet, L. 'The EEC/EU as an Evolving Compromise between French Dirigism and German Ordoliberalism (1957–1995)', *Journal of Common Market Studies* 57 (2019): 77–93.

9

Commercial Banks, the Eurodollar Market and the Beginnings of Monetary Integration

CARLO EDOARDO ALTAMURA

Introduction

The decade-long process of European monetary integration has been the most ambitious, and probably the most controversial, project of its type.[1]

The Eurozone crisis of the early 2010s reinforced the scepticism toward monetary integration experienced not only by populist politicians but also by disillusioned academics. Belke and Verheyen, for example, argued in 2012 that: 'It is time to admit that under the prevailing structure and membership, the euro area simply does not work successfully.'[2]

Now that the European Union has survived the Eurozone debt crisis, it is the right time to retrace the origins of the process of European monetary integration from the mid-to-late 1940s until the end of the 1960s. The period analysed in this chapter was not, on the surface, a period of major achievements or accomplishments, but it was nonetheless a foundational moment in European economic history, from being a war-torn continent Europe gradually started rebuilding its payment, trade and monetary infrastructure.

The chapter will deviate from current historiography by showing how the process of European monetary integration was not only a process managed by politicians and policymakers (i.e., managed from above), but also a process that involved a much wider variety of actors from the private sector such as bankers. The chapter will show how the issues related to monetary integration at the level of high politics translated into the practices of financial actors to illustrate how these actors were not simply passive actors but active

---

1 P. B. Kenen and E. E. Meade, *Regional Monetary Integration* (Cambridge and New York, NY, Cambridge University Press, 2008), p. 41.
2 A. Belke and F. Verheyen, 'Doomsday for the Euro Area: Causes, Variants and Consequences of Breakup', *International Journal of Financial Studies* 1, no. 1 (2013): 1–15.

promoters of European integration. Thanks to primary sources collected from one of the major European banks, the Midland Bank, the chapter will be able to include the voice of neglected actors in the process of monetary integration and illustrate the contribution of European bankers towards a more integrated European monetary and financial framework. This was achieved through the creation of banking clubs, organisations of commercial banks from multiple European countries willing to cooperate in order to expand their operations abroad and share knowledge about foreign markets in Europe and beyond.

Literature Review

European monetary integration in the mid 1940s, at the time of the Bretton Woods conference in July 1944, looked like a chimera. Bretton Woods was, mostly, an Anglo-American affair that officialised the United States as the world hegemon in the Western world. The Bretton Woods negotiations have been the subject of several books.[3] In practice, though, the power of the United States was so great that the settlement 'largely reflected American interests'.[4] The main preoccupation of European and American policy-makers after the end of the Second World War was how to integrate Germany into Europe and Europe into Germany, and how Europe could avoid another war. In this sense, since the immediate post-war period, the process of European monetary integration has been as much an economic process as a political one.[5] The process of economic and monetary integration was initially led by the United States with the goal of restoring 'open, multilateral trade'.[6] The main problem with the initial American approach towards European monetary and economic integration was a coordination problem; European countries could import more (as the Americans wished) only if they exported more, and this required them to act in a coordinated way to liberalise their currencies and trade system.

3 See, for example, R. N. Gardner, *Sterling–Dollar Diplomacy in Current Perspective*, expanded ed. (New York, NY, Columbia University Press, 1980); B. Steil, *The Battle of Bretton Woods: John Maynard Keynes, Harry Dexter White, and the Making of a New World Order* (Princeton, NJ, Princeton University Press, 2013); E. Helleiner, *Forgotten Foundations of Bretton Woods: International Development and the Making of the Postwar Order* (Ithaca, NY, Cornell University Press, 2014).
4 H. James, *Making the European Monetary Union* (Cambridge, MA and London, Harvard University Press, 2012), p. 37.
5 P. Minkkinen and H. Patomäki (eds.), *The Politics of Economic and Monetary Union* (Heidelberg, Springer, 1997).
6 B. Eichengreen, *Globalizing Capital: A History of the International Monetary System* (Princeton, NJ and Oxford, Princeton University Press, 2008).

The weakness of European finances and the coordination problem became evident in the late 1940s, during the sterling crisis of 1947 and the realignment of European currencies in 1949.

In 1946, the United Kingdom (UK) negotiated a US$3.75 billion loan repayable over 50 years at 2 per cent interest from the United States on condition that the UK would restore current account convertibility within a year (i.e., by 15 July 1947). As Eichengreen pointed out, 'the six weeks of convertibility were a disaster'.[7] Dollar reserves were exhausted and the UK was forced to suspend convertibility on August 20. The extent of European economies' dollar shortage had started to disquiet American policymakers earlier in 1947.[8]

American fears resulted in the speech made by Secretary of State George C. Marshall at Harvard University on 5 June 1947. Economic support for the European continent had been under discussion in Washington, DC, but Marshall's proposal had not yet been approved by Congress; then the sterling crisis crucially weakened domestic opposition.[9]

Over the next 4 years, the United States transferred to European countries US$13 billion through the Marshall Plan. Unfortunately, what was given was, at least partly, taken away by the 1948–9 recession in the United States.[10] The recession was the main reason behind the devaluations of 1949. Despite the comparatively mild character of the recession compared with those of 1929 and 1938, lower prices for American products enabled European countries to import a greater quantity of American goods while making European goods less competitive in overseas markets. Increasing imports and declining exports put European finances under renewed strain.

Although the devaluations moderated the dollar shortage, they did not eliminate it. European countries recognised that, in order to complete the transition to convertibility, extraordinary measures had to be taken. These extraordinary measures resulted in the European Payments Union (EPU), which was created in September 1950 (and applied retroactively to July 1950). The goal was 'to move from the bilateral trade patterns of the immediate post-Second World War period to a multilateral trade of peacetime reconstruction'.[11]

---

7 Eichengreen, *Globalizing Capital*, p. 101.
8 C. C. S. Newton, 'The Sterling Crisis of 1947 and the British Response to the Marshall plan', *The Economic History Review* 37, no. 3 (1984): 391–408, 394.
9 Newton, 'The 1949 Sterling Crisis', 169.   10 Eichengreen, *Globalizing Capital*, p. 102.
11 E. Mourlon-Druol, *A Europe Made of Money: The Emergence of the European Monetary System* (Ithaca, NY, Cornell University Press, 2012), p. 22. On the EPU, see also A. O. Hirschman, 'The European Payments Union. Negotiations and the Issues', *The Review of Economics and Statistics* 33, no. 1 (1951): 49–55; D. Jones, 'The European

The EPU addressed the biggest issue affecting European economies notwithstanding Marshall aid, that is, the dollar shortage or gap, by providing an effective way to limit the use of dollars for intra-European transactions and facilitate intra-European trade growth by replacing a multitude of bilateral payment arrangements with a single, multilateral arrangement.[12] In the context of the EPU, participating countries agreed to accept overdraft credits as means of settlement up to the limit scheduled with their allocated quotas. Once a country's quota had been exhausted, the debtor was supposed to settle its debts with dollars or gold. Responsibility for clearing payments was given to the Bank for International Settlements (BIS), based in Basel. The Union was started with an initial working capital fund of US$350 million provided by the United States. In its 6 years of existence, until 1958, the EPU was remarkably successful in expanding intra-European trade by integrating European economies into a common market[13] and in providing the background for the gradual liberalisation of payments. Between 1949 and 1956, Europe more than doubled its dollar holdings,[14] and on 27 December 1958 eight countries declared their currencies convertible for current account transactions. The liberalisation of current account transactions was preceded in 1957 by the signing of the Treaty of Rome, establishing the European Economic Community (EEC), which required authorisations for exchange transactions to be granted in the most liberal manner (Article 68) and established the creation of the Monetary Committee of the European Community composed of representatives of finance ministers and central banks under Article 105(2) to monitor economic and financial conditions.[15] Importantly, the Treaty of Rome did not deal specifically with monetary issues, focusing more on the creation of a customs union and the Common Agricultural Policy (CAP).[16] This lapse was

Monetary Agreement, the European Payments Union, and Convertibility', *The Journal of Finance* 12, no. 3 (1957): 333–47; J. Ljungberg and A. Ögren, 'Discipline or International Balance: The Choice of Monetary Systems in Europe', *The European Journal of the History of Economic Thought* 29, no. 2 (2022): 218–45.

On the pre-EPU schemes, see A. Faudot, 'The European Payments Union (1950–58): The Post-war Episode of Keynes' Clearing Union', *Review of Political Economy* 32, no. 3 (2020): 371–89.

12 Kenen and Meade, *Regional Monetary Integration*, p. 43.

13 M. Segers, 'Eclipsing Atlantis: Trans-Atlantic Multilateralism in Trade and Monetary Affairs as a Pre-history to the Genesis of Social Market Europe (1942–1950)', *Journal of Common Market Studies* 57, no. 1 (2018): 60–76, 70.

14 J. Gillingham, *European Integration, 1950–2003: Superstate or New Market Economy?* (Cambridge and New York, NY, Cambridge University Press, 2003), p. 39.

15 H. James, *Making the European Monetary Union* (Cambridge, MA and London, Harvard University Press, 2012), p. 41.

16 H. K. Scheller, 'Le comité des gouverneurs des banques centrales de la CEE et l'unification monétaire européenne', *Histoire, économie et société* 4 (2011): 79–99.

one of the issues addressed in the second phase of the EEC, starting with the Memorandum of the Commission on the Action Programme of the Community for the Second Stage published in October 1962, informally known as the 'Marjolin Memorandum', after the vice-president of the EEC in charge of economic and monetary affairs.[17]

The Marjolin Memorandum can be seen as a premature attempt at expanding the scope of the EEC to monetary affairs. The most concrete result of the memorandum was the creation of the Committee of Governors of the Central Banks of the Member States of the European Economic Community, or, more simply, the Committee of Governors (CoG), in May 1964 that would play a crucial role in the European Monetary Union. The CoG would be based in Basel at the BIS, which already served as the centre of international monetary discussions. In the inaugural session of the CoG in July 1964, Marjolin asked the governors how they would differentiate their activities from those of the Monetary Committee, to which the governors responded that the two committees were fundamentally different, referring to the nature of the discussions taking place in Basel being more technical than in Brussels.[18] Marjolin had a rather ambitious vision for the CoG, setting out three main areas of work, namely action to stop fluctuation in agricultural prices, anti-inflationary action and determining the usefulness of capital controls that had been implemented in West Germany to limit capital inflows.[19]

In reality, Marjolin's ambitious vision would be frustrated, because the tasks of the CoG were fairly limited, namely to stimulate exchanges of view on differing monetary policies, to encourage consultations between economic and financial leaders and to improve the collection of monetary statistics.[20] A close relationship existed between the Monetary Committee and the CoG as the governors' alternates in the CoG would sit as representatives of central banks in the Monetary Committee, but, because the work of the Committee was impacted negatively by, for example, the absence of France in 1965–6 as a part of France's 'empty chair' policy, the CoG would establish itself as a forum for monetary cooperation. At the European level the main issues addressed by the CoG in the second half of the 1960s were the

---

17 European Commission, 'Memorandum of the Commission on the Action Programme of the Community for the Second Stage' (1962), http://aei.pitt.edu/1327/1/memoran dum_1962_second_stage.pdf.
18 Scheller, 'Le comité des gouverneurs', 87.
19 James, *Making the European Monetary Union*, p. 54.
20 G. Toniolo, *Central Bank Cooperation at the Bank for International Settlements, 1930–1973* (Cambridge, Cambridge University Press, 2005).

balance-of-payments weakness of Italy, the UK and, later in the decade, of France at least partially aggravated by destabilising capital flows from the unregulated Eurodollar market.

By the beginning of July 1968, France's reserves had been exhausted. In Basel the governors agreed to a US$600 million credit, coming mainly from Germany and Italy (US$200 million each), with the remainder from Belgium and the Netherlands. While speculation and monetary imbalances were creating havoc in the fabric of European monetary cooperation, Marjolin had been succeeded by Raymond Barre as Commissioner responsible for economic and financial affairs and as vice-president. During his tenure, he witnessed the sterling and French franc crises and left office 2 months before speculation forced the Deutsche Mark (DM) to be revalued.[21]

Barre provided a crucial contribution to the early phase of economic and monetary union at a time of increasing pressure under the Bretton Woods system.[22] The first Barre Memorandum presented in February 1969 at the ECOFIN (the Economic and Financial Affairs Council) was the first of the two plans presented by Barre and focused on three main lines of action. First, a medium-term convergence of the Group's economic policies in order to reconcile differing national preferences. Secondly, the coordination of short-term economic policies. Thirdly, a progressive narrowing of the margin of fluctuations among EEC currencies. Compared with the Plan of Action of 1962, the first Barre Memorandum or Plan was much more modest, but it still attracted the scepticism of central bankers, because many of them were perplexed at the possibility of European convergence.[23] Nonetheless, in February 1970 a Community Mechanism for Short-Term Monetary Assistance was created, and in March 1971 ECOFIN agreed to create a medium-term financial assistance facility to assist countries suffering from balance-of-payments difficulties. Following the Hague summit of December 1969, Barre started working on a second memorandum or plan,[24] presented to ECOFIN in

21 D. Howarth, 'Raymond Barre. Modernizing France through Monetary Cooperation', in K. Dyson and I. Maes (eds.), *Architects of the Euro: Intellectuals in the Making of the European Monetary Union* (Oxford, Oxford University Press, 2016).
22 J. Bille, 'Raymond Barre et l'Europe', *Commentaire* no. 171 (2020): 697–700; I. Maes, 'History of Economic Thought and Policy-Making at the European Commission', in H. Badinger and V. Nitsch (eds.), *Routledge Handbook of the Economics of European Integration* (Abingdon, Routledge, 2015).
23 Maes, 'History of Economic Thought', p. 43.
24 European Commission, 'Communication de la Commission sur l'élaboration d'un plan par étapes vers une union économique et monétaire (Bruxelles, 27 février 1970)', www.cvce.eu/ obj/communication_de_la_commission_sur_l_elaboration_d_un_plan_par_etapes_ver s_une_union_economique_et_monetaire_bruxelles_27_fevrier_1970-fr-a167b413-bab9-4b e9-a461-635db9031b3f.html.

March 1970, in which he proposed three main steps and a 10-year working calendar for the move to European Monetary Union. Despite the vagueness with regard to the implementation of some of its proposals, such as the harmonisation of fiscal policies, it contained several crucial elements that would be reprised in the Werner Plan, the EMS and the Single European Act of 1985. As other scholars have argued, if the Werner Plan is to be considered the founding act of the EMS, the two Barre Plans represented the conceptual foundations of monetary integration.[25]

Bankers as Agents of Integration

The path towards European monetary integration is often analysed through the analytical lens of the actions of great thinkers, visionary politicians or milestone events of other kinds. Nonetheless, European monetary and economic integration was also made by individuals and corporations. In this sense, the rest of the chapter relates to historiographical works aiming at including the roles of a multiplicity of actors in the process of European economic integration. In this historiography, and despite the illuminating contributions by scholars such as Ludlow, Kaiser, Knudsen and, more recently, Mourlon-Druol,[26] the role of bankers and agents of integration remains largely unexplored. Partly this is explained by the more limited and complex access to banking archival sources; and it is partly owing to the more limited attention that the process of European economic and monetary integration in the pre-1970s period has received in existing narratives.[27] Monetary and economic aspects have often been eclipsed by other achievements, such as the CAP, which is considered by many scholars to have been the 'EU's first major policy'.[28]

In our view, banking actors played a prominent role both as *followers* of the movement towards integration and also, perhaps more crucially, as *influencers* of the same process in the form of 'banking clubs' and 'banking

---

25 Howarth, 'Raymond Barre'.
26 W. Kaiser, *Christian Democracy and the Origins of the European Union* (Cambridge, Cambridge University Press, 2007); W. Kaiser, B. Leucht and M. Rasmussen (eds.), *The History of the European Union: Origins of a Trans- and Supranational Polity, 1950–72* (London, Routledge, 2009); A.-C. L. Knudsen, *Farmers on Welfare: The Making of Europe's Common Agricultural Policy* (Ithaca, NY, Cornell University Press, 2009); N. P. Ludlow, *The European Community and the Crises of the 1960s: Negotiating the Gaullist Challenge* (Abingdon, Routledge, 2005).
27 For a partial exception, see N. P. Ludlow, *The European Community*.
28 N. P. Ludlow, 'The Making of the CAP: Towards a Historical Analysis of the EU's First Major Policy', *Contemporary European History* 14, no. 3 (2005): 347–71.

consortia'. It is this second aspect as influencers or agents of integration that is analysed in this section.

Moments of optimism in European integration tended to be reflected in enthusiasm for closer banking cooperation taking the form of more or less formal associations of commercial banks willing to share knowledge and expertise on specific topics and markets. As narrated by Ross, when the first of these clubs, known as the Club des Célibataires (Bachelors' Club), was created in 1959 by the Banque de la Société Générale de Belgique, Deutsche Bank and the Amsterdamsche Bank N.V., the founders explicitly wished to participate in the 'economic and perhaps also political integration of Europe'.[29] Compared with the actors in the political arena involved in the integration process, the absence of any French bank from the club might appear quite remarkable. This absence can be explained by the fact that the banks involved in the club were all in private hands and were suspicious of institutions with public ownership or participation; in the case of France, four commercial banks and the Banque de France had been nationalised by General de Gaulle in 1945.

Banking clubs and, later, banking consortia (Table 9.1) were not only a response to the ongoing process of European integration, but also represented an original response to the increasing influence of American banks on the European continent. As pointed out by Battilossi, the number of American banks with branches in London increased from ten in 1958 to fifty-five in the early 1970s.[30]

Finally, banking associations like clubs and consortia were a response to increasing financial innovation in the form of Eurodollars, dollars held outside American legislation, and the products derived from the Eurodollar market such as long-term Eurobonds and, by the end of the 1960s, medium-term Euroloans.[31]

29 D. M. Ross, 'European Banking Clubs in the 1960s: A Flawed Strategy', *Business and Economic History* 27, no. 2 (1998): 353–66.
30 S. Battilossi, 'Introduction: International Banking and the American Challenge in Historical Perspective', in S. Battilossi and Y. Cassis (eds.), *European Banks and the American Challenge: Competition and Cooperation in International Banking under Bretton Woods* (Oxford, Oxford University Press, 2002), pp. 1–35, 15.
31 On the Eurodollar market, see C. E. Altamura, *European Banks and the Rise of International Finance: The Post-Bretton Woods Era* (Abingdon, Routledge, 2017); C. E. Altamura, 'The Paradox of the 1970s: The Renaissance of International Banking and the Rise of Public Debt', *Journal of Modern European History* 15, no. 4 (2017): 529–53; S. Battilossi, 'Financial Innovation and the Golden Ages of International Banking 1890–1931 and 1958–81', *Financial History Review* 7 (2000): 141–75; C. R. Schenk, 'The Origins of the Eurodollar market in London: 1955–1963', *Explorations in Economic History* 35 (1998): 221–38. On the American challenge, see Battilossi and Cassis (eds.), *European Banks*.

Table 9.1 European banking consortia

Group	Members	Country	Assets in US$ Billion	Total
ABECOR	Algemene Bank Nederland	Netherlands	10.2	132.6
(established 1972,	Banca Nazionale del Lavoro	Italy	22.7	
reconstituted	Banque de Bruxelles	Belgium	7.5	
1974)	Banque Nationale de Paris	France	29.9	
	Barclays Bank Limited	UK	28.3	
	Hypobank	Germany	9.5	
	Dresdner Bank	Germany	21.0	
	Banque Internationale à Luxembourg (Associated)	Luxembourg	0.8	
	Österreichische Länderbank (Associated)	Austria	2.1	
	Banque de la Société Financière Européenne (Associated)	Consortium	0.6	
EAC/EBIC	Amsterdam–Rotterdam Bank	Netherlands	9.7	104.0
(established 1963)	Banca Commerciale Italiana (1973)	Italy	16.8	
	Creditanstalt Bankverein (1971)	Austria	3.0	
	Deutsche Bank	Germany	24.7	
	Midland Bank	UK	19.1	
	Société Générale (1971)	France	21.6	
	Société Générale de Banque	Belgium	9.1	

ABECOR, Associated Banks of Europe Corporation; EAC/EBIC, European Advisory Committee/European Banks' International Company SA.
Source: C. E. Altamura, *European Banks and the Rise of International Finance: The Post-Bretton Woods Era*, 1st ed. © 2017 Routledge. Reproduced by permission of Taylor & Francis Group.

Banking clubs have been especially criticised for their apparent ineffectiveness in the long run, but we must not forget how politically fragmented Europe was when these arrangements were created. In a European context of heterogeneity in norms and regulations, where 'even the largest commercial banks had little experience in international banking'[32] and the integration process was still in its infancy, banking clubs represented a seminal step to limit the risks involved in establishing a presence abroad by allowing the

32 R. Roberts (with C. Arnander), *Take Your Partners: Orion, the Consortium Banks and the Transformation of the Euromarkets* (Basingstoke and New York, NY, Palgrave Macmillan, 2001), p. 20.

systematic exchange of information, in a cost-effective way, between member banks through meetings and joint study groups.

In what follows, we are going to focus on the Midland Bank, at that time one of the four largest commercial banks in the UK, and its participation in the association known as the European Advisory Committee (EAC) which succeeded the Club des Célibataires. We will rely on a wide range of archival documents relating to the EAC from about 1964 to the end of the decade, available at the archives of the Hongkong and Shanghai Banking Corporation in London.

The European Advisory Committee and the Quest for European Banking Integration

The Club des Célibataires gradually opened up to new members in the early 1960s, and the Midland Bank was formally accepted in 1963. By 1964 the bank had become a full member and was participating in the club's regular meetings. Interestingly, during the same years the efforts of the UK to join the European project were abandoned under French pressure.[33] As anticipated, the old name Club des Célibataires was also replaced with a new one, the EAC, to reflect the association's somewhat more ambitious scope with regard to continental cooperation. Meetings took place at regular intervals every 3 months; the location of each meeting alternated amongst the member banks. It must be noted that the officialisation of the association, like the creation of the Club des Célibataires in 1958, took place in an especially fertile moment of European economic integration following the publication of the Marjolin Memorandum in 1962 and the creation of the CoG in early 1964.

The first meeting of the EAC, informally known by its members as the 'Club of Four', took place in Düsseldorf in February 1964. After some practical arrangements had been made with regard to the following meetings, the selection of secretaries and so on, the main issue discussed was the admission of other European banks. Several potential new members, notably from France, Switzerland and Sweden, were discussed. With regard to France, despite the symbolic importance of adding a French representative to the Club, it was decided to postpone the decision; with regard to Swiss banks, Swiss Bank Corporation had applied, but it was decided that 'Switzerland should retain its neutral position' and not join. With regard to the admission of a Swedish bank, the group was divided between the Midland

---

33 A. Moravcsik, 'De Gaulle between grain and *Grandeur*: The Political Economy of French EC Policy, 1958–1970 (Part 2)', *Journal of Cold War Studies* 2, no. 3 (2000): 4–68.

Bank, which opposed the admission of Marcus Wallenberg's Stockholms Enskilda Bank, and the remaining members, who viewed the addition of a Swedish member with a favourable eye. Interestingly, the American investment bank Kuhn, Loeb & Co. had approached the EAC to ask about the possibility of inclusion, to which the committee replied that 'the Group's policy is to strengthen the new co-operation between European banks first'.[34]

The second meeting took place in Amsterdam in May 1964. The main issue at stake was again the admission to the EAC of banks in other European countries. The natural candidate was a French bank, but a decision as to the admittance of a French bank was again postponed, particularly in view of arguments put forward by the representatives of Midland Bank; according to the Midland Bank, the Club of Four 'should for the time being remain at its own and concentrate first on consolidation of the co-operation amongst themselves'.[35] We can assume that the reticence of the Midland Bank towards inviting a French partner at least partly mirrored the skirmishes of the preceding years between the British government, with its proposal for a free-trade area, and de Gaulle; those skirmishes continued for the rest of de Gaulle's presidency.[36] Deutsche Bank, represented by Hermann Josef Abs, argued that, although the EAC should be careful about admitting new members, excessive delays in admitting a French bank could result in Crédit Lyonnais or Société Générale, two of the three large nationalised banks, potentially joining a new club.

In the September 1964 meeting, Abs spoke to the Committee about the potential French new members. He had approached Crédit Lyonnais, which was 'still interested' in joining the EAC. In the ensuing exchange of views, it was felt that other banks, notably the Banque de Bruxelles, were trying to compete with the EAC and had approached other banks in several European capitals, albeit, for the time being, to no avail. Swiss Bank Corporation ultimately decided to remain neutral, provided that neither of the two other large Swiss banks was admitted in the Club. Swedish banks were also put on hold. Abs was especially keen on considering a French bank for possible inclusion, notably Crédit Lyonnais or Société Générale as, despite their nationalisation, they operated largely as private banks. Again, the Midland Bank insisted that the time was not ripe yet to include new members.

---

34 European Advisory Committee, Minutes of the Meeting held at Düsseldorf on 19 February 1964, Midland Bank Archives (henceforth MBA), 0200/190.
35 European Advisory Committee, Minutes of the Meeting held at Amsterdam on 15 May 1964, MBA, 0200/190.
36 See, for example, Moravcsik, 'De Gaulle between grain and *Grandeur*'.

During the same meeting, Abs spoke about the reactions in London with regard to the admission of the Midland Bank to the Club, the 'most upset' being Barclays Bank, followed by Westminster, Lloyds and National Provincial. Barclays Bank was so annoyed that it reduced the volume of business directed to Deutsche Bank. The meeting was relevant also because, for the first time, the committee discussed what they perceived as the 'aggressiveness of U.S. banks in Europe',[37] mirroring the political debate around what would eventually be known as the *défi américain* (the American challenge).

American activism reflected the new Kennedy administration and a reinforced interest in keeping communism at bay by spending substantial amounts of dollars abroad. As noted by Gillingham:

> Between 1963 and 1966 nearly $1.4 billion flowed annually into Europe, $837 million of it into the EEC countries. The money went largely into direct investment but not (as was widely believed) into the fearsome mega-enterprises conjured up by Servan-Schreiber [in *Le défi américain*, published in 1967] that captured imaginations and could realize the economies of scale created by the opening of the Common Market.[38]

The issue was 'not new' but it had been gaining in acuteness 'certainly in Germany and in Switzerland', where American banks were competing with domestic ones on interest rates paid on credit balances, on interest and commissions charged on loans and other facilities. A certain number of American banks were singled out as especially aggressive, namely First National City Bank followed by Morgan Guaranty Trust, the Bank of America and Chase Manhattan Bank. The committee reached the conclusion that 'some form of positive action' had to be elaborated to 'defend themselves' and to 'counteract the American banks' actions'. The final meeting of 1964 decided that new admissions should not be considered for the time being as 'although the co-operation between the members had been valuable so far, it had not been spectacular'.[39] Consequently, the club 'should gain more substance' before admitting new members. The rest of the meeting was devoted to the issue of 'United States banks in Europe' and each member bank described its domestic experience with American competition. The situation in Germany, Belgium and the Netherlands was fairly similar, with

---

37 European Advisory Committee, Minutes of the Meeting held at Brussels on 28 September 1964, MBA, 0200/190.
38 Gillingham, *European Integration*, p. 58.
39 European Advisory Committee, Minutes of the Meeting held in London on 14 December 1964, MBA, 0200/190.

long-established and newcomer banks 'adopting an increasingly aggressive attitude'. The competition of American banks was the result of the growth of American companies in Europe, coupled with the ability of American banks of transferring funds between their branches in different countries, in some cases free of commission or at better exchange rates than domestic banks.

Again, the situation for the Midland Bank was different, because the American presence was largely confined to London and, although the American banks undoubtedly 'transgressed from the accepted business code from time to time', the Midland Bank felt that matters could usually be rectified by 'persuasion'. It is extremely interesting to note the radically different attitude towards the American challenge in the banking domain versus what was happening in the political and economic field. Commercial banks showed a proactiveness, an ability to respond in a coordinated manner to the challenge represented by American banks in a way that was completely different from the inability to devise common solutions to the challenge in other fields. For example, Kuisel, referring to the debate about the influx of American capital in Europe in the first half of the 1960s, pointed out that, 'without a common policy among the Six, American capital found havens elsewhere within the Common Market'.[40] In fact, American companies such as General Motors or Phillips Petroleum easily moved from France to Belgium once bureaucratic delays or political issues undermined their investment plans. In this sense, banks were a step ahead in their efforts to coordinate a response to the American challenge.

The American Challenge and Monetary Turbulence

The creation of the EAC coincided with the mandate of Walter Hallstein as the first president of the European Commission (1958–67) and, as mentioned above, the emergence of the American challenge in the economic and political sphere, which meant increasing European exposure to world markets, initiating structural changes and prompting defensive measures on the part of the Commission.[41]

Much of the capital invested in Europe was represented by direct investments in the manufacturing sector,[42] but a sizeable amount did flow into the coffers of American banks that fuelled the burgeoning Eurodollar market. The rise of the Eurodollar market was the result of several overlapping factors: increasing investments and a strengthening balance of payments in Europe, Soviet fears of expropriation of their assets detained in the United States, increased activity of

40 R. F. Kuisel, 'De Gaulle's Dilemma: The American Challenge and Europe', *French Politics and Society* 8, no. 4 (1990): 13–24.
41 Gillingham, *European Integration*, p. 58.   42 Kuisel, 'De Gaulle's Dilemma'.

US-based multinational companies in Europe and American regulation of inter-est rates. These elements – plus the restrictions on the external use of sterling by the Bank of England in 1957 and the fundamental return to current account convertibility by the major European countries in December 1958 – allowed foreign banks in London in particular to accept deposits in dollars offering higher rates to depositors than in the United States.

Eurodollar transactions also held another crucial competitive advantage. They were not constrained either by the capital controls imposed in the United States after the end of the Korean War to counter the gradual balance of payment deterioration, such as the Interest Equalization Tax, the Voluntary Foreign Credit Restraint Program and the Foreign Direct Investment Program, or by monetary regulations imposed since the Great Depression such as Regulation Q.

Without regulations and limitations, banks operating in the Eurodollar market were able, on the one hand, to pay higher rates to depositors at very short maturities and, on the other, to lend at lower interest rates than domestic banks. It comes as no surprise, then, that the Eurodollar business became a privileged tool at the disposal of a new generation of bankers born after the Great Depression, to open a wide breach in the restrictive order built in Bretton Woods.

Until the early 1960s, when the BIS started to collect data from reporting countries, there were no comprehensive and credible statistics for the Eurodollar market. Italy, Switzerland, the UK, Canada and Japan were the largest sources of Eurodollar deposits. The first year of systematic analysis of the Eurocurrency market is 1963, and during that year the gross (i.e., includ-ing interbank deposits) dollar liabilities of ten reporting countries amounted to US$10.475 billion.

In 1965, the EAC informed Crédit Lyonnais that no changes in the com-position of the club were in sight. Crédit Lyonnais took notice and expressed interest in knowing the club's stance with regard to US banks operating in Europe, especially with regard to their transactions on European capital markets. Discussion then shifted to the working groups that had recently been created to analyse several issues. The committee had decided that the 'first priority' of the Economic Research Group was to prepare a study on the chemical industry 'in particular in view of the strong American competition'.[43] The Eurodollar market continued to attract the attention of

43 European Advisory Committee, Minutes of the Fifth Meeting of the Committee held in Frankfurt am Main on 15 March 1965, MBA, 0200/190.

member banks and 'the future development of the Eurodollar market in particular ought to be watched closely by the member banks'.

National issues often dominated the discussions within the EAC. In the October 1965 meeting, Mr Karsten of the Amsterdam-Rotterdam Bank spoke about the difficulties in getting contracts for the Organisation Européenne de Recherches Spatiales, which 'the French are clearly controlling [. . .] to such an extent that for projects originating from its studies only guarantees of French banks are accepted', saying that, in order to do something about that, 'it is our intention to protest against this situation through the intermediary of the Dutch Ministry of Foreign Affairs'.[44]

In 1966, the expansion of American banks in Europe continued to worry the members of the EAC greatly. In the first annual meeting, it was reported that:

> It was felt by all those present that the larger American banks that have embarked on expanding their branches network in Continental Europe are doing so quite resolutely with deliberate absence of regard for the illwill [sic] this may cause among the national banking communities, and that apart from going after the business generated by the local American interests, they are also competing with the local banks for the international business of the latter's more important customers.[45]

With regard to membership extension, although the committee agreed that it was 'still premature to approach any other bank', the committee decided, 'with respect to France, which is considered most important in the European scene', that each member 'should watch the development of the French banking situation very carefully'.[46] The committee also exchanged information on European capital markets and on the activities of American banks, in this regard, EAC banks raised the question of whether it would be opportune to open up banking activities in the United States. Potential 'countermeasures' against American activities were widely discussed in the subsequent meeting in September 1966. The group reached the conclusion that, 'if it were to be at all successful, any joint venture in the United States on the part of European banks should [. . .] carry considerable weight to cope with fundamental conditions in the U.S. such as the size of the territory and

---

44 European Advisory Committee, Minutes of the Fifth Meeting of the Committee held in Amsterdam on 18 October 1965, MBA, 0200/190.
45 European Advisory Committee, Minutes of the Ninth Meeting of the Committee held in Brussels on 14 March 1966, MBA, 0200/190.
46 European Advisory Committee, Minutes of the Tenth Meeting, held in Frankfurt/Main on 20 June 1966, MBA, 0200/190.

the strength of local home-based competition'. This precondition would require European banks to join their forces, which 'would involve considerable if not insuperable difficulties'. Some EAC members also felt that such a move into US territory would most probably constitute 'an additional excuse for increased competition of American banks in Europe and would, in any event, not counteract such competition'.[47] German banks, supported by Dutch and Belgian banks, described the 'forceful and often hardly ethical competition of American banks'. Mr Karsten of Amsterdam-Rotterdam Bank stressed the 'seriousness of U.S. banks' competition in Europe and internationally', fearing that 'time is running out for European banks'. The most worrisome element in the strategy of American banks was the participation in European banks; amongst the potential defence mechanisms figured, according to Karsten, cooperation with American banks not yet established in Europe, or entering into cooperation with banks operating in 'underdeveloped countries' to forestall the influence of American banks.

The extension of membership continued to encounter serious problems. Deutsche Bank 'recommended' the entry of Crédit Lyonnais as the latter was anxious to extend its relationship with Deutsche Bank in such areas as trade promotion, publicity and investment research. Nonetheless, Karsten of Amsterdam-Rotterdam Bank expressed reservations in view of his bank's close ties with a competing French bank, Société Générale. Mr Crombé of Société Générale de Banque also expressed reservations on the ground that Crédit Lyonnais was a nationalised bank, that Crédit Lyonnais was in direct competition given his four branches in Belgium and, finally, on the ground of existing ties with private banking groups in France such as Crédit Industriel et Commercial. Given the opposition within the group, it was decided that member banks should continue to foster their relationships independently with French banks and that a final decision with regard to the admission of a French bank should be postponed.[48]

The discussions within the group continued to be dominated by the need to address the aggressive and 'unethical' stance of American banks. The main advantages of American banks were the circumvention of minimum tariff and rate agreements; extremely advantageous interest rates offered to the subsidiaries of US companies, compensated by good margins at home; and, finally, their ability to offer multiple currency loans through their

---

47 European Advisory Committee, Minutes of the Eleventh Meeting held in Brussels on 26 September 1966, MBA, 0200/190.
48 European Advisory Committee, Minutes of the Twelfth Meeting of the Committee held in London on 13 December 1966, MBA, 0200/190.

international branch network.[49] The group agreed that, at the domestic level, the only effective policy would be meeting 'aggression with aggression', although the members recognised that the counter-actions taken so far were 'inadequate'. The Foreign Managers Group edited a major study in July 1967 titled 'The Competition of the U.S. Banks in Europe' to describe the 'handicaps' EAC banks were suffering from and submit propositions 'on how best to counteract such handicaps'.[50] The study identified thirty American banks represented in fifteen European countries with ninety-nine branches and sixty-one 'participations'. American banks could base their business on contacts with American subsidiaries in Europe, foreign exchange dealings conducted independently, operation on the Euromarket and on orders received from the head office and from branches of the same bank located in other countries. The core business of American banks was represented by the lending business, the international payment business and operations in the money and foreign exchange market. Target customers included large American multinational companies and internationally oriented European companies. Overall, although American banks could count on certain advantages such as easy access to dollars, the study recognised that EAC banks had 'very substantial advantages' and it was crucial to impress on existing and new customers this domestic advantage and 'superiority'.

In 1967, a joint venture to operate on the Euromarket was established under the name Banque Européenne de Crédit à Moyen Terme.

A reworked version of the study on the presence of American banks in Europe was prepared in November 1967. In this new version, it was recognised that the main advantage of American banks resided in their international organisation as they offered 'multinational companies world-wide parallel service for the activities of these latter and they are in practice the only banks in the world to do so'.[51]

The report also outlined two tendencies with long-lasting consequences for European banks. On the one hand, European banks had to adapt themselves to the 'increasing liberalisation of trade, services and capital transfers'; on the other, 'growing economic integration in Europe and elsewhere'. American competition was a direct consequence of a world-wide trend towards 'concentration'.

49 European Advisory Committee, Minutes of the Foreign Managers' Meeting at Amsterdam on 10 January 1967, MBA, 0200/190.
50 'The Competition of U.S. Banks in Europe', 3 July 1967, MBA, 0200/190.
51 'EBIC's International Policies with Special Reference to the Competition of American Banks', November 1967, MBA, 0200/190.

Nonetheless, by 1968, intra-community investments were twice those coming from the United States, and the American challenge was slowing[52] at a time when the club had to face a period of monetary instability across Europe centred around the 'startling emergence' of the DM as an object of 'fevered speculation'.[53] German industrial production in the first quarter of 1968 had been 7 per cent, and orders received by industry were 13 per cent up on the levels reported for the same period of 1967, while Germany's trade account surplus had reached DM5.4 billion. As a result of the strong performance of the German economy, the liquid reserves of the banking system continued to increase, in part as a consequence of the inflow of 'hot money' from the Eurodollar market, as a study prepared by Deutsche Bank in May 1968 reported.[54] Speculation on a revaluation of the DM continued throughout 1968, especially in the summer of 1968 when German Minister of Economy Karl Schiller travelled to London in late August. Some US$359 million entered West Germany between 27 and 29 August. In an emergency meeting in Bonn in November 1968, the Americans and European governments pushed for a revaluation of the DM, but the move was firmly resisted by Schiller and his colleague at the Ministry of Finance, Franz Josef Strauss. The fact that French banks were in the hands of the French state continued to represent an obstacle to their admission into the club. During 1968, the EAC was approached by Banco Hispano-Americano of Spain and Creditanstalt-Bankverein from Austria, but the club decided that 'no action' should be taken for the time being. In 1968, the EAC decided to open a joint representative office in Djakarta (now known as Jakarta). In 1969, the monetary turbulence continued to have an impact on European countries and EAC member banks. Pressure on the DM did not stop after the November 1968 meeting; on the contrary, the West German federal elections scheduled for September 1969 offered an ideal scenario for increasing speculation.

During that year, German monetary authorities recognised that restraining measures would be needed for domestic purposes. Foreign and domestic demand for West German goods was rising rapidly, labour shortages were developing despite a large inflow of foreign workers, order backlogs were growing alarmingly long and prices were beginning to rise.[55] According to the

52 Kuisel, 'De Gaulle's Dilemma', 21.
53 W. G. Gray, '"Number One in Europe": The Startling Emergence of the Deutsche Mark, 1968–1969', *Central European History* 39 (2006): 56–78.
54 Deutsche Bank, 'Some Aspects of Latest Developments in the Financial Markets of the Federal Republic of German', 27 May 1968, MBA, 0200/190.
55 L. Krause, 'Private International Finance', *International Organization* 25, no. 3 (1971): 523–40, 526.

Bundesbank, throughout the first three quarters of 1969, the inflow of new orders from abroad increased by 18 per cent.[56]

Initially, fiscal policy was used to restrain the domestic economy as the government was able to achieve a cash surplus in its domestic budget, but fiscal policy could not do the entire job, and monetary policy was needed to reinforce the restraint.

The Bundesbank tried to increase monetary stringency by a series of moves, including increasing the reserve ratios of the banks and raising the central bank interest rate. As monetary tightness began to be felt, however, West Germans became less willing to lend to foreigners, and private foreign money was attracted into Germany. As long as foreign funds were available, the liquidity of German firms could not be effectively squeezed by the Bundesbank.

Speculation on a revaluation of the DM acquired further momentum at the end of the first quarter of 1969 when a speech by Strauss about a possible revaluation of the DM to cool off the German economy set off a rush of funds into the DM, which was greatly facilitated by the unregulated Eurodollar market. Between 1 and 9 May, an estimated US$4 billion flowed into West Germany through the Eurodollar market.[57] Unfortunately for speculators, Strauss announced on 9 May that the DM would not be revalued. In the days after the announcement only US$1.5 billion left West Germany.

The Bundesbank continued to implement a restrictive monetary policy by raising twice the banks' minimum reserve ratios, first in June by about 15 per cent, and then again in August by a further 10 per cent. Furthermore, the central bank's interest rate was increased in April, June and September from 3 per cent to 6 per cent. The effort of the Bundesbank continued to be nullified in 'greater part' by the inflows coming from abroad. After a short break, speculation on the DM continued as the general election on September 28 approached. Ultimately, the Bundesbank realised that 'restrictive measures without alteration of the exchange rate [. . .] largely cancelled each other out'.[58]

The official foreign currency exchanges were closed on the last two business days before the election, and the Bundesbank decided to stop intervening on the foreign exchange market. The mark was allowed to float briefly between September 30 and October 24, before being re-pegged

56 Bundesbank Annual Report 1969, p. 1.
57 Confidential Report of the Economic Intelligence Unit, 'Euro-Currency Market', 4 June 1969, Bank of England Archives, 6A123/6.
58 Bundesbank Annual Report 1969, p. 13.

upward (after consultation with the International Monetary Fund and the Monetary Committee of the European Economic Community) on October 24 by 9.3 per cent at DM 3.66 per US dollar instead of the former DM 4.00, the largest revaluation since the creation of the Bretton Woods system. The choice of a high revaluation rate was justified by the need to look convincing and by the need to check internal economic activity and domestic price increases.

The speculation on the DM deeply upset the Bundesbank. For the first time since the Great Depression, it showed how international capital markets could facilitate speculative flows by providing a more sophisticated and quicker mechanism to reflect confidence flows. Consequently, after many years of benign neglect, starting from 1969, the attitude of the Bundesbank became gradually but decisively critical for the Eurocurrency market, as German monetary authorities became the most active opponents of these funds that were free to roam from one country to another with dire consequences on domestic (anti-inflationary) monetary and credit policies. Ultimately, the resurgence of capital mobility was making it more difficult for regulatory authorities to pursue domestic goals and the 'eurocurrency market flows seemed to work against German monetary policy'.[59]

Insofar as the EAC was concerned, after the one in Djakarta another representative office was opened in South Africa (in Johannesburg) in 1969 and another one in Toronto in 1971. No new members were accepted until 1971, when Creditanstalt from Austria and Société Générale from France joined the club. In September 1970, EAC members together with the Commercial Bank of Australia, Fuji Bank of Japan and United California Bank International created the Euro-Pacific Finance Corporation as an investment bank active in medium- and long-term lending.

The year 1970 proved to be especially important both for European monetary integration and for banking clubs. During that year, the ambitious Werner Plan was announced. The plan contained proposals for 'currency unification, a common fiscal policy and coordination of regional and structural policies, as being ancillary to economic integration'.[60] The plan envisaged a European monetary union by 1980, which would be gradually achieved through a three-step process. Ultimately the ambitious plan failed to deliver, although several of its items of advice were followed by European countries. In March 1972, exchange-rate fluctuations were

59 Toniolo, *Central Bank Cooperation*, p. 464.
60 N. Acocella, *The European Monetary Union: Europe at the Crossroads* (Cambridge and New York, NY, Cambridge University Press, 2020), p. 6.

reduced by limiting the swings in bilateral exchange rates to a 2.25 per cent band (an arrangement known as the 'snake in the tunnel') and a European Monetary Cooperation Fund was established in Basel in 1973 to increase cooperation between member states working towards Economic and Monetary Union.[61]

The Werner Plan was presented in an extremely convoluted period in contemporary history when the Bretton Woods system, which had been in place since 1944, was crumbling and the post-war miracle partly based on cheap oil and post-war reconstruction was ending.

In 1970 a new banking club, named Europartners, saw the light of day thanks to the initiative of Crédit Lyonnais and Germany's Commerzbank. The original idea of the club was to become one big European unified bank. The rationale for creating Europartners was the idea that Europe was definitely moving towards becoming a unified political entity: Crédit Lyonnais and Commerzbank (and in 1971 Banco di Roma from Italy) imagined Europe in the late 1970s as being 'marked by individualisation of European monetary space with reduced fluctuations between currencies of member countries', by 'harmonisation in the fiscal, legal and social domains', by the 'convergence of cyclical and monetary policies' and by 'some progress in the freedom of capital movements between member states but increased capital controls between member countries and third parties'.[62]

Once Crédit Lyonnais, one of the three large nationalised French banks, had created its own club, the resistance to accepting a nationalised bank in the EAC started to fade. In a special meeting convoked in Amsterdam, in November 1970, Karsten of Amsterdam-Rotterdam Bank argued that 'with increasing grouping taking place between European banks, there was now a real danger that we could find ourselves left without a major French or Italian partner'.[63] Consequently, Karsten felt that it was finally time to invite two large nationalised banks, such as Société Générale from France and Banca Commerciale Italiana from Italy. The former would join in 1971 to respond to Crédit Lyonnais, and Banca Commerciale Italiana would become a member in 1973. A Europe of banks was finally taking shape.

61 Kenen and Meade, *Regional Monetary Integration*, p. 46.
62 'Perspectives de la coopération interbancaire: Réflexions préliminaires concernant les besoins de services bancaires et financiers', probably 1972, Crédit Lyonnais Archives, 143AH8.
63 European Advisory Committee, Special Meeting in Amsterdam, 18 November 1970, MBA, 0200/0267.

Conclusion

The period from the Bretton Woods conference to the Barre Memoranda is not considered to have been the most fruitful in terms of European monetary integration compared with what would happen in the following decades, namely the Werner Plan of 1970, the European Monetary System of 1979, the Maastricht Treaty of 1992 and the adoption of the euro in 2002.[64] Nonetheless, the two-and-a-half decades that followed 1944 should be analysed as a foundational moment in the history of European monetary unification, creating 'an adaptable framework of institutions that would, over decades, make progress possible toward free trade, open markets, stable currencies, and liberal societies'.[65]

The integrational process, the chapter has shown, was a multifaceted process which involved a multiplicity of actors from the public but also from the private sphere. The role and agency of the latter have been underappreciated by existing narratives. The chapter has shown how bankers reacted to, and sometime anticipated, progress towards European integration, for example by creating formal banking associations with the intent of creating a unified European banking conglomerate. Bankers were also capable of developing innovative responses to perceived challenges from abroad, namely from American multinational banks, something that was much more complex to realise in the political field.

European banks reacted to each milestone in the integration process, such as the Rome Treaty or the creation of the Committee of Governors, by creating new tools to cooperate and reinforce this cooperation. Banking clubs such as the EAC constitute a fitting example; although they were criticised for their apparent ineffectiveness, banking clubs proved to be a valuable tool to share knowledge about European and international markets, enter the burgeoning and unregulated Eurodollar market and devise potential strategies to counteract the competition of American banks. Banking clubs also show the challenges of the European project. Accepting new members proved to be contentious and the source of multiple discussions because the nationalised status of French and Italian banks posed a problem to most of the EAC members. Challenges came from within, but also from outside. The American challenge coming from American banks presented a constant

64 See, for example, K. Dyson and K. Featherstone, *The Road to Maastricht: Negotiating Economic and Monetary Union* (Oxford and New York, NY, Oxford University Press, 1999); K. Dyson (ed.), *European States and the Euro: Europeanization, Variation, and Convergence* (Oxford and New York, NY, Oxford University Press, 2002).
65 Gillingham, *European Integration*, p. 76.

threat over the heads of European banks, but their response, partly based on banking clubs and banking consortia, allowed European banks to lay the foundations for a strong international expansion starting in the 1970s and continuing until the debt crisis of 1982.[66] Banking clubs and consortia allowed European banks to open international offices in a cost-effective way in a world with high costs of information, communication and transport.

At a time when European monetary integration was still in its infancy, private actors provide a useful lens through which we can better appreciate not only the opportunities that the process of monetary integration was opening to them but also the many challenges looming on the horizon.

Recommended Reading

Altamura, C. E. *European Banks and the Rise of International Finance: The Post-Bretton Woods Era* (Abingdon, Routledge, 2017).

Battilossi, S. and Y. Cassis (eds.). *European Banks and the American Challenge: Competition and Cooperation in International Banking under Bretton Woods* (Oxford, Oxford University Press, 2002).

Dyson, K. and K. Featherstone, *The Road to Maastricht: Negotiating Economic and Monetary Union* (Oxford and New York, NY, Oxford University Press, 1999).

Eichengreen, B. *Globalizing Capital: A History of the International Monetary System* (Princeton, NJ and Oxford, Princeton University Press, 2008).

James, H. *Making the European Monetary Union* (Cambridge, MA and London, Harvard University Press, 2012).

Mourlon-Druol, E. *A Europe Made of Money* (Ithaca, NY, Cornell University Press, 2012).

---

66 On the expansion of European banks in the post-1973 period, see Altamura, *European Banks*; Altamura, 'Global Banks and Latin American Military Dictators, 1974–1982', *Business History Review* 95 (2021): 301–32. On the debt crisis see, for example, C. E. Altamura and J. Flores Zendejas, 'Politics, International Banking, and the Debt Crisis of 1982', *Business History Review* 94 (2020): 753–78; W. Cline, *International Debt: Systemic Risk and Policy Response* (Washington, DC, Institute for International Economics, 1984); R. Devlin, *Debt and Crisis in Latin America* (Princeton, NJ, Princeton University Press, 1989).

From the Werner Report to the Start of EMU

HUBERT ZIMMERMANN

From the Werner Plan to the Snake

In November 1968, the finance ministers of the Group of Ten, comprised of the leading industrial nations, convened in Bonn for an emergency meeting. It focused on recent monetary turbulence in the markets, particularly the rampant speculation against the French franc and the British pound, but also on the weakness of the American dollar, a core issue of international monetary diplomacy throughout the 1960s. The finance ministers of France, the United Kingdom (UK) and the United States, representing the major Western allies of the Federal Republic of Germany (FRG), exerted strong pressure on the Germans to revalue their currency so as to stop the speculative movements against the weaker currencies. (Throughout this chapter, unless specified otherwise, 'Germany' and 'Germans' refer to the FRG.) Their efforts were to no avail. The proceedings, humorously described in many ex-post accounts, soon bordered on the farcical and ended with complete disagreement.[1]

This blatant failure of monetary cooperation underlined that the transatlantic management characterising Western monetary diplomacy after the Bretton Woods conference in 1944 was at its last gasp. Monetary imbalances had undermined the system of fixed-but-adjustable exchange rates as postwar capital controls were removed. Constant disruptive spillovers from a volatile American monetary policy and the dogged pursuit of a conservative, anti-inflationary currency policy by Germany were to remain core factors in the following three decades that witnessed the slow and convoluted emergence of a common European currency and, thus, the

---

1 A. Wilkens, 'L'Europe et sa première crise monétaire. Bonn et Paris en novembre 1968', *Journal of European Integration History* 18, no. 2 (2012): 221–43.

replacement of a transatlantic monetary order by a regional, that is, European order.[2]

The extremely negative international reaction to their stance at the Bonn Conference intensified the concern of many German policy-makers that a go-it-alone policy, geared predominantly towards domestic objectives, would undermine both the transatlantic and the European framework of alliances that had sustained the nation's political and economic rise from the ashes. Despite continued currency turmoil after the conference, a coalition of German industry and farming interests, along with the majority Christlich Demokratische Union (CDU)/Christlich-Soziale Union alliance of parties in the ruling coalition, managed to hold off revaluation until the federal elections of October 1969.[3] The institutionally entrenched fixation of the German economy on export-led growth was to become one of the most serious and persistent underlying causes of monetary instability in Europe, lasting until today.[4] As a result of Germany's refusal to revalue, Franco-German relations reached a new low. The French franc had become the epicentre of speculation due to the unstable political situation in France after the unrest of May 1968. Reeling under costly and inefficient efforts to stabilise the currency and afraid that the Common Agricultural Policy (CAP), the core French economic interest in the European Communities (EC), would be irreparably damaged, the French government repeatedly urged Germany to agree to a European solution that could deal with the situation.[5] The Franco-German dynamic playing out in this episode was a constant feature of European monetary integration, leaving other countries such as Britain (by its own choice), Italy (weakened by political and economic troubles) or the Benelux countries (due to their small size) with comparatively little influence.

After another year of turbulence, involving a devaluation of the franc and a revaluation of the Deutsche Mark (DM), the newly elected Chancellor of Germany, Willy Brandt, announced his support for monetary union and a European reserve fund at the EC Hague Summit of

2 H. Zimmermann, 'The Fall of Bretton Woods and the First Attempt to Construct a European Monetary Order', in L. Magnusson and B. Stråth (eds.), *From the Werner Plan to the EMU: In Search of a Political Economy for Europe* (Brussels, Peter Lang, 2001), pp. 49–72.

3 W. G. Grey, '"Number One in Europe": The Startling Emergence of the DM, 1968–69', *Central European History* 39 (2006): 56–78.

4 A. Nölke, 'Exportism as an Ideology in World Politics', in K.-G. Giesen (ed.), *Ideologies in World Politics* (Wiesbaden, Springer, 2020), pp. 125–43.

5 Akten zur Auswärtigen Politik Deutschlands (henceforth AAPD) 1969, I: Doc. 147, Conversation of Chancellor Kiesinger with French Ambassador Seydoux, 7 May 1969, pp. 559–62.

December 1969.[6] This placed the issue of a common currency, which until then had been a topic for technocrats and political visionaries, firmly on the agenda of European heads of state.

The idea reflected the fear that the monetary problem would damage European integration. As early as in January 1969, the Head of the Economic Department in the German Federal Chancellery had outlined the dilemma clearly:

> Germany is confronted with two options: (1) according to its stability policy priority over European politics (i.e., the preservation and further development of the Community). A consequential stability policy which is shielded from external influences will inevitably set in motion tendencies favouring dissolution of the EC; or (2) rather according to its European policy a certain priority over stability policy and accepting higher inflation than hitherto, be it through a renunciation of certain external economic preferences or through a common growth and economic policy.[7]

Brandt chose the second option. He was about to set in motion a policy of reconciliation with the East (the so-called Ostpolitik) that needed a strong anchoring in European institutions as an antidote to lingering fears of German hegemony, an obvious parallel to Chancellor Helmut Kohl's reasoning prior to Maastricht.[8]

The French enthusiastically embraced Chancellor Brandt's proposal, since it offered them three major advantages: first, getting closer to their longstanding aspiration of more independence from dollar hegemony;[9] secondly, preserving advantageous EC policies, such as the CAP; and thirdly, getting the Germans to assume some of the burden of adjustment in future intra-European imbalances. However, this obligation, probably even more constraining than the by now quite onerous political commitment to intervene under the Bretton Woods system, led the Germans to

---

6 Statement by W. Brandt at the Hague Summit, 1 December 1969, www.cvce.eu/en/col lections/unit-content/-/unit/02bb76df-do66-4c08-a58a-d4686a3e68ff/a4b76b9e-9b8b-4752-9657-05e26c5a1f5d/Resources#840ec5a1-a449-4822-9662-49e92450c706_en&overlay.
7 Bundesarchiv (henceforth BA), B 136/3332, Dept. III/1 (Meyer) to Chancellor Kiesinger, 8 January 1969.
8 For the genesis of this proposal, see A. Wilkens, 'Der Werner-Plan. Währung, Politik und Europa, 1968–1971', in F. Knipping and M. Schönwald (eds.), *Aufbruch zum Europa der zweiten Generation: Die europäische Einigung 1969–84* (Trier, Wissenschaftlicher Verlag Trier, 2004), pp. 217–44; H. Zimmermann, 'Der unschlüssige Hegemon: Deutschland und die Anfänge der europäischen Währungsintegration', in Knipping and Schönwald (eds.), *Aufbruch zum Europa der zweiten Generation*, pp. 203–16.
9 D. J. Howarth, *The French Road to European Monetary Union* (Basingstoke, Palgrave Macmillan, 2001).

take a very cautious stance in the ensuing negotiations. These were pursued in a Committee under the chairmanship of Luxembourg's Prime Minister Pierre Werner,[10] where two groups emerged. Adherents of the so-called coronation theory, particularly the German and Dutch governments, argued that monetary union could only constitute the final step in a long-term process of economic convergence among the participating economies. Presaging a lasting intra-European debate, they focused particularly on low inflation rates and the elimination of excessive government deficits and debts. German negotiators carefully avoided binding commitments as long as their European partners were not willing to share Germany's basic economic philosophy and to implement structural changes in their economic policies.[11] In contrast, France, Belgium and Italy argued that a monetary union would impose the necessary convergence and thus should be the first step to be taken, with a European Reserve Fund tackling any imbalances. However, this proposal was rejected. At the same time, the French government remained opposed to a form of political union which most experts regarded as a precondition for a working monetary union and which was mentioned explicitly in the Werner Plan. This asymmetry between monetary and political union remained the central problem at the heart of the common currency.

Despite these fundamental differences, the experts presented their plan in October 1970.[12] The authors of the Werner Report, foreshadowing Alan Milward's well-known argument,[13] made it explicit that the core idea was to regain monetary sovereignty for Europe and its member states: 'The increasing interpenetration of the economies has entailed a weakening of autonomy for national economic policies. The control of economic policy has become all the more difficult because the loss of autonomy at the national level has not been compensated by the inauguration of Community policies.'[14] Their plan foresaw a monetary union in stages, involving a parallel coordination of monetary and macroeconomic policies among the participating nations. The fundamental differences between the monetarist camp and the economist camp were

10 E. Danescu, *Pierre Werner and Europe: The Family Archives behind the Werner Report* (Cham, Palgrave Macmillan, 2019).
11 Political Archive, Foreign Office Germany (henceforth PA-AA), III A 1, 590, Memorandum by State Secretary Schöllhorn, 23 April 1970.
12 'Werner Report' (1970), https://ec.europa.eu/economy_finance/publications/pages/publication6142_en.pdf.
13 A. Milward, *The European Rescue of the Nation State* (Berkeley, CA, University of California Press, 1992).
14 'Werner Report', p. 8.

papered over by the text.[15] In particular, the core question of who should bear the burden of adjustment in the case of monetary imbalances was left unresolved. The first stage was supposed to begin in January 1971, and to last for 3 years. It was the only clearly defined stage, and projected a narrowing of the margins of fluctuation of the exchange rates of European currencies as well as the establishment of a European Monetary Cooperation Fund.

The Werner Plan was accepted by the EC governments, but it faced an extremely unstable economic environment, as vividly demonstrated by the events of May 1971. Once more, Germany was confronted with a massive speculative influx of dollars and the Bundesbank reeled under its obligations to intervene in the market. Combating inflation was its mantra, and it regarded the neutralisation of speculative money as 'imported inflation'. The bank's governing council was split over whether the FRG should float the DM or whether it should try to stem the tide with capital controls and a temporary float.[16] The government was concerned about the detrimental impact on the EC: 'A unilateral German monetary action without prior consultation would throw the EC into a crisis and give rise to doubts about Germany's adherence to the treaties.'[17] It tried to persuade the other European nations to implement a temporary joint float against the dollar, thereby creating a common currency bloc against the dollar. France and Italy refused to participate and advocated strict capital controls, which was in turn resisted by the German Minister of Economics, Karl Schiller. In the end, the DM floated unilaterally, effectively putting an end to any prospect of achieving the objectives set out by the Werner Committee in the near future. Soon, however, the Germans had to realise that such an isolated course would imperil the whole European framework within which its economic and security policies were embedded.

Thus, despite its quick demise, the Werner Plan paved the way for the breakthrough of the European option. The talks institutionalised a constant European dialogue, which first complemented but then increasingly supplanted the established transatlantic forums. The regular meetings of the Monetary Committee of the EC (composed of two representatives of the Commission and two of each member state), the Committee of Governors,

---

15 A. Verdun, 'The Political Economy of the Werner and Delors Reports: Continuity amidst Change or Change amidst Continuity?', in Magnusson and Stråth (eds.), *From the Werner Plan to EMU*, pp. 73–96.

16 D. Heisenberg, *The Mark of the Bundesbank* (Boulder, CO, Lynne Rienner Press, 1999), p. 31.

17 PA-AA, IIIA1, vol. 585, Memorandum by von Bismarck-Osten, 6 May 1971.

which assembled the central bank governors of all EC member states, and the working parties established by these committees led to the emergence of an increasing transnational consensus. Slowly, this consensus converged on the monetary philosophy of the Bundesbank as the central bank which was perceived to be most successful. Finally, the Werner Plan also contained the blueprint of a mechanism to narrow the fluctuations among European currencies: the so-called 'Snake'.

The Snake

Richard Nixon's decision to dissolve the gold–dollar link in August 1971 set into motion the last stage of the unravelling of the transatlantic order of monetary cooperation, progressively removing the cocoon which had shielded the Europeans from the necessity to solve monetary disagreements primarily among themselves.[18] Sharp divisions on how to react to this American challenge emerged in Europe. Instead of agreeing on a common strategy, most European countries still hoped for a transatlantic solution. After some weeks of uncertainty, the United States, Europe and Japan came to the Smithsonian agreement of December 1971 which realigned their currencies and created a 'tunnel' of ±2.25 per cent within which the newly agreed par values would fluctuate. However, it soon became obvious that the Americans were unwilling to intervene decisively in defence of the parities reached at the end of 1971. As a result, European exchange rates once more experienced turbulence. The Germans finally resorted to capital controls, resulting in the resignation of Schiller and his replacement with former Defence Minister Helmut Schmidt.[19] Attempts to narrow intra-European differences as prescribed by the Werner Plan were restarted and led to the so-called Snake, an attempt to stabilise European exchange rates within the tunnel provided by the Smithsonian agreement.

The Snake started in April 1972, with Belgium, France, Germany, Luxemburg, Italy and the Netherlands as members. One week later, the UK, Ireland and Denmark, which were about to enter the EC in January 1973, also joined. To support the arrangement, Commission Vice President Raymond Barre proposed a European Fund for Monetary Cooperation,

---

18 E. Mourlon-Druol, 'European Monetary Integration', in S. Battilossi, Y. Cassis and K. Yago (eds.), *Handbook of the History of Money and Currency* (Singapore, Springer, 2020), pp. 809–32.

19 H. James, *International Monetary Cooperation since Bretton Woods* (Oxford, Oxford University Press), p. 240.

which should provide funds to countries that had to intervene due to their currencies reaching the margins prescribed by the Snake. This idea, however, was resisted by the hard currency countries, and a European equivalent of the International Monetary Fund (IMF) would remain but a dream, even after the creation of the common currency.

The Snake experienced a rocky start due to the continuing instability created by the dollar. The UK soon left, in June 1972, and floated the pound. Nonetheless, the EC heads of government reaffirmed their determination to press ahead with the future objective of monetary union and the goal of creating some kind of European Monetary Fund, as they did at the Paris EC summit of October 1972. In early 1973, the final crisis of the Bretton Woods system erupted as the United States devalued the dollar by another 10 per cent. Once again, huge sums of money moved to Germany, since the DM was the most likely candidate for further appreciation. Faced with this prospect, the resulting damage to German exporters as well as a collapse of the 'Snake', Chancellor Brandt urgently appealed to Nixon to support German efforts to stem speculation and restart negotiations for a new monetary system.[20] However, Nixon just reminded Brandt that the United States was not obliged under the Smithsonian agreement to intervene in markets.[21] Resorting once more to capital controls was seen by the Bundesbank as ineffective and impossible to implement.[22] Another isolated float was ruled out. Finance Minister Helmut Schmidt stated in an interview soon after the crisis: 'The Federal Government had at no point during the February and March crises of the dollar the intention to embark on monetary unilateralism, either through autonomous revaluation or isolated floating.'[23] The paramount consideration by now was cooperation with European partners. The Germans told the EC members that the FRG was prepared 'to pay a high price' if they would join them in a common float that would take the 'Snake' out of the tunnel.[24] They tried hard to elicit the participation of the British, whose Prime Minister Edward Heath was in Bonn during the height of the crisis. However, the British posed conditions (large-scale unconditional credits) which, according to one observer,

---

20 AAPD 1973, I, Doc. 44, Brandt to Nixon, 9 February 1973.
21 Declassified Documents Reference System 2006, Nixon to Brandt, 10 February 1973, Doc. nr. CK3100519753.
22 Bundesbank Archive (henceforth BBA), B 330, 6702/2, Minutes 381st Central Bank Council Meeting, 7 February 1973.
23 Der Spiegel no. 12 (1973): 73.
24 AAPD 1973, I, Doc. 69, German–British Summit Meeting, 1 March 1973, p. 336, n. 2.

amounted to 'a humorous way of rejecting participation'.[25] Italy, which had left the Snake in February 1973, also shied away from a common float with the DM. France, however, while at first adamant it would not join a DM zone without partners to balance German dominance, finally gave up its resistance to bloc floating. After all, this offered one way towards the long-term French objective of escaping dollar hegemony, and a better chance to work towards a more symmetrical monetary system, even if dollar constraints were replaced by the need to follow German policies. The bitter pill of bloc floating was sweetened by a small German revaluation and helped along by the unspoken, but quite obvious, threat of unilateral German action with unforeseeable consequences for the Common Market. Schmidt gave the EC partners 10 days to arrive at a solution.[26] In an emergency meeting on 11 March 1973, six EC members (later joined by Norway and Sweden) decided on a common float and on the termination of buying dollars. One month later, a European Monetary Cooperation Fund was established, which, although it did not have its own resources and played only an advisory role, would become 'the kernel of the future organisation of central banks at the Community level'[27].

Despite the commitment in principle to common European solutions, it proved difficult to stabilise intra-European exchange rates, given the economic turmoil, which was compounded by the oil-price crisis and economic stagflation in the EC. Strongly diverging economic policies doomed the arrangement almost from its inception. Inflation rates in most of Europe soared above the German benchmark (see Figure 10.1), and in May 1974 France was forced out of the Snake after it lost almost a fifth of its reserves in a futile attempt to stabilise the franc. In March 1975, former Commissioner Robert Marjolin published an influential report for the Commission on Economic and Monetary Union 1980, which noted the disappointing progress of monetary integration since the Werner Plan talks and emphasised the importance of more coordination in terms of fiscal policy, labour and capital markets and industrial policies.[28]

25 E. Hoffmeyer, *The International Monetary System: An Essay in Interpretation* (Amsterdam, North-Holland, 1992), p. 105.
26 AAPD 1973, Ambassador Sachs (EC, Brussels) to Auswärtiges Amt, 5 March 1973, p. 356, n. 8.
27 Danescu, *Pierre Werner and Europe*, p. 317.
28 'Report of the Study Group "Economic and Monetary Union 1980"' (1975), www .cvce.eu/content/publication/2010/10/27/93d25b61-6148-453d-9fa7-9e220e874dc5/pub lishable_en.pdf.

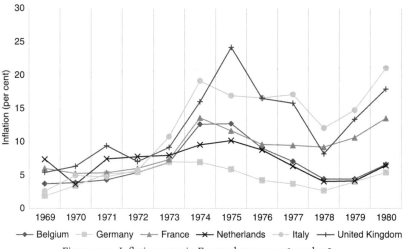

Figure 10.1   Inflation rates in Europe between 1969 and 1980.

Despite this less than stellar progress and the unstable economic environment, monetary integration continued. In a historical accident, the respective finance ministers ascended at the same time to the highest office in both France and Germany: Helmut Schmidt became Chancellor in May 1974, while Valéry Giscard d'Estaing, who had been the French minister of economics and finance since 1969, was elected as President. Thus, two heads of government with intimate knowledge of the failure of the transatlantic order and the complicated attempts to find a European alternative came to lead the two most important countries in a prospective monetary union.[29]

For Germany, the political relevance of European monetary coordination continued to grow in parallel with increasing resignation regarding the American position. The Germans also were clearly aware of their advantageous position due to the asymmetrical effects of adjustment pressures within the Snake, which they felt much less than the deficit countries, as Schmidt explained to Prime Minister Wilson: 'Those countries remaining in the Snake were forced to take care that their own

29 G. Thiemeyer, 'Helmut Schmidt und die Gründung des Europäischen Währungssystems', in F. Knipping (ed.), *Zwischen Aufbruch und Krise: Die Europäische Integration 1970–1984* (Trier, Wissenschaftlicher Verlag Trier, 2004), pp. 245–68; F. A. W. J. van Esch, 'The Rising of the Phoenix: Building the European Monetary System on a Meeting of Minds', *L'Europe en Formation* no. 353–4 (2009): 133–48.

currency would not limp behind general developments. With regard to inflation, they would therefore have to aspire to the same economic goals as the other participants. It is a loss of prestige for a country to be forced to leave the Snake. Second, the Snake has a psychological effect: the public gets the impression that governments act.'[30] The Bundesbank also supported the effort to achieve closer intra-European margins as long as this did not constrain the Bundesbank's autonomy; however, it noticed the continuous high-level consultations of EC heads of government on monetary issues with unease, wary of having to compromise the Bundesbank's priority of price stability for the sake of the government's European preferences. The inflation rate differentials among member states, which had led to frequent exchange rate adjustments, reflected in their reading the heterogeneity of national political economies and economic philosophies. For this reason, the Bundesbank's reaction to various plans for monetary union, such as the Fourcade Plan of May 1975, the All Saints' Day Manifesto of November 1975 and the Tindemans Report of December 1975, was very hesitant.[31]

Although France rejoined the Snake in July 1975 at the same rate as that at which it had left it a year previously, it was forced to exit again 8 months later. In effect, the Snake became a DM zone with the Benelux countries and the non-EC countries Norway and Sweden as members. The unhappy experience of France with the Snake opened a window of opportunity for the Giscard government to reorient economic policy towards a stronger emphasis on domestic stabilisation and a restrictive monetary policy, emulating the German model and attempting to narrow the gap in terms of economic performance. Membership in a European currency arrangement was useful as an external constraint in this respect.[32] However, this policy turn was intensely contested in domestic politics. To Giscard, it was obvious that a system with more obligations for Germany was necessary in order to achieve a more equitable sharing of the burden of intervention, which fell disproportionally on the weaker currencies. A replacement for the Snake seemed imperative.[33]

---

30 AAPD 1975, I, Conversation Schmidt–Prime Minister Wilson, May 29, 1975, p. 637.
31 H. Tietmeyer, *Herausforderung Euro: Wie es zum Euro kam und was er für Deutschlands Zukunft bedeutet* (Munich, Hanser Verlag, 2004), pp. 79–80; Heisenberg, *The Mark of the Bundesbank*, p. 44.
32 K. Dyson and K. Featherstone, *The Road to Maastricht: Negotiating Economic and Monetary Union* (Oxford, Oxford University Press, 1999), pp. 115–19.
33 V. Giscard D'Estaing, *Le pouvoir et la vie*, vol. 1: *La rencontre* (Paris, Compagnie 12, 1998).

The Rise and Fall of the European Monetary System (EMS)

In October 1977, Commission President Roy Jenkins gave a speech at the European University Institute in Florence in which he proposed monetary union as a central goal of the EC.[34] The speech was one of the highlights of the Commission's increasing advocacy for a common approach to intra-European monetary problems that time and again had derailed the efforts to ensure a smooth working of intra-European trade and of EC policies such as the CAP. It was also a response to the diverging reactions of EC members to the economic crises of the 1970s, which had created a deep malaise affecting the whole project of European integration. The speech was received with little enthusiasm as, unbeknownst to Jenkins, the Big Three, namely France, Germany and Britain, had already established a secret troika of high-level officials to work towards this goal.[35]

In April 1978, plans for the establishment of an EMS were presented to partly surprised, partly worried participants at the Copenhagen EC summit of April 1978. The proposal had been coordinated in confidential consultations between Schmidt and Giscard, the former having deliberately kept the Bundesbank in the dark about his intention to present a new initiative in the field of monetary integration. While not prepared to go as far as Jenkins' proposal for monetary union, Schmidt wanted to achieve a common European Unit of Account which would move jointly against the dollar and restore a bigger degree of European autonomy in the face of volatile US policies.[36] At Copenhagen, he proposed a European Monetary Fund following the example of the IMF, which would pool 15–20 per cent of the reserves of the participating countries.[37] The negotiations on the EMS reignited the clashes between the Bonn government and the Bundesbank, but in the end the latter had to accept the proposal. Nonetheless, it succeeded in getting an important commitment: in the case of fundamental conflict with

34 R. Jenkins, 'Europe's Present Challenge and Future Opportunity' (1977), www.cvce.eu /obj/address_given_by_roy_jenkins_on_the_creation_of_a_european_monetary_u nion_florence_27_october_1977-en-98bef841-9d8a-4f84-b3a8-719abb63fd62.html.
35 On the EMS negotiations, see E. Mourlon-Druol, *A Europe Made of Money: The Emergence of the European Monetary System* (Ithaca, NY, Cornell University Press, 2012); H. James, *Making the European Monetary Union: The role of the Committee of Central Bank Governors and the origins of the European Central Bank* (Cambridge, MA, Harvard University Press, 2012), p. 154.
36 'EMS: Callaghan Note of EMS Discussion (at Copenhagen European Council ?Dinner [sic])' (1978), www.margaretthatcher.org/document/111533.
37 James, *Making the European Monetary Union*, p. 154.

its core monetary objective, that is, domestic price stability, the Bundesbank would be permitted to suspend its intervention obligations.[38]

In December 1978, the European Council in Brussels agreed on the establishment of the EMS. Five months later, the system started with eight participating nations. Its core element, the Exchange Rate Mechanism (ERM), pegged national currencies to the value of a unit of account within a fluctuating band of ±2.25 per cent. This unit of account was named the European Currency Unit and was defined by a basket of the currencies of the member countries, reflecting their share in intra-European trade and the size of each country's gross domestic product (GDP). Once the market value of currencies reached a point close to the limits, the participating banks were obliged to intervene, by either buying or selling their currencies, to correct the exchange rate. If these interventions, which were supported by a European Monetary Cooperation Fund, turned out to be insufficient to keep the parity of a currency within the band, participating members would negotiate a realignment. Some members, such as Italy, were granted more leeway (6 per cent). The Italians, with an inflation rate substantially above the average in the Community, initially had been very reluctant to join the system, in case it did not provide for a substantial aid mechanism during currency crises. However, the fear of being excluded from the core of the European integration process and the potential of an external constraint to support the government in its efforts to implement domestic reforms finally led to Italy's participation.[39]

Britain also became a nominal member of the EMS; however, it decided to stay outside the ERM until 1990. Although the UK had initially participated in the confidential working group set up to sketch a first plan for the new monetary scheme, the British representative, in a situation reminiscent of the negotiation of the EEC Treaty in the 1950s, soon became a rather distant observer. Distrustful of German and also French motives, the UK remained on the sidelines of the path towards monetary union. Denis Healey, Britain's Chancellor of the Exchequer at the time, claimed that 'the fundamental reason'

---

38 The so-called Emminger letter is attached to a record of a long meeting between Schmidt and the Bundesbank on 30 November 1978; BBA, N2/267. For the English translation, see 'EMS: Bundesbank Council Meeting with Chancellor Schmidt (Assurances on Operation of EMS)' (1978), www.margaretthatcher.org/document/11 1554. See also D. Marsh, *The Euro: The Politics of the New Global Currency* (New Haven, CT, Yale University Press, 2009), pp. 83–6.

39 G. Bentivoglio, 'The Tentative Alliance? Britain, Italy and Participation in the European Monetary System', *Journal of European Integration History* 22, no. 1 (2016): 85–106, 96.

why Britain did not join the EMS was not due to any economic considerations, but rather its relationship with the United States, a relationship 'infinitely more important than our relationship with Europe'.[40] Given the potent spillover effects of the continuing attempts to harmonise intra-European exchange rates, the British decision was momentous.

The EMS represented a major step in monetary cooperation, with considerable symbolic importance, and was touted by the participating governments as a huge achievement in European integration. Compared with the Snake, it was more flexible and had a more potent credit mechanism. However, it contained no instruments to force economic convergence among the participating economies, and no really effective European monetary fund was created. The EMS also lacked a lender of last resort in the form of a common central bank. As a discretionary monetary system, it preserved the option of exchange rate adjustments in the case of fundamental problems. This factor has led scholars to argue that this more flexible system would have been much more adequate for a heterogeneous currency area such as the current eurozone and its single currency.[41] The exchange rate instrument certainly reduces the need for painful domestic adjustment measures that are imposed on unwilling societies and possess dubious legitimacy, as in the case of Greece during the euro crisis. However, it leaves the currency area vulnerable to asymmetrical shocks, requiring incessant political negotiations about the coordination of diverging responses. Furthermore, the objective of creating an alternative global currency to the US dollar, which, in the French reading, bestowed an 'exorbitant privilege' on the United States, was unobtainable in this way.

The EMS had a less than auspicious start. In its first 4 years, seven exchange rate adjustments were necessary. As soon as 6 months after its starting date, the DM was revalued for the first time, while the Danish krone was devalued. As it turned out, the intervention obligations in the EMS mainly fell on the weaker members. The DM became the anchor currency which allowed the Bundesbank to preserve its autonomy. This forced other countries to either mirror Germany's anti-inflationary policies, regardless of domestic conditions, or to negotiate a change in parities. This usually conflict-prone exercise became a regular feature of the EMS (Figure 10.2 shows how the participating currencies diverged over time).

---

40 Marsh, *The Euro*, p. 87.
41 M. Höpner and A. Spielau, 'Better Than the Euro? The European Monetary System (1979–1998)', *New Political Economy* 23, no. 2 (2018): 160–73.

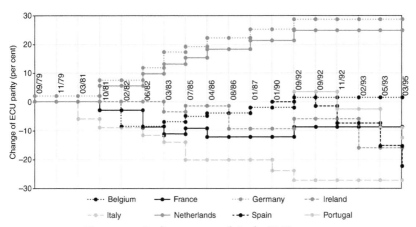

Figure 10.2   Realignment rounds in the EMS, 1979–95.

A core moment in the history of European monetary integration came after the French presidential elections of 1981 produced a socialist government under François Mitterrand. He broke with the orthodox policies of his predecessor and pursued an expansionist policy. Almost immediately, the currency markets reacted and put the parity of the franc under pressure. Despite two devaluations in 1981 and 1982, the pressure on the French did not abate. Faced with the choice of exiting the EMS altogether or discontinuing his economic policy, Mitterrand chose the latter course in March 1983. In terms of the overall economic philosophy of the European integration process, this decision for the *franc fort* (strong franc) and a policy of austerity was fundamental. A helpful DM revaluation of 5.5 per cent coupled with a smaller franc devaluation managed to stabilise the situation. The French U-turn inaugurated a trend for more economic convergence and less frequent exchange rate adjustments, which paved the way for the completion of the Common Market in the wake of the Single European Act of 1988 and the design of monetary union.[42]

Between 1987 and 1992, it seemed that the EMS had reached a certain equilibrium, though the French and Italians continued to criticise the asymmetry in the system. New members were added (Spain in 1989, the UK in 1990 and Portugal in 1992) and Italy moved to a narrower band. The Basle–Nyborg Agreement of September 1987, drafted by the Committee of Central Bank Governors, introduced limited changes aimed at increasing convergence through strengthened surveillance mechanisms and reform of the

42 Howarth, *The French Road to European Monetary Union*, pp. 55–82.

intervention mechanism, which facilitated earlier intervention and extended credit periods for the financing of foreign exchange operations.

The EMS also played a major role in the strengthening of transnational elites which disseminated what were to become the core ideas on which monetary union was founded: anti-inflationary policies, budgetary discipline, credibility towards financial markets and central bank independence.[43] What was missing once again was a mechanism for economic harmonisation and/ or resource transfer. Thus, the friction-free functioning of the mechanism was short-lived. Höpner and Spielau[44] suggest that, while the EMS made economic sense as an exchange rate mechanism, the core problem was the political costs associated with the negotiation of exchange rate alignments. In fact, these adjustments regularly led to sharp domestic and intra-European disputes. The solution for these political conflicts was obvious: an irrevocable fixing of exchange rates through monetary union.

Towards the Common Currency

In July 1987, the Single European Act, the first major revision of the Rome Treaties, came into effect. Among its goals was the free movement of capital by 1992. This prospect gave renewed impetus to ideas towards completing monetary union. The new Commission President, Jacques Delors, a former French finance minister under Mitterrand who was to become one of the most activist Commission presidents in the history of the EU, saw a monetary union as the logical complement to the Single Market.[45] He also was sensitive to the long-term French concern with France's vulnerability to the strength of the DM. A solution to this never-ending problem was also seen as increasingly necessary in the German foreign ministry. In February 1988, German Foreign Minister Hans-Dietrich Genscher came out in favour of a deepening of monetary integration and proposed the creation of a European Central Bank (ECB). Though the finance ministry and the Bundesbank urged caution, Kohl supported the idea, influenced also by its favourable reception in the media and by the business community.

In June, the Hannover European Council, on the basis of a prior under-standing between France and Germany, established a Committee com-posed of the central bank presidents of the twelve member states under

43 K. R. McNamara, *The Currency of Ideas: Monetary Politics in the European Union* (Ithaca, NY, Cornell University Press, 1998); Mourlon-Druol, *A Europe Made of Money*.
44 Höpner and Spielau, 'Better Than the Euro?'.   45 J. Delors, *Mémoires* (Paris, Plon, 2004).

the chairmanship of Delors. The participation of the central bankers made sure that these decisive actors, who had formed a core epistemic community[46] since the early days of the Werner Plan, were supportive of the eventual outcome (tellingly, the Bundesbank's president, Karl Otto Pöhl, initially refused to participate). It also ensured a common outlook among participants regarding the 'fundamental principles' underpinning an eventual monetary union: 'price stability, open and efficient markets, the free play of competition and budgetary discipline'.[47] The meetings were held at the Bank of International Settlements in Basle, a bastion of orthodox thinking.

The committee published its plan 9 months later.[48] Like the Werner Plan, which was a source of inspiration, it consisted of a proposal for the achievement of monetary union in stages, but without a fixed timetable.[49] The first stage, with a starting date of 1 July 1990, foresaw the full liberalisation of capital markets and the participation of the currencies of all member countries in the ERM. In addition, interest rate and inflation differentials among the member states were to be lessened, while budgetary discipline in prospective member states should be established. In a second stage, a European Monetary Institute, later the ECB, would be established. Its mandate would give it an independence modelled on and even surpassing the Bundesbank – a key element of the proposal which was necessary to achieve the support of central bank governors. The third stage would irrevocably fix exchange rates, culminating in a single currency for all participating nations. Distinct national economic policies, however, were to be retained, in the hope that some kind of common discipline could be imposed in the process. Intergovernmental Conferences (IGCs) on monetary and economic as well as on political union were to work out the exact steps. The talks about a political union reflected the German thesis that a strengthening of the institutions governing the EMU was necessary to ensure its democratic legitimacy.[50] Against a resistant Mitterrand, Kohl pushed for more competences for the European

---

46 A. Verdun, *European Responses to Globalization and Financial Market Integration: Perceptions of Economic and Monetary Union in Britain, France and Germany* (Houndmills, Palgrave Macmillan, 2000).

47 Monetary Committee of the EC, 'Economic and Monetary Union beyond Stage I' (1989), https://ec.europa.eu/archives/emu_history/documentation/chapter13/19891 020eno3ecomonetaryunion.pdf.

48 Committee for the Study of EMU, 'Report on Economic and Monetary Union in the European Community' (1989), https://ec.europa.eu/archives/emu_history/docu mentation/chapter13/19890412en235repeconommetary_a.pdf.

49 Delors, *Mémoires*, pp. 332–40.

50 M. Segers and F. Van Esch 'Behind the Veil of Budgetary Discipline: The Political Logic of the Budgetary Rules in EMU and the SGP', *Journal of Common Market Studies* 45, no. 5 (2007): 1089–1109.

parliament[51] as he needed to demonstrate to his domestic audience that the surrender of monetary sovereignty would be at least compensated for by more parliamentary control on the supranational level.

Widespread scepticism greeted the Delors report for both economic and political reasons. The influential Optimum Currency Area theory, formulated by Mundell[52] and refined by others (for example, McKinnon[53]), stated that a monetary union could work only under conditions such as mobility of labour and capital, symmetry of external shocks and convergence of inflation rates.[54] Many economists argued that the prospective euro members were far from constituting an optimum currency area, particularly the southern countries.[55]

Such economic arguments, however, were unable to stop the momentum. Overshadowed by the fall of the Berlin Wall and after very strong pressure by the French, the Strasbourg European Council in December 1989 established the date for the IGCs on monetary and political union. All of the member states, except the UK, accepted the recommendations of the Delors report, and by November 1991 the EMU negotiations were concluded, despite the spectacular events that in parallel had precipitated the end of the Cold War.

The results were put into treaty form at the summit in Maastricht in December 1991. Admission to the monetary union would depend on satisfying certain criteria to measure economic convergence: price stability (the inflation rate of potential members should not exceed by more than 1.5 per cent the average of the three members with the lowest inflation), debt stability (government deficits should not exceed 3 per cent of GDP and their overall debt should be below 60 per cent of GDP) and exchange rate stability (in the 2 years prior to EMU, interest rates should be no more than 2 per cent above those of the three countries with the lowest rates). As it turned out, these criteria were not set in stone.

To assuage German concerns about the use of monetary policies for political purposes, the independence of the newly created central bank was enshrined in the treaty, emulating the example of the Bundesbank. A 'no-bailout' clause,

51 Letters Kohl to Mitterrand, 27 November and 5 December 1989, in H. J. Küsters and D. Hofmann (eds.), *Dokumente zur Deutschlandpolitik: Deutsche Einheit: Sonderedition aus den Akten des Bundeskanzleramtes 1989–90* (Munich, Oldenbourg, 1998), pp. 565–7, 614–15.
52 R. A. Mundell, 'A Theory of Optimum Currency Areas', *American Economic Review* 51, no. 4 (1961): 657–65.
53 R. I. McKinnon, 'Optimum Currency Areas', *American Economic Review* 53, no. 4 (1963): 717–25.
54 M. J. Artis, 'Reflections on the Optimal Currency Area (OCA) Criteria in the Light of EMU', *International Journal of Finance and Economics* 8, no. 4 (2003): 297–307.
55 T. Sadeh, 'Who Can Adjust to the Euro?', *The World Economy* 28, no. 11 (2005): 1651–78.

stating that neither the Community nor any member state should be liable for the commitments of other members, was included to put a brake on the use of the printing press to finance government deficits.

Historians and political scientists have since debated what made this success possible. An influential and still widely cited argument is that one should see EMU as a strategy, particularly by France, to embed the reunited Germany in a European framework by neutralising its most powerful instrument, the DM.[56] In their communications with the German government, the French made it clear that there was indeed a link between their support for German reunification and monetary union.[57] Germany's Chancellor Helmut Kohl, mindful of the French apprehensions, went along with this strategy.[58] Domestic opposition to relinquishing the DM was overcome by Kohl's dogged determination to deepen European integration. Thus, EMU can be explained as a political deal between the biggest member states instead of by invoking economic arguments that, in fact, provide no clear-cut motivation.[59]

Moravcsik[60] and others argue that domestic interests were decisive for the Maastricht compromise. Only the convergence of the domestic economic self-interest of the various states made cooperation possible and led to a bargain which reflected the strength of the respective member states representing their domestic preferences. Institutionally entrenched domestic actors limited the bargaining space of the negotiators.[61] Another influential explanation has been the argument that the economic crises of the 1970s and 1980s caused a convergence of ideas around the paradigm of sound money, which had been disseminated by expert committees and transnational elites.[62]

The Maastricht deal left lots of ambiguities and unanswered questions on the table. It was in particular the 'economic' component of EMU which remained underdeveloped. The talks on economic union went nowhere,

---

56 M. J. Baun, *An Imperfect Union: The Maastricht Treaty and the New Politics of European Integration* (Boulder, CO, Westview, 1996).

57 See Küsters and Hofmann (eds.), *Dokumente zur Deutschlandpolitik*, pp. 596–600.

58 T. Pedersen, *Germany, France and the Integration of Europe: A Realist Interpretation* (London and New York, NY, Pinter, 1998).

59 T. Sadeh, and A. Verdun, 'Explaining Europe's Monetary Union. A Survey of the Literature', *International Studies Review* 11, no. 2 (2009): 277–301.

60 A. Moravcsik, *The Choice for Europe: Social Purpose and State Power from Messina to Maastricht* (Ithaca, NY, Cornell University Press, 1998).

61 K. Kaltenthaler, *Germany and the Politics of Europe's Money* (Durham, NC, Duke University Press, 1998).

62 McNamara, *The Currency of Ideas*; M. Marcussen, *Ideas and Elites: The Social Construction of Economic and Monetary Union* (Vilborg, Aalborg University Press, 2000); A. Verdun, *European Responses to Globalization*.

since they reproduced the same cleavages that had bedevilled the Werner Plan. While the French argued for a *gouvernement économique* (economic government) which would rein in the autonomy of the monetary authorities, the Germans wanted a common political structure which would have democratically legitimate powers to enforce the harmonisation of divergent economic policies. Fiscal policy, banking supervision, labour market regulation, wage setting and so on remained national competences and imposed a reliance on 'implicit' coordination.[63] In 1997, the so-called Euro-Group of finance ministers from euro members was created as an informal gathering to discuss the general direction of economic policy in the Eurozone and to serve as a potential counter-weight to the ECB.

Hopes for a smooth ratification process, however, were dashed when a Danish referendum on the treaty unexpectedly produced a negative vote. The 'permissive consensus' and the reliance on 'output legitimacy' which had served as popular legitimation for European integration was blown away.[64] The Danish political system, based on strong parliamentary oversight, was a bad fit for a monetary union which, despite some token civil participation through the European Parliament, suffered from an overwhelmingly technocratic design. After the Danish government had obtained an opt-out from parts of the treaty, including monetary union, a second referendum was held, which produced a positive result. Ratification of the Maastricht Treaty turned into a nail-biter when French president Mitterrand also decided to call a referendum, which was initially expected to pass with a comfortable majority. However, the French electorate approved the treaty in September by the slightest of margins, 51 per cent to 49 per cent. The referendum showed the strength both on the right and on the left of the political spectrum of an anti-globalist, sovereigntist sentiment, which reappeared with a vengeance during the euro-crisis, and not only in France. Britain, where public opinion has been persistently unfavourable to participation in EMU, set strict conditions on potential membership, and Prime Minister Tony Blair ruled it out in 1997.

The fundamental uncertainty about the fate of the project was compounded by the concomitant effects of the end of the Cold War, in particular German reunification. These were too much of a strain for the system and produced a massive crisis in the EMS. In response to the short-lived economic

---

63 K. Dyson, *The Politics of the Euro-Zone: Stability or Breakdown?* (Oxford, Oxford University Press, 2000).

64 F. Scharpf, *Governing in Europe: Effective and Democratic?* (Oxford, Oxford University Press, 1999).

reunification boom and the resulting inflationary pressure, the Bundesbank raised its interest rates to an extremely high level, forcing other central banks to follow suit in order to avoid destabilising capital flows into Germany. The result was a recession in other member states of the EMS.

The EMS Crisis 1992–1993 and the Stability and Growth Pact

The liberalisation of capital markets had progressed in a way that allowed speculators to target perceived weak currencies in the EMS with enormous sums and little risk. They focused particularly on the Italian lira and the British pound. The latter had only recently joined the ERM, at a rate that many economists and central bankers considered too high, and central banks were forced to intervene on a massive scale in an attempt to keep fluctuations within the prescribed bands. In September 1992, the Italian and British governments capitulated, and both countries were forced out of the EMS.[65] The Bundesbank, in particular, was subjected to intense criticism because of its interest rate policy and the refusal to intervene with its full strength. Further devaluations occurred, involving Spain, Portugal and Ireland. In July 1993, the bandwidths were increased to ±15 per cent, amounting to a de facto suspension of the EMS. After almost a year of on–off pressure, the French franc was saved only by a statement from Bundesbank President Karl Otto Pöhl who, under pressure by the German government, declared that the bank would do everything possible to defend the franc. Recalling earlier episodes in post-war European monetary history such as the 1968–9 DM-revaluation debate, the events strained German–French relations to breaking point, only to underline in the end the pivotal importance of mutually cooperative relations.[66] The crisis dramatically demonstrated the vulnerability of other currencies to German policies and served as a stark reminder of the advantages of a currency union. It also reminded sceptical economic actors in the hard currency countries that exchange rate volatility remained a major threat to their export-dependent economies. The realignments resulting from the EMS crisis produced an overvaluation of the DM, which led to a period of sluggish growth and later to far-reaching reforms in an attempt to improve the competitiveness of German products. At the same time, converging interest rates (Figure 10.3) among the prospective currencies

---

65 For an inside perspective on the crisis, see Marsh, *The Euro*, pp. 132–75.
66 E. Aeschimann and P. Riché, *La guerre de sept ans: Histoire secrète du franc fort 1989–1996* (Paris, Calmann-Lévy, 1996).

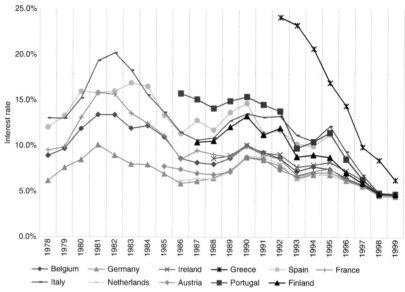

Figure 10.3   Convergence of European interest rates prior to EMU.

entering the euro allowed member countries with previously low ratings to borrow at unprecedented rates, planting the seeds for long-term imbalances, which would erupt in the second decade of the euro.

The lack of a fiscal union nurtured increasing doubts about the sustainability of the commitment to the convergence criteria once monetary union was achieved. The German domestic debate, in particular, was dominated more and more by voices which expressed serious doubts that the stability-oriented policies required in the run-up to the common currency would last once countries with a less orthodox monetary culture than Germany had gained accession to EMU. Monetary union threatened to become a contested electoral issue. As a consequence, German Finance Minister Theo Waigel launched a proposal for a binding framework which should prevent fiscal misbehaviour.[67] The so-called Stability and Growth Pact (SGP) reinforced the limits on annual government deficits to 3 per cent of GDP and the overall debt level at 60 per cent of GDP. It strengthened surveillance procedures and mandated possible fines after the Commission had given an early warning and ECOFIN had initiated the so-called excessive deficit procedure. At the

67 M. Heipertz and A. Verdun, *Ruling Europe: The Politics of the Stability and Growth Pact* (Cambridge, Cambridge University Press, 2010).

December 1995 Madrid European Council, the assembled leaders accepted the principle of such a stability pact. After acrimonious discussions, the German insistence on the automatic application of sanctions was relaxed. The French managed to obtain additional resolutions on growth and employment when the SGP was adopted at the 1997 Amsterdam European Council. After its adoption, the pact was criticised for restricting the use of fiscal policy in the absence of a common European budget. However, France and Germany would soon prove it to be a toothless tiger. Despite these disagreements, the member states agreed to start the third stage of monetary union in 1999 and settled on the name for the new currency, the euro, as well as on the location for the ECB.

Heterogeneity and Democratic Deficit

One of the core questions after Maastricht was which countries would actually qualify for membership in the monetary union. The convergence criteria presented supposedly objective benchmarks, but it soon became obvious that these would be subject to political interpretation. The experiences of the Snake and the EMS, both of which quickly shed members as soon as economic fundamentals diverged, served as a strong warning. In 1994, the German finance minister and foreign policy spokesman of the CDU, Karl Lamers, published a proposal which suggested starting monetary union with a 'hard core' of countries with a relatively high degree of convergence. This hard core, according to the author, would encompass France, Germany and the Benelux countries.[68] However, despite regular reports about attempts to keep laggards such as Italy out of EMU, the political will to demonstrate European cohesion, represented above all by Helmut Kohl, triumphed.

Countries used various tricks to fulfil the convergence criteria, as former Bundesbank president Hans Tietmeyer lamented in his memoirs.[69] Overall, political objectives rather than objective economic factors were decisive in ensuring that eleven of the fifteen member states joined the third stage. Belgium and Italy, for example, were nowhere near the debt-to-GDP ratios prescribed by the convergence criteria. In a perceptive article, David Bearce found 'surprisingly little evidence of euro area policy convergence in terms of

---

68 K. Lamers and W. Schäuble, 'Reflections on European Policy, September 1', in B. F. Nelsen and A. Stubb (eds.), *The EU: Readings on the Theory and Practice of European Integration* (Basingstoke, Macmillan, 1994), pp. 71–81.
69 Tietmeyer, *Herausforderung Euro*.

economic growth, employment, and inflation.'[70] The same was true for government spending. This result was not surprising to many scholars working in the field of comparative political economy. Höpner and Schäfer[71] have documented the existing heterogeneity of EU member states, showing in detail that the six founding members were (and still are) most homogeneous with respect to indicators such as tax rates, union density or social expenditure. The introduction of the euro combined two different growth models in one currency, a northern export-led model and a southern demand-led model.[72] They had been able to coexist under a more flexible structure, but monetary union led to enormous external imbalances, which, in the absence of a common debt instrument, had a dramatic impact on the creditworthiness of debtor nations. The attempts to strengthen the 'E' in EMU foundered on deeply entrenched structural differences in Europe's 'varieties of capitalism'.[73] The larger the membership in the monetary union, the greater this potential for economic divergence, creating a dilemma which can be solved only by dissolution or at the cost of democratic legitimacy.[74]

The lack of stable popular support for a single currency was another flaw. Dyson and Featherstone's monumental *The Road to Maastricht* is still the most comprehensive history of the process. They argue that the establishment of monetary union was the result of the collaboration of core executives and monetary and financial elites. The result was a focus on financial and monetary aspects, but a neglect of issues of legitimacy. This turned out to be particularly ominous with regard to the southern members, which not only lost core components of their capacity to adjust to shifting economic conditions, but also became locked into a stable and strong currency at a time when many of their industries faced increasing competition from China and other emerging economies.[75] Only a few voices in this period cautioned

70 D. H. Bearce, 'EMU: The Last Stand for the Policy Convergence Hypothesis?', *Journal of European Public Policy* 16, no. 4 (2009): 582–600, 584.

71 M. Höpner and A. Schäfer, 'Integration among Unequals. How the Heterogeneity of European Varieties of Capitalism Shapes the Social and Democratic Potential of the EU', Max Planck Institute for the Study of Societies Discussion Paper (2012), www .econstor.eu/bitstream/10419/60484/1/720803926.pdf http://www.mpifg.de/pu/mpi fg_dp/dp12-5.pdf.

72 A. Johnston and A. Regan, 'European Monetary Integration and the Incompatibility of National Varieties of Capitalism', *Journal of Common Market Studies* 54 (2016): 318–36.

73 P. Hall and D. Soskice, *Varieties of Capitalism: The Institutional Foundations of Comparative Advantage* (Oxford, Oxford University Press, 2001).

74 H. Zimmermann, 'The Euro Trilemma, or: How the Eurozone Fell into a Neofunctionalist Legitimacy Trap', *Journal of European Integration* 38, no. 4 (2016): 425–40.

75 A. Hassel, 'Adjustments in the Eurozone: Varieties of Capitalism and the Crisis in Southern Europe' (2014), https://papers.ssrn.com/sol3/papers.cfm?abstract_id=2426198.

against such potential constraints, which were mitigated in the first decade of the euro by low borrowing costs. The governor of the Italian central bank, Antonio Fazio, for example, warned about the competitiveness of Italian industry if it was inextricably linked to more dynamic economies in a monetary union.[76] As has been argued in many influential articles,[77] with accession to EMU, governments have increasingly given up policy instruments which allowed them to influence growth and employment policies. This created a deficit in governing capacity that leads straight into the heart of the democratic deficit debate.

Notwithstanding these fundamental problems, the Commission stated in the convergence reports that eleven countries would join. The UK, Denmark and Sweden would opt out; Greece would join later. On 31 December 1998, the euro was created by irrevocably locking the exchange rates of eleven currencies.

Recommended Reading

Dyson, K. and K. Featherstone. *The Road to Maastricht: Negotiating Economic and Monetary Union* (Oxford, Oxford University Press, 1999).

Johnston, A. and A. Regan. 'European Monetary Integration and the Incompatibility of National Varieties of Capitalism', *Journal of Common Market Studies* 54 (2016): 318–36.

Marsh, D. *The Euro: The Politics of the New Global Currency* (New Haven, CT, Yale University Press, 2009).

McNamara, K. R. *The Currency of Ideas: Monetary Politics in the European Union*. (Ithaca, NY, Cornell University Press, 1998).

Mourlon-Druol, E. *A Europe Made of Money: The Emergence of the European Monetary System* (Ithaca, NY, Cornell University Press, 2012).

Mourlon-Druol, E. 'European Monetary Integration', in S. Battilossi, Y. Cassis and K. Yago (eds.), *Handbook of the History of Money and Currency* (Singapore, Springer, 2020), pp. 809–32.

Zimmermann, H. 'The Fall of Bretton Woods and the First Attempt to Construct a European Monetary Order', in L. Magnusson and B. Stråth (eds.), *From the Werner Plan to the EMU: In Search of a Political Economy for Europe* (Brussels, Peter Lang, 2001), pp. 49–72.

---

76 Marsh, *The Euro*, p. 193.
77 See, for example, F. Scharpf, 'Monetary Union, Fiscal Crisis, and the Pre-emption of Democracy', *Zeitschrift für Staats- und Europawissenschaften* 9, no. 2 (2011): 163–98.

The Euro Area Crisis: From Pre-history to Aftermath

AMY VERDUN

Introduction

On 26 July 2012, Mario Draghi declared in front of a group of about 200 London business people that he would do 'whatever it takes to save the euro'.[1] These seven words have been analysed to have made all the difference.[2] By doing so, the European Central Bank (ECB) effectively ended a long period of uncertainty and indecisiveness. The markets needed a strong signal so that they knew that the young European currency would be supported politically and economically.

After summer 2012, the euro area did not experience the same level of crisis, although the sovereign debt crisis was truly resolved only in 2015 and there were still challenging times until then.[3] Furthermore, early on, at the onset of the Covid-19 pandemic the euro area was once again put to the test, when the words spoken by President Lagarde, 'we are not here to close spreads', on 12 March 2020, sent the Italian stock exchange into a tailspin, as financial markets took them to mean that the ECB would not support all of

---

1 M. Draghi, 'Verbatim of the Remarks Made by Mario Draghi', Speech at the Global Investment Conference, London (2012), www.ecb.europa.eu/press/key/date/2012/ht ml/sp120726.en.html.
2 M. Baldassarri, 'What Would Have Happened in Europe if Mario Draghi Had Not Been There?', in M. Baldassarri, *The European Roots of the Eurozone Crisis: Errors of the Past and Needs for the Future* (Cham, Palgrave Macmillan, 2017), pp. 425–41; A. Verdun, 'Political Leadership of the European Central Bank', *Journal of European Integration* 39, no. 2 (2017): 207–21; S. Wanke, 'Five Years of "Whatever It Takes": Three Words That Saved the Euro', KfW Research (2017), www.kfw.de/PDF/Download-Center/Konzernthemen/Research/PDF-Dokumente-Volkswirtschaft-Kompakt/One-Pager-2017-EN/VK-No.-13 9-July-2017-Whatever-it-takes_EN.pdf.
3 On the end of the sovereign debt crisis and difficulties until the end of 2014, see, inter alia, M. Chang and P. Leblond 'All in: Market Expectations of Eurozone Integrity in the Sovereign Debt Crisis', *Review of International Political Economy* 22, no. 3 (2015): 626–55; D. Howarth and L. Quaglia 'The Political Economy of the Euro Area's Sovereign Debt Crisis: Introduction to the Special Issue of the *Review of International Political Economy*', *Review of International Political Economy* 22, no. 3 (2015): 457–84.

the member states. Within a week, however, by launching a major Pandemic Emergency Purchase Programme – an asset purchase programme of private and public sector securities – the ECB Governing Council was able to quickly rectify this initial misstep. The ECB once again signalled clearly to financial markets that the euro area would receive full support from the ECB.[4] It was a momentous occasion when the euro area received full support. Throughout its pre-history, during its conception, Economic and Monetary Union (EMU) had not always received this kind of support.

Pre-history

At the end of the twentieth century, the European Union (EU), and before it the European Community (EC), had witnessed numerous attempts to create an EMU. A process that only a few years prior might have seemed 'pie in the sky' was slowly becoming reality. The history leading up to the start of stage three of EMU had taken place over numerous decades. At the Hague Summit of 1969, which gave rise to the Werner Plan of 1970[5] to draft a plan for EMU, the heads of state or government declared 'the political will to establish an economic and monetary union'.[6] Furthermore, some European countries collaborated on exchange rates throughout the 1970s, with some member states participating in the so-called 'Snake' (a European exchange rate system).[7] Later in that decade, the MacDougall Report of 1977 discussed the progress that would be necessary in the fiscal domain to advance towards deeper integration.[8] The MacDougall Report examined the need for a centralised budget to accompany EMU. Drawing on insights from mature

---

4 C. Lagarde, 'Extraordinary times require extraordinary action. There are no limits to our commitment to the euro. We are determined to use the full potential of our tools, within our mandate', tweet (2020), https://twitter.com/lagarde/status/1240414918966 480896?lang=en; A. Verdun, 'Women's Leadership in the European Central Bank', in H. Müller and I. Tömmel (eds.), *Women and Leadership in the European Union* (Oxford, Oxford University Press, 2022), pp. 290–307; ECB, 'ECB Announces €750 Billion Pandemic Emergency Purchase Programme (PEPP)' (2020), www.ecb.europa.eu/pres s/pr/date/2020/html/ecb.pr200318_1~3949d6f266.en.html.
5 Council and Commission of the EC, Werner Report, 'Report to the Council and the Commission on the Realization by Stages of Economic and Monetary Union in the Community', *Bulletin of the EC*, Supplement 11, Doc 16.956/11/70 (8 October 1970).
6 Committee for the Study of Economic and Monetary Union, 'Report on Economic and Monetary Union in the European Community' (henceforth 'Delors Report') (Luxembourg, Office for Official Publications of the EC, 1989), p. 7.
7 T. Oatley, *Exchange Rate Cooperation in the European Union* (Ann Arbor, MI, University of Michigan Press, 1998).
8 Commission of the European Communities, Report of the Study Group on the Role of Public Finance in European Integration, 2 vols. (henceforth 'MacDougall Report') (Brussels, Commission of the European Communities, 1977).

federal states, it concluded that public finance could be used to cushion the effects of a recession or reducing differences in per capita income.[9] It called for an initial Community budget of 2–2.5 per cent of gross domestic product (GDP), whereas higher percentages were specified for subsequent economic integration scenarios.[10] The European Monetary System (EMS) of 1979 and the creation of the European Currency Unit were important building blocks.[11] Eventually, the 1989 Delors Report relaunched the process and provided another major blueprint for the creation of Europe's monetary union. Despite the difficulty in achieving EMU in the early decades, this activity also indicated a rather strong commitment, in principle, to the goal. Furthermore, by the time the single currency was created, more member states than initially expected ended up being part of it from the outset.[12]

However, when EMU was incorporated into the Maastricht Treaty, its institutional set-up was still incomplete.[13] The institutional architecture of EMU was based on an understanding of what was feasible at the time, rather than an ideal typical 'model'. EMU was launched in three stages.[14] The first was based on the achievements which had already been attained in the area of completing the single market. Stage two would start right after capital markets had formally been liberalised in 1994. Regarding economic market regulation and redistribution, however, only modest developments occurred, and deeper integration in this area was not foreseen prior to the launch of the final stage of EMU. It relied on coordination of policies by national authorities. By design, EMU had not been accompanied by more

[9] Ibid., vol. I, p. 12.   10 Ibid., vol. I, p. 17.

[11] F. Giavazzi, S. Micossi and M. Miller, *The European Monetary System* (Cambridge, Cambridge University Press, 1988); P. De Grauwe, 'Is the European Monetary System a DM-Zone?', in A. Steinherr and D. Weiserbs (eds.), *Evolution of the International and Regional Monetary Systems* (London, Macmillan, 1991), pp. 207–27; B. Herz and W. Roger, 'The EMS Is a Greater Deutschmark Area', *European Economic Review* 36 (1992): 1413–25.

[12] T. Risse, D. Engelmann-Martin, H.-J. Knopf and K. Roscher, 'To Euro or Not to Euro? The EMU and Identity Politics in the European Union', *European Journal of International Relations* 5, no. 2 (1999): 147–87; K. Dyson and K. Featherstone, *The Road to Maastricht: Negotiating Economic and Monetary Union* (Oxford, Oxford University Press, 1999); A. M. S. Watson, *Aspects of European Monetary Integration: The Politics of Convergence* (Basingstoke, Macmillan, 1997).

[13] A. Verdun, 'An "Asymmetrical" Economic and Monetary Union in the EU: Perceptions of Monetary Authorities and Social Partners', *Journal of European Integration* 20, no. 1 (1996): 59–81; A. Verdun, 'The Increased Influence of the EU Monetary Institutional Framework in Determining Monetary Policies: A Transnational Monetary Elite at Work', in B. Reinalda and B. Verbeek (eds.), *Autonomous Policy Making by International Organizations* (London, Routledge, 1998), pp. 178–94.

[14] A. Verdun, 'Institutional Architecture of the Euro Area', *Journal of Common Market Studies* 56, no. S1 (2018): 74–84.

fiscal federalism. Instead, the design of EMU envisaged that each member state would take care of its own finances. In fact, an agreement was made to the effect that member states would consider macroeconomic policy-making as a matter of 'common concern'. Thus, EMU was asymmetrical: a centralised EU-level monetary policy and decentralised economic policies.[15] The level of European integration achieved prior to the onset of EMU did have a number of mechanisms that enabled financial transfers: a major part of the EU budget was spent on policies such as the Common Agricultural Policy and Regional (or Cohesion) Policy. Yet these were not set up with the intent that they would act as so-called automatic stabilisers, an example of which would be unemployment benefits. Furthermore, the funds were capped – at a level intended to stay close to about 1 per cent of the gross national income of the EU – an insufficient amount for the EU to serve as a fiscal authority. The central governments of most federal systems have at least 15 per cent of GDP to work with. The ECB was to serve as a supranational monetary authority, whose mandate was to secure price stability. Without prejudicing that goal, the ECB would support the economic objectives of the EU's 1992 Maastricht Treaty. Most advanced economies can use monetary policy or fiscal policy to influence the economic well-being of their citizens. A central bank's typical instrument is interest rates, which can be used to stimulate the economy. Another instrument is government spending. This is the role of the fiscal authority. It taxes and spends. In the EU context, the latter authority is very weak. Therefore, in the euro area the coordination between monetary and fiscal policy is between the ECB, on the one hand, and the national governments, on the other. It was not always conceptualised that way.

In 1999 the exchange rates of eleven of the then fifteen EU member states were irrevocably fixed. EMU was built on previous experiences with economic and monetary cooperation and integration: the single market, including the free movement of capital, and the EMS, with at its core its exchange rate mechanism in which all countries except the United Kingdom (UK) participated. Under the leadership of Jacques Delors, the then president of the European Commission, a blueprint had been designed by a committee of mostly central bank presidents.[16] This thought piece eventually formed an

---

15 Verdun, 'An "Asymmetrical" Economic and Monetary Union'. See also D. Howarth and A. Verdun, 'Economic and Monetary Union at Twenty: A Stocktaking of a Tumultuous Second Decade: Introduction', *Journal of European Integration*, 42, no. 3 (2020): 287–93.

16 Delors Report.

important basis for the wording incorporated in the Maastricht Treaty.[17] Some member states, in particular Germany and the Netherlands, had been concerned that, if many countries joined the euro early on, particularly those countries that had a tradition of loose monetary policy, exchange rate volatility and high debt, then those countries might have the ability to destabilise EMU and jeopardise the low inflation objective of the euro area. The Maastricht Treaty envisaged that the European System of Central Banks (ESCB) would have as its overarching mandate maintaining price stability. The statute of the ESCB states that

> In accordance with Article 127(1) and Article 282(2) of the Treaty on the Functioning of the European Union, the primary objective of the ESCB shall be to maintain price stability. Without prejudice to the objective of price stability, it shall support the general economic policies in the Union with a view to contributing to the achievement of the objectives of the Union as laid down in Article 3 of the Treaty on European Union.[18]

Inflation had been a challenge in the European Community throughout the 1970s and 1980s.

Germany had demonstrated over the decades, before the irrevocable fixing of the exchange rates on 1 January 1999, that it was able to keep inflation low and lead the group of EC countries towards deeper coordination.[19] It was the lead country in the EMS regime,[20] and its policy success had given it credibility. Seeing that member states had voluntarily converged around that system, including the German emphasis on price stability, meant that this system had de facto support.

In order to ensure a system of rules that would keep budgetary deficits and public debt under control, a so-called Stability and Growth Pact (SGP) was invented that provided rules so that the Council of the EU could ultimately even impose monetary fines on member states. However, once they were in EMU, member states (notably France and Germany) did not comply with the

---

17 Ibid.
18 Protocol (No 4) on the Statute of the European System of Central Banks and of the European Central Bank, as annexed to the consolidated versions of the Treaty on European Union and the Treaty on the Functioning of the European Union (2010/C 83/01) OJ C 83, 30.3.2010, p. 230.
19 M. L. L. Segers and F. A. W. J. Van Esch, 'Behind the Veil of Budgetary Discipline. The Political Logic of the Budgetary Rules in EMU and SGP', *Journal of Common Market Studies* 45, no. 5 (2007): 1089–1109.
20 P. Ludlow, *The Making of the European Monetary System: A Case Study of the Politics of the European Community* (London, Butterworth Scientific, 1982); E. Mourlon-Druol, *A Europe Made of Money: The Emergence of the European Monetary System* (Ithaca, NY, Cornell University Press, 2012); Herz and Roger, 'The EMS Is a Greater Deutschmark Area'.

budgetary and fiscal policy rules.[21] There was a concern that some governments might tax and spend more than others, and in particular that some member states might run high levels of budgetary deficits and fiscal debt. It was foreseen that long-term interest rates would converge over time. Thus, if some member states had higher debt than others, the thinking was that they might be pushing long-term interest rates up, and so imposing cost on others to pay for the higher interest rates. To avoid such free riding, the SGP would provide discipline. Member states would not be permitted to have budgetary deficits any higher than 3 per cent of GDP. Public debt (the accumulated budgetary deficits) would ideally be about 60 per cent of GDP. If they had started with higher debt levels, member states would need to try to reduce them gradually and consistently over time.

EMU was also a particularly European response to global developments.[22] The pre-existing set-up of EU institutions facilitated the creation of this particular EMU. Furthermore, two countries played a particularly large role. EMU was at its core a compromise between France and Germany – both of these countries used EMU to balance national interests. The continued survival and institutional development of the edifice that supports the EU single currency relies on France and Germany remaining committed to the political goal of deeper integration. Furthermore, the type of EMU that was created focused on price stability – which some have labelled 'sound money'.[23] This particular set of ideas gave the euro area a compass during the various decades of EMU. Those who had a harder time in EMU have a more difficult time making their grievances heard in EU institutions.

Outline of the Chapter

This chapter consists of three parts, concerning the crisis, the aftermath and the origins – making sense of the crisis from a scholarly point of view by including a reflection on its origins. The first part includes a historical

---

21 M. Heipertz, and A. Verdun, 'The Dog That Would Never Bite? On the Origins of the Stability and Growth Pact', *Journal of European Public Policy* 11, no. 5 (2004): 773–88; M. Heipertz and A. Verdun, 'The Stability and Growth Pact – Theorizing a Case in European Integration', *Journal of Common Market Studies* 43, no. 5 (2005): 985–1008; M. Heipertz and A. Verdun, *Ruling Europe: Theory and Politics of the Stability and Growth Pact* (Cambridge, Cambridge University Press, 2010); Segers and Van Esch, 'Behind the Veil'.

22 L. W. Pauly, 'The Politics of European Monetary Union: National Strategies, International Implications', *International Journal* 47, no. 1 (1992): 93–111; T. Sadeh and A. Verdun, 'Explaining Europe's Monetary Union: A Survey of the Literature', *International Studies Review* 11, no. 2 (2009): 277–301.

23 K. R. McNamara, *The Currency of Ideas: Monetary Politics in the European Union* (London, Cornell University Press, 1998).

reconstruction and analysis of the euro crisis. The second examines the developments that took place in the aftermath of the euro crisis. what plans were developed to deal with the state of affairs and what reports were written about the next steps to be taken, on the basis of lessons learned. Finally, in the third part of the chapter I look back at the developments that preceded the crisis. Here I offer a historiography and theorise how EMU emerged by examining its creation from various perspectives and at various levels of analysis. By shedding light on its origins, I attempt to make more sense of the euro area crisis and the present state of affairs.

The remainder of the chapter is structured as follows. The next section examines the euro area crisis as it unfolded and the responses of political leaders. The following section examines the creation of institutional structures (the European Financial Stability Facility (EFSF), European Stability Mechanism (ESM), Banking Union and Capital Markets Union and road maps (the Four Presidents' Report and the Five Presidents' Report) and the plans of 2017 (the March 2017 White Paper on the Future of Europe and the May 2017 Reflection Paper on EMU). The next section examines current developments, including the changes incurred because of Brexit and the reduction in support for multilateralism as a result of the election of Donald Trump as president of the United States. The penultimate section provides an overarching analysis of these developments. The final section draws conclusions and speculates about the road ahead.

The Euro Area Crisis

EU member states started experiencing difficulties related to the financial crisis that had first erupted in the United States in 2007 and then blew over to Europe soon after. The 2007–8 financial crisis, followed by the economic crisis of 2009 and the sovereign debt crisis of 2010–12, put the euro to the test. The euro edifice showed cracks in its architecture during the entire duration of the euro area crisis.

The Outbreak of the Financial Crisis

In 2007, when the financial crisis took hold of Europe, when there was insufficient money to go around, the ECB was fast to react – making overnight lending easily available.[24] This ECB support was necessary because, as the money dried up, banks were increasingly reluctant to lend

---

24 A. Verdun, 'Economic Developments in the Euro Area', *Journal of Common Market Studies* 46 (2008): 215–32.

to one another, and these ECB measures facilitated the parking of their funds with the ECB.[25] This bold and innovative step on the part of the ECB had not been expected, and few realised that the ECB was prepared to do this. The ECB rose to the occasion, and it would do so a few more times subsequently when credit was tight or bond markets worried.

The financial crisis brought to the fore the incomplete nature of European integration in economic and monetary affairs. Fiscal policy remained firmly in the hands of national authorities, and there was no collective fund or responsibility to come to the aid of member states in need. Indeed, the crisis did not merely expose the weaknesses in fiscal policy architecture; banking supervision was also weak.[26] Or, as the British economist Charles Goodhart[27] put it, 'a crossborder bank is international in life but national in death.'[28] This meant that, in the face of a severe banking crisis and subsequently major downward corrections of the stock exchanges, EU countries found themselves not knowing what strategy the EU would take and national governments turned to domestic solutions. A fortnight after the Lehman collapse, Ireland decided, unilaterally, to secure consumer bank deposits.[29] The German government criticised the Irish government for taking such unilateral action, but a week later followed suit with a similar unilateral policy.[30] It took until November 2008 for the EU to furnish a European response that focused on having the member states and the EU inject €200 billion into the EU economy (1.5 per cent of GDP) and on ways to improve competitiveness.[31] However, the EU's central budget did not have access to such large funds. First, the EU does not have a large budget to spend (the EU manages about 1 per cent of the GDP of the EU's member states); and secondly, the Commission would have only a very small proportion of that amount to allocate to crisis management.

---

25 F. Drudi, A. Durré and F. P. Mongelli, 'The Interplay of Economic Reforms and Monetary Policy: The Case of the Eurozone', *Journal of Common Market Studies* 50, no. 6 (2012): 881–98.

26 P. Schure, 'European Financial Market Integration', in A. Verdun and A. Tovias (eds.), *Mapping Economic Integration* (Basingstoke, Palgrave Macmillan, 2013), pp. 105–24.

27 C. A. E. Goodhart, 'Procyclicality and Financial Regulation', Banco de España, *Estabilidad Financiera* no. 16 (2009), www.bde.es/f/webbde/Secciones/Publicaciones/InformesBol etinesRevistas/RevistaEstabilidadFinanciera/09/May/Fic/iefo116.pdf, p. 16.

28 House of Lords, European Union Committee, *The Future of EU Financial Regulation and Supervision: 14th Report of Session 2008–2009, vol. II: Evidence* (London, Her Majesty's Stationary Office, 2009), p. 30.

29 J. Murray-Brown and N. Dennis, 'Ireland Guarantees Six Banks' Deposits', *Financial Times*, 30 September 2008, www.ft.com/content/2124f8f4-8eb9-11dd-946c-0000779fd18c.

30 B. Benoit and G. Parker, 'Berlin Shrugs Off Attack on Savings Pledge', *Financial Times*, 6 October 2008, http://web.archive.org/web/20081008012423/http://www.ft.com/c ms/s/0/389588ae-93ce-11dd-9a63-0000779fd18c.html.

31 European Commission, Communication from the Commission to the European Council, 'A European Economic Recovery Plan', COM (2008) 800 final.

In autumn 2008, the Commission had access to no more than a small amount of loans to deal with crisis management. Thus, what it did in November 2008 was offer to act as a 'clearing house', a broker for a coordinated response by member state governments. In fact, after this decision, the proposal still needed to go to national parliaments for approval. This episode exposed the problem that the EU lacked a sufficiently large central budget or other fund to be tapped into at a time of crisis. It also showed the vulnerability of collective action in the EU, it being so reliant on national parliamentary approval.

In 2009, the EU was in recession.[32] However, lacking an EU budget of suitable proportion, the member states of the EU sought to combat the crisis by finding domestic solutions. Governments in these countries spent vast amounts of public money to keep the economy going. Fearing a repeat of the recession of the 1930s, which followed the stock exchange crash of 1929 and subsequent banking crisis, the spending of national governments led to a considerable increase in public debt and budgetary deficits in most EU countries.[33] In 2008 the average public debt of the seventeen countries of the euro area was below 70 per cent of GDP; by 2009 it was steeply on the rise.[34]

The Euro Area Crisis and the Sovereign Debt Crisis

The actual euro area crisis, in particular the sovereign debt crisis component of it, can be traced back to autumn 2009. But, from January 2010 onwards, the EU found itself in the worst crisis since the Maastricht Treaty entered into force in 1993. In October 2009, the newly elected government of Greece under George Papandreou informed the world that its budgetary deficit was much larger than reported by the previous government, namely 12.8 per cent instead of 3.6 per cent of GDP.[35] The EU rules stipulated that member states should maintain budgetary deficits no larger than 3 per cent of GDP. Prior to 2009, excessive deficit decisions were focusing on excesses of perhaps 0.5 per cent or 1 per cent difference from the norm. Thus, this large discrepancy, and the seemingly major disregard by the Greek government of the euro area's fiscal governance rules, took many by surprise.[36] The result was a chain reaction of

---

32 European Commission, *Autumn Economic Forecast: Statistical Annex of European Economy* (Brussels, European Commission, 2012), p. 43, table 7.

33 See J.-C. Trichet, 'Shaping a New World: The Crisis and Global Economic Governance', Lecture at Bocconi University, Milan (2010), www.youtube.com/watc h?v=UPhVVcOVQBo.

34 European Commission, 'European Economic Forecast – Autumn 2009', https://ec.europa .eu/economy_finance/publications/pages/publication16055_en.pdf, p. 214, table 42.

35 See also K. Featherstone, 'The Greek Sovereign Debt Crisis and EMU: A Failing State in a Skewed Regime', *Journal of Common Market Studies* 49, no. 2 (2011): 193–217.

36 Featherstone, 'The Greek Sovereign Debt Crisis'.

responses ranging from rating agencies downgrading Greek debt to an increase in the cost of lending for the Greek government.

Member state governments had a hard time deciding how to respond to this problem. They were facing two possible scenarios. They could decide not to do anything because Article 125 of the Treaty on the Functioning of the European Union (TFEU) does not allow the EU to bail out a member state that is running a large debt and has difficulties refinancing its debt. Furthermore, there was a concern about moral hazard – by assisting a country that is blatantly flouting the rules, one might be unwillingly encouraging more such behaviour. Alternatively, the EU member states could decide to help out collectively, as provided for by Article 122 TFEU. Considering all these points, German Chancellor Angela Merkel was initially reluctant to help. But, by May 2010, it became apparent that the problems were too large to ignore.

Rating agencies and financial markets responded increasingly negatively.[37] Neither the member states' government leaders nor EU institutions were able to come up with a timely response that would halt a negative spiral of lack of confidence in EMU governance. As the crisis evolved, an increasing number of media commentators and academics forecast that a country such as Greece might have to leave the euro. Some even warned that complications related to the euro crisis would undermine the entire euro area edifice through a process of contagion.[38] Demands for austerity were the main proposal for overcoming the sovereign debt crisis, leading to protests in the streets and concern about the risk of a deflationary spiral.

The Creation of New Institutional Structures

None of these interventions, or the extent of the support for member states in need, were planned for, in the original architecture of EMU, as per the Maastricht Treaty or in the reform of the SGP.[39] As we saw above, the experience of France and Germany having failed to meet the SGP deficit rules had given the scheme a credibility problem. With Greece violating the

---

37 S. C. W. Eijffinger. 'Rating Agencies: Role and Influence of Their Sovereign Credit Risk Assessment in the Eurozone', *Journal of Common Market Studies* 50, no. 6 (2012): 912–21.

38 P. Krugman, 'Greece and the Euro: Is the End Near?', Truthout (2012), http://truth-out.org/opinion/item/9358-greece-and-the-euro-is-the-end-near; W. Münchau, 'The Eurozone Really Has Only Days to Avoid Collapse', *Financial Times*, 27 November 2011, www.ft.com/content/d9a299a8-1760-11e1-b00e-00144feabdc0; 'Ten Crucial Days in Race to Save the Euro', *Financial Times*, 29 November 2011, www.ft.com/content/66bc845c-1aae-11e1-bc34-00144feabdc0; J. Randall, 'Whatever Germany Does, the Euro as We Know It Is Dead', *The Telegraph*, 29 August 2011, www.telegraph.co.uk/finance/comment/jeffran dall/7746806/Whatever-Germany-does-the-euro-as-we-know-it-is-dead.html.

39 Heipertz and Verdun, *Ruling Europe*.

rules so blatantly, the Germans were having difficulties accepting that they might need to step up to the plate and assist Greece. The problem was that, with Germany responding so slowly and refusing to send a clear signal that it would act, the sovereign debt crisis quickly escalated. As financial markets were not sure whether Greece was going to be assisted by the other member states or the EU, the cost of borrowing for Greece increased sharply. The yield spreads for Greek government debt rapidly went up, making it increasingly difficult (bordering on impossible) for the Greek government to refinance its debt. Eventually, in May 2010, the situation reached a climax when EU leaders needed to decide whether they would let Greece default or would provide Greece with enough funds for it to renew its loans. They opted for the latter and created a new institutional structure: the EFSF.[40] In the first instance the EFSF received €750 billion. The Troika made up of the European Commission, ECB and IMF made €110 billion available to assist Greece.

It was not enough, however. The sovereign debt crisis continued. The difficulties in refinancing debt (attracting capital at an affordable rate) also affected other countries in the periphery of Europe. By November 2010, Ireland had been given a financial support package of loans amounting to €85 billion, with contributions from the euro area member states through the EFSF, bilateral loans from Denmark, Sweden and the UK (three countries that were not in the euro area), assistance from the IMF and even an Irish contribution (from the national pension fund). In May 2011, Portugal too was provided with a 'financial and economic support package', of €78 billion, again a mix of loans or lines of credit from the IMF, the EU and the euro area, managed by the IMF, the EFSF and the European Financial Stability Mechanism. On 8 October 2012, a new permanent mechanism for dealing with crises, the ESM, was inaugurated. This was administered by an inter-governmental organisation set up by the euro area member states to ensure financial stability in the euro area.

In July 2011 and again in November 2011, the costs of refinancing government debt in Greece and, to a lesser extent, Italy (and to some extent Spain) were making headlines. Financial markets and analysts were worried about the health of the euro area, because the situation in Greece was bad enough, but, if a similar situation happened in either Italy or Spain individually, but especially in both together, these countries would be considered too big to

---

40 L. Gocaj and S. Meunier, 'Time Will Tell: The EFSF, the ESM, and the Euro Crisis', *Journal of European Integration* 35, no. 3 (2013): 239–53; A. Verdun, 'A Historical Institutionalist Explanation of the EU's Responses to the Euro Area Financial Crisis', *Journal of European Public Policy* 22, no. 2 (2015): 219–37.

bail out.[41] In July 2011, Greece was offered a €109 billion rescue package. This time there was some 'restructuring' of debt (meaning that effectively Greece went through a partial default). Some investors were informed that they would not be receiving their money back on part of the loans. This is referred to as a 'haircut'. Forgiving some debt meant that a plan could be made whereby Greece would be able to pay back its debt, but keeping the total amount reasonable.

The sovereign debt crisis had an impact on national politics. National governments in a number of EU member states experienced difficulties. In some countries, governments fell and early elections were called or a technocratic government was installed temporarily. In other countries, ruling parties lost regularly scheduled elections. Examples of the former are the Netherlands, Slovakia and Slovenia – where the crisis, arguably, led to early elections in those countries. In Greece, the electoral process was very turbulent. In Italy, a technocratic government was installed. Examples of the latter are France and Spain, where the ruling candidate or ruling party lost in scheduled national elections.

The Role of the ECB

Throughout all of this turmoil, the ECB played an important role in stabilising markets. As mentioned above, the ECB made credit readily available in August 2007. In autumn 2008, it collaborated actively with other major central banks to respond to the financial crisis. In the May 2010 period, it was one component of the Troika created to assist countries in need. In December 2011, it enabled long-term refinancing by making nearly €489 billion in loans available (at a 1 per cent interest rate) to 500 banks. The ECB made another €530 billion available to 800 banks in its second long-term refinancing operation in February 2012.[42] In June 2012, Spain requested €100 billion in soft loans from the EFSF, and later that month Cyprus too requested support. In June 2012, the first steps were taken to devise a so-called banking union, for which the role of supervisor would be given to the ECB. Member states' heads of state and government agreed in 2013 that more collaboration on banking supervision was necessary.[43] The role of

---

41 'The Spanish Bail-out: Going to Extra Time', *The Economist* 403, no. 8789 (2012): 26–8.
42 C. Wyplosz, 'The ECB's Trillion Euro Bet', VoxEU (2012), https://cepr.org/voxeu/columns/ecbs-trillion-euro-bet.
43 D. Howarth and L. Quaglia, 'Banking Union as Holy Grail: Rebuilding the Single Market in Financial Services, Stabilizing Europe's Banks and "Completing" Economic and Monetary Union', *Journal of Common Market Studies* 51, no. S1 (2013): 103–23; D. Howarth and L. Quaglia, 'The Steep Road to European Banking Union:

supervisory authority was given to the ECB.[44] The ECB expanded its number of positions so that these new regulators could maintain oversight over the banking sector. In addition, a Capital Markets Union was conceived of. Its role was to remove barriers to investment and facilitate capital provision throughout the single market.[45]

In summer 2012, when the yield spreads between countries of the periphery and the euro area core were widening too much – due to speculation of a euro area collapse and unsustainable finances – the ECB took another major step. It introduced a programme called Outright Monetary Transactions. This policy meant that the ECB would buy an unlimited quantity of bonds (less than 3 years' maturity) from a country whose debt market appeared not to be functioning because of financial speculation. The ECB announced that it would make these funds available only to those countries that had applied for assistance from the ESM and agreed to the economic conditionality.[46] In this way, the ECB took numerous bold steps to act during the euro debt crisis. Indeed, the many daring decisions made under the leadership of ECB President Mario Draghi earned him the 'Person of the Year 2012' award of the *Financial Times*.[47]

The Aftermath

Even during the euro crisis, initiatives were being undertaken to 'complete' EMU. At the highest leadership level, roadmaps were put forward.

Presidents' Reports, the 2017 White Paper and the Reflection Paper

In 2012, a so-called Four Presidents' Report aimed to kick start a process of producing a vision for the future of EMU entitled Towards a Genuine Economic and Monetary Union. The idea was that national policies had

Constructing the Single Resolution Mechanism', *Journal of Common Market Studies* 52, no. S1 (2014): 125–40; S. De Rynck, 'Banking on a Union: The Politics of Changing Eurozone Banking Supervision', *Journal of European Public Policy* 23, no. 1 (2016): 119–35.
44 B. Nielsen and S. Smeets, 'The Role of the EU Institutions in Establishing the Banking Union. Collaborative Leadership in the EMU Reform Process', *Journal of European Public Policy* 25, no. 9 (2018): 1233–56.
45 For an analysis, see R. Epstein and M. Rhodes, 'From Governance to Government: Banking Union, Capital Markets Union and the New EU', *Competition & Change* 22, no. 2 (2018): 205–24.
46 See Drudi et al., 'The Interplay of Economic Reforms and Monetary Policy'.
47 L. Barber and M. Steen, 'FT Person of the Year: Mario Draghi', *Financial Times*, 13 December 2012, www.ft.com/content/8fca75b8-4535-11e2-838f-00144feabdco.

to be put in line with EMU. The report stated that member states would have to 'act and coordinate according to common rules'.[48] Ideas were put forward to ensure responsibility for supervision at the EU level, including mechanisms to prevent the failure of banks and guarantee consumer deposits (Banking Union). Another element was to develop an integrated budgetary framework that would encompass coordination and joint decision-making. These ideas had already been incorporated in the Treaty on Stability, Coordination and Governance, and steps were taken towards the European Semester, a system of economic policy coordination that started in 2011. Over time it has become more established.[49] There was also some language about more fiscal integration and democratic issues.

A few years later, in 2015, the so-called Five Presidents' Report picked up where the Four Presidents' Report left off and announced bolder plans for deeper integration.[50] It focused on the future of EMU and provided a set of steps to be taken between 2015 and 2025 in the areas of economic union, financial union, fiscal union, democratic accountability, legitimacy and institutional strengthening. The headings followed closely those of the previous Four Presidents' Report. The Five Presidents' Report was bold about the later stages, recommending the creation of an EU-level treasury.

The Five Presidents' Report anticipated two major reports that would assist in further institutional changes: a White Paper and a Reflection Paper.[51] It was intended that they would be issued in 2017 and, indeed, both of them were issued at the agreed time. However, some major developments in the interim curtailed their impact.

48 H. Van Rompuy (in close cooperation with J. M. Barroso, J.-C. Juncker and M. Draghi), 'Towards a Genuine Economic and Monetary Union' (henceforth Four Presidents' Report) (2012), www.bankingsupervision.europa.eu/about/milestones/shared/pdf/2 012-06-26_towards_genuine_economic_and_monetary_union.pl.pdf, p. 2.

49 For more details, see A. Verdun and J. Zeitlin 'Introduction: The European Semester as a New Architecture of EU Socioeconomic Governance in Theory and Practice', *Journal of European Public Policy* 25, no. 2 (2018): 137–48.

50 J. Juncker (in close cooperation with D. Tusk, J. Dijsselbloem, M. Draghi and M. Schultz), 'Completing Europe's Economic and Monetary Union' (henceforth Five Presidents' Report) (2015), www.ecb.europa.eu/pub/pdf/other/5presidentsreport .en.pdf.

51 European Commission, 'White Paper on Future of Europe: Reflections and Scenarios for the EU27 by 2025' (2017), https://op.europa.eu/en/publication-detail/-/publication/b a81f70e-2b10-11e7-9412-01aa75ed71a1/language-en; European Commission, 'Reflection Paper on the Deepening of the Economic and Monetary Union' (2017), https://commis sion.europa.eu/publications/reflectionpaper-deepening-economic-and-monetary-union_en.

The Changing Political Landscape

In June 2016, eligible voters in the UK voted by a small margin to leave the EU. This situation caused the EU a lot of trouble. Not only did the EU member states need to keep focusing on speaking with one voice, but there was concern that other member states (and other domestic groups in member states) would start to copy the UK stance. This situation made it difficult for the EU's leaders to steam ahead with EMU plans. In fact, marking the anniversary of the Treaty of Rome, the 25 March 2017 report included different scenarios as a basis for a conversation about the next steps. For instance, the first two scenarios included 'carrying on' and 'nothing but the single market'. The report also included a more differentiated perspective, as the third scenario was called 'those who want more do more'. The fourth scenario was 'doing less more efficiently' and the final scenario (unsurprisingly) was 'doing much more together'. This last scenario includes steps towards deepening EMU. This included developments such as further transferring sovereignty to the EU level on matters such as international trade and giving the European Parliament (rather than national parliaments) the final say on international trade agreements. It also included greater coordination on 'fiscal, social and taxation matters, as well as European supervision of financial matters [. . .] EU financial support is made available to boost economic development and to respond to shocks at regional, sectoral and national level'.[52]

Eventually, Brexit was resolved at the eleventh hour: there was agreement on an interim package that would avoid a hard border between the Republic of Ireland and Northern Ireland. The UK had effectively left the customs union and the single market. It had renegotiated a deal with the EU which left the UK with considerably less access to the EU. But it had 'taken back control'. The situation with the UK needed to be resolved before the EU as a whole would be ready to consider deeper integration. The one advantage of the UK having left is that it was often the one member state that was profoundly critical of deeper integration, and indeed objected to it. With the UK gone, further attempts to deepen integration were once again possible.[53] For instance, the response to the coronavirus crisis, which, as we will see below, included an innovation in terms of seeking funds on

52 European Commission, 'White Paper on the Future of Europe' (2017), https://commission.europa.eu/content/future-europe/white-paper-future-europe_en, p. 24.
53 M. Cini and A. Verdun, 'The Implications of Brexit for the Future of Europe', in B. Martill and U. Staiger (eds.), *Brexit and Beyond: Rethinking the Futures of Europe* (London, CL Press, 2018), pp. 63–71.

international markets to support member states in need, might not have been something to which the UK would have been favourable. (But that is a counterfactual exercise that remains a supposition.) The developments in the UK took place against the context of the term of office of US President Donald Trump (2016–20), who ran on a platform that was much less sympathetic to the EU. All these factors meant that the EU needed to focus once again on how the economic and monetary side of the integration process may need to be strengthened to deal with the incomplete edifice of EMU. The EU dealt with these issues by providing its views on the completion of EMU in reports.[54]

Finally, in 2020, with the outbreak of the Covid-19 pandemic, the EU was both slow and fast to respond. The EU was criticised for having been insufficiently swift in an early stage to reach a helping hand to Italy that was the first country to struggle with Covid-19 infections, in particular in the northern regions. Yet it was able in summer 2020 to come up with an agreement in principle to borrow money from international markets to spend on EU member states' pandemic recovery plans – both with loans and with grants. Although the institutional structure created to set up the financial backing for the support package is temporary, most observers speak of an unprecedented step forward for the EU.[55]

A Historiography of the Euro Area Crisis

There are a number of ways to offer a historiography of the causes of EMU and its ability to persist over time.[56] One is to classify contributions in the literature along a scale running from rationalist theories to gradualist theories.[57] A classical political-economic distinction is between Marxist and market-based explanations. Another possible method of classification is a distinction

54 European Commission, 'Completing Europe's Economic and Monetary Union –Policy Package' (2017), https://economy-finance.ec.europa.eu/publications/completing-europes-economic-and-monetary-union-policy-package_en.
55 V. D'Erman and A. Verdun, 'An Introduction: "Macroeconomic Policy Coordination and Domestic Politics: Policy Coordination in the EU from the European Semester to the Covid-19 Crisis"', Journal of Common Market Studies 60, no. 1 (2022): 3–20; F. Fabbrini, 'The Legal Architecture of the Economic Responses to COVID-19: EMU beyond the Pandemic', Journal of Common Market Studies 60, no. 1 (2022): 186–203; M. Rhodes '"Failing Forward": A Critique in Light of Covid-19', Journal of European Public Policy 28, no. 10 (2021): 1537–54.
56 This section draws on Sadeh and Verdun, 'Explaining Europe's Monetary Union'.
57 A. Verdun, 'Why EMU Happened: A Survey of Theoretical Explanations', in P. M. Crowley (ed.), Before and beyond EMU: Historical Lessons and Future Prospects (London, Routledge, 2002), pp. 71–98.

between high and low politics.[58] Possibly, one could use philosophical distinctions, such as the underlying ontological and epistemological logics of the different approaches to EMU.[59] Finally, some scholars of the political economy of EMU prefer to analyse the causes of EMU, which made it happen and affect its ability to persist over time, using four levels of analysis: EU, national, domestic and global. Here 'domestic' means political developments inside nation states and within their institutional context. 'Domestic' is to be distinguished from 'society', which can develop outside the nation state's institutions, even if within its territory, and is too wide a concept to apply in this case. 'National' is taken to mean at the level of nation states.[60] Compared with some of the other categorisations, the levels-of-analysis method has two advantages. First, it is well established in the discipline of international relations. While the theoretical divisions suggested above reflect important disagreements among scholars, it is generally accepted that any issue can be analysed at a number of levels. Secondly, rather than presenting various approaches as irreconcilable ends of a given continuum, it presents them as compatible arguments, coming at the issue from a number of angles. It offers a useful framework within which this literature review on EMU can elaborate on the various theoretical arguments and diverse methodological tools used in the study of European monetary integration.

Global-Level Explanations of EMU

Global-level explanations of EMU usually include a discussion of the role of a hegemon. Robert Gilpin argued convincingly that any international regime, including a monetary regime, requires that a major power is willing and able to use its influence to support the regime.[61] Economic factors alone cannot do the trick.[62] In the pre-1992 period, the United States was considered the

58 K. Kaltenthaler, 'German Interests in European Monetary Integration', *Journal of Common Market Studies* 40, no. 1 (2002): 69–87.
59 E. Adler. 'Seizing the Middle Ground: Constructivism in World Politics', *European Journal of International Relations* 3, no. 3 (1997): 319–63.
60 See B. Eichengreen and J. Frieden, 'The Political Economy of European Monetary Unification: An Analytical Introduction', *Economics and Politics* 5, no. 2 (1993): 85–104; B. Eichengreen, J. Frieden and J. von Hagen, 'The Political Economy of European Integration: Introduction', in B. Eichengreen, J. Frieden and J. von Hagen (eds.), *Monetary and Fiscal Policy in an Integrated Europe* (New York, NY, Springer, 1995), pp. 1–11; J. A. Frieden and E. Jones, 'The Political Economy of European Monetary Union: A Conceptual Overview', in J. Frieden, E. Gross and E. Tones (eds.), *The New Political Economy of EMU* (Lanham, MD, Rowman & Littlefield, 1998), pp. 163–86.
61 R. Gilpin, *The Political Economy of International Relations* (Princeton, NJ, Princeton University Press, 1987).
62 B. J. Cohen, *The Geography of Money* (Ithaca, NY, Cornell University Press, 1998); B. J. Cohen, 'Beyond EMU: The Problem of Sustainability', in B. Eichengreen and

global hegemonic power. However, Europeans disliked the way the US policies dominated the international political economy. In particular, the French, going back to Robert Triffin, felt that the United States had abused its role.[63] To some extent, the European monetary integration process can be seen as responding in some way to the dollar politics and a sense that the EU could do better if only it had its own currency and thus was less dependent on the US dollar.[64] Since the hegemonic power at the global level did provide monetary stability, EU member states sought to include this goal when creating EMU.

Another factor that played a role was that by 1989 the global balance of power had changed, as the Berlin Wall came down, the central and eastern European countries formerly in the Warsaw Pact sought a new destiny and the Soviet Union disintegrated. Germany experienced the greatest change as the German Democratic Republic was incorporated to form an enlarged Federal Republic of Germany. This country was now larger than the other three large member states of the EU of twelve member states. Prior to 1989 four member states had roughly the same population (about 58 million); with Germany reunified, it was suddenly the most populous country (about 80 million). Member states wanted to make sure that Germany was firmly embedded in European integration. The creation of EMU within the Maastricht Treaty ensured that there would be a European Germany (rather than a German Europe). Various scholars have pointed out that ultimately Germany agreed to EMU in return for international legitimacy for its unification and to prepare the EC, as it was then called, for its eventual enlargement to the east.

A further element related to global factors is that trade and financial flows were expanding. These forces of 'globalisation' were increasingly constraining state policies and influenced decision-making. Globalisation had already limited the autonomy of national monetary policy and

J. Frieden (eds.), *The Political Economy of European Monetary Unification*, 2nd ed. (Boulder, CO, Westview, 2000); B. J. Cohen, *The Future of Money* (Princeton, NJ, Princeton University Press, 2004).

63 J. Story and M. de Cecco, 'The Politics and Diplomacy of Monetary Union: 1985–1991', in J. Story (ed.), *The New Europe: Politics, Government and Economy since 1945* (Oxford, Blackwell, 1993), pp. 328–54, 329–33; D. J. Howarth, *The French Road to European Monetary Union* (Basingstoke, Palgrave, 2001); A. Verdun, *European Responses to Globalization and Financial Market Integration: Perceptions of Economic and Monetary Union in Britain, France and Germany* (Basingstoke, Palgrave, 2000).

64 C. R. Henning, 'Systemic Conflict and Regional Monetary Integration: The Case of Europe', *International Organization* 52, no. 3 (1998): 537–73; C. R. Henning, *Tangled Governance: International Regime Complexity, the Troika, and the Euro Crisis* (Oxford, Oxford University Press, 2017).

lowered the opportunity cost of giving up the national currency, especially for small states.[65] Hence EMU could be used to influence monetary policy that many had accepted as no longer under the control of national governments.[66] The emergence of the type of EMU which came into being in the 1990s can therefore also be explained in terms of a global ideological shift away from the Keynesian paradigm, changing ideas about the government's proper role in monetary policy-making and rising capital mobility.[67] The 'sound money' idea was gaining terrain: there was a growing consensus among the advanced liberal economies that more market-oriented policies were the key to lower rates of inflation and unemployment, as well as higher growth rates.[68] Constructivists argue that the 1970s oil-price shocks challenged the shared knowledge structure on macroeconomic issues and prompted decision-makers to look for new knowledge to structure, inform and legitimise their discourse and action.[69] This enabled transnational experts and epistemic communities, such as central banks, to influence policy-makers and to diffuse 'sound money' ideas from the late 1970s onwards.[70] Some authors argued that, rather than being based on consensual knowledge, powerful interests used EMU to impose these ideas on the European public. Thus, they expected a legitimacy problem for EMU.[71] These cognitive shifts were not confined to Europe; and they coincided with the global rise in capital mobility and the above-mentioned loss of monetary policy autonomy.

65 E. Jones, J. Frieden and F. Torres, *Joining Europe's Monetary Club: The Challenges for Smaller Member States* (New York, NY, St Martin's Press, 1998).

66 Verdun, *European Responses*.

67 See, inter alia, K. R. McNamara, *The Currency of Ideas: Monetary Politics in the European Union* (London, Cornell University Press, 1998); K. R. McNamara, 'Economic Governance, Ideas and EMU: What Currency Does Policy Consensus Have Today?', *Journal of Common Market Studies* 44, no. 4 (2006): 803–21.

68 See D. R. Cameron, 'From Barre to Balladur: Economic Policy in the Era of the EMS', in G. Flynn (ed.), *Remaking the Hexagon: The New France in the New Europe* (Boulder, CO, Westview, 1995), pp. 117–57; K. Dyson, *Elusive Union: The Process of Economic and Monetary Union in Europe* (London, Longman, 1994); M. Marcussen, 'The Role of "Ideas" in Dutch, Danish and Swedish Economic Policy in the 1980s and the Beginning of the 1990s', in P. Minkkinen and H. Patomäki (eds.), *The Politics of Economic and Monetary Union* (Kluwer, Dordrecht, 1997), pp. 75–103; Verdun, *European Responses*.

69 Adler, 'Seizing the Middle Ground'.

70 Dyson, *Elusive Union*; M. Marcussen, *Ideas and Elites: The Social Construction of Economic and Monetary Union* (Vilborg, Aalborg University Press, 2000); A. Verdun, 'The Role of the Delors Committee in the Creation of EMU: An Epistemic Community?', *Journal of European Public Policy* 6, no. 2 (1999): 308–28.

71 P. Minkkinen and H. Patomäki (eds.), *The Politics of Economic and Monetary Union* (Kluwer, Dordrecht, 1997).

EU-Level Explanations

EU-level explanations of the creation of EMU and the challenges of its design point to studies that focus their attention on the EU level. Rather than emphasising that leaders of nation states seek to optimise their interests, EU-level explanations suggest some systemic or structural logic or process that turns membership in EMU into some kind of inevitability for the states. As mentioned above, for a number of reasons, Germany was a dominant player in the monetary policy realm in the EU. Indeed, during the 1970s and 1980s, it was common to describe the European monetary regime as being dominated by Germany. Much was written on the asymmetry in the EMS of the 1980s, the ability of the German authorities to set their monetary policy independently from other member states and the tendency of the latter to follow the German policy.[72] It can also be argued that the rules of EMU reflect German views and interests.[73]

Yet, despite these observations and the persistent beliefs, the German monetary authorities did not try to 'lead': they did not attempt to influence other monetary authorities (unless there was a crisis). In securing their commitment to the EMS, other monetary authorities simply followed (or paid close attention to) German monetary policies.[74] Furthermore, the Bundesbank was from the outset rather cautious about EMU – even lukewarm or critical of it. Many members of the German public, both laymen and experts, were sceptical of EMU at the time it was being created.[75] Germany also never had the power to coerce EU member states into accepting its rules,

---

72 See, for example, O. Bajo-Rubio and M. D. Montáves-Garcés, 'Was There Monetary Autonomy in Europe on the Eve of EMU? The German Dominance Hypothesis Re-examined', *Journal of Applied Economics* 5, no. 2 (2002): 185–207; T. Congdon, 'The ERM: Incompatible with Domestic Policies', in P. Temperton (ed.), *The European Currency Crisis* (Cambridge, Probus, 1993), pp. 73–90; P. De Grauwe, 'Is the European Monetary System a DM-Zone?', in A. Steinherr and D. Weiserbs (eds.), *Evolution of the International and Regional Monetary Systems* (London, Macmillan, 1991), pp. 207–27; M. Fratianni and J. Von Hagen, 'On the Road to EMU', in M. Baldassarri and R. Mundell (eds.), *Building the New Europe: The Single Market and Monetary Unification*, vol. 1 (New York, NY, St Martin's Press, 1993), pp. 253–79; Herz and Roger, 'The EMS Is a Greater Deutschmark Area'; H. D. Smeets, 'Does Germany Dominate the EMS?', *Journal of Common Market Studies* 29 (1990): 37–52; J. Story, 'The Launching of the EMS: An Analysis of Change in Foreign Economic Policy', *Political Studies* 36, no. 3 (1988): 397–412.

73 Dyson, *Elusive Union.*

74 I. Maes and A. Verdun, 'The Role of Medium-Sized Countries in the Creation of EMU: The Cases of Belgium and the Netherlands', *Journal of Common Market Studies* 43, no. 2 (2005): 327–48.

75 See J. S. Barkin, 'Hegemony without Motivation: Domestic Policy Priorities and German Monetary Policy', *German Politics and Society* 14, no. 3 (1996): 54–72; S. Bulmer and W. Paterson, 'Germany in the European Union: Gentle Giant or

or to punish those who broke the rules.[76] The only sanction available to Germany at the outset was not to agree to the establishment of EMU or to stay outside.

If Europe was lacking a power structure that would force EU member states into establishing EMU, might there have been a technical or functional structure that worked to this effect? Neo-functionalists argue that trade integration among the EU member states created technical spillover for monetary integration. After the completion of the internal market project, national currencies were responsible for some of the few remaining trade barriers, such as exchange commissions and exchange rate risk. Since full capital mobility, national monetary autonomy and exchange rate stability form an incompatible triangle, the liberalisation of capital flows as part of the internal market meant that exchange rate stability could come only at the expense of national autonomy. Thus, a currency union was a natural extension to the internal market project.[77] Neo-functionalist arguments were especially prominent in EU documents supporting the cause of a single currency.[78] Neo-functionalist accounts have more difficulty explaining periods of stagnation in integration, or the exact timing of processes. If the power and technical structure did not make EMU inevitable, perhaps EMU should be understood in the context of the EU's broader institutional structure. Issue linkages allow a country to explicitly or implicitly trade concessions in one issue area for gains in another. The poorer EU member states accepted EMU, which was important to post-unification Germany, for the sake of greater European political and economic integration. In return, they would receive transfer payments from the wealthier member states through the Cohesion Fund.[79] And these binds still left

Emergent Leader?', *International Affairs* 72, no. 1 (1996): 9–32; A. Markovits and S. Reich, *The German Predicament* (Ithaca, NY, Cornell University Press, 1997).

76 McNamara, *The Currency of Ideas*, pp. 26–7.

77 T. Padoa-Schioppa, *The Road to Monetary Union in Europe: The Emperor, the Kings, and the Genies*, 2nd ed. (Oxford, Oxford University Press, 2000).

78 See D. R. Cameron, 'Economic and Monetary Union: Underlying Imperatives and Third-Stage Dilemmas', *Journal of European Public Policy* 4, no. 3 (1997): 455–85; Commission of the European Communities, 'One Market, One Money', *European Economy* no. 44 (1990), https://ec.europa.eu/economy_finance/publications/pages/publication7454_en.pdf; Delors Report; T. Padoa-Schioppa, *Efficiency, Stability, and Equity: A Strategy for the Evolution of the Economic System of the European Community* (New York, NY, Oxford University Press, 1987); Pauly, 'The Politics of European Monetary Union', p. 101; W. Sandholtz, 'Choosing Union: Monetary Politics and Maastricht', *International Organization* 47, no. 1 (1993): 1–39; W. Sandholtz, 'Money Troubles: Europe's Rough Road to Monetary Union', *Journal of European Public Policy* 3, no. 1 (1996): 84–101, p. 94; Verdun, *European Responses*.

79 L. L. Martin, 'International and Domestic Institutions in the EMU Process', *Economics and Politics* 5, no. 2 (1993): 125–44.

sufficient national room for manoeuvre, because of the decentralised configuration of the European System of Central Banks.[80] Other scholars argue that stronger EU institutions (perhaps a European economic government) are needed in order to bind the commitment of member states to EMU, especially given their diversity, and possibly to spread more evenly the costs and benefits of EMU.[81] The sustainability of EMU may also depend on strengthening the European Parliament, in order to reduce the democratic deficit of the EU,[82] the accountability problem of the ECB[83] or the fact that EMU is based on output legitimacy.[84] The EMU system may be too focused on the German model and be inappropriate for other member states.[85] There is also a role for supranational institutions in this view: the Commission, and its president in his personal capacity, was important in promoting the idea of EMU. As we saw in the previous chapter, the Commission was involved in the establishment of the committee of governors, in supporting the Barre plans and in launching the 1977 Jenkins initiative.[86] The Commission insisted on the inclusion of the vision of EMU in the preamble to the Single European Act, mediated between European leaders and was important in overcoming British opposition to EMU. The Commission kept the vision of monetary union in Europe on the agenda at times when governments

80 D. J. Howarth and P. H. Loedel, *The European Central Bank: The New European Leviathan*, 2nd ed. (Basingstoke, Palgrave Macmillan, 2005).
81 See I. Begg (ed.), *Europe: Government and Money: Running EMU: The Challenge of Policy Coordination* (London, Federal Trust, 2002); C. Crouch (ed.), *After the Euro: Shaping Institutions for Governance in the Wake of Monetary Union* (Oxford, Oxford University Press, 2000); A. Verdun, 'La nécessité d'un "gouvernement économique" dans une UEM asymétrique. Les préoccupations françaises sont-elles justifiées?', *Politique Européenne* no. 10 (2003): 11–32.
82 Martin, 'International and Domestic Institutions'.
83 W. H. Buiter, 'Alice in Euroland', *Journal of Common Market Studies* 37, no. 2 (1999): 181–209; Verdun, 'The Role of the Delors Committee'.
84 A. Verdun and T. Christiansen, 'Policies, Institutions and the Euro: Dilemmas of Legitimacy', in Crouch (ed.), *After the Euro*, pp. 162–78; A. Verdun and T. Christiansen, 'The Legitimacy of the Euro: An Inverted Process?', *Current Politics and Economics of Europe* 10, no. 3 (2001): 265–88.
85 See K. R. McNamara, and E. Jones, 'The Clash of Institutions: Germany in European Monetary Affairs', *German Politics and Society* 14, no. 3 (1996): 5–30; H. Kaufmann, 'The Importance of Being Independent: Central Bank Independence and the European System of Central Banks', in C. Rhodes and S. Mazey (eds.), *The State of the European Union: Building a European Polity* (Boulder, CO, Lynne Rienner, 1995).
86 D. M. Andrews, *Organizing Principals: The European Commission as an Agent for Monetary Integration* (Claremont, CA, European Union Center of California, 2002); K. Dyson and L. Quaglia, *European Economic Governance and Policies*, vol. 1: *Commentary on Key Historical and Institutional Documents* (Oxford, Oxford University Press, 2010), pp. 176–7; R. Jenkins 'Europe's Present Challenge and Future Opportunity' (1977), http://aei.pitt.edu/4404/1/4404.pdf.

were opposed to the idea.[87] European central bankers promoted consensus over the merits of macroeconomic discipline, price stability as the prime policy objective and central bank independence from politicians. These ideas became the foundation for EMU.[88] EMU was also supported by more subtle processes involving non-governmental organisations and the emerging European civil society.[89] Thus, EMU is neither the result of German monetary dominance nor an inevitable and necessary evolution of the general process of European integration. However, the EU's general institutional set-up helped the creation of EMU.

National-Level Explanations of EMU

Classical political science explains international relations as a reflection of the selfish pursuit of national interests. Let us start with the economic national interests. Optimum currency area (OCA) theory posits that currency unions enhance trade and income by reducing the exchange rate trade barrier, at the expense of independent macroeconomic policies.[90] Thus, currency unions would be efficient among major trade partners with coordinated business cycles, open economies, flexible prices, high labour mobility and financial market integration.[91] The 'new optimum currency area' theory, which developed in the 1980s, argues that fixing a weak currency to a strong currency also benefits the credibility and increases the chance of success of disinflation policies, and reduces the

---

87 See also Pauly, 'The Politics of European Monetary Union'; W. Sandholtz and A. Stone Sweet (eds.), *European Integration and Supranational Governance* (Oxford, Oxford University Press, 1998); A. Verdun, 'The Institutional Design of EMU: A Democratic Deficit?', *Journal of Public Policy* 18, no. 2 (1998): 107–32; A. Verdun, 'Governing by Committee: The Case of the Monetary Committee', in T. Christiansen and E. Kirchner (eds.), *Committee Governance in the European Union* (Manchester, Manchester University Press, 2000), pp. 132–44.

88 K. Dyson, K. Featherstone and G. Michalopoulos, 'Strapped to the Mast: EC Central Bankers between Global Financial Markets and Regional Integration', *Journal of European Public Policy* 2, no. 3 (1995): 465–87; W. Sandholtz, 'Monetary Bargains: The Treaty on EMU', in A. W. Cafruny and G. G. Rosenthal (eds.), *The State of the European Community: The Maastricht Debates and Beyond* (Boulder, CO, Lynne Rienner, 1993) 125–42.

89 S. Collignon and D. Schwarzer, *Private Sector Involvement in the EMU: The Power of Ideas* (London, Routledge, 2003).

90 R. Mundell, 'A Theory of Optimum Currency Areas', *American Economic Review* 51 (1961): 657–75.

91 For the so-called OCA criteria, see M. J. Artis, 'Currency Interdependence: What Economics Has to Say', *Journal of Public Policy* 22, no. 2 (2002): 111–18; G. S. Tavlas, 'The "New" Theory of Optimum Currency Areas', *The World Economy* 16, no. 6 (1993): 663–85.

costs of capital.[92] Economists argue that inefficient currency unions are costly to their member states and unsustainable in the long run.

According to the endogenous optimum currency theory of Frankel and Rose,[93] currency unions can potentially triple trade among their members and secure price stability among the member states. Balancing EMU's credibility gains against its adjustment costs, the non-Mediterranean pre-2004 member states have been potentially unstable members of the euro bloc, as are a few of the new EU member states.[94] The OCA theory and other economic analyses have many critics, who argue that it is irrelevant to explain EMU, because EMU is mostly a political project, which is not driven by considerations of efficiency.[95] Indeed, regions within many countries (which are currency areas in themselves) often also do not form an OCA,[96] but the lack of an OCA within state boundaries usually does not call into question the stability of those currencies. In fact, one does not need to go that far to admit that there are many stable political arrangements that involve economic inefficiency. Jones goes even further, arguing that the diversity of the countries participating in EMU is a strength rather than a weakness and that Europe's single currency helps to maintain such diversity rather than tending to eliminate it.[97] If

92 See F. Giavazzi and M. Pagano, 'The Advantage of Tying One's Hands: EMS Discipline and Central Bank Credibility', *European Economic Review* 32 (1988): 1055–82; M. Kaelberer, *Money and Power in Europe: The Political Economy of European Monetary Cooperation* (Albany, NY, State University of New York Press, 2001); P. B. Kenen, *Economic and Monetary Union in Europe: Moving beyond Maastricht* (Cambridge, Cambridge University Press, 1995); W. Schelkle, 'The Theory and Practice of Economic Governance in EMU Revisited: What Have We Learnt about Commitment and Credibility?', *Journal of Common Market Studies* 44, no. 4 (2006): 669–86; A. Steinherr (ed.), *Thirty Years of European Monetary Integration: From the Werner Plan to EMU* (London, Longman, 1994); Tavlas, 'The "New" Theory'.

93 J. A. Frankel and A. K. Rose, 'The Endogeneity of the Optimum Currency Area Criteria', *Economic Journal* 108, no. 449 (1998): 1009–25; J. A. Frankel and A. K. Rose, 'An Estimate of the Effect of Common Currencies on Trade and Income', *The Quarterly Journal of Economics* 117, no. 2 (2002): 437–66.

94 T. Sadeh, 'Who Can Adjust to the Euro?', *The World Economy* 28, no. 11 (2005): 1651–78.

95 D. M. Andrews and T. D. Willett, 'Financial Interdependence and the State: International Monetary Relations at Century's End', *International Organization* 51, no. 3 (1997): 479–511; Eichengreen et al., 'The Political Economy of European Integration'; T. D. Willett, 'Some Political Economy Aspects of EMU', *Journal of Policy Modeling* 22, no. 3 (2000): 379–89. For a nuanced analysis of the UK and EMU, see M. J. Artis, 'Reflections on the Optimal Currency Area (OCA) Criteria in the Light of EMU', *International Journal of Finance and Economics* 8, no. 4 (2003): 297–307.

96 B. Eichengreen, *European Monetary Unification: Theory, Practice and Analysis* (Cambridge, MA, MIT Press, 1997).

97 E. Jones, *The Politics of Economic and Monetary Union: Integration and Idiosyncrasy* (Lanham, MD, Rowman and Littlefield, 2002).

EMU is not about gains to the national economy, what political ends does it serve?

State-centrists, such as Moravcsik reject economic efficiency as an explanation of the establishment of EMU.[98] They argue that national governments acted rationally in negotiating each of the steps in the evolution of the EU. Rejecting neo-functionalist, transnational and constructivist arguments about the origins of EMU, Moravcsik argues that the establishment of the EMS at the end of the 1970s and the Maastricht Treaty in the early 1990s resulted from careful negotiations and bargaining of national governments, reflecting in particular the interests of the most powerful member states.[99] National governments ceded only as much sovereignty as they calculated it was in their interest to cede.[100]

Moravcsik's intergovernmental approach differs from traditional political realism in accepting that foreign policy goals of national governments vary in response to shifting pressures from domestic societal groups.[101] However, he asserts that domestic politics merely act as a filter between the international economy and national governments. Since he attributes agency in international affairs to national governments, his approach can still be considered state-centred.

Most state-centred explanations of EMU analyse specific member states. The most common argument here is based on some Franco-German deal. Indeed, some German policy-makers may have considered EMU as a mechanism for sharing the costs of unification with other EU member states,[102] just as the EMS was argued to be a shock-absorber mechanism, distributing shocks coming from the rest of the world among its member states.[103] For France and the Mediterranean member states, EMU was meant to disguise a softening of their currency link with Germany, because policy

98 A. Moravcsik, 'Taking Preferences Seriously: A Liberal Theory of International Politics', *International Organization* 51, no. 4 (1997): 513–53; A. Moravcsik, *The Choice for Europe: Social Purpose and State Power from Messina to Maastricht* (Ithaca, NY, Cornell University Press, 1998); A. Moravcsik, 'A New Statecraft? Supranational Entrepreneurs and International Cooperation', *International Organization* 53, no. 2 (1999): 267–306.

99 Moravcsik, *The Choice for Europe*.

100 M. Levitt and C. Lord, *The Political Economy of Monetary Union* (Basingstoke, Palgrave Macmillan, 2000).

101 A. Moravcsik, 'Preferences and Power in the European Community – A Liberal Intergovernmentalist Approach', *Journal of Common Market Studies* 31, no. 4 (1993): 473–524, 481.

102 Sandholtz, 'Monetary Bargains', pp. 113–14.

103 D. Gros and N. Thygesen, *European Monetary Integration*, 2nd ed. (Harlow, Longman, 1998), pp. 150–5.

discipline would be enforced by a committee rather than the rigours of the market.[104] In other words, in addition to their aversion to US hegemony, French decision-makers also sought European monetary integration since the late 1960s in order to limit German economic and monetary dominance for the benefit of greater freedom to manage domestic redistributive policies.[105] Kaltenthaler argues that the French made it clear to German government officials that, as an occupying power, France could actually block or delay German unification if its interests were not taken into account.[106] However, it is hard to imagine that France, or any other EU member state, could really have prevented German unification. These country studies allow a nuanced look at specific forces and interests that gave birth to EMU and help sustain it, but their weakness is, of course, their external validity. What can we learn about EMU from looking at a single country or a subset of countries? And, as Jones argues, the costs and benefits of EMU may be associated with cross-border cleavages more than with individual countries.[107] This suggests that some inconsistency is built into the structure of EMU, where decisions are derived from national policies, but costs and benefits are not accrued at the national level. Perhaps EMU is better explained at the domestic level than at the national one? Indeed, the more nation-specific the analysis gets, the more prominent domestic-level explanations become.

Domestic-Level Explanations of EMU

Domestic-level explanations of EMU include a focus on the ability of EU member states to set their exchange rates, with attention focused on competing domestic interest groups. Other factors are the political business cycle, the influence of domestic institutions and cabinet duration, partisan policies and populist arguments. Exchange rate policies, including currency unions, redistribute income among interest groups. What determined the stances of various groups in relation to EMU? Frieden argues that European producers and trade unions in the tradable goods sector, favored manipulating the exchange rate.[108] In contrast, consumers, workers and producers of non-tradable goods,

---

104 G. Garrett, 'The Politics of Maastricht', *Economics and Politics* 5, no. 2 (1993): 105–23.
105 Howarth, *The French Road*.   106 Kaltenthaler, 'German Interests', p. 80.
107 Jones, *The Politics of Economic and Monetary Union*.
108 J. A. Frieden, 'The Impact of Goods and Capital Market Integration on European Monetary Politics', *Comparative Political Studies* 29, no. 2 (1996): 193–222; J. Frieden, 'The Euro: Who Wins? Who Loses?', *Foreign Policy* no. 112 (1996), 25–40; J. A. Frieden, 'Making Commitments: France and Italy in the European Monetary System, 1979–1985', in Eichengreen and Frieden (eds.), *The Political Economy of European Monetary Unification*, pp. 25–46.

multinationals, international investors and producers of hi-tech products preferred fixing the exchange rate. In the 1980s, changes in the balance of power among French and Italian political parties that represent these cleavages explain the evolution of exchange rate policies of each of these countries, in favour of greater monetary integration. German industry also gained from fixed exchange rates with its competitors in southern European inflationary countries.[109]

Frieden links direct gains from exchange rate changes to policy attitudes. EMU can also be explained as a result of domestic cleavages;[110] in Germany, the relationship between its government and the Bundesbank.[111] Some scholars combine national-level game theory with bureaucratic cleavages to explain major decisions on the path to EMU. If these decisions can be characterised as coordination games, in which the prime preference of the national actors was to cooperate rather than cheat each other, the distributional conflicts on the specific format of cooperation were settled by domestic-level factors.[112] Elsewhere, I argue that monetary authorities in France, Germany and the UK wanted to be part of the process, to contain the Bundesbank and to model EMU on German monetary institutions.[113] Employers' organisations in all three member states were cautiously in favour of EMU, provided that it gave birth to a strong currency and did not involve more regulations or high transfer payments to poor countries. Trade unions saw EMU as a way to improve growth and employment prospects in Europe and were concerned that it would be created with or without their consent. They believed that supporting EMU offered an opportunity for

109 C. Hefeker, *Interest Groups and Monetary Integration: The Political Economy of Exchange Regime Choice* (Boulder, CO, Westview, 1997); Eichengreen and Frieden, 'The Political Economy of European Monetary Unification'; B. Eichengreen and J. Frieden (eds.), *The Political Economy of European Monetary Unification*, 2nd ed. (Boulder, CO, Westview, 2000); Kenen, *Economic and Monetary Union*.

110 R. Youngs, 'The Politics of the Single Currency: Learning the Lessons of Maastricht', *Journal of Common Market Studies* 37, no. 2 (1999): 295–316.

111 M. Kaelberer, 'Hegemony, Dominance or Leadership? Explaining Germany's Role in European Monetary Cooperation', *European Journal of International Relations* 3, no. 1 (1997): 35–60; D. Heisenberg, *The Mark of the Bundesbank: Germany's Role in European Monetary Cooperation* (Boulder, CO, Lynne Rienner, 1999); P. H. Loedel, *Deutsche Mark Politics: Germany in the European Monetary System* (London, Lynne Rienner, 1999).

112 M. O. Hosli, 'The Creation of the European Economic and Monetary Union (EMU): Intergovernmental Negotiations and Two-Level Games', *Journal of European Public Policy* 7, no. 5 (2000): 744–66; D. Wolf and B. Zangel, 'The European Economic and Monetary Union: Two-Level Games and the Formation of International Institutions', *European Journal of International Relations* 1, no. 3 (1996): 355–93.

113 Verdun, 'An "Asymmetrical" Economic and Monetary Union'; Verdun, *European Responses*.

them to remain serious negotiation partners in a Europe in which unions were losing their importance.

The political business cycle literature stresses the role of interest groups and the electorate during the electoral cycle, focusing on the timing of elections and the importance of governments seeking re-election. Governments try to avoid inflation and devaluation of the currency before elections, and delay them until after the elections in order to finance perks that the incumbents enjoy in office or transfers to their constituents. Pre-election inflation and devaluation are avoided by accumulating debt, which is visible to the electorate only after a time lag. Therefore, pegs are especially hard to sustain around the time of elections.[114] The extent to which policy-makers are sensitive to interest groups depends on institutional features: the preferences and political influence of interest groups. In countries with credit-based financial institutions, such as France, Germany and Italy, where capital is typically raised through bank loans, the industrial and banking sectors should in theory support a strong currency policy and membership in EMU in order to make debt repayments easier. In contrast, in the UK, where capital is raised mainly through issues of bonds and equities, there should be little support for EMU.[115] However, in reality France and Italy persistently differed from Germany in their preferences regarding the institutional make-up of EMU.

Other domestic political institutions also play a role: for example, multi-party government coalitions in unitary rather than federal systems may give up monetary autonomy because it is hard for each player to target the benefits of monetary policy directly at its constituencies.[116] Political uncertainty is related to cabinet duration. According to the literature, cabinet duration in Europe is associated with exchange rate variation. On the one hand, fixed exchange rates cause political stability, serving as focal points for policy agreement and bargaining or as credibility anchors, thereby helping politicians to manage intra-party and intra-coalition conflicts.[117] On the other

---

114 A. Alesina and N. Roubini, *Political Cycles and the Macroeconomy* (Cambridge, MA, MIT Press, 1997).

115 L. S. Talani, *Betting for and against EMU: Who Wins and Who Loses in Italy and in the UK from the Process of European Monetary Integration* (London, Ashgate, 2000); J. I. Walsh, 'National Preferences and International Institutions: Evidence from European Monetary Integration', *International Studies Quarterly* 45, no. 1 (2001): 59–80.

116 M. Hallerberg, 'Veto Players and the Choice of Monetary Institutions', *International Organization* 56, no. 4 (2002): 775–802.

117 W. Bernhard and D. Leblang, 'Democratic Institutions and Exchange-Rate Commitments', *International Organization* 53, no. 1 (1999): 71–97; J. A. Frieden, 'Real Sources of European Currency Policy: Sectoral Interests and European Monetary Integration', *International Organization* 56, no. 4 (2002): 831–60.

hand, stable cabinets would be more likely to fix exchange rates in the first place, because maintaining a fixed exchange rate may require politically difficult adjustments and long decision-making horizons.[118]

The two-way causal relation between cabinet duration and exchange rate variation makes it difficult to tell whether EMU is a cause of greater cabinet duration or a result of it. Sadeh, by studying a sample of forty-three member states and candidate and neighbourhood countries during 1992–8, shows that the effect of cabinet duration on EMU can be isolated after controlling for that two-way causality, as well as for OCA variables.[119] However, cabinet duration and various domestic institutions are more likely to have been features that facilitated EMU rather than a driving motive for its establishment. The choice of exchange rate policy is also part of a political agenda, sensitive to the ideological or constituency bias of the ruling coalition. Is EMU a project for right-wing governments? Scholars see EMU and the history of the EMS as reflecting a monetarist agenda, redistributing income from labour to capital.[120] Under the rules of the SGP, such policies are supposed to be more difficult to pursue (although in recent years, during the Covid-19 pandemic, the rules have been relaxed). The fiscal constraints imposed by EMU, central bank independence and setting price stability as a policy goal isolate policy-makers from the pressures of domestic politics and accountability, promote a hospitable investment climate and maximise the power of capital. Furthermore, some argue that EMU was created by elite males in large financial houses and firms, government bureaucracies and EU organisations. EMU is part of a process of deepening social inequality to the detriment above all of women and children.[121] Perhaps unsurprisingly, there are gendered differences in attitudes to EMU.[122] Some of the confusion with regard to partisan exchange rate policies can be clarified by

---

118 W. Bernhard and D. Leblang, 'Democratic Processes, Political Risk and Foreign Exchange Markets', *American Journal of Political Science* 46, no. 2 (2002): 316–33.

119 T. Sadeh, *Sustaining European Monetary Union: Confronting the Cost of Diversity* (Boulder, CO, Lynne Rienner, 2006).

120 J. Grahl, *After Maastricht: A Guide to European Monetary Union* (London, Lawrence and Wishart, 1997); T. Oatley, *Exchange Rate Cooperation in the European Union* (Ann Arbor, MI, University Michigan Press, 1998).

121 S. Gill, 'The Emerging World Order and European Change: The Political Economy of European Union', *The Socialist Register* (1992): 157–96; S. Gill, 'An EMU or an Ostrich? EMU and Neo-liberal Globalisation; Limits and Alternatives', in Minkkinen and Patomäki (eds), *The Politics of Economic and Monetary Union*, pp. 207–31.

122 S. Banducci and P. Loedel, 'Gender, Austerity, and Support for EMU across Generations', *Journal of European Integration* 42, no. 3 (2020): 415–31.

controlling for institutional features, such as the strength of trade unions and transnational business.[123] All in all, domestic factors have played an important role.

Conclusion

This chapter examined the euro area crisis, by looking at its pre-history, the unfolding of the crisis and its aftermath, and provided a historiography of the origins of EMU – making sense of the crisis from a scholarly point of view by including a reflection on its origins. It chronicled the pre-history of the euro crisis by reviewing and examining its chequered path towards its institutional set-up. In reviewing the sequence of events that led to the immediate outbreak of the euro area crisis, the chapter identified a number of challenges that the EU was faced with. The institutional set-up, the norms underlying EMU and the dominance of Germany made it initially difficult for the EU to respond. The crisis worsened as the leaders took their time to identify a way out. Most of the initial responses were too little, too late, leading the euro area to the brink of collapse. Once unconditional support had been given, the EU started a process of institutional change – identifying different institutional structures to deepen European integration, in particular in the economic and monetary domain. Structures such as the EFSF, the ESM and the Banking Union were intended to deepen EMU. Political leadership was also signalled when considering further road maps spelled out in the Four and Five Presidents' Reports and the 2017 White Paper on the Future of Europe and Reflection Paper on EMU. Some recent developments have thrown the EU a curve ball: it had been challenging to develop EMU further whilst also dealing with Brexit and US President Donald Trump's diminished support for multilateralism. Upon examining the origins of EMU, we find explanations on four levels of analysis: the global level, EU level, member state (national) level and domestically within the member states.

In the context of the Covid-19 crisis, however, new opportunities have arisen. On the one hand, the member states' first reaction to challenges posed by the Covid-19 crisis were national. Yet, within a few months, the EU's leaders agreed to far-reaching temporary measures to help out those countries in need. Although it is too soon to say whether these initiatives will have

---

123 A. Bieler, 'Labour and the Struggle over the Future European Model of Capitalism: British and Swedish Trade Unions and Their Positions on EMU and European Co-operation', *British Journal of Politics and International Relations* 10, no. 1 (2008): 85–105.

a lasting impact on the institutional structure of the EU, the practice of helping out, and finding EU means to address the issues, may foreshadow deeper integration.

Recommended Reading

Chang, M. *Economic and Monetary Union* (Basingstoke, Palgrave Macmillan, 2016).

Dyson, K. and K. Featherstone. *The Road to Maastricht: Negotiating Economic and Monetary Union* (Oxford, Oxford University Press, 1999).

Dyson, K. and L. Quaglia. *European Economic Governance and Policies*, vol. 1: *Commentary on Key Historical and Institutional Documents* (Oxford, Oxford University Press, 2010).

Jones, E. *The Politics of Economic and Monetary Union: Integration and Idosyncrasy* (Lanham, MD, Rowman and Littlefield, 2002).

McNamara, K. R. *The Currency of Ideas: Monetary Politics in the European Union* (London, Cornell University Press, 1998).

Mourlon-Druol, E. *A Europe Made of Money: The Emergence of the European Monetary System* (Ithaca, NY, Cornell University Press, 2012).

Sadeh, T. *Sustaining European Monetary Union: Confronting the Cost of Diversity* (Boulder, CO, Lynne Rienner, 2006).

Verdun, A. *European Responses to Globalization and Financial Market Integration: Perceptions of Economic and Monetary Union in Britain, France and Germany* (Basingstoke, Palgrave Macmillan, 2000).

———

12

The Institutional and Legal Culture
of European Integration

PHILIP BAJON

Introduction

This chapter sets out to conceptualise the institutional and legal evolution of the European Communities (EC) over time from the Treaties of Paris and Rome to the Treaty of Maastricht.

The founding treaties of Paris and Rome were essentially open-ended efforts for integration, despite their undeniable differences in nature. At the moment of negotiating the founding treaties and during the first years of the Communities, it was unforeseeable whether the Communities would go through a process of gradual and increasing federalisation, or whether member states would eventually manage to dominate the Communities. The balance between these contradictory tendencies inherent in the founding treaties was clarified only through the open political battles in the 1960s. In a sense, the battle between federalist and intergovernmentalist streams has continued beyond Maastricht to the present day.

The chapter is divided into three major sections. The first section will deal with the original institutional setting and balance proposed by the Treaties of Paris and Rome. The second section will consider the rise and dominance of the intergovernmental pillar in the institutional setting of the European Economic Community (EEC). It will pay particular attention to three elements that crucially shaped the institutional and legal culture of European integration: first, the Comité des Représentants permanents (Committee of Permanent Representatives, known under its French abbreviation COREPER); secondly, the Gaullist challenge to the EEC from 1963; and thirdly, the establishment of summitry and of the European Council by the mid 1970s. Finally, the third section will look at how the Single European Act (SEA) and the Maastricht

Treaty transformed the European institutional and legal system and whether the major treaty reforms of the 1980s and early 1990s did or did not amount to 'changing the game' with regard to the projects of gradual federalisation and a deepening of legal integration.

Origins of the Institutional Culture of the Communities

In his famous declaration of 9 May 1950, French foreign minister Robert Schuman proposed a pooling of French and West German coal and steel production under the umbrella of a strong supranational High Authority (HA). The plan had been elaborated by a small group around Jean Monnet, the 'statesman of interdependence'.[1] In the subsequent negotiations, a common assembly was added to the scheme to increase democratic control over the HA. Then, in response to Benelux concerns about potential excesses of the HA, the idea of also introducing a Council of member state ministers as a counterweight to the HA emerged. The West German delegation proposed a classical separation of powers, with a common assembly and a permanent court of justice, because the delegation leader Walter Hallstein and his main legal adviser Friedrich Ophüls regarded the emerging institutions as the embryo of a future federal organisation. Hallstein highlighted the benefits of a strong constitutional court of justice to Monnet as early as in July 1950.[2] In the four-pillar institutional structure of the European Coal and Steel Community (ECSC), Monnet's original conception prevailed. The HA enjoyed extensive administrative powers to apply well-defined rules, and the institutional balance between the HA and the Council clearly leaned towards the former. The ECSC Court included elements of international law, French administrative law and, somewhat more discretely, also constitutional law. Although the Court hardly met Hallstein's hopes and expectations, the ECSC legal system nevertheless broke with classical international public law.[3]

1 F. Duchêne, *Jean Monnet: The First Statesman of Interdependence* (New York, NY, W. W. Norton, 1994).
2 I. Pernice, 'Begründung und Konsolidierung der Europäischen Gemeinschaft als Rechtsgemeinschaft', in M. Zuleeg (ed.), *Der Beitrag Walter Hallsteins zur Zukunft Europas: Referate zu Ehren Walter Hallsteins* (Baden-Baden, Nomos, 2003), pp. 56–70.
3 A. Boerger-De Smedt, 'Negotiating the Foundations of European Law, 1950–57: The Legal History of the Treaties of Paris and Rome', *Contemporary European History* 21 (2012): 339–56; B. Davies and M. Rasmussen, 'From International Law to a European Rechtsgemeinschaft: Towards a New History of European Law, 1950–1979', in J. Laursen (ed.), *The Institutions and Dynamics of the European Community, 1973–83* (Baden-Baden, Nomos, 2014), pp. 97–130.

In the Treaties of Rome of 1957, negotiators handled the institutional questions in a pragmatic way to ensure ratification in France. This was consistent with a general trend of softening the supranational nature of further integration projects after the proposals to set up the European Defence Community and the European Political Community were defeated in the French Assemblée nationale in 1954. The experience of the ECSC showed that the supranational HA greatly depended on member state support from the ECSC Council, with the Council members blocking parts of the ECSC's agenda, such as the competition policy. Having learned this lesson, the treaty drafters gave the member states a more prominent role in the institutional set-up of the Treaties of Rome.[4] Therefore, the committee chaired by Belgian foreign minister Paul Henri Spaak, who had to elaborate a roadmap for the Common Market and the European Atomic Community, proposed on 21 April 1956 a four-pillar structure, in which the Council was to receive the role of decision-making centre and the HA (now identified as 'the Commission') was relegated to merely holding the legislative initiative, acting as a supranational co-executive.

The intergovernmental conference (IGC) held at Val Duchesse in Brussels confirmed this institutional scheme, which subsequently became part of the treaty. Although the jurists' committee, the famous *'groupe de rédaction'*, was able to introduce a limited number of constitutional 'injections' into the Treaties of Rome, the two new treaties were clearly designed to secure the centrality of the member states. At the same time, the EEC treaty did not provide a well-defined roadmap like the *'traité de loi '* of Paris. Instead, it simply established the core principles, the objectives and the means to achieve them. Thus, it was essentially an open-ended and flexible framework treaty.[5]

Federalist assumptions seriously affected the agenda and political style of the newly created supranational executives, the HA from 1951 and the Commission from 1958, and the worldviews of their officials. Prominent examples were the first president of the HA, Jean Monnet, and the first EEC Commission president, Walter Hallstein. While the former can be seen as a pragmatic bureaucrat in favour of a supranational technocracy,

---

4 D. Sindbjerg Martinsen and M. Rasmussen, 'EU Constitutionalisation Revisited. Redressing a Central Assumption in European Studies', *European Law Journal* 25 (2019): 1–22, 6; T. Witschke, *Gefahr für den Wettbewerb? Die Fusionskontrolle der Europäischen Gemeinschaft für Kohle und Stahl und die 'Rekonzentration' der Ruhrstahlindustrie 1950–1963* (Berlin, Akademie Verlag, 2009).

5 Boerger-De Smedt, 'Negotiating the Foundations of European Law'.

the latter – as a lawyer – was much more a European federalist in theory, holding strong beliefs about the nature of European integration, the role of Community institutions and the status of European law.[6] Hallstein worked towards establishing the Commission as 'a new element in international diplomacy'[7] on the same level as the member state governments. The European Parliament (EP) was a second stronghold of federalist ideology. The double-mandate system before 1979 ensured that the political centre provided a majority of members of the EP (MEPs), while politicians from the political fringes tended to be excluded from the EP, leading to a much larger pro-European majority than was seen in most national parliaments.[8] In some cases however, the 'political fringes' first became strong in the European elections and later 'went national'. Regarding support for EEC federalisation at the national level, the picture was more ambivalent. Member state parliaments in the Benelux countries and Italy were generally positive about federalist-inspired institutional reform of the EEC. However, the governments of these pro-European countries did not always share the enthusiasm of their parliaments for further developing the federalist character of the EEC. A striking example was provided by Italian MEPs favouring majority voting in the Community, while Italian governments appreciated and employed the informal veto right of the Luxembourg Compromise on several occasions.

Despite the obvious presence and relevance of federalist ideas in the supranational institutions and the member state political systems, the definitive reform towards political and institutional deepening of the EEC in a federal sense never occurred. The Communities never produced fully fledged federal institutions running European public policies, because the advocates of such a reform were eventually unable to overcome the resistance in most member states. Yet, the backing for federalisation inside the supranational institutions became a driving force for what is termed the 'constitutional interpretation' of European law.[9]

---

6 W. Loth, W. Wallace and W. Wessels (eds.), *Walter Hallstein – Der vergessene Europäer?* (Bonn, Europa Union, 1995); W. Hallstein, *Der unvollendete Bundesstaat: Europäische Erfahrungen und Erkenntnisse* (Düsseldorf and Berlin, Econ, 1969).
7 See W. Hallstein, 'Die Kommission – ein neues Element im internationalen Leben, British Institute of International and Comparative Law, London, 25. März 1965', in W. Hallstein and T. Oppermann (eds.), *Europäische Reden* (Stuttgart, DVA, 1979), pp. 545–59.
8 V. Herman and J. Lodge, 'The Dual Mandate', in V. Herman and J. Lodge (eds.), *The European Parliament and the European Community* (London, Palgrave Macmillan, 1978), pp. 141–56.
9 Sindbjerg Martinsen and Rasmussen, 'EU Constitutionalisation Revisited', 7.

In Hallstein's view, the replacement of power politics with the rule of law was a core element of integration and made the EEC a 'Community of Law'. Already in 1955, the Legal Service of the HA adopted a federal understanding of the ECSS treaty and of the role of the ECSC Court, interpreting European law and the role of the Court *as if* they were aiming at the construction of a federal Europe. As president of the EEC Commission, Hallstein promoted the federalist understanding of European law and encouraged the European Court of Justice (ECJ) to assume the role of a constitutional court.[10] However, throughout the 1950s the constitutional interpretation was largely rejected by member state governments, experts, scholars and the ECJ itself.[11] The ECJ did not embrace the federal vision of European law until the milestone cases of the early 1960s, *Van Gend en Loos* of 1963 and *Costa v E.N. E.L.* of 1964, in which the Court developed the new legal doctrines of direct effect and primacy.[12]

The Rise and Dominance of Intergovernmentalism

The Striving for Consensus

The rise of EEC intergovernmentalism was a complex and wider development, facilitated by the aforementioned ambiguities of the treaties. A core element of it was the gradual expansion of the role of the Council pillar and a drift towards consensus in the management and decision-making of the Council. From the outset of EEC integration, the build-up of major public policies following the EEC framework treaty, such as the Common Agricultural Policy (CAP) or tariff harmonisation, urged member states to work towards a high degree of consensus concerning the objectives to be achieved and the methods to be employed. Because the Communities were still in a fragile and formative period, member states hesitated to entirely

---

10 For the support of the ECJ's new legal doctrines by Hallstein and other high officials, see M. Rasmussen, 'Rewriting the History of European Public Law: The New Contribution of Historians', *American University International Law Review* 28 (2013): 1187–1221, 1209–10; A. Boerger and M. Rasmussen, 'The Making of European Law: Exploring the Life and Work of Michel Gaudet', *American Journal of Legal History* 57 (2016): 1–32, 25–6; A. Vauchez, 'The Transnational Politics of Judicialization: Van Gend en Loos and the Making of EU polity', *European Law Journal* 16 (2010): 1–28; A. Vauchez, *Brokering Europe: Euro-lawyers and the Making of a Transnational Polity* (Cambridge, Cambridge University Press, 2015), pp. 133–46.

11 M. Rasmussen, 'Establishing a Constitutional Practice of European Law: The History of the Legal Service of the European Executive, 1952–65', *Contemporary European History* 21 (2012): 375–97.

12 M. Rasmussen, 'Revolutionizing European Law: A History of the Van Gend en Loos Judgement', *International Journal of Constitutional Law* 12 (2014): 136–63.

delegate the administrative business to Community institutions. Instead, they involved their national administrations to a very high degree. There was no alternative to this initial choice also for purely technical reasons, because only national administrations had at their disposal the specific competences and resources to deal with some of the technical challenges at Community level.

The most important phenomenon illustrating the consensus search among member states was the emergence of new committee structures in the Council pillar and beyond. COREPER was formally established on 24 January 1958 to organise the work of the General Affairs Council and to set up various working groups preparing Community legislation.[13] The permanent representatives, in daily Community business often labelled 'ambassadors', acted as deputies to the ministers of the member states. They were accompanied by national experts who served both in the permanent representation and in national ministries. Complex technical issues were usually delegated to the expert working groups and committees, in which also the Commission was present. COREPER's function thus was to counterbalance the supranational bodies of the Commission and also of the EP.

With the creation of specialised Council compositions, such as the Agricultural Council, a 'functional division of labour' became apparent in the Council pillar, which helped to cope with the complexity of the Community agenda. The Special Committee for Agriculture took over much of the Council's workload in the field. Following this model, many subcommittees and technical working groups – composed of supranational as well as national officials and experts – saw the light of day in the early 1960s, for example the Special Committee for Article III, monitoring the Community's Kennedy Round negotiations within the General Agreement on Tariffs and Trade. Likewise, management and advisory committees were also set up in support of the Commission to implement CAP legislation. These 'comitology committees' were composed of Commission officials, national experts and social partners. Through the emerging committee structures, national administrations became integrated both in the agenda-setting and in the administrative tasks of the Commission. This seriously questioned the political and administrative autonomy of the Commission, which had originally been conceived as a safeguard for the interests of smaller member states. However, comitology structures also encouraged a less

13 M. Dumoulin, 'The Interim Committee (April 1957 to January 1958)', in M. Dumoulin (ed.), *The European Commission, 1958–1972: History and Memoirs* (Luxembourg, Office for Official Publications of the European Communities, 2007), pp. 37–49.

confrontational and rather deliberative bargaining style between the supranational and national actors involved.

On the one hand, the emergence and increasing involvement of COREPER and of various other committee structures in Community affairs were the result of the member states' desire to monitor the activist Commission. On the other hand, those committee structures can more broadly be understood as the governments' attempt to control the vast integration process of the EEC, which was far more confusing than the highly specialised coal and steel integration. Monthly Council meetings were simply insufficient to supervise the multiplicity of Community activities and tasks. COREPER, with its expertise and seat in Brussels, addressed the problem and gave crucial support to the Council. However, the advocates of the 'community method' – from the Benelux states in particular – warned that the rise of COREPER would risk the EEC's 'slide into unaccountable technocracy'.[14]

The Political and Institutional Battles of the 1960s

Strictly opposed to the federalists were the advocates of intergovernmental European cooperation, most prominently French President General Charles de Gaulle. Throughout his various governments from 1958 to 1969, he made a number of proposals for western European cooperation as an intergovernmental alternative to the EEC model, first in the Fouchet Plans of 1960–2, then in the French–West German Elysée Treaty of 1963 and finally in his proposal to the West German government of July 1964 for participation in the *force de frappe* (France's nuclear strike force).[15] The EEC was about to reach a point of no return by the mid 1960s, with the near-completion of the CAP, the agreement on the common price level for cereals of December 1964, the decision on the

14 N. P. Ludlow, 'The European Commission and the Rise of Coreper: A Controlled Experiment', in W. Kaiser, B. Leucht and M. Rasmussen (eds.), *The History of the European Union: Origins of a Trans- and Supranational Polity 1950–72* (London, Routledge, 2009), pp. 189–205; N. P. Ludlow, 'Mieux que six ambassadeurs. L'émergence du COREPER durant les premières années de la CEE', in L. Badel, S. Jeannesson and N. P. Ludlow (eds.), *Les administrations nationales et la construction européenne: Une approche historique (1919–1975)* (Brussels, Peter Lang, 2005), pp. 337–56; A.-C. L. Knudsen and M. Rasmussen, 'A European Political System in the Making 1958–1970: The Relevance of Emerging Committee Structures', *Journal of European Integration History* 14 (2008): 51–68; P. H. J. M. Houben, *Les Conseils des Ministres des Communautés européennes* (Leiden, A. W. Sijthoff, 1964); F. Hayes-Renshaw and H. Wallace, *The Council of Ministers*, 2nd ed. (Basingstoke, Palgrave Macmillan, 2006).

15 M. Vaïsse, *La grandeur: Politique étrangère du général de Gaulle 1958–1969* (Paris, Fayard, 1998); E. Roussell, *Charles de Gaulle* (Paris, Gallimard, 2002); W. Loth, 'De Gaulle und Europa. Eine Revision', *Historische Zeitschrift* 253 (1991): 629–60; W. Loth, 'Hallstein und de Gaulle: Die verhängnisvolle Konfrontation', in Loth, Wallace and Wessels (eds.), *Walter Hallstein*, pp. 171–88; W. Loth, *Charles de Gaulle* (Stuttgart, Kohlhammer, 2015).

fusion of the executives in spring 1965 and the extension of majority voting from January 1966. France had dominated the Community agenda and had enormously benefited from the CAP during the preceding years. However, French supremacy provoked the other member states, which increasingly developed a quid-pro-quo attitude towards Community business.[16]

Hallstein's audacious attempt of spring 1965 to strengthen the spillover dynamic and the supranational institutions at the expense of the Council pillar crystallised the tensions and overall distrust among member states. In the Commission proposals of spring 1965 for CAP financing in the period 1965–70, Hallstein linked agricultural financing to a general strengthening of supranationality. Throughout spring and summer 1965, the Council remained divided over the Commission proposals, and Hallstein for his part refused to soften the proposals.[17] Guided by his geopolitical vision of intergovernmental cooperation, annoyed by the EEC partners' quid-pro-quo politics and provoked by the activist Commission, de Gaulle decided to boycott the EEC Council from early July 1965 onwards, and also to withdraw France's ambassador.[18] The unfolding crisis was named after France's 'empty chair' at Brussels. In one of his eccentric press conferences, de Gaulle revealed that France would return to the Council only if ambitious Commissioners – above all Hallstein – were replaced by obedient bureaucrats, if the Commission were turned into a European technical secretariat and if majority voting in the Council were suspended or replaced by a national veto right.[19] De Gaulle later focused on his claim for a national veto, when he realised that the other member states would protect the Commission.[20]

In several respects, the element of rising state power became a central feature of the 'empty chair crisis'. First, it rapidly became common sense among national and Community officials that the crisis was deeply political in

16 N. P. Ludlow, *The European Community and the Crises of the 1960s: Negotiating the Gaullist Challenge* (London, Routledge, 2006), pp. 52–8; N. P. Ludlow, 'Challenging French Leadership in Europe: Germany, Italy, the Netherlands and the Outbreak of the Empty Chair Crisis of 1965–66', *Contemporary European History* 8 (1999): 31–48.

17 P. Bajon, '"The Human Factor". French–West German Bilateralism and the "Logic of Appropriateness" in the European Crisis of the Mid-1960s', *Diplomacy & Statecraft* 29 (2018): 455–76.

18 J.-M. Palayret, H. Wallace and P. Winand, *Visions, Votes and Vetoes: The Empty Chair Crisis and the Luxembourg Compromise Forty Years On* (Brussels, Peter Lang, 2006); J. Newhouse, *Collision in Brussels: The Common Market Crisis of 30 June 1965* (New York, NY, W. W. Norton, 1967); M. Camps, *European Unification in the Sixties: From the Veto to the Crisis* (New York, NY, McGraw-Hill, 1966); P. Bajon, *Europapolitik 'am Abgrund': Die Krise des 'leeren Stuhls' 1965–66* (Stuttgart, Franz Steiner, 2012).

19 C. de Gaulle, *Pour l'effort 1962–1965* (Paris, Plon, 1970), pp. 372–92.

20 Bajon, *Europapolitik 'am Abgrund'*, pp. 239–43.

nature and could be overcome only by negotiations 'between the member state governments'. The Legal Service of the Commission under Michel Gaudet underlined that legal instruments (i.e., taking France to court for treaty infringement) would be unhelpful in the attempt to end the empty chair politics.[21] De Gaulle did not make any claims regarding the European legal order or the ECJ during the crisis,[22] nor did France's partners try to bring France before the ECJ for breaching the law of the treaty, although MEPs from the Netherlands publicly demanded this.[23]

Secondly, the supranational institutions such as the Commission and the EP were largely marginalised when the crisis increasingly turned into a classical 'concert' and power play between the governments. Internal expertise from the West German government and from the Legal Service of the Commission suggested that majority votes and even unanimous decisions were legitimate and feasible in France's absence.[24] This was grist to the mills of France's EEC partners and gave them a welcome pretext to reaffirm their leadership in the Community and to increase the diplomatic pressure on France. Politicians and officials from the Benelux and Italian governments urged West Germany's Foreign Minister Gerhard Schröder to counteract de Gaulle's brinkmanship more systematically and to bring France back to the EEC Council. Without much public attention, Schröder built a coalition against de Gaulle, and he urged the partner governments to consult each other and to resist French attempts to manipulate, confuse, weaken and split the so-called *bloc des cinq* (bloc of five). Schröder's campaign

---

21 Memo by Gaudet 'Absence d'un Etat membre [. . .]', 12 July 1965, BAC 49 2013 18; Gaudet to Hallstein 'Annahme der Tagesordnung durch den unvollständig besetzten Rat', 26 July 1965, BAC 49 2013 18; record of Commission session of 30 January 1978, undated, BAC 49 2013 18; Telex 1403 Sachs (Brussels) to Carstens and Lahr, 15 September 1965, document 351, in H.-P. Schwarz, *Akten zur Auswärtigen Politik der Bundesrepublik Deutschland 1965* (Munich, Oldenbourg, 1966), p. 1442. See also Rasmussen, 'Establishing a Constitutional Practice', 15.

22 A. Bernier, *La France et le droit communautaire 1958–1981: Histoire d'une réception et d'une co-production* (Ph.D. thesis, University of Copenhagen, 2017), pp. 112–18.

23 Telex Obermayer (The Hague) to German Foreign Office, 15 July 1965, PAAA, B20 1321.

24 Record of talks between Schröder and Spaak, 26 July 1965, document 303, in Schwarz, *Akten zur Auswärtigen Politik 1965*, p. 1275; note by Meyer-Lindenberg, 'Verfahrensfragen [. . .]', 16 July 1965, PAAA, B20 1321; note by Carstens, 'EWG', 7 September 1965, PAAA, B20 1322; Kölble (Ministry of Interior) to Foreign Office, 22 September 1965, PAAA, B20 1323; memo by Ophüls, 'Fragen der Beschlußfähigkeit des Rates bei der EWG bei Mitwirkungs-Weigerung eines Ratsmitglieds [. . .]', 16 September 1965, PAAA, B20 1322; German Foreign Office memo, 'Die Rechtsfolgen des französischen Fernbleibens aus den Gemeinschaften', c. autumn 1965, BAC 49 2013 18; note of German Ministry of Economics, 'Einstimmige Beschlußfassung im Rat der Fünf', 28 October 1965, p. 1, PAAA, B20 1325; memo by Hans-Joachim Glaesner, 'Beschlüsse des Rates bei Fernbleiben eines Mitgliedstaates', 12 November 1965, BAC 49 2013 18.

was designed to provoke and to pressurise de Gaulle, therefore he also briefed the partner governments about the West German legal expertise.[25]

Thirdly, despite the obvious polarisation between France and the Five, an anti-supranational consensus emerged amongst all six member states, which consolidated and locked-in the intergovernmental tendency that characterised EEC politics for several years. Although de Gaulle initially demanded the relegation of the Commission to a mere secretariat, the subsequent conflict was less about the Commission powers. As mentioned above, the Commission and the EP were marginalised anyway by the intergovernmental style of the crisis management. Instead, the conflict centred around the functioning of the Council pillar, that is, the transition to majority voting scheduled for January 1966 in the Treaties of Rome. While the Rome Treaties primarily emphasised the role of member states, they still offered a certain perspective for federalisation (e.g., the independent role of the Commission and of the EP, the option for direct elections to the EP and above all the gradual extension of voting procedures at Council level).[26] The eventuality of being outvoted over a 'vital interest' necessarily raised questions about the sovereignty of the member state.

At the Luxembourg conference in January 1966, which formally ended the empty chair crisis, France and its partners reached a clearly anti-supranational agreement over how to handle voting. On the one hand, de Gaulle gave up his original maximalist demand for formal treaty revision. Instead, the French government agreed to negotiate a 'political arrangement', or, in Couve's words, 'Le droit reste inchangé. Il y a les consequences politiques.' ('The law remains unchanged. There are political consequences.').[27] French diplomats pointed out to de Gaulle that the Council had always dealt with important questions by seeking unanimity, and that this consensual working style was likely to prevail even after the formal transition to voting.[28] On the other hand, France's partners – maybe with the exception of the Dutch – did their

---

25 P. Bajon, 'De Gaulle Finds His "Master". Gerhard Schröder's "Fairly Audacious Politics" in the European Crisis of 1965–66', *Journal of European Integration History* 17 (2011): 253–69; PAAA, B1 214, Schröder to Schmücker, 3 January 1966; record of Schröder's talk before the Bundestag Foreign Affairs Committee of 23 September 1965, p. 21, ADBT, 3104, 4 Legislative Period, Protocol 87; article in 'Europe' entitled 'La politique francaise de la chaise vide: Une analyse des problèmes juridiques', 20 November 1965, BAC 49 2013 18.

26 Boerger-De Smedt, 'Negotiating the Foundations of European Law'.

27 Memo 'Une réunion a eu lieu à Luxembourg[. . .]', 29 January 1966, p. 2, MAE, DE-CE, 1113.

28 Memo (presumably by Jean-Pierre Brunet) entitled 'Règles de majorité dans le Traité de Rome', 21 May 1965, p. 5, MAE, DE-CE, 1111. See also N. P. Ludlow, 'The Eclipse of the Extremes. Demythologising the Luxembourg Compromise', in W. Loth (ed.), *Crises and Compromises: The European Project 1963–1969* (Baden-Baden, Nomos; Brussels, Bruylant, 2001), pp. 247–64, 248; Newhouse, *Collision in Brussels*, p. 67.

utmost to accommodate French concerns. They provided the French government with reassuring statements about how 'desirable' consensus was, and they made a number of proposals for strengthening unanimous decision-making at the expense of qualified majority voting.[29] Schröder in particular shared de Gaulle's preferences in terms of sovereignty of the nation-state and agreed with the general that the member states should ultimately control the process of European integration, while the independent role of the supranational institutions had to be strictly limited.[30] Both the Commission and the EP were only marginally involved in the crisis management or in the conference at Luxembourg in January 1966. The Commissioners, most prominently Hallstein and his influential *chef de cabinet* Karl-Heinz Narjes, in their bilateral talks with the French and the West German governments, did their utmost to defend the principle of voting and EEC supranationality, without success.[31] At Luxembourg, France's partners tolerated the French unilateral declaration that no member state must be outvoted when 'very important national interests' were at stake, and that each member state was free to define its 'vital interests' independently.

The arrangement found at Luxembourg delivered the pretext for a more aggressive veto culture in which a Council minority could refer to the informal arrangement or allude more generally to the empty chair crisis to block new legislation favoured by a majority of the other member states.[32] Voting on important non-budgetary questions did not take place during the

29 Note by Meyer-Lindenberg, 'Vorschläge Außenminister Spaaks zur Mehrheitsregel', 26 January 1966, PAAA, B20 1330. See also the decision for the 'stopping of the clock' regarding the Council agenda: Protocol of EEC Council 17–18 and 28–29 February 1966, 29 April 1966, p. 120, HACM, CM2 1966 1; Commission paper 'Décisions ayant dû être prises en 1966 mais qui ont dû être remises en raison de la crise', 26 January 1966, BAC 49 2013 19.

30 Bajon, 'De Gaulle Finds His "Master"'.

31 Jazke to Narjes, 17 September 1965, BAK, NH, 1187; Lanzke to Narjes, 16 September 1965, BAK, NH, 1187; Manuscript Noel of Commission session of 26 January 1966, HAEU, EN, 761; memo of Hallstein cabinet, 'Ich danke sehr [. . .]', c. mid-January 1966, BAK, NH, 1119; Narjes to Hallstein, 2 March 1965, BAK, NH, 1119; memo Narjes, 'Gespräch in Bonn vom 23.–26. November', 22 November 1965, BAK, NH, 1114; note Narjes, 'Gespräch mit dem Bundeskanzler am 10. Dezember', 9 December 1965, BAK, NH, 1114; note Narjes, 'Ihr Gespräch mit Bundesminister Schröder', 9 December 1965, BAK, NH, 1090; Hallstein to Wagner (BDI), 5 February 1966, BAK, NH, 1194.

32 Memo 'Effets indirects de la règle de la majorité', undated, HAEU, EN, 807; R. Streinz, *Die Luxemburger Vereinbarung: Rechtliche und politische Aspekte der Abstimmungspraxis im Rat der Europäischen Gemeinschaften seit der Luxemburger Vereinbarung vom 29. Januar 1966* (Munich, Florentz, 1984); Palayret et al., *Visions, Votes and Vetoes*; Hayes-Renshaw and Wallace, *The Council of Ministers*; R. Lahr, 'Die Legende vom Luxemburger Kompromiß', *Europa-Archiv* 38 (1983): 223–32; W. Nicoll, 'The Luxembourg Compromise', *Journal of Common Market Studies* 23 (1984): 35–43;

remaining years of the 1960s, and was rarely used in the first half of the 1970s, despite the newly experienced dynamic of the integration process during those years.[33]

While the element of state power experienced a breakthrough in the empty chair crisis, the original open nature of the treaties with regard to the ultimate goal of the integration project faded. The immediate or mid-term development of the EEC into highly federalised Communities was by that point in time no longer conceivable. Crucially, the crisis of the mid 1960s was also significant in terms of the eventual disappearance of the federalist rhetoric which the advocates of supranationality had employed throughout the 1950s and in the early 1960s.[34]

The Consolidation of the Intergovernmental Dynamic in the 1970s

The empty chair crisis concluded the formative period of European integration, which produced winners and losers among the Community institutions. The Council demonstrated an excellent performance and implemented most of the initial EEC agenda, including the CAP and the customs union. Nonetheless, the Communities lacked dynamic leadership. This was not only a result of the continuous disagreement over UK membership, but also due to the fact that the efforts for negative integration, which had been so characteristic for the formative years of the Communities, had to a large extent been completed. In contrast, de Gaulle had successfully frustrated the Commission's striving for power and federalisation. Following the clash of 1965–6, the Commission lost its original federalist impetus and pursued a policy of maintaining a low profile. Weakened as an agenda setter, the Commission hardly assumed the role that Hallstein claimed for it, namely to be an 'engine, guardian and honest broker'.[35]

A. Teasdale, 'The Life and Death of the Luxembourg Compromise', *Journal of Common Market Studies* 31 (1993): 567–79; D. Heisenberg, 'Informal Decision-Making in the Council: The Secret of the EU's Success?', in S. Meunier and K. R. McNamara (eds.), *Making History: European Integration and Institutional Change at Fifty* (Oxford: Oxford University Press, 2007), pp. 67–87.

33 Memo 'Nombre de décision [. . .]', 9 March 1967, HAEU, Emile Noel, 807; memo UE (82)19 rev, 'Vote à la majorité qualifiée dans le Conseil. Note du Secrétariat general', 22 March 1982, HAEU, Klaus Meyer, 220.

34 Ludlow, *Crises of the 1960s*, pp. 122–4.

35 On the Commission's role as described by Hallstein himself, see Hallstein, *Der unvollendete Bundesstaat*, p. 56.

At the same time, with the political, economic and institutional challenges of the late 1960s and 1970s, the impact of the Luxembourg Compromise of 1966 on the Community's institutions and procedures came to the fore. Both the Commission and the Council adopted a more cautious approach to legislative proposals, so as to avoid the crystallisation of controversies and invocations of the Luxembourg formula by member states.[36] As a consequence, EEC institutions seemed to 'underperform'. Federalist-inclined observers of European integration, such as the members of the European Movement, tended to identify the Luxembourg arrangement as the main obstacle to further progress in the Community and as the major origin of the inefficiency and *'lourdeur'* ('heaviness') of Community decision-making, the so-called 'Eurosclerosis' of the 1970s. However, the contribution of the Luxembourg Compromise to the overall malfunctioning of the EEC's institutional machinery is difficult to substantiate empirically. Researchers have been unable to document a legislative setback as a result of utilisation of the Luxembourg formula.[37] Contemporary observers, such as the 'three wise men' in their report on institutions in 1979, pointed out that the inefficient management of Community business was a complex and wider phenomenon, which was to a large extent the result of external challenges and of fundamental disagreements among member states about the *finalité politique* (political finality) of European integration.[38]

The accession of the UK, Ireland and Denmark in 1973, and of Greece in 1981, clearly fostered the intergovernmental dimension of the Communities. The governments in London, Copenhagen and Athens shared the French government's preference for an intergovernmental approach to European integration. Under the label of the 'Luxembourg Compromise Club' they frequently invoked the informal right to a veto and insisted on their freedom to define what they regarded as 'vital national interests'. At the same time, summitry experienced a renaissance during the late 1960s and 1970s. Its institutionalisation through the European Council further cemented the member states' collective government in the Council

36 Memo UE(82)19 rev, 'Vote à la majorité dans le Conseil'.
37 J. Golub, 'Did the Luxembourg Compromise Have Any Consequences?', in Palayret et al. (eds), *Visions, Votes and Vetoes*, pp. 279–99.
38 J. Frowein, 'Zur institutionellen Fortentwicklung der Gemeinschaft', in Institut für das Recht der EG der Universität Köln (ed.), *Die institutionelle Entwicklung der Europäischen Gemeinschaften in den siebziger Jahren* (Cologne, Berlin, Bonn and Munich, Heymanns, 1973), pp. 83–105.

pillar.[39] The first influential summit meeting at The Hague in December 1969 had the ambition of overcoming the policy-making deadlock of the Gaullist era. Under the auspices of the new French president, Georges Pompidou, the summit addressed three major topics, namely enlargement, economic and monetary union, and European political cooperation.[40] While the following summits at Paris 1972 and at Copenhagen 1973 were regarded as somewhat unsuccessful, a breakthrough occurred after Valéry Giscard d'Estaing and Helmut Schmidt had become president in France and chancellor in West Germany. At the Paris summit of December 1974, the heads of state and government decided to institutionalise their meetings under the name European Council.[41] The 'provisional European government' (Jean Monnet) not only seized control of a large number of minor questions and leftovers from the Council (of Ministers), but also, crucially, assumed a broader leadership role and became the primary agenda-setter and initiator of grand reforms in the Communities. Its central role in the institutional set-up of the EEC was confirmed first in the SEA and later in the treaty of Maastricht.[42]

Member States and Constitutional Practice in European Law

When the ECJ developed its new constitutional doctrines in the 1960s and the governments presented their positions in the key cases before the ECJ, a majority of them was opposed to any new doctrinal breakthroughs, like

39 M. Westlake, *The Council of the European Union* (London, John Harper, 1995); W. Wessels, *Der Europäische Rat: Stabilisierung statt Integration? Geschichte, Entwicklung und Zukunft der EG-Gipfelkonferenzen* (Bonn, Europa Union, 1980); S. Bulmer, 'The European Council's First Decade: Between Interdependence and Domestic Politics', *Journal of Common Market Studies* 24 (1985): 89–104; E. Mourlon-Druol and F. Romero, *International Summitry and Global Governance: The Rise of the G7 and the European Council, 1974–1991* (London, Routledge, 2014).
40 Jan van der Harst (ed.), special issue 'The Hague Summit of 1969', *Journal of European Integration History* 9, no. 2 (2003); J. van der Harst, *Beyond the Customs Union: The European Community's Quest for Deepening, Widening and Completion, 1969–1975* (Brussels, Bruylant; Baden-Baden, Nomos, 2007).
41 Mourlon-Druol and Romero, *International Summitry*; E. Mourlon-Druol, 'Steering Europe. Explaining the Rise of the European Council, 1975–1986', *Contemporary European History* 25 (2016): 409–37.
42 N. P. Ludlow, 'European Integration in the 1980s: On the Way to Maastricht?', *Journal of European Integration History* 37 (2013): 11–23; N. P. Ludlow, 'Jacques Delors (1985–1995): Navigating the European Stream at Full Flood', in J. van der Harst (ed.), *An Impossible Job? The Presidents of the European Commission 1958–2014* (London, John Harper, 2015), pp. 173–96; Y.-S. Rittelmeyer, 'The Institutional Consecration of the European Council: Symbolism beyond Formal Texts', in Y.-S. Rittelmeyer and F. Foret (eds.), *The European Council and European Governance: The Commanding Heights of the EU* (London, Routledge, 2014), pp. 25–42.

France in the *Bosch* case,[43] the Netherlands, Belgium and West Germany in the *Van Gend en Loos* case[44] and Italy in *Costa v. E.N.E.L.*[45]

The late 1960s and early 1970s were a period of great political dynamic – inter alia due to de Gaulle's resignation, the summit at The Hague, and the imminent enlargement of the EEC towards northwestern Europe. In this context and encouraged by the triptych 'completion, enlargement, deepening' of the Hague summit, the newly composed 'Court of 1967', led by French judge Robert Lecourt, attempted to push the boundaries of European law and extended its case law to new fields such as the external competences of the Community and human rights.[46] Member states' governments and administrations were well aware of the dynamic nature of European law, and it was also in this period that several of the most important national courts began to react, as the West German Bundesverfassungsgericht (Constitutional Court) did in the *Solange* case.[47] In particular, the preliminary reference mechanism, which was so instrumental in the development of the ECJ's constitutional case law, became a point of contention.[48]

However, European law and ECJ reform never reached top priority on the agenda of any of the member states. The only partial exception was the negotiations over the Treaty of Maastricht discussed below. Although the British government, after northwestern enlargement in 1973, joined the sceptical French point of view, ECJ reform never became a central foreign policy objective of the UK or France, despite both governments occasionally raising the question of the ECJ's doctrinal advances. There were two major reasons for the limited saliency of ECJ reform at the European level. First, the

---

43 Judgment of the Court of 6 April 1962, *Kledingverkoopbedrijf de Geus en Uitdenbogerd v. Robert Bosch GmbH and Maatschappij tot voortzetting van de zaken der Firma Willem van Rijn*, Reference for a preliminary ruling: Gerechtshof 's-Gravenhage, Netherlands, Case 13-61, ECLI:EU:C:1962:11.

44 Judgment of the Court of 5 February 1963, *NV Algemene Transport- en Expeditie Onderneming van Gend & Loos v. Netherlands Inland Revenue Administration*, Reference for a preliminary ruling: Tariefcommissie, Netherlands, Case 26-62, ECLI:EU:C:1963:1.

45 Judgment of the Court of 15 July 1964, *Flaminio Costa v. E.N.E.L.*, Reference for a preliminary ruling: Giudice conciliatore di Milano, Italy, Case 6-64, ECLI:EU:C:1964:66.

46 W. Phelan, *Great Judgments of the European Court of Justice: Rethinking the Landmark Decisions of the Foundational Period* (Cambridge, Cambridge University Press, 2019).

47 B. Davies, *Resisting the European Court of Justice: West Germany's Confrontation with European Law, 1949–1979* (Cambridge, Cambridge University Press, 2013).

48 M. Rasmussen, 'How to Enforce European Law? A New History of the Battle over the Direct Effect of Directives, 1958–1987', *European Law Journal* 23 (2017): 290–308; V. Fritz, 'The First Member State Rebellion? The European Court of Justice and the Negotiations of the "Luxembourg Protocol" of 1971', *European Law Journal* 21 (2015): 680–99.

legal, political and economic consequences of the constitutional case law remained limited in the period before the SEA. Secondly, national administrations and courts could easily contain the various consequences of ECJ case law until the 1980s.

From the early 1960s throughout the first Community enlargement until the late 1970s, the member state governments united in the Council remained divided over how to assess and deal with the ECJ's constitutional case law. This often resulted in deadlock when the Council responded directly to the ECJ. One minority protected the Court, while another minority actually ensured that advances in ECJ case law would not be codified. In particular, when larger member states attacked the Court, governments of smaller member states such as the Benelux countries or Denmark defended the ECJ against the assault. Paradoxically, those smaller states (which occasionally defended the Court) were often at the same time limiting the ECJ's constitutional case law on an administrative level.[49] As a consequence of this peculiar constellation in the Council, the ECJ was never threatened by a Council majority in favour of curbing or reforming the Court.

The SEA and the Treaty of Maastricht

The SEA became the first major treaty reform since 1958. The Act not only envisaged the creation of a Single Market by 1992, but also formalised the foreign policy cooperation initiated in the early 1970s, granted the EP genuine powers in the legislative process through the cooperation procedure and made majority voting a standard for future legislation concerning the Single Market. Despite their obvious relevance, these innovations were far from what more federalist-inclined politicians had hoped for, and they were crucially accompanied by a confirmation of the European Council as the leading agenda-setting institution.

---

49 P. Bajon, 'Intergovernmentalism on the Rise – the Council Pillar in the Battle over the Constitutional Practice of European Law', in M. Rasmussen and B. Davies (eds.), *The History of European Law 1950 to 1993: The Battles over the Constitutional Practice* (publisher not yet known for certain, 2024); K. van Leeuwen, 'Blazing a Trail. The Netherlands and European Law, 1950–1983', in Davies and Rasmussen (eds.), *The History of European Law 1950 to 1993: The Battles over the Constitutional Practice* (publisher not yet known for certain, 2024); J. Langeland Pedersen, *Constructive Defiance? Denmark and the Effects of European Law, 1973–1993* (Ph.D. thesis, University of Aarhus, 2016); M. Rasmussen, 'At the Vanguard? Belgium and European Law 1950 to 1993', in Rasmussen and Davies (eds.), *The History of European Law 1950 to 1993: The Battles over the Constitutional Practice* (publisher not yet known for certain, 2024); Bernier, *La France et le droit communautaire*, pp. 222–4; Rasmussen, 'How to Enforce European law', 304–5; Sindbjerg Martinsen and Rasmussen, 'EU Constitutionalisation Revisited'.

However, the SEA became a real 'game changer' with regard to the European legal order developed by the ECJ. Before the Act, the Common Market was anything but unitary because of national protectionism in the form of different standards, taxation schemes, hidden state aid and so on. The quite advanced case law on the four freedoms, which the ECJ developed from the 1970s onwards, had only limited impact since national administrations and courts could simply ignore the ECJ rulings. However, when the Single Market acquired more importance in the second half of the 1980s, member state governments were under increasing pressure to accept the constitutional legal order built by the ECJ. The SEA legislative programme provoked a rise in litigation and confronted national administrations and courts with the wider scope and consequences of European law. Furthermore, the broad political support for the Act and for the project of the Single Market made it more difficult for member states to oppose the Act and the European legal order in the way they had done during the period before 1984.[50]

The Commission under Jacques Delors' presidency took advantage of the new political dynamic of the mid 1980s. His Commission distinguished itself with its activism in various policy fields such as the budget, monetary union, competition and the environment, as well as regional and social policy, and it gained international profile by successfully dealing with German reunification and acquiring a leadership role in the Group of Seven. The dynamic and performance demonstrated by the Delors Commission created hopes for a move towards a federalised Europe through a reform that would also finally codify the ECJ's doctrinal advances and the proto-federal legal order which had come into being by the end of the 1980s. The committee of the twelve independent central bank presidents under Delors' chairmanship delivered a report on monetary union in April 1989, in which it clearly suggested that national sovereignty be transferred to a federal monetary institute as a step towards a single currency. With German reunification lying ahead in 1989–90, Delors continued to publicly demand a significant transfer of executive authority to the Commission. His proposals to the IGC of February 1991 suggested not only a substantial strengthening of the Commission, but also the codification of ECJ case law and an overall increase of supranationality in the new European Union that was based on a single treaty. This package was rejected by the member states' governments.

---

50 Sindbjerg Martinsen and Rasmussen, 'EU constitutionalisation revisited', 15–16; Langeland Pedersen, *Constructive Defiance?*, pp. 137–230.

To further counteract Delors' claim for more Commission power, the French government introduced the idea of intergovernmental treaty pillars. This idea was picked up in a treaty draft by the Luxembourg Council presidency in April 1991. However, the pillar design was criticised by the Netherlands, Belgium, Italy and Germany. In September 1991, the Dutch Council presidency tabled its own, more federalist-styled draft treaty, which proposed to bring the pillars under Community law as well as to strengthen the EP.[51] The Dutch draft was supported only by Delors and the Belgian government, because it downplayed the role of the common foreign and defence policy, something which was not appreciated by the advocates of institutional strengthening. Despite those controversies over the pillar design, the negotiations that ultimately led to the Treaty of Maastricht placed the important policy fields of Justice and Home Affairs as well as the Common Foreign and Security Policy in the intergovernmental second and third pillars. Delors managed to avert the downgrading of the Commission, but the member states clearly rejected the federalist treaty design he advocated.[52] In the context of the Treaty of Maastricht, the member states also seriously challenged the ECJ. In the so-called Barber Protocol (which referred to the ECJ's Barber ruling of 17 May 1990 on UK private pension schemes, and which was added to the Treaty of Maastricht), the governments interpreted an EEC treaty article before the ECJ was able to clarify a detail of its ruling.[53] The way the member states overturned the Court raised the question of whether the 'Masters of the Treaty' had 'hijacked the Acquis Communautaire'.[54]

By the time of the Maastricht treaty, the EU had acquired a hybrid character. On the one hand, the SEA had locked in a proto-federal European legal order, which the member states de facto accepted as a necessary foundation for the Singe Market. On the other hand, the

---

51 Dutch proposal for a draft treaty, 23 September 1991, in *Agence Europe*, Documents, Nr. 1733/1734, 3 October 1991. For a closely related text, see 'Draft Treaty towards European Union by the Dutch Presidency (Maastricht, 24 September 1991)', www.cvce.eu/en/obj/draft_treaty_towards_european_union_by_the_dutch_presidency_maastricht_24_september_1991-en-d39ea094-caef-4bab-a345-f8ba104bb740.html.

52 Ludlow, 'European Integration in the 1980s'; W. Loth, 'Negotiating the Maastricht Treaty', *Journal of European Integration History* 37 (2013): 67–85; Ludlow, 'Jacques Delors'; C. J. Bickerton, D. Hodson and U. Puetter (eds.), *The New Intergovernmentalism: States and Supranational Actors in the Post-Maastricht Era* (Oxford, Oxford University Press, 2015).

53 D. Curtin, 'The Constitutional Structure of the Union. A Europe of Bits and Pieces', *Common Market Law Review* 30 (1993): 17–69; B. Fitzpatrick, 'Community Social Law after Maastricht', *Industrial Law Journal* 21 (1992): 199–213.

54 Curtin, 'The Constitutional Structure of the Union', 44–61.

member states dominated the EU politically and rejected or limited the ECJ's constitutional claim. The ambiguities of the member states' attitudes were reflected by judgments of the supreme courts of three major EEC member states between 1989 and 1993 – the Corte Costituzionale (in 1989), the Conseil d'État (in 1989) and the Bundesverfassungsgericht (in 1993).[55] Although the supreme courts accepted the operation of the European legal order, they dismissed the ECJ's claim for constitutional autonomy and argued that the competences of the EU were delegated by the member states, on the basis of their respective national constitutions.

Concluding Remarks

This chapter has demonstrated that, despite the strong presence of federalist ideas and rhetoric in the supranational institutions and in national parliaments, the member states' governments gradually reinforced their political control over the process of European integration and rejected or limited the ECJ's constitutional case law. The openness of the founding treaties with regard to either a federal or an intergovernmental outcome allowed the member states' governments to strengthen the intergovernmental Council pillar. Historically, the institutional and legal culture of the EEC reflected the rise of intergovernmentalism in various ways. In response to the broad nature and complexity of integration in the EEC, member states opted for a consensual approach to Community business, and it led to the emergence of various committee structures, most notably COREPER, which had not originally been foreseen in the treaty. Around 1963–6, the Gaullist challenge to EEC-Europe triggered a massive political battle, which locked in the consensus trend and further consolidated the drift towards intergovernmentalism. From the mid 1970s, the EC developed into the leading agenda-setter of the EEC, illustrating the centrality of the member states in a period of perceived institutional inefficiency, the so-called 'Eurosclerosis'. Even during the *relance européenne* (European revival) of the 1980s, core member states maintained their long-term scepticism towards gradual federalisation, which deeply affected the design of the

---

55 Corte Costituzionale, decision No. 232 of 21 April 1989, *S.p.a. Fragd v. Amministrazione delle Finanze*; Conseil d'État, 20 October 1989, Nicolo, Dalloz, 136; Bundesverfassungsgericht Urteil vom 12. Oktober 1993, Az. 2 BvR 2134, 2159/92. See also B. de Witte, 'Sovereignty and European Integration: The Weight of Legal Tradition' in A.-M. Slaughter, A. Stone Sweet and J. H. H. Weiler (eds.), *The European Court and National Courts – Doctrine and Jurisprudence: Legal Change in Its Social Context* (Oxford, Hart, 1998), pp. 277–304.

Treaty of Maastricht. With the pillar structure of the Treaty of Maastricht, member states clearly rejected the Delors Commission's federalist vision and its proposal for a substantial transfer of member state sovereignty to supranational institutions.

In the period under scrutiny, a proto-federal European legal order slowly emerged over time. However, member states rejected or limited the constitutional case law of the ECJ and the Court's attempt to push the boundaries of European law. At the same time, the Council members remained divided over how to deal with the ECJ's constitutional claim and practice. They neither systematically challenged the Court and tried to revise the status quo of European law, nor did they codify the ECJ's constitutional advances (e.g., in the Treaty of Maastricht).

While historians have frequently pointed to the rising importance of intergovernmentalism throughout the history of European integration, scholars of the history and evolution of European law have mostly focused on the expanding role of the supranational institutions and how the federalist assumptions of their members shaped the emergence of a constitutional European legal order. In contrast, this chapter has illustrated that the most remarkable development in the legal history of the Communities between the Treaties of Rome and the Treaty of Maastricht was probably the rise of the member states' collective government in the Council and more generally the cementation of state power in the intergovernmental pillar of the Communities.

The reinforcement of intergovernmentalism in the post-SEA period, culminating in the member states' rejection of the federalist project around 1990, was to a certain extent motivated by member states' concerns about the introduction of majority voting in the Single Market, as suggested by Joseph Weiler.[56] However, the above analysis of the institutional and legal culture of integration since the 1950s suggests that member states were primarily driven by long-term trends of resistance against the ECJ's constitutional claim. Added to this was the profound scepticism, if not aversion, of most of the member states towards the vision of a gradual federalisation of the Communities through supranational institutions.[57]

---

56 J. H. H. Weiler, 'The Transformation of Europe', The Yale Law Journal 100 (1991): 2403–83; J. H. H. Weiler, 'A Quiet Revolution: The European Court of Justice and Its Interlocutors', Comparative Political Studies 26 (1994): 510–34.

57 Sindbjerg Martinsen and Rasmussen, 'EU Constitutionalisation Revisited', 15–17, 22.

Recommended Reading

Bajon, P. *Europapolitik 'am Abgrund': Die Krise des 'leeren Stuhls' 1965–66* (Stuttgart, Franz Steiner, 2012).

Loth, W. *Building Europe: A History of European Unification* (Berlin, De Gruyter, 2015).

Ludlow, N. P. *The European Community and the Crises of the 1960s: Negotiating the Gaullist Challenge* (London, Routledge, 2006).

Patel, K. K. *Project Europe: A History* (Cambridge, Cambridge University Press, 2020).

Rasmussen, M. and B. Davies, *The History of European Law 1950 to 1993: The Battles over the Constitutional Practise* (publisher not yet known for certain, 2024).

Weiler, J. H. H. 'The Transformation of Europe', *The Yale Law Journal* 100 (1991): 2403–83.

13

The Formation of the Migration Regime of the EU

EMMANUEL COMTE

Introduction

International migration regimes refer to the way states interact when there are flows or pressures for flows of people with the prospect of lasting settlement across their borders. States generally enforce border checks, recognise only a limited right of residence, reduce social security rights outside the country of employment and deny civic rights for migrants. In Europe in the late 1940s, states routinely responded to migration flows with such cumbersome and arbitrary administrative practices. Today, in contrast, the regime of migration between the member states of the European Union (EU) displays openness. Migrants' social security rights are exportable, and they benefit from civic rights. Deep closure towards low-skilled migration from outside Europe also characterises this regime, however. During the post-war decades, change has defied continuity, and today's liberal migration regime has achieved depth, width and longevity, making it without equivalent in modern history. The emergence of this unique free migration space within Europe has been neither a generic nor a linear process, and deepening has been the enemy of widening. The crucial turning point occurred in 1955 in the preparation of the Treaty of Rome. In 1992, the Treaty of Maastricht completed the second period of intense change. No determinism produced this outcome. Several actors favoured alternative scenarios. The United Kingdom (UK), in particular, recently decided to exit this liberal regime and the Union altogether.

Literature Review

The political scientist Kenneth A. Dahlberg published the first significant study on the formation of this regime in 1968. According to him, 'the particular constellation of the labour market of the Six [member states of the European Community (EC)] in 1958' partly explained their project of liberalising the movement of labour. Italy was suffering from unemployment and West Germany from a lack of workforce.[1] Regarding the actors of this change, he concluded that while, 'with a strong treaty text, the Commission can make the most of its bureaucratic strengths and achieve a great deal within a limited sphere [. . .] it is the member states which control the degree of spillover which they will allow'.[2] Dahlberg could not explain the contours of this 'limited sphere', defined by the member states, although its definition constituted the primary political choice.

A breakthrough occurred with the work of the political scientist Ronald Stanley Klein in 1981.[3] He sought to understand the politics between governments, the outcome of which would constitute this 'limited sphere' within which non-intergovernmental international institutions would operate. He considered European integration as a set of regional arrangements aiming to solve problems between governments, issue area by issue area. He used the concept of an *international legal regime* to refer to the outcome of negotiations between governments. Klein drew on the records of the meetings of the EC Council of Ministers: 'The approach to study [. . .] the Council-level [. . .] isolates the battle over issues at the highest political level [. . .], a battle which may lead to multinational regulation for some issues and national reaction [. . .] for others.'[4] Klein, therefore, introduced an intergovernmental approach, using the minutes of the meetings of the Council in the first instance.

The historian Federico Romero continued this approach. He was interested in international interdependence. Post-war economic growth required migration flows, creating interdependence between European labour markets. Romero recognised 1947 as a turning point because the onset of the Cold War led European states to favour flows within each bloc.[5] West European governments needed to organise this interdependence. Romero was interested in the 'forms of organisation of interdependence'.[6] He explained these

1 K. A. Dahlberg, 'The EEC Commission and the Politics of the Free Movement of Labour', *Journal of Common Market Studies* 6, no. 4 (1968): 310–33, 310.
2 Dahlberg, 'The EEC Commission', 333.
3 R. S. Klein, 'The Free Movement of Workers: A Study of Transnational Politics and Policy-Making in the European Community' (Ph.D. thesis, George Washington University, 1981).
4 Klein, 'The Free Movement of Workers', 96.
5 F. Romero, 'Migration as an Issue in European Interdependence and Integration: The Case of Italy', in A. S. Milward, F. M. B. Lynch, R. Ranieri, F. Romero and V. Sørensen, *The Frontier of National Sovereignty: History and Theory 1945–1992* (London, Routledge, 1993), pp. 33–58, 35–6.
6 F. Romero, *Emigrazione e integrazione europea, 1945–1973* (Rome, Edizioni Lavoro, 1991), p. 83.

forms as the result of negotiations between governments seeking to maximise economic prosperity. He deeply investigated Italian positions. The Italian government wanted a new organisation of European interdependence: 'Italy [...] had a fundamental interest in opening up the European labour market for its own unemployed. From the end of the Second World War, Italy's apparent overpopulation and scarcity of capital generated a widespread political consensus on the urgency of a vast emigration.'[7] However, to understand the outcome of the negotiations, it was necessary, as the historian Simone Alberdina Wilhelmina Goedings proposed, to consider also the strategies of Italy's partners and their confrontation.[8]

The reciprocal openness to migration within the EU is exceptional in the international governance of migration, whereas the presence of an emigration state favouring such openness is common. The position of the Italian government finds equivalents in other regions where migration closure has prevailed. Within the North American Free Trade Agreement, Mexico failed to achieve freedom of movement for workers, despite the intense capacity of the US labour market to absorb immigrant workers. The relationship of Turkey with the EU is another example. Also, despite German needs for workers from the mid 1950s, some authors have emphasised that the German–Italian recruitment agreement signed on 20 December 1955 strictly followed the prevailing administered migration regime.[9] In that regime, destination states created selective and temporary openings, which allowed them to reconcile the contradictory domestic pressures of employers and unions. West Germany was not interested in setting up the free movement of workers in a bilateral framework. However, it was interested in establishing a multilateral framework. As reported by the historian Roberto Sala, during the June 1955 Messina Conference initiating the negotiations for the Treaty of Rome, 'the German government proposed the formula that established the institution of freedom of movement among the objectives of the Community'.[10] The specificity of the German strategy explains the singularity of today's EU regime. Until recently, this specificity remained little known.

Similarly, until recently there was little archive-based knowledge on migration negotiations after the early 1970s – in particular, the negotiations

7 Romero, 'Migration as an Issue', p. 36.
8 S. A. W. Goedings, *Labor Migration in an Integrating Europe: National Migration Policies and the Free Movement of Workers, 1950–1968* (The Hague, Sdu Uitgevers, 2005), p. 16.
9 Romero, *Emigrazione e integrazione europea*, pp. 49–50; R. Sala, 'Il controllo statale sull'immigrazione di manodopera italiana nella Germania federale', *Annali dell'Istituto Storico Italo-Germanico in Trento* 30 (2004): 119–52, 125–8.
10 Sala, 'Il controllo statale', 138.

of the 1985 and 1990 Schengen agreements. The latest works of the historian Simone Paoli have contributed to filling this gap.[11] Until recently, we possessed little archive-based knowledge on the negotiations concerning the social security of migrant workers, the right of establishment in independent professions (including agriculture), migration from third countries and relevant debates in frameworks other than the EC or the Organization for European Economic Co-operation (OEEC).

Research

Today, we have a better and more complete picture of the formation of the migration regime of the EU, from the late 1940s onwards.

Blockages and Tensions

In the late 1940s, the migration regime in western Europe involved cumbersome bureaucratic procedures, and destination states could select and restrict immigration according to their evolving needs and preferences. They generally required visas, including for short-term stays, from the nationals of lower-income countries in western Europe – Turkey, Greece and Portugal – but also for Germans and Austrians, as a result of the Second World War. Germans and Austrians needed visas to enter all other west European countries. In Germany, the consulates of France, Belgium and Sweden – three significant destinations of German emigration – could not deliver entry visas to Germans without the prior consent of their central administration, whereas the consulates of these countries elsewhere could deliver entry visas directly.[12] The persisting fear of German subversion in Alsace and Moselle meant the French Ministry of the Interior forbade new settlements of German nationals in those parts of French territory in principle.[13] Germans were not welcome in French border regions even as frontier workers: whereas there were 53,000 Belgian frontier workers in France in 1950, there were only 700 German workers.[14]

This situation did not satisfy all parts of the French government. The Planning Commission and the Labour Ministry demanded more foreign

---

11 S. Paoli, *Frontiera Sud: L'Italia e la nascita dell'Europa di Schengen* (Florence, Le Monnier, 2018).
12 Archives of the OECD, Paris (henceforth AOECD), film 49, C(50)060, 6 March 1950, annex.
13 *Journal officiel de la République française* (henceforth *JORF*), 19 March 1946, p. 2264.
14 Archives historiques de l'Union européenne, Florence (henceforth AHUE), MAEI, PS20, France.

workers. The Ministry of Foreign Affairs was receptive to US calls to foster cooperation in western Europe. In the negotiations to allocate Marshall Plan aid and create the OEEC, in 1947, the French declared a need for 300,000 foreign workers for the following years. However, no other countries declared significant labour needs – in a framework that included all west European countries. The UK, in particular, declared a need for only 24,500 foreign workers for the following years.[15] Soon afterwards, British unemployment rose and British workers, in particular in coal mines, became more hostile to foreign workers.[16] Facing the protest of the British National Union of Mineworkers, the British government suspended an agreement for recruitment of miners that it had signed with the Italian government.[17] Within the OEEC, the British stressed the risk of 'the failure of any immigration plan' without 'more effective demand for foreign labour'.[18] Unions would prevent immigrants from taking jobs, they argued.

France would not commit itself to more liberal migration arrangements in the long term in a setting where it would be the only country of immigration. As French Foreign Minister Georges Bidault summarised the siuation as early as 1947: 'If the union is limited to France and Italy, we will lose.'[19] As the British withdrew, the French tried to secure the support of the Benelux states, in particular Belgium – a country of significant immigration then. By the end of 1948, however, Belgium experienced high unemployment and suspended immigration.[20] By the beginning of 1950, the negotiations to liberalise migration were breaking down within the OEEC. The delegates of the few countries of immigration were pointing out that a 'policy of total freedom would mean public opinion and the trade unions contesting the hiring of foreign workers much more forcefully than at present'.[21]

The deadlock came against the rising need for emigration in West Germany – the strategic fulcrum of the Cold War. At the end of the Second World War, 9.4 million German expellees had immigrated to West Germany, increasing the population by 20 per cent.[22] Immigration from East

---

15 AOECD, film 124, MO(49)14, 8 February 1949, annex.   16 AOECD, film 125, MO(54)49.
17 Romero, 'Migration as an Issue', pp. 41, 45.
18 AOECD, film 124, MO(53)25, 26 June 1953.
19 V. Auriol and P. Nora, *Journal du septennat, 1947–1954*, vol. 1: *1947* (Paris, Armand Colin, 1970), p. 391.
20 A. Martens, *Les immigrés: Flux et reflux d'une main-d'œuvre d'appoint: La politique belge de l'immigration de 1945 à 1970* (Leuven, Presses universitaires de Louvain, 1976), pp. 74–6, 78.
21 AOECD, film 124, MO(50)4, 1 February 1950.
22 Auswärtiges Amt, Politisches Archiv, Berlin (henceforth AAPA), B10, 412-00, 2365, January 1950, p. 59.

Germany continued. The 1948 monetary reform in West Germany, aiming at tackling inflation, made real wages stickier and was immediately responsible for increasing unemployment in a context of rising labour supply. By March 1950, 1.85 million were unemployed.[23] German policy-makers had to accept emigration, but they favoured destinations in Europe rather than overseas. They considered the division of Germany temporary and predicted that there would later be a need for German farmers to repopulate the eastern territories which were becoming emptied of Germans. Emigration to nearby countries would more certainly allow Germans to return once the division had been ended.[24] In July 1950, German diplomats called for European solidarity to accommodate the emigration of 450,000 German workers.[25] The German calls remained unanswered, however. The United States then promoted broader cooperation at the western level to deal with European emigration by sending migrants overseas.[26] Even though this emigration contributed to easing tensions in Europe, the United States – which enforced restrictive immigration policies – did not have the capacity to transform the migration regime in Europe.

German Strategy

The Federal Republic of Germany (FRG) was committed to promoting the principle of the free movement of persons within the frameworks of western cooperation – including those not of immediate relevance to German emigration. In 1950, France, West Germany, the Benelux states and Italy started negotiations in Paris for a European Coal and Steel Community (ECSC). Vast resources in coal and steel gave the Germans bargaining power. In September, the German Labour Ministry official Julius Scheuble pushed successfully to arrange the free movement of skilled coal miners and steel-workers within this Community.[27] Even though there was a shortage of such workers in West Germany, the goal was to create a precedent likely to foster free movement – and German emigration – in other sectors.

On 1 July 1953, the West German government unilaterally abolished all visa requirements for stays of less than 3 months for the nationals of member states of the OEEC or the Council of Europe.[28] This decision was intended to

---

23 AAPA, B10, 412-00, 2365, January 1950.
24 AAPA, B10, 412-00, 1877, 'Grundsätzliche Fragen einer Auswanderung'.
25 AAPA, B10, 412-00, 1877, 28 July 1950.
26 E. Comte, 'Waging the Cold War: The Origins and Launch of Western Cooperation to Absorb Migrants from Eastern Europe, 1948–57', *Cold War History* 20, no. 4 (2020): 461–81.
27 AAPA, B15, 120 (4), 19 September 1950 meeting, p. 2.
28 Archives centrales du Conseil de l'Union européenne, Bruxelles (henceforth ACCUE), CM1 1953 61, Suppression des visas à compter du 1er juillet 1953.

obtain reciprocity and facilitate German movements in Europe. Other governments granted reciprocity in 1954. In the OEEC Council in October 1953, German Minister of Economic Affairs Ludwig Erhard declared himself in favour of 'the total liberalisation of labour movements in Europe'.[29] German Minister of Labour Anton Storch repeatedly affirmed in 1954 that the principle of the free movement of labour was 'profoundly just'.[30] European agreements including this principle should apply to all German nationals under the German Basic Law – therefore, also to East German immigrants, whose swift integration in densely populated West Germany remained a challenge.[31]

Despite success in the ECSC and for short-stay visas, German actions could not overhaul the migration regime in western Europe until 1954. From 1955, however, West Germany drove a gradual transformation of the European migration regime. The rise in labour demand in West Germany strengthened West Germany's capacity to convince other states to relax migration rules. The unemployment rate in West Germany fell to 5 per cent in 1955 – it was as low as 2.2 per cent in Baden-Württemberg and 2.9 per cent in North-Rhine Westphalia.[32] The national unemployment rate for men was as low as 1.8 per cent, creating a shortage of male workers. As migrants were predominantly men, West Germany was about to become the leading country of immigration in Europe. Why, then, did German policy-makers maintain their support for the free movement of people?

The chief concern of German diplomats was the cohesion of western Europe. According to the German Ministry of Foreign Affairs in May 1955, 'Europe cannot be successful in negotiations with the East unless it presents itself as united. The FRG is particularly interested in this, in the prospect of German reunification.'[33] For German Chancellor Konrad Adenauer, 'if integration [of western Europe] is successful, we can throw the weight of a united Europe in the balance [. . .] during the negotiations on [. . .] reunification'.[34] For

---

29 AOECD, film 107, C/M(53)030, 29–30 October 1953 meeting.
30 AHUE, CM1 1954 196, 27 October 1954 meeting; AHUE, CM1 1954 194, 27–28 July 1954 meeting.
31 AAPA, B10, 224-23-00, 871, 12 February 1954.
32 U. Herbert, *Geschichte der Ausländerpolitik in Deutschland: Saisonarbeiter, Zwangsarbeiter, Gastarbeiter, Flüchtlinge* (Munich, C. H. Beck, 2001), p. 202.
33 AAPA, B10 225-10-01, 900, p. 1, note for the session of the Bundestag Foreign Affairs Committee of 3 May 1955.
34 'Anweisung von Konrad Adenauer an die Bundesminister (19. Januar 1956)', www .cvce.eu/en/obj/directive_issued_by_chancellor_konrad_adenauer_to_member s_of_the_german_government_19_january_1956-en-b763087b-2c4c-407e-99d9-9baf7 de1f904.html.

Adenauer, 'a great impetus to the Communist Parties in France and Italy' would strike a blow to west European integration.[35] In Italy, the Communist Party benefited electorally from unemployment. A permanently open migration regime in western Europe would send Italian workers a signal regarding opportunities in non-communist Europe, which could reduce their support for communism. Also, West German leaders still considered that a liberal migration regime in western Europe could help them absorb more swiftly a sudden inflow of German immigrants in the case of a political crisis in eastern Europe.

The Secretary of State in the German Ministry of Foreign Affairs, Walter Hallstein, favoured the limited framework of the ECSC to develop 'close ties and solid forms of organisation'.[36] In June 1955, the Messina Conference aimed to deepen cooperation between the six member states. The German Memorandum proposed a 'gradual introduction of the free movement of labour'.[37] Given the new German influence over migration, the final resolution of the Conference considered, in the same terms, 'the gradual introduction of the free movement of labour'.[38]

After Messina, officials from the German Ministry of Economic Affairs then took over German representation in the detailed negotiations of the Treaty of Rome. They got a working group set up to 'define the particular problems of the free movement of physical persons whose occupational activity [was] not a salaried job'. They obtained an agreement that the new liberal regime would 'take into consideration all the people [. . .] who [wished] to exercise an independent profit-making activity'.[39] This definition could include independent workers, such as farmers or independent professionals, but also firms. The principle of free movement could thus also favour the expansion of German firms, by removing obstacles to their right of establishment and fostering the mobility of auxiliary professionals, such as lawyers, doctors or architects.

The Contours of an Opening

On 25 March 1957, the Six signed the Treaty of Rome, which provided for the free movement of persons by 1970. Articles 48 and 49 dealt with workers, while other articles dealt with the right of establishment for the

---

35 K. Adenauer, *Memoirs, 1945–1953*, trans. B. Ruhm von Oppen (London, Weidenfeld & Nicolson, 1966), p. 387.
36 ACCUE, CM3 NEGO 6, 1–3 June 1955 meeting.
37 R. Ducci and B. Olivi, *L'Europa incompiuta* (Padua, Cedam, 1970), pp. 276–9.
38 ACCUE, CM3 NEGO 6, Messina resolution.
39 ACCUE, CM3 NEGO1 45, MAE/CIG Doc. no. 193, 1 September 1955.

self-employed. One of the first points of discussion concerned the actual beneficiaries and geographical limits. Member states diverged over the overseas possessions of France, Belgium and the Netherlands – vast territories with dozens of millions of inhabitants in Africa, south-east Asia and the Caribbean. Their inclusion could cement their ties with their metropoles. However, such a prospect did not match German goals, which focused on the cohesion of western Europe and potential outlets for Germans in Europe. The poverty and potential number of emigrants from overseas threatened to transform the entire project. Even before the Messina Conference, in May 1955, the German Labour Ministry had called on the Ministry of Foreign Affairs to make sure that 'extra-European possessions of member states remain outside the planned [. . .] freedom of movement'.[40] Eventually, German support for development programmes overseas led the French to back down. The member states did not include the inhabitants of their overseas possessions among the beneficiaries of free movement, although some territories intimately associated with France – the French overseas *départements* – were accorded the prospect of inclusion at a later stage.

In exchange for German financial participation in development programmes, German negotiators wished nevertheless to liberalise movements from Europe to overseas. They aimed at facilitating the access of their companies' staff and independent workers to the overseas resources. For instance, in April 1959, the German winegrower Richard Matuschka-Greiffenclau – the president of the Deutscher Weinbauverband (German Viticulture Association) – defended in the EC's Economic and Social Committee the interests of the 'young forestry workers [from the member states] keen to help develop African forests'.[41] It was not clear whether he was referring only to forestry or to deforestation in order to promote viticulture. In November 1959, the EC Council adopted a directive granting firms and independent professionals of the member states the right of establishment in the overseas territories.[42] A declaration of the Council also lifted visa requirements in those territories for the nationals of the member states.[43] The regime of free movement would thus be limited to Europe, but the Germans could extract migration and economic opportunities from their development programmes overseas.

40 AAPA, B10 225-10-01, 900, 27 May 1955.
41 ACCUE, CM2 1959 857, CES 38 f/59, 8 April 1959.
42 *Official Journal of the European Communities* (henceforth *OJEC*), 147/60, 10 February 1960.
43 ACCUE, CM2 1959 858, Council meeting, 23–24 November 1959.

In Europe, the Germans wished to extend the freedom of movement beyond the Six, to all of western Europe. Free movement among the Six could reduce emigration opportunities in other strategic countries, such as Greece and Turkey. The United States – albeit not prepared to absorb migrants itself – shared similar concerns. In December 1956, the US government submitted a plan to the OEEC for the extension of free movement of labour to all of western Europe. Once again, the OEEC failed to be an operative framework due to British opposition. The British delegate, Edward Redston Warner, declared that his government would 'by no means agree that it [might be] possible to [...] put [US proposals] into practice'.[44] The transformation of the migration regime in western Europe would take place not through a transatlantic framework, but through German actions. Reaching a west European dimension would need a gradual extension of the scheme among the Six.

This process started soon after the Six signed the Treaty of Rome. In Athens on 9 July 1961 and Ankara on 12 September 1963, the Community signed two association agreements, with Greece and Turkey, respectively. The Community and Greece would implement the free movement of workers 'as per [...] the Treaty establishing the Community' and the right of establishment of the treaty.[45] The Community and Turkey only 'agreed to be inspired by [...] the Treaty establishing the European Economic Community to realise the free movement of workers among them gradually'.[46] In 1970, an additional protocol completed the association agreement with Turkey. Article 36 specified more clearly that 'The member states of the Community and Turkey will realise the free movement of workers between them' by 1986.[47]

Despite those commitments, the Community achieved little in the short run. Greece and Turkey did benefit from more migration opportunities, but only through traditional bilateral agreements with Germany. Greek emigration grew from around 20,000 people a year in the 1950s to 100,000 in 1963. In 1964, 70 per cent of Greek emigrants headed for West Germany.[48] Similarly, Turkish emigration grew steadily, and there were 450,000 Turkish workers in the Community in 1971 – most of them in West Germany.[49]

---

44 AOECD, film 177, C/M(56)43.   45 AHUE, CM2 1967 1112, 20/03/1967, I/III/2914/67.
46 ACCUE, CM2 1966 1044, 29 October 1965, S/802/65 (NT 18), annex.
47 Archives historiques de la Commission européenne, Bruxelles (henceforth AHCE), BAC 15 1993 34 1976, 26 October 1976.
48 AHUE, CM2 1967 1113, V/2997/66 rév.
49 ACCUE, CM7 ASS1 260, Rec. 2/71, 15–18 March 1971.

French Reluctance

Inside the Community, the implementation of the freedom of movement succeeded, despite French reluctance, thanks to German support and the intense labour demand in West Germany. The number of jobs offered by employers for each outstanding request by workers went from 1.1 in October 1959 to 2.2 a year later. In Baden-Württemberg, it even reached 83 in 1960.[50] As German employers were starting to hire workers from outside the Community – in particular from Greece and Turkey – the French supported the Italian demand for priority hiring of workers from within the Community. This would ensure that German employers would hire Italian workers as a priority, so that the latter would not turn to France. In February 1961, French delegates in the Council wanted to avoid member states 'slowing down the commitments they [had] made with [. . .] Articles 48 and 49' of the treaty by recruiting workers in third countries.[51] Despite the delays for German employers that a Community priority procedure could entail, the Germans backed down after the intervention of the president of the Commission, Walter Hallstein – the former Secretary of State in the German Ministry of Foreign Affairs. In August 1961, the member states agreed to 'try hard [. . .] to fill available jobs in priority [. . .] with workers from the member states [. . .] before resorting to workers from third countries'.[52]

This commitment did not extinguish French fears. In March 1964, the member states implemented the free movement of workers with Regulation 38/64. The French resorted to a provision in the regulation to impose a 2-week period after a company had advertised a job before Community nationals could take it.[53] This period served to give priority to French workers. France applied this restriction to all vacancies for unskilled office and retail employees across the country.

Meanwhile, West Germany was absorbing the bulk of Italian migrants in the Community. In October 1968, the French accepted, with Regulation 1612/68, the abolition of any priority for French workers. French unions remained concerned. In May 1969, the secretary-general of the Confédération générale du travail (the largest French confederation of trade unions, at that time close to the Communist Party) pointed out to the president of the EC Council that the member states and the Community 'should never consider

50 ACCUE, CM2 1961 375, COM(61)100 final, 12 July 1961.
51 AHUE, CM2 1961 379, GSQ meetings, 2–3 February 1961, annex 1.
52 OJEC, 26 August 1961, pp. 1073–84.
53 AHCE, BAC 144 1992 250 (1964–1965), SEC (65) 2483, 30 July 1965.

the free movement of labour as a way to resolve existing unemployment in some regions of the Community'.[54] The free movement of workers nevertheless drastically changed the migration pattern of Italians. Whereas, until the 1950s, Italian emigrants had divided equally between European and overseas destinations, in the 1960s over 80 per cent of Italian emigrants remained in Europe – the majority heading for West Germany.[55]

French reluctance did not concern just immigrants' access to jobs. Regarding social security transfers too, Germany drove a new regime of exportable social security rights in the Community by transferring the bulk of social security benefits for migrants and their families. In 1961, Germany paid allowances to 47,925 such families; France to eight times fewer. In 1964, healthcare benefits paid in Italy to families of migrant workers amounted to 394.2 billion Belgian francs on behalf of Germany and 89.5 billion Belgian francs on behalf of France.[56] The reason for this discrepancy was that France had achieved temporary derogations. In 1969, West German social security institutions paid 88 per cent of benefits for the families in Italy of Italian migrant workers in the Community.[57]

French reticence impaired the opening for independent workers and the professions. Even though France possessed the largest surface of cultivable land and the lowest population density in the Community, the immigration of new farmers created alarm. In 1963, the French made sure the first measures for the right of establishment in agriculture would apply only to land that had been abandoned or had remained unfarmed for more than 2 years and to persons who had worked as farm employees in the destination country for 2 years without interruption.[58] German support for the Common Agricultural Policy – which benefited France enormously – meant that the opening proceeded. French rural circles nevertheless expressed concern regarding the access of farmers from other countries to their local mutual funds.[59] They also wished that the government could suspend the right of establishment in times of economic difficulty. The vice-president of the

---

54 AHUE, CM2 1968 1018, 19 May 1969.
55 E. Recchi, *Mobile Europe: The Theory and Practice of Free Movement in the EU* (London, Palgrave Macmillan, 2015), p. 50.
56 Commission administrative pour la sécurité sociale des travailleurs migrants, *Rapports sur la mise en œuvre des règlements concernant la sécurité sociale des travailleurs migrants* (Luxembourg, Office des publications officielles des Communautés européennes, 1961–5).
57 AHUE, CM2 1971 1264, 1072/69 (SOC 98), GSQ meeting, 1 July 1969.
58 *OJEC*, 20 April 1963, 1323/63–1328/63.
59 AHUE, CM2 1968 875, 179/68 (ES 7), COREPER meetings of 12–13 July and 13–15 December 1967.

Centre National des Jeunes Agriculteurs (National Centre for Young Farmers), Hilaire Flandre, warned the Economic and Social Committee that it was worth 'planning an appropriate Community procedure rather than risking that at some point, a member state [would] not respect the directive'.[60] French farmers, therefore, suggested that they would not respect in practice the right of establishment.

Member states still did not recognise their respective qualifications and diplomas and – as a result – the right of establishment in the professions. In some cases, governments created new certifications to prevent workers from other states in the Community from taking jobs. In France, the government decided to require a qualification from all sailors. In December 1972, Transport Minister Robert Galley tried to reassure workers in maritime navigation about the freedom of movement by emphasising that 'The French government does not recognise, and does not intend to recognise, the equivalence of foreign qualifications.' As a result, he stressed, such freedom would not 'have big consequences in practice'.[61] In 1974, the European Court of Justice recalled that the right of establishment had been directly applicable since the end of the transition period in 1969.[62] Nevertheless, in the absence of recognition of qualifications and diplomas, member states could still deny the right of establishment to the holders of foreign degrees.

Closure and Appeal after 1973

The downturn starting in 1973 affected the movement towards a more liberal migration regime in western Europe. In September 1973, the German authorities increased the tax employers paid to hire foreign workers from outside the Community. In November, they completely halted immigration from outside the Community.[63] By December 1981, the number of foreign workers in West Germany had fallen from 2.6 million to 1.8 million.[64] The UK, which joined the Community in 1973, and France adopted similar measures. With the 1971 Immigration Act, the British government had stopped issuing work

---

60 AHUE, CM2 1970 1023, CES 591/69, ESC meeting, 29 October 1969.
61 *JORF*, 1972-3, no. 113; E. Comte, 'Xénophobie en mer: Marins français contre étrangers dans la Communauté européenne, 1971–1975', *Le Mouvement Social* 264, no. 3 (2018): 41–59.
62 Case 2-74, 21 June 1974, *European Court Reports*, 1974, 631.
63 H. Werner, 'Migration and Free Movement of Workers in Western Europe', in P. J. Bernard (ed.), *Les travailleurs étrangers en Europe occidentale* (Paris, Mouton, 1976), pp. 65–85, 68.
64 ACCUE, Liste Rouge 31316, SEC (77) 3954.

permits to unskilled or low-skilled workers from outside the Community.[65] In July 1974, the French government suspended the immigration of workers and put a cap on family immigration from outside the Community.[66]

In the following years, the member states deepened their cooperation to stem immigration from Africa and the Middle East. Within the United Nations (UN), lower-income countries of emigration – which constituted a majority in the UN General Assembly – started the negotiation of a Convention on migrant workers. EC member states coordinated their positions, and the European Commission stated in March 1981 that 'the new international economic order should mean that labour migration – as experienced in the last twenty-five years [. . .] – should no longer occur'.[67] Against the provisions in the draft convention, EC member states considered that they should 'keep their entire freedom regarding the right to expel migrants illegally present on their territories'.[68] Likewise, the Community prepared a new Convention of Lomé III with the African, Caribbean and Pacific associated countries. EC member states made sure to focus the debate on the return of migrants to their countries of origin – rather than on new opportunities for migration.[69]

These restrictive immigration policies did not affect the liberal regime within the Community. The freedom of movement in the Community shielded Italian migrants to Germany from the restrictive shift in migration policy. These developments, therefore, radically differentiated migrants from inside and outside the Community. The proportion of Italians among immigrants in Germany rose steeply after 1973. Consequently, it became even more urgent for Greece, Portugal, Spain and Turkey to join the Community. Negotiations with the first three were successful. Greece and Portugal each had a small population. All three countries were experiencing sluggish demographic growth. They had reached gross domestic products per capita not that much lower than those in the Community and had developed a small middle class. Accordingly, the likelihood of significant migration flows was low. Nevertheless, given the high unemployment rate in Germany and the rest of the Community, the treaties for the accession of all three countries included a 7-year transition period before the free movement of workers would come into force.[70]

65 Werner, 'Migration and Free Movement', p. 71.
66 G. P. Tapinos, L'immigration étrangère en France: 1946–1973 (Paris, Presses universitaires de France, 1975), p. 119 fn. 3.
67 ACCUE, Liste Rouge 68488, SEC (81) 466.
68 ACCUE, Liste Rouge 68488, 6008/81 SOC 101, GSQ meeting.
69 ACCUE, Liste Rouge 83948, CES 691/82.
70 OJEC, 19 November 1979; OJEC, L 302, 15 November 1985, Accession Treaty, Articles 56, 58, 60, 216, 218, 220.

Turkey started those negotiations in a position as good as Greece and better than Spain and Portugal, given the plans included in the 1963 association agreement and its 1970 additional protocol. Nevertheless, the Europeans found ways to delay the implementation of their commitments to Turkey, pretexts to infringe them and, finally, the resolve to violate them. European policy-makers were wary about the likelihood that the Turkish population would reach 80 million by the end of the century. Turkish living standards were much lower than those in the Community, generating a risk of mass migration.[71] In Ankara in July 1976, Community representatives informed their Turkish counterparts that 'the realisation of the objective pursued [would be] a difficult task'. They put forward 'the [. . .] employment situation' and the 'restrictive immigration policy' that the member states had been 'forced' to adopt.[72] In October 1980, after the army had installed a military government, France and West Germany took advantage of the political instability in Turkey to introduce obligatory visas for Turkish nationals.[73] Article 41 of the additional protocol had, however, committed the contracting parties to 'refrain from introducing [. . .] any new restrictions on the freedom of establishment and the freedom to provide services'.[74] Eventually, on 1 June 1981, German Minister of Foreign Affairs Hans-Dietrich Genscher informed the president of the Commission, Gaston Thorn, that 'as of 1986, we cannot grant Turks a general right to take up employment in the Community'.[75] He put forward unemployment problems, the difficulties of integration and the growth of the Turkish population in Germany. In 1984, the Community informed Turkey that it would not implement freedom of movement.

Change Resuming

The liberal deepening of the internal migration regime resumed in the mid 1980s. After the downturn following the second oil-price shock, German policy-makers aimed to promote exports to accelerate economic recovery. Eliminating internal border controls for persons, they believed, would ease cross-border trade flows. Chambers of Trade and Industry in border regions were other important pressure groups, as eliminating those obstacles could foster their economic development.[76] The president of the Permanent

71 AHCE, BAC 15 1993 34, CEE-TR 6/76, 1–2 March 1976.
72 ACCUE, Liste Rouge 74138, S/1244/76 (NT 17), addendum 2, 13 July 1976.
73 ACCUE, Liste Rouge 74141, 8510/82, ASSRE 218, 8 July 1982.
74 ACCUE, Liste Rouge 74141, 13 October 1980.
75 ACCUE, Liste Rouge 74534, 1 June 1981.
76 ACCUE, Liste Rouge 1842, 15 February 1983.

Conference of Chambers of Commerce and Industry of the Community, Herbert Pattberg, considered that 'the administrative obstacles at borders [meant] a harmful waste of time and money that it [was advisable] to eliminate as soon as possible'.[77] West Germany started negotiating agreements to abolish border controls for persons with all its western neighbours, from Denmark to Austria.

In parallel, as early as November 1981, the Germans called for the completion of the Common Market in a German–Italian proposal – the Genscher–Colombo Plan. After the Fontainebleau Summit in 1984, British Prime Minister Margaret Thatcher also endorsed this project. The French were isolated.[78] Completing the Common Market entailed the recognition of standards, diplomas and certificates. It also entailed the full mobility of capital. After 15 years of depreciation of the French franc relative to the Deutsche Mark, French policy-makers could not accept the full mobility of capital without the development of a European currency. Monetary integration would prevent outflows driven by speculation regarding further depreciation of the franc. Such a project required treaty revisions, which the British refused to countenance, in order to avoid further integration.

French President François Mitterrand's tactic was to get closer to the Germans on the abolition of border controls – which were of little interest to the UK as an island country – in order to isolate the British and obtain treaty revisions.[79] In May 1984, Chancellor Kohl and President Mitterrand agreed on the principle of abolishing formalities at land borders between France and West Germany for Community citizens.[80] On 14 June 1985, 2 weeks before the European Council in Milan, which would discuss treaty revisions, France signed with Germany and the Benelux states the Schengen agreement, on the abolition of all controls of persons at their internal borders.[81] This agreement seemed to create a first step towards the completion of the Common Market without the UK. Accordingly, the British backed down and accepted majority voting at the European Council in Milan, which called for an intergovernmental conference to revise the treaty. In 1986, the Single European Act referred to monetary union and planned 'an area without internal frontiers in which the free movement of goods, persons,

---

77 ACCUE, Liste Rouge 1842, telex no. 074.
78 Archives Nationales, Paris (henceforth AN), 5 AG 4 4767, Archives of Jacques Attali, European Council, Milan, 28–29 June 1985.
79 AN, 5 AG 4 EG 41, dossier 1, déjeuner 12 June 1985.
80 AN, 5 AG 4 CM 41, dossier 4, sous-dossier 2, Conseil des ministres du 20 juin 1984, Communication du ministre des Affaires européennes.
81 ACCUE, Liste Rouge 1842, accord.

services and capital [would be] ensured'.[82] The British interpreted this provision as meaning that the free movement of persons applied only to member state nationals and controls could continue.

Both the Schengen agreement and the Single European Act were declarations of intent, which required detailed implementation. British reticence impaired the abolition of border controls among the twelve member states of the Community under the Single European Act in the following years. The Germans were then in favour of the Schengen framework of five member states moving ahead faster. Deepening was again the enemy of widening. The French tactical decision to accept the Schengen agreement did not mean they were enthusiastic about it. The growth of asylum requests and illegal immigration from third countries made them concerned about giving up their controls.[83] Chancellor Kohl's Minister for Schengen Affairs, Lutz Stavenhagen, strove to accelerate work among the Five. In December 1989, he pointed out to President Mitterrand's technical advisor for European Affairs, Élisabeth Guigou, that negotiating a convention to implement the Schengen agreement had already taken 4 years. In contrast, it had taken 'very little time to reach an agreement on the principles of economic and monetary union'.[84] France obtained a common and restrictive visa policy and strengthened controls at external borders. The list of countries subject to visas eventually included 102 countries. The Five were able to sign the Schengen Convention on 19 June 1990.[85]

Southern European member states would have to accept the Convention in its entirety if they wished to join the area without border controls. In May 1990, the French emphasised 'the need to consider membership as a commitment without particular rules, since the text of the Convention formed an integral whole and the bloc of countries subject to common visa provisions could not be reduced'.[86] The Schengen framework thus enhanced French power to lead southern European governments to harden their immigration policies towards third countries. Italy, Spain, Portugal and Greece adapted their legislation and signed the Schengen Convention between November 1990 and November 1992.

---

82 *OJEC*, L 169/1–28, 29 June 1987.
83 R. King, 'Migration and the Single Market for Labour: An Issue in Regional Development', in M. Blacksell and A. M. Williams (ed.), *The European Challenge: Geography and Development in the European Community* (Oxford, Oxford University Press, 1994), pp. 218–41, 237.
84 AN, 5 AG 4 EG 69, dossier 1, É. Guigou to Président, 13 December 1989.
85 *OJEC*, 22 September 2000, Schengen Convention.
86 AN, 5 AG 4 AH 18, dossier 1, minutes of the meeting of the Central Negotiating Group, 31 May 1990.

Among the Twelve, the only output of cooperation in this area was the Dublin Convention, signed on 15 June 1990, which determined the state responsible for examining each asylum application lodged in the Community.[87] Member states considered such a mechanism to be a prerequisite for the abolition of internal border controls, in order to avoid third-country nationals moving across the Community and presenting successive asylum applications to benefit from a prolonged right of residence.

Maastricht Culmination

Schengen negotiations slightly deepened the liberal internal migration regime by abolishing internal border controls, but more importantly deepened the coordinated restrictions to third-country immigration. Alongside those negotiations, the Twelve also achieved a series of new bargains, culminating with the Treaty of Maastricht, which transformed the EC into the EU. Those various bargains decisively deepened the liberal migration regime inside the Union. Around the Single European Act, the trend towards completion of the Common Market entailed finding an agreement on the mutual recognition of diplomas and qualifications. The stake was the international expansion of companies. The capacity to move qualified members of staff and executives across countries and cooperate with co-national independent professionals would foster growth. Lawyers, doctors and architects were strategic professionals. In January 1985, German representatives in the Committee of Permanent Representatives (COREPER) called for the abolition of obstacles created by the problems arising from the lack of mutual recognition of diplomas, certificates and other qualifications. To move more swiftly, they recommended giving up efforts to harmonise training. They looked for an easy way to achieve a 'breakthrough for a large number of professions'.[88] In December 1988, the Association of European Chambers of Commerce and Industry also supported a 'correspondence of professional qualifications'.[89] On 21 December 1988, the Council adopted Directive 89/48 on a general system for the recognition of higher-education diplomas.[90] It applied both to employed and to self-employed workers. The member states had to let Community nationals holding a certification issued in another member state practise a regulated profession.

In June 1987, the member states created the Erasmus programme, with the same ultimate goal of supporting mobile, transnational executives and

---

87 *OJEC*, C 254, 19 August 1997, pp. 1–12.
88 ACCUE, Liste Rouge 40866, 4471/85 ETS 2, annex, 28 January 1985.
89 ACCUE, Liste Rouge 1850.   90 ACCUE, Liste Rouge 35136.

qualified professionals who would contribute to the internationalisation of companies.[91] The programme should foster students' mobility across European countries. It targeted university students who had demonstrated their capacity to complete their academic education. It targeted not language students, but students in science, engineering or business who would become the future executives of European companies. By the end of December 1989, the Council had decided to extend the programme, earmarking 192 million European Currency Units for the following 3 years.[92]

The fall of the Berlin Wall on 9 November 1989 and the demise of communism in eastern Europe started another dynamic that contributed to deepening the liberal migration regime inside the Community. West German leaders were determined to use this opportunity to incorporate East Germany as soon as possible. At this crucial turning point, they wanted to use the liberal migration regime within western Europe to absorb the hundreds of thousands of Germans suddenly coming from the east more swiftly. They arranged that these German nationals could benefit from their right of free movement and free circulation in the Community directly with their East German documents, to alleviate the burden on West German administrative services.[93]

In this turbulent context, west European leaders feared that the Soviet leaders would use force on a large scale to prevent the disintegration of their empire. West European governments hastened their efforts to create a Common Foreign and Security Policy (CFSP) to deter the Soviet Union from escalating the crisis. On 18 April 1990, Kohl and Mitterrand delivered a joint message to the president of the Council. In parallel with the creation of the CFSP, they wanted 'to reinforce the democratic legitimacy of the Union', from which a form of European citizenship could emerge.[94] In the Council on 4 December 1990, several representatives of the member states declared that 'European citizenship [would be] one of the basic elements of the credibility of the CFSP.[95] Two days later, on 6 December 1990, Kohl and Mitterrand sent a joint letter to the president of the Council, Giulio Andreotti. They accepted 'the institution of proper European citizenship' in the Treaty of Maastricht, based on the 'proposals of the Spanish government,' which had

---

91 ACCUE, Liste Rouge 34831, Decision 87/327.
92 *OJEC*, 30 December 1989, L 395/23, Decision 89/663.
93 AN, 5 AG 4 AH 18, dossier 1, É. Guigou to Président.
94 'Message conjoint de François Mitterand et Helmut Kohl (Paris, 18 avril 1990)', www .cvce.eu/obj/message_conjoint_de_francois_mitterrand_et_helmut_kohl_pari s_18_avril_1990-fr-89369c53-5d93-4e56-8397-825ca92c86f5.html.
95 ACCUE, Liste Rouge 62273, 10356/90 REVTRAT 18, 30 November 1990.

referred to the possibility of a European 'military service'.[96] Creating a form of European citizenship implied giving rights to European citizens to foster their feeling of belonging and their resolve to support the CFSP. Three directives of the EC Council had just, on 28 June 1990, granted the nationals of the member states the right to reside wherever they wanted in the Community, independently of the exercise of economic activity.[97] Article 8 of the Treaty Establishing the European Community, as defined by the Treaty of Maastricht, added the right to vote and stand for local and European elections in the country of residence.[98]

Magnetic Attraction and the Enlargements

Adenauer had considered that European integration, German prosperity and the opportunities they would create for East Germans and other east Europeans would constitute a magnetic attraction (*Sogwirkung*).[99] In their risings against communism, the east Europeans wanted to move to the West, where a vast area of free migration existed. Kohl and Mitterrand declared in Munich on 18 September 1990 that 'the process of European union has been a determining factor in favouring upheavals in central and eastern Europe and German unification'.[100] As the historian N. Piers Ludlow underlines, 'European integration [. . .] contributed to that image of western European success, stability and prosperity that did so much to destabilise Communist rule in eastern Europe as the Cold War came to an end.' The participants in the risings against communism in eastern Europe were 'conscious of the way in which the quality of life within the other half of their continent vastly outstripped their own'.[101] The risings in eastern Europe were as much against communism as they were about the opportunity to move westwards. West German leaders understood the importance of sending signals that would encourage this perspective. Besides facilitating the access of East Germans to their right of free movement inside the Community, West German

---

96 Presse- und Informationsamt der Bundesregierung (ed.), *Bulletin des Presse- und Informationsamtes der Bundesregierung* no. 144 (Bonn, Deutscher Bundesverlag, 1990), p. 1513.
97 ACCUE, Liste Rouge 2381, Directive 90/366; Liste Rouge 2385, Directive 90/364; Liste Rouge 2387, Directive 90/365.
98 *OJEC*, C 224, EU Treaty, 31 August 1992.
99 T. Pedersen, *Germany, France, and the Integration of Europe: A Realist Interpretation* (London, Pinter, 1998), p. 73.
100 *Agence Europe*, 19 September 1990, p. 4.
101 N. P. Ludlow, 'European Integration and the Cold War', in M. P. Leffler and O. A. Westad (eds.), *The Cambridge History of the Cold War*, vol. II: *Crises and Détente* (Cambridge, Cambridge University Press, 2010), pp. 179–97, 195.

negotiators insisted during the ultimate phase of the negotiation of the Schengen Convention on lifting visa requirements for the nationals of Hungary and Czechoslovakia. Only French insistence explains why the Five maintained visa requirements for other countries of central and eastern Europe.[102]

In Europe, massive migration flows from east to west followed the end of the Cold War. Whereas in 1986 three-quarters of asylum seekers in West Germany came from the Global South, by 1993 three-quarters came from eastern Europe.[103] Massive migration both manifested the attraction of western Europe and anticipated the formal enlargements of the EU eastwards. Most central European countries became part of the EU in 2004; Romania and Bulgaria joined in 2007, and Croatia in 2013. The high emigration rate from new member countries led the number of EU citizens living in a country other than their own to jump from 5.9 million in 1999 to 13.6 million in 2012. The number of Romanians residing in western Europe increased tenfold between 2000 and 2012. By then, nearly 11 per cent of Romanians had moved to another European country.[104] Migration flows demonstrated the magnetic effect that the vast area of free migration within Europe created in formerly communist countries.

The Challenge of Polarity

The contradictory trends of deepening both the openness inside Europe and the restrictions towards non-European immigration resulted in a strong polarity that became increasingly challenging to manage. The Twelve included in the Treaty of Maastricht, as the Justice and Home Affairs pillar, the common visa policy which the Schengen Convention had defined. The Council could decide with a qualified majority as of 1 January 1996 on the list of third countries whose nationals should need to hold a visa when crossing the external borders of the Union.[105] The Schengen Convention became part of EU law with the Treaty of Amsterdam, which came into force on 1 May 1999 – forcing the new members of eastern Europe to accept it in its entirety when joining. The UK and Ireland nevertheless benefited from an opt-out, which allowed them to exercise the border controls they deemed necessary.[106]

---

102 AN, 5 AG 4 AH 18, dossier 1, SGCI, 11 May 1990.
103 K. J. Bade, *Migration in European History* (Oxford, Blackwell, 2003), p. 284.
104 Recchi, *Mobile Europe*, pp. 52, 56.
105 *OJEC*, C 224, 31 August 1992 Treaty on European Union, Article 11, new Article 100C.
106 *Official Journal of the European Union*, C 340, 10 November 1997, 'Protocol Integrating the Schengen *Acquis*'; 'Protocol on the Application of Certain Aspects of Article 7a to the United Kingdom and Ireland'.

Despite the transfer into EU law of the intergovernmental Schengen cooperation, the management of the EU's external borders, the visa policy and the distribution of asylum seekers among EU members remained unresolved points of contention. The rising migration pressure led EU border states to complain that they lacked EU support to manage the waves of third-country migrants. Meanwhile, in contrast, other member states were trying to avoid responsibility for the problem.

Things came to a head in 2015, when 1.3 million migrants arrived in the EU without proper documentation and claimed asylum. The majority, about 800,000, arrived via Greece; 180,000 came via Italy. In August 2015 – just 1 month – nearly 200,000 entered the EU.[107] On 13 September 2015, after more than 13,000 had arrived in Munich in 1 day, Germany decided to restore controls at its south-eastern border with Austria temporarily.[108] German policy-makers wanted to stem the inflow of immigrants, who had often circulated unregistered across the member states of south-eastern Europe. The German border authorities also suspended any trains between Austria and Germany temporarily. The German decision created a domino effect in the area without internal border controls, with all countries likely to end up as a dead-end for the flow of immigrants restoring border checks. The crisis culminated when Austria dispatched tanks to the Brenner Pass and started building a fence and a registration centre there in April 2016 to stop the inflow of immigrants.[109]

The EU's leaders renewed their efforts to manage the growing migration pressure at the EU's external borders while safeguarding the liberal migration regime inside the EU. Efforts to improve cooperation on third-country immigrants have not produced new results so far. In particular, the negotiation of a new Dublin system to allocate asylum seekers among EU member states is still in negotiation at the time of writing. Consequently, EU policy-makers have further deepened the closure to third-country immigrants. In June 2015, the EU launched a maritime force operation in the Mediterranean to intercept the boats transporting irregular immigrants. Previous operations had only entailed

---

107 Frontex, '710 000 Migrants Entered EU in First Nine Months of 2015' (2015), https://frontex.europa.eu/media-centre/news/news-release/710-000-migrants-entered-eu-in-first-nine-months-of-2015-NUiBkk.
108 'Migrant Crisis: Germany Starts Temporary Border Controls', *BBC News*, 14 September 2015, www.bbc.com/news/world-europe-34239674.
109 'Italy Must Stop Refugee Flow, or We'll Shut Brenner Pass', *The Local*, 14 April 2016, www.thelocal.at/20160414/italy-must-stop-refugee-flow-or-well-shut-brenner-pass-austria.

surveillance and rescue. EU vessels could then board, search, divert and seize ships used to transport immigrants.[110] The EU's leaders also developed new cooperation with Turkey, according to which Turkey agreed to stabilise the flow of migrants from Syria and the Middle East. On 18 March 2016, the EU–Turkey statement indicated that it was planned to grant up to €3 billion to non-governmental organisations in Turkey working to stabilise the flow of migrants. In exchange for Turkish cooperation, EU leaders also pledged to make progress on visa liberalisation for Turkish citizens and in the talks related to Turkish accession to the Union.[111]

Brexit

Besides the challenge of polarity, the magnetic effect too ended up threatening the liberal migration regime inside the EU. After the first enlargement to central and eastern European countries, Germany used the maximum restrictions provided for in the transition periods of those enlargements, to cope with high unemployment after the reunification, which lasted until the mid 2000s. Germany did not fully open its labour market to Polish immigrant workers until 2011. In contrast, the UK opened up swiftly. As a result, the annual flow of immigrant workers from the new member states of central and eastern Europe to the UK jumped from 25,000 in 2003 to 337,000 in 2007.[112] The number of Polish-born residents in the UK increased from 95,000 in 2004 to 679,000 in 2013.[113] The Great Recession of 2008 and 2009 spurred resentment against immigrants. The Conservatives campaigned against immigration and the EU and returned to power in 2010. British voters criticised the impact of European and non-European immigrants on the labour market, the payment of benefits to European immigrants and the apparent loss of control over non-European immigration.[114] According to Prime Minister David Cameron, 'around 40 per cent of all

---

110 'Migrant Crisis: EU to Begin Seizing Smugglers' Boats', *BBC News*, 07 October 2015, www.bbc.com/news/world-europe-34461503.
111 'EU–Turkey statement, 18 March 2016', www.consilium.europa.eu/en/press/press-releases/2016/03/18-eu-turkey-statement.
112 Recchi, *Mobile Europe*, pp. 52–76.
113 Office for National Statistics, 'International Migration: A Recent History' (2015), www.ons.gov.uk/peoplepopulationandcommunity/populationandmigration/internationalmigration/articles/internationalmigrationarecenthistory/2015-01-15. Cited by M. Corrales, 'Fear and Loathing in the UK: How the Fear of Immigration from Central and Eastern Europe Influenced the Brexit Referendum Result' (Master's thesis, University of Vienna, 2019), p. 14.
114 C. Boswell and A. Geddes, *Migration and Mobility in the European Union* (Basingstoke, Palgrave Macmillan, 2011), pp. 91, 185.

recent European Economic Area migrants [were] supported by the UK benefits system'. Moreover, 'each family claim[ed] on average around [£] 6,000 a year of in-work benefits alone [. . .] and over 10,000 recently-arrived families claim[ed] over [£]10,000 a year'.[115]

The Conservative government organised a referendum on British membership of the EU in June 2016. During the referendum campaign, immigration was the key concern for 'Leave' voters.[116] According to data collected by the Centre for Social Investigation, the reason to vote 'Leave' that ranked the highest was 'to regain control over EU immigration'.[117] Anti-EU politicians orchestrated anti-immigration sentiment among British voters to secure a negative outcome in the referendum. In April 2016, British MP Nigel Farage – the leader of the UK Independence Party – decided to focus his Brexit campaign on immigration: 'We have to, in this campaign, make people understand that EU membership and uncontrolled immigration are synonymous with each other.'[118]

The victory of 'Leave' ushered in a first episode of disintegration in the history of the EU's liberal migration regime. Nevertheless, this episode did not threaten the continued existence of this regime. Starting even before the referendum, Germany re-emerged as the major country of immigration in the EU by far. It absorbed the majority of migrants from central and eastern Europe and thus stabilised migration flows across the EU. Germany's unemployment rate dropped sharply, from more than 12 per cent in early 2006 to about 4.5 per cent in 2015. Germany's net migration balance in relation to EU countries reached 295,000 in 2013, 304,000 in 2014 and 333,000 in 2015.[119] This situation alleviated tensions in other immigration countries. Regarding migration flows from outside the EU too, Germany was a leading country of immigration, thereby contributing to alleviating the challenge of polarity for other EU countries. The British ended up isolated in their decision to leave the EU, insofar as Brexit has not yet triggered any domino effect of disintegration.

115 Speech on Europe, 10 November 2015, cited by Corrales, 'Fear and Loathing', p. 26.
116 C. Prosser, J. Mellon and J. Green, 'What Mattered Most to You When Deciding How to Vote in the EU Referendum?', *British Election Study*, 11 July 2016, www.britishelectionstudy.com/bes-findings/what-mattered-most-to-you-when-deciding-how-to-vote-in-the-eu-referendum/#.WJ9OgxjMxE4.
117 N. Carl, 'CSI Brexit 4: Reasons Why People Voted Leave or Remain', Centre for Social Investigation (2018). Cited by Corrales, 'Fear and Loathing', p. 4.
118 Corrales, 'Fear and Loathing', p. 53.
119 Statistisches Bundesamt, Wiesbaden, 2014–2017.

Concluding Remarks

The guiding thread in the formation of the migration regime of the EU has been the support Germany has provided. By fostering more liberal migration arrangements, the Germans aimed to stabilise and unify western Europe in the context of the Cold War. The opportunities associated with the regime were limited to European populations. Those opportunities could also serve for short-term German emigration – a convenient instrument to manage the demographic and territorial upheavals taking place in the eastern part of the continent. Last but not least, an open migration regime in Europe for independent workers and skilled professionals favoured the penetration of foreign markets by German firms. The size of the West German labour market stabilised this regime and won the support of other countries of immigration in most decades during this period. When that market ran into difficulties in the 1970s and early 1980s, and again in the 2000s, the regime weakened. The UK and France played a minor role. The European migration regime has, therefore, been the product of a form of German cooperative and benevolent hegemony. Germany has arranged equally legally binding agreements with other states. It has, so far, mostly provided benefits rather than imposing costs. This regime has been a way to promote German interests in Europe – encouraging the demise of the Soviet Union, German reunification and the evaporation of borders to foster German economic and social expansion.

Recommended Reading

Comte, E. 'La rupture de 1955 dans la formation du régime européen de migrations', *Relations Internationales* 166 (2016): 137–58.

Comte, E. *The History of the European Migration Regime: Germany's Strategic Hegemony* (Abingdon and New York, NY, Routledge, 2018).

Comte, E. and S. Lavenex, 'Differentiation and De-differentiation in EU Border Controls, Asylum and Police Cooperation', *The International Spectator* 57, no. 1 (2022): 124–41.

Lucassen, L. A. C. J. 'The Rise of the European Migration Regime and Its Paradoxes (1945–2020)', *International Review of Social History* 64, no. 3 (2019): 515–31.

Paoli, S. *Frontiera Sud: L'Italia e la nascita dell'Europa di Schengen* (Florence, Le Monnier, 2018).

14

The Constitutional Dimension: Centralisation, Democratisation and the Rule of Law

ANDRÁS JAKAB AND LANDO KIRCHMAIR

Introduction: Does the European Union Have a Constitutional Dimension?

The constitutional dimension of the European Union (EU) has to account for the fact that the Treaty Establishing a Constitution for Europe (TECE) seems to have failed in 2005 in the Dutch and French referenda. Thus we are unlikely to have a legal document officially called a 'constitution' in the foreseeable future. Yet, the designation is not decisive on its own (cf. the German Grundgesetz or the Hungarian Basic Law). Treaties can also be constitutions, as the examples of Cyprus (1960, Treaty of Establishment),[1] the Constitution of Württemberg (1819), the Constitution of Saxony (1831)[2] and the Norddeutsche Bund (1867) show.[3] The fact that there was no (successful) constitution-making procedure (or that the treaty draftings and amendments were not meant to be constitution-making) is also of secondary importance: in Israel, for example, there was no constitution-making procedure at all, as the formal constitution was created by judicial case law out of ordinary statutes. Finally, constitutionalism depends not only on specific legal documents, but also on informal elements and respective ideas. And such elements and ideas are the basis of European constitutionalism.[4]

---

1 K. Doehring, 'Staat und Verfassung in einem zusammenwachsenden Europa', *Zeitschrift für Rechtspolitik* 3 (1993): 98–103.
2 E.-W. Böckenförde, 'Geschichtliche Entwicklung und Bedeutungswandel der Verfassung', in E.-W. Böckenförde, *Staat, Verfassung, Demokratie* (Frankfurt am Main, Suhrkamp, 1991), pp. 29–52, 38 with further references.
3 C. Möllers, 'Pouvoir constituant – Constitution – Constitutionalism', in A. von Bogdandy and J. Bast (eds.), *Principles of European Constitutional Law*, 2nd ed. (Oxford, Hart, 2010), pp. 169–205, 176.
4 For more details on this issue, tracing European constitutionalism back even before the European Coal and Steel Community in 1951 and explaining how modern constitutionalism developed (in Europe) as a response to absolutism, see A. Jakab, *European Constitutional Language* (Cambridge, Cambridge University Press, 2016), pp. 118–22.

It seems that the EU *does* have a constitution: the founding treaties serve as its constitution (in the formal sense). In this sense referring to the founding treaties, see the European Court of Justice (ECJ) already in several cases.[5] If we understand a constitution as one or several legal documents which are more difficult to amend than 'ordinary' laws, and against which one can measure the validity of the 'ordinary' laws, the founding treaties can be qualified as the Constitution of the EU.[6] These treaties are procedurally more difficult to amend than 'ordinary' laws (the two most important categories of which are regulations and directives); and the validity of these ordinary measures is examined against the founding treaties (Article 263 of the Treaty on the Functioning of the European Union (TFEU)).

The EU Constitution is more rigid than constitutions usually are in terms of amendment requirements. On the one hand, however, since the Treaty of Lisbon we also have simplified treaty revision procedures (Article 48(6)–(7) of the Treaty on the EU (TEU)). On the other hand, EU primary law was more frequently amended than the US Constitution was during the same period – at least as long as the group of EU member states was still rather small. And flexibility can be and has successfully been assured in both entities usually through judicial interpretation of the respective Constitution.

The treaties constitute the powers of the EU institutions and (for the concept of a constitution, more importantly) serve at the same time the function of limiting this power as well as that of the member states. They can serve even as a limitation of the constitutional autonomy of the member states.[7] Insofar as the symbolic function is concerned, the EU Constitution seems deficient, however. On the one hand, numerous acts (most of them called protocols) enjoy the same rank as the treaties (making primary law almost as opaque as Austrian constitutional law). Austrian constitutional law is to be found also in simple 'statutes'. Therefore, the Austrian Constitution has been described as

---

5 Case 294/83 *Parti écologiste 'Les Verts' v. Parliament* EU:C:1986:166, para 23; Opinion 1/91 *European Economic Area* EU:C:1991:490, para 21; 'constitutional principle' and 'constitutional guarantee' in Cases C-402/05 P and C415/05 P. *Kadi et al. v. Council and Commission* EU: C:2008:461, paras 285, 290. For a sceptical view on this terminology of the ECJ, see A. Somek, 'Constitutional Treaty: A Comment on the Legal Language of the European Union', *Annual of German & European Law* 1 (2003): 310–22. See also generally on this question J. H. H. Weiler, *The Constitution of Europe* (Cambridge, Cambridge University Press, 1999).

6 For more details, see Jakab, *European Constitutional Language*. See also in the affirmative S. Griller, 'Is This a Constitution? Remarks on a Contested Concept', in S. Griller and J. Ziller (eds.), *The Lisbon Treaty: EU Constitutionalism without a Constitutional Treaty?* (Vienna, Springer, 2008), pp. 21–56, 50.

7 See C. Antpöhler, J. Dickschen, S. Hentrei, M. Kottmann, M. Smrkolj and A. von Bogdandy, 'Reverse Solange – Protecting the Essence of Fundamental Rights against EU Member States', *Common Market Law Review* 49, no. 2 (2012): 489–519; G. C. Rodríguez Iglesias, 'Zur "Verfassung" der Europäischen Gemeinschaft', *Europäische Grundrechte-Zeitschrift* (1996): 125–31, 125–6.

a ruin.[8] On the other hand, the symbolic content of the EU Constitution is rather slim. The values of modern constitutionalism and constitutional principles (mentioned in the preamble; e.g., the rule of law, democracy) can have symbolic force, but no explicit references are made to the anthem, flag or coat of arms.[9] The failure of the TECE is partly to be explained by the rejection of this symbolic content (the Lisbon Treaty is more or less the TECE without the symbolic content of, and the designation as, a constitution). This is not unique either, as some national constitutions also lack these elements, but it is still a deficiency, if we expect a constitution to be a symbol of a political community.

As (legal) scholars, we cannot entirely substitute the symbolic side. But if we call the founding treaties (including the Charter of Fundamental Rights of the European Union) the 'Constitution of Europe'[10] (or, somewhat more precisely, but less enthusiastically, the 'Constitution of the EU') and if we conceptualise legal issues as constitutional issues,[11] then we are forming the public discourse by vesting some symbolic force in these documents. There are numerous handbooks and textbooks containing in their respective titles mention of the 'constitutional law' of the EU.[12] Consequently, the decoupling of state and constitution[13] and expressions like 'postnational constitutionalism',[14] 'unity of

---

8 H.-R. Klecatsky, 'Bundes-Verfassungsgesetz und Bundesverfassungsrecht', in H. Schambeck (ed.), *Das österreichische Bundes-Verfassungsgesetz und seine Entwicklung* (Berlin, Duncker & Humblot, 1980), pp. 83–110. For the critique that EU treaties contain too much in the way of substantive rules for typical constitutions, see D. Grimm, *The Constitution of European Democracy* (Oxford, Oxford University Press, 2017), p. 195.

9 On the symbols of the EU and their (sometimes questionable) legal basis, see M. Röttinger, 'Die Hoheitszeichen der Europäischen Union – ein paar vielleicht nicht nur theoretische Rechtsfragen', *Europarecht* 6 (2003): 1095–108.

10 See, for example, J. Habermas, *Zur Verfassung Europas* (Berlin, Suhrkamp, 2011).

11 For a missed opportunity where the ECJ did not conceptualise a legal issue as a constitutional issue, see Case C-364/10, *Hungary v. Slovakia*, EU:C:2012:630.

12 Among the latest ones, see, for example, R. Schütze, *European Constitutional Law*, 2nd ed. (Cambridge, Cambridge University Press, 2015); von Bogdandy and Bast, *European Constitutional Principles*; A. Rosas and L. Armati, *EU Constitutional Law* (Oxford and Portland, OR, Hart, 2012), especially pp. 1–6 with further references.

13 F. Amtenbrink and P. A. J. van den Berg (eds.), *The Constitutional Integrity of the European Union* (The Hague, T. M. C. Asser, 2010); G. Martinico, *The Tangled Complexity of the EU Constitutional Process: The Frustrating Knot of Europe* (London, Routledge, 2012); U. K. Preuß, 'Disconnecting Constitutions from Statehood', in P. Dobner and M. Loughlin (eds.), *The Twilight of Constitutionalism?* (Oxford, Oxford University Press, 2010), pp. 23–46; J. H. H. Weiler and M. Wind (eds.), *European Constitutionalism beyond the State*, (Cambridge, Cambridge University Press, 2003); P. Craig, 'Constitutions, Constitutionalism, and the European Union', *European Law Journal* 7 (2001): 125–50, A. Peters, *Elemente einer Theorie der Verfassung Europas* (Berlin, Duncker & Humblot, 2001), with further references; A. Weber, *Europäische Verfassungsvergleichung* (Munich, C. H. Beck, 2010), pp. 17–18.

14 A. Albi, 'Introduction: The European Constitution and National Constitutions in the Context of "Post-national Constitutionalism"', in A. Albi and J. Ziller (eds.), *The European Constitution and National Constitutions: Ratification and Beyond* (Alphen an

European and national constitutional law',[15] 'transnational constitutionalism',[16] 'multilevel constitutionalism'[17] and 'constitutional pluralism'[18] are all to be welcomed, as they soften the traditional national state-centred paradigm (even if they seem somewhat confusing).[19] They all contribute to constitutionalising the legal terminology of the EU, which (through implied connotations, besides the legal situation, which is not directly influenced by the terminology) (1) can help strengthen the EU in public discourse (the constitutional language can enhance public attention, which leads to better political accountability; the new language can also contribute to the formation of a European polity);[20] and (2), even more importantly, can help to stop constitutional changes in member states, if these changes contradict the principles of the Constitution of the EU (both by forming EU discourse and awakening responsibility at EU level and by forming domestic discourses and making it clear that not everything that would be a procedurally possible constitutional amendment can be done).[21]

Three Intertwined Stories: Federalist Centralisation, Democratisation and Strengthening the Rule of Law

The institutional history of the EU begins with France, Germany, Italy and the Benelux countries ratifying the Treaty of Paris, establishing the European Coal and Steel Community led by its own executive branch, the High Authority, in

den Rijn, Kluwer Law International, 2007), pp. 1–14; J. Shaw, '"Postnational Constitutionalism" in the European Union', *European Public Policy* 6 (1999): 579–97.

15 I. Pernice, 'Europäisches und nationales Verfassungsrecht',*Veröffentlichungen der Vereinigung der Deutschen Staatsrechtslehrer* 60 (2001): 149–93, especially 172–6.

16 N. Tsagourias (ed.), *Transnational Constitutionalism: International and European Models* (Cambridge, Cambridge University Press, 2007).

17 I. Pernice, 'Multilevel Constitutionalism in the European Union', *European Law Review* 27 (2002): 511–29.

18 N. Walker, 'The Idea of Constitutional Pluralism', *Modern Law Review* 65 (2008): 317–59; N. W. Barber, *The Constitutional State* (Oxford, Oxford University Press, 2010), pp. 172–83; M. Avbelj and J. Komárek (eds.), *Constitutional Pluralism in the European Union and Beyond* (Oxford and Portland, OR, Hart, 2012) with further references.

19 For opposing views, using mainly arguments based on the historical origins and inherent meaning of the word 'constitution', see O. Beaud, *La puissance de l'État* (Paris, Presses universitaires de France, 1994), p. 209; D. Grimm, 'Does Europe Need a Constitution?', *European Law Journal* 1 (1995): 282–302, 292; M. Loughlin, 'What Is Constitutionalisation?', in Dobner and Loughlin (eds.), *The Twilight of Constitutionalism?*, pp. 47–70, especially 69–70.

20 See M. Poiares Maduro, 'The Importance of Being Called a Constitution', *International Journal of Constitutional Law* 3 (2005): 332–56, 354–5.

21 See especially Antpöhler et al., 'Reverse Solange', 130.

1951.[22] This development continued when in 1957 the foundation of the European Economic Community (EEC) was – besides the Euratom Treaty – laid out by the so-called Treaty of Rome. Both treaties founded organisations which enjoyed autonomous powers and featured important and innovative legal elements such as the doctrine of direct effect, distinguishing these supranational communities from other international organisations. Importantly, the history of the constitutional dimension of EU law arguably unfolded and continues to unfold in three intertwined stories: federalist centralisation, democratisation and the rule of law. The ECJ was and continues to be an essential part of all these stories, which are not isolated and did not happen in a strict chronological order, but have important overlaps and mutually influence each other in the respective story line.

Federalist Centralisation

Federalist centralisation concerns the development of the relationship between EU law and member state law, namely the division of competences between the EU and its member states, and is, thus, an important element of the (early) constitutional dimension of the EU. This dimension, originating in the early stages of the EU, which was further back in time framed as the European Communities, hinges on a particular structural legal architecture of the Communities. The chief architect of this structure is the ECJ, which is responsible for the evolution of the doctrines of direct applicability and supremacy.

Establishing the Autonomous EU Legal Order

In 1963 the ECJ postulated the autonomy of the Community legal order, which was accompanied by the direct effect of EU law on the national laws of the member states,[23] just like the primary application of EU law.[24] This arguably was the foundation on which the subsequent development of the EU could successfully be based, establishing a strong and effective autonomous legal system.[25] The landmark judgment in this regard was *Van Gend & Loos*, in which the ECJ famously declared as early as 1963 that the

---

22 See, for example, Schütze, *European Constitutional Law*, pp. 12ff.
23 See Case 26/62 *Van Gend & Loos* EU:C:1963:1.
24 See Case 6/64 *Costa v. E.N.E.L.* EU:C:1964:66; Case 11/70 *Internationale Handelsgesellschaft mbH gegen Einfuhr- und Vorratsstelle für Getreide und Futtermittel* EU:C:1970:114, paras. 3–4; Case 106/77 *Amministrazione delle Finanze dello Stato v. Simmenthal SpA* EU:C:1978:49.
25 See E. Stein, 'Lawyers, Judges, and the Making of a Transnational Constitution', *American Journal of International Law* 75 (1981): 1–27; J. H. H. Weiler, 'The Transformation of Europe', *Yale Law Journal* 100 (1991): 2403–83.

'Community constitutes a new legal order of international law for the benefit of which the states have limited their sovereign rights, albeit within limited fields, and the subjects of which comprise not only the Member States but also their nationals'.[26] In this case, the ECJ stipulated that EU law enjoys direct effect and thus creates individual rights which member states and their courts must respect.[27] Only a year later, the ECJ added something important to this finding. In *Costa v. E.N.E.L.*, the Court stated that the law of the European Community is itself a legal order by postulating the 'autonomy of the Community legal order' when holding that, '[i]n contrast with ordinary international treaties, the EEC Treaty has created its own legal system which, on the entry into force of the Treaty, became an integral part of the legal systems of the Member States and which their courts are bound to apply'.[28] The autonomous EU legal order thus was born and important constitutional elements were already present.[29]

Moreover, the ECJ continued by saying that '[t]he integration into the laws of each Member State of provisions which derive from the Community, and more generally the terms and the spirit of the Treaty, make it impossible for the States, as a corollary, to accord precedence to a unilateral and subsequent measure over a legal system accepted by them on a basis of reciprocity'.[30] The primacy of EU law over member state law was thereby established.

Primacy of EU Law over Member State Constitutional Law

On the basis of this foundation, some years later, in 1970, in the case *Internationale Handelsgesellschaft* the Court explicitly claimed the primacy of EU law even over the constitutional law of its member states, no matter whether fundamental rights or structural principles are concerned:

> [T]he law stemming from the Treaty, an independent source of law, cannot because of its very nature be overridden by rules of national law, however

---

26 Case 26/62 *Van Gend & Loos*, p. 12.   27 Ibid., pp. 13, 16.
28 Case 6/64 *Costa v. E.N.E.L.*, p. 593; the German version uses the term *Rechtsordnung*; the French version uses *ordre juridique*; cf. Opinion 1/91 *European Economic Area*, para. 2 postulated the 'autonomy of the Community legal order', whereas the German version postulated the 'Autonomie des Rechtssystems der Gemeinschaft'. For more on this, see W. Schroeder, *Das Gemeinschaftsrechtssystem: Eine Untersuchung zu den rechtsdogmatischen, rechtstheoretischen und verfassungsrechtlichen Grundlagen des Systemdenkens im Europäischen Gemeinschaftsrecht* (Tübingen, Mohr Siebeck, 2002), pp. 104–5, with further references in notes 6 and 7. For a more recent example, see Case C-284/16 *Slovak Republic v. Achmea BV* EU:C:2018:158, para. 33.
29 See Jakab, *European Constitutional Language*, Chapter 3.
30 Case 6/64 *Costa v. E.N.E.L.*, pp. 593–4.

framed, without being deprived of its character as Community law and without the legal basis of the Community itself being called in question. Therefore the validity of a Community measure or its effect within a Member State cannot be affected by allegations that it runs counter to either fundamental rights as formulated by the constitution of that State or the principles of a national constitutional structure.[31]

In 1978, in the case *Simmental II*, this primacy of EU law over conflicting member state law was finally explicitly spelled out in positive terms. The court stated that, beyond rendering conflicting member state law automatically inapplicable, also the adoption of new national legislation which conflicts with EU law is precluded.[32]

Implied Powers and the EU 'Constitutional Charter'

In 1971, the ECJ had developed in addition the implied powers doctrine, stipulating that the powers conferred upon the EU in relation to its member states (the internal dimension) would imply also an external power to conclude international treaties.[33] This competence, which was succinctly developed in further case law, has been included in the Treaty of Lisbon, Article 216(1).

Furthermore, in 1986, the ECJ referred to the EEC Treaty as 'the basic constitutional charter' of the Community.[34] This was confirmed in 1991: '[T]he [EU] Treaty, albeit concluded in the form of an international agreement, none the less constitutes the constitutional charter of a [Union] based on the rule of law.'[35]

In 1998, in the judgment *IN.CO.GE. '90 and others*, the ECJ finally clarified the legal consequences of a conflict between EU law and member state law. According to the ECJ, EU law enjoys *Anwendungsvorrang* (primacy) but not *Geltungsvorrang* (i.e., it does not invalidate conflicting member state law).[36]

In 2008 and 2013, respectively, the ECJ firmly established the constitutional dimension of the EU also with regard to international law when deciding that EU regulations freezing the assets of certain terror suspects as instructed by

---

31 Case C-11/70 *Internationale Handelsgesellschaft*, para. 3. See in this regard also Case C-409/06 *Winner Wetten GmbH v. Bürgermeisterin der Stadt Bergheim* EU:C:2010:503, para. 61: 'Rules of national law, even of a constitutional order, cannot be allowed to undermine the unity and effectiveness of Union law.' See also Case C-399/11 *Stefano Melloni v. Ministerio Fiscal* EU:C:2013:107, para. 59.
32 Case 106/77 *Amministrazione delle Finanze dello Stato v. Simmenthal SpA*, para. 17.
33 Case 22/70, *Commission of the European Communities v. Council of the European Communities* EU:C:1971:32.
34 Case 294/83, *Parti ecologiste 'Les Verts' v. European Parliament*, p. 1365.
35 Opinion 1/91 *European Economic Area*, para. 21.
36 Case C-10/97 *Ministero delle Finanze v. IN.CO.GE. '90 and others* EU:C:1998:498, para. 21.

UN Security Council Resolutions violate EU fundamental rights and therefore violate the constitutional character of the EU.[37]

This development, together with the evolution of the European treaties, for instance in 1986 through the Single European Act, the first major revision of the Treaty of Rome, and the Treaty of Lisbon in 2009, besides many other minor but nevertheless important developments which must be left out here, such as the phenomenon of agencification,[38] constitutes the federalist centralisation of the EU and thus is an important pillar of the constitutional dimension of the EU.[39]

Most Recent Developments and Ruptures in the Story Line

In the recent Rimšēvičs case handed down in 2019, the ECJ has potentially taken another major step in the process of European integration, advancing federalist centralisation yet again. For the first time in the history of the EU, the ECJ declared void an act of a member state, namely the decision of the Republic of Latvia to remove the Governor of the Latvian Central Bank, Ilmārs Rimšēvičs, from office.[40] Commentators have already described this judgment as a 'constitutional moment'[41] which 'should send shockwaves through the circles participating in the discourse on European constitutional law'.[42] For this 'Mephistophelian power of a court to nullify an act of public authority has always been regarded as the ultimate expression of its superior position'.[43] This is certainly true in symbolic terms. However, considering the primacy of EU law and the so-called Rechtsbereinigungspflicht (obligation to

---

37 Joined Cases C-402/05 P and C-415/05 P *Kadi v. Council and Commission* EU:C:2008:461 para. 285; Cases C-584, C-593 and C-595/10P *Commission v. Kadi* EU:C:2013:518.

38 See P. Weismann, *European Agencies and Risk Governance in EU Financial Market Law* (London, Routledge 2016).

39 See K. Lenaerts, 'Constitutionalism and the Many Faces of Federalism', *American Journal of Comparative Law* 38 (1990): 205–63; F. Mancini, 'The Making of a Constitution for Europe', *Common Market Law Review* 26 (1989): 595–614. For the argument that 'by the early 1970's all major constitutional doctrines were already in place', see Weiler, 'The Transformation of Europe', 2413, n. 22.

40 Cases C-202/18 and C-238/18 *Ilmārs Rimšēvičs and European Central Bank v. Republic of Latvia* EU:C:2019:139, para. 66.

41 D. Sarmiento, 'Crossing the Baltic Rubicon', *Verfassungsblog* (2019), https://verfassungs blog.de/crossing-the-baltic-rubicon.

42 J. Bast, 'Autonomy in Decline? A Commentary on Rimšēvičs and ECB v Latvia', *Verfassungsblog* (2019), https://verfassungsblog.de/autonomy-in-decline-a-commen tary-on-rimsevics-and-ecb-v-latvia.

43 Bast, 'Commentary on Rimšēvičs'. On the specificities of this which provide context for this decision, see J. Weinzierl, 'Der EuGH erklärt erstmalig nationales Recht für ungültig – Anmerkung zum Urteil des EuGH v. 26.2.2019, Rs. C-202/18 (Rimšēvičs)' *Europarecht* 54 (2019): 434–58.

bring their laws into conformity with EU law) of member states, this is not that different from the ECJ simply declaring that the member state had not acted in conformity with EU law. It was already settled case law that national legislators must not enact new national law conflicting with EU law, which includes the duty to adjust national law to EU law.[44] Yet, it is an important showcase for the constitutional dimension of the federalist centralisation of the EU.

Primacy in its typical form as developed by the ECJ is by now settled case law.[45] However, 'for all its uniqueness and despite the fact that most legal actors have accepted it to a large extent, primacy remains sensitive and contested. This is witnessed by the fact that the attempt to codify it in the Constitutional Treaty failed.'[46] Only Declaration No. 17 concerning primacy annexed to the Treaty of Lisbon provides an anchor for this concept in EU primary law. This declaration unambiguously states that 'The Conference recalls that, in accordance with well settled case law of the Court of Justice of the European Union, the Treaties and the law adopted by the Union on the basis of the Treaties have primacy over the law of Member States, under the conditions laid down by the said case law.'

What is more, after the sixtieth anniversary of *Van Gend & Loos* and *Costa v. E.N.E.L.* and with the help of hindsight, another driving force behind the success of European integration has been detected in the preliminary reference procedure and the ready acceptance of important players in member state legal orders which apply EU law to give it its designed effect within member state legal orders.[47] (For instance, the Austrian Constitutional Court is quite active in this regard and sent its first preliminary reference request just 4 years after Austria's accession to the EU, VfSlg 15.450/1999.) Hence, the strong position of the ECJ claiming the unconditional primacy of EU law over member state (constitutional) law depends in a way on the organs applying national law. While basically member states accept the primacy of EU law concerning non-constitutional member state law, a lack of knowledge of EU law and more trivial reasons might actually undermine the basic acceptance

---

44 See, for example, Case C-290/94 *Commission v. Greece* EU:C:1996:265, para. 2; Case 104/86 *Commission v. Italy* EU:C:1988:171, para. 12.

45 See, for example, Case C-409/06 *Winner Wetten GmbH*, para. 55 with further reference.

46 M. Claes, 'The Primacy of EU Law in European and National Law', in D. Chalmers and A. Arnull (eds.), *The Oxford Handbook of European Union Law* (Oxford, Oxford University Press, 2015), pp. 178–211, 178.

47 See in this regard M. Rasmussen, 'Revolutionizing European Law: A History of the *Van Gend en Loos* Judgment', *International Journal of Constitutional Law* 12 (2014): 136–63, 136.

of the primacy of EU law, at least to some extent.[48] Especially with regard to self-confident national constitutional courts, this adds another perspective. Indeed, various national constitutional courts have made rulings to establish 'counterlimits' of EU primacy, indicating the existence of a 'two-dimensional reality'.[49]

In this vein, the story of federalist centralisation is not over yet. The history of enforcement and supremacy conflicts between the ECJ and the member states, especially in the light of the recent rule of law and democracy crisis, but also taking into account the replies by the ECJ concerning the concept of 'constitutional identity'[50], what is 'ultra vires' and the '*Solange* fundamental rights protection', all developed by the German Constitutional Court (Bundesverfassungsgericht),[51] and analogous concepts such as the doctrine of '*controlimiti* '[52] developed by the Italian Constitutional Court, show that we are still in the midst of an ongoing process of federalist centralisation with ups and downs in its story line. Indeed, until 5 May 2020, the relationship between the ECJ and the German Constitutional Court could be described – despite all the vicissitudes and small ruptures – as a 'fruitful dialogue'.[53] Yet, this harmonious relationship has been shaken to the core by the judgment of the German Constitutional Court on the Public Sector Purchase Programme (PSPP) of the European Central Bank.[54] For the first time in the history of the EU, the German Constitutional Court declared a judgment of the ECJ *ultra vires*, stating that the ECJ had acted 'objectively arbitrarily' when 'interpreting the treaties in

48 See Claes, 'The Primacy of EU Law', pp. 187–93 for examples and further references.

49 See B. De Witte, 'Direct Effect, Primacy and the Nature of the Legal Order', in G. de Búrca and P. Craig (eds.), *The Evolution of EU Law* (Oxford, Oxford University Press, 2011), pp. 323–62, 352–6.

50 On the concept and its origin in German law, see M. Polzin, *Verfassungsidentität* (Tübingen, Mohr Siebeck, 2018). See also C. Calliess and G. Van der Schyff (eds.), *Constitutional Identity in a Europe of Multilevel Constitutionalism* (Cambridge, Cambridge University Press, 2019).

51 For a good overview, see M. Wendel, *Permeabilität im europäischen Verfassungsrecht: Verfassungsrechtliche Integrationsnormen auf Staats- und Unionsebene im Vergleich* (Tübingen, Mohr Siebeck, 2011).

52 For an analysis of the 'Taricco saga', see, for example, G. Piccirilli, 'The "Taricco Saga": The Italian Constitutional Court Continues Its European Journey', *European Constitutional Law Review* 14 (2018): 814–33.

53 In this vein, see A. Paulus, 'Horizontale und vertikale Aufgabenteilung beim Grundrechtsschutz in Europa', in T. Groh, F. Knur, C. Köster, S. Maus and T. Roeder (eds.), *Verfassungsrecht, Völkerrecht, Menschenrechte: Vom Recht im Zentrum der Internationalen Beziehungen. Festschrift für Ulrich Fastenrath zum 70. Geburtstag* (Heidelberg, C. F. Müller, 2019), pp. 79–88, 86.

54 Bundesverfassungsgericht, Judgment of the Second Senate 5 May 2020 No. 2 BvR 859/ 15 (*PSPP*).

a way which was no longer comprehensible'.[55] Despite the lengthy judgment and this qualification, it is, however, more than questionable whether the PSPP judgment of the ECJ must actually be mandatorily qualified as *ultra vires* in terms of structurally expanding the competences of the EU.[56] On this point, the critique of the PSPP judgment of the German Constitutional Court is largely justified. It has been asked whether we are on the way to the 'law of the jungle of judges'.[57] Jakab and Sonnevend conclude that it is 'more than likely that this new sort of judicial politics' introduced by the PSPP judgment, which amounts to 'flagrantly giving up on a paradigm that ensured peace between two of the most important courts in Europe. The paradigm that maintaining one's theoretical position can be combined with a practical way of living together. The paradigm that the rule of law is diminished if state agencies are exposed to contradicting legal obligations both seeking to be supreme over the competing one, and the agencies are forced to make a choice that will inevitably be illegal, one way or another', 'will equally hurt European integration and the rule of law'.[58] It seems that, by declaring the ECJ judgment *ultra vires*, the German Constitutional Court has finally proven that the *ultra vires* control by member states should not be in the hands of quite a small number of judges speaking in the name of democracy but rather in the sphere of politics. Hence, when a member state holds that an EU act is *ultra vires*, this should rather be expressed by a democratic decision of the member state because the ECJ has, judicially speaking, the last word on matters of EU competence. Before coming back to the rule of law and democracy crisis below, we will first revisit another constitutional dimension of the EU: democratisation.

Democratisation

Every step towards federalist centralisation made the need for democratic legitimacy greater, that is, federalist centralisation actually led to democratisation. This development is key to understanding how the relationship between the institutions of the EU and the legislation procedures changed

---

55 Bundesverfassungsgericht, Judgment of the Second Senate 5 May 2020 No. 2 BvR 859/15 (*PSPP*) paras. 112, 116.
56 ECJ, Case C-493/17 *Weiss et al.* EU:C:2018:1000.
57 See F. C. Mayer, 'Auf dem Weg zum Richterfaustrecht? Zum PSPP-Urteil des BVerfG' (2020), *Verfassungsblog*, https://verfassungsblog.de/auf-dem-weg-zum-richterfaustrecht.
58 A. Jakab and P. Sonnevend, 'The Bundesbank Is under a Legal Obligation to Ignore the PSPP Judgment of the Bundesverfassungsgericht' (2020) *Verfassungsblog*, https://verfassungsblog.de/the-bundesbank-is-under-a-legal-obligation-to-ignore-the-pspp-judgment-of-the-bundesverfassungsgericht. See also the critical analysis offered in the special issue 'The German Federal Constitutional Court's PSPP Judgment', *German Law Journal* 21 (2020).

over the decades. The democratisation narrative is more helpful for the explanation of these inter-institutional changes than the separation of powers narrative (which is otherwise often used in the legal literature).[59] We will pay special attention both to the so-called democratic deficit of the EU and to the recent democracy crisis of some of its member states, while necessarily, again, neglecting other important developments, such as the enlargement process integrating different national histories, including those of former dictatorships (like Greece, Spain and Portugal) as well as the central and eastern European countries, which had to adapt to the EU's market economy and democracy in very little time.[60]

The Evolution of Democratic Legitimacy in the EU

By democratisation we mean the establishment and the process of enhancing the effectiveness of political accountability of political decision-makers both in the executive (the Commission) and in the legislative (the EP and Council) branch. The debates on the lack of democratic legitimacy of the EU led to the creation of the first direct elections to the EP in 1979. In contrast to federalist centralisation, the most significant improvements of the democratic legitimacy of the EU actually came with modifications by European treaties. Also, in terms of democratisation, the Single European Act in 1986, and even more so the Maastricht Treaty in 1992 and in particular the Treaty of Lisbon in 2009, improved the status and the powers of the EP. The political accountability of the Commission, however, despite some legal control by the EP, still remains questionable. The battleground topic is the so-called '*Spitzenkandidaten*' system. In other words, the question of whether the EP should actually have the final say on the composition of the Commission.[61] The nomination of the current Commission President, Ursula von der Leyen, showcased – despite some preceding positive development – that the democratisation story is still unfinished in an important sense, especially concerning political accountability.

---

59 Yet, for the concept of an institutional balance of powers, see ECJ, Case C-9/56 *Meroni* EU:C:1958:7 and subsequent case law.

60 See, for example, G. Pridham, *Designing Democracy: EU Enlargement and Regime Change in Post-Communist Europe* (New York, NY, Palgrave Macmillan, 2005).

61 See A. Jakab, 'Why the Debate between Kumm and Armstrong Is about the Wrong Question' (2014) *Verfassungsblog*, https://verfassungsblog.de/debate-kumm-armstrong-wrong-question. See also M. Diaz Crego, 'Parliamentary Hearings of the Commissioners-Designate: A Decisive Step in the Investiture Process' (2019), www.europarl.europa.eu/EPRS/EPRS-Briefing-640131-Parliamentary-hearings-Commissioners-designate-FINAL.pdf.

A Homogeneous Demos?

A common topic in the debate on EU democracy is whether there is a European demos which could be the bearer of EU popular sovereignty.[62] The argument has two forms: (1) it can concern the factual homogeneity of the EU; and (2) it can concern the feeling of togetherness (national identity) of European citizens. Both forms have a soft ('not yet') and a radical ('there will never be a European demos') version.[63] The latter form will be dealt with in the next subsection; here we analyse only the former.

There are numerous counter-arguments against *homogeneity*. (1) According to a well-known classic argument, it is not homogeneity, but rather the opposite, *heterogeneity*, that is necessary for democracy. In Madison's faction theory,[64] the existence of different social factions guarantees that none of them will have full power and none of them will be oppressed. (2) Another argument is that heterogeneity itself need not be a problem, but might be one if the heterogeneous groups are fixed (e.g., along ethnic or religious lines).[65] In this case, elections are not elections in a meaningful sense, but function merely as population censuses. But European elections have not seemed so far to move towards this dead-end, so a fear of it would be premature. (3) A third counter-argument emphasises the point that even European nation states are no longer as homogeneous as some would like them to be. We are currently living in multicultural societies (not only in the United States or in Switzerland, but in most EU member states).[66] The requirement of homogeneity (if it goes further than the requirement to accept the rule of law and democracy) would bring the danger of an emphasis on assimilation and exclusion, or even a friend–enemy distinction within society.[67] (4) A fourth argument is based on history, stating

---

62 For an affirmative answer, see A. Verhoeven, *The European Union in Search of a Democratic and Constitutional Theory* (The Hague, Kluwer Law International, 2002), pp. 159–89. For opposition to the idea of a European demos, see J. H. H. Weiler, 'European Democracy and Its Critics: Polity and System', in J. H. H. Weiler, *The Constitution of Europe* (Cambridge, Cambridge University Press, 1999), pp. 264–85, 265.

63 See C. Closa, 'Some Foundations on the Normative Discussion on Supranational Citizenship and Democracy', in U. K. Preuß and F. Requejo (eds.), *European Citizenship, Multiculturalism and the State* (Baden-Baden, Nomos, 1998), pp. 105–124, 113.

64 J. Madison, 'Federalist No. 10: The Same Subject Continued: The Union as a Safeguard against Domestic Faction and Insurrection', *New York Daily Advertiser*, 22 November 1787, National Archives, https://iowaculture.gov/history/education/educator-resources/primary-source-sets/american-political-parties/federalist-paper.

65 C. Gusy, 'Demokratiedefizite postnationaler Gemeinschaften unter Berücksichtigung der EU', *Zeitschrift für Politik* 45 (1998): 267–81, 279; Peters, *Theorie der Verfassung Europas*, p. 712.

66 Verhoeven, *Democratic and Constitutional Theory*, p. xi.

67 Peters, *Theorie der Verfassung Europas*, p. 704.

that most of today's nation-states were not formed along ethnic lines: it was rather the other way around. First there was the political unit, and thereafter it formed the population into one cultural and linguistic unit. The traditional opposing idea originates from Johann Gottfried von Herder, Friedrich Carl von Savigny and Friedrich Meinecke among others and is based on the rather peculiar German case, where actually a common identity came into being first and political unity came later.[68] At the time of the French Revolution (1789) half of the population of France did not speak French (but spoke Italian, German, Breton, English, Occitan, Catalan, Basque, Dutch), and only 12–13 per cent spoke it correctly. At the time of Italian unification, in 1861, only 2.5 per cent(!) of the population spoke the Italian that we know today.[69] (5) A fifth argument concentrates on the logic of democracy: it is based on *individuals* (and not on collectivist units), and the popular unity will be formed first by the democratic procedure itself.[70] A classic form of this idea is to be found in Emmanuel Joseph Sieyès' *Qu'est-ce que le Tiers État?* of 1789 and remained strong in the French republican tradition.[71] So *ethnos* and *demos* are analytically different.[72]

In the light of the above arguments, it is very difficult to say that it is conceptually impossible to have a democracy on the EU level because of cultural differences. We can reason, though, that a simple Westminster-style majoritarian parliamentarism would not be the right choice for the pluralist EU, but a consensual coalition-style parliamentarism is better.[73] Hence, what remains is a generally expressed scepticism, which, however, is conceptually unfounded. The main reason for the claim that democracy at the EU level would not work in practice is mostly a somewhat dubious claim that the European peoples just would not want it, because they simply would not have the feeling of togetherness with other European peoples.

---

68 See Peters, *Theorie der Verfassung Europas*, p. 653. In public law scholarship, for an early formulation of the necessity of a pre-legal cultural unit of people for state formation, see G. Jellinek, *Die Lehre von den Staatenverbindungen* (Vienna, Hoelder, 1882), p. 263. For a contemporary formulation in the context of the EU, see E.-W. Böckenförde, *Welchen Weg geht Europa?* (Munich, Carl-Friedrich-von-Siemens-Stiftung, 1997), pp. 40–1.

69 E. J. Hobsbawm, *Nations and Nationalism since 1780: Programme, Myth, Reality* (Cambridge, Cambridge University Press, 1990), pp. 60–1. For more details, see Jakab, *European Constitutional Language*, pp. 224–41.

70 Peters, *Theorie der Verfassung Europas*, pp. 649 n. 86, 704, 707.

71 E. J. Sieyès, 'What Is the Third Estate?', in *Political Writings: Including the Debate between Sieyès and Tom Paine in 1791*, ed. and trans. M. Sonenscher (Indianapolis, IN, Hackett, 2003), pp. 92–162.

72 E. K. Francis, *Ethnos und Demos* (Berlin, Duncker & Humblot, 1965), p. 77.

73 On the difference between majoritarian and consensus government, see A. Lijphart, *Democracies* (New Haven, CT, Yale University Press 1984), especially pp. 1–36.

Political Identity

The critics of the idea of a European demos as formed by procedures can easily point out that separatist Catalan or Scottish nationalists were not impressed by the Spanish or British procedures either, and national identity in general does not necessarily flow from procedures. So the problem is not factual similarity or dissimilarity, but rather the identity.[74] And identity still primarily belongs to the nation states.[75]

It is all very true. (1) One possible counter-argument is that national identity is fading in general in the world,[76] so in time the feeling of togetherness will lose its relevance. This would, however, be a weak counter-argument. We do not have exact and convincing empirical data about fading national identities, and examples of the opposite can also be presented – especially in the light of the coronavirus crisis.[77] But, even if we had data for it, it would be very difficult to project a certain level of fading to the future as a continuous development. (2) A more convincing argument says that, even in the United States, when the famous words 'We the people' were put on paper, it was nothing more than wishful thinking, or rather political manipulation. So we could similarly attempt it in the EU.[78] We can also point out that nations are imagined or even mythical communities, so the nation is not a fixed fact; it can even change over time (as happens when an ethnic minority assimilates into the majority).[79] Peaceful methods of identity-building are possible (like having EU sport teams competing against the Americans or the Chinese winning most of the medals by far if we were to count the EU as a nation), which could be used in the future. The development of EU citizenship is very important in this regard and might become even more important.[80] We have some doubts about whether it

---

74 Grimm, 'Does Europe Need a Constitution', 297.

75 For an empirical survey proving this, see M. Deflem and F. C. Pampel, 'The Myth of Postnational Identity: Popular Support for European Unification', *Social Forces* 75 (1996): 119–43.

76 M. Sandel, *Democracy's Discontent* (Cambridge, MA, Belknap Press of Harvard University Press, 1996), p. 344.

77 For an empirical study on national in-group satisfaction versus collective narcissism during the Covid-19 pandemic, see, for example, C. M. Federico, A. Golec de Zavala and T. Baran, 'Collective Narcissism, In-Group Satisfaction, and Solidarity in the Face of COVID-19', *Social Psychological and Personality Science* 12, no. 6 (2020): 1071–81.

78 M. Zuleeg, 'What Holds a Nation Together? Cohesion and Democracy in the United States of America and in the European Union', *American Journal of Comparative Law* 45 (1997): 505–26, 526.

79 Shown for the example of France by E. Weber, *From Peasants into Frenchmen: The Modernization of Rural France, 1880–1914* (Stanford, CA, Stanford University Press, 1976).

80 See, for example, E. Guild, *The Legal Elements of European Identity: EU Citizenship and Migration Law* (The Hague, Kluwer, 2004). For the argument on EU citizenship

could work in the foreseeable future. But it is less relevant here, as our actual point would be that national identity in this strong substantive sense is not absolutely necessary. (3) What we need is only loyalty towards the system, towards the procedures of democracy (such a loyalty is possible only, of course, if the procedures work). Specifying national identity as a precondition for democracy is methodologically biased, as it reconstructs the concept of democracy in terms of the concrete sociological features of some democracies.[81] This helps to maintain the effectiveness of law (and hence the rule of law), and, with adherence to these basic constitutional values (and the connecting emotional identification), the system can survive crisis situations too.

Therefore, the existence of a unified and dominant European political identity is not necessary in order to have a functioning European democracy. There is no doubt that it would be useful, but it is not necessary. Further preconditions for the democratisation of the EU, such as the formation of a democratic mentality and interested public opinion (media coverage), have been discussed.[82]

The Direct Link between Election and Responsibility: The Effectiveness of Popular Will

Where the actual problem lies is rather in what Anne Peters calls 'the missing correlation between election and responsibility'.[83] In other words, there are elections, and also a new government (Commission) is set up, but the direct link between the two acts is missing. There seem to be only two institutional solutions to ensure the virtues of democracy (both loyalty and self-correction): one possibility would be to transform the EU into a presidential system (similar to the United States), the other would be to parliamentarise it.[84] The latter seems to be a more viable option, as the current system is much nearer to the parliamentary system, so only minor institutional changes would be necessary in order to achieve it.[85]

---

without duties, see D. Kochenov, 'EU Citizenship without Duties', *European Law Journal* 20 (2014): 482–98; C. Rumford, 'European Civil Society or Transnational Social Space? Conceptions of Society in Discourses of EU Citizenship, Governance and the Democratic Deficit: An Emerging Agenda', *European Journal of Social Theory* 6 (2003): 25–43.

81 See J. Habermas, 'Remarks on Dieter Grimm's "Does Europe Need a Constitution?"', *European Law Journal* 1 (1995): 303–7.

82 See Jakab, *European Constitutional Language*, pp. 192–4.

83 Peters, *Theorie der Verfassung Europas*, p. 627.

84 The advantages of various institutional sub- and in-between types are considered by W. van Gerven, *The European Union: A Polity of States and Peoples* (Oxford and Portland, OR, Hart, 2005), pp. 318–32.

85 Ibid., pp. 344–5.

An important step to solve the problem would thus be to make the EP alone responsible for the election of the Commission, whereas the European Council could have a ceremonial role similar to that of monarchs or presidents in parliamentary systems.[86] The idea goes back almost to the beginning of the EEC, quoting Walter Hallstein, the first president of the Commission, on this issue: '[a]s a parliamentary democracy, the Community is still imperfect [. . .] because the European Parliament has not yet acquired its full role'.[87] Jean Monnet had a different (functionalist) view on the issue.[88]

The State of the Art of European Democracy

The above-mentioned solution is a nice plan, but what actually should be done right now? First of all, future Members of the EP have to be convinced that this is a viable way. Strong, willing and able politicians who will have enough ambition to make this change are needed in the EP. As politicians are mostly not lacking in ambition, we are optimistic that sooner or later this will happen, and that this tendency will regain its impetus. Whereas in 2014 the *Spitzenkandidat* was indeed the later President Juncker, in 2019 intergovern-mental backdoor politics trumped the connection between the electoral outcome and the Commission. The right moment when the political colour of the EP and that of the Council will be different in order for this conflict to play out will nevertheless arrive sooner or later and the 2019 setback might well be overcome.

In the words of John Markoff, 'One might anticipate a recapitulation of Europe's nineteenth-century struggles over democratisation on a larger scale, in which the power of the EP in Strasbourg in relation to the European bureaucracy becomes a central point of contention.'[89] It is happening here and now, and the outcome is likely to be the same as in the nineteenth century. The sooner, the better.

As (legal) scholars, we can contribute to this in one way: by using 'democracy' and 'democratic' in the EU context in a sense which helps the realisation

---

86 For more details, see Jakab, *European Constitutional Language*. For a similar approach, see F. E. Bignami, 'The Democratic Deficit in European Community Rulemaking: A Call for Notice and Comment in Comitology', *Harvard International Law Journal* 40 (1999): 415–515, 463; van Gerven, *The European Union*, pp. 350.

87 W. Hallstein, *Europe in the Making* (London, Allen & Unwin, 1972), pp. 40–1.

88 See K. Featherstone, 'Jean Monnet and the Democratic Deficit in the European Union', *Journal of Common Market Studies* 32 (1994): 149–70.

89 J. Markoff, *Waves of Democracy: Social Movements and Political Change* (London, Pine Forge, 1996), p. 135.

of the purpose of this concept, that is, which helps the improvement of the self-correction capacity and the induction of loyalty. The EU's political power is a fact, and if we want to run the EU in the most useful way for its citizens, then accountability has to be improved. The most viable means to this end seems to be the parliamentarisation of the EU. Future story lines which inhibit this should thus be rejected; stories which help this should be embraced.

Strengthening the Rule of Law

The development of the rule of law includes not just questions of the formal rule of law such as judicial independence, enforceability, clarity of legal norms, stability and foreseeability, and certain procedural requirements, but in a wide (thick or substantive) sense also the protection of human rights. Thus, the inclusion of the Charter of Fundamental Rights (CFR) in the rank of EU primary law, the origins of which can be traced back to yet another important judgment of the ECJ in the Stauder case, acknowledging in 1969, for the first time in the EU's history, that fundamental rights formed part of the unwritten general principles of EU law,[90] is an important climax of this story. By the rule of law, we thus mean a list of requirements, aimed at inhibiting the arbitrary use of public authority. The constitutional dimension of the history of the EU is constituted also, and increasingly so since the recent rule of law crisis, by the question of the rule of law both within the EU and as a tool to correct shortcomings at the member state level. Hence, the constitutional dimension of the EU rule of law is not merely that at the (horizontal) level of the EU the separation of powers is given, but also that, on a vertical level, the EU's member states need to justify to the EU that their rule of law remains intact. Precisely this element is an essential and still heavily contested aspect of the constitutional dimension of the EU.

The Recent Decline of the Rule of Law in EU Member States

In the past few years, the rule of law has been declining in many countries of the world,[91] including several member states of the EU.[92] The fear that more stable democracies could take such a turn is pervasive in public debate and

90 ECJ, Case 29/69 *Stauder* EU:C:1969:57.
91 M. A. Graber, S. Levinson and M. Tushnet (eds.), *Constitutional Democracy in Crisis?* (Oxford, Oxford University Press, 2018).
92 A. Jakab and D. Kochenov (eds.), *The Enforcement of EU Law and Values: Ensuring Member States' Compliance* (Oxford, Oxford University Press, 2017); A. von Bogdandy and P. Sonnevend (eds.), *Constitutional Crisis in the European Constitutional Area: Theory, Law and Politics in Hungary and Romania* (Oxford, Hart; Munich, C. H. Beck; Baden-Baden, Nomos, 2015); M. Brusis, 'Illiberale Drift und Proliferation – BTI-Regionalbericht

scholarly discourse.[93] The study of legal rules, nevertheless, yields only partial insight into the state of the rule of law. In particular, in the case of erosion (i.e., slow, step-by-step degradation) of the rule of law, the main problem is exactly the slow demise of the normativity of constitutional law, that is, the growing chasm between the constitution and constitutional reality.[94] Amendments to formal legal acts have little to say about what and how things will change. If we do not want to remain blind to erosion, besides considering the formal rules, we must also examine the de facto conduct of addressees of these rules and the narrative accompanying it (the latter includes the social mentality, or the political rhetoric regarding constitutional institutions).[95] Fine-tuned constitutional law doctrine is always capable of identifying a de facto breach of the general requirements of the rule of law by the addressees of constitutional rules. However, the question regarding the gravity of such breaches cannot be captured with the standard tools of legal doctrine alone. In order to fully grasp reality, one should also resort to rule of law indices.[96]

Especially recent events in Hungary, Poland and Romania proved that it is far from obvious that, once a state becomes a member of the EU, it will follow the principles of the rule of law without any external enforcement mechanism.[97] This section is, however, not about those countries, but about the constitutional dimension of the rule of law.[98] In this regard, a general

Ostmittel- und Südosteuropa', Bertelsmann Stiftung (2018), https://mbrusis.eu/wp-content/uploads/2018/04/BTI18_OMESOE.pdf.

93 See, for example, E. Luce, *The Retreat of Western Liberalism* (Boston, MA, Little, Brown, 2017).

94 A. Jakab, 'What Can Constitutional Law Do against the Erosion of Democracy and the Rule of Law? On the Interconnectedness of the Protection of Democracy and the Rule of Law', *Constitutional Studies* 6 (2020): 5–34; K. Albrecht, L. Kirchmair and V. Schwarzer, 'Introduction', in K. Albrecht, L. Kirchmair and V. Schwarzer (eds.), *Die Krise des demokratischen Rechtsstaats im 21. Jahrhundert* (Stuttgart, Franz Steiner, 2020) pp. 11–20.

95 For such an analysis, see, for example, A. Jakab, 'What Is Wrong with the Hungarian Legal System and How to Fix It', Max Planck Institute for Comparative Public Law & International Law (2018), https://ssrn.com/abstract=3213378, pp. 2ff.

96 For a showcase of combining empirical research based on indices with doctrinal rule of law questions, see T. Ginsburg and M. Versteeg, 'Constitutional Correlates of the Rule of Law', in M. Adams, A. Meuwese and E. Hirsch Ballin (eds.), *Constitutionalism and the Rule of Law Bridging Idealism and Realism* (Cambridge, Cambridge University Press, 2017), pp. 506–25.

97 For more details, see von Bogdandy and Sonnevend, *Constitutional Crisis in the EU*, pp. 5–190.

98 However, on the point that democracy at EU level is also being compromised by EU elections in authoritarian member states, see A. Jakab, 'How to Defend the Integrity of the EP Elections against Authoritarian Member States', *Verfassungsblog* (2019), https://verfassungsblog.de/how-to-defend-the-integrity-of-the-ep-elections-against-authoritarian-member-states.

legal problem which is convincingly put forward by Jan-Werner Müller is noteworthy. He basically states that the Copenhagen criteria cannot efficiently be enforced against member states (and their enforcement was deficient even against candidate countries).[99] Requirements of the thick concept of the rule of law can be systematically breached, and the EU is unable to handle the situation efficiently. If, however, the EU does not want to lose its credibility and we want to conceptualise the legal order of the EU as a constitutional order, it has a duty to defend the rule of law (cf. Article 2 TEU) to the greatest possible extent, at least within Europe, and especially within the EU.[100] This tension between the enforcement impotence of the EU, on the one hand, and the moral and (implied) legal duty to enhance the rule of law within its territory, on the other hand, lies at the heart of this section.

The Value of the Rule of Law

Every society is held together by certain values, which are at least rhetorically unquestionable. For example, in Europe in the Middle Ages, it was Christianity, and heretics had to face serious consequences as they breached religious taboos. Since the end of the Second World War, in western Europe, and since the end of communism in the whole of Europe, the integrating values have been the secular values of constitutionalism. The twentieth century in Europe can also be viewed as being a period of experimentation and failure with what were considered at the time new secular taboo systems, such as nationalism or socialism. Nowadays, democracy and the protection of fundamental rights (i.e., the purposes of the Council of Europe) seem to be the only credible options when it comes to organising society in Europe. Of course, there are never-ending debates about what these concepts actually mean.[101] But at the same time, there is a final institutionalised arbiter in Europe for these questions: the European Court of Human Rights (ECHR). Or, to put it differently: the Vatican is today in Strasbourg. There were and

---

99 See J.-W. Müller, 'Should the EU Protect Democracy and the Rule of Law inside Member States?', *European Law Journal* 21 (2015): 141–60; D. Kochenov, *EU Enlargement of the Failure of Conditionality* (Alphen aan den Rijn, Kluwer, 2008).

100 See C. Hillion, 'Overseeing the Rule of Law in the EU. Legal Mandate and Means', in C. Closa and D. Kochenov (eds.), *Reinforcing Rule of Law Oversight in the European Union* (Cambridge, Cambridge University Press, 2016), pp. 59–81.

101 See W. B. Gallie, 'Essentially Contested Concepts', *Proceedings of the Aristotelian Society* 56 (1956): 167–98. Concerning Article 2 TFEU, see L. Kirchmair, 'Demokratische Legitimität, die EU-Rechtsstaatlichkeitskrise und Vorüberlegungen zu einer transnationalen Gewaltengliederung', *Zeitschrift für praktische Philosophie* 6 (2019): 171–212.

there will be heretical attempts to question these values, but, if we want to believe that European integration has a chance, then we have to stop all such attempts before it becomes too late. If it is allowed to happen in one EU member state, then it will also be possible in another member state and, before you know it, the European edifice built on these values will fall apart surprisingly quickly. Through the use of creative reinterpretation, the European constitution in its current form already presents opportunities to stop dangerous tendencies. The ECJ can use the moral authority of the ECHR in order to enforce the values of European integration, and, via the preliminary procedure, it can make all member state courts into local agents which profess and enforce these values.

Enforcing the Rule of Law in EU Member States

Obviously it is not sufficient for a court to simply refer to values when it makes a decision. A good lawyer always thinks in two layers: on the one hand, they try to provide a doctrinal justification for the decision, but, on the other hand, they have to make a decision which is acceptable from a social and/or moral point of view.[102]

As we have seen, the history of the ECJ is full of activist moves where decisions were made which – to say the least – were not obvious from the text of the treaties.[103] How was the Court able to get away with this? What common features can be derived from these successful instances of competence expansions?

We note six such common features. (1) The arguments used in these cases were normally teleological arguments relying either on the main purpose of the European integration or on the purpose of specific rules/institutions. This is exactly the situation when expansively interpreting Article 51(1) CFR, delineating the scope of application of the CFR, in the light of the above: the purpose is to protect fundamental rights as a fundamental value according to Article 2 TEU.[104] (2) Institutionally, it was generally the Commission which first adopted a particular stance,

---

102 On P. Magnaud, *le bon juge*, see A. Jakab, 'What Makes a Good Lawyer? Was Magnaud Indeed Such a Good Judge?', *Zeitschrift für öffentliches Recht* 62 (2007): 275–87.

103 See, for example, K. Alter, *Establishing the Supremacy of European Law: The Making of an International Rule of Law in Europe* (Oxford, Oxford University Press, 2001).

104 For such a proposal, see A. Jakab, 'Application of the EU CFR by National Courts in Purley Domestic Cases', in Jakab and Kochenov (eds.), *The Enforcement of EU Law and Values*, pp. 252–62; A. Jakab and L. Kirchmair, 'Two Ways of Completing the European Fundamental Rights Union: Amendment to vs. Reinterpretation of Article 51 of the EU Charter of Fundamental Rights', *Cambridge Yearbook of European Legal Studies* 24 (2022): 239–61.

which was then followed by the ECJ.[105] In our case, it means an explicitly stated aim of the Commission to abolish the limits of Article 51(1) CFR. This has already actually happened: Viviane Reding, then the commissioner responsible for justice, fundamental rights and citizenship, explicitly proposed this in her Tallinn speech, but she wanted to achieve this via a formal treaty amendment.[106] (3) The third factor which makes expansions more likely is if political law-making seems to be inoperative.[107] This is also an obvious tick in the box: we see only the pretext of real action (e.g., in the form of the so-called rule of law mechanism)[108] – the necessary majority by the member states is obviously missing. (4) A usual method for expanding judicial competences is to establish the competence but not to use it, or to use it in a way which does not lead to conflict with any government. This was famously done in *Marbury v. Madison*, but also in *Costa v. E.N.E.L.*, in which 'the ECJ declared the supremacy of EC law' but 'found that the Italian law [...] did not violate EC law'.[109] The first step of strengthening the EU rule of law should also probably be a *Costa v. ENEL* type of decision establishing the full applicability of the Charter without establishing an actual violation of it. (5) As a second step – after the establishment of the competence in a case without the establishment of a violation – a violation also has to be established. For this second case, the more obvious a violation of fundamental rights is and the more isolated the 'convicted' member state, the more likely it is that the judgment establishing the violation will be accepted by member states.[110] There are similarities between certain interpretations of Article 51 CFR and the US constitutional law 'doctrine of incorporation'.[111] It is very probable that ECJ will have to deal with

---

105 E. Stein, 'Lawyers, Judges, and the Making of a Transnational Constitution'.

106 Viviane Reding, 'Observations on the EU Charter of Fundamental Rights and the future of the European Union', XXV Congress of FIDE (Fédération Internationale pour le Droit Européen) (2012), https://ec.europa.eu/commission/presscorner/det ail/en/SPEECH_12_403.

107 Weiler, 'Transformation of Europe'.

108 European Commission, 'A New EU Framework to Strengthen the Rule of Law' (2014), https://eur-lex.europa.eu/legal-content/EN/ALL/?uri=celex% 3A52014DC0158.

109 K. Alter, 'Who Are the "Masters of the Treaties"? European Governments and the European Court of Justice', *International Organization* 52 (1998): 121–47, 131.

110 See X. Groussot, L. Pech and G. T. Petursson, 'The Scope of Application of Fundamental Rights on Member States' Action: In Search of Certainty in EU Adjudication' (2011), www.readcube.com/articles/10.2139/ssrn.1936473.

111 See M. Cartabia, 'Article 51 – Field of Application', in W. B. T. Mock and G. Demuro (eds.), *Human Rights in Europe: Commentary on the Charter of Fundamental Rights of the European Union* (Durham, NC, Carolina Academic Press, 2010), pp. 315–21, 318–19.

such cases in the near future. (6) Parallel to (4) and (5), in order to avoid becoming unnecessarily involved in domestic politics concerning questions which are far from obvious, the ECJ would also need to develop a margin of appreciation doctrine, similar to that of the ECHR.[112] This would result in a situation where the ECJ would be able to intervene only in those cases where the common minimum level of fundamental rights protection was being violated. Concerning its deferential function, it would be similar to the concept of 'systemic deficiency',[113] but the decision about this would remain with a judicial and not with a political body (i.e., the Commission).

To sum up, the cards for playing a more activist role are in the hands of the ECJ.[114] European institutions do not seem to want to stop this move by the ECJ, and member states have no means to do so (except for quite unlikely treaty amendments in this regard). Member state coalitions against ECJ judgments and warnings about a judicial Armageddon are highly unrealistic. If the European integration process fails, then it will not be because of stronger protection of fundamental rights. It will either be for purely economic reasons or it will be because of anti-constitutionalist and illiberal attempts within some of the member states.

With judicial statesmanship, patience in waiting for the right cases and a conscious strategy, the decisive move towards a community of fundamental rights can be achieved in the very near future. For this purpose, the ECJ has to reassert its responsibility in both enhancing European integration and promoting the values of the EU. The ECJ has not been inactive.[115] If we seek

---

112 On the margin of appreciation doctrine as a special type of deference doctrine, see A. Legg, *The Margin of Appreciation in International Human Rights Law* (Oxford, Oxford University Press, 2012), pp. 17–66.

113 See A. von Bogdandy, C. Antpöhler and M. Ioannidis, 'Protecting EU Values: Reverse Solange and the Rule of Law Framework', in A. Jakab and D. Kochenov (eds.), *The Enforcement of EU Law and Values*, pp. 217–51.

114 M. Höreth, 'Warum der EuGH nicht gestoppt werden sollte – und auch kaum gestoppt werden kann', in U. Haltern and A. Bergmann (eds.), *Der EuGH in der Kritik* (Tübingen, Mohr Siebeck, 2012), pp. 73–112. On the practical impossibility of the revision of ECJ rulings by member states, see M. Höreth, 'The Least Dangerous Branch?,' in M. Dawson, B. De Witte and E. Muir (eds.), *Judicial Activism at the European Court of Justice* (Cheltenham, Edward Elgar, 2013), pp. 32–55, especially 39–40.

115 See, for instance, Case C-619/18 *Commission v. Poland* EU:C:2019:531; C-192/18 *Commission v. Poland* EU:C:2019:924 on effective judicial protection by independent courts as a matter of the rule of law. See also Case C-64/16 *Associação Sindical dos Juízes Portugueses v. Tribunal de Contas* EU:C:2018:117; Case C-216/18 PPU *LM Minister of Justice and Equality* EU:C:2018:586; Case C-619/18 R *Commission v. Poland* EU: C:2018:852; Case C-619/18 *Commission v. Poland* EU:C:2019:531. See also A. von

a happy end of this story line and an adequate response to the current historical challenge of dismantling the rule of law in EU member states, then this seems to be the only viable route and therefore the necessary one.

Concluding Remarks

We recounted the constitutional dimension of the history of the EU as three intertwined stories, which are, however, not without ruptures. While the federalist centralisation is probably the most complete story (despite some reservations), democratisation and even more so the development of a vertical rule of law are stories involving many struggles and even minor setbacks. The development from a confederal (international) organisation into a state-like, centralised (federal) organisation particularly concerns the development of the relationship between EU law and member state law, and the division of competences between the EU and its member states. Both have been clarified especially by the ECJ in the process of European integration, particularly when installing the doctrines of direct applicability and supremacy. In this vein, the ECJ proved to be the most important institutional driving force of European constitutionalism – despite some setbacks displayed through a history of enforcement and supremacy conflicts with constitutional courts of member states.

Every step towards federalist centralisation made the need for democratic legitimacy stronger, that is, federalist centralisation actually led to democratisation. This development is key to understanding how the relationship between the institutions of the EU and the legislation procedures changed over the decades. Democratisation concerns the establishment and the process of enhancing the effectiveness of political accountability of political decision-makers both in the executive (the Commission) and in the legislative (the EP and Council) branches and some form of political identity. This dimension of the EU constitution has also seen considerable improvement during the process of European integration. Important treaty revisions strengthening the EP and bringing about increasing parliamentarisation of the EU are considerable developments. Yet, this story is still not

Bogdandy and L. Spieker, 'Countering the Judicial Silencing of Critics: Article 2 TEU Values, Reverse Solange, and the Responsibilities of National Judges', *European Constitutional Law Review* 15 (2019): 391–426, 412 for the qualification, in particular, of the judgment *Associação Sindical dos Juízes Portugueses* as 'a veritable stepping stone towards a "Union of values" as important as *van Gend en Loos* and *Costa/ENEL*'.

over. Important developments such as the nomination of the Commission by the EP (instead of the Council) are still in the midst of their evolution. Authoritarian politics in some EU member states are a particular challenge, as undemocratic EU member states might compromise also the elections to the EP (if EU member states which do not meet democratic standards organise these elections).

The rule of law, by which we mean a list of requirements aimed at inhibiting the arbitrary use of public authority, is the most recent complementation of the constitutional dimension of the EU. Again, spearheaded by the ECJ, this includes not just questions of the formal rule of law such as judicial independence, enforceability, clarity of legal norms, stability and foreseeability, and certain procedural requirements, but also, in a wide (thick or substantive) sense, the protection of human rights within the EU and its member states. This story, however, has experienced disruptions and is the most unfinished of the three inter- twined stories we identified as constituting the constitutional dimension of the history of the EU.

The evolution of the constitutional dimension of the EU was (and will be) highly dependent on the ECJ, which has contributed to the EU consti- tution in a step-by-step manner. Thus, neither Maastricht nor other import- ant instances of constitutional codifications during the process of European integration seem to have been 'constitutional moments' in the sense of turning points in EU constitutional history. Instead, continuous develop- ment and adaptation of the judicial component is decisive for constitutional developments (given the existence of a large number of players with a veto in treaty modification procedures). Treaty modifications (or a corresponding silence by new treaties with regard to formerly proactive case law) were often just a codification of (or tacit consent to) previous judicial case law (or secondary law). The dilemmas of deepening versus widening have become particularly visible through the recent rule of law and democracy crisis in some of the new central and eastern European member states. On the one hand, this crisis inhibits deeper cooperation. On the other hand, exactly the challenge that it poses also sheds light on the need to develop new areas of cooperation and strengthen existing ones (such as anti-corruption measures, as well as democracy and the rule of law). The outcome of this challenge is as yet uncertain. However, what we are witnessing already in recent case law of the ECJ, precisely addressing this crisis, might be another major leap in the constitutional dimension of the EU towards a more centralised polity along the lines of the constitutional principles of liberal democracies.

Recommended Reading

Jakab, A. *European Constitutional Language* (Cambridge, Cambridge University Press, 2016).
Schütze, R. *European Constitutional Law*, 2nd ed. (Cambridge, Cambridge University Press, 2015).
von Bogdandy, A. and J. Bast. *Principles of European Constitutional Law* (Oxford, Hart, 2011).

15

EU Enlargement: Origins and Practice

MARC MARESCEAU

Introduction

The treaties establishing the European Coal and Steel Community (ECSC), the European Economic Community (EEC) and the European Atomic Energy Community (Euratom) contained, from their very beginning, the possibility of enlarging the initial number of six member states. Article 98 ECSC provided that '[a]ny European State may request to accede to the present Treaty' and laid down the enlargement procedure. When the EEC and Euratom Treaties were concluded in 1958, no ECSC enlargements had occurred. The main elements of the enlargement procedure of Article 98 ECSC would not only remain the principal features of the accession provision in the EEC Treaty (Article 237) and Euratom Treaty (Article 205), but also continue to be the key references in the unique accession provision in later versions of the Treaty on European Union (TEU). The current Article 49 TEU of the Lisbon Treaty reads as follows:

> Any European State which respects the values referred to in Article 2 and is committed to promoting them may apply to become a member of the Union. The European Parliament and national Parliaments shall be notified of this application. The applicant State shall address its application to the Council, which shall act unanimously after consulting the Commission and after receiving the consent of the European Parliament, which shall act by a majority of its component members. The conditions of eligibility agreed upon by the European Council shall be taken into account.
>
> The conditions of admission and the adjustments to the Treaties on which the Union is founded, which such admission entails, shall be the subject of an agreement between the Member States and the applicant State. This agreement shall be submitted for ratification by all the contracting States in accordance with their respective constitutional requirements.

To date seven enlargements have taken place in the European Community (EC)/European Union (EU): (1) with the United Kingdom (UK), Ireland and Denmark in 1973; (2) with Greece in 1981; (3) with Spain and Portugal in 1986; (4) with Austria, Sweden and Finland in 1994, (5) with Poland, Hungary, the Czech Republic, Slovakia, Estonia, Latvia, Lithuania, Slovenia, the Republic of Cyprus and Malta in 2004; (6) with Bulgaria and Romania in 2007; and (7) with Croatia in 2013.

Since Article 49 TEU and its predecessors provide the only available legal framework for EU accession, all enlargements have necessarily gone through this provision. This chapter is an analytical and synthetic overview of the history, context and practice of that provision. It examines in particular the main political, institutional and legal steps which have taken place in the history of the EU's enlargement and aims to provide insight into the complex enlargement labyrinth. It first explores the conditionality requirements for EU membership for candidate states and then goes into the various stages of the accession process, from application for membership to entry into force of the accession treaty.

A contribution on EU enlargement cannot ignore the fact that the UK left the EU on 1 February 2020. Brexit, the counterpart of EU accession, is covered in a separate contribution in this volume.[1] It should also be mentioned that, before Brexit took place, an exit from the EC had already occurred when Greenland left. In contrast to the Faroe Islands, which were never part of the EU, Greenland, which was part of Denmark when Denmark joined, also became part of the EC on 1 January 1973. In 1979, Greenland was granted 'home rule', and in 1982 a proposal for withdrawal of Greenland from the EC obtained 52 per cent of the votes in a referendum. This led in 1984 to a treaty between the EC member states and Greenland to the effect that application of the EC Treaties to Greenland would cease, while new arrangements governing relations between the contracting parties were being introduced.[2]

Conditionality Requirements for Candidate States

Article 49 TEU formulates a double conditionality requirement for candidate states. The applicant must be a 'European State' and be prepared to respect and promote the values on which the EU is founded. These conditions are

---

1 See Chapter 6 by N. Piers Ludlow in this volume.
2 See 'Treaty Amending, with Regard to Greenland, the Treaties Establishing the European Communities and Protocol on Special Arrangements for Greenland', *Official Journal of the European Union* (1985): L 29/1.

examined on the basis of the existing practice.[3] In the early 1990s, the EU also embarked on an ambitious enlargement policy for the countries of central and eastern Europe (CEECs), known as 'pre-accession strategy'. This new approach had a tremendous impact on EU policy-making and led to the 'big bang' enlargement of 2004 and the subsequent enlargements of 2007 and 2013. The main ingredients of this enlargement strategy are briefly examined here.

'Any European State' May Apply for EU Membership

Article 49 TEU does not provide a third country with a legal right to join the EU. It establishes a procedure for a state to apply for EU membership, nothing more and nothing less. If a candidate state, in the EU's view, fully respects the conditions laid down in that provision, it 'may apply to become a member of the Union', but there is no guarantee that the applicant will be accepted as a new member state. The expression '[a]ny European State', used in all versions of the provision on accession since the ECSC Treaty, has never been reformulated or worked out in the basic treaties themselves, and the EC/EU institutions have not really tried to elucidate its wording.

However, one notable exception must be mentioned. At the 1991 Maastricht European Council, the Commission had been asked to prepare an in-depth reflection on possible future EU enlargement. In its report, published in 1992, surprisingly and for the first time, the Commission explicitly addressed the issue of 'the limits of Europe' and noted that the term 'European' used in the treaty combined 'geographical, historical and cultural elements which all contribute to the European identity'. In the Commission's view, '[t]he shared experience of proximity, ideas, values, and historical interaction cannot be condensed into a simple formula, and is subject to review by each succeeding generation'. Consequently, the conclusion was that it was 'neither possible nor opportune to establish now the frontiers of the European Union whose contours will be shaped over many years to come',[4] and no further attempt was made to define in a more precise way the concept of a 'European State'. This careful wording of 'the limits of Europe' might have been influenced by the then pending application for EU accession by the Republic of Cyprus, an island in the eastern Mediterranean Sea and

---

3 For an introduction to this practice, see M. Maresceau, 'E comme élargissement', in *Abécédaire de droit de l'Union européenne: En l'honneur de Catherine Flaesch-Mougin* (Rennes, Presses universitaires de Rennes, 2017), pp. 173–86.
4 'Europe and the Challenge of Enlargement', *Bulletin of the European Communities*, Suppl. 3/92 (1992): 11.

geographically part of the Middle East, for which the Commission was preparing an opinion (see below).

The question regarding the meaning and scope of the 'European State' condition has hardly ever been an issue in the EC/EU's long enlargement practice. In most past enlargements, the position of all or virtually all applicant states did not raise doubts about their 'European character'. That said, the 'European State' conditionality deserves special attention with regard to the application for EC/EU membership of Morocco, Turkey and Cyprus.

The Application of Morocco

For the 1984 Fontainebleau Summit, President Mitterrand invited King Hassan II as a special guest, and the latter used this occasion to send the French President a letter informing him of Morocco's intention to apply for membership of the EC. It was afterwards formalised in an official application submitted on 8 July 1987.[5] The rapid response of the President of the Council to this application, on 1 October 1987, was very evasive.[6] While Morocco was recognised as a special partner of the Community,[7] the bilateral agreements which were being negotiated 'devraient assurer la poursuite d'une coopération renforcée et plus étendue, tenant compte de la spécificité de nos relations et de nos intérêts communs' ('should ensure the pursuit of a strengthened and more extended cooperation, taking account of the specificity of our relations and of our common interests').[8] In other words, even if the president's response did not explicitly state that Morocco did not satisfy the 'European State' condition of (what was then) Article 237 EEC Treaty, the Community was not prepared to place the ongoing negotiations in a context of possible future accession of Morocco to the Community. The Council had already decided not to submit the Moroccan application to the Commission for an opinion, which would have been the essential first step in the accession procedure (see below). In practical terms, this meant that, for Morocco, the accession procedure in the EEC Treaty was discontinued

---

5 See *Bulletin of the European Communities* (1987): 7–8, point 2.2.35.
6 For a comprehensive overview of the historical background of the Moroccan application, see V. Ipek, *North Africa, Colonialism and the EU* (Cham, Pivot, 2020), pp. 53–86, who also provides the texts of the Moroccan application and the answer of the President of the Council, see p. 79, note 9 and p. 83, note 33.
7 See *Bulletin of the European Communities* (1987): 9, point 2.2.19.
8 See also 'XXIst General Report on the Activities of the European Communities 1987' (1988), http://aei.pitt.edu/31714, p. 306, no. 794.

before it even properly started. This also explains why the Commission did not publish a formal opinion on Morocco's application.

The Application of Turkey

Another application for accession where the question of the 'Europeanness' of the candidate state could have been a major issue is that of Turkey. However, the 1987 Turkish application for accession received a treatment different from that of Morocco. Both countries are neighbours of the EU, and might present similarities, but there are also many differences. Morocco, despite being very close to Spain, is geographically clearly separated from the European continent. Turkey, with about 95 per cent of its territory located in Asia and with its capital, Ankara, in Asian central Turkey, has its most important city, Istanbul, largely in Europe. In 1987, Turkey formally applied for accession to the Community. The Council, in accordance with the accession provision in the EEC Treaty and in contrast to what had happened with Morocco's application, asked the Commission for an opinion. The Commission delivered in 1989 a negative opinion on the Turkish application, but not for reasons relating to the 'European State' conditionality. While the Commission considered that, for political and economic reasons, the Community could not open accession negotiations with Turkey, it emphasised that this negative response was not 'casting doubt' on Turkey's 'eligibility for membership of the Community'. Consequently, the Commission seemed to be of the opinion, even though this was not expressed in so many words, that Turkey did satisfy the 'European State' conditionality (see below).

In order to understand why Turkey could fall within the concept of a 'European State', one must go back to the history of EU–Turkey relations. In 1963, the EEC signed an association agreement with Turkey. This agreement was mixed, which means that, on the side of the Community, it was signed by the EEC and by the member states, and it contained in its preamble and in Article 28 a vague but explicit reference to possible future accession of Turkey to the EC. In the preamble, the contracting parties recognised 'that the support by the European Economic Community to the efforts of the Turkish people to improve their standard of living *will facilitate the accession of Turkey to the Community at a later date*' (emphasis added), while Article 28 held that '[a]s soon as the operation of this Agreement has advanced far enough to justify envisaging full acceptance by Turkey of the obligations arising out of the Treaty establishing the Community, the Contracting parties *shall examine the possibility of accession of Turkey to the Community*' (emphasis added). This wording, copied word for word from the association agreement concluded with Greece 2 years earlier,[9] could only be understood as meaning that Turkey, as a third state, was at least 'eligible' for EEC membership. The Greek request for such an agreement had been launched on 8 June 1959, that of Turkey on 31 July 1959. However, a coup d'état in Turkey on 27 May 1960 against the Menderes government, which in 1961 had led to the execution of the Turkish prime minister and two other ministers of his cabinet, delayed but did not prevent the signature of the association agreement with Turkey. The impact of the EEC's association with Greece had an accelerating effect on the conclusion of the Ankara Agreement. Certainly, neither in the Athens nor in the Ankara Agreement had the explicit reference to accession to be understood that future accession was guaranteed, but what it did indicate was that for Turkey, at least implicitly, the 'European State' condition of Article 237 EEC Treaty was considered by the EEC and its member states to have been satisfied. Another interpretation, implying that Turkey did not fall within the 'European State' concept, would have meant that the 1963 Agreement, with its specific wording, could simply never have been signed. In other words, with the signature of the 1963 Agreement, and by explicitly using the wording 'accession' twice in that agreement, the EEC and its member states had removed the strongest possible obstacle to a later Turkish application for accession.

It is not clear whether, at the moment of signing the agreement with Turkey, the EEC and its member states fully realised the important political and legal implications of their signature. Perhaps the references to accession had a merely symbolic meaning for the EEC and its member states. In this pioneering phase of EEC treaty-making practice, where the agreement with Turkey, after that with Greece, was the second bilateral agreement ever concluded by the EEC with a third state. such a reference might have appeared unreal and therefore have been easier to make than if there had been a clear prospect of accession. But the eventuality of a later accession could also have been taken seriously and regarded as something not to be ruled out either. At the ceremony for the signing of the Ankara Agreement, Walter Hallstein, then President of the Commission, strongly emphasised that 'Die Türkei gehört zu Europa' ('Turkey belongs to Europe'), an expression which was even repeated three times in his famous speech. He also

---

9 See the preamble and Article 72 in the 1961 Athens Association Agreement, https://eur-lex.europa.eu/legal-content/EN/TXT/PDF/?uri=CELEX:31963D0106&from=EN.

explicitly recalled the memory and personality of Atatürk, who had given Turkey a modern and European character.[10]

There is no doubt that, at the moment of signing the Ankara Agreement, with an ideologically divided European continent, there was a strong incentive to enhance the relationship between Turkey and the West. In this context it is also useful to recall that Turkey and Greece had already joined the North Atlantic Treaty Organization (NATO) in 1952, and the conclusion of an association agreement between the EEC and Turkey was seen as a powerful signal and even proof of Turkey's solid integration with the West. All this helped to pave the way for the inclusion of an explicit reference to the possible accession of Turkey in the association agreement itself. While insisting on solid German support for a rapid association with Turkey, some commentators note that there was serious hesitation and even reluctance regarding such an agreement, particularly in France and Italy. The initial lack of support from those two member states appeared to be primarily economically motivated, since the envisaged customs union in the association agreement could adversely affect their economic interests. In addition, in France, in contrast to the perception in West Germany and the United States, the rapprochement with Turkey was not perceived as an important strategic necessity for the West.[11] In this context, Charles Rutten, a prominent Dutch diplomat closely involved in the negotiations for the Ankara Agreement, provides an interesting explanation. He recalls in his memoirs that, in the negotiations for the association agreement, the Turkish negotiators were, in accordance with the ideas of Atatürk, very 'Westernised'. Religious and cultural differences in these negotiations, in particular between Islam and Western culture, were, according to Rutten, hardly or even not at all touched upon. He observes that today this can perhaps be seen as 'kortzichtig' ('short-sighted'), but, in the early 1960s, the broader geopolitical context 'overshadowed' all other aspects of the bilateral relationship. He also adds that he accompanied Joseph Luns to Ankara for the ceremony of the signing of the association agreement. Luns was in Ankara not only to represent the Dutch

---

10 The original version in German (and a French translation) of the Hallstein speech is available at the European University Institute, Florence, Archives historiques de la Commission, 1963, CEAB 5, no. 1152.
11 For an in-depth analysis, based on original sources, see E. Krieger, *Die Europakandidatur der Türkei: Der Entscheidungsprozess der Europäischen Wirtschaftsgemeinschaft während der Assoziierungsverhandlungen mit der Türkei 1959–1963* (Zurich, Chronos, 2006), pp. 76–108, 152–62; E. Krieger, 'Turkey's Fragile EU Perspectives since the 1960s', in H.-L. Kieser (ed.), *Turkey beyond Nationalism: Towards Post-nationalist Identities* (London and New York, NY, I. B. Tauris, 2006), pp. 167–74.

Government as Minister of Foreign Affairs, but also as the President in Office of the Council of the EEC. According to Rutten, Luns was an 'admirer of Atatürk' and their journey to Ankara was perceived as a success.[12]

Strangely enough, in early specialised EC legal writing on the origins of the 1963 Ankara Agreement, the inclusion of the explicit reference to possible future accession of Turkey receives little or no attention. In other words, it is as if the conclusion of the association agreement was taken for granted and, in the early 1960s, the question of the possible accession of Turkey to the Community was largely treated in a similar manner to that of Greece by political and legal scholars.[13] Seen in this context, it is not astonishing that, notwithstanding its large geopolitical impact, the ratification of the Ankara Agreement in the EEC member states was not much more than a formality, and the reference in the association agreement to a later possible accession of Turkey to the EC was not an issue anywhere. Fifteen months after its signature, the agreement with Turkey entered into force. In this regard, it is equally useful to draw attention to Turkey's membership of the Council of Europe. As early as in 1949, a few months after the signature of the Statute of the Council of Europe, Turkey, together with Greece and Iceland, had been invited by the Committee of Ministers of the Council of Europe to become members.[14] Nobody in the Council of Europe raised the question of whether Turkey was sufficiently European to be part of a European organisation whose purpose, according to its preamble, was to bring 'European States' into a closer association. Apparently, for all its members, there was no doubt that Turkey was a state belonging to this category.

While there might be a variety of reasons and justifications for why the EU and its member states currently are of the opinion that Turkey does not satisfy the political and/or economic conditions for accession, the argument that it cannot be considered to be a 'European State' is problematic. This is particularly so in the light of the explicit references to accession in the 1963 Association Agreement, the confirmation on various occasions of Turkey's 'eligibility for EU membership' and the EU's formal and explicit recognition of Turkey as 'a candidate State destined to join the Union' (see below).

---

12 See C. Rutten, *Aan de wieg van Europa en andere Buitenlandse Zaken: Herinneringen van een diplomaat* (Amsterdam, Boom, 2005), p. 77.

13 For more details on this point, see M. Maresceau, *Bilateral Agreements Concluded by the European Community* (Leiden and Boston, MA, Martinus Nijhoff, 2006), pp. 328–31.

14 A. H. Robertson, *The Council of Europe: Its Structure, Functions and Achievements* (London, Stevens, 1956), p. 20.

The Application of Cyprus

The application for EU membership by the Republic of Cyprus on 4 July 1990 was, for a number of reasons, a complex matter. This was not only because of the de facto split of the island after the Turkish military operations of 1974 (see below), but also because of the 'European State' conditionality for EU membership laid down in Article 49 TEU.

The geographical location of the island is such that Cyprus is part of Asia rather than of the European continent. This special characteristic could have been a serious obstacle hindering the application by Cyprus. However, neither the EU institutions nor any of the member states formally questioned the applicant's 'Europeanness'. It is striking how, in its 1993 Opinion on the application of the Republic of Cyprus for EU membership,[15] the Commission avoided addressing directly the issue of the geographical dimension of the concept of a 'European State' and confined itself to designating Cyprus as 'an island strategically located in the north-east Mediterranean'.[16] The Commission's final conclusion was that 'Cyprus's geographical position, the deep-lying bonds which, for two thousand years, have located the island at the very fount of European culture and civilization, the intensity of the European influence apparent in the values shared by the people of Cyprus and in the conduct of the cultural, political, economic and social life of its citizens, the wealth of its contacts of every kind with the Community, all these confer on Cyprus, beyond all doubt, its European identity and character and confirm its vocation to belong to the Community.'[17] In other words, after simply noting the 'geographical position' of Cyprus, the Commission emphasises the history, culture, civilisation and values of the people of Cyprus, declaring that all these elements, taken together, confer on Cyprus 'its European identity and character'. Consequently, the Commission did not see the need to define Cyprus as a 'European State' in so many words, but rather described it as a state which has the 'vocation to belong to the Community', a view which was naturally also shared by the government of the Republic of Cyprus, for which there could be no doubt that 'Cyprus has always been Europe'.[18]

---

15 For the text, see Commission Communication COM(93)313 final.   16 Ibid., point 13.
17 Ibid., point 44.
18 See, for example, the profusely illustrated publication published by the Government of the Republic of Cyprus, *Cyprus Has Always Been Europe* (Nicosia, Press and Information Office, 2006).

Respect for and Promotion of the Values on Which the Union
Is Founded

Eligibility for EU membership depends not only on the answer to the question of whether the application for membership is made by a 'European State', but also, as is now laid down in Article 2 TEU, on respect by the candidate state for the values on which the Union is based.

It was Article F, paragraph 1 of the Treaty of Maastricht which introduced for the first time the provision stating that the systems of government of EU member states 'are founded on the principles of democracy'. The Treaty of Amsterdam added another clause in the TEU, stipulating that the Union is founded on the principles of liberty, democracy, respect for human rights and fundamental freedoms, and the rule of law (then Article 6). It also defined these basic principles as 'common to the Member States'. Consequently, it was a logical move to require respect of these principles by future candidates for EU accession.[19] This was all the more so since the 1993 Copenhagen European Council had already identified these principles as 'political conditions' which CEECs had to satisfy in order to become EU member states[20] (see below).

In the Treaty of Lisbon, the basic principles, as expressed in the Amsterdam version of Article 49 TEU, were slightly reformulated and became 'values' on which the Union was founded. Moreover, the EU expected candidates to be 'committed to promoting them'. These 'values' refer to respect for human dignity, freedom, democracy, equality, the rule of law and respect for human rights, including the rights of persons belonging to minorities.[21] The explicit reference to 'rights of persons belonging to minorities' was a new reference in the TEU, but, as will be explained in the next section, it had already been included in the 1993 Copenhagen European Council political conditionality principles for EU accession. It was the

---

19 See C. Hillion, 'Overseeing the Rule of Law in the European Union. Legal Mandate and Means', Swedish Institute for European Policy Studies (2016), www.sieps.se/en/publi cations/2016/overseeing-the-rule-of-law-in-the-european-union-legal-mandate-and-means-2016iepa/Sieps_2016_1_epa, p. 6; C. Hillion, 'Enlarging the European Union and its Fundamental Rights Protection', in I. Govaere, E. Lannon, P. Van Elsuwege and S. Adam (eds.), *The European Union in the World: Essays in Honour of Marc Maresceau* (Leiden and Boston, MA, Martinus Nijhoff, 2014), pp. 557–73.

20 For an overview, see P. Balázs, 'Enlargement Conditionality of the European Union and Future Prospects', in Govaere et al. (eds.), *The European Union in the World*, pp. 523–40.

21 See D. Kochenov, *EU Enlargement and the Failure of Conditionality: Pre-accession Conditionality in the Fields of Democracy and the Rule of Law* (Austin, TX and Boston, MA, Wolters Kluwer, 2008), pp. 67–82; D. Kochenov, 'Overestimating Conditionality', in Govaere et al. (eds.), *The European Union in the World*, pp. 541–56.

prospect of accession to the EU by the CEECs which led to the introduction of the explicit requirement for candidate states to comply with the basic democratic principles/values on which the EU had been founded. The unfolding crisis of the early 1990s in former Yugoslavia, leading to the disintegration of that country, was the catalyst for the move in that direction.

The reference to protection of minorities could have been a sensitive topic in the compliance review of the Copenhagen conditionality (see the next section), all the more so since in a number of applicant CEECs there were complaints of infringements of rights of persons belonging to minorities. In particular, the position of the large Russian-speaking minority in Estonia and Latvia raised significant challenges as a result of these countries' strict citizenship and language legislation. After the re-establishment of their independence, Estonia and Latvia proceeded from the principle of state continuity in international law to restore their pre-war citizenship legislation, leading to the creation of a large number of so-called 'non-citizens'.[22] The EU, in particular the European Commission, has been criticised for not handling this issue with sufficient attention and care in its yearly reporting in the pre-accession process and in the follow-up after EU accession.[23] Comparable criticism has also been raised with regard to the Hungarian minority in Slovakia, something which was explicitly noted in the Commission's Opinion of 15 July 1997.[24] In addition, regarding Slovakia's application for EU membership, the Commission observed that the government did not sufficiently respect the powers devolved by the constitution to other bodies and that the rights of the opposition were too often disregarded.

---

22 On the background of this issue, see P. Van Elsuwege, 'State Continuity and Its Consequences: The Case of the Baltic States', *Leiden Journal of International Law* 16 (2003): 377–88.

23 The most comprehensive study on this question is that of P. Van Elsuwege, *From Soviet Republics to EU Member States: A Legal and Political Assessment of the Baltic States' Accession to the EU*, 2 vols. (Leiden and Boston, MA, Martinus Nijhoff, 2008), especially pp. 69–80, 240–4, 269–88, 421–49. See also D. Kochenov, *EU Enlargement and the Failure of Conditionality*; D. Kochenov, V. Poleshchuk and A. Dimitrovs, 'Do Professional Linguistic Requirements Discriminate? A Legal Analysis: Latvia and Estonia in the Spotlight', in *European Yearbook of Minority Issues Online* (Leiden, Brill, 2013), pp. 137–87; M. Maresceau, 'Quelques réflexions sur l'origine et l'application de principes fondamentaux dans la stratégie d'adhésion de l'Union européenne', in *Le droit de l'Union européenne en principes. Liber amicorum en l'honneur de Jean Raux* (Rennes, Éditions Apogée, 2006), pp. 71–3; M. Maresceau, 'The EU Pre-accession Strategies: A Political and Legal Analysis', in M. Maresceau and E. Lannon (eds.), *The EU's Enlargement and Mediterranean Strategies: A Comparative Analysis* (Basingstoke, Palgrave Macmillan, 2001), pp. 3–28, 17–19; M. Maresceau, 'Bilateral Agreements Concluded by the European Community' (Leiden and Boston, MA, Martinus Nijhoff, 2006), pp. 435–7.

24 COM(97) 2004 final.

Copenhagen Conditionality and Pre-accession Strategy

The 1993 Copenhagen European Council is crucial to the understanding of conditionality for EU membership. The preparatory works, the results of the summit itself and their follow-up, which brought into the picture the concept of 'pre-accession strategy', led to the most resounding and spectacular event in the history of EU enlargement. Eleven years after that European Council, on 1 May 2004, the fifth EU enlargement became reality. This enlargement had an enormous geopolitical impact, by including in the EU a large number of new member states from behind the former Iron Curtain and by bringing the number of EU member states from fifteen to twenty-five in one accession wave.

The fifth enlargement was different from previous enlargements not only because of its geopolitical dimension and size, but also because of the methodology followed in the process of its preparation. A largely comparable, but enhanced, monitoring methodology was used with regard to the subsequent enlargements which brought Bulgaria, Romania and Croatia into the EU.[25] The accession treaty with Croatia was signed in 2011. The act of accession requested that the Commission closely monitor Croatia's fulfilment of its commitments.[26] Moreover, this enhanced monitoring is even more pronounced for currently pending or other enlargement applications. This is essentially the result of the evolving context and the growing understanding that the EU's accession negotiations in the past insufficiently covered fundamental issues such as respect for the rule of law, democracy and human rights (see below).

The following section addresses first the historical background of the EU's changing perception on enlargement with the CEECs; it then briefly examines the main characteristics of the pre-accession phenomenon.

Background and German Unification

When Gorbachev introduced *Glasnost* and *Perestroika* in the Union of Soviet Socialist Republics (USSR) in 1985, it was expected and unavoidable that these new policies would have far-reaching political and economic implications in

---

25 For details on the accession of Bulgaria and Romania, see the Commission's 'Communication on Comprehensive Monitoring on the State of Preparedness for EU Membership of Bulgaria and Romania', COM(2005)534 final. See also A. F. Tatham, *Enlargement of the European Union* (Austin, TX and Boston, MA, Wolters Kluwer, 2009), pp. 112–15.

26 See Commission Communication COM(2012) 601 final; Commission Communication COM(2013) 171 final.

the CEECs.[27] The governments of various countries involved in these reforms were of the opinion that their 'return to Europe' could best be achieved by acceding to the EC. As early as in 1989 this became the prevailing opinion in Hungary, Poland and Czechoslovakia (at that time still one country), the so-called 'forefront States' on the path of reform.

On 15 July 1989, in the context of the festivities celebrating the 200th anniversary of the French Revolution, the Group of Seven (G7) met in Paris under the chairmanship of President Mitterrand. The G7 pledged support for political and economic reforms in central and eastern Europe and invited the European Commission to coordinate this support. At the Paris November 1989 European Summit, Mitterrand reiterated the EC's commitment to support changes in central and eastern Europe 'au prix, *conditio sine qua non*, du retour vérifié à la démocratie' ('at the price, *conditio sine qua non*, of a verified return to democracy'). The combination of the multilateral approach with a rapidly growing steering role for the European Commission to underpin the reforms would prove to be an efficient strategy.[28] One of the first initiatives launched was the Poland–Hungary Action for Reform (PHARE). Right from the start of this project, which also involved considerable financial support, assistance was made conditional on organising free elections, establishing a multiparty system, respect for human rights and introducing a market economy. These 'PHARE conditions' would, a few years later, largely coincide with the 1993 Copenhagen conditions for EU membership.[29]

Almost simultaneously with the launching of PHARE, the EC also initiated a policy of developing bilateral 'trade and commercial and economic cooperation agreements' with countries from the Council for Mutual Economical Assistance (Comecon). In 1988, that is, even before political reforms in Hungary had been achieved, the EC had already signed such an agreement with that country, and a series of more or less similar agreements were signed

---

27 On this episode of European history, see contributions in M. Maresceau (ed.), *The Political and Legal Framework of Trade Relations between the European Community and Eastern Europe* (Dordrecht and Boston, MA, Martinus Nijhoff–Kluwer Academic, 1989), in particular P. Benavides, 'Bilateral Relations between the European Community and Eastern European Countries', pp. 21–5; J. Maslen, 'European Community–CMEA: Institutional Relations', pp. 85–92 and the concluding observations by V. Sychev, 'East–West European Trade: The CMEA View' and W. De Clercq, 'East–West European Trade: The EC View', pp. 311–18.

28 *Agence Europe*, 20–21 November 1989, p. 3. See also J. Werts, *The European Council* (London, John Harper, 2008), pp. 88–90.

29 For the first PHARE initiative, see 'Council Regulation 390/89 of 18 December 1989', *Official Journal of the European Union* (1989): L 375/11, which was afterwards extended to other CEECs.

afterwards, in 1989 with Poland and the USSR and in 1990 with other Comecon countries. But the rapidity and intensity of the political changes in most of these countries made the bilateral trade and cooperation agreements almost obsolete before they entered into force. This explains why the EC was prepared for a serious upgrade of the bilateral frameworks that had just been agreed and was willing to envisage the conclusion of 'association agreements'.[30] While the EC was supportive towards the process of political and economic transformation, it was at the same time cautious regarding speedy enlargement for the CEECs. Were the changes and reforms in these countries genuine? Would they last, and was the EC itself in a position to enlarge, in other words to absorb those countries in an orderly manner? Who would be included in this move and who would not? Many questions remained on the table while everything was moving so rapidly and so drastically.

Before examining the negotiations with the 'forefront States' for the conclusion of association agreements, called 'Europe Agreements', it is useful to add a brief comment on the incorporation in 1990 of the five *Länder* of the former German Democratic Republic (GDR) into the EC. In its Communication 'The Community and German Unification', the Commission explained that 'the integration of the German Democratic Republic into the Community through unification, therefore, does not amount to accession in formal terms'.[31] From a strictly legal point of view this was indeed correct; the inclusion of the new German *Länder* was not an operation subject to the accession provision of Article 237 EEC (now Article 49 TEU). The integration of the GDR was achieved in stages and with transitional periods, but without formal revision of the basic treaties. In this context, it might be useful to recall that the 1957 EEC Treaty contained a 'Protocol on Internal German Trade and Connected Problems' which

---

30 See Commission Communication of 27 August 1990, 'Association Agreements with the Countries of Central and Eastern Europe: A General Outline', COM(90)398. An earlier policy paper from the Commission on a possible 'association' with CEECs (the not-so-well-known Communication of 18 April 1990, 'The Development of the Community's Relations with the Countries of Central and Eastern Europe', SEC (90) 717 final) already contains the principal elements for the Communication of 27 August 1990; in the Communication of 18 April 1990, Yugoslavia is twice explicitly mentioned as one of the CEECs which could benefit from multilateral support from the G24; reference to Yugoslavia disappears in the Communication of 27 August 1990.
31 See Communication 'The Community and German Unification' (based on) SEC (90) 751, 20 April 1990. See also *Bulletin of the European Community*, (1990): suppl. 4/90. For more details, see Tatham, *Enlargement of the European Union*, pp. 48–56; A. Mayhew, *Recreating Europe: The European Union's Policy towards Central and Eastern Europe* (Cambridge, Cambridge University Press, 1998), pp. 18–20.

exclusively concerned trade between the FRG and the GDR. For the five other EEC member states, the GDR was a third country.

Insofar as the negotiations for the conclusion of association agreements with the 'forefront States' were concerned, they quickly proved to be more complicated than expected for the EC.[32] The three states concerned saw Europe Agreements as real 'pre-accession agreements' and asked for an explicit and unambiguous reference to possible future accession in the agreements they were negotiating, although such a far-reaching approach was not shared by the EC itself. References to future accession in bilateral association agreements, after the experience with the 1963 Association Agreement with Turkey (see above), was something which the EC wished to avoid, as much as possible. After the failed coup d'état against Gorbachev in August 1991, a compromise would soon be reached. In the last section of the preamble of these agreements, the parties recognised that it was the associated country's 'ultimate objective . . . to become a member of the European Union' and that these agreements would 'help [the associated countries] to achieve this'. However, this careful formulation, which already implied a serious concession from the EC, could not hide the fact that Europe Agreements did not, in themselves, imply a clear political commitment and certainly not a legal one of the EC to admit the associated country as a member state. In its important Communication of 27 August 1990 on the conclusion of Association Agreements, the Commission provided the following explanation: 'Several governments have referred to their interest in eventual membership for their countries in the Community. This, however, is not among the objectives of the association agreements discussed in this Communication. These agreements, as the Commission has pointed out, have a special value in themselves and should be distinguished from the possibility of accession to the Community as provided for by article 237 of the EEC Treaty. This possibility would not be affected by the conclusion of association agreements.'[33] Thus, in

---

32 For a detailed historical analysis of the Europe Agreements, see J. I. Torreblanca, *The Reuniting of Europe: Promises, Negotiations and Compromises* (Aldershot, Ashgate, 2001). On the legal dimension of these agreements, see the contributions in P.-C. Müller-Graff (ed.), *East Central European States and the European Communities: The Legal Adaptation to the Market Economy* (Baden-Baden, Nomos, 1993). See also P.-C. Müller-Graff, 'Legal Framework for Relations between the European Union and Central and Eastern Europe: General Aspects', in M. Maresceau (ed.), *Enlarging the European Union: Relations between the EU and Central and Eastern Europe* (London and New York, NY, Longman, 1997), pp. 27–40; M. Maresceau, 'On Association, Partnership, Pre-accession and Accession', in Maresceau (ed.), *Enlarging the European Union*, pp. 1–22.

33 European Commission, 'Association Agreements with the Countries of Central and Eastern Europe', COM(90)398.

the Commission's view, Europe Agreements, as association agreements, were not 'pre-accession agreements', but rather an alternative to such agreements.

In the end, Europe Agreements were signed in 1991 with Hungary, Poland and the Czech and Slovak Federal Republic (the last Europe Agreement had not yet been ratified at the moment of the dissolution of the Czech and Slovak Federal Republic; its initial version was adapted in 1993 and then signed with, on the one hand, the Czech Republic and, on the other hand, Slovakia as contracting parties). Further Europe Agreements were signed with Romania in 1993 and Bulgaria in 1994. The conclusion of Europe Agreements with Estonia, Latvia and Lithuania – which had been part of the Soviet Union for 50 years – was not an evident option at the beginning of the 1990s. Initially, only Denmark and Germany supported such a step. The absence of a short-term NATO accession perspective, the unstable situation in Russia and the agenda-setting of the Danish Presidency in the second half of 1993 all played important roles in the decision in 1995 to include the three Baltic states within the group of associated CEECs.[34] Finally, a Europe Agreement was also signed with Slovenia in 1996, the only country from former Yugoslavia to be included in this list of agreements. In contrast to what happened with Slovenia, with Croatia no Europe Agreement could be signed. The 1995 Croat military offensive, the expulsion of the Serb population of the Krajina and other issues prevented the signature of such an agreement. After the death of President Tuđman, a Stabilisation and Association Agreement with Croatia was signed in 2001. This agreement entered into force in 2005.[35]

All the countries just mentioned, together with Cyprus and Malta (see above), later joined the EU. Unfortunately, as has already been mentioned, within the limits of this chapter, it is impossible to enter into the specificities of each individual enlargement.

EU Accession: A Joint Objective

The turning point in the EU's position on accession came with the 1993 Copenhagen European Council. Germany, and in particular Chancellor Helmut Kohl, had played a pivotal role in the reorientation of the EU's policy towards the CEECs. Looking back, it was a tremendous achievement that he managed to take on board President Mitterrand. Without this historical

---

34 For more details, see Van Elsuwege, *From Soviet Republics to EU Member States*, pp. 187–92.
35 See *Official Journal of the European Union* (2005): L 26.

alliance and personal friendship between Kohl and Mitterrand, it is very unlikely that EU enlargement eastwards would have taken place the way it has.

It is worth recalling the wording of the conclusions of that important summit. After welcoming 'the courageous efforts undertaken by the associated countries' in the modernisation of their economies and their clear commitment to ensure a rapid transition, the Copenhagen European Council 'agreed that the associated countries in Central and Eastern Europe that so desire shall become members of the European Union'. This was a bold formulation of the Council's new political message which, if realised, could change the destiny of the European continent.

Seen in this context, the conclusion of 'association agreements' became for the CEECs an indispensible first step to go ahead with the procedure for enlargement.[36] Article 49 TEU did not and does not contain, even today, such a condition, and in the past accessions had taken place without being preceded by an association agreement, but from now onwards applications for accession by CEECs would necessitate the conclusion of such an agreement. In reality, however, this new condition was itself not a serious obstacle for candidates aspiring to become EU members, except for Slovenia, which, after opposition by Italy as a result of unresolved issues related to the Second World War and its aftermath, was not able to sign a Europe Agreement – the *conditio sine qua non* to move forward – until 10 June 1996, while *in extremis* applying for EU membership on the same day.[37]

The most important statement in the Copenhagen European Council conclusions was that '[a]ccession will take place as soon as an associated country is able to assume the obligations of membership by satisfying the economic and political conditions required'. EU membership did require 'that the candidate country has achieved stability of institutions guaranteeing democracy, the rule of law, human rights and respect for and protection of minorities, the existence of a functioning market economy, as well as the capacity to cope with competitive pressure within the Union'. Moreover, membership presupposed 'the candidate's ability to take on the obligations of membership including adherence to the aims of political, economic and monetary union'. The introduction of these conditions necessarily implied

---

36 On the fifth and sixth enlargements, see Tatham, *Enlargement of the European Union*, pp. 71–116.
37 On this question, see P. Vehar, 'The Osimo Agreements in the Europe Agreements', in A. Ott and K. Inglis (eds.), *Handbook on European Enlargement: A Commentary on the Enlargement Process* (The Hague, T. M. C. Asser Press, 2002), pp. 367–8.

a close follow-up of the reform process in the CEECs, and it rapidly became clear that the Commission would have to play the key role in this operation. The Commission was indeed the only institution with the capacity and expertise to assume such a demanding and delicate role.

Finally, in the Copenhagen Conclusions, the European Council held that '[t]he Union's capacity to absorb new members, while maintaining the momentum of European integration, is also an important consideration in the general interest of both the Union and the candidate countries'. In the later stages of the accession preparation process, however, not enough attention has been paid to this 'last condition' – the forgotten condition of Copenhagen – which was addressed not to the candidate states but to the EU itself. In reality, this condition introduced an existential dilemma on the fundamental choices which had to be made between, on the one hand, enlarging the EU and, on the other hand, deepening of the EU itself. In order to illustrate this point, it is useful to explain here Margaret Thatcher's view on EU enlargement. She maintained that

> during the 1980s and most of the 1990s, Britain was in the forefront of those urging a widening of Community membership [. . .] Enlargement of the Community eastwards has traditionally been attractive to both the British and the Germans, but has been a good deal less so to the French and to the countries of Southern Europe. There is no great secret as to why this is so. Alongside our wish to see the ex-communist countries encouraged to create successful Western-style economies, British governments have hoped that, as the EU jargon has it, *widening* would be at the expense of *deepening*. With the prospect of enlargement to include as many as twenty-seven members – counting in all the candidate countries – it seemed to us a plain impossibility to proceed with creating a federal superstate. The differences and potential conflicts between the members would be just too great.

But she also expressed doubts about this approach:

> One may question whether this policy still makes much sense. All that has been seen of developments within the European Union over the last decade confirms that 'deepening' – that is the persistent accumulation of more and more powers by European institutions to override national wishes and interests – will go ahead, however much membership 'widens' [. . .] For all these reasons, I am now unpersuaded by the case for further EU expansion.[38]

---

38 See M. Thatcher, *Statecraft: Strategies for a Changing World* (London, HarperCollins, 2002), pp. 338–40.

Coexistence between 'widening' and 'deepening', at first sight seemingly opposing objectives, required, and still requires today, walking a thin line in EU enlargement decision-making.[39]

At this point, it might be useful to come back to the crucial question of why the EC/EU committed itself to enlarge by incorporating the CEECs and to add a reflection on the geopolitical impact of this commitment. At the 1992 Edinburgh European Council, the Commission presented a report which, building on its Communication of 27 August 1990, strongly pleaded in favour of closer association with the CEECs, but this policy paper did not address the impact of enlargement on the EU's eastern neighbours that had formerly been members of Comecon and were not involved in the association process.[40] The 1992 Edinburgh European Council took good note of the Commission's position and seemed also to share the Commission's approach that there was a pressing need for greater political stability on the European continent after the collapse of the USSR. Seen from this perspective, the subsequent 1993 Copenhagen European Council constituted the evident confirmation of this new orientation. At the 1995 Madrid European Council, EU enlargement was presented as 'both a political necessity and a historic opportunity for Europe', which 'will ensure the stability and security of the continent and will thus offer both the applicant States and the current members of the Union new prospects for economic growth and general well-being'. In other words, enlargement assumed a meaning which went beyond the applicant states directly involved in the ongoing operation. In the EU's vision, European stability and prosperity remained the highest political goals of enlargement. Consequently, at the 1999 Helsinki European Council, reference was made to the benefits of enlargement for 'the entire European continent',[41] and the 2002 Copenhagen European Council defined EU enlargement as 'an ambitious process to overcome the legacy of conflict and division in Europe'.[42] Seen from this angle, EU enlargement had 'become the driving force for peace, democracy, stability and prosperity on our continent'.[43] No doubt, these objectives are most noble, but the EU seems to have overlooked that EU enlargement can work efficiently only if those of the EU's eastern neighbours which are not involved

---

39 On this question, see the report by MEP A. Stubb, 'The Institutional Aspects of the European Union's Capacity to Integrate New Member States', P6 TA(2006)0569, European Parliament, 13 December 2006.
40 See European Commission, 'Towards a Closer Association with the Countries of Central and Eastern Europe'.
41 Ibid., point 3.   42 Ibid., point 3.   43 Ibid.

in the accession operation largely share this vision. Under the Yeltsin administration, when EU enlargement was mainly perceived as a domestic EU affair, the EU should have deployed considerable efforts to assess the impact of pre-accession policies and of EU accession on Russia and other eastern European neighbours and should not have treated this as if it were Pandora's box. Important questions here are, for example, NATO enlargement, since this seemed to go hand in hand with EU enlargement, the situation of the Russian-speaking minorities in the Baltic states and the impact of accession on the position of Kaliningrad (for which a solution was found). These issues and others relevant for European and global security go far beyond the limits of the present chapter and cannot be further addressed here,[44] but need nevertheless to be recalled if one is to understand the broader political context of the EU's enlargement process and its ramifications for the development of EU–Russia relations. This chapter does not deal with the issue of NATO enlargement.[45]

Pre-accession

An important follow-up to the 1993 Copenhagen European Council was the 1994 Essen European Council. A lot was expected from this summit organised under the German Presidency. It is not astonishing that the 'pre-accession strategy' was formally launched and the expression 'pre-accession strategy' used for the first time at this European Council (strangely enough, in a somewhat 'hidden' way in Annex IV of the Essen Conclusions).[46] This would not prevent the phenomenon of pre-accession from rapidly becoming the leading point of reference in the preparation for accession of the CEECs,

---

44 On geopolitical concerns of EU enlargement for Russia, see, for example, R. Sakwa, *Russia against the Rest: The Post-Cold War Crisis of World Order* (Cambridge, Cambridge University Press, 2017), pp. 249–76; P. Van Elsuwege and F. Bossuyt, 'From Strategic Partner to Strategic Challenge: In Search of an EU Policy towards Russia', in F. Bossuyt and P. Van Elsuwege (eds.), *Principled Pragmatism in Practice: The EU's Policy towards Russia after Crimea* (Boston, MA and Leiden, Brill–Nijhoff, 2021), pp. 1–13. See also P. Van Elsuwege, 'The Legal Framework of EU–Russia Relations: *Quo Vadis?*', in Govaere et al. (eds.), *The European Union in the World*, pp. 443–60; M. Maresceau, 'EU Enlargement and EU Common Strategies on Russia and Ukraine: An Ambiguous Yet Unavoidable Connection', in C. Hillion (ed.), *EU Enlargement: A Legal Approach* (Oxford and Portland, OR, Hart, 2004), pp. 189–90.

45 For possible interconnections between NATO enlargement and EU enlargement, see M. E. Sarotte, *Not One Inch: America, Russia, and the Making of Post-Cold War Stalemate* (New Haven, CT and London, Yale University Press, 2021), especially pp. 140, 185, 189, 198–9.

46 For an overview, see M. Maresceau, 'Pre-accession', in M. Cremona (ed.), *The Enlargement of the European Union* (Oxford, Oxford University Press, 2003), pp. 9–42.

and, as has already been mentioned, the Commission assumed the bulk of the conceptual and strategic thinking for this new approach.[47] Clearly, the Commission played a pivotal role in the pre-accession process and 'promoted, and controlled, the future members' progressive application of the wider *EU acquis*'.[48] The main message behind the pre-accession strategy concept was to bring the CEECs closer to the EU, in political, economic and, above all, legal terms, *before* accession took place, in order to avoid the prospect of a 'confrontational' accession scenario.

In this reorientation, paradoxically, Europe Agreements, which had not been conceived as pre-accession instruments by the EU, now themselves became an important vehicle, institutionally as well as substantially, in the move towards accession. Institutions of the Europe Agreements (the Association Council, Association Committees, specialised technical subcommittees etc.) were increasingly being used to achieve pre-accession objectives, and substantive chapters of these agreements, such as the ones on establishing free trade, became particularly relevant in this respect.

As emphasised in Annex IV of the Essen Conclusions, the two new pillars for pre-accession were, on the one hand, the so-called 'Structured Dialogue' and, on the other hand, the setting up of an intensive programme for the approximation of laws. The 'Structured Dialogue' aimed to allow candidate states to become more familiar with the work of the EU institutions, through joint meetings of representatives of the EU and officials of the applicant states. Notwithstanding its laudable objective, this part of the pre-accession strategy was in fact difficult to organise. 'Joint meetings', unless operated within the framework of the Europe Agreements, had little practical significance and could never acquire 'decision-making' status. The 'Structured Dialogue' initiative was therefore abandoned and replaced, in 1998, by the 'enhanced pre-accession strategy'.[49] The second pillar, focusing pre-accession on the adaptation of domestic laws of the CEECs to the legal

---

47 See Commission Communication 'The Europe Agreements and Beyond: A Strategy to Prepare the Countries of Central and Eastern Europe for Accession', COM(94)320 final, 13 July 1994 and follow-up Commission Communication COM(94) 361 final, 27 July 1994.

48 See C. Hillion, 'The EU's Neighbourhood Policy towards Eastern Europe', in A. Dashwood and M. Maresceau (eds.), *Law and Practice of EU External Relations: Salient Features of a Changing Landscape* (Cambridge, Cambridge University Press, 2008), p. 312. For more details, see K. Inglis, 'The Pre-accession Strategy and Accession Partnerships', in A. Ott and K. Inglis, *Handbook on European Enlargement*, pp. 103–11.

49 On this concept, see Van Elsuwege, *From Soviet Republics to EU Member States*, pp. 289–91.

acquis of the EU's internal market, was an effective tool in creating an environment propitious to accession, and the Commission rapidly became the institution in charge of the management of the pre-accession phase.

In 1990 the Republic of Cyprus and Malta applied for EU accession while Hungary, on 1 April 1994, was the first of the CEECs to do so, soon followed by Poland. Eight other CEECs (the Czech Republic, Slovakia, Estonia, Latvia, Lithuania, Bulgaria, Romania and Slovenia) would do the same, and in 2003 Croatia too applied for EU membership. All these applications put into motion *de jure* and *de facto* the various procedural mechanisms which had already been laid down in the general procedural rules and practices of the existing Article 49 TEU.

From Applying for Accession to Ratification of the Accession Treaty

The dominant political players in the enlargement process, the European Council and the Council (of Ministers), are composed of the member states of the Union. National visions and approaches may therefore be the determining factor in any enlargement decision-making. Member states also have an important additional means of ultimate control, and it should be kept in mind that accession treaties must go through national ratification procedures.

Initiating the Accession Procedure

The application for accession by a candidate state constitutes the very first formal step in the procedure for EU membership and is addressed to the Council.[50] It is possible to move forwards in the procedure only if the Council, acting unanimously, asks the Commission to provide an opinion on the application, as was already made clear by the fate of the Moroccan failed application for accession explained above. A more recent example of a failed application is that of Switzerland. After having signed the agreement establishing the European Economic Area (EEA) on 2 May 1992, Switzerland also applied, on 20 May 1992, for membership of the EC. However, at the referendum on EEA membership, organised on 6 December 1992, the EEA, to everybody's astonishment, was rejected by a majority of the Swiss population with 50.3 per cent of the votes. Shortly afterwards, Switzerland

---

50 For a first in-depth legal analysis of the accession procedure, see J. Raux, *Les relations extérieures de la Communauté économique européenne* (Paris, Éditions Cujas, 1966), pp. 461–523.

suspended, until further notice, the procedure for accession to the EEC which it had initiated. While accession negotiations with Switzerland were not opened, neither was the Swiss application for EU accession withdrawn, and it remained for more than two decades in an 'inactivated' state. However, domestic Swiss political pressure for a formal withdrawal increased considerably and, finally, on 27 July 2016, Switzerland informed the EU that the application for accession had to be considered withdrawn. The President of the EU Council could only take note of this request.[51] Other examples where the accession procedure had been duly initiated but, for different reasons, failed to lead to accession, are provided by the applications for EU membership by Iceland (see below) and Norway (see below).

Notwithstanding the explicit wording of Article 49 TEU that the 'Council' acts unanimously after consulting the Commission, the decision to open accession negotiations is now 'decided' at the highest possible EU institutional level, that is, the 'European Council'.[52] In reality, this does not greatly change the situation: the Council (of Ministers) has always been closely involved in the preparation of the ultimate decision of the European Council.

On the whole, the history of EU enlargement shows an increasing presence of the European Council in the accession process. Notwithstanding the fact that, before the Lisbon Treaty, the European Council was not even explicitly mentioned in Article 49 TEU, that institution has gradually emerged as the main political authority for determining the political and economic conditionality principles for EU membership. Of course, this does not mean that, before the 1993 Copenhagen Summit, European Councils had been absent from the enlargement agenda. For example, note the 1984 Fontainebleau and Dublin European Council Conclusions preparing for the accessions of Spain and Portugal, which faced Greek opposition, inter alia concerning the common market organisation for wine. Prominent developments in the field of EU enlargement can easily be retraced through the 'Conclusions of the European Council', which in fact constitute leading points of reference in any overview of EU enlargement. That said, the now explicit mentioning of the European Council, in the Lisbon version of Article

---

51 See the letter sent by the President of the Council on 19 October 2016 to the President of the Swiss Confederation, www.eda.admin.ch/dam/europa/fr/documents/bundes rat/161019-Lettre-UE-retrait-adhesion-CH_en.pdf.

52 On the role of the European Council preparing for the 2004 Enlargement, see Werts, *The European Council*, pp. 112–17. In his recently published new edition, Werts emphasises the crucial role of the European Council as a 'constitutional architect', in particular in shaping EU enlargement, see J. Werts, *The European Council in the Era of Crises* (London, John Harper, 2021), pp. 109, 137, 182.

49 TEU, remains discrete: that provision merely holds that 'the conditions of eligibility agreed upon by the European Council shall be taken into account'.

After the Council has requested an opinion, it is the Commission's task to examine the candidate's state of preparation and ability to become an EU member state. The Commission sends a detailed questionnaire to the applicant and collects as much relevant data as possible. The Commission's opinion also builds on know-how and expertise acquired in previous enlargements. In its opinion, the Commission presents an overall analysis of the candidate's position in the light of political and economic criteria set by the EU and is not binding. However, examples in the EU's enlargement practice where, after a negative opinion and without the Commission reviewing formally its opinion, negotiations for accession have nevertheless been opened are very rare. An example is the Commission's negative opinion of 20 January 1976 on the application of Greece, which was 'ignored' by the Council.[53] Nonetheless, the expression of a positive opinion by the Commission does not necessarily lead to a rapid initiation of accession negotiations, as illustrated by the Commission's positive opinion of 9 November 2005 on the application for EU accession by the Former Yugoslav Republic of Macedonia, which was afterwards, for more than a decade, blocked by Greece. The Greek obstacle has finally been removed (see below), but afterwards a new one has emerged, this time imposed by Bulgaria, which was recently also removed (see below). All this is an illustration of the European political and legal reality that all member states must agree to formally open accession negotiations. But, even if accession negotiations have been opened, a member state can, in the course of these negotiations, exert considerable pressure on the orientation or pace of the negotiations and may even block them and, in the last instance, refuse ratification.

Mention should also be made of the practice of granting 'candidate status' to applicant states before the formal opening of accession negotiations. This is a political intervention which involves various EU institutions. Notwithstanding this, from a strictly legal point of view, it would appear that every country which formally applies for EU membership is a 'candidate State'. Article 49 TEU itself does not mention the procedure of granting 'candidate status' as a special phase or special recognition in the accession process. Nevertheless, the explicit granting of 'candidate status' may have

---

53 C. Hillion, 'Accession and Withdrawal in the Law of the European Union', in A. Arnull and D. Chalmers (eds.), *The Oxford Handbook of European Union Law* (Oxford, Oxford University Press, 2015), pp. 126–52, 129, note 15.

considerable symbolic weight. The European Council may wish to express satisfaction with ongoing reforms and adaptations undertaken by the applicant state, while at the same time using this opportunity to identify those domains which might need substantial additional efforts by applicant states. This approach was chosen for a number of western Balkans applicants, when the European Council assessed the state of the rule of law, judiciary, police, electoral process, fight against corruption and organised crime, and efficiency of public administration. Applicants perceive the formal granting of 'candidate status' as a stimulating political signal in their approach to the EU, but, as such, it is not necessarily a guarantee of quick accession. At the 1999 Helsinki European Council, Turkey was the first applicant state on which this status was explicitly conferred. 'Candidate status' had already been granted to the Former Yugoslav Republic of Macedonia (2005), now North Macedonia, Montenegro (2010), Serbia (2012), Albania (2014) and, very recently, also to Ukraine, Moldova and Bosnia and Herzegovina (2022). In addition, the EU is prepared to grant 'candidate status' to Georgia 'once the priorities specified in the Commission's opinion on Georgia's membership application have been addressed'[54] (see below). At the 1999 Helsinki European Council, Turkey was the first applicant to explicitly receive such status.

Accession Negotiations

Once the Commission has recommended that the Council should open accession negotiations, the applicant presents its 'Negotiating Position' and the Commission prepares a 'Draft Common Position', which is further assessed and finally adopted by the Council. The EU Common Position highlights specific benchmarks to which a candidate might be urged to show special attention during the negotiations. The green light for the formal start of accession negotiations is provided at a bilateral intergovernmental accession conference.

The Commission fulfils from the early phase of the negotiations onwards an important screening task and acts in principle as facilitator and supervisor in the ensuing accession process. 'Screening' means carrying out a detailed review of the compatibility of the national laws of the applicant state with the requirements of the EU *acquis* and goes hand in hand with monitoring. Through regular reporting, at least on a yearly basis, progress or hindrance in the ongoing negotiations is assessed. Over the years, the strategic

---

54 See 'Council Conclusions, Enlargement and Stabilisation and Association Process', 13 December 2022, 15935/22, point 8.

importance of the Commission's role in the preparation for accession has become increasingly formalised, particularly after the launching of the pre-accession strategy. A member of the Commission was put in charge of overseeing relations with the CEECs,[55] a function which initially was combined with other responsibilities, but evolved towards being a full-time position as Commissioner for Enlargement under the Prodi Commission. After the 2004 enlargement, the person in this position was given the title Commissioner for European Neighbourhood Policy and for Enlargement Negotiations.[56] This implied, at least at the level of the Commission, a visible and proactive approach in which developments relating to enlargement would be followed closely during the pre-accession phase. After the 2004 enlargement, the amount of attention paid to the conditionality requirements for pending or newly introduced applications increased considerably, in particular for chapters of the *acquis* which are considered particularly sensitive such as Chapters 23 (Judiciary and Fundamental Rights) and 24 (Justice, Freedom and Security). This led to a further strengthening of the Commission's monitoring task.[57] These chapters are now put on the negotiation table in the earliest phase of the negotiations for accession and will not leave that table until the accession negotiations have been concluded (see below).

For the negotiations which led to the successful accessions of 2004, 2007 and 2013, the Commission had delivered final formal favourable opinions in 2003, 2005 and 2011. For example, the (first) opinion of 20 April 2004 on the opening of accession negotiations with Croatia was followed by the favourable final opinion of 12 October 2011, whereby the Commission considered 'that Croatia meets the political criteria and expects Croatia to meet the economic and *acquis* criteria and to be ready for membership by 1 July 2013'.[58] Such interventions by the Commission are, in fact, opinions, which are not explicitly foreseen in Article 49 TEU and must not be confused with the 'opinion' to which Article 49 TEU refers, which comes in the early phase of the accession procedure.

---

55 For more details on the screening process, see Tatham, *Enlargement of the European Union*, pp. 254–6, 444–6.
56 On the impact of the 2004 enlargement on the structure of the European Commission with ten new Commissioners, see comments by the first Hungarian Commissioner, Peter Balázs, 'Enlargement Conditionality of the European Union', in Govaere et al. (eds.), *The European Union in the World*, p. 538.
57 See Hillion, 'Accession and Withdrawal', pp. 130–2.
58 See Commission Communication COM(2004) 257 final; Commission Communication COM(2011) 667 final.

In negotiations for accession, the stakes are high. Applicants must be able and willing to accept not just the principles and political objectives laid down in the basic EU Treaties, but also the whole body of EU primary and secondary law, including existing international agreements concluded by the EU with third countries. This set of rules, as interpreted by the European Court of Justice, including acts in the field of CFSP as well as justice and home affairs, together with a great variety of other legal and political acts, which are not always easy to qualify, becomes the *acquis* of the Union for the acceding third state. Seen from this perspective, accession negotiations are something that is unique and truly different from classical bilateral or multilateral negotiations between the EU and third states. The reason is simply that, in negotiations for accession, ultimately, the objective of the candidate state is to become part of the group of member states on the other side of the negotiating table.

In past accessions, as well as for applications for accession which have formally been opened (see below), the classical negotiation model used by the EU for examining compliance with the *acquis* is composed of thirty-five chapters and comprises not only specific substantive policies (agriculture, justice etc.) and institutional, financial and budgetary matters but above all the classical hard-core EU internal market *acquis*: free movement of goods, persons, services and capital as well as competition law and policies. In addition, the *acquis* has a very wide coverage. It includes 'horizontal policies' that are relevant to the achievement of the internal market without having, strictly speaking, a 'free movement' character (for example consumer protection, protection of the environment, company law) as well as 'flanking policies', which fall outside the four classical freedoms and include areas such as research and technological development, information services and policies regarding youth. Often in the course of the negotiations, applicants realise that they will not be in a position to fully apply the whole of this vast and substantive EU *acquis* immediately in their legal order and may thus ask for 'transition periods', which are temporary derogations from the application of the *acquis*. This constitutes the main workload of the negotiating teams, where negotiations focus on how far and under what circumstances requests for derogations from the *acquis* can be accepted by the EU and, if accepted, how long they might last.

'Transition periods' had not been invented in 1972 when the first accession treaty was signed; they already existed in an intra-Community relationship in the first basic Community Treaties. In the EEC Treaty, transition periods of a general nature had been foreseen for the achievement of the customs union; sometimes specific transitional arrangements have been accepted for a particular member state, such as, for example, for Luxembourg in relation to free movement of workers. However, their increasing use in enlargement negotiations led to growing concerns. This can easily be understood: an internal market which is not applied in a homogeneous manner is doomed to become rapidly unworkable. Consequently, as a general rule, temporary derogations need to follow a strict timeframe and supervision by the Commission is fundamental. That said, numerous transition periods have nevertheless in practice been granted to new member states, in particular for the enlargements involving the CEECs.[59] In the Fifth Accession Treaty, probably the longest derogation was until 31 December 2017 (for Poland, regarding emissions from large combustion plants).

Transition periods are one thing, 'permanent derogations' from the basic principles of the EU's internal market are another. In the history of the EU's enlargement, only a handful of such derogations have ever been accepted by the EU. They are so exceptional that they deserve special mention. They are to be found in the 2004 Protocol 6 on the acquisition of secondary residences in Malta and in Protocol 2 on the Åland Islands. Protocol 6 allows Malta, as a very small state, to continue to apply, under certain conditions, its restrictive legislation on the acquisition and holding of immovable property for secondary residence purposes by nationals of EU member states who have not legally resided in Malta for at least 5 years.[60] Protocol 2 on the Åland Islands allows restrictions on the right to acquire and hold real estate as well as restrictions on the right of establishment and the right to provide services.[61] Another, very unusual, permanent derogation from the basic principles of the internal market is that allowing Denmark to maintain its existing discriminatory legislation on the acquisition of second homes. This exception was accepted in the Maastricht Treaty and afterwards explicitly reconfirmed in the Lisbon Treaty.[62] Its origin is to be found in a transition measure of the 1972 Accession Treaty, which, in principle, should have been brought to an end once the transition period had elapsed. But, after the initial

59 For numerous illustrations of transitional derogations, see, for example, in the field of the environmental *acquis*, K. Inglis, *Evolving Practice in EU Enlargement: With Case Studies in Agri-food and Environment Law* (Leiden and Boston, MA, Martinus Nijhoff, 2010), pp. 271–331.
60 For the text of Protocol 6 Act of Accession, see *Official Journal of the European Union* (2003): L 236/947.
61 For the text of Protocol 2 Act of Accession, see *Official Journal of the European Union* (1994): C 241/352.
62 Treaty of Lisbon, Protocol 32.

rejection of the Maastricht Treaty in a first referendum, Denmark obtained a number of 'opt outs', including a permanent derogation for the acquisition of secondary residences. In a second referendum, the Danish population accepted the adapted version of the Maastricht Treaty.

Finally, unforeseen events can occur in the course of accession negotiations, which may prevent a successful outcome of these negotiations. This is what happened with Iceland's application for EU membership. In the aftermath of the world-wide financial crisis of 2008–9, Iceland applied for EU membership on 17 July 2009. Notwithstanding the intensity of the crisis, or perhaps because of it, the EU reacted very promptly. On 24 February 2010, the Commission delivered a positive opinion, and on 17 June 2010 the European Council agreed to open accession negotiations. But things would not evolve as expected. A worrying signal was the Fifth Ministerial Accession Conference of 18 December 2012, where it was noted that challenging chapters of the *acquis* still lay ahead.[63] On 17 December 2013, Iceland informed the Council that negotiations were to be put on hold. As a consequence, one of the most important substantive chapters of the accession negotiations, that on fisheries, could not even be opened. On 12 March 2015, the Minister for Foreign Affairs of Iceland informed the EU that the government no longer intended to resume negotiations and that commitments made by the previous government in the negotiations had been 'superseded by the present policy'.[64] In the future, close relations with the EU would continue to be developed, mainly through the EEA Agreement. The EU could not do much more than take note of this letter. So far, Iceland's application for membership has not been formally withdrawn.

Also Malta's application for EU membership experienced difficulties. In 1993, together with Cyprus, Malta had received a positive opinion from the Commission. However, after elections in October 1996, the Maltese government, elected on a political platform against EU accession, decided to 'freeze' its application for membership. In 1998, after new elections, the Maltese government was eager to 'defrost' the 'frozen' application. Accession negotiations were opened in 2000 and culminated in the accession of Malta to the EU on 1 May 2004.

---

63 See Council, 18 December 2012, 17894/12 Presse 543.
64 See www.europa-nu.nl/9353000/1/j4nvih7l3kb9irw_j9vvj9idsjo4xr6/vjs6nohrs7ll/f=/
verklaringijsland.pdf; 'Government Considers Iceland No Longer an EU Candidate'
(2015), www.europarl.europa.eu/meetdocs/2014_2019/documents/deea/dv/07_mf
a_news_eu_candidate_150416/07_mfa_news_eu_candidate_150416en.pdf. See also
H. Þ. Hilmarsson, 'Should Iceland Seek European Union and Euro Area membership?',
Regional Formation and Development Studies 21, no. 1 (2017): 53–67.

Accession Negotiations Currently Pending

It is an almost impossible task to provide, within the limits of the present chapter, a concise overview of the ups and downs of the EU–Turkey relationship. Any such exercise must necessarily be incomplete and fragmentary. Moreover, this is perhaps even more the case when attempting to provide elements of the EU's relationship with the countries in the western Balkans which are not part of the EU.

Negotiations for accession have formally been opened with Turkey, with Montenegro, Serbia and, in 2022, with North Macedonia and Albania. For the moment, no opening of accession negotiations with Bosnia and Herzegovina and Kosovo has occurred (see below).

Turkey

Attention has already been drawn to the specific position of Turkey with regard to the 'European State' conditionality requirement of Article 49 TEU. Besides the explicit reference to accession (see above), the 1963 Association Agreement with Turkey also included the rare objective of establishing a customs union (as did also the agreement with Greece). Furthermore, in the 1963 agreement, the parties also explicitly agreed 'to be guided by' the relevant provisions of the EEC Treaty for progressively securing free movement of workers and abolition of restrictions on freedom of establishment and provision of services. The main legal aspects of the EU–Turkey relations are not included in the present chapter.[65]

However, the promising general picture created in the initial phases of the bilateral relationship between the EU and Turkey has not materialised. Instead, over the years, the relationship has become increasingly strained. Some of the main elements of the growing confrontational atmosphere between the EU and Turkey must be put in historical perspective and are briefly addressed in the present section.

---

65 For a general overview of EU–Turkey relations, see H. A. Kabaalioğlu, 'The Turkish Model of Association: Customs Union before Accession', in P. Demaret, J. F. Bellis and G. Garcia Jiménez (eds.), *Regionalism and Multilateralism after the Uruguay Round: Convergence, Divergence and Interaction* (Brussels, European Interuniversity Press, 1997), pp. 115–60. For an overview of the vast case law of the European Court of Justice, see C. Kaddous, 'Le rôle de la Cour de justice dans l'interprétation de l'accord d'association CEE–Turquie', in B. Bonnet (ed.), *Turquie et Union européenne: État des lieux* (Brussels, Bruylant, 2012), pp. 79–103; M. Maresceau, 'Turkey: A Candidate State Destined to Join the Union', in N. N. Shuihne and L. W. Gormley (eds.), *From Single Market to Economic Union: Essays in Memory of John A. Usher* (Oxford, Oxford University Press, 2012), pp. 315–40.

After the 1989 negative opinion of the European Commission on the Turkish application for membership (see above), a new difficult moment in the history of EU–Turkey relations occurred when in 1993 the Commission granted a positive opinion on the application for EU membership by the Republic of Cyprus, notwithstanding the de facto division of the island after the 1974 Turkish military operations in Cyprus. The Commission expeditiously believed 'that the result of Cyprus's accession to the Community would be increased security and prosperity and that it would help bring the two communities on the island closer together'.[66] In the Commission's view, the preparation of the island for accession would contribute to create the momentum for 'a peaceful, balanced and lasting settlement of the Cyprus question'.[67] During the same period the EU also launched its new political orientation on rapprochement with the CEECs. In fact, the efforts deployed by the EU in developing its pre-accession strategy for the CEECs rapidly overshadowed the EU–Turkey relations, even though, in the course of this new orientation, Turkey could not be completely ignored, as was for example demonstrated by the establishment of the final phase of the EU–Turkey customs union.[68] Nonetheless, the reality of the EU's pre-accession strategy was such that Turkey was left aside, something which, understandably, became a cause of growing frustration for Turkey. This is clearly demonstrated by the failed 1998 'European Conference' initiative, which was launched at the 1997 Luxembourg European Council, aiming at bringing together the EU member states and 'the European States aspiring to accede to it and sharing its values and internal and external objectives'.[69] Prime Minister Tony Blair, who held the EU Presidency in the first half of 1998, had strongly promoted the inclusion of Turkey in the group of European states aspiring to accede to the EU.[70]

In 1999, rather unexpectedly, in the middle of a terrible earthquake in Turkey or perhaps even because of this atrocious calamity, bilateral relations between Greece and Turkey saw moments of genuine improvement. On 10–11 December 1999, one of the most important European Councils in the history of EU–Turkey relations took place in Helsinki. Certainly, in the Helsinki conclusions, the EU did reiterate that everything possible would need to be done to reach a comprehensive settlement on the Cyprus question

---

66 Commission Communication COM(93) 313 final, point 46.   67 Ibid., point 47.
68 See Le Monde, 8 February 1995, 'L'Union européenne se rapproche de la Turquie. La Grèce lève son veto à l'union douanière'.
69 See Conclusions of 12–13 December 1997, point 4.
70 See Maresceau, 'The EU Pre-accession Strategies', pp. 5–7.

before the conclusion of the ongoing accession negotiations, but a settlement of this issue was not a hard precondition for EU accession of Cyprus. After the rejection of the Annan Plan by a large majority (75.38 per cent) of the Greek Cypriot population on 24 April 2004, the accession of the Republic of Cyprus to the EU, without a solution of the Cyprus issue, became a reality on 1 May 2004.

Nonetheless, in Helsinki, Turkey, for the first time, was labelled as 'a candidate State destined to join the Union on the same criteria as applied to other candidate States'. This meant that Turkey did satisfy the 'European State' conditionality of Article 49 EU. In the words of Turkish Prime Minister Bülent Ecevit, the official recognition in Helsinki of Turkey's candidate status for full EU membership constituted 'a landmark event not only for Europe, but for the world as well' and 'the road to full membership [was] hereby opened'.[71] Consequently, Turkey became an integral part of the EU's pre-accession strategy as applied to other candidate states. In 2001, the EU formalised this important upgrade through the Accession Partnership for Turkey, while Turkey, for its part, following the model used for the CEECs, laid down its own National Programme for the Adoption of the *Acquis*.[72]

In 2002, after new elections in Turkey, the political landscape changed drastically, and the Erdoğan government and the Adalet ve Kalkınma Partisi (Justice and Development Party) came to power. In the first phase of this new domestic political constellation, Turkey continued to support proactively the approach towards the EU, while the EU backed the political and economic reforms in Turkey under the new government, but signals of domestic reorientation towards a less secular Turkey and a growing impact of Islam in political life would soon emerge and did not necessarily create the most propitious atmosphere for 'enhanced pre-accession'. Perhaps even more worrying for the EU–Turkey relationship was the fact that the EU would gradually find itself in a deep domestic political and institutional crisis, which came to a first climax through the rejection of the Treaty on the European Constitution in 2005. Before this rejection, the December 2004 Brussels European Council had decided to open accession negotiations with Turkey on 3 October 2005 and, in addition, in the middle of this crisis, under Austrian

---

71 See 'Statement of Prime Minister Bülent Ecevit in Helsinki on Turkey's Candidacy to the EU December 11, 1999', www.mfa.gov.tr/statement-of-prime-minister-bulent-ecevit-in-helsinki-on-turkey_s-candidacy-to-the-eu_br_december-11_-1999-.en.mfa.
72 See 'Council Decision 2001/235/EC', *Official Journal of the European Union* (2001): L 85/13.

pressure, the EU had also decided to open accession negotiations with Croatia.

No doubt, the fiasco of the European Constitution increasingly triggered existential questions on the EU's accession strategy for Turkey. How could the EU incorporate Turkey when it found itself in such a deep crisis? As a consequence of the 2004 Enlargement, the EU had urged Turkey to sign an additional protocol to the 1963 association agreement recognising the enlargement which had just taken place. Since the 2004 enlargement also included the Republic of Cyprus among the new EU members, Turkey was initially not prepared to sign such a protocol. After heavy pressure from the EU, Turkey did finally sign, but simultaneously published a unilateral declaration emphasising that the Republic of Cyprus referred to in the new additional protocol 'was not the original partnership State established in 1960'. Consequently, Turkey would 'thus continue to regard the Greek Cypriot authorities as exercising authority, control and jurisdiction only in the territory south of the buffer zone, as is currently the case, and as not representing the Turkish Cypriot people and will treat the acts performed by them accordingly'. Moreover, Turkey also made clear that its signature, ratification and implementation of the 2005 additional protocol did not amount 'to any form of recognition of the Republic of Cyprus referred to in the Protocol'.[73] The EU's reaction to Turkey's unilateral statement was sharp and unequivocal: it had no legal effect and, in the words of the Council of the EU, 'the Republic of Cyprus became a Member State of the European Union on 1st May 2004'. The EU and its member states added 'that they recognise only the Republic of Cyprus as a subject of international law' and in addition, the EU also urged Turkey to open its ports and airports to Cyprus. Clearly, these two different approaches looked irreconcilable, and the opening of accession negotiations, 5 weeks later, did not have a calming effect on the dispute.

Since then, the follow-up of EU–Turkey relations has gone from bad to worse and is now largely characterised by stagnation and decline.[74] On 11 December 2006, as a consequence of the Cyprus dispute, the Council of the EU decided that eight chapters directly or indirectly related to the rejection by Turkey to open its ports and airports could not be opened for negotiation. After 2006, only three chapters have been opened (Monetary

---

73 See 'Declaration by Turkey on Cyprus, 29 July 2005', www.mfa.gov.tr/declaration-by-turkey-on-cyprus_-29-july-2005.en.mfa.

74 On the follow-up, see M. Müftüler-Baç, 'External Differentiated Integration: The Modalities of Turkey's Opting into the European Union' (2021), https://papers.ssrn.com/sol3/papers.cfm?abstract_id=3807363.

Policy, Regional Policy and Coordination of Structural Instruments and Financial and Budgetary Provisions), while all important substantive chapters remain hermetically sealed. It is understandable that, under these circumstances, the Commission's global impression is that 'Turkey's accession negotiations have effectively come to a standstill' and 'no further chapters can be considered for opening or closing'.[75] This view is shared by other EU institutions.[76]

In the present contribution not much more can be done than to take note of this state of affairs and only the most pressing EU concerns can be provided, all the more so since, so far, Turkey has shown little sign of being amenable to cooperation. In the EU's view, Turkey has continued to move further away from basic EU values 'with backsliding in the areas of democracy, rule of law, fundamental rights and the independence of the judiciary'.[77] All these concerns and many others are reiterated in various recent Council Conclusions.[78] For its part, the Commission observes that '[t]he continued arrest and pre-trial detention under broad anti-terrorist legislation of opposition leaders, human rights activists, journalists, civil society and academics is deeply worrying'[79] and Turkey's reaction to the 2016 failed coup d'état is considered very disproportionate. In the Joint Communication by the Commission and the High Representative of the Union for Foreign Affairs and Security of 22 March 2021 a new attempt was made to sum up the main components of the deteriorating state of the bilateral relationship. Certainly, the EU continues to reaffirm its 'strategic interest in the development of a cooperative and mutually beneficial relationship with Turkey' and insists that it continues to be in favour 'of a positive EU-Turkey agenda' and prepared 'to engage with Turkey in a phased, proportioned and reversible manner to enhance cooperation in a number of areas of common interest', but this requires from Turkey at least 'readiness to promote a genuine partnership'. In particular, Turkish actions in the eastern Mediterranean challenging the rights of the Republic of Cyprus, its actions against Greece and its assertive interventions in regional conflicts are unacceptable and the

75 See European Commission, Staff Working Document, Turkey Report, SWD(2019) 220 final.
76 See, for example, the European Parliament resolution of 13 March 2019 calling for the suspension of the accession negotiations with Turkey, P8_TA(2019)0200.
77 See European Commission, '2020 Communication on EU Enlargement Policy', 6 October 2020, Commission Communication COM(2020) 660 final, p. 4.
78 See Council Conclusions, 'Enlargement and Stabilisation and Association Process', 13 December 2022, 15935/22, where the Council also expresses its deep regret with regard to Turkey's non-alignment with EU sanctions against Russia, see point 51.
79 See Commission Communication COM(2020) 660 final.

EU expects from Turkey 'de-escalation'. [80] While this chapter was being finalised new direct contacts between the EU and Turkish political leadership are taking place, which may perhaps bring signals of "de-escalation" but it is, for the moment, unclear how this will be achieved. Anyway, one is far away from the promising 1999 Helsinki Statement that Turkey is 'a candidate State destined to join the Union on the same criteria as applied to other candidate States'. Today, the situation is simply that Turkey's commitments are not matched by corresponding measures and reforms. Therefore, it is also not surprising that, under such circumstances, nothing has been achieved 'to re-energise the accession process', as was proclaimed in the famous EU–Turkey Statement of 18 March 2016 in the midst of the refugee crisis.[81] Even if the statement itself has been subjected to criticism from various sides, on the whole, the arrangements have, in the EU's view, delivered results and massive humanitarian aid has been channelled to Turkey, but multiple problems remain.[82]

The Western Balkans

In this section only some general elements of the EU's approach towards accession of the western Balkan countries can be provided. Unfortunately, in the present contribution, details of the complex state of play of the current negotiations and current bilateral relations between the EU and the individual western Balkan States cannot be examined. It is also useful to note that after the completion of the present chapter in this book, the EU has updated certain aspects with regard to its relations with the western Balkans.[83]

The EU has on multiple occasions expressed strong support for 'a credible European perspective for the Western Balkans' and for 'an enhanced accession process'.[84] EU enlargement to incorporate the western Balkan countries is presented as a crucial and effective foreign policy goal to establish a sound neighbourhood relationship. In the EU's view, this enlargement would extend the reach of the Union's fundamental values of respect for human dignity, freedom, democracy, the rule of law, peacebuilding and respect for human rights. Certainly, nobody expects that meeting these standards for accession would be easy, and each application is to be judged on its own

---

80 See JOIN(2021) 8 final, 20 March 2021; 'Statement of the Members of the European Council', 25 March 2021, SN 18/21; Council Conclusions of 13 December 2022.

81 Council, Press Release, 144/16, 18 March 2016.

82 See Commission Communication of 12 October 2022, COM(2022) 528 final.

83 Ibid.; Council Conclusions, 'Enlargement and Stabilisation and Association Process', 13 December 2022, 15935/22.

84 See Commission Communication COM(2020) 57 final; Commission Communication COM(2018) 65 final.

merits. Moreover, it is true that the EU's objectives for the western Balkans have to be achieved in a very complex and fragmented historical, geographical, political and legal environment wherein not just candidate states and EU institutions have their word to say. After the 'big bang' enlargement of 2004, critical voices on further EU enlargement have increasingly been heard, and signals of enlargement fatigue have become increasingly prevalent in various member states. In particular, the growing uneasiness, if not irritation, in a number of member states and EU institutions concerning the 'rule of law' discussion, particularly insofar as Poland and Hungary are concerned, is tending to hinder further accession initiatives, particularly in the western Balkans.

As explained above, member states occupy a key position in the enlargement process, and they have indeed, politically as well as legally, the final say on each individual accession. This is a reality which stems directly from the basic treaties, and the importance of the weight of the member states in this procedure has in the past long been neglected, but, apparently, the situation is changing.

It is against this background that the European Commission's Communication of 5 February 2020, 'Enhancing the Accession Process – A Credible EU Perspective for the Western Balkans', has to be understood. In that policy paper, the Commission came up with a proposal to reinvigorate the enlargement strategy,[85] after the French government had published in November 2019 its 'Non-paper Reforming the European Union Accession Process', which was strongly critical of the ongoing enlargement.[86] The 'non-paper' suggested that the future EU accession process should be based not simply upon opening and closing thirty-five chapters of the *acquis*, as had been the case before, but on stringent conditionality and much more on thematic clustering to bring about effective convergence towards European norms and standards as well as on 'reversibility', allowing the EU to stop the enlargement process if a candidate was no longer in a position to meet the basic criteria for membership or ceased to fulfil the commitments which it had undertaken. The timing of the French initiative was not innocent, since the decision on the opening of accession negotiations with Albania and North Macedonia was then a top priority of the EU's official political

---

85 Ibid. For more details, see C. Rapoport, 'Une perspective européenne enfin crédible pour les Balkans?', *Revue trimestrielle de droit européen, Action extérieure de l'Union européenne. Chroniques* (2020): 695–700.
86 For the text, see Politico, www.politico.eu/wp-content/uploads/2019/11/Enlargement-nonpaper.pdf.

neighbourhood agenda (see below). Moreover, some of the other member states, without saying this loudly, seemed to share the French approach.

In its Communication, the Commission, without copying word for word the French policy paper, followed nevertheless its main message on 'clustering' chapters of the *acquis*, but was also keen to emphasise that it was not aiming to change, as such, the Copenhagen criteria. What the Commission did was in the first place to propose making the enlargement process more comprehensive. In the Commission's words, there is a 'firm merit-based prospect for full EU membership for the Western Balkans', which is 'indispensable for the EU's credibility, for the EU'[s] success and for the EU's influence in the region and beyond, especially at times of heightened geopolitical competition'.

In the Commission's revised methodology, updated in the Commission's Communication on EU Enlargement Policy of 12 October 2022,[87] the new cluster on 'the fundamentals', that is, the one on the rule of law, economic criteria and public administration reform, occupies a central place. Progress in these 'fundamentals' is an essential prerequisite for going ahead in other clusters and '[n]egotiations on each cluster will be opened as a whole – after fulfilling the opening benchmarks – rather than on an individual chapter basis'. The leading principles of the revised enlargement strategy can be summarised under the following policy options: reinforced credibility, with strong focus on fundamental reforms; solid political steering; and a stronger dynamic process, creating opportunities for early alignment and increased predictability both for the candidate states and for the EU. The EU is prepared to provide incentives to support the reform process but, in the event of serious prolonged stagnation or backsliding, the possibility of taking restrictive measures is not ruled out. Of course, all this needs to be further refined and worked out, and the envisaged strategy does not necessarily create the impression of a rapid and smooth achievement of the set accession objectives. Today, whether one likes it or not, the enlargement process is much more demanding than used to be the case in the past.

Notwithstanding the fact that in this section no examination of the state of play of the relations of the various western Balkans countries to the EU is provided, it might nevertheless be useful to recall that the EU is currently negotiating accession with Montenegro and Serbia and that the first intergovernmental conferences opening the accession negotiations with North Macedonia and Albania were held on 18 and 19 July 2022, after a solution had

---

87 See COM(2022) 528 final.

been found for pending bilateral issues between Bulgaria and North Macedonia. As has already been mentioned, Bosnia and Herzegovina received candidate status in 2022, but accession negotiations have not yet been opened. Kosovo, which has not applied for EU membership and does not have candidate status, has concluded a non-mixed Stabilisation and Association Agreement with the EU, but is not recognised by five EU member states (Cyprus, Greece, Romania, Slovakia and Spain). A lot will depend on achieving a comprehensive legally binding settlement between Serbia and Kosovo in order to move forward.

The Recent Applications for EU Accession by Ukraine,
Moldova and Georgia

Since the termination of writing of the chapter on EU enlargement in this volume on 1 February 2022, Ukraine, Moldova and Georgia have, in the aftermath of the Russian invasion of Ukraine of 24 February 2022, applied for EU membership. This deserves a word of explanation, which initially was not foreseen in this section. This explanation is not much more than a presentation of a short timeline of events relevant for understanding procedure for EU accession by the three countries concerned. Unfortunately, it is not feasible to provide a substantive epilogue to this chapter.

Certainly, the association agreements which Ukraine, Moldova and Georgia have concluded with the EU already had a far-reaching integration-oriented character.[88] The preamble of these agreements acknowledges 'the European aspirations' of these countries and the 'European choice' they have made. The three association agreements also state that they do not prejudice future bilateral developments. Furthermore, the agreements with Ukraine and Moldova recall that they are European countries which '[share] a common history'; while the preamble of the agreement with Georgia recognises that Georgia is 'an Eastern European country'. In addition, in the case of Ukraine, the country's constitution was amended in February 2019 in order to include an explicit political commitment for Ukraine to become a member of the EU and NATO.[89] However, no reference to possible future accession could be found anywhere in these association agreements, as was

---

88 For a thorough analysis of the association agreement with Ukraine, see G. Van der Loo, *The EU–Ukraine Association Agreement and Deep and Comprehensive Free Trade Area: A New Legal Instrument for EU Integration without Membership* (Leiden and Boston, MA, Brill–Nijhoff, 2016), especially pp. 23–7 on the 'integration-oriented' character.
89 For more details, see R. Petrov, 'Challenges of the EU–Ukraine AA's Effective Implementation into the Legal Order of Ukraine', in S. Lorenzmeier, R. Petrov and C. Vedder (eds.), *EU External Relations: Shared Competences and Shared Values in*

the case in the 1963 Association Agreement with Turkey. In other words, the EU's approach towards these countries was a very cautious one and the Eastern Partnership countries concerned had in their association agreements with the EU also not been defined as 'potential candidates for EU membership', a qualification which was explicitly used for the western Balkan states. All this can easily explain why the chapter on EU enlargement in this book was very concise with regard to the Eastern Partnership states. In the prevailing geopolitical constellation, a scenario whereby the EU would be considering preparing for the accession of those states in the near future appeared highly hypothetical, almost surrealistic to contemplate. But the 2022 Russian military intervention changed that picture drastically. Indeed, very rapidly after the beginning of the war, Ukraine formally applied for EU membership on 28 February 2022; Moldova and Georgia followed less than a week later on 3 March. As early as 17 June 2022, the European Commission presented its opinions on the applications for membership, in which it noted 'the European perspective' of the three applicant states.[90] Insofar as Ukraine and Moldova, were concerned, the Commission emphasised that the two applicants should be granted candidate status if a number of conditions were fulfilled. According to the Commission, candidate status could not yet be granted to Georgia; that country was encouraged to fully address the long list of priorities which the Commission had identified in its opinion of 17 June 2022. The Commission's strategic options on this matter were endorsed by the European Council Conclusions of 23–24 June 2022 and the Commission was invited to report on the fulfillment of the conditions specified in its opinions. Further steps had to be envisaged by the European Council 'when all the conditions are fully met'. In some recent comments on the Commission's choice, it has been argued that the granting of candidate status to Ukraine can be seen as 'essentially an act of moral support, to boost the country's resistance to the aggression and, perhaps more than ever in the history of EU enlargement, as a (geo)political decision rather than a scrupulous legal application of the conditions related to Article 49 TEU'.[91]

Agreements between the EU and Its Eastern European Neighbours (Cham, Springer, 2021), pp. 129–46, 138–9.

90 For the Commission's opinion on Ukraine's application, see COM(2022) 407 final. For Moldova's application, see COM(2022) 406 final. For Georgia's application, see COM (2022) 405 final.

91 See R. Petrov and C. Hillion, 'Guest Editorial, Accession through War. Ukraine's Road to the EU. Applying for EU Membership in Times of War', *Common Market Law Review* 59 (2022): 1289–1300, 1291.

This may indeed be the case, but, at the end of the day, a close legal scrutiny remains indispensable in an accession procedure.

In its opinions of 17 June 2022, the Commission addressed the question of democracy in the applicant states, focusing on respect for the rule of law, the state of the judiciary, the fight against corruption and the issue of organised crime, all topics which, in one way or another, had their relevance for the applicant states. Another aspect, equally relevant for the three candidates, concerns the issue of fundamental rights. Insofar as Ukraine is concerned, a difficult topic could be that of rights of persons belonging to minorities in the field of education and language.

On 12 October 2022, the Commission published its yearly 'Communication on EU Enlargement Policy',[92] but this does not add much to what was already known. In the words of the Commission '[t]he Russian aggression has demonstrated more clearly than ever that the perspective of membership of the European Union is a strong anchor not only for prosperity, but also for peace and security', something which was also shared by the Council.[93] The task that now lies ahead for the EU institutions is huge and will necessarily take considerable time. A lot will depend on the will and mood of the member states to pursue the path which the EU leadership has chosen in 2022.

The European Very Small States

Also the special case of the very small European states Liechtenstein, Andorra, San Marino and Monaco deserves to be mentioned. Today, only Liechtenstein is a member of the European Economic Area (EEA) and already fully participates in the internal market, but does not envisage applying for EU membership. San Marino organised a referendum on possible application for EU membership, held on 20 October 2013. A majority of those of the San Marino population who participated in the vote was in favour of such an application, but the required quorum of 32 per cent of registered voters was not met. That meant the end of San Marino's attempt to apply for EU membership, and this will probably not change soon. There are, for the moment, no indications that either Andorra or Monaco is interested in applying for EU membership. Since 2015, Andorra, San Marino and Monaco have been negotiating a far-reaching association agreement on their participation in the internal market, but these negotiations are, for a variety of reasons, particularly complex and have so far not yet been

92 COM(2022) 528 final.   93 See Conclusions, 13 December 2022, 15935/22.

finalised. This complexity has to do with, on the one hand, the specific nature of these countries as very small states, something which is not always well understood by the EU, and, on the other hand, the very far-reaching dimension, institutionally and substantially of the envisaged agreement(s). Notwithstanding the fact that the very small European states are legally entitled to apply for EU membership, the EU is not necessarily an ardent proponent of EU accession by these states because of the institutional complications which such an accession could entail.[94] A final remark about very small states and EU membership is that it is often overlooked that Malta is a very small state, which in area (but not in population) is smaller than Andorra, but Malta is already a full-fledged EU member state.

Consent of European Parliament, Final Council Decision and Ratification by the Member States

Since the European Parliament has to give its consent to accession of an applicant state (Article 49 TEU), it is logical that it is formally informed of each application for accession. Article 49 provides that the European Parliament as well as national parliaments shall be notified of an application for accession. Since the entry into force of the Lisbon Treaty, national parliaments too are notified of an application for accession. This is understandable, since most, if not all, parliaments of the member states are involved in the respective national ratification procedures of an accession treaty. In the various enlargements which have taken place so far, the impact of national parliaments in this operation has been minimal. However, now that EU enlargement is becoming more politically sensitive than it used to be in the past, it is possible that in the future, at least in some member states, further EU enlargement might be subject to closer scrutiny or controversy.

The first EC treaties contained no mention of the (parliamentary) Assembly in the accession procedure. It was only in the Single European Act (1987) that assent of the European Parliament was introduced as a procedural requirement in the accession procedure before enlargement could take place. Notwithstanding this important competence, whereby the European Parliament can refuse to give its consent, its impact on the various enlargements which have taken place afterwards, including the 2004 enlargement, has so far been minimal.

---

94 See European Commission, 'Relations with the Principality of Andorra, the Principality of Monaco and the Republic of San Marino. Options for Closer Integration with the EU', COM(2012) 680 final, 20 November 2012.

In the accession procedure, the ultimate step from the Council's perspective is its formal decision accepting the application for admission, the conditions for admission and the necessary adjustments to the treaties. Conditions and adjustments are subject to an agreement between the member states and the applicant state.

Once accession negotiations are concluded, the final drafting of the various legal instruments for accession takes place. These instruments are the Treaty of Accession and the Final Act which are international treaties between the EU member states and the applicant state. The Treaty of Accession stipulates that the applicant will become a member state once the ratification procedures have been completed. The most important substantive part of these legal instruments is the Act of Accession, which itself forms an integral part of the Treaty of Accession. The Act of Accession contains inter alia the substantive arrangements regarding transitional measures. The Final Act takes the form of a Table of Contents of the commitments undertaken and provides a list of Declarations of the parties.[95]

Ratification by all contracting parties is required before the Treaty of Accession can enter into force. In the applicant states, this is, generally speaking, no problem since one might expect that candidates are in principle eager to become EU members. Nevertheless, an accession treaty has twice been rejected by Norway, in 1972 and 1994, in a referendum after that country had negotiated and even signed the accession treaty. In the 1972 referendum 53.5 per cent of those who participated rejected the accession treaty. This rejection did not prevent the accession of the three other applicants: the UK, Denmark and the Republic of Ireland; in the 1994 referendum the 'no' vote was 52.2 per cent. Again, this did not prevent the accession of the other applicants: Austria, Finland and Sweden.

The Treaty of Accession is a classical international law treaty signed by states. The EU itself is not a contracting party to an accession treaty. If one EU member state does not ratify the accession treaty, it cannot enter into force. Such a scenario has never occurred, and only once in the history of EU enlargement has a member state organised a referendum to approve an accession treaty. This happened in France in 1972 with the first accession treaty. In the light of what had happened in the 1960s in relation to the application of the UK to join the EC, this can easily be understood. General de Gaulle had on various occasions vetoed the UK's attempts to join the EC. His

95 On the instruments of accession, see Tatham, *Enlargement of the European Union*, pp. 260–1.

successor, Georges Pompidou, was in favour of the UK's accession, but was of the opinion that the political backing of the population for such a radical reversal of the French position was indispensible. A referendum offered the possibility of acquiring democratic support for this move and, with a majority of 68.31 per cent of the votes cast, the French population accepted the accession treaty which had been negotiated.[96] Later, in 2005, in the aftermath of the failure of the project for a Constitution for Europe, which had led to a negative outcome of the referendum in France, an amendment to the French constitution has been proposed, whereby, as a matter of principle, for future EU enlargements, a referendum is required, unless accession treaties are approved through the *procédure du Congrès*, that is, a joint meeting of the members of the Assemblée nationale (National Assembly) and the Senate. Needless to say, under this new procedure, which was introduced into the French constitution in 2008, future enlargements could face additional difficulties in France.

Conclusion

This chapter aimed to provide an analytical overview of the EU's approach towards the phenomenon of 'enlargement'. It focused on the structure and contents of the provision on enlargement in the EU Treaty and examined closely its practice. This approach, which necessarily concentrated on the EU inter-institutional reality of the enlargement phenomenon, allowed the inclusion of precious elements of the often complex historical background on a variety of issues which are directly related to the topic examined. Consequently, the current contribution made a complex journey through the various steps of the process of enlargement from the moment of application for accession to the entry into force of the treaty of accession.

The conclusion of this chapter returns, for some final comments, to the conditionality requirements for EU membership. The 'European State' condition, which the enlargement provision of the TEU imposes, has in most cases not given rise to difficulties, since virtually all applications originated from 'European States' and this did not need further clarification. Morocco's application was swiftly set aside by the Council. That of Turkey could have been a more serious stumbling block, but that was already, in a very early phase of the EC's treaty practice, dissipated with the 1963 signature of the

---

96 See F. Decaumont, 'Le référendum du 23 avril 1972', in J.-R. Bernard, F. Caron, M. Vaïsse and M. Woimant (eds.), *Georges Pompidou et l'Europe* (Brussels, Éditions Complexe, 1995), pp. 583–601.

association agreement, which in its preamble stipulated that the agreement could 'facilitate the accession of Turkey to the Community at a later date'. Of course, that did not mean that Turkey's accession was guaranteed or would be easy, but at least Turkey's 'eligibility' for membership seemed to have been recognised, and that is today, notwithstanding all the difficulties of the present EU–Turkey relationship, still the case.

The second conditionality test, introduced rather late in the history of the EU's enlargement, which requires respect for European values and principles, is more of a problem for certain applicants. Currently, the biggest difficulty focuses again on Turkey, and accession negotiations with that country are for the moment at a complete standstill. Paradoxically, in some ways this suits the EU. The EU has no clear vision regarding what to do with the Turkish application for membership. Moreover, the EU itself has been going through an uneasy period which includes, among other things, Brexit, problems with certain member states from central and eastern Europe regarding European values, the migration crisis and increasing enlargement fatigue in a number of member states. All this, unavoidably, may also affect pending and future applications for accession from western Balkan countries and the very recent applications for EU membership of Ukraine, Moldova and Georgia. A key aspect here, which could not be properly addressed in this contribution, is the position of Russia, the most important neighbour of the enlarged EU. What went wrong in this relationship and why? Whatever the answer to these questions may be, one thing is certain: further EU enlargement eastwards remains, under the present circumstances, an extremely difficult challenge. Real change would probably be possible only with a workable EU–Russia relationship, but, unfortunately, that is something which, for the moment, is very far from being the reality.

Recommended Reading

Hillion, C. 'The EU's Neighbourhood Policy towards Eastern Europe', in A. Dashwood and M. Maresceau (eds.), *Law and Practice of EU External Relations: Salient Features of a Changing Landscape* (Cambridge, Cambridge University Press, 2008), pp. 309–33.

Maresceau, M. 'Pre-accession', in M. Cremona (ed.), *The Enlargement of the European Union* (Oxford, Oxford University Press, 2003), pp. 9–42.

Ott, A. and K. Inglis (eds.). *Handbook on European Enlargement: A Commentary on the Enlargement Process* (The Hague, T. M. C. Asser Press, 2002).

Petrov, R. 'Challenges of the EU–Ukraine AA's Effective Implementation into the Legal Order of Ukraine', in S. Lorenzmeier, R. Petrov and C. Vedder (eds.), *EU External*

Relations: Shared Competences and Shared Values in Agreements between the EU and Its Eastern European Neighbours (Cham, Springer, 2021), pp. 129–46.

Tatham, A. F. *Enlargement of the European Union* (Austin, TX and Boston, MA, Wolters Kluwer, 2009).

Van Elsuwege, P. *From Soviet Republics to EU Member States: A Legal and Political Assessment of the Baltic States' Accession to the EU*, 2 vols. (Leiden and Boston, MA, Martinus Nijhoff, 2008).

Van der Loo, G. *The EU–Ukraine Association Agreement and Deep and Comprehensive Free Trade Area: A New Legal Instrument for EU Integration without Membership* (Leiden and Boston, MA, Brill–Nijhoff, 2016).

PART III

*

NARRATIVES AND OUTCOMES

16

A Global Perspective on European Cooperation and Integration since 1918

ANNE-ISABELLE RICHARD

Introduction

European integration as the solution that brought peace and democracy after the devastating wars ravaging Europe in the early twentieth century: this is still one of the most widespread narratives about European cooperation. It is, and was, also the pivot of the discourse of the European Union (EU) and its predecessors to justify their existence and create their success in a bold form of self-fashioning.[1] Just like the German *Stunde Null* (zero hour) and the international caesura that the United Nations emphasised between itself and the League of Nations, European cooperation projects after the Second World War emphasised the novelty of their endeavours and the break with the preceding, violent era.[2]

The post-1945 literature often feels obliged to provide a nod to the inter-war period in referencing Richard Coudenhove-Kalergi or Aristide Briand as European visionaries. This nod implicitly confirms a 'novelty narrative'. The historiography on inter-war European cooperation has nuanced this narrative, not in providing a teleology, but in mapping out longer developments and, sometimes, continuities. The recent historiography on European integration after 1945 has been nuancing the 'benign narrative' of peace, democracy and human rights, for example highlighting the imbrication of European integration in colonialism, which is generally not acknowledged in the EU's narratives. This chapter will build on these literatures and situate the impetus for European cooperation and integration in a changing global context from

---

1 See K. K. Patel, 'Provincialising European Union: Co-operation and Integration in Europe in a Historical Perspective', *Contemporary European History* 22 no. 4 (2013): 649–673, 665.
2 R. Overy, 'Interwar, War, Postwar: Was There a Zero Hour in 1945?', in D. Stone (ed.), *The Oxford Handbook of Postwar European History* (Oxford, Oxford University Press, 2012), pp. 60–78, 77; M. Mazower, *Governing the World: The History of an Idea* (London, Penguin, 2012).

the First World War onward. As a result of this global perspective, the colonial dimension of European projects and narratives, as well as (perspectives on) developments in Africa and in Asia, will play a significant role.

War and peace were catalysts for structural changes taking place since the turn of the century. As the French publicist Georges Duhamel put it, 'it was during the War that we became very conscious of what Europe was and what it represented in the world'.[3] After the First World War, the position of Europe in the world changed profoundly and an intense sense of crisis swept across Europe. This was not just the result of the war in Europe, it was also the result of developments in other parts of the world. Concerns over the rise of the United States since the late nineteenth century, the creation of the Soviet Union (USSR), the growing economic and political importance of the British Dominions and Latin America and the rise of Japan were coupled with fear about the large-scale unrest that was spreading around the colonial world. Particularly the latter fears were linked to the future of European colonial empires and concomitantly the economic and geopolitical future and civilisational standing of Europe in the world. When studied from this perspective, it becomes clear that many of the actors examined in the inter-war literature argued for various forms of European cooperation inspired both by their experience of the Great War in Europe and by a form of existential fear that Europe might lose its position at the top of the geopolitical, civilisational and racial ladder. The rise of the extra-European world provided a rationale for European cooperation. In turn, European colonies, in particular the African colonies, were seen as essential to European recovery. Within a changing world order, calls for European cooperation in the inter-war period were aimed at maintaining the global status quo. The period after 1945 is often pointed to as the period when the big shift in Europe's global position took place and as a result solutions to these challenges needed to be found. However, this chapter argues that these changes were already under way and that answers to existential questions were already being discussed in the inter-war period. Without an understanding of these discussions, the answers of the post-1945 period cannot be understood.

This chapter will therefore take a global view that includes an examination of colonial thought in Europeanist circles for three interlinked reasons: to fully understand the fundamental challenge from all corners of the globe that was already being felt at the end of the First World War; how the idea of Europe – in civilisational and racial terms – was heavily informed

---

3 G. Duhamel, in *Entretiens: L'avenir de l'esprit européen* (Paris, Institut International de Coopération Intellectuelle, 1934), p. 128.

by non-European interactions; how Africa and Asia came to be understood differently and thus why Eurafrica became relevant. For some, the colonial community of interest was the reason why a united Europe would be impossible; for others colonial ties were no less important, but constituted the reason why it was necessary to integrate overseas territories in a European project. This chapter will thus demonstrate how colonies were an essential part of inter-war European projects and indicate how they continued to be so well up to (and, in a certain way, after) decolonisation.

The chapter will focus on four frameworks: geopolitics, economics, civilisational ideas and racial beliefs, that played a predominant role in the writings of many Europeanists, across Europe. Their emphases differed, but aspects of these frameworks can be found in almost all of their conceptions of global order and the role of Europe and European states in that order. In analysing the writings and projects both of state actors and of non-state actors, the chapter will highlight the plurality of Europeanist projects explored and launched in the inter-war period that are commonly understood as constituting 'European integration' and indicate the continuity between inter-war and post-war projects. In understanding European cooperation projects as possible answers to the question of how to deal with a changing global order, this chapter will also nuance exceptionalist or *sui generis* arguments about European cooperation. Finally, a comment on terminology. European cooperation; integration; federation; Union; Pan-Europa; United States of Europe: all of these terms were used to describe some form of cooperation between the European states in the inter-war period. I will use 'European cooperation' as an umbrella term, which also points to the plurality of European projects, since these terms were not used very precisely and cooperation was the most generic word used. I will follow common practice in the literature and use 'European integration' for the process of cooperation in the EU and its direct predecessors after 1945.[4]

Historiography

The historiography on European integration is often associated with a focus on state actors and chasing the 30-year rule. Indeed, inter-state and inter-institutional relations have played a prominent role.[5] However, the 'early'

---

4 See A. G. Harryvan and J. van der Harst, *Documents on European Union* (Basingstoke, Palgrave Macmillan, 1997), p. 2.
5 For an overview, see W. Kaiser, 'From State to Society? The Historiography of European Integration', in M. Cini and A. K. Bourne (eds.), *Palgrave Advances in European Union Studies* (Basingstoke, Palgrave Macmillan, 2006), pp. 190–208.

literature, represented by someone such as Walter Lipgens, forced to wait for state archives to open, made a virtue out of necessity. If we look beyond the ideological component of this 'Federalist hurray historiography',[6] we see a transnational approach that has become more popular in the last 20 years, which combines state/institutional archives with civil society sources examining activist networks across borders.[7]

This approach is perhaps even more pronounced when it comes to the inter-war literature. 'No more war' and Franco-German relations are important themes in this literature, but it also has a strong focus on the *variety* of initiatives proposed and implemented. As a result, it highlights the role of non-state actors, such as business leaders, economists, publicists, intellectuals and lobby groups, more than the post-1945 literature does. In foregrounding the interaction between state and non-state actors the inter-war historiography used a multilevel governance lens *avant la lettre*. Both the attention to the diversity of projects and the range of actors facilitate the making of connections to developments in the late 1940s.

There are multiple strands that can be methodologically and thematically (reflecting the variety of projects) distinguished in the inter-war literature. First, there is a host of 'national' histories as well as biographical studies. Examples of national histories include Duchenne's study of Belgian and Holl's study of German Europeanist networks.[8] Amongst the biographies, we see a mix of types of actors: besides statesmen such as French foreign minister Aristide Briand, or diplomats such as Jacques Seydoux, activists such as Paneuropa-founder Richard Coudenhove-Kalergi, publicists such as Francis Delaisi and trade unionists such as Edo Fimmen have been the subject of biographical studies.[9] Some of these cross the Second World War divide,

6 W. Kaiser, 'From Isolation to Centrality: Contemporary History Meets European Studies', in W. Kaiser and A. Varsori (eds.), *European Union History: Themes and Debates* (Basingstoke, Palgrave Macmillan, 2010), pp. 45–65, 45.

7 For types of sources, see particularly W. Lipgens, *Sources for the History of European Integration (1945–1955): A Guide to the Archives in the Countries of the Community* (Leiden, Sijthof, 1980); K. K. Patel, 'Widening and Deepening? Recent Advances in European Integration History', *Neue Politische Literatur* 64 (2019): 327–57; P. Clavin, 'Defining Transnationalism', *Contemporary European History* 14, no. 4 (2005): 421–39.

8 G. Duchenne, *Esquisses d'une Europe nouvelle: L'Europeisme dans la Belgique de l'entre-deux-guerres (1919–1939)* (Brussels, Peter Lang, 2008); K. Holl, 'Europapolitik im Vorfeld der deutschen Regierungspolitik: Zur Tätigkeit proeuropäischer Organisationen in der Weimarer Republik', *Historische Zeitschrift* 219, no. 1 (1974): 33–94.

9 J. Bariéty (ed.), *Aristide Briand, la Société des Nations et l'Europe, 1919–1932* (Strasbourg, Presses universitaires de Strasbourg, 2007); A. Ziegerhofer-Prettenthaler, *Botschafter Europas: Richard Nikolaus Coudenhove-Kalergi und die Paneuropa-Bewegung in den zwanziger und dreißiger Jahren* (Vienna, Böhlau, 2004); S. Jeannesson, *Jacques Seydoux: Diplomate, 1870–1929* (Paris, Presse de l'université Paris-Sorbonne, 2013); E. Bussière,

such as Deighton's study of the British Labour politician Ernest Bevin.[10] Closely related to more state-centric studies are the works that examine the Briand proposal for European cooperation of 1929–30.[11]

A strand of research that at times draws genealogical lines well beyond the inter-war period, going back to the nineteenth century or even further, focuses on ideas of Europe and the role of culture and intellectuals. While the projects studied in the other strands did emphatically aspire to 'practical politics', this was not always the case here.[12] Examples of the intellectual strand are the work by Pegg, Chabot or, more recently, Greiner, who examines newspapers.[13] Bailey's study of German visions of Europe, moreover, connects developments on either side of the Second World War.[14]

Economic or technical projects for European cooperation are also well represented in the literature. Studies of economic projects for European cooperation have a long pedigree and connect economic and business history with the history of European cooperation, regularly crossing the Second World War divide.[15] The technological historiography is more recent, with the studies coming out of the Tension of Europe network, such as that of Lagendijk, definitively putting the field on the map.[16] Political party families,

O. Dard and G. Duchenne (eds.), *Francis Delaisi, du dreyfusisme à 'l'Europe nouvelle'* (Brussels, Peter Lang, 2015); W. Buschak, *Edo Fimmen: Der schöne Traum von Europa und die Globalisierung* (Essen, Klartext, 2002).

10 A. Deighton, 'Ernest Bevin and the Idea of Euro-Africa from the Interwar to the Postwar Period', in M.-T. Bitsch and G. Bossuat (eds.), *L'Europe unie et l'Afrique: De l'idée d'Eurafrique à la Convention de Lomé I* (Brussels, Bruylant, 2005), pp. 97–118.

11 W. Lipgens, 'Europäische Einigungsidee 1923–1930 und Briands Europaplan im Urteil der deutschen Akten', *Historische Zeitschrift* 203, no. 1 (1966), part 1: 46–89, part 2: 316–63; A. Fleury and L. Jilek (eds.), *Le Plan Briand d'Union fédérale européenne: Perspectives nationales et transnationales, avec documents* (Bern, Peter Lang, 1991).

12 A. I. Richard, 'Huizinga, Intellectual Cooperation and the Spirit of Europe, 1933–1945', in M. Hewitson and M. D'Auria (eds.), *Europe in Crisis: Intellectuals and the European Idea, 1917–1957* (Oxford, Berghahn, 2012), pp. 243–56.

13 C. H. Pegg, *Evolution of the European idea, 1914–1932* (Chapel Hill, NC, University of North Carolina Press, 1983); J.-L. Chabot, *Aux origines intellectuelles de l'Union européenne: L'idée d'Europe unie de 1919 à 1939* (Grenoble, Presses universitaires de Grenoble, 2005 [1978]); F. Greiner, *Wege nach Europa: Deutungen eines imaginierten Kontinents in deutschen, britischen und amerikanischen Printmedien, 1914–1945* (Gottingen, Wallstein, 2014).

14 C. Bailey, *Between Yesterday and Tomorrow: German Visions of Europe, 1926–1950* (Oxford, Berghahn, 2013).

15 E. Bussière, *La France, la Belgique, et l'organisation économique de l'Europe, 1918–1930* (Paris, Imprimerie Nationale, 1992); R. Boyce, *The Great Interwar Crisis and the Collapse of Globalization* (Basingstoke, Palgrave Macmillan, 2009); L. Badel, *Un milieu libéral et européen: Le grande commerce français 1925–1948* (Paris, Imprimerie Nationale, 1999); I. J. Blanken, *Geschiedenis van Koninklijke Philips Electronics N.V.*, vol. III *De ontwikkeling van de N.V. Philips' gloeilampenfabrieken tot elektrotechnisch concern (1922–1934)* (Leiden, Martinus Nijhoff, 1992).

16 V. Lagendijk, *Electrifying Europe: The Power of Europe in the Construction of Electricity Networks* (Amsterdam, Aksant, 2008).

such as Catholic networks, have been analysed by Kaiser.[17] Buschak's work shows that leftwing ideas, projects and support for European cooperation deserve more attention in the literature, particularly since the questions that inter-war leftwing movements posed are still making the headlines today.[18]

The study of networks plays a prominent role in the inter-war European cooperation literature. Recent work on international organisations such as the League of Nations has strengthened this approach. The overlap in and circulation of personnel, practices and ideas of these institutions and networks situates European initiatives in a wider framework of (re)organising the world, both after the First World War and after the Second World War.[19]

While the 'novelty narrative' of the EU has come up against the inter-war literature, the 'benign narrative' of peace, democracy and human rights has also been corrected in the literature. This has been done in a number of ways, for example in studies that examine national socialist or fascist projects for European cooperation.[20] The following will focus on another corrective to the 'benign narrative': the literature that analyses the entanglement between European cooperation and colonialism. Ageron's 1975 article put Eurafrica and inter-war Franco-German colonial debates on the agenda.[21] Since then the concept of Eurafrica has remained a focal point for studies that address colonialism and European cooperation, although the bulk of attention has been directed towards the post-1945 period and to France.

Most of the strands mentioned above can be discerned in this Eurafrican subfield too. Some of these studies focus on specific empires, such as Leikam on the British, Deschamps on the Belgian or Montarsolo and Migani on the French empire, or Kottos on all of these together.[22] While most works are based on European perspectives, some works also bring in African

---

17 W. Kaiser, *Christian Democracy and the Origins of European Union* (Cambridge, Cambridge University Press, 2007).

18 W. Buschak, *Die Vereinigten Staaten von Europa sind unser Ziel – Arbeiterbewegung und Europa im frühen 20. Jahrhundert* (Essen, Klartext, 2014).

19 Mazower, *Governing the World*.

20 B. Bruneteau, *L'Europe nouvelle de Hitler: Une illusion des intellectuels de la France de Vichy* (Monaco, Éditions du Roche, 2003).

21 C.-R. Ageron, 'L'idée d'Eurafrique et le débat colonial franco-allemand de l'entre-deux-guerres', *Revue d'Histoire Moderne et Contemporain* 22, no. 3 (1975): 446–75.

22 F. Leikam, *Empire, Entwicklung und Europa: Die Europapolitik Großbritanniens und die Entwicklungsländer im Commonwealth, 1945–75* (Augsburg, Wißner-Verlag, 2011); E. Deschamps, 'Entre héritage colonial et destin européen. La Belgique, le Congo et la problématique de l'outre-mer dans le processus d'intégration européenne (1945–1960)' (Ph.D. thesis European University Institute, 2016); G. Migani, *La France et l'Afrique sub-saharienne, 1957–1963: Histoire d'une décolonisation entre idéaux eurafricains et politique de puissance* (Brussels, Peter Lang, 2008); Y. Montarsolo, *L'Eurafrique*

perspectives.[23] In this respect, the historiography on Africa is also of interest, given how, for example, Cooper and Wilder have examined alternatives to the nation-state in the lead up to decolonisation.[24] An interdisciplinary approach can be found in the special feature of *EuropeNow*.[25] Dimier focuses on the perspective of the European bureaucracy and shows how former French colonial officials have continued to impact development policy in Africa.[26] A number of works are of a more general nature, including the edited collection by Bitsch and Bossuat and the studies by Moser and Garavini.[27] Technology and development are strongly represented in this subfield, as shown by Davies as well as Diogo and Van Laak.[28] Most recently, Hanssen and Jonsson have collated this literature in a persuasive call to integrate Eurafrica into our understanding of European integration.[29] Patel has done this in his encompassing study of the EU and its predecessors.[30]

Although Wagner and the contributors to the volume edited by Davis and Serres have enriched the Eurafrica field by analysing visions of Europe in colonial parties and from the colonies, a broader, primary-source-based, field,

    contrepoint de l'idée d'Europe: Le cas français de la fin de la deuxième guerre mondiale aux négociations des Traités de Rome (Aix-en-Provence, Presses universitaires de l'Université de Provence, 2010); L. Kottos, *Europe between Imperial Decline and Quest for Integration: Pro-European Groups and the French, Belgian and British Empires (1947–1957)* (Brussels, Peter Lang, 2016).

23 M. Rempe, *Entwicklung im Konflikt: Die EWG und der Senegal, 1957–1975* (Cologne, Böhlau, 2012); A. I. Richard, 'The Limits of Solidarity. Europeanism, Anti-colonialism and Socialism at the Congress of the Peoples of Europe, Asia and Africa at Puteaux, 1948', *European Review of History* 21, no. 4 (2014): 519–37.

24 F. Cooper, *Citizenship between Empire and Nation: Remaking France and French Africa, 1945–1960* (Princeton, NJ, Princeton University Press, 2014); G. Wilder, *Freedom Time: Negritude, Decolonization and the Future of the World* (Durham, NC, Duke University Press, 2015).

25 H. B. Ducros (ed.), special feature 'Beyond Eurafrica: Encounters in a Globalized World', *EuropeNow* 15 (2018), www.europenowjournal.org/2018/02/28/introduction-2.

26 V. Dimier, *The Invention of a European Development Aid Bureaucracy: Recycling Empire* (Basingstoke, Palgrave Macmillan, 2014).

27 M.-T. Bitsch and G. Bossuat (eds.), *L'Europe unie et L'Afrique: De l'idée d'Eurafrique à la Convention de Lomé I* (Brussels, Bruylant, 2005); T. Moser, *Europäische Integration, Dekolonisation, Eurafrika: Eine historische Analyse über die Entstehungsbedingungen der Eurafrikanischen Gemeinschaft von der Weltwirtschaftskrise bis zum Jaunde-Vertrag, 1929 1963* (Baden-Baden, Nomos, 2000); G. Garavini, *After Empires: European Integration, Decolonization and the Challenge from the Global South, 1957–1986* (Oxford, Oxford University Press, 2012).

28 M. H. Davis, *Markets of Civilization: Islam and Racial Capitalism in Algeria* (Durham, NC, Duke University Press, 2022); M. P. Diogo and D. van Laak, *Europeans Globalizing: Mapping, Exploiting, Exchanging* (Basingstoke, Palgrave Macmillan, 2016).

29 P. Hanssen and S. Jonsson, *Eurafrica: The Untold History of European Integration and Colonialism* (London, Bloomsbury Academic, 2014).

30 K. K. Patel, *Project Europe: A History* (Cambridge, Cambridge University Press, 2020).

that takes colonialism and relations to Asia into account as well, is still in its infancy.[31]

Europe in the Global Order

These days, Europe is no longer the power political, the economic or the cultural centre of the world. The world has emancipated itself from Europe.[32]

This quote from Richard Coudenhove-Kalergi, founder of the Paneuropa Union, immediately indicates the relevance to European cooperation of the four frameworks mentioned in the introduction: (geo)politics, economics, civilisational ideas and racial beliefs. In the rest of this chapter, each of those frameworks will be analysed in turn, before sketching the role of Eurafrica in European cooperation. It will draw on examples from across the European movement. French and Dutch sources are well represented due to the fact that they were both important continental colonial powers and later founders of the European Coal and Steel Community, but with empires that were quite different in terms of location (mainly in Africa versus mainly in Asia) and economic approach (a variety of tariffs in the French empire, in contrast to the Open Door policy in the Dutch East Indies). This difference makes it possible to present a range of viewpoints, rather than suggesting a hermetic argument.

Coudenhove-Kalergi is also well represented. While he is often portrayed as exceptional, the reason why he is of interest in this chapter is the opposite. Like many of the actors examined here, he was an intermediate thinker. He was not a systemic thinker; his views were eclectic and he borrowed from everyone. At the same time, he was a great propagandist – who also antagonised many people. Thus, he became a point of reference, positively or negatively. His ideas can be seen as representative of the spirit of the age. In this way, this chapter is a form of intellectual history in practice, exploring how ideas were negotiated in day-to-day practice.[33]

---

31 F. Wagner, 'Kolonialverbände in Deutschland, Frankreich, Spanien und Belgien. Von der kolonialpraktischen Kooperation zum "europäischen Ideal" (1880–1914)', in F. Bösch and F. Greiner (eds.), *Europabilder im 20. Jahrhundert: Entstehung an der Peripherie* (Göttingen, Wallenstein, 2012), pp. 27–53, M. H. Davis and T. Serres (eds.), *North Africa and the Making of Europe: Governance, Institutions and Culture* (London, Bloomsbury, 2018).

32 R. N. Coudenhove-Kalergi, *Paneuropa* (Vienna, Paneuropa-Verlag, 1923), pp. 13–14. All translations are my own.

33 R. Koekkoek, A. I. Richard and A. Weststeijn, 'Introduction. Intellectual History in Imperial Practice', in R. Koekkoek, A. I. Richard and A. Weststeijn (eds.), *The Dutch Empire between Ideas and Practice, 1600–2000* (Basingstoke, Palgrave Macmillan, 2019), pp. 1–15.

Geopolitics

Various geopolitical developments that influenced thinking about European cooperation were mentioned in the introduction. These ideas about the rise of other centres of power and the need for Europe to cooperate are illustrated in the map that Coudenhove-Kalergi used widely (Figure 16.1).

On this map Coudenhove-Kalergi divided the world into five force fields: Paneurope (including its colonies), the British Empire, the USSR, East Asia and Panamerica. Coudenhove-Kalergi was not alone in seeing the world like this. In 1929–30, a French magazine, the *Revue des Vivants*, ran a contest about how to organise the peoples of Europe. Foreshadowing 'Third Force' ideas from the 1940s, the editors argued that 'the time had come for humanity [. . .] to organise itself in continents'. The United States was very clearly independent of Europe. The awakened Asia had Moscow as its capital. There was only one guarantee for European nations aiming to protect their heritage: a Federation of European States.[34] The 502 projects that the *Revue* received from across France and Europe generally supported Coudenhove-Kalergi's division of the world, although the position of Britain remained a point of discussion, also for Coudenhove-Kalergi.[35] Although he was to change his opinion after the Italian invasion of Abyssinia (now Ethiopia) in 1935, Coudenhove-Kalergi argued that, with its empire spread over the globe and particularly with the growing independence of the Dominions, Britain had different interests from the continental European countries. Leopold Amery, British colonial secretary and member of the Round Table Movement and Paneuropa, also stressed the growing importance of the Dominions.[36] He argued that the British Empire and Paneurope were roughly equal in size: Britain and the Dominions combined were similar to the European states, if they cooperated; and both had a colonial empire.[37]

If Britain should, could or would not want to join because of its empire, it would nonetheless be an ally to Europe. This was the prevalent view amongst many Europeanists. In the Netherlands, opinion was more hesitant, however, on account of that country being strategically and economically dependent on the British Empire in Europe and in Asia. While more grassroots activists

---

34 Les Vivants, 'Le prix de la *Revue des Vivants*', *Revue des Vivants* 3, no. 3 (1929): 442.
35 J. Gracy, 'Résumé des cinquante études suivantes', in *La Fédération Européenne: Les meilleures des cent cinq projets soumis au concours de La Revue des Vivants* (Paris, Éditions de La Revue des Vivants, 1930), pp. 427–38.
36 A. Bosco, *The Round Table Movement and the Fall of the 'Second' British Empire (1909–1919)* (Newcastle-upon-Tyne, Cambridge Scholars, 2017).
37 L. S. Amery, 'The British Empire and the Pan-European Idea', *Journal of the Royal Institute of International Affairs* 9, no. 1 (1930): 1–22.

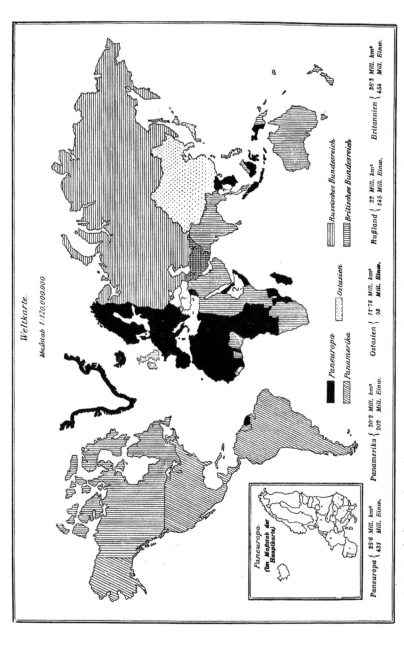

Figure 16.1   R. N. Coudenhove-Kalergi, the Paneuropa *Weltkarte* (world map), from *Paneuropa* (Vienna, Paneuropa-Verlag, 1923).

followed Coudenhove-Kalergi's model, more high-profile actors tended to argue for the inclusion of Britain until the early 1930s, when Britain adopted imperial preference.[38] Overall, the British empire played a pivotal role in discussions on British participation in a European project, as the Commonwealth continued to do up to and beyond the Brexit referendum in 2016.

In discussions about the position of the USSR, the Russian Revolution and anti-communism played important roles. They were invoked to argue, on the one hand, why Europeans should cooperate and, on the other, why the USSR could not be part of such an endeavour. Furthermore, the USSR had become a champion of the Asian peoples, according to Coudenhove-Kalergi.[39] These views were widely shared across Europe. Well before the start of the Cold War, anti-communism was a very significant factor – and it was so both for what it meant directly within Europe and also for what it meant in the colonies and concomitantly the repercussions for Europe. For most Europeanists, the Russian Revolution strengthened their Europeanism. Colonial unrest and communist uprisings, particularly in Asia in the mid-to-late 1920s, played an important role in the arguments about colonial investment and European cooperation of French minister Albert Sarraut, for example.[40]

Panamerica was regarded both as an inspiration and as a challenge to Europe. The Americas were very much in the public eye in the early 1920s. This was the result of the role of the United States and President Woodrow Wilson during and after the First World War, but also because of the 1923 centenary of the Monroe Doctrine, which in Europeanist circles was often (not necessarily correctly) understood as a model for continental organisation.[41] Beckert has analysed the rise of the Americas and the challenge this posed to the existing global order with an emphasis on the period up to the First World War.[42] These developments amplified after the war.

---

38 A. I. Richard, 'Les boutiquiers idéalistes. Federalism in the Netherlands in the interwar period', in G. Duchenne and M. Dumoulin, *Générations de fédéralistes européens depuis le XIXe siècle: Individus, groupes, espaces et réseaux* (Brussels, Peter Lang, 2012), pp. 93–108.

39 Coudenhove-Kalergi, *Paneuropa*, p. 14.

40 A. Sarraut, *Les possibilités de conflit entre l'Europe et les races de couleur et les conditions de la paix du monde* (Boulogne: Comité national d'études sociales et politiques, 1925); T. N. Harper, *Underground Asia: Global Revolutionaries and the Assault on Empire* (London, Allan Lane, 2020).

41 R. N. Coudenhove-Kalergi, *Paneuropa ABC* (Vienna, Paneuropa-Verlag, 1931), p. 1, A. H. Fried, *Pan-Amerika: Entwicklung, Umfang und Bedeutung der zwischenstaatlichen Organisation in Amerika (1810–1916)* (Zurich, Orell Füssli, 1918).

42 S. Beckert, 'American Danger: United States Empire, Eurafrica, and the Territorialization of Industrial Capitalism, 1870–1950', *The American Historical Review* 122, no. 4 (2017): 1137–70.

Latin American countries were gaining influence, while Coudenhove-Kalergi already considered the United States 'the richest, most powerful and most advanced Empire in the world'.[43] The relationship between the United States and Latin America was often compared to the increasingly equal relationship between Britain and the Dominions, for example by the French economist Francis Delaisi.[44] The threat the Americas posed was mainly in terms of economic competition, as will be discussed below, and in cultural terms, in which the Americas were seen as superficial and commercial.

The most profound challenge to Europe's position in the world came from Asia, as will be further developed in the section on hierarchies of civilisation and race. While this is not an argument that has received a lot of attention in the literature, it was of existential importance for many. Japan's victory over Russia in 1905 was understood as a turning point in European conceptions of global order. This was reinforced by Japan's economic development, its activities in Korea and China and its position among the victors of the First World War. The widespread unease with Japanese claims for a race equality clause at Versailles and the many anti-Asian immigration laws were further expressions of Yellow Peril ideas.[45] Moreover, just like the Russian Revolution, the rise of Japan was linked to anti-colonial uprisings across Asia. While for Coudenhove-Kalergi, whose mother was Japanese, Japan was becoming a 'regular' great power, for many others, such as the above-mentioned Sarraut or Dutch prime minister and old colonial hand Hendrik Colijn, this was of great concern.[46] Although this changed in the 1930s with Japan's actions in China, in the 1920s the pan-Asiatic conferences were considered of not too much concern by the Europeanist press.[47]

While concern about the rise of Japan was common, there was much less consensus on the fate of the European colonies in Asia. Some, such as Colijn, were concerned about outside influences, from communism, Japan or events in other colonies, and as a result argued that, if the European colonial empires did not cooperate, they would 'perish together'.[48] Others, such as

---

43 Coudenhove-Kalergi, *Paneuropa*, p. 16.

44 F. Delaisi, *Les deux Europes* (Paris, Payot, 1929).

45 N. Shimazu, *Japan, Race and Equality: The Racial Equality Proposal of 1919* (London, Routledge, 1998).

46 H. Colijn, 'L'exposition internationale coloniale de Paris et la coopération internationale européenne' (1930), Historisch Documentatiecentrum Nederlandse Politieke Partijen, Vrije Universiteit, Amsterdam, Colijn, 0577, 054, Doos 13, Map losse stukken 1930.

47 See, for example, 'La conférence panasiatique de Nagasaki (1ᵉʳ août 1926)', *L'Europe Nouvelle*, 2 October 1926; 'Conférence panasiatique à Changhai', *L'Europe Nouvelle*, 6 January 1928; S. Pistocchi, 'Les États Fédérés d'Europe', *Revue des Vivants* (1926): 133–262.

48 Colijn, 'L'exposition internationale coloniale de Paris'.

Coudenhove-Kalergi, went one step further and forecast the end of these European colonies. While Indians may have seen this very differently, Coudenhove-Kalergi and quite a few others in various foreign policy circles saw British India on the road to becoming a Dominion.

Although it was not mentioned on Coudenhove-Kalergi's map, the League of Nations played a pivotal role in the thinking of and the planning for a European future on at least three different levels. This was, first of all, the case in terms of personal connections. Many activists were simultaneously active in the League and Europeanist organisations, and continued to be so after 1945. Jean Monnet is probably the most prominent example as Deputy Secretary General of the League of Nations as well as President of the High Authority of the Coal and Steel Community. Secondly, the experiences of the League in how to organise an international bureaucracy and to develop policy provided for lively exchanges between League and Europeanist organisations and in turn are essential to understand future European bureaucracies and policy-making practices.[49] Finally, the League was also pivotal in terms of how European cooperation was conceived of, given that the member states of the League of Nations were predominantly European nations. The discussions centred on the question of whether to understand European cooperation as competition or as a complement to the League. Three broad approaches were put forward by Europeanists. First, there were those who supported the League and European cooperation and saw them as complementary. They often justified this by referring to Article 21 of the League Covenant that was designed to accommodate the Monroe Doctrine.[50] Secondly, there were those who grew increasingly disillusioned. As it became progressively clear that the League could not safeguard the (economic, political or military) peace, ideas for European cooperation became an option that seemed worthwhile to explore, as Walter Lipgens already argued in 1966.[51] This was, for example, the case for quite a few Dutch activists.[52] Finally, there were those who had

---

49 K. Gram-Skjoldager, H. A. Ikonomou and T. Kahlert (eds.), *Organising the 20th-Century World: International Organizations and the Emergence of International Public Administration, 1920–1960s* (London, Bloomsbury Academic, 2020); P. Clavin, *Securing the World Economy: The Reinvention of the League of Nations, 1920–1946* (Oxford, Oxford University Press, 2013).
50 A. I. Richard, 'Competition and Complementarity: Civil Society Networks and the Question of Decentralising the League of Nations', *Journal of Global History* 7, no. 2 (2012): 233–56; J. M. Guieu, 'Le discours Européen des militants pour la Société des Nations dans l'entre-deux-guerres', *Études Germaniques* 2, no. 254 (2009): 349–62.
51 Lipgens, 'Europäische Einigungsidee'.
52 A. I. Richard, 'Between the League of Nations and Europe: Multiple Internationalisms and Interwar Dutch Civil Society', in R. van Dijk, S. Kruizinger, V. Kuitenbrouwer and

always been sceptical about the League; this was especially true for grassroots activists and for Coudenhove-Kalergi. They first of all criticised the League for not having any real power.[53] Secondly, with its global aspirations, the League neglected European questions, while at the same time Article 10 of the Covenant could entangle Europeans in conflicts elsewhere. Coudenhove-Kalergi argued that the League should be reorganised along the lines of the five global empires. Paneurope would then be a regional group in terms of Article 21.[54]

Coudenhove-Kalergi's critique of the League made the Paneuropean project an easy target for its critics. On the one hand, it reinforced general objections to the Paneuropean idea which argued that Paneuropa created antagonisms between continents. On the other hand, it fed ideas about European cooperation constituting competition to the League. Even though Coudenhove-Kalergi went against the grain in starting to support the League in the aftermath of the Abysinnia crisis, by then, his critique of the League had alienated internationalists who might otherwise have been sympathetic to his ideas and more generally to ideas of European cooperation.

Economics

The inter-war period saw a very vivid discussion of how economic and political cooperation related to each other. This debate has not ceased since, going from neo-functionalism to recent discussions on fiscal union. In the inter-war period this debate came to a head around French Foreign Minister Aristide Briand's speech to the General Assembly of the League in September 1929, which seemed to put economic cooperation first, and his subsequent Memorandum of May 1930 that prioritised political cooperation.[55] While the change from economics to politics was probably due to the wish to forestall objections by the United States and concomitantly Britain and Germany,[56] activists and policy-makers were quite taken aback by the shift as they generally saw economic union as preceding political cooperation. Only a few grassroots activists argued for the creation of a full-blown political federation as a first

R. van der Maar (eds.), *Shaping the International Relations of the Netherlands, 1815–2000: A Small Country on the Global Scene* (Abingdon, Routledge, 2018), pp. 97–116.

53 R. N. Coudenhove-Kalergi, 'Agonie des Völkerbundes', *Paneuropa* 8, no. 7 (1932): 205–2011, 209.

54 Coudenhove-Kalergi, *Paneuropa ABC*, p. 9.

55 League of Nations, *Journal of the Tenth Assembly* (Geneva, 1929) no. 4, 5 September 1929, 51–55; 'Memorandum du gouvernement francais', 1 May 1930, Archives du Ministère des Affaires Etrangères, Papiers 1940, Leger, 3.

56 R. W. D. Boyce, 'Britain's First "No" to Europe: Britain and the Briand Plan, 1929–1930', *European Studies Review* 10, no. 1 (1980): 17–45, 33–4.

step.[57] The preference for economic cooperation was also expressed in the 502 projects submitted to the competition organised by the *Revue des Vivants* in 1930.[58] While economic cooperation was thus prioritised by most, the types of economic cooperation that were proposed ranged widely.

Nonetheless, there were a number of recurring points and the starting point was clear: the interconnectedness of the world economy. Delaisi explored this theme extensively in his massive work *Les contradictions du monde moderne*. He illustrated the contradiction between political nationalism and economic interdependence as follows:

> The Congo [. . .] is nothing more than an annex of our car factories, Japan of the Samurai is a competitor to Manchester, the negro from the banks of Lake Tanganyika extracts the copper for our telephones, the worker in Rouen weaves the cotton goods for the coolies of the banks of the Mekong, and the French *petit bourgeois* lets his money work on the banks of Yang-Tse-Kiang or in the nitrate-areas of the *cordillera* of the Andes.[59]

This globalised interconnectedness was a product of the later part of the nineteenth century.[60] As Beckert has shown, profound changes were taking place, and after the First World War many of them came to a head.[61] One of the most obvious changes in Europe was the rise of tariff walls, following the creation of many new states. The rise of tariffs was perceived by many as one of the foremost economic problems of the period and the one that aggravated problems of overproduction and underconsumption most. Envious eyes were cast on the United States 'with its large uninterrupted market'. The introduction of the Smoot Hawley tariff by the United States in 1930, however, amplified global trade barriers and was used as an argument in favour of European cooperation, although some were simultaneously worried that a European customs union would start a global tariff war.

The relationship to colonial empire was not straightforward as there were many different colonial tariff regimes. The Dutch, for example, practised an Open Door policy in the Indies. This meant that they were initially not very enthusiastic about European cooperation as that might compromise this Open Door. However, when the Tariff Truce Conference of 1929–30 failed and Britain turned to Imperial Preference (after it had already left the gold standard), the Dutch started to explore plurilateral conventions that the

57 Richard, 'Les boutiquiers idéalistes'.   58 Gracy, 'Résumé des cinquante études suivantes'.
59 F. Delaisi, *Les contradictions du monde moderne* (Paris, Payot, 1925), p. 172.
60 M. Daunton, 'Britain and Globalisation since 1850: 1 Creating a Global Order, 1850–1914', *Transactions of the Royal Historical Society* 16 (2006): 1–38.
61 Beckert, 'American Danger'.

League approved of. The 1932 Convention of Ouchy with Belgium and Luxemburg provides a clear stepping stone to the later creation of the Benelux grouping. Given the diversity in tariff regimes applicable to the various colonial territories of, for example, the French empire, it was hard to make a clear argument in relation to cooperation, beyond noting that the rest of the world was developing more quickly than Europe, divided as it was by tariff walls.

Concerns over rapid economic development outside Europe were accompanied by the realisation that world trade could flow around Europe, as the First World War had proven. The United States, the Dominions and Latin America were part of what Delaisi called the 'Third Europe'. The literature on inter-war European cooperation often refers to Delaisi's book *Les deux Europes*. However, it does this in a different context. It focuses on the two Europes mentioned in the title and Delaisi's argument that industrialised Europe, the first Europe, and agricultural Europe, the second Europe, complemented each other. However, Delaisi arrived at this argument about the two Europes only as a second-best solution. He spent two-thirds of the book explaining how the *third* Europe, everywhere where Europeans (whites) could work without the aid of the indigenous population, was his preferred choice, but that, since it was emancipating itself, the two Europes needed to find a way to work together. This global reasoning, however, is not mentioned in the literature.[62]

Another major change following the First World War took place in the relationship between the state and the economy, with a much larger role for the state following the war experience. In certain circles, particularly in France, planning became all the rage in attempts to address economic difficulties. Delaisi and the Union Douanière Européenne are examples of those that developed 5-year plans.[63] Planning was, however, not just a state initiative; indeed, planning by business leaders was also a significant component, since some neoliberals *avant la lettre* argued that private initiative was superior to state planning. The International Steel Cartel and the Phoebus Lightbulb Cartel are examples of cartels in which the companies which participated supported European cooperation.[64] Planning was of great

62 Bussière et al., *Francis Delaisi*.
63 See, for example, L. Coquet, 'Un plan quinquennal pour l'Europe', *Journal des Nations*, 7/13 November 1931.
64 W. Kaiser and J. Schot, *Writing the Rules for Europe: Experts, Cartels, and International Organizations* (Basingstoke, Palgrave Macmillan, 2018); Blanken, *Geschiedenis van Koninklijke Philips*, vol. III, p. 240.

importance in the colonial sphere as well, of course. We can think, for example, of Sarraut's plan for the *mise en valeur* of the French empire or of Eurafrican projects where planning and cartels were supposed to facilitate colonial development and the civilising mission.

Civilisation and Race

Across the board, all activists agreed that civilisation was what defined Europe. The various incarnations of ideas of European civilisation and culture are well covered in the literature. It is, however, both important and perhaps superfluous to note the paradox that, despite ideas about European decline following the First World War, European civilisation was still commonly regarded as the most advanced civilisation.[65] This understanding was strongly influenced by the thinking of European civilisation in relation to non-European cultures – most strongly in the colonial context. Rather than emphasising the diversity of European culture, as was common in an intra-European setting, in the colonies, the concept of a sameness of European cultures and civilisation prevailed. European civilisation was the undisputed universal civilisation.[66] Despite imperial competition between the European states, the confrontation with a non-European 'Other' highlighted the common civilisation that bound Europeans together. Sometimes couched in civilisational terms, these sentiments often drew on discourses about the superiority of the white race. The perceived contrast between, on the one hand, peoples supposedly living in a state of nature or decadent 'civilised' peoples, as suggested by Orientalist discourse, and, on the other hand, 'European modernity' worked to reinforce the belief in a supremacy of European civilisation and thus the justification of and need for colonial projects. At the same time, this supremacy discourse and fears about challenges to that supremacy fed into European projects.[67]

---

65 For European decline, see P. Valéry, *La crise de l'esprit* (Paris, La nouvelle revue française, 1919); O. Spengler, *Der Untergang des Abendlandes: Umrisse einer Morphologie der Weltgeschichte*, 2 vols. (Vienna, Braumüller, 1918; Munich, C. H. Beck, 1922), J. Ortega y Gasset, *La rebelión de las massas* (Barcelona, Espasa Lobros, 1929).

66 D. Chakrabarty, *Provincialising Europe: Postcolonial Thought and Historical Difference* (Princeton, NJ, Princeton University Press, 2000).

67 See A. L. Conklin, *A Mission to Civilize: The Republican Idea of Empire in France and West Africa, 1895–1930* (Stanford, CA, Stanford University Press, 1997); P. Duara, 'The Discourse of Civilization and Pan-Asianism', *Journal of World History* 12, no. 1 (2001): 99–130, M. Adas, 'Contested Hegemony: The Great War and the Afro-Asian Assault on the Civilizing Mission Ideology', *Journal of World History* 15, no. 1 (2004): 31–63; C. Aydin, *Politics of Anti-Westernism in Asia: Visions of World Order in Pan-Islamic and Pan-Asian Thought* (New York, NY, Columbia University Press, 2007); S. Dulucq, *Écrire l'histoire de l'Afrique à l'époque coloniale (XIXᵉ–XXᵉ siècles)* (Paris, Karthala, 2009).

These ideas were based on entwined conceptions of hierarchies of civilisation and race. Not all of the actors involved subscribed to the same understandings, but broad lines can be distinguished. The mandate system divided the A, B and C Mandates also along these lines.[68] Certain territories were seen as more developed than others. Asia, often understood as encompassing the area between Casablanca and Tokyo,[69] might be seen as decadent, but Japanese, Chinese, Indian and Muslim culture were generally understood as being part of a civilisational order. This capacity of civility, however, thus also entailed a potential danger to European civilisation, which was considered to be in decline. In discussing Sarraut's *Grandeur et servitude coloniales*, the reviewer in *L'Europe Nouvelle* made the point that, 'if Asia awakens, it is necessary that Europe, in response, unites'.[70]

Africa, and particularly sub-Saharan Africa, was viewed quite differently from Asia. Sub-Saharan Africa was not part of the civilisational map of the world; the African peoples were supposedly backward and without history. As a result, Africa was generally viewed through a racial lens. The bulk of public opinion regarding Europe's role vis-à-vis colonised peoples, and particularly Africans, oscillated between paternalistic and biological racism.

The French publicist Gaston Riou is an example of the latter. One of his books had the telling title *S'unir ou mourir (Unite or Perish)*.[71] He was strongly motivated by ideas about the destiny of the white race. Despite its deficiencies, the importance of the white race was paramount in the world because of its 'profound and durable humanist values'. For Riou, friendships between kindred spirits of different races could not bridge the racial gap that separated them: 'the distance is much smaller between Romain Rolland and Henri Massis, the enemies, than between Rolland and Rabindranath Tagore, the friends'.[72]

Coudenhove-Kalergi was somewhere in between these two extremes. Some racial theories were problematic for him, with a Jewish wife and a Japanese mother. According to him, there could not be two types to the white race, because the real opposition was between black and white.[73] He thus did subscribe to racial theories when it came to Africans. In relation to

68 S. Pedersen, *Guardians: The League of Nations and the Crisis of Empire* (Oxford, Oxford University Press, 2015), p. 29.
69 See, for example, R. N. Coudenhove-Kalergi, 'Rings um Europa, Pan-Asien, pan-asiatische Propaganda', *Paneuropa* 11, no. 3 (1935): 85–6, 85.
70 'Compte rendu, *Grandeur et servitude coloniales*', *L'Europe Nouvelle*, 4 July 1931.
71 G. Riou, *S'unir ou mourir* (Paris, Librairie Valois, 1929).
72 G. Riou, *Europe ma patrie* (Paris, Librairie Valois, 1928), p. 75.
73 R. N. Coudenhove-Kalergi, 'Europäische Rasse', *Paneuropa* 10, no. 5 (1934): 99–101.

Africa, he was convinced that racial solidarity trumped state solidarity. The Belgians, British, French and Portuguese had to recognise that they were more tightly linked to their 'white neighbours than to their black subjects'.[74]

The paternalistic kind of racism was almost omnipresent in the inter-war period, except perhaps in anti-colonial circles. 'Modern colonial practice' was propagated by many, for example Sarraut and most of the Dutch groups, but also the circle around the journal *L'Europe Nouvelle*. While in the literature this is generally depicted as a peace and Europeanist journal, it devoted a lot of space in its columns to colonialism and argued, for example, that France was 'the tutor of the indigenous populations' and had to assure itself of 'their effective collaboration' in order to develop 'the still unexplored immense riches of our colonies'.[75]

The combination of these civilisational and racial ideas in relation to Asia and Africa, as well as geopolitical and economic analyses about the rise of Japan, developments in British India, the influence of communism and unrest in the colonies meant that, although for the time being Asian colonies were generally included in projects for European cooperation, they were seen differently from how colonies in Africa were perceived. Although this view was not widely shared in, for example, the Netherlands, with its largest colony in Asia, the future emancipation of the Asian colonies (at an, admittedly, unspecified time) was expected and instead Eurafrican cooperation was promoted.[76] The French politician Joseph Caillaux expressed this view, which would continue to play an important role well into the 1960s, as follows:

> I have become convinced that Europe will reconcile itself through Africa. The more I see the retreat from Asia, the chosen isolation of the United States, the more I am convinced that Africa is the great reserve – of raw materials and of markets – of the Europeans.[77]

Eurafrica

Africa had a particular importance in Europeanist discourse that derived in part from the relationship between Europe and Africa and in part from the analysis of Europe's position in the world, and in particular its relations with

74 R. N. Coudenhove-Kalergi, 'Afrika', *Paneuropa* 5, no. 2 (1929): 1–19, 5.
75 'La France et ses colonies sont solidaires', *L'Europe Nouvelle*, 1 May 1926.
76 Note, for instance, the 1957 Dulles–Adenauer exchange, used by the latter to argue for the Eurafrique fund as an indispensable part of the EEC. K. Adenauer, *Teegespräche 1955–58* (Munich, Siedler, 1986), pp. 178–82. I thank Mathieu Segers for the reference.
77 J. Caillaux, *D'Agadir à la grande pénitence* (Paris, Flammarion, 1933), p. 125.

Asia, as discussed above. Europe and Africa were seen as interdependent and complementary continents, in terms of levels of civilisation and resources. Rather than thinking of Africa as the continent where the great powers competed to plant their own flag, the advocates of Eurafrica argued that the European states should 'develop' Africa together. The benefits of this cooperation would be enormous. Geopolitically, Eurafrican cooperation would end internal divisions and buttress Europe's position vis-à-vis the United States, the USSR, the British empire and Asia. Economically, Africa could provide Europe with 'raw materials for its industry, food stuffs for its population, lands to settle for its surplus population, employment for its unemployed and markets for its products'.[78] Africa, on the other hand, would benefit from European humanitarian efforts. These would bring modern medicine, education, economic development and, above all, civilisation. These arguments were, of course, standard colonial rhetoric, but applied at the European level.

Eurafrican projects came in many guises. The most far-reaching projects argued for a common European government for all African colonies. These projects were generally proposed by more grassroots activists or seen as an objective for the future. They built on ideas of internationalisation of the colonies, inspired by the Congo and the mandate system. The least far-reaching projects argued for access for all European citizens and companies, regardless of nationality, to all European colonies, a so-called European Open Door policy. In this context, the Belgian socialist Jules Destrée proposed an African citizenship for all Europeans so that they would have free access.[79] In almost all projects, infrastructure played a central role, with plans for roads, railways and river navigation connecting various parts of Africa to Europe abounding.[80] The rationale was that these investments were too big for individual countries, whereas their impact, if executed, would be enormous: for the development of Africa, but, for example, also in addressing the unemployment problem in Europe. Sarraut, whose plan for the *mise en valeur* of the French empire in the aftermath of the First World War had not been funded, came to support Eurafrican plans in the 1930s. If joint funding were to make these development projects possible, this would benefit the local populations, who would be less likely to revolt.

78 Coudenhove-Kalergi, 'Afrika als Tatsache', 3.
79 J. Destrée, *Pour en finir avec la guerre* (Brussels, L'Églantine, 1931).
80 D. von Laak, *Imperiale Infrastruktur: Deutsche Planungen für eine Erschließung Afrikas 1880 bis 1960* (Paderborn, Schöning, 2004).

Similar reasoning was put forward after the Second World War in the discussions over the Council of Europe's Strasbourg plan in 1952. The future president of Senegal and member of the Consultative Assembly of the Council Léopold Senghor used the idea of Eurafrica to argue for African interests. To achieve this, he did not eschew language Eurafricanists had been using since the 1920s and which circumstances in the early 1950s had given new prominence: 'Europe [had] let the hour of Eurasia slip', would the Assembly 'fail to grasp the opportunity of achieving Eurafrica?'[81] Kottos has shown that, although the Strasbourg plan was ultimately rejected by the Council of Ministers, transnational pressure groups secured its revival at the Treaties of Rome in 1957.[82] Eurafrica played a pivotal role in European cooperation projects involving a global analysis in the inter-war period. The conclusions from that analysis only became more acute after 1945, and Eurafrica remained part of European integration projects.

Conclusion

This chapter has adopted a global perspective to analyse the question of European cooperation in the inter-war period. The world order was changing profoundly in this period. Many in Europe sought solutions to what they felt were geopolitical, economic, civilisational and racial challenges from all corners of the world. Europeanists argued that some form of European cooperation would be the best answer, particularly if the cooperation extended to the African colonies. When the changes under way in this period were further amplified after the Second World War and Europe had to come to terms with its changing position even more, a significant number of the answers formulated in the inter-war period were repurposed to fit the situation in the late 1940s. These findings suggest that both the 'novelty' and the 'benign' narratives used by the EU need adjusting.

A global perspective shows that, besides the experience of the war itself and Franco-German relations, developments in other parts of the world played an important role in discussions on European cooperation. Within these, empire was of particular significance. It could act as a brake, as in the case of Britain or the Netherlands in the 1920s, but preventing the loss of colonies could also be the reason why Europeans needed to cooperate.

81 L. S. Senghor, *Conseil de l'Europe Assemblée Consultative: Deuxième session, 7–28 août 1950. Comptes rendus*, vol. II: *Séances 13 à 21* (Strasbourg, Commission Européenne, 1950), pp. 494–5.
82 Kottos, *Europe between Imperial Decline and Quest for Integration*, pp. 167–204.

Regardless, colonial ideologies of civilisational and racial hierarchies were fundamental to European self-perceptions. These ideologies led to a different understanding of Asia and Africa: regarding Asia, civilisational aspects predominated; regarding Africa, racial aspects. Imperialism in Asia was understood to have an end, albeit in the distant future, whereas for Africa this argument was barely made in the inter-war period. This difference explains the enthusiasm for Eurafrican projects. Eurafrican cooperation, in whatever form, would diminish European competition and buttress Europe's global position, both after the First World War and after the Second World War. These non-European foundations of the European cooperation story have to be addressed as well in order to properly understand the European project.

Recommended Reading

Adas, M. 'Contested Hegemony: The Great War and the Afro-Asian Assault on the Civilizing Mission Ideology', *Journal of World History* 15, no. 1 (2004): 31–63.

Chabot, J. L. *Aux origines intellectuelles de l'Union européenne: L'idée d'Europe unie de 1919 à 1939* (Grenoble, Presses universitaires de Grenoble, 2005 [1978]).

Clavin, P. *Securing the World Economy: The Reinvention of the League of Nations, 1920–1946* (Oxford, Oxford University Press, 2013).

Hanssen, P. and S. Jonsson, *Eurafrica: The Untold History of European Integration and Colonialism* (London, Bloomsbury Academic, 2014).

Harper, T. N. *Underground Asia: Global Revolutionaries and the Assault on Empire* (London, Allan Lane, 2020).

Montarsolo, Y. *L'Eurafrique contrepoint de l'idée d'Europe: Le cas français de la fin de la deuxième guerre mondiale aux négociations des Traités de Rome* (Aix-en-Provence, Presses universitaires de l'Université de Provence, 2010).

Patel, K. K. *Project Europe: A History* (Cambridge, Cambridge University Press, 2020).

Ziegerhofer-Prettenthaler, A. *Botschafter Europas: Richard Nikolaus Coudenhove-Kalergi und die Paneuropa-Bewegung in den zwanziger und dreißiger Jahren* (Vienna, Böhlau, 2004).

17

War, Peace and Memory: Franco-German Reconciliation

CARINE GERMOND

Introduction

In 'Göttingen', the French singer Barbara, who as a Jewish child hid in German-occupied France during the Second World War, celebrated Franco-German reconciliation after the bloodshed and hatred that had marked bilateral relations in the past. The song, recorded in 1964 first in French and later in German, was hailed as a hymn to Franco-German reconciliation and credited for improving post-war Franco-German relations. The song's melancholic tunes certainly captured the Zeitgeist of an era: it was recorded roughly a year after the signature of the Élysée 'friendship' treaty on 22 January 1963. The treaty was instrumental in forging a narrative of how the two countries overcame a shared history of conflict and rivalry to become a driving force of European integration.

Although the word reconciliation does not feature in the text of the Élysée treaty, the elaborated dramatisation that preceded the treaty's signing made for powerful symbolic politics and provided the ground-work for a novel storyline of bilateral relations. This new narrative, with its symbolic elements and emotional gestures, reordered and trans-formed a shared history with its memory of war, feuds and hostility into one of friendship and partnership. It tells a success story often portrayed as a model for other countries and is one of the best export items in Franco-German history.[1] Over the years, Franco-German reconciliation has become a near-idyllic example in the wider European pursuit of a lasting peace, following the bloodshed and destruction of two world wars. Today, the depth and breadth of relations and mutual

---

1 C. Defrance, 'Die Meistererzählung von der deutsch-französischen "Versöhnung"', *Aus Politik und Zeitgeschichte* 63 (2013): 1–3.

trust and cooperation achieved by the Franco-German dyad have no parallel in the world and international relations. Given its uniqueness, it is perhaps not surprising that Franco-German reconciliation would also grow into a constitutive fixture of the classic peace narrative of post-war European integration.

Narratives are formed by events or developments that are told along a storyline.[2] They do not just describe what happened but, more importantly, (re)construct how we remember and tell them. In essence, they involve the selection, linkage and ordering of historical actions, decisions and events to create an overarching framework of meaning. Narratives are thus deliberate constructs that mobilise emotions and are fundamental and powerful elements of history telling. They help us to trace, explain and remember the development of society; they tell us how the past is officially and privately constructed and commemorated. They convey or frame a specific message and imbue events with meaning, importance or emotional identification. They are also practical and political tools that explain the formation and evolution of inter-state relations and shape collective memory over time.

Relations between France and Germany provide a fascinating example of the discursive power of narratives. Historical narrative production was influential in nation-building and state-formation processes in Europe in the nineteenth century. Whether centred on bilateral hostility or partnership, narratives have supported and legitimised domestic and European political agendas in France and Germany throughout that period and up to the twentieth century. While antagonism and conflicts were defining features of the two countries' histories and memory, the framing of a narrative about a shared (conflictual) history and norms of cooperation has been an essential part of the process of creating a joint, bilateral memory to support Franco-German reconciliation in the post-war era. In addition, Franco-German reconciliation is no longer discussed merely as a process and an outcome, but has spawned its own narrative.

This chapter weaves together different strands of literature on Franco-German relations in/and Europe to analyse the history of the bilateral relationship through the narrative lenses of war, reconciliation and memory. It is essential to study how these narratives affected and transformed the bilateral relationship to fully understand its narrative complexity and

---

2 W. Kaiser, 'Clash of Cultures: Two Milieus in the European Union's "A New Narrative for Europe" Project', *Journal of Contemporary European Studies* 23, no. 3 (2015): 364–77, 365.

comprehend how it was instrumentalised to legitimate political, domestic and European agendas over time.

The first section charts the main scholarly trends that have shaped how Franco-German history was and is told, interpreted and remembered. The second section explores the transformation of antagonistic French and German memories into shared memories of wars and peace that form the linchpin of the present-day close partnership. The third section examines how the 1963 treaty functions as a foundational narrative of the Franco-German reconciliation. The final section delves into the mythologisation of the Franco-German engine and its role in shaping and steering post-war European integration.

Telling the Story: Dominant Trends in the Literature on Franco-German Relations

Franco-German relations are among the most extensively studied special or privileged relationships between two countries, with the spectacular transformation of their relations after 1945 especially. This literature has often produced a narrative that emphasises a century-old history of political, economic and military rivalry and conflict, whose devastating consequences could only be overcome through the parallel processes of Franco-German reconciliation and European integration after 1945.[3]

A significant feature of this literature is the prevalence of a teleological approach, which stresses the linear transformation and emotional quality of bilateral relations. Generally, the authors who adopt this approach study the development from a hereditary enmity to reconciliation to a special relationship that enabled France and Germany to shape and lead Europe. The images of the 'motor', 'linchpin', 'engine' or 'axis' attempt to capture this pivotal role,[4] while the imagery of the 'couple', 'duo' and 'tandem' stresses the personal entente of their leaders.[5] These various labels also emphasise Franco-German

3 See, for example, A. Cole, *Franco-German Relations* (Harlow, Pearson, 2001); C. Germond and H. Türk, *A History of Franco-German Relations in Europe: From 'Hereditary Enemies' to Partners* (New York, NY, Palgrave Macmillan, 2008).

4 R. Picht and W. Wessels (eds.), *Motor für Europa: Deutsch-französischer Bilateralismus und europäische Integration* (Bonn, Europa Union Verlag, 1990); J. Friend, *The Linchpin: Franco-German Relations 1950–1990* (New York, NY, Praeger, 1991); D. P. Calleo and E. R. Staal, *Europe's Franco-German Engine* (Washington, DC, Brookings Institution Press, 1998); G. Hendriks and A. Morgan (eds.), *The Franco-German Axis in European Integration* (Cheltenham and Northampton, Edward Elgar, 2001).

5 H. Ménudier (ed.), *Le couple franco-allemand en Europe* (Paris, Presses Sorbonne Nouvelle, 1993); C. Germond, 'Franco-German Dynamic Duos', in A. Menon, E. Jones and S. Weatherill (eds.), *The Oxford Handbook of the European Union* (Oxford, Oxford University Press, 2012), pp. 193–205.

contacts' political or diplomatic nature, their high degree of institutionalisation and the relationship's internal cohesion. This cohesion, however, may be more assumed than real. This conceptualisation of bilateral relations has been criticised for following too closely official discourses on both sides of the Rhine and failing to capture the complexity and scope of bilateral relations fully.[6]

Another essential characteristic of the literature on Franco-German relations is its emphasis on crucial disruptive turning points in the historical timeline, especially big moments of high politics that are indicators of continuity or change in the relationship. Accordingly, there is broad public and political consensus to break down the relationship into three grand periods, which also overlap with specific master narratives: hereditary enmity (before 1945), reconciliation (1945–63) and privileged cooperation (since 1963). These periods are seen as marking epochal caesurae and showing identifiable patterns of bilateral interactions and thematic unity.

Generally, the practice of categorising Franco-German relations in this manner has had three main effects. The first is a tendency to generate heavily state-centric literature that stresses cooperation between states and governments and neglects cross-border exchanges between civil societies. The second is a frequent disregard for slow-paced, subtle political and societal changes. Bilateral conflicts or rivalry did not necessarily mean an absence of trans-border exchange and influence. Political elites, social movements and intellectuals also looked to the other side of the Rhine for inspiration, role models and resources to promote change in their own country, despite, and especially during, periods of heightened inter-state rivalry as in the late nineteenth century.[7] Instead, periods of mutual attraction and repulsion alternated during the long nineteenth century and the first half of the twentieth century.[8] The third is a reduced interest in the role of narratives in Franco-German history telling.[9]

---

6 See, for example, E. Sangar, *Diffusion in Franco-German Relations: A Different Perspective on a History of Cooperation and Conflict* (Cham, Palgrave Macmillan, 2020).

7 W. Kaiser, 'Transnational Mobilization and Cultural Representation: Political Transfer in an Age of Proto-globalization, Democratization and Nationalism 1848–1914', *European Review of History* 12 (2005): 403–24.

8 R. Marcowitz, 'Attraction and Repulsion. Franco-German Relations in the "Long Nineteenth Century"', in Germond and Türk (eds.), *A History of Franco-German Relations*, pp. 13–26.

9 For exceptions, see, for example, C. Defrance, 'Die Meistererzählung'; C. Buffet and B. Hauser, *Haunted by History: Myths in International Relations* (Oxford, Berghahn, 1998); U. Pfeil (ed.), *Mythes et tabous des relations franco-allemandes aux XXe siècle/Mythen und Tabus der deutsch-französischen Beziehungen im 20. Jahrhundert* (Bern, Peter Lang, 2012).

Turning Foes into Friends: Narrating
Franco-German Relations

War and rivalry for territories and supremacy on the European continent were constitutive features of France and Germany's history. Still, antagonism took on a different significance with the advent of the French Revolution and nationalism. The birth of the French and German national movements, often in violent opposition to the neighbouring country, added national fervour to the traditional power-political rivalry and territorial conflicts of earlier centuries.[10]

Since the nineteenth century, France and Germany have repeatedly occupied each other's territories. The occupation of German territory by French Emperor Napoleon I's troops and the subsequent wars of liberation from Napoleonic rule established France as Germany's principal enemy and rival. The enmity further solidified when Prussia defeated France in 1871 and annexed the eastern French provinces of Alsace and Lorraine. The Franco-Prussian war of 1870–1 was the first of three major wars involving both countries in a span of 75 years. These successive wars entrenched the idea of an age-old, ingrained animosity opposing the two countries that became popular in public opinion and among the political classes.

Nevertheless, the concept of hereditary enmity did not arise from a legacy of conflict. Instead, it was primarily a construct to strengthen German national identity and popularise the demand for a German nation-state at the onset of the nineteenth century. In Germany, anti-French national sentiments solidified into the notion of a long-term hereditary enmity at this earlier point. In contrast, the concept did not take root in France until the country's humiliating defeat in the Franco-Prussian war, where these national, revanchist desires would come to coalesce around the reintegration of the annexed provinces of Alsace-Lorraine into the French motherland.

The Franco-Prussian war marked in both countries the completion of nationalising the enemy.[11] The political class and dominant historiography of national apologetics supported an historicised, albeit largely anachronistic, concept of 'hereditary enemies' that helped unify national forces against a designated enemy. Prominent historians such as Heinrich von Treitschke in Germany and Jacques Bainville in France conceptualised the (mainly national) history of the relations between their countries as one of perennial conflict. Both historians created 'traditions of hate' and used the term

---

10 See Marcowitz, 'Attraction and Repulsion'.　11 Ibid., p. 20.

'hereditary enmity' as a metaphor to characterise the natural condition of Franco-German relations.[12]

The development of the 'hereditary enemy' master narrative was part and parcel of a process of Othering that legitimised German and, later, French national purposes. It crystallised distinct, yet mutually antagonistic, French and German memories and national narratives. The creation of enemies was closely associated with other nationalist symbols and political rhetoric to foster national identity, sentiments and patriotism, which could be mobilised in times of national crisis.

In France, unsurprisingly, the narrative of the hereditary enemy features predominantly in literary and historical works after the Franco-Prussian War (Figure 17.1) and until 1945, albeit with significant fluctuations. In Germany, it grew more potent in the wake of the Rhine crisis of 1840, although its popularity appears to have been more variable between 1862 and 1932 (Figure 17.2). The coming to power of Adolf Hitler in 1933 occasioned a revival of the narrative of hereditary enmity in Germany. Figures 17.1 and 17.2 were created with Google Books Ngram Viewer. They report the frequency with which the phrases '*ennemis héréditaires*' and '*Erbfeindschaft*' are mentioned in French- and German-language books scanned by Google. Although Ngram may not cover the totality of the literary and scholarly production, it is nevertheless useful to exemplify broad trends over time. The year 1800 is the earliest starting date.

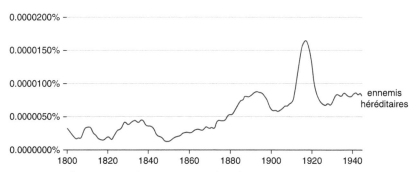

Figure 17.1 The narrative of Franco-German hereditary enemies (*ennemis héréditaires*) in the French-language literature (1800–1945).
Source: Google Books Ngram Viewer

---

12 H. Frey and S. Jordan, 'Traditions of Hate among the Intellectual Elite: The Case of Treitschke and Bainville', in Germond and Türk (eds.), *A History of Franco-German Relations*, pp. 61–72.

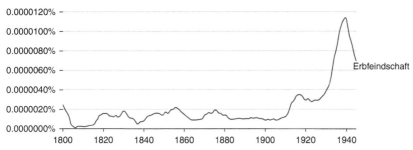

Figure 17.2   The narrative of Franco-German hereditary enemies (*Erbfeindschaft*) in the German-language literature (1800–1945).
Source: Google Books Ngram Viewer

Territorial annexation, experiences of occupation and humiliated national sentiments had thus nurtured a deep-seated distrust and resentment on both sides of the Rhine, which was disseminated by intellectual and political elites and continued to mould relations after 1945. In the first 10 years after the Second World War, the measures taken by France in its zone of occupation to ensure that Germany would not disturb the peace in Europe again were driven by a policy that prioritised security against its former foe. The seemingly harsher conditions of exploitation imposed by the French in their zone of occupation and the contentious issue of the coal-rich Saar region, which had been integrated into the French economy, nurtured German resentment well into the post-war period. In such conditions, how could France and Germany escape geopolitical rivalry and replace hostility with friendship? How did the two countries transcend war and competition and become a symbol of European cooperation?

Unquestionably, the challenges of the post-1945 period – the emerging Cold War, pressures from the United States to guarantee the economic and political stability of western Europe and Germany's anchoring in the West, the universal material devastation, population loss and moral legacy of the Holocaust – called for a new approach to Franco-German relations. At its heart, this new approach consisted of embedding West Germany within western European cooperation structures, like the European Coal and Steel Community (ECSC) founded in 1951 and the European Economic Community (EEC) founded in 1957. Both states saw in European integration a means to break the cycle of Franco-German wars and provide a concrete solution to specific French and German problems. When the issue of German rearmament and North Atlantic Treaty Organization (NATO) membership came onto the agenda with the outbreak of the Korean War in 1950, the

French response was also to Europeanise the problem by proposing the creation of a European Defence Community (EDC). When French parliamentarians voted down the project in 1954, a fully sovereign Federal Republic of Germany joined NATO and the Western European Union in 1955. Yet, domestic and international factors alone do not fully explain the dramatic transformation from enmity to amity.

Charles Kupchan provides another explanation that could be applied for Franco-German reconciliation. According to him, reconciliation first requires the removal of a country's insecurity by the unilateral exercise of strategic restraint and concession to its adversary. Secondly, each state practises reciprocal restraint to move away from competition and lay the ground for cooperation. Thirdly, as interactions among governing officials, private sector elites and ordinary citizens increase in frequency and intensity, societal integration steps in and provides additional reconciliation incentives. The last phase entails the generation of new narratives that create a new shared identity and a shared sense of solidarity.[13] Interestingly, Kupchan excludes Franco-German rapprochement from his argument because the stable peace that emerged between the two countries after the Second World War developed as the direct product of war, occupation and reconstruction and is thus a 'somewhat "artificial"'[14] construct.

Nevertheless, after a long period of deep-rooted bellicose relations, reconciliation radically redefined the Franco-German relationship in the second half of the twentieth century. It essentially shifted a narrative that had memorialised war and antagonism – the infamous hereditary enemy – to one in which memory, peace rhetoric and symbolism were used to bolster friendship and cooperation. Old narratives centred on war and antagonism were repressed, suppressed or delegitimised and replaced with new ones centring on and celebrating reconciliation and friendship. The establishment of a collective memory of war and conflicts thus served as a basis for rapprochement after 1945.

This process also had constitutive links with European integration, which removed traditional and familiar objects of fear while also disrupting the established societal narratives about the two countries. The transformation of an antagonistic relationship into exemplary amity served as a Franco-German master narrative and underpinned the grand narrative of European integration as a peace-building process. Peace-making between

---

13 C. A. Kupchan, *How Enemies Become Friends: The Sources of Stable Peace* (Princeton, NJ, Princeton University Press, 2010), p. 6.
14 Ibid., p. 33.

these two former enemies was the prerequisite for establishing and main-taining a stable peace in Europe, which facilitated political and societal rapprochement and reconciliation.

In this context, bottom-up initiatives also played a critical role for bringing the French and German societies closer. After 1945, a few pioneers would act as reconciliation entrepreneurs by championing cultural and societal contacts. Popular initiatives such as the town partnerships fostered the widespread acceptance of reconciliation among the French and German populations.[15] Anticipating the economic gains that could arise from the complementary nature of the two economies and wagering on the reconstruction of historical economic links disrupted by the war, business and industrial interests were other important actors in cementing the transformation of bilateral relations. Growing civil society contacts and a developing economic interdependence were crucial factors that made the use of military force for solving bilateral disagreements or conflicts inconceivable and redundant.

Literary and scholarly works once again served to propagate and popular-ise the new master narrative of bilateral relations and Franco-German recon-ciliation. Figures 17.3 and 17.4 chart the ebbs and flows of the reconciliation narrative in the francophone and germanophone literature. Figures 17.3 and 17.4 report the frequency with which the phrases '*réconciliation franco-allemande*' and '*deutsch-französische Versöhnung*' ('Franco-German reconcili-ation') are mentioned in French- and German-language books scanned by Google. The starting date of the horizontal axis reflects the earliest mention

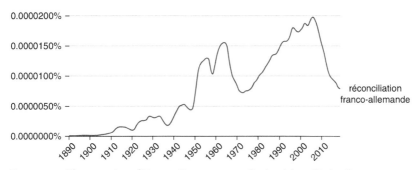

Figure 17.3 The narrative of Franco-German reconciliation (*réconciliation franco-allemande*) in French-language books (1890–2019).
Source: Google Books Ngram Viewer

15 See, for example, E. Campbell, 'The Ideals and Origins of the Franco-German, Sister Cities Movement, 1945–70', *History of European Ideas* 8 (1987): 77–95.

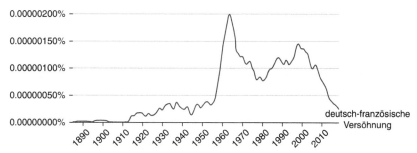

Figure 17.4 The narrative of Franco-German reconciliation (*deutsch-französische Versöhnung*) in German-language books (1885–2019).
Source: Google Books Ngram Viewer

of the phrase for which the search was performed. These figures display similar trends, with a slow increase in usage of the phrase 'Franco-German reconciliation' during the inter-war period, with two peaks roughly around 1960–5 and 2000–5. The first peak reflects the twofold impetus of the early post-war steps towards European integration and efforts creating political, economic, societal and cultural linkages between France and Germany, culminating in the signing of the Élysée Treaty in 1963. In the years after, Franco-German reconciliation, although less prominent, remained alive and was regularly re-emphasised at critical bilateral and European junctures. The narrative of Franco-German reconciliation grew to a crescendo in the run-up to the introduction of the euro, the single currency introduced by the European Union (EU) in the early 2000s, only to decrease sharply after that. Figures 17.3 and 17.4 clearly show the decisive momentum that the Élysée Treaty gave to the reconciliation narrative.

Institutionalising and Ritualising Reconciliation:
The Élysée Treaty as a Foundational Narrative
of Franco-German Friendship

The Élysée Treaty was signed on 23 January 1963 under the aegis of French President Charles de Gaulle and German Chancellor Konrad Adenauer. The document occupies a place of choice in the literature, which describes it as the fleuron or jewel in the crown of Franco-German reconciliation policies.[16] It is often portrayed as a decisive turning point in the countries' shared

---

16 C. Defrance and U. Pfeil, 'Au service du rapprochement franco-allemand. Dialogue d'historiens de part et d'autre du Rhin', in G. Mink and L. Neumayer (ed.), *L'Europe et ses passés douloureux* (Paris, La Découverte, 2007), pp. 91–103, 101.

history, the starting point of reconciliation and the foundation stone of their present-day friendship and collaboration. The treaty is thus located within a narrative evoking the end of a centuries-old ancestral enmity that eventually gave way to peaceful cooperation and friendship. The combined reference to and usage of friendship and solidarity in the joint declaration preceding the treaty elevated it beyond diplomatic rhetoric, while the text itself served to qualify the new exclusive and contractual relationship established between the two countries. Although scholars are more critical of this narrative, the treaty is part and parcel of a politically salient amity symbolism that revolves around three central tropes: the narrative of Franco-German reconciliation, the image of the Franco-German couple and socialising among young people.[17]

As its most essential function, the treaty set out to define the terms of Franco-German political and diplomatic cooperation. It laid the groundwork for a unique, resilient and adaptable relationship characterised by a complex web of regularised institutional interactions between states and societies. In addition, the treaty's multilayered system of consultations provided a forum in which Paris and Bonn (and later Berlin) learned to negotiate and reach compromises, whereby the Franco-German dialogue became established as a pivotal element of post-war European politics. Moreover, organising voluntary cooperation between state and civil society actors guaranteed a high degree of continuity and intensity in bilateral relations. Over the decades, the treaty evolved in scope and purview, with several modifications that expanded or adapted the existing consultation mechanisms.

The 1963 treaty departed from earlier practices of bilateral relations. In the 1950s, officials on both sides of the Rhine viewed bilateral cooperation in Europe pragmatically. While there was a mutual recognition that resentment needed to be removed in order for the two countries to cooperate fruitfully, few officials mentioned reconciliation as a goal. When the idea was present, as in the 1950 Schuman Declaration, it was framed as a means towards creating a unified and peaceful Europe, not as an end in itself. Mutual distrust continued to inhibit official rapprochement, even though local initiatives by cultural and civil societal actors promoted bilateral exchanges and dialogue. Although it remained limited in practice, this early rapprochement period laid the foundation stone for a newly defined relational pattern.

17 M. Delori, 'Amity Symbolism as a Resource for Conflict Resolution. The Case of Franco-German Relations', in A. Frieberg and C. K. Martin Chung (eds.), *Reconciling with the Past: Resources and Obstacles in a Global Perspective* (Abingdon, Routledge, 2017), pp. 29–53, 32.

The policy that de Gaulle and Adenauer initiated was a defining moment of change. Grandiloquent speeches and symbolic gestures became fixtures of the practice and narrative of bilateral relations.[18] These new practices, often combined with idealistic references to Franco-German friendship and reconciliation, appealed to emotions and reason. Particularly illustrative of this are de Gaulle's speech to German youth in Ludwigsburg in 1962, the iconic photographs of de Gaulle and Adenauer standing in Reims Cathedral in 1962 and their embrace after the signing of the treaty. It is no accident that these dramatic gestures continue to resonate strongly decades later. The deliberate likeness between French President François Mitterrand and Chancellor Helmut Kohl holding hands in front of the memorial to the Battle of Verdun in 1984 and the silent commemoration of French President François Hollande and German President Joachim Gauck holding hands during a joint visit at the martyr village of Oradour-sur-Glane is entirely intentional.

Neither was the choice of the sites for these events incidental. Rather, all are emblematic *lieux de mémoire* (sites of memory) of the bellicose Franco-German history. In Pierre Nora's sense, the term *lieu de mémoire* may refer to a place, object or concept vested with historical significance in the popular collective memory. It can also signify a cultural landmark, place, practice or expression stemming from a shared past. The Cathedral of Reims had been the traditional crowning place of French kings, but was nonetheless shelled by the Germans during the First World War. The burning cathedral left a lasting imprint on bilateral and European memory,[19] as had the other sites themselves when employed. Reims is doubly significant as it is where the German military surrendered at the end of the Second World War. Likewise, the Battle of Verdun in 1916 involved predominantly French and German forces and was one of the longest and bloodiest battles of the First World War. Finally, Oradour-sur-Glane's population was massacred by the Waffen-SS Division Das Reich during the liberation of France in June 1944.

In these instances, memory (and remembrance) of the war legitimised and bolstered the reconciliation narrative as a core component of the 'new'

18 Buffet and Hauser, *Haunted by History*; V. Rosoux, *Les usages de la mémoire dans les relations internationales: Le recours au passé dans la politique étrangère de la France à l'égard de l'Allemagne et de l'Algérie de 1962 à nos jours* (Brussels, Bruylant, 2002); C. Nourry, *Le couple franco-allemand: Un symbole européen* (Brussels, Bruylant, 2005).

19 T. W. Gaehtgens, *Reims on Fire: War and Reconciliation between France and Germany* (Los Angeles, CA, Getty Publications, 2018). See also J. Grossmann, 'Der Erste Weltkrieg als deutsch-französischer Erinnerungsort? Zwischen nationalem Gedenken und europäischer Geschichtspolitik', *Cahiers d'Études Germaniques* no. 66 (2014): 207–20.

Franco-German relationship established by the Élysée Treaty. It also drew attention to the shared elements of bilateral history. This semantic continuity is also visible in the commemorations of treaty anniversaries, whose regular celebrations have become critical political rites and have ritualised the treaty's original symbolism. In 2003, for the treaty's fortieth anniversary, French and German parliamentarians gathered in the Palace of Versailles, a place with great historical significance for both countries. In 2019, the fifty-sixth commemoration of the 1963 treaty and the simultaneous signing of a new cooperation treaty in Aachen, a border town steeped in Franco-German history, celebrated the countries' shared Carolingian heritage. Defrance argued that this new treaty made a common heritage site of Franco-German reconciliation, imbued with positive connotations.[20]

The Élysée Treaty thus gave birth to political symbolism, myths and narratives that still constitute the semantic and semiotic base of today's Franco-German relationship. Moreover, its symbolic practices have been influential in establishing and maintaining a mythicised atmosphere celebrating reconciliation and friendship, even if it is not always reflected in reality.[21] At the same time, these practices have become part of a Franco-German shared identity. The organisation of regular bilateral summits and meetings, the creation of a Franco-German Youth Office to facilitate youth exchanges, town twinnings, personal connections, ceremonial events, symbolic gestures and commemorations instituted collectively perpetuate (and ritualise) the narrative of Franco-German amity. The reconciliation symbolism established by the treaty facilitated the conversion of public opinion and the normalisation of mutual representations. That is, of course, not to say that stereotypes or clichés have all disappeared, but positive stereotypes have replaced negative stereotypes.

Rosoux explained how political leaders utilised various narratives to alleviate the memory of the conflictual past, naturalise Franco-German rapprochement and help transform mutual representations.[22] This includes, for example, the First World War as a shared martyrdom (the Verdun ceremony, 1984), Franco-German wars as European civil wars (Valéry Giscard d'Estaing, 1975) and reconciliation as a return to or celebration of the original and mythical

20 C. Defrance, 'Debating the History of Franco-German Reconciliation with Third-Party Countries: A Review', in N. Colin and C. Demesmay (eds.), *Franco-German Relations Seen from Abroad: Post-war Reconciliation in International Perspectives* (Cham, Springer, 2020), pp. 223–36, 234.
21 See, for example, G. Ziebura, *Die deutsch-französischen Beziehungen seit 1945: Mythen und Realitäten* (Pfullingen, G. Neske, 1970); Rosoux, *Les usages de la mémoire.*
22 Rosoux, *Les usages de la mémoire.*

union of the Carolingian empire (de Gaulle, 1966; the Treaty of Aachen, 2019). According to Delori, another measurable effect of this change has been a change in the commonplace understanding of the role of Franco-German bilateral cooperation within the European framework.[23]

As the notion of reconciliation became entrenched in public discourses and opinions, Franco-German relations ceased to be a mere instrument of European unity and acquired a value of their own. The Élysée Treaty of 1963 did not solely codify Franco-German institutionalised bilateralism, but also effectively supported the two countries' claim to leadership in Europe. In effect, 'more than any other bilateral treaty, the Élysée treaty has become a kind of common theme, an obligatory reference, not only for Franco-German relations but also for the creation of the European Community'.[24] It has been instrumental in turning a history of feuds and rivalry into a success story of cooperation through symbolism, narrative and discursive power. Frank thus raised the question of whether the Franco-German treaty of 1963 can itself be considered a Franco-German *lieu de mémoire*.[25] Although his answer remains inconclusive, he notes that the treaty has produced symbols that emotionally underpin a Franco-German community, not unlike other sites of remembrance.

The extent of the treaty's legacy and its symbolic impact, however, are not limited to the bilateral level. Rather, the treaty, with its symbolism of reconciliation and friendship, is internationally recognised as a blueprint for conflict resolution in international relations. The fascination and admiration for the historic turnaround from enmity to amity, the effective functioning of bilateral cooperation in Europe, the successful mythicisation of the Franco-German success story and its close association with the classic European integration narrative all explain the powerful significance ascribed to Franco-German reconciliation.

The idea of the Franco-German reconciliation process as a model that could be exported is neither novel nor uncommon,[26] and is underscored by literature both for and against. Existing scholarship has considered conflicts between neighbouring states in Europe, Asia and Africa with similarly deep-seated antagonism or historically fraught relations in the light of the Franco-German experience and practice of reconciliation and conflict resolution.[27]

---

23 Delori, 'Amity Symbolism', p. 35.
24 Ménudier, *Le couple franco-allemand*, p. 5.
25 R. Frank, 'Der Élysée-Vertrag: Ein deutsch-französischer Erinnerungsort?', in C. Defrance and U. Pfeil (eds.), *Der Élysée-Vertrag und die deutsch-französischen Beziehungen 1945–1963–2003* (Munich, Oldenburg, 2005), pp. 237–47.
26 Defrance, 'Debating the History'.
27 See, for example, V. Rosoux, *Les usages de la mémoire*; M. M. Mirza and S. Bhutto, 'Franco-German and India–Pakistan Reconciliation: A Comparative Study', *Journal of*

Even among those critical of the notion of reconciliation, specialists have extensively debated the actors, vehicles and mechanisms of Franco-German reconciliation, the different features and contexts of the process, the structuring elements that make them generalisable and transferable, and also their limits.[28] They have pointed out the differences between rapprochement and reconciliation. There is a broad agreement among specialists that the transferability of the Franco-German reconciliation process to other regions of the world marked by inter-state and international conflicts is limited owing to the different historical, cultural, political, societal or institutional contexts. While most reject the idea that the Franco-German model can be exported and adopted, many do argue for a Franco-German 'toolbox', whose devices could be used to ease tensions and facilitate the establishment of peaceful and cooperative relations.[29]

The 1963 Élysée Treaty played an influential role in establishing a narrative centred on reconciliation and friendship. This narrative has become a crucial rhetorical tool used to emphasise bilateral unity and solidarity. Through discourses, rituals and symbols, the construction of Franco-German friendship and reconciliation was a slow and non-linear process. Still, it has been instrumental in emphasising the role of France and Germany in European regional integration.

Between Myth and Narrative: The Franco-German Engine and European Integration

One of the most enduring assumptions in European (Union) studies is that France and Germany are the two powerhouses driving the economic and political integration of Europe. The numerous metaphors (motor, engine, axis, tandem, locomotive) used to describe their bilateral partnership suggest a capacity to provide momentum and steer European integration.[30] The engine narrative has served to justify a *primus inter pares* role for both countries in Europe. The Franco-German claim to leadership in Europe is underpinned by rhetoric, symbolic and mediatised commemorations, and other ritualised events, which bolster the Franco-German community of

---

Management and Social Sciences 2 (2013): 42–56; L. Ren, *Rationality and Emotions: Comparative Studies of the Franco-German and Sino-Japanese Reconciliations* (Berlin, Springer, 2014).

28 See, for example, S. Seidendorf, *Le modèle franco-allemand: Les clés d'une paix perpétuelle? Analyse des mécanismes de coopération* (Paris, Presse universitaire du Septentrion, 2013).

29 Defrance, 'Debating the History', p. 224.

30 W. Paterson, 'Did France and Germany Lead Europe? A Retrospect', in J. Hayward (ed.), *Leaderless Europe* (Oxford, Oxford University Press, 2009), pp. 89–110; J. Schild, 'Mission Impossible? The Potential for Franco-German Leadership in the Enlarged EU', *Journal of Common Market Studies* 5 (2010): 1367–90.

interest and purpose and keep alive the myth of the engine. Treaty anniversaries, bilateral summits, joint communiqués and other bilateral encounters have fuelled a great deal of myth-making and symbolism about the two states' essential role in Europe and the unique nature of their relationship. Even if the Franco-German engine has been repeatedly pronounced dead, stalled or broken in the last three decades, its reputation for driving integration forward endures.

The close bilateral relationship of France and Germany has been inextricably entwined with Europe's post-war developments from the beginning. In its most simplistic form, the mainstream narrative is that the reconciliation of the former enemies cleared the way for economic integration, which provided multiple occasions for the two countries to work together, deepen their bilateral partnership, provide leadership and steer the course of European integration. Their close cooperation frequently proved instrumental in advancing or deepening European union. Krotz and Schild have described this unique interdependence as 'embedded bilateralism', which is the 'inter-related reality of Franco-German bilateralism and multilateral European integration'.[31]

Franco-German relations have, furthermore, shaped the early narrative legitimising the project of uniting Europe along with its eventual institutional form. This narrative centred on the necessity of safeguarding peace, security and economic recovery in Europe following the Second World War and in the context of the emerging Cold War. The treaties concluded during the 1950s established institutions whose primary purpose was to substitute for longstanding rivalries, primarily between France and Germany, a common European destiny and to find novel ways of achieving common interests in order to make war unthinkable and materially impossible. This early choice of sectoral, economic and supranational integration as the way to peace and prosperity was thus to provide a vehicle for and justify Franco-German reconciliation.

The narrative of France and Germany acting as the main driving force of European union has become an intrinsic element of the countries' agency in Europe over the years. Although feared or complained about by EU partners at times, Franco-German cooperation is deemed essential for reaching bilateral and European compromises. Nevertheless, the engine's heart is not the constant harmony and convergence of interests it might otherwise be

---

31 U. Krotz and J. Schild, *Shaping Europe: France, Germany, and Embedded Bilateralism from the Élysée Treaty to Twenty-First Century Politics* (Oxford, Oxford University Press, 2013), p. 1.

portrayed to be. Instead, it is the two countries' capacity to overcome diverging interests and bridge differing positions that has been the greatest contributor. When the two countries find common ground, the resulting bilateral compromise is likely to meet their EU partners' needs and interests. This idea is subsumed in the widespread belief that, when the two countries agree and act together, Europe thrives; when they struggle, so does Europe.

The narrative on the dominant role of the Franco-German engine is primarily grounded in state-centric theoretical approaches. From a rational choice perspective, the Franco-German engine's role is rooted in both states' (assumed or real) need to cooperate to solve joint, bilateral and/or European problems. Intergovernmental approaches assume that the French and German governments have been influential in determining the outcome of intergovernmental bargaining. Accordingly, the ability of the Franco-German engine to matter and propel forward integration is most visible and best documented when 'history-making' or 'big bang' decisions, such as treaty revisions, are at stake.[32] Those accounts stress the essential role of states in international bargaining.

Several instances of Franco-German bilateral leadership seem to confirm the conclusions in many of these approaches. The leading role played by France and Germany in the creation of the ECSC and during the negotiations of the Rome Treaties instituting the EEC and the European Atomic Energy Community is well established.[33] Other well-documented instances of bilateral leadership are the creation of the European Monetary System,[34] the Single European Act[35] and the negotiations of the Maastricht and Amsterdam Treaties.[36] These examples illustrate the importance of the

---

32 D. Leuffen, H. Degner and K. Radtke, 'Which Mechanics Drive the "Franco-German Engine"? An Analysis of How and Why France and Germany Have Managed to Shape Much of Today's EU', *L'Europe en Formation* 4 (2012): 45–83; Cole, *Franco-German Relations*, pp. 61–71.

33 See, for example, H. J. Küsters, *Die Gründung der Europäischen Wirtschaftsgemeinschaft* (Baden-Baden, Nomos, 1982); K. Schwabe, *Die Anfänge des Schuman-Plans 1950/51/The Beginnings of the Schuman-Plan* (Baden-Baden, Nomos, 1988); P. Gerbet, 'Le rôle du couple franco-allemand dans la création et le développement des Communautés européennes', in Picht and Wessels (eds.), *Motor für Europa*, pp. 69–119.

34 See, for example, N. P. Ludlow, *The Making of the European Monetary System: A Case Study of the Politics of the European Community* (London, Butterworths, 1982); H. Simonian, *The Privileged Partnership: Franco-German Relations in the European Community 1969–84* (Oxford, Clarendon Press, 1985).

35 See, for example, A. Moravcsik, *The Choice for Europe: Social Purpose and State Power from Messina to Maastricht* (Ithaca, NY, Cornell University Press, 1998).

36 See, for example, C. Mazzuccelli, *France and Germany at Maastricht: Politics and Negotiations to Create European Union* (New York, NY, Garland, 1997); M. J. Geary, C. Germond and K. K. Patel, 'The Maastricht Treaty: Negotiations and Consequences in Historical Perspective: Introduction', *Journal of European Integration History* 19, no. 1 (2013): 5–11.

bilateral relationship, because it provided the necessary leadership or acted as a mechanism for mediating other bilateral and European differences. In addition, Franco-German relations have shaped constitutive bargains in EU policy fields, especially the Common Agricultural Policy.[37]

Yet this seemingly impressive track record of bilateral leadership conceals historical occasions when the two countries behaved as a brake rather than as a motor of European integration.[38] Franco-German dissensions account in large part for the demise of the EDC in 1954, while the Benelux countries were the main driving forces behind the European relaunch of the mid 1950s that led to the signature of the Rome Treaties in 1957. Likewise, monetary cooperation within the 'Snake' crumbled in an atmosphere of bilateral divergences in the second half of the 1970s. The Snake was the first attempt at European monetary cooperation. Its aim was to limit exchange rate fluctuations between European currencies within an upper and lower band, which provided a tunnel within which European currencies could trade. As Cole notes, the metaphor of the Franco-German motor tends to overshadow the role of other crucial actors such as European partners, supranational institutions and other societal actors.[39]

Although the prior examples highlight the complexity of Franco-German bilateralism, the (at least partially fictional) 'motor' and 'engine' narratives have nevertheless served several discursive purposes. Myths and narratives frequently involve specific characters. A first purpose has been to stress the personal dimension of bilateral relations and emphasise the engine role played by its primary actors, the notorious Franco-German 'couples' formed by the political leaders. This personification is a product of the treaty itself, which gives the heads of state and government a prominent role in breathing life into the relationship. The ups and downs of personal relations are often taken as a general indicator of the bilateral relationship and its traction potential.[40] History has lent strength to this standard view of the Franco-German engine. Functional, dynamic couples have often proven influential in bringing about crucial European integrationist advances, whereas problematic tandems struggled to overcome their disagreements and act for Europe's good.[41]

---

37 D. Weber, 'Franco-German Bilateralism and Agricultural Politics in the European Union: The Neglected Level', *West European Politics* 22 (1999): 45–67; C. Germond, 'The Agricultural Bone of Contention. The Franco-German Tandem and the Making of the CAP, 1963–1966', *Journal of European Integration History* 32 (2010): 25–44.

38 See Paterson, 'Did France and Germany Lead Europe', pp. 89–110.

39 Cole, *Franco-German Relations*, p. 62. 40 Ibid., pp. 47–9.

41 See, for example, K. Seidel and C. Germond, 'The Franco-German Relationship at the Heart of EU history', in B. Leucht, K. Seidel and L. Warlouzet, *Reinventing Europe: The History of the European Union, 1945 to the Present* (London, Bloomsbury Academic, 2023), pp. 299–316; C. Germond, 'Franco-German Relations and the European Integration

Simultaneously, leaders have instrumentalised their close personal relations to cultivate public support at home and for the benefit of both partners and European integration.

As a term of referral, the so-called Franco-German 'couple' has come to epitomise the close personal relations between leaders on opposite sides of the Rhine. A Google Books Ngram Viewer analysis displays a similar upward trend in the term's usage in the anglophone, francophone and germano-phone scholarly literature from its inception in the 1960s, with an especially noticeable growth c. 1990 and a sharper decrease from the mid 2000s (Figures 17.5(a), 17.6(a) and 17.7(a)). A search replacing 'couple' with 'engine' (Figures 17.5(b), 17.6(b) and 17.7(b)) reveals a comparable evolution, albeit

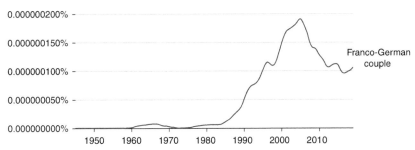

Figure 17.5(a) The narrative of the Franco-German couple in the anglophone literature (1945–2019).
Source: Google Books Ngram Viewer

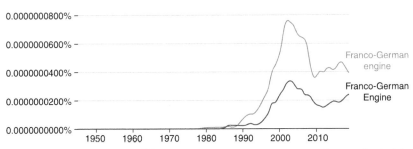

Figure 17.5(b) The narrative of the Franco-German engine (or Franco-German Engine) in the anglophone literature (1945–2019).
Source: Google Books Ngram Viewer

Process since 1989', in K. Larres, H. Moroff and R. Wittlinger (eds.), *The Oxford Handbook of German Politics* (Oxford, Oxford University Press, 2022), pp. 491–508.

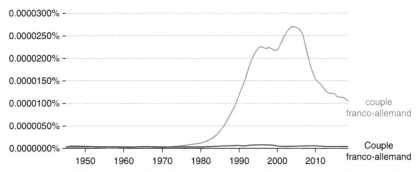

Figure 17.6(a) The narrative of the Franco-German couple (*couple franco-allemand* and *Couple franco-allemand*) in the francophone literature (1945–2019).
Source: Google Books Ngram Viewer

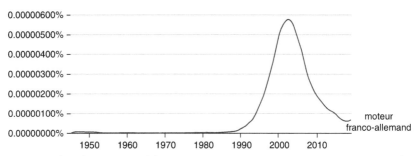

Figure 17.6(b) The narrative of the Franco-German engine (*moteur franco-allemand*) in the francophone literature (1945–2019).
Source: Google Books Ngram Viewer

with an increased frequency for 'engine.' This would suggest that these two terms tend to be used interchangeably. Reflecting on this differentiated usage, George-Henri Soutou concluded that historians favour the term engine, while the media prefer the more eye-catching image of the couple.[42]

Now commonly applied to all Franco-German pairs, the term 'couple' began to be used in the 1960s in the context of de Gaulle's and Adenauer's policy of rapprochement. Incidentally, de Gaulle and Adenauer are often portrayed as the ideal-typical duo, whose close and friendly relations, sometimes likened to a 'geriatric romance',[43] left a blueprint for their successors.

42 G.-H. Soutou, 'L'émergence du couple franco-allemand: Un mariage de raison', *Politique étrangère* 4 (2012): 727–38.
43 R. J. Granieri, 'More Than a Geriatric Romance. Adenauer, de Gaulle and the Atlantic Alliance', in Germond and Türk (eds.), *A History of Franco-German Relations*, pp. 189–98.

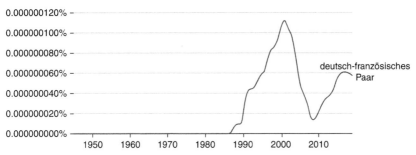

Figure 17.7(a) The narrative of the Franco-German couple (*deutsch-französisches Paar*) in the germanophone literature (1945–2019).
Source: Google Books Ngram Viewer

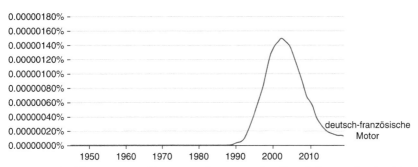

Figure 17.7(b) The narrative of the Franco-German engine (*deutsch-französische Motor*) in the germanophone literature (1945–2019).
Source: Google Books Ngram Viewer

Adenauer's invitation to de Gaulle's family home, La Boisserie, was to mark symbolically that this was not just a relationship between two nations but also one between two men. If this prominence given to the two elderly statesmen as the original Franco-German couple overshadowed the early achievements of bilateral rapprochement, it did nevertheless establish the Franco-German duo as a cornerstone of European politics.

The relative concomitance of changes at the top political levels in the two countries from the late 1960s–early 1970s onwards facilitated the association of Franco-German couples with specific phases of European integration. Historically too, the most influential couples have often been those in which the leaders belonged to different political families and started from different ideological positions. Scholars have suggested that this is an essential condition for their ability to strike comprehensive compromises acceptable to their fellow European states,[44] since effective Franco-German leadership is never based on a unity of preferences. Instead, the two countries' capacity to overcome diverging interests, bridge differing positions and thus embrace their partners' preferences is essential for advancing European integration.

The two duos formed by Valéry Giscard d'Estaing and Helmut Schmidt in the 1970s and François Mitterrand and Helmut Kohl in the 1980s stand out for their role in developing the partnership and European integration. In addition to sharing excellent personal relations, they agreed on the necessity of close cooperation to lead Europe. This enabled them to take advantage of opportunities arising from the European and international context.[45] In consequence, it is no coincidence that the notion of a Franco-German engine – and all its associated derivatives – began to be used when collaboration between Giscard and Schmidt proved decisive for the advancement of political cooperation and for laying the groundwork of the community's early economic and monetary governance. Mitterrand and Kohl also purposefully used the influence of the Franco-German partnership to push forward various bilateral initiatives to develop further integration in the economic, monetary and defence areas. Increased bilateral cooperation in these areas also underpinned European initiatives. In these instances, bilateral deals prefigured and shaped what would be later agreed upon at a European level.

When Mitterrand and Kohl left the political scene, the Franco-German couple became more elusive and lacked the closeness and trust that had characterised prior years. The ascent of a new generation of political leaders who had not directly experienced the Second World War partly accounts for the change in the nature of the bilateral partnership since the 1990s. German reunification, moreover, altered the equilibrium of bilateral relations that rested on a trade-off between Germany's economic prowess and France's political power. Previously, this shared leadership had given France and Germany the credibility, clout and capacity to steer Europe. But German reunification tilted the balance of power, favouring a demographically more significant, economically more robust German state positioned at the heart of an enlarging EU. The new tandem was now one of relative equals with increasing competition for its leadership. As bilateral relations came under strain from the 1990s onwards, French and German leaders were tempted to seek closer cooperation with other European partners, Great Britain first among them. Yet, the Élysée Treaty tied the two countries together

44 D. Webber, *The Franco-German Relationship in the European Union* (London, and New York, NY, Routledge, 1999), pp. 167–81.
45 Germond, 'Franco-German Dynamic Duos', pp. 197–9.

institutionally, while the narrative of Franco-German amity constrained their ability to seek 'special relationships' elsewhere.

The recent, Hollywood-inspired, trend of nicknaming Franco-German couples by contracting their leaders' name into one – Merkozy, short for Merkel and Sarkozy, and Merkron, short for Merkel and Macron – has become another discursive means to underscore both France's and Germany's continued starring role in Europe and the symbiotic personal relations of their leaders. These nicknames bespeak deep personal cooperation that goes beyond the traditional confines of the Élysée Treaty and affirms a kind of Franco-German duumvirate in Europe. While these patterns of intense bilateral concertation are not new, they are conspicuous by virtue of their public salience, intensity and overt claim to joint leadership in the EU.

The use of these labels by the media closely follows the crisis-solving, broker role played by these duos at critical junctures in the EU's most recent history. Accordingly, a peak in the Merkozy narrative (Figure 17.8(a)) coincides with the pair successfully working together to rescue the EU from the euro and sovereign debt crisis in the early 2010s. The search criteria used were all sources, all authors, all companies, all subjects, all industries, all regions and all languages. Searches limited to sources in French, German and English display similar trends. The chapter uses for its analysis data made available publicly by Factiva, accessed through an institutional academic (Norwegian University of Science and Technology – NTNU) subscription to the Factiva database. The new treaties to reform and improve Eurozone governance agreed in 2010 and 2012 bore the hallmarks of Franco-German compromises.[46] The Merkron tandem was (and portrayed itself as) instrumental in managing the historical crises of Britain's departure from the EU, Donald Trump's norm-shredding US presidency and the Covid-19 pandemic, with its economic and social-impact fallouts. The mediatic popularisation of the nickname Merkron (Figure 17.8(b)) coincided also with the attempt by newly elected French President Emmanuel Macron to revive the narrative of the Franco-German engine to support his plans for an ambitious European initiative and a new narrative for Europe centred on 'a Europe that protects'. In his mind, France and Germany should be at the vanguard of promoting this new Europe.

The growing popularity of these labels is not due merely to their catchiness. They effectively convey a twofold message that encapsulates the discursive essence of what the Franco-German couple is (or should be)

46 J. Schild, 'Leadership in Hard Times: Germany, France, and the Management of the Eurozone Crisis', *German Politics & Society* 31, no. 1 (2013): 24–47.

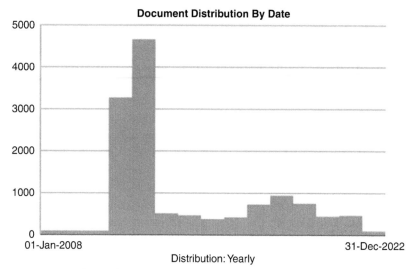

Figure 17.8(a) The Merkozy narrative in the media (2008–22).
Source: the table reports the frequency with which the term 'Merkozy' appears in Factiva's global news database, in 12,800 documents across the timespan concerned.

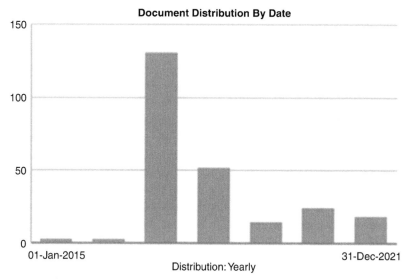

Figure 17.8(b) The Merkron narrative in the media (2015–21).
Source: the table reports the frequency with which the term 'Merkron' is mentioned in news media accessible in Factiva's global news database, in 240 documents across the timespan concerned.

about: the French and Germans stand together and share a broad agreement on critical issues, and they fulfil a leadership role in the EU. In addition, these labels articulate four crucial features of Franco-German bilateralism. First, they reflect the new internal balance of the couple: the two parties are equal partners. Secondly, they describe a bilateral coalition, united in the desire to drive EU decision-making and in the exertion of joint leadership – one often dependent on the leaders' individual willingness to cooperate as Europe's engine. In effect, the Merkozy and Merkron couples are simply further iterations of Franco-German institutionalised bilateralism. Thirdly, they suggest an 'institution of decentralized bargaining',[47] which helped the French and German governments strengthen their bargaining position vis-à-vis the EU's supranational institutions and partners. Fourthly, as some scholars have argued, these labels denote a successful 'discursive double game', where agreement is possible only if both leaders can legitimise their standard solution simultaneously at home and in relation to other EU decision-makers.[48]

There exists yet another discursive purpose of the Franco-German engine narrative, which is cultivated by both capitals. This is to preserve the image of bilateral cohesion and unity, and emphasise the convergence of national interests and mutual trust (these being considered the cement of the bilateral relationship). Accordingly, a function of the mythic engine is to substantiate the closeness and vitality of the bilateral partnership, even though national self-interest remains the main driving force behind policies on both sides of the Rhine. A function of the engine narrative is thus to gloss over momentary disagreements and project bilateral cohesion and cooperation even – or especially – when there is little of it to hand.

For example, relations with NATO and the American ally remained contentious for a long time as French foreign policy abided by the Gaullist tenets of French and European independence. Disagreements over transatlantic relations and France's absence from NATO's integrated military structures (1966–2009) constituted a serious obstacle to a deepening of Franco-German defence and security collaboration.[49] Conflicts throughout the European integration

---

47 M. Guidi and Y. Karagiannis, 'The Eurozone Crisis, Decentralized Bargaining and the Theory of EU Institutions', SOG Working Paper (2013), www.researchgate.net/publi cation/275339276_The_Eurozone_Crisis_Decentralized_Bargaining_and_the_Theor y_of_EU_Institutions.

48 A. Crespy and V. Schmidt, 'The Clash of Titans: France, Germany and the Discursive Double Game of EMU Reform', *Journal of European Public Policy* 21 (2014): 1085–1101.

49 R. Laird (ed.), *Strangers and Friends: The Franco-German Security Relationship* (New York, NY, St Martin's Press, 1989); S. A. Kocs, *Autonomy or Power: The Franco-German Relationship and Europe's Strategic Choices (1955–1995)* (Westport, CN, Praeger, 1995).

process have also regularly strained relations. Splits on European issues largely account for the steady deterioration of the bilateral relationship during the 1990s. Long periods of 'cohabitation' in France – the cooperation of a conservative president with a socialist prime minister, or vice versa – further hampered bilateral cooperation on European matters, too. Enlargement has also been a major topic of contention. Where France initially resisted enlargement, instead prioritising the deepening of European integration over its widening, Germany favoured pursuing both aims in parallel for economic and geopolitical motives. France, by necessity, did unenthusiastically accept enlargement when it seemed to have become inevitable. The EU's successive enlargements have made it even more difficult for the two countries to steer Europe forward. These and treaty revisions have provided another arena to display the potentially contentious Franco-German bilateral relations.[50]

Conclusion

The chapter has analysed the history of the Franco-German relationship by examining how narratives of war, peace and memory shaped and reshaped it in the past and present. It sheds novel light on a history of conflict and cooperation.

The chapter first discussed the emergence of the hereditary enemy narrative which celebrated war and antagonism in the nineteenth century and was closely linked to the birth of the French and German nation-states. After 1945, the old narrative of a hereditary enmity was repressed, suppressed or otherwise delegitimised and replaced with new ones focusing on reconciliation, friendship and a shared history. Literary and scholarly production played a critical role in popularising and circulating mainstream narratives among societies and in enabling widespread acceptance. At the same time, it also contributed to disrupting established discourses about the two countries' history and shifting the narrative from war to peace, reconciliation and cooperation.

The chapter also demonstrated how the 1963 Élysée Treaty functioned as a foundational narrative of present-day relations. The new relationship it defines used reconciliation and amity symbolism through personal connections, symbolic gestures, ceremonial events and anniversaries.

50 C. Mazzucelli, U. Guérot and A. Metz, 'Cooperative Hegemon, Missing Engine or Improbable Core? Explaining French–German Influence in European Treaty Reform', in D. Beach and C. Mazzucelli (eds.), *Leadership in the Big Bangs of European Integration* (Basingstoke, Palgrave Macmillan, 2006), pp. 158–77.

They ritualised political and societal cooperation and perpetuated the narrative of Franco-German reconciliation. They reinterpreted the countries' conflict-ridden past into a shared memory of their bellicose history. Beyond the treaty's institutional provisions, state and civil society actors were instrumental in guaranteeing a high degree of continuity in bilateral relations.

Furthermore, the chapter examined the narrative that consistently emphasised the role played by the Franco-German duo as a 'central engine' that shaped post-war European cooperation. The chapter showed that the mythic Franco-German engine had been constructed to emphasise the convergence of national interests and mutual trust. Even so, enduring self-interest remained a powerful driving force in policy- and decision-making on both sides and justified France and Germany's *primus inter pares* role in Europe. Moreover, contrary to what the mainstream engine narrative suggests, Franco-German leadership in Europe was exerted neither consistently nor continuously, nor was it based on a unity of preferences. Instead, the countries' capacity to bridge diverging interests and positions enabled them to act as Europe's engine. This has not changed. The still unparalleled Franco-German institutionalised bilateralism remains a critical instrument for shaping the EU's agenda and building compromises.

Arguably, though, the most formidable achievement of reconciliation is to have made cooperation an uncontested cornerstone of France and Germany's policy in Europe. The time of bloodshed and hatred that Barbara sang about belongs irreversibly to the past.

Recommended Reading

Germond, C. and H. Türk (eds.). *A History of Franco-German Relations in Europe: From 'Hereditary Enemies' to Partners* (New York, NY, Palgrave Macmillan, 2008).

Hendriks, G. and A. Morgan (eds.). *The Franco-German Axis in European Integration* (Cheltenham and Northampton, Edward Elgar, 2001).

Krotz, U. and J. Schild. *Shaping Europe: France, Germany, and Embedded Bilateralism from the Élysée Treaty to Twenty-First Century Politics* (Oxford, Oxford University Press, 2013).

Pedersen, T. *Germany, France, and the Integration of Europe: A Realist Interpretation* (London, Pinter, 1998).

Sangar, E. *Diffusion in Franco-German Relations: A Different Perspective on a History of Cooperation and Conflict* (Cham, Palgrave Macmillan, 2020).

18

The 'Saints' of European Integration: From Visionaries to Architects

MICHAEL GEHLER

Basic Questions, Categories and Structure

Integration research has dealt with 'founding fathers' of the European Union (EU)[1] as an ambiguous subject in order not to speak of 'saints' right away. Is that an appropriate term? If yes and this notion is taken seriously, who should be considered for it? In fact, there are different categories. This issue is about recognising, naming and valuing reference persons and personalities in the history of Europe's unification, but is it really about 'saints'? Further questions arise. How far back should we focus? Should we go back to the nineteenth century, or should we start after the First World War, or even after the Second World War? Is it about those who gave us the idea of Europe's unification or about the founders of the communities?[2]

If we turn to the first category, it is necessary to briefly present those whom we might label 'idealistic masterminds and visionary precursors of European ideas in modern history' such as Victor Hugo (1802–85), Giuseppe Mazzini (1805–72) and Charles Mackay (1814–89) from the nineteenth century.

If we look at the first half of the twentieth century, we could consider as a second category political actors and lobbyists after the First World War

---

1 R. T. Griffiths, 'The Founding Fathers', in E. Jones, A. Menon and S. Weatherill (eds.), *The Oxford Handbook of the European Union* (Oxford, Oxford University Press, 2012), pp. 181–92. For 'the founding fathers' and 'the "heroic" phase of European integration and the emergence of the enlightened elite', see A. Varsori, 'A Historical Interpretation of the Process of European Integration', in J. M. Magone (ed.), *Routledge Handbook of European Politics* (London and New York, NY, Routledge, 2014), pp. 97–115, 97–98, 100–2.

2 For many of the personalities presented in this chapter, see W. Böttcher (ed.), *Klassiker des europäischen Denkens: Friedens- und Europavorstellungen aus 700 Jahren europäischer Kulturgeschichte* (Baden-Baden, Nomos, 2014); W. Böttcher, *Europas vergessene Visionäre: Rückbesinnung in Zeiten akuter Krisen* (Baden-Baden, Nomos, 2019).

who held various offices, performed particular functions in various institutions, had more concrete ideas and gave political impulses such as Aristide Briand (1862–1932) in the inter-war years, during wartime and in exile. As a third category we can also think of Richard N. Coudenhove-Kalergi (1894–1972), or of Jean Monnet (1888–1979), who acted as a bridge builder and liaison between pre-war ideas and new conceptions as well as being a decisive source of ideas for Robert Schuman.

After 1945, and especially in the 1950s, a fourth category would be the 'founders of the European Communities', such as – in chronological order – Robert Schuman (1866–1963), Konrad Adenauer (1876–1967), Alcide De Gasperi (1881–1954) and Paul-Henri Spaak (1899–1972). Then, as a fifth category, one could think of the following outstanding actors, who could be called 'initiators of a second generation', such as Pierre Werner (1913–2002), Valéry Giscard d'Estaing (1926–2020) and Helmut Schmidt (1918–2015). Our sixth category, or a third generation of 'builders of the European Union' would include François Mitterrand (1916–96), Jacques Delors (1925–) and Helmut Kohl (1930–2017), the last two of whom were named Honorary Citizens of Europe after Monnet by a unanimous decision of the heads of state and governments. It is not surprising that many of these protagonists have become winners of the Charlemagne Prize.

Criticism, Beatification and Further Guiding Questions

If we limit the reference personalities to the so-called 'saints' around whom there have been forms of a cult, around whom a myth exists and a real veneration has been created, we will be able to name the aforementioned political actors Monnet, Schuman, Adenauer and De Gasperi, in that order, although criticism of such categories has been voiced in a heretical position on the 'founding fathers' held by Alan S. Milward.[3]

We should also mention the possibility of beatification, which is practised in the Roman Catholic Church and used as a preliminary to canonisation. De Gasperi and Schuman are particularly at issue here. The latter was awarded the honorary title 'Father of Europe' by the EU Parliament. The Italian daily newspaper *La Stampa* reported in 2002 that Adenauer was to be beatified. The Holy See, however, remained silent on the matter, while for De Gasperi and

---

3 A. S. Milward, 'The Lives and Teachings of the European Saints', in A. S. Milward, *The European Rescue of the Nation State* (London, Routledge, 1992), pp. 318–44.

Schuman beatifications are already pending at the Vatican. The Archdiocese of Trento initiated the diocesan process of the beatification of De Gasperi in 1993. A process of beatification by the Catholic Church for the French statesman and 'EU founding father' Schuman was completed in 2004 at the diocesan level in Metz and has since then also been dealt with in the Vatican.[4]

So what should we focus on and which personalities should we concentrate on? Starting from the biographies, it is necessary to answer the following questions. What led to these personalities being honoured, revered and valued? Does this stand up to scrutiny, and what did they achieve in terms of Europe's unification? Who made the protagonists mentioned into 'saints' and praised them as 'fathers' of Europe? How was this publicly expressed and institutionally manifested, for example through monuments, honours, commemorative publications and the naming of buildings, foundations and publications? What place do these 'saints' occupy in the historiography of European integration, apart from being the subjects of an apologetic and euphemistic literature of veneration? Would it not be better to use terms such as 'architects', 'master builders', 'idea givers', 'initiators', 'pioneers' and 'visionaries'?

When speaking of 'saints', a historiographical, that is, de-sacralising-rationalising and factual-historical approach, should be chosen, especially since we are not dealing with European church history and theology, but with European integration politics. Therefore, in order to de-sacralise, contextualise and relativise the 'saints', a step-by-step approach and a differentiated methodology would seem to make sense.

Idealistic Masterminds and Visionary Precursors of European Ideas in Modern History

In the 1848 pre-revolutionary period a republican Europeanism emerged, with exponents such as the Italian Risorgimento representative Giuseppe Mazzini or the French writer Victor Hugo, who coined the motto of the 'United States of Europe' for the continent's future. Mazzini's activities were remarkable, with the founding of 'Young Italy' (1831) in Marseille and 'Young Europe' (1834) in Berne, where politically liberal ideas and romantic-literary writing were combined.[5] Mazzini considered Europe to be the 'lever of the

---

4 Concerning Schuman, see https://archives.eui.eu/en/fonds/153157?item=HALK. For De Gasperi, see www.santiebeati.it/dettaglio/92035.
5 H. Gollwitzer, *Europabild und Europagedanke: Beiträge zur deutschen Geistesgeschichte des 18. und 19. Jahrhunderts* (Munich, C. H. Beck, 1964), p. 244; L. Piccardo, *Dalla patria all'umanità: L'Europa di Giuseppe Mazzini* (Bologna, il Mulino, 2020). See also P. M. Lützeler, *Die Schriftsteller und Europa: Von der Romantik bis zur Gegenwart* (Munich, Piper, 1992), pp. 144–89.

world' – for him it was not from the United States that the struggle for freedom and humanity could be expected.[6]

The Scottish journalist and politician Charles Mackay claimed to be the first to have brought the slogan of the 'United States of Europe' into the world and thus made it public. On 1 February 1848, he articulated the appropriate combination of words in the radical democratic newspaper *The London Telegraph* of the English democratic movement.[7] In 1849–50, he presented motions in the House of Commons in London for the introduction of international arbitration and general disarmament. Mackay assumed that only Europe was the haven of freedom, not North America, where slavery still prevailed.[8] With this motto, he promoted a political reconstruction of the continent as a confederal peace league.[9]

Comparable ideas and considerations circulated in circles of international exiles in France (Paris and Strasbourg), Switzerland (Berne and Geneva) and the United Kingdom (London).[10] The common experience of emigration created a climate of democratic European solidarity, which, however, remained inhomogeneous and fragile, as it did among the European Christian socials, but especially among the Catholic conservatives, represented by the 'Black International' in Geneva.[11]

Mackay's slogan found its way into German and French newspapers. On the continent, it was a catchphrase directed against the 'neo-absolutism' of the 'Holy Alliance of Princes' (1815) by the liberal-democratic movement, which wanted to see it replaced by a future 'Holy Alliance of the Peoples'. The slogan had primarily a societal and domestic dimension in the sense of being a social and political term of struggle. It was far less connected to a constitutional programme for a politically united Europe.[12]

---

6 Gollwitzer, *Europabild und Europagedanke*, p. 245.

7 A. Ernstberger, 'Charles Mackay und die Idee der Vereinigten Staaten von Europa im Jahre 1848', *Historische Zeitschrift* 146 (1932): 263–303.

8 Gollwitzer, *Europabild und Europagedanke*, p. 245.

9 *London Telegraph*, 1 April 1848, 2 e f, quoted after Ernstberger, 'Charles Mackay', 277. On this relevant topic as well as on linguistic history, see also N. Schumacher, *Der Wortschatz der Europäischen Integration: Eine onomasiologische Untersuchung des sog. 'europäischen Sprachgebrauchs' im politischen und institutionellen Bereich* (Düsseldorf, Schwann, 1976), pp. 167–71.

10 Gollwitzer, *Europabild und Europagedanke*, p. 244.

11 E. Lamberts (ed.), *The Black International: 1870–1878: The Holy See and Militant Catholicism in Europe/L'Internationale noire 1870–1878: Le Saint-Siège et le Catholicisme militant en Europe* (Leuven, Leuven University Press, 2002); J. Großmann, *Die Internationale der Konservativen: Transnationale Elitenzirkel und private Außenpolitik in Westeuropa seit 1945* (Munich, Oldenbourg, 2014).

12 P. Renouvin, *Les idées et les projets d'Union européenne au XIXe siècle* (Paris, Conciliation Internationale, 1931), pp. 35–6.

On 21 August 1849, Victor Hugo had declared in his opening speech as president of the World Peace Congress in Paris thus: 'Un jour viendra où l'on verra ces deux groupes immenses, les États-Unis d'Amérique, les États-Unis d'Europe, placés l'un en face de l'autre, se tendant la main par-dessus les mers.' ('The day will come when one will see these two immense groups, the United States of America, the United States of Europe, facing each other, holding out their hands across the seas.').[13] On 17 July 1851, as a deputy in the French National Assembly, Hugo stated: 'Le peuple français a taillé dans un granit indestructible et posé au milieu même du vieux continent monarchique la première pierre de cet immense édifice de l'avenir, qui s'appellera un jour les États-Unis d'Europe' ('The French people have carved out of indestructible granite and laid in the very midst of the old monarchical continent the first stone of that immense edifice of the future which will one day be called the United States of Europe.').[14]

Concrete Sources of Ideas and Political Impulses in Inter-war, Exile and Post-war Times

Pan-European by Conviction and Passion: Richard Coudenhove-Kalergi

Richard Nikolaus Count Coudenhove-Kalergi (1894–1972) was a tireless champion and promoter of the idea of European unification in the inter-war period and accordingly proud of his cosmopolitanism and internationalism. His ancestors were Flemish nobles and Greeks; his father was a diplomat of the Habsburg Monarchy in Tokyo and his mother Japanese. The experience of the First World War[15] led Coudenhove-Kalergi to the idea of Pan-Europe[16] because he recognised the economic rise of the United States as

---

13 J. ter Meulen, *Der Gedanke der Internationalen Organisation in seiner Entwicklung*, 3 vols. (The Hague, Martinus Nijhoff, 1917–40), vol. II, p. 318.

14 V. Hugo, *Œuvres complètes de V. Hugo. Actes et paroles: Avant l'exil, 1841–1851*, vol. I (Paris, J. Hetzel & Cie, 1882), p. 425. See also M. Gehler, 'Vom Schlagwort der "Vereinigten Staaten von Europa" zur Realität des Europas der vereinigten Staaten im 21. Jahrhundert', in M. Lützeler and M. Gehler (eds.), *Die Europäische Union zwischen Konfusion und Vision: Interdisziplinäre Fragestellungen* (Vienna, Cologne and Weimar, Böhlau, 2022), pp. 161–81.

15 Despite upsurges of nationalism, ideas and visions for Europe existed also during the First World War, see M. Hewitson, 'The Legacy of War and the Idea of Europe in the 1920s', in M. D'Auria and J. Vermeiren (eds.), *Visions and Ideas of Europe during the First World War* (London and New York, NY, Routledge, 2020), pp. 238–53.

16 W. Loth, *Europas Einigung: Eine unvollendete Geschichte*, 2nd ed. (Frankfurt am Main and New York, NY, Campus, 2020 [2014]), p. 10; M. Gehler, *From Saint-Germain to Lisbon: Austria's Long Road from Disintegrated to United Europe 1919–2009*, trans. P. Isenberg (Vienna, ÖAW Verlag, 2020), pp. 66–8.

a challenge for Europe and the looming threat of Bolshevism, which he saw as a 'European cultural catastrophe'.[17] He wondered whether, in view of the millions of war victims, Europe would still be able to maintain peace and independence in the face of the growing non-European world powers despite Europe's political and economic fragmentation, or whether it would be forced to organise itself into a confederation of states in order to save its existence. He saw the danger that Europe would be 'pulverised' between the Soviet Union and the United States.[18]

In 1923, he published an influential political book entitled *Paneuropa*, in which he advocated the unification of Europe from Portugal to Poland with twenty-seven countries (but without Great Britain, which he saw as a world power) and prophetically called for Franco-German cooperation. The demand was clear: 'The Pan-European movement wants the establishment of the United States of Europe as a European confederation of states and customs union.'[19] Explicitly he demanded a 'European Monroe doctrine' according to the motto 'Europe for the Europeans!'[20] Coudenhove-Kalergi initially took the Pan-American Union as a model. 'The crowning of European aspirations would be the constitution of the United States of Europe on the model of the United States of America',[21] he stated in the founding and formation phase of the Pan-European Union. However, he later considered the model of the US federal state to be too centralistic for Europe. The 'United States of Europe' should develop separately from the League of Nations. According to Coudenhove-Kalergi, two chambers were envisaged for the Paneuropa Union, a House of Nations and a House of States, the former consisting of 300 deputies, one for every million Europeans, and the latter of 27 government representatives.[22] He then founded an eponymous movement that operated as an interest group and maintained offices in many European countries. The Union had its

---

17 A. Ziegerhofer, 'Entweder sich dem Bolschewismus zu unterwerfen – oder ihn abzu-
wehren! Coudenhoves Paneuropa als "Speerspitze" gegen den Kommunismus?', in
M. Gehler, A. Brait and P. Strobl (eds.), *Geschichte schreiben – Geschichte vermitteln: Inner-
und interdisziplinäre Perspektiven auf die Europaforschung* (Hildesheim, Zurich and
New York, NY, Georg W. Olms, 2020), vol. II, pp. 97–119.
18 R. Coudenhove-Kalergi, *Kampf um Europa*, vol. III (Vienna and Leipzig, Paneuropa
Verlag, 1928), p. 4.
19 Ibid., p. 3.
20 Ibid., p. 139; R. Coudenhove-Kalergi, *Kommen die Vereinigten Staaten von Europa?*
(Glarus, Paneuropa Verlag, 1938). See also A. Ziegerhofer-Prettenthaler, *Botschafter
Europa: Richard Nikolaus Coudenhove-Kalergi und die Paneuropa-Bewegung in den zwanziger und dreißiger Jahren* (Vienna, Cologne and Weimar, Böhlau, 2004).
21 R. N. Coudenhove-Kalergi, *Paneuropa*, 2nd ed. (Vienna, Paneuropa Verlag, 1924), p. 151.
22 Ibid., pp. 140–2.

headquarters in the Hofburg in Vienna. It organised Paneuropa congresses in
Vienna, Basel and Berlin. The Nazis fought against his ideas and banned his
writings. In 1938 Coudenhove-Kalergi had to escape from Austria. He spent
the Second World War in US exile, where he taught at New York University
and tried in vain to persuade the Roosevelt administration to incorporate
a suborganisation on Europe in the future United Nations. He returned to
Switzerland after the war, but was not part of the mainstream of the
European movement, serving instead as a top representative of the
European Parliamentarians' Union, which was founded in 1947. He was
awarded the Charlemagne Prize on 18 May 1950 'in recognition of his life's
work in shaping the United States of Europe'[23] and was Honorary President
of the European Movement (1952–65). In 1952 he re-established the Pan-
European Union and had sympathies with the idea of a 'Europe of the
Fatherlands' allegedly formulated by Charles de Gaulle.[24]

Europe Pioneer in the Weimar Republic: Wilhelm Heile

Wilhelm Heile of the German Democratic Party (Deutsche Demokratische
Partei) was the first German post-First World War politician to take up the
idea of a 'United States of Europe' in the weekly *Die Hilfe*,[25] whereby he, in
competition with Coudenhove-Kalergi, advocated the formation of
a European confederation, seeing in it a basis for the pacification of Europe
and thus also a possibility for the elimination of the peace order for the
German Reich established by the Treaty of Versailles.[26] With his conception
of future supranational integration in the form of a federal state, he was 'one
of the most active of the leading pro-Europeans in the Weimar Republic',
being in this sense ahead of his time.[27] Heile was oriented less strongly to the
Pan-American Union and the United States than Coudenhove, being aligned
rather to the Greater German idea of central Europe (*Mitteleuropa*) of

23 'Charlemagne Prize Laureate 1950 Richard Nikolaus Graf Coudenhove-Kalergi', www
.karlspreis.de/en/laureates/richard-nikolaus-graf-coudenhove-kalergi-1950/
biography.
24 A. Ziegerhofer-Prettenthaler, 'Richard Nikolaus Coudenhove-Kalergi (1894–1972)', in
Böttcher (ed), *Klassiker des europäischen Denkens*, pp. 592–8.
25 W. Heile, 'Die Vereinigten Staaten von Europa', *Die Hilfe* no. 18 (1922): 274–6.
26 H. Greve, 'Wilhelm Heile. Portrait eines Gründervaters der Europa-Union', in Europa-
Union Deutschland (ed.), *70 Jahre Einsatz für ein föderales Europa* (Berlin, Europa Union
Verlag, 2016), pp. 6–26, 14–16.
27 J. C. Heß, 'Europagedanke und nationaler Revisionismus. Überlegungen zu ihrer
Verknüpfung in der Weimarer Republik am Beispiel Wilhelm Heiles', *Historische
Zeitschrift* 225 (1977): 572–622.

Friedrich Naumann, without sharing the latter's hegemonic power-political intention for Germany in its entirety.[28]

In 1925, the radical socialist and French Prime Minister Édouard Herriot (1924–5) had spoken out in favour of a united Europe before the French Chamber after the electoral victory of the left-wing alliance Cartel des gauches. On 5 September 1929, the new Prime Minister Aristide Briand, a founding member of the Parti Républicain Socialiste who served as Honorary President of the Pan-European Union, took up the old idea of an ever closer union of European states before the League of Nations Assembly in Geneva. He appealed to the twenty-seven European members of the League of Nations to cooperate in a 'European federal order'. Their deputies asked for a concretisation of his proposal. Briand then proposed the 'organisation of a regime of European federal union' in a memorandum on 17 May 1930. In contrast to previous proposals for the formation of customs unions, internal tariffs were to be retained, giving priority to politics over economics.[29]

A political framework was to provide security for the 'European Union'. The term *union* was deliberately used instead of *unité*, that is, 'unification', but not 'unity'. Briand thought of a 'European Conference' as the governing body, consisting of representatives of the national governments who were to be members of the League of Nations. In addition, there was to be an executive body in the manner of a 'Standing Political Committee' and a secretariat as administrative support. The relationship to the League of Nations remained unclear. Briand repeatedly referred to cooperation, but in practice his ideas amounted to a European regional pact, which would probably have caused problems for the League of Nations with unclear political functions as a competitor. Although the majority of European governments expressed a generally positive opinion, concrete proposals were criticised. In September 1930, due to the criticism of several members in the League of Nations Assembly, only a 'Study Commission for the European Union' was set up, which did not produce any further results, so that the project ended unsuccessfully.[30] The idea lived on, however, and provided a point of reference for Robert Schuman's declaration on the

---

28 Greve, 'Wilhelm Heile', 15.
29 A. Elisha and R. Cassin, *Aristide Briand, la paix mondiale et l'union européenne* (Groslay, Éditions Ivoire-Clair, 2003); G. Unger, *Aristide Briand: Le ferme conciliateur* (Paris, Éditions Fayard, 2005).
30 O. Keller and L. Jílek (eds.), *Le Plan Briand d'union fédérale européenne: Documents* (Geneva, Fondation Archives européennes, 1991); D. Hammer and I. Kögl, 'Aristide Briand (1862–1932)', in Böttcher (ed.), *Klassiker des europäischen Denkens*, pp. 452–8.

formation of the European Coal and Steel Community (ECSC) on 9 May 1950. Now politics was to follow economics, and the latter was apparently to take precedence.

The Archfather of Europe's Integration: Jean Monnet

The Frenchman Jean Monnet can be considered the 'forefather of Europe' because he was the architect, impetus, advisor and strategist in the years after 1945, when the profile of the ECSC was being defined. Although he was a businessman and neither an academic nor an intellectual, he acted as a political thinker for the 'founding fathers'. He was one of the few who, above all, defined the values of a new community. His career as a political innovator was unusual because he was never an elected politician, but acted mostly behind the scenes and therefore enjoyed the reputation of an éminence grise.

Monnet's Biographical Background

To understand the actions of this personality better, we have to go back to the time of the First World War. Monnet was born in Cognac on 9 November 1888. His father Jean Gabriel came from a peasant family and became president of a cooperative of small farmers to compete with the giants of the brandy industry in 1896. Jean grew up in this mercantile patrician home, hated school, rejected books and went to the City of London to learn English at sixteen. He then travelled around the world for family business. He was a practitioner, even though he theorised on the basis of his own experiences. According to him, politics was supposed to bring people together.

Declared unfit in 1914, he became an advisor to Étienne Clémentel, the French minister of commerce and postal services a year later, and worked for various ministries until 1918, when he was practically in charge of the civil economy. As Clémentel's appointee, Monnet was responsible for cooperation with the Allies in London and in 1917 participated in the formation of the Allied Maritime Transportation Executive, which controlled shipping and rationed all supplies to the Allies. After the war, Monnet became assistant secretary-general of the League of Nations (1920–3) in charge of economic affairs. He mediated the conflict over Upper Silesia in 1920–1 and negotiated a League of Nations loan for Austria in 1922. However, he then gave up this function in order to save the family business in Cognac, which was in turmoil.[31]

---

31 F. Knipping, 'Jean Monnet (1888–1979)', in Böttcher (ed.), *Klassiker des europäischen Denkens*, pp. 574–81.

In 1926, Monnet advanced to head the European office of the Wall Street investment bank Blair & Coy and worked for them until 1939. After making profits and losses between 1929 and 1932, he negotiated loans for Blair & Coy in 1927–8 to initiate reconstruction programmes in Poland and Romania. Attempts to form Sino-Western joint ventures to invest in railroads and modernise China were thwarted by the Great Depression.[32]

Influenced by these experiences, Monnet learned that international cooperation alone was not enough to prevent economic crises and threats of war, especially if national vetoes were not lifted. After France's military defeat in 1940, he worked as an official in the British Supply Council in Washington (1940–3), which was responsible for war purchases. He subsequently prepared the 'Victory Program', which formulated US arms production goals. Monnet established a vast network and close ties, for example, with John J. McCloy, later High Commissioner for the US Zone in West Germany, and the US Secretaries of State Dean Acheson and John Foster Dulles. Monnet's insider knowledge was both an invisible and an invaluable asset to his post-war career. In 1943–4, he was a member of the French National Liberation Committee in Algiers. This exile cooperation with de Gaulle set the stage for Monnet's positioning as head of planning in the first post-war French government of 1945–6, a role which he continued to exercise even after de Gaulle's resignation in 1946.

In January 1946, with the support of de Gaulle, he launched a 5-year plan for investment and modernisation of the French economy. As 'Chef du Plan' (1946–50), he was able to obtain aid from the United States when the Lend–Lease programme expired. Monnet's plan was the first step in rebuilding France into a modern industrial state.[33]

Monnet's Political Breakthrough

When the Anglo-Americans set up the Federal Republic of Germany (FRG) as a frontline state in the Cold War against the East and the German western state seemed to gain 'sovereignty', France's control of the International Ruhr Authority was threatened by failure. This forced a change of attitude. Foreign Minister Robert Schuman's proposal of 9 May 1950, to form a federal coal and

---

32 H. Su, 'The Father of Europe in China: Jean Monnet and the Creation of the C.D.F.C. (1933–1936)', *Journal of European Integration History* 13, no. 1 (2007): 9–24.

33 J. Monnet, *Mémoires* (Paris, Fayard, 1976); J. Monnet, *Memoirs* (London, W. Collins and Son Ltd, 1976); É. Roussel, *Jean Monnet 1888–1979* (Paris, Fayard, 1996); K. Schwabe, *Jean Monnet: Frankreich, die Deutschen und die Einigung Europas* (Baden-Baden, Nomos, 2016), pp. 55–127.

steel community between France and the FRG open to other countries, was based on Monnet's suggestions. Since the Schuman Plan meant joint control not only of the Ruhr region but also of the French coal and steel sector, this signified equal rights. Monnet thus laid the basis for further treaties and peace between the two states as the core of western European unification.[34]

He was awarded the Charlemagne Prize of the City of Aachen on 17 May 1953 as 'creator of the first sovereign supranational European institution'.[35] On the basis of his experience as president of the High Authority of the ECSC, Monnet believed that other communities should be established in the same way in order for them to grow together into a European federation. After the failure of the European Defence Community (EDC) in 1954, French political opposition focused on Monnet as the 'champion of supranationality'. Owing to growing domestic criticism, on 9 February 1955 he finally gave up his post as President of the High Authority, which he had held since 10 August 1952.[36] The ECSC, however, served as an institutional model for further integration. Monnet feared that after the EDC fiasco a successful Common Market would require more European federalism than was politically possible.

In October 1955, he founded the Action Committee for the United States of Europe (ACUSE) as a lobbying tool, with top representatives from all political parties and trade unions in the Community states except communists and Gaullists.[37] A plan for a European monetary union had already been developed in November 1957, but it came into being much later. From 1958 onwards, Monnet saw the common market as a means to the end of a political union. With de Gaulle's return to power in June 1958, Monnet gradually lost his influence on French governments. In 1959 he was honoured with the Grand Cross of the Order of Merit of the FRG.

Monnet sympathised with de Gaulle's Fouchet Plans of 1961–2 for political cooperation among heads of state and government. The ACUSE

---

34 G. Bossuat and A. Wilkens (eds.), *Jean Monnet, l'Europe et les chemins de la paix* (Paris, Publications de la Sorbonne, 1999); G. Grin, *Shaping Europe: The Path to European Integration According to Jean Monnet* (Lausanne, Jean Monnet Foundation for Europe, 2017).

35 'Charlemagne Prize Laureate 1953 Jean Monnet', www.karlspreis.de/en/laureates/jean-monnet-1953/biography. See also F. J. Fransen, *The Supranational Politics of Jean Monnet: Ideas and Origins of the European Community* (Westport, CN, Greenwood Press, 2001).

36 G. Goedert, 'Vers quelle Europe? Propos de Jean Monnet', *Nos cahiers. Lëtzebuerger Zäitschrift fir Kultur* 38, no. 3–4 (2017): 9–28.

37 P. Fontaine, *Le Comité d'action pour les États-Unis d'Europe de Jean Monnet* (Lausanne, Centre de recherches européennes, 1974).

promoted not only British accession to the European Community (EC) but also an 'equal partnership' between Europe and the United States. In 1962, Monnet was elected to the American Academy of Arts and Sciences and in 1963 he received the Presidential Medal of Freedom from US President Lyndon B. Johnson for his services to the unification of Europe and the effectiveness of cooperation among the Atlantic nations. Monnet supported the idea of a European Council, which was created in 1974 and brought together heads of state and government, though not on the basis of community treaties. In 1975, at the age of eighty-six, Monnet dissolved the ACUSE. He was made the first Honorary Citizen of Europe by the Heads of Government of the EC in 1976.

Monnet's Legacy

On 16 March 1979 Monnet died in Bazoches-sur-Guyonne. His mortal remains were transferred to the Panthéon and interred in a grave of honour in 1988 at the instigation of French President Mitterrand and by decision of the French National Assembly. Today Monnet is regarded as an unusual statesman of interdependence and mutual solidarity,[38] whose methodology is still being used and thus has remained current.[39]

The 'Monnet method'[40] is interpreted in different ways. Its core elements include elite decisions being taken behind the scenes ('clandestine integration') and the generation of spillover effects in economic integration. It generated less, however, in terms of synergies from the economy for politics. Later the Commission's President Jacques Delors used this method to transform the EC into the EU. Owing to some democratic shortcomings, it lost its persuasive power as the single market programme also had a greater impact on people's everyday lives.

Not all of Monnet's initiatives and proposals were realised in his time, but his close collaborator Max Kohnstamm later helped Jacques Delors to prepare for the Economic and Monetary Union (EMU) in the 1980s with a new Action Committee. In this way, Monnet's ideas continued to have an impact. The 'forefather of Europe' was a man of action who had been not a theorist

---

38 F. Duchêne, *Jean Monnet: The First Statesman of Interdependence* (New York, NY and London, Norton & Co., 1994); S. Brown Wells, *Jean Monnet: Unconventional Statesman* (Boulder, CO and London, Lynne Rienner, 2011).

39 P. Fontaine, *Jean Monnet: Actualité d'un bâtisseur de l'Europe unie* (Paris, Economica, 2013).

40 G. Grin, *Méthode communautaire et fédéralisme: Le legs de Jean Monnet à travers ses archives* (Lausanne, Fondation Jean Monnet pour l'Europe, 2014).

but a practitioner. It is repeatedly claimed that Monnet said that, if he could begin again, he would start with culture. However, the veracity of this quote is unproven and this claim seems surprising, since he was a technocrat, a man concerned with coal and steel, not a man of culture. Nevertheless, Monnet left behind a mature vision not only of what a united Europe should look like, but also of how world politics would be determined by a lasting partnership between the United States and Europe, consisting of a European federation and a European–American alliance.[41]

Founders of the European Communities: Robert Schuman, Konrad Adenauer, Alcide De Gasperi and Paul-Henri Spaak

Starting with a 'Non-European': Winston S. Churchill

After the Second World War, the catchword and idea of a 'United States of Europe'[42] took on increased significance due to the beginning of the Cold War and the intensification of East–West antagonism in the wake of a further increase of anti-communism. Winston S. Churchill made explicit reference to Coudenhove-Kalergi[43] in his famous lecture at the University of Zurich on 19 September 1946. The speech of the British opposition politician contained the demand to 'create a kind of United States of Europe', whereby Great Britain was on the one hand to promote this initiative, but on the other wanted to remain outside.[44]

Historical research on Europe speaks of the 'Churchill moment',[45] which was certainly more than just a moment, namely a certain period-specific hype that lasted for a few years, from 1946 to probably the early 1950s, especially among academics and intellectuals, but also among citizens, who, however,

41 H. Su, 'Jean Monnet's Grand Design for Europe and Its Criticism', *Journal of European Integration History* 15, no. 2 (2009): 29–46.

42 D. W. Unwin, 'From a Europe of States to a State of Europe? An Historical Overview of the Uniting of Western Europe', in J. Gower (ed.), *The European Union Handbook*, 2nd ed. (London and Chicago, IL, Fitzroy Dearborn Publishers, 2002), pp. 3–13; V. A. Schmidt, 'The Role of Ideas and Discourse in European Integration', in H. Heinelt and S. Münch (eds.), *Handbook of European Policies: Interpretive Approaches to the EU* (Cheltenham and Northampton, MA, Edward Elgar, 2018), pp. 35–54.

43 R. S. Churchill, *The Sinews of Peace: Post-war Speeches by Winston S. Churchill 1947–1948* (London, Cassell and Company, 1948), p. 82.

44 Auswärtiges Amt (ed.), *Europa: Dokumente zur Frage der europäischen Einigung*, 3 vols. (Munich, Oldenbourg, 1962), vol. I, p. 113; 'Address Given by Winston Churchill (Zurich, 19 September 1946)', www.cvce.eu/de/obj/address_given_by_winston_ch urchill_zurich_19_september_1946-en-eacb02e7-ea6b-4299-aa43-10819fod44bf.html.

45 W. Schmale, *For a Democratic 'United States of Europe' (1918–1951): Freemasons – Human Rights Leagues – Winston S. Churchill – Individual Citizens* (Stuttgart, Franz Steiner, 2019), pp. 11–16, 125–48.

received a clear response with the founding of the ECSC. The establishment and institutionalisation of the ECSC by a European technocracy was tantamount to a rejection of the European civil society that was also just forming. The architects of the Montanunion, as the ECSC was also called, thus understood how to distance themselves from the ideas of the federalist–idealist-oriented European associations.[46]

Churchill's speech was a stirring one, although it was not always entirely clear to contemporaries who should be part of the United States of Europe, which was to be a continental and fortress Europe without Great Britain and not a federal Europe, in the Cold Warrior's opinion.[47] Parallel to his speech, European federalists met in Hertenstein, Switzerland, from 15 to 22 September 1946, and advocated a federal unification of the continent.[48] Boosted by Churchill's appeal, on 17 December 1946, the Union Européenne des Fédéralistes (UEF) under Hendrik Brugmans in Paris was counting on a social democratic Europe as a 'third force' to preserve Europe's 'autonomy'.[49]

Brugmans was the first president of the UEF and gave the opening speech at the Hague European Congress on 7 May 1948. Two years later, he founded the Collège d'Europe in Bruges, where he served as rector until 1972.[50] The UEF propagated a 'theory of dynamic federalism' in Montreux in 1947.[51] This conception envisaged a dynamism that would successfully adapt to new social orders despite new challenges and have universal applicability, achieving progress in stages. Therefore, federalism was not the goal, but the path. That has remained the case.[52] A European constitution was to gradually emerge from economic development.[53] To the question 'What is Europe?', posed to Churchill in 1947, he is said to have replied: 'A pile of rubbish,

46 C. Norwig, *Die erste europäische Generation: Europakonstruktionen in der Europäischen Jugendkampagne 1951–1958* (Göttingen, Vandenhoeck & Ruprecht, 2016), pp. 331–42. See also M. Burgess, 'Federate or Perish. The Continuity and Persistence of the Federal Idea in Europe, 1917–1957', in M. Hewitson and M. D'Auria (eds.), *Europe in Crisis: Intellectuals and the European Idea, 1917–1957* (New York, NY and Oxford, Berghahn, 2012), pp. 305–22.
47 P.-H. Spaak, *Memoiren eines Europäers* (Hamburg, Hoffmann & Campe, 1969), pp. 263–4.
48 M. Behne, 'Wilhelm Heile und das föderale Europa', in Europa-Union Deutschland (ed.), *75 Jahre Einsatz für ein föderales Europa* (Berlin, Europa-Union Verlag, 2021), pp. 33–41, 37–38 with appendix p. 52.
49 Loth, *Europas Einigung*, p. 14.
50 K. Brummer, *Der Europarat: Eine Einführung* (Wiesbaden, Springer, 2008), p. 22.
51 L. Herbst, 'Die zeitgenössische Integrationstheorie und die Anfänge der europäischen Einigung 1947–1950', *Vierteljahrshefte für Zeitgeschichte* 34, no. 2 (1986): 161–205, 198.
52 See www.federalists.eu/de/uef/was-ist-foederalismus.
53 Herbst, 'Die zeitgenössische Integrationstheorie', 198.

a charnel house, a breeding ground for pestilence and hatred.'[54] Churchill cannot be seen as pro-European.[55]

Christian democratic parties played an even more important role after 1945 than after 1918. In the founding states of the European Economic Community (EEC), they contributed to shaping the idea of Europe after the Second World War, which was to find expression in the much-cited 'triumvirate' of Adenauer, De Gasperi and Schuman.[56] The Christian democratic vision of Europe was combined with the idea of the Occident (*Abendland*) of the Christian West, which was supported by anti-communist, anti-liberal and anti-materialist principles in order to gain momentum in the context of the emerging Cold War in a defensive stance against the Stalinist Soviet Union and to support the project of western European integration.[57]

Father of the European Union: Robert Schuman

The deeply religious French Christian democrat Robert Schuman is considered to be the 'patron saint', if not a 'saint', of the EU. Born in Clausen close to Luxembourg on 29 June 1886, he returned with his family at a young age to the German-speaking part of the province of Lorraine, which Germany had annexed in 1871. His mother was from Luxembourg, his father from Lorraine. As a Reich German, his mother tongue was Mosel-Franconian German, as spoken in Luxembourg and German-speaking Lorraine. During the First World War, he worked in the German administration. After the return of Lorraine to France in 1918, he became a French citizen. After the German occupation of France in 1940, he was deported to the German Reich, but managed to escape in 1942 and joined the resistance, becoming a co-founder of the Christian social party Mouvement Républicaine Populaire in 1944.[58]

His greatest political achievement was the Franco-German rapprochement, thus creating the preconditions for western European unification. As foreign minister, he served in ten successive governments from July 1948 to

---

54 W. D. Gruner and W. Woyke, *Europa-Lexikon: Länder – Politik – Institutionen*, 2nd ed. (Munich, dtv Verlag, 2007 [2004]), p. 44.

55 A. Nötzold, 'Winston Churchill (1874–1965)', in Böttcher (ed.), *Klassiker des europäischen Denkens*, pp. 493–9, here 497–9.

56 W. Kaiser, *Christian Democracy and the Origins of European Union* (Cambridge, Cambridge University Press, 2007).

57 R. Forlenza, 'The Politics of the *Abendland*: Christian Democracy and the Idea of Europe after the Second World War', *Contemporary European History* 26, no. 2 (2017): 261–86.

58 F. Roth, *Robert Schuman: Du Lorrain des frontières au père de l'Europe* (Paris, Fayard, 2008).

December 1952. He thus embodied continuity and stability in French policy.[59] His historic proposal of 9 May 1950 was to place 'Franco-German coal and steel production under a common "higher authority" within the framework of an organisation open to participation by the other European countries'.[60] Via moral rehabilitation, Germany should become democratic, with Schuman showing the two historical arch-enemies a pragmatic and concrete path to understanding.[61] After receiving cabinet approval on the morning of 9 May 1950 and the support of Acheson and Adenauer beforehand, Schuman announced the bold proposal at a hastily called press conference in the Quai d'Orsay clock room that afternoon, the day before the Three Power Conference of Foreign Ministers in London.[62]

Schuman took advantage of Monnet's bold idea to achieve the goal of Franco-German understanding and to create a framework for the integration of West Germany. French politics and public opinion were shocked by the radical political change of course, all the more so because Schuman signalled France's willingness to set aside its national sovereignty for the European common good. He invited neighbouring states to join. His declaration became the impetus for change. Wisely, he asked Monnet to lead the negotiations to implement the proposal with a detailed and contractual plan. Schuman took political responsibility, advocated the policy in government and prevailed against the resistance of the steel manufacturers.[63]

His remarkable tenure as foreign minister ended in December 1952, but he still supported René Pleven's EDC plan, which had been signed by the ECSC member states in May. Its rejection by the Assemblée Nationale on 30 August 1954 was a painful setback for Schuman. He returned to the government as Minister of Justice (1955–6) and was elected the first President of the European Parliament (EP) on 19 March 1958, serving until his resignation for health reasons in 1963. His book *Pour l'Europe* was published a few days after his death on 4 September 1963 in Scy-Chazelles

---

59 R. Poidevin, *Robert Schuman: Homme d'État, 1886–1963* (Paris, Édition Beauchesne, 1988).
60 P. Gerbet, 'La genèse du plan Schuman. Des origines à la déclaration du 9 mai 1950', *Revue française de Science politique* 6, no. 3 (1956): 525–53; H. Rieben, M. Nathusius, F. Nicod and C. Camperio-Tixier, *Un changement d'espérance: La Déclaration du 9 mai 1950, Jean Monnet – Robert Schuman* (Lausanne, Fondation Jean Monnet pour l'Europe, 2000).
61 J.-P. Rioux, *The Fourth Republic, 1944–1948* (Cambridge, Cambridge University Press, 1987), pp. 142–3.
62 Duchêne, *Jean Monnet*, pp. 190–220; Rioux, *The Fourth Republic*, p. 142.
63 H. Maier, 'Der Mann, der Europa entworfen hat: Ohne Robert Schuman gäbe es keine EU. Heute gehört er zu den grossen Vergessenen der Nachkriegsgeschichte', *Neue Zürcher Zeitung*, 31 October 2021, www.nzz.ch/feuilleton/robert-schuman-der-mann-der-europa-gestaltet-hat-ld.1651974?reduced=true.

(Département Moselle) close to Metz. Despite the East–West political divide after 1945, Schuman, due to personal experiences, had counted the states of central and eastern Europe in his image and vision of Europe. They were to join the common Europe as soon as they were able to do so.[64]

Schuman is regarded in France and beyond as the 'Père de l'Europe',[65] although it was also perfectly clear to him that France's nationhood (*l'état nation*) should remain largely untouched.[66] His clever, diplomatic and courageous policies served as a source of inspiration, strength and motivation for French–German rapprochement, understanding and reconciliation and contributed to peaceful change in western Europe. With the ECSC, on which the EEC and Euratom were built, he helped to lay the foundation for the later EU.

On 10 January 1958, Schuman received an honorary doctorate from the Catholic University of Louvain for his services to the unification of Europe. On 15 May of the same year, he was awarded the International Charlemagne Prize of the city of Aachen 'in recognition of his great services to the first practical foundations of the European federation in the political and economic field and to a common future of Germany and France in peace and security'.[67] With Karl Jaspers, he received the Erasmus Culture Prize the following year. On 24 October 1966, a Robert Schuman Monument was inaugurated in Luxembourg. In 2007, Schuman's home in Scy-Chazelles was awarded the 'European Heritage' label by the French state. As a champion of Franco-German understanding, Schuman was a model of moral values in politics for Catholic and other Christian churches. Schuman had remained a bachelor and lived almost like a monk, with daily church services and regular study of the missal. A beatification process was initiated in Schuman's home diocese of Metz and has been pending at the Vatican since 2004. The German Christian Democrat and Member of the EP (MEP) Hans August Lücker from the European People's Party (EPP), Executive President of the German Committee for the Beatification of Schuman, had deposited a collection of documents in the Historical

64 F. Gergely, 'Les visites de Robert Schuman dans le bassin du Danube', in S. Schirmann (ed.), *Robert Schuman et les Pères de l'Europe: Cultures politiques et années de formation* (Brussels, Peter Lang, 2008), pp. 69–84; S. Koppelberg and C. Frohn, 'Robert Schuman (1886–1963)', in Böttcher (ed.), *Klassiker des europäischen Denkens*, pp. 554–60.
65 R. Lejeune, *Robert Schuman (1886–1963): Père de l'Europe* (Paris, Fayard, 2000).
66 A. Wilkens (ed.), *Le Plan Schuman dans l'Histoire: Intérêts nationaux et projet européen* (Brussels, Bruylant, 2004).
67 'Charlemagne Prize Laureate 1958 Robert Schuman', www.karlspreis.de/en/laureates/robert-schuman-1958/biography.

Archives of the European University Institute in Florence. Pope Francis granted Schuman the heroic degree of virtue on 19 June 2021 as a preliminary step to beatification.[68] Schuman's residence in Scy-Chazelles is part of the Robert Schuman Museum of the Département Moselle.[69]

Western Integration in Favour of West German Partial Sovereignty: Konrad Adenauer

As the Cold War escalated, the Western occupiers in Germany merged their zones. As former mayor of Cologne, dismissed by the Nazis, and chairman of the Christlich Demokratische Union (CDU) in the British zone, Konrad Adenauer became the first chancellor (1949–63) of the FRG by a majority of one vote (his own). He was one of the co-founders of the Communities and saw Franco-German cooperation as a means of recognising West Germany's position. Thus, he worked closely with Schuman and Monnet in founding the ECSC. Adenauer's image of Europe was essentially focused on western Europe. His ideas on integration fluctuated. He had already gained international recognition as party chairman of the CDU in the western European framework in the early years by participating in the meetings of the Christian democrats' Geneva Circle (organised by Georges Bidault's close confident Victor Koutzine), to which Adenauer continued to send his confidants Herbert Blankenhorn and Otto Lenz.[70] Through Jean Monnet, Walter Hallstein and Max Kohnstamm, Adenauer realised the unique opportunities presented by the Schuman Plan (1950–2) and the EEC (1955–8). This network was extended by Louis Armand, Franz Etzel, Carl Friedrich Ophüls, Franz Josef Strauß and others when it came to Euratom and the negotiations on the trilateral nuclear power (1956–8), and in the following years Adenauer met de Gaulle at the highest level and was able to maintain close contact with the French president's entourage through Monnet's intermediary. Even if Adenauer acted on the same level, de Gaulle ultimately remained the 'strong man' of Europe who alone could decide on the EEC and the North Atlantic Treaty Organization (NATO) at the decisive moment. When de Gaulle returned to power in France in 1958, Adenauer developed good relations

---

68 'Promulgazione di Decreti della Congregazione delle Cause dei Santi, 19.06.2021', https://press.vatican.va/content/salastampa/it/bollettino/pubblico/2021/06/19/0 395/00862.html.

69 'À Bruxelles, Robert Schuman reste une référence', www.la-croix.com/Religion/A-B ruxelles-Robert-Schuman-reste-reference-2021-06-19-1201162067.

70 M. Gehler, 'The Geneva Circle of West European Christian Democrats', in M. Gehler and W. Kaiser (eds.), *Christian Democracy in Europe since 1945*, vol. II (London and New York, NY, Routledge, 2004), pp. 207–20.

with him. He saw the post-war world as divided between the democratic and capitalist West and the communist and dictatorial East. Although 18 million Germans remained under Soviet control in East Germany, Adenauer rejected any compromise with the Soviet Union and any suggestions for the subservience of West Germany, at the cost of thereby preventing German unification. He staunchly supported US secretary of state John Foster Dulles' 'policy of strength' against the Soviet bloc, in which policy West Germany served as a frontline state. The division of Germany was ultimately symbolised by the erection of the Berlin Wall in 1961.[71] Schuman's voice met with an open ear from Adenauer.[72]

With de Gaulle, Adenauer had not only arranged his own political and personal relationship, but also intensified it. In the wake of the disappointment about the 'passively tolerated position' of the Anglo-American powers against the background of the Berlin crisis in 1958–61,[73] the chancellor moved step by step ever closer to the French president and his policy, which culminated in the signing of the so-called Treaty of Friendship, or Élysée Treaty, between the FRG and France on 22 January 1963.[74]

The chancellor was responsible for not only creating, but also realising, leading and consolidating the new West German state that achieved its sovereignty in a step-by-step manner within the growing western European economic community. These historical merits are lasting and undisputed. However, the promise of realising German reunification via the FRG's policy of Western integration was not kept. On the contrary: the division of Germany solidified and the division of Europe deepened. The 'priority of the freedom of the partial state over the unity of the total state in a possible lack of freedom'[75] was a fundamental motif of Adenauer's policy concerning the two Germanies. In the end, his motto

71 K. Adenauer, *Memoirs* (Chicago, IL, Regnery, 1966); H. P. Schwarz, *Konrad Adenauer: A German Politician and Statesman in a Period of War, Revolution, and Reconstruction* (Providence, RI, Berghahn Books, 1995); M. Gehler, 'Adenauer's Ideas on Europe and Western European Integration Policy within the Context of Private and Political Networks', in J.-D. Durand (ed.), *Christian Democrat Internationalism: Its Action in Europe and Worldwide from post World War II until the 1990s*, vol. II: *The Development (1945–1979): The Role of Parties, Movements, People* (Brussels, Peter Lang, 2013), pp. 201–41;
72 L. van Middelaar, *The Passage to Europe: How a Continent Became a Union* (New Haven, CT and London, Yale University Press, 2013), pp. 137–43.
73 R. Steininger, *Berlinkrise und Mauerbau 1958 bis 1963: Mit einem Kapitel zum Mauerfall 1989* (Munich, Olzog, 2009).
74 U. Lappenküper, *Die deutsch-französischen Beziehungen 1949–1963: Von der 'Erbfeindschaft' zur 'Entente élémentaire'*, 2 vols. (Munich, Oldenbourg, 2001).
75 R. Morsey and K. Repgen (eds.), *Adenauer-Studien*, vol. I (Mainz, Matthias Grünwald Verlag, 1971); W. Weidenfeld, 'Konrad Adenauer', in Böttcher (ed.), *Klassiker des europäischen Denkens*, pp. 537–42.

of 'no experiments' led to a lack of alternatives and of solutions with his policy regarding the two Germanies. The construction of the Berlin Wall in 1961 was the most visible expression of its failure. The FRG's room for manoeuvre in foreign policy in general and policy regarding the two Germanies in particular remained limited. The FRG could essentially manoeuvre only within the framework of the Atlantic alliance and the western European integration association. Changes had to take place in the east and emanate from there in order for there to be any movement in a situation that had become frozen. Despite all the criticisms of him, it cannot be overlooked that, with his policy of integration with the West, Adenauer created the basis of the fundamental framework (the German Basic Law) of the FRG at the time and what would become the preconditions (membership in NATO and the EC/ EU) for German unification. These were the foundations that set the country on course for integration with the West in the 1950s. In that respect, the founding chancellor of the West German partial state was immortalised in the forms and methods of the creation of German unification in 1990.

A Convinced European in His Last Period of Government: Alcide De Gasperi

Alcide De Gasperi was born on 3 April 1881, in Pieve Tesino, a small village in the Trentino region of Austria-Hungary, a mixed-language border region. He began his political career as a co-founder of the Partito Popolare Trentino (Trentino People's Party) and was elected a member of the Reichsrat in Vienna in 1911. In 1918 he received Italian citizenship when Trentino became part of Italy. Three years later he was elected to the Italian Parliament. In 1923 he became the general secretary of the Partito Popolare Italiano (PPI, Italian People's Party), which he had entered in 1919 as a close collaborator of its founder, the priest Don Luigi Sturzo. The PPI was the forerunner of the Democrazia Cristiana (Christian Democracy), which was co-founded by De Gasperi on 15 December 1943 together with Attilio Piccioni, Giovanni Gronchi and Mario Scelba (of the PPI), Aldo Moro and Giulio Andreotti (of Azione Cattolica, Catholic Action), Amintore Fanfani and Giuseppe Dossetti (of the Federazione Universitaria Cattolica Italiana, Italian Catholic Federation of University Students) and Giuseppe Alessi from Sicily. Under the fascists, De Gasperi was arrested and sentenced to prison in 1927 because of his continued political opposition to Mussolini. After his early release, he spent his time in internal exile in the Vatican Library for 14 years. From December 1945 to July 1953, he served as prime minister in eight successive coalitions and devoted himself primarily to foreign policy.[76]

At the Paris Peace Conference in 1946, he represented Italy's interests as a loser of the Second World War, winning over the United States, United Kingdom and France to join the club of the democratic West. De Gasperi, like his political friend Adenauer,[77] recognised that close ties with western European countries and the United States would help Italy's political stability and economic welfare.[78] Therefore he advocated his country's participation in the Marshall Plan (1948), NATO (1949) and the ECSC (1952). After the departure of Foreign Minister Carlo Sforza, De Gasperi was solely responsible for European policy and supported a deepening of integration. His demand in late autumn 1951 for the formation of a European political authority was intended to prevent an exclusively military partial integration.[79] An integrated army was inconceivable without a common foreign policy, which is why the Common Assembly received a mandate from the ECSC foreign ministers to prepare a draft treaty for a European Political Community (EPC). When the Treaty on the EDC was signed on 27 May 1952, De Gasperi saw it as a 'new light of hope'. In his mind, Article 38 established an important point for the future: the goal of a supranational and politically integrated Europe.[80]

De Gasperi's ideas on Europe had various origins. He had a deep Christian faith and believed that social solidarity should transcend national boundaries. According to him, a federalist Europe was already spiritually united by a common history and civilisation.[81] In 1952 he was awarded the prestigious Charlemagne Prize 'in recognition of his constant promotion of European unification [. . .] tireless devotion, borne of a sense of reality, to the political and economic cooperation of the European peoples with the ultimate goal of supranational union [which] has achieved significant

76 M. Cau, 'Alcide De Gasperi (1881–1954)', in Böttcher (ed.), *Klassiker des europäischen Denkens*, pp. 510–16; S. Lorenzini and B. Taverni (ed.), *Alcide De Gasperi e la stabilizzazione della Repubblica 1948–1954* (Bologna, il Mulino, 2009).

77 T. Di Maio, *Alcide De Gasperi e Konrad Adenauer: Tra superamento del passato e processo d'integrazione europea (1945–1954)* (Turin, Giappichelli, 2004).

78 N. Perrone, *De Gasperi e l'America: Un dominio pieno e incontrollato* (Palermo, Sellerio Editore, 1995); N. Perrone, *La svolta occidentale: De Gasperi e il nuovo ruolo internazionale dell'Italia* (Rome, Castelvecchi, 2017).

79 R. Magagnoli, 'Anregungen zu einer Neubewertung der Europapolitik Alcide De Gasperis', *Journal of European Integration History* 4, no. 1 (1998): 27–54.

80 'Alcide De Gasperi: Demokratie ohne Grenzen', www.europarl.europa.eu/RegData/ etudes/BRIE/2018/621874/EPRS_BRI(2018)621874_DE.pdf.

81 D. Preda, *Alcide De Gasperi, federalista europeo* (Bologna, il Mulino, 2004).

practical results'.[82] Being inspired by the Christian democrat European federalist ideas of the Italian State President Luigi Einaudi (1948–55), De Gasperi had been a particularly strong advocate of the EPC. His areas of responsibility included foreign policy, defence, economic and social integration, and respect for human rights. The creation of a federal organisation was proposed, which would combine the ECSC and the EDC within 2 years.[83] On 11 May 1954, a few months before De Gasperi's death in Sella/Borgo di Valsugana on 19 August 1954, he was elected President of the ECSC Common Assembly. Just 11 days after his death, the French National Assembly decisively rejected the proposed EDC.[84] That was the end of the project.

De Gasperi's daughter Maria Romana kept alive the memory of his legacy and served as Honorary President of the De Gasperi Foundation in Rome, which she founded in 1982.[85]

Christian Democratic publications (e.g., the *Rheinische Merkur*), other various foundations (e.g., the Fondation Robert Schuman and the Konrad-Adenauer-Stiftung), ecclesiastical circles and the Roman Catholic Church highlighted the importance of the Christian Democratic founding fathers, who came from border regions such as Lorraine, Luxembourg, the Rhineland and Trentino, with corresponding publicity.[86] The EPP, which is committed to a stronger Europe, argues as follows: 'Our roots go back to the founding fathers of Europe – Robert Schuman, Alcide De Gasperi and Konrad Adenauer – and our members come from all the member states of Europe.'[87]

For Europe's socialists, veneration as 'saints' is less pronounced, as the example of Spaak shows.

---

82 'Charlemagne Prize Laureate 1952 Alcide de Gasperi', www.karlspreis.de/en/laure ates/alcide-de-gasperi-1952/biography.

83 A. Santagostino, 'Luigi Einaudi: The Architect of Europe?', *Rivista di Studi Politici Internazionali* 80, no. 3 (2013): 429–40.

84 É. Arnoulx de Pirey, *De Gasperi: Le père italien de l'Europe* (Paris, Téqui, 1991); E. A. Carrillo, *De Gasperi: The Long Apprenticeship* (Notre Dame, IN, University of Notre Dame Press, 1965); M. R. De Gasperi (ed.), *De Gasperi e l'Europa* (Brescia, Morcelliana, 1979); G. Petrilli, *La politica estera ed Europea di De Gasperi* (Rome, Edizioni Cinque Lune, 1975).

85 See www.fondazionedegasperi.org/inglese.

86 'Pères de l'Europe', www.robert-schuman.eu/fr/doc/divers/Peres_de_l_Europe.pdf; T. Jansen, 'Alcide de Gasperi und Konrad Adenauer, Italien und Deutschland in Europa', www.kas.de/de/einzeltitel/-/content/alcide-de-gasperi-und-konrad-adenauer -italien-und-deutschland-in-europa; 'Drei Männer – ein Ziel', www.domradio.de/arti kel/fuer-ein-vereintes-europa-schuman-de-gasperi-adenauer.

87 'Über uns', www.eppgroup.eu/de/ueber-uns; 'Unsere Geschichte', www .eppgroup.eu/de/ueber-uns/geschichte.

Mediator between Germans and French: Paul-Henri Spaak

Paul-Henri Spaak played a leading role in the post-war period for western Europe's integration. Before the war, he had already occupied a prominent position in Belgian politics as a government minister since 1935, with terms as prime minister in 1938 and 1939. During his time in government, Spaak had advocated Belgian neutrality and tried to keep the country out of the Second World War. Belgium's surrender in May 1940 and the 4 years of German occupation that Spaak spent in exile in London completely changed his international outlook. He became a staunch supporter of international alliances and European integration. In the immediate post-war years, Spaak served several times as prime minister and foreign minister of his country, sometimes in parallel. He also served as chairman of the Organisation for European Economic Co-operation (OEEC) and as president of the Consultative Assembly of the Council of Europe. He emerged as a prominent proponent of the Schuman Plan and the Pleven Plan.[88]

His most important contribution to integration policy was as chairman of the Intergovernmental Conference (IGC) following the Messina Conference on 1–3 June 1955 to draw up plans for extending integration. Because of his high reputation and conviction, he proved to be the ideal choice to lead the difficult negotiations. As chairman of an IGC in Brussels, Spaak coordinated various committees and subcommittees that prepared specific parts of a definitive proposal. His report was presented to the ECSC foreign ministers at a conference in Venice on 29–30 May 1956, which addressed the two concerns of sectoral integration (atomic energy) and broader economic integration (common market) in their own separate organisations, resulting in the signing of the EEC and Euratom Treaties on 25 March 1957.[89] Spaak can therefore with good reason be called one of the 'fathers of the Rome Treaties'.[90]

On 30 May 1957, Spaak was awarded the International Charlemagne Prize of the City of Aachen because of his 'great services to the federal unification of the European states, their common economic future and their security'.[91] Shortly

88 M. Winter, 'Paul-Henri-Spaak (1899–1972)', in Böttcher (ed.), *Klassiker des europäischen Denkens*, pp. 613–19.

89 P.-H. Laurent, 'Paul-Henri Spaak and the Diplomatic Origins of the Common Market, 1955–1956', *Political Science Quarterly* 85, no. 3 (1970): 373–96; P.-H. Laurent, 'The Diplomacy of the Rome Treaty, 1956–57', *Journal of Contemporary History* 7, no. 3–4 (1972): 209–20.

90 M. Gehler, *The Signing of the Rome Treaties 65 Years Ago: Origins, Provisions and Effects* (Bonn, ZEI, 2022).

91 'Charlemagne Prize Laureate 1957 Paul Henri Spaak', www.karlspreis.de/en/laure ates/paul-henri-spaak-1957/biography.

before, Spaak had become Secretary General of NATO, and he held this office until 1961. In 1966, he retired from politics, but in the same year he assumed the office of President of the Atlantic Treaty Association, which he held until 1969.

Initiators of a Second Generation in the 1970s: Pierre Werner, Valéry Giscard d'Estaing and Helmut Schmidt

Benelux Mediator and Namesake for the Preliminary Stage of the Euro: Pierre Werner

As a Christian democrat, Prime Minister and Minister of Finance of Luxembourg Pierre Werner shaped the political future of his country for several decades and was one of the few statesmen who made attempts to advance European integration from the 1970s to the mid 1980s. Each founding member also seems to have had its own fathers of the communities, as the example of Luxembourg shows, especially when it came to the question of the seat of community institutions, when thinking of the High Authority, the European Court of Justice or the European Investment Bank.[92]

Werner played a major role in regional integration (Benelux) and in EC policy-making, and gained a strong reputation for forging a political consensus between larger powers (Germany and France) and between diametrically opposed positions ('economists' versus 'monetarists'). In this way he succeeded in defending Luxembourg's vital interests, ranging from the financial centre to the location of the seats of the European institutions. Werner was involved in the major ideological debates of the time.[93]

At their summit on 1 December 1969, as part of an effort to deepen European integration at a time of impending enlargement, the EC's heads of state and government asked Werner to prepare a report on a monetary union to deepen integration even before the forthcoming enlargement. Although he was initially in favour of a monetary approach, Werner was one of the first to develop arguments for a symmetrical EMU. The careful balance he imagined reappeared in the Werner Report – a precursor to a full EMU in the EU. On 8 October 1970, he presented a seven-step plan to achieve the project through institutional reforms and closer political cooperation over the next 10 years. The plan proposed parallel action through economic policy coordination and monetary policy measures, with differences arising

92 C. Barthel, 'Trois chefs de la diplomatie, un défi commun. Joseph Bech, Eugène Schaus et Pierre Werner face à la question du siège européen à Luxembourg (1952–1965/67)', *Nos cahiers. Lëtzebuerger Zäitschrift fir Kultur* 38, no. 3–4 (2017): 29–151.
93 E. Danescu, 'A Pragmatic Visionary through a Century of Change – Pierre Werner', *Journal of European Integration History* 24, no. 1 (2018): 9–29.

between Paris and Bonn over the pace and scope. Nevertheless, at the Paris Summit on 19–20 October 1972, the heads of state and government called for the formation of an EMU by 1980. However, the plan fell victim to the changing global economic environment of the 1970s: high inflation and increasing economic divergence made the goal unrealistic. It was not until the late 1980s that EMU was coupled with the Single Market programme under much more favourable conditions. Pierre Werner's thinking and political action and his vital input contributed to the European monetary integration.[94]

France's Pioneer for a European Currency: Valéry Giscard d'Estaing

Valéry Giscard d'Estaing (1926–2020), president of France from 1974 to 1981, together with his friend German Chancellor Helmut Schmidt (1918–2015), in office from 1974 to 1982, were personalities who decisively advanced European integration. Giscard's most important contribution was the establishment of the European Council, which he launched at a meeting of heads of state and government in Paris in December 1974, combined with regular meetings of heads of state and government of member states without officials to resolve outstanding problems of the EC and give it a new direction. As France's finance minister for 10 years, he possessed economic expertise and organised the annual summits of major industrialised countries (the Group of Seven) using the same exclusive concept according to the Monnet method in small and elite groups of politicians and statesmen. 'VGE', as his name is sometimes abbreviated in France, was the politician who most consistently advocated Franco-German rapprochement in the 1970s and at the same time strove for European integration. On the basis of parity with the FRG, France was to regain its influence on the international stage.[95]

After Mitterrand's victory in the 1981 presidential election, Giscard retired and went to the Assemblée Nationale and to the EP for one term under the leadership of the Liberal group. There he advanced to become a proponent of more competence for the EC and supranationality. As an elder statesman, Giscard was President of the European Constitutional Convention (2002–3). In 2003, he was awarded the Charlemagne Prize as President of the European Convention 'in recognition of his work in drafting a constitution for a united

---

94 A. Steinherr (ed.), *30 Years of European Monetary Integration: From the Werner Plan to EMU* (London, Longman, 1994).
95 M. Weinachter, *Valéry Giscard d'Estaing et l'Allemagne: Le double rêve inachevé* (Paris, Éditions L'Harmattan, 2004); G. Valance, *VGE* (Paris, Flammarion, 2011).

Europe that would bring the Union closer to its citizens', because he 'has driven the unification process for decades in various capacities and, together with the members of the Convention, has become a decisive driving force for the "new" Europe in recent months'.[96]

Priority for Security and Currency for Europe: Helmut Schmidt

Helmut Schmidt was a social democrat and German Finance Minister from 1972 to 1974. Although he was initially reluctant to join the EEC, he saw the EC developing as an instrument for promoting prosperity and increasing the international influence of western Europe. However, as Chancellor (1974–82) he had little access to the Commission and was a representative of inter-governmentalism. Schmidt was more a world politician than a European politician and more a realist than an idealist.[97]

In the late 1970s, the Franco-German axis strengthened as the engine of the Community. Going beyond the framework of the Élysée Treaty (1963), Giscard and Schmidt exchanged views regularly as well as collaborating in or on the margins of the European Council to make the German's initiative for a European Monetary System (EMS) a success. At the Bremen summit in July 1978, his energetic chairmanship, despite Britain's unwillingness to participate, contributed to the agreement of the other EC members to join the EMS, which took off on 13 March 1979. With the EMS, a starting point was created for the later euro. Both Giscard and Schmidt can be considered its 'initiators'. Schmidt also campaigned for the NATO Double-Track Decision (1979–82), like hardly any other German politician. He can thus be described as a stability, security and currency European.[98] The Giscard–Schmidt duo

---

96 'Begründung des Direktoriums der Gesellschaft für die Verleihung des Internationalen Karlspreises zu Aachen an den Präsidenten des Europäischen Konvents Valéry Giscard d'Estaing', www.karlspreis.de/de/preistraeger/valery-giscard-destaing-2003/begruen dung-des-direktoriums.

97 K. Spohr, *Helmut Schmidt: Der Weltkanzler* (Darmstadt, Theiss, 2016); M. Haeussler, 'The Convictions of a Realist: Concepts of "Solidarity" in Helmut Schmidt's European Thought, 1945–82', *European Review of History/Revue européenne d'histoire* 24, no. 6 (2017): 955–72; M. Haeussler, *Helmut Schmidt and British–German Relations: A European Misunderstanding* (Cambridge, Cambridge University Press, 2019).

98 G. Thiemeyer, 'Helmut Schmidt und die Gründung des Europäischen Währungssystems 1973–1979', in F. Knipping and M. Schönwald (eds.), *Aufbruch zum Europa der zweiten Generation* (Trier, Wissenschaftlicher Verlag, 2004), pp. 245–68; M. Waechter, *Helmut Schmidt und Valéry Giscard d'Estaing: Auf der Suche nach Stabilität in der Krise der 70er Jahre* (Bremen, Edition Temmen, 2011).

was followed almost seamlessly by the Kohl–Mitterrand duo,[99] which was supplemented by an active Commission President to form a trio that developed comparable integration dynamics.

Builders of the European Union in the late 1980s and the First Half of the 1990s: Helmut Kohl, François Mitterrand and Jacques Delors

'German Unity and European Unification Are Two Sides of the Same Coin': Helmut Kohl

Helmut Kohl (1930–2017) was born in Ludwigshafen in a German–French border region on the Rhine. An up-and-coming Christian democrat, he was the youngest member of the Rhineland-Palatinate state parliament in 1959, the youngest chairman of the state parliament in 1963, prime minister in 1969 and the youngest chancellor of the FRG in 1982. Despite his political successes, he was repeatedly underestimated. He established close contacts with the French socialist François Mitterrand. Both were convinced supporters of integration and, together with Commission President Jacques Delors, formed a triangle between Bonn, Brussels and Paris. Kohl saw German unity in 1990 as one side of the European coin. His advocacy of greater involvement of a unified Germany in European integration met with Mitterrand's approval.[100]

Kohl stressed the need for progress in a political union, especially with regard to the development of a common foreign and security policy and the strengthening of the powers of the EP. The outcome of the IGC, however, was only half a success. While considerable progress was made on the EMU, none was made on Europol and the political union favoured by Kohl. His main efforts were then devoted to establishing the euro, which he saw as 'a matter of war and peace' in Europe. Although German public opinion was less than enthusiastic about abandoning the D-Mark, there was confidence in Kohl's European policy. Without his willingness and support to prepare for its introduction, the euro could not have been brought in after Kohl's term in office (1982–98).[101] At the Vienna Council summit in December 1998, the

99 C. Germond, 'Dynamic Franco-German Duos: Giscard–Schmidt and Mitterrand–Kohl', in Jones, Menon and Weatherill (eds.), *The Oxford Handbook of the European Union*, pp. 194–205.

100 H. Kohl, *Erinnerungen 1982–1990* (Munich, Droemer Verlag, 2005).

101 H. Stark, *Helmut Kohl, l'Allemagne et l'Europe: La politique d'intégration européenne de la République Fédérale 1982–1998* (Paris, Éditions L'Harmattan, 2004); H.-P. Schwarz, *Helmut Kohl: Eine politische Biographie* (Munich, DVA Verlag, 2012), pp. 797–855, especially 800–19; W. Loth, 'Helmut Kohl und die Währungsunion', *Vierteljahrshefte für Zeitgeschichte* 61, no. 4 (2013): 455–80.

heads of state and government awarded Kohl the title of Honorary Citizen of Europe after Monnet.

The European Union as a Response to German Unification:
François Mitterrand

During his time as French president (1981–95), Mitterrand was willing to help intensify European integration. His attitude early on was European, but not necessarily focused on the EEC. As a member of parliament, he voted for the Treaty of Rome but believed that Africa, not Europe, should be the focus of French foreign policy.[102] In the 1960s, he criticised de Gaulle's vetoes of British EEC membership. Differences in the Socialist International in the 1970s made Mitterrand wary of taking a strongly pro-European stance as leader of the Socialist Party (Parti Socialiste). At the 1981 Luxembourg EC summit, he called for the creation of an 'espace social européen' ('European social space'), which met with little affection from his counterparts. In the wake of the crisis in the French economy and the twofold devaluation of the franc, Mitterrand understood the importance of the European market and Franco-German relations in securing France's prosperity. In 1983, he announced that the franc would remain in the EMS and signalled his willingness to pursue a conservative fiscal and monetary policy. For Mitterrand, European policy became a top priority, which he actively followed from then on. France's 'greatness' seemed possible only together with the FRG. His re-election in 1988 was made possible by a campaign for EMU, a common defence policy and a social charter. On 1 November the same year, Kohl and Mitterrand were simultaneously awarded the Charlemagne Prize 'in recognition of their uninterrupted and successful striving for lasting friendship between their countries and for the preservation and consolidation of the European Community'.[103]

Mitterrand's further European policy which, in the French foreign policy tradition, encompassed the entire continent, then developed in response to changes in Europe, such as the opening of the east in 1989 and German unification in 1990.[104] After a brief period of mistrust and scepticism about the re-emerging German question, when Mitterrand wanted to return to the

102 A. Cole, *François Mitterrand: A Study in Political Leadership* (New York, NY, Routledge, 1994), p. 117.
103 'Charlemagne Prize Laureates 1988 François Mitterand and Helmut Kohl', www .karlspreis.de/en/laureates/francois-mitterrand-and-helmut-kohl-1988/biography.
104 F. Schotters, 'Mitterrand's Europe: Functions and Limits of "European Solidarity" in French Policy during the 1980s', *European Review History/Revue européenne d'history* 24, no. 6 (2017): 973–90.

classic balance of powers, he concluded that German unification would be inevitable. More than ever, the Communities were to serve as an instrument to protect and strengthen France's European and global position. Mitterrand finally used the unalterable fact of German unification to bind Germany more closely to Europe and to ensure progress towards deeper European integration under Franco-German leadership. The result was the 1992 EU Treaty of Maastricht. Mitterrand's reputation as a European statesman is linked to his vision for France and Europe, which was based on strengthened Franco-German partnership with deeper integration. He is considered, along with Delors and Kohl, the master builder of the EU and instilled in the citizens of his country a conviction in support of the idea of unifying the continent.[105]

The Most Active Commission President after Hallstein: Jacques Delors

As Commission President from 1985, Delors took on the role of initiator and pacesetter of European integration. Born in Paris in 1925 as the son of a bank clerk, he became involved in the progressive Catholic youth movement. Like Monnet, Delors did not attend university, but worked at the Banque de France immediately after graduating from high school. In the 1960s, he became a member of Monnet's planning commission. As an advisor on social affairs to Gaullist Prime Minister Jacques Chaban-Delmas in 1969, he encouraged social reforms. Delors saw the market as an indispensable allocator of resources, decision-maker and source of economic dynamism, but believed that the market alone could not ensure social justice or a moral social order. During Mitterrand's presidency, Delors became finance minister and played a central role in the reorientation of the EMS in 1983, coupled with French reform and austerity policies. As Commission President, Delors developed the most ambitious programme to date for deepening European integration since the EEC Treaty, with the aim of completing the single market established therein and generating spillover effects in the process. Delors used the Monnet method of 'stealth integration' by promoting spillovers from the market to policy areas, benefiting European institutions, including the EP.

---

105 P. Favier and M. Martin-Roland, *La Décennie Mitterrand*, vol. I: *Les ruptures (1981–1984)* (Paris, Éditions du Seuil, 1990); P. Favier and M. Martin-Roland, *La Décennie Mitterrand*, vol. II: *Les épreuves (1984–1988)* (Paris, Éditions du Seuil, 1991). Differing views on Mitterrand and German unification can be found in U. Lappenküper, *Mitterrand und Deutschland: Die enträtselte Sphinx* (Munich, Oldenbourg, 2011); T. Schabert, *Mitterrand et la réunification allemande: Une histoire secrète (1981–1995)* (Paris, Grasset, 2005); T. Schabert, *France and the Reunification of Germany: Leadership in the Workshop of World Politics* (Cham, Springer Nature/Palgrave Macmillan, 2021).

The construction of the European market was to succeed, but the political union did not, mainly because of the negative and passive attitude of the heads of state and government. Delors is a member of the board of trustees of the initiative A Soul for Europe and the Spinelli Group, which is committed to European federalism, and heads the think tank Notre Europe (Our Europe). The realisation of the single market in 1993 is closely associated with Delors' name. After Monnet and Kohl, he became the third Honorary Citizen of Europe in 2015.[106]

Conclusion

In European integration history, federalism always had its possibilities and limits.[107] Most of the exponents mentioned in this chapter, as well as the so-called 'saints', were not pure federalists, but were forced to be pragmatists and realists due to national policy interests, be it as masterminds, ministers or heads of state and government. Convinced federalists, those who remained idealists and true supranationals were outsiders who had a lot to say but not always much to decide. Examples include forgotten pro-Europeans such as Walter Hallstein,[108] who did not want to continue his term in office in 1967, because of de Gaulle's rejection, among other things, and the Italian MEP

106 J. Delors, *Changer* (Paris, Stock, 1975); J. Delors with P. Alexandre, *En sortir ou pas* (Paris, Grasset, 1985); J. Delors, *La France par l'Europe* (Paris, Clisthène-Grasset, 1988), English translation J. Delors, *Our Europe: The Community and National Development*, trans. B. Pearce (London, Verso, 1991); J. Delors, *Le nouveau concert européen* (Paris, Odile Jacob, 1992); B. Maris, *Jacques Delors: Artiste et martyr* (Paris, Alben Michel, 1993); A. Rollat, *Delors* (Paris, Flammarion, 1993); J. Delors, *L'unité d'un homme: Entretiens avec Dominique Wolton* (Paris, Odile Jacob, 1994); C. Grant, *Delors: Inside the House That Delors Built* (London, Nicholas Brealey, 1994); G. Ross, *Jacques Delors and European Integration* (Cambridge, MA, Polity Press, 1995); N. P. Ludlow, 'Jacques Delors (1985–1995): Navigating the European Stream at Full Flow', in J. van der Harst and G. Voerman (eds.), *An Impossible Job? The Presidents of the European Commission 1958–2014* (London, John Harper, 2015), pp. 173–96.
107 S. Saurugger, 'The European Union and Federalism: Possibilities and Limits', in G. Grin, F. Nicod and B. Altermatt (eds.), *Formes d'Europe/Forms of Europe* (Paris, Éditions Economica, 2018), pp. 173–200.
108 G. Fragnière, *Walter Hallstein ou ... une pédagogie politique pour la Fédération européenne* (Brussels, Presses Interuniversitaires Européennes, 1995); W. Loth, W. Wallace and W. Wessels (eds.), *Walter Hallstein: The Forgotten European?* (Houndmills, Macmillan, 1998); W. Loth, *Walter Hallstein: Un européen déterminé, en La Commission européenne 1958–1972. Histoire et mémoires d'une institution* (Luxembourg, Communautés Européennes, 2007); J. Elvert, 'Walter Hallstein (1901–1982)', in Böttcher (ed.), *Klassiker des europäischen Denkens*, pp. 635–40.

Altiero Spinelli,[109] who was not to get his way in 1984 with a draft constitution drawn up by the EP on setting up a political European Union.

Historical integration research has dealt extensively with the 'founding fathers' of the EU, speaking not of 'saints' but of 'architects', 'master builders', 'idea generators', 'initiators', 'pioneers' and 'visionaries'. The fact that they were *governmental Europeans* and only at times *community Europeans* was related to domestic and party-political constraints.

The German Christian Democrat Adenauer had in mind the sovereignty of the West German state, which he tried to link with western European integration, cementing the political division of the continent. Giscard and Mitterrand, on the one hand, saw the link with the FRG as an opportunity to strengthen France's position; Kohl, on the other hand, saw German unity as the other side of the coin of the reunification of the whole of Europe. Certainly, however, Monnet can be called the 'forefather' and Schuman the 'founding father' of Europe. This is the view held by the Fondation Robert Schuman.[110] Other founders were grouped around them,[111] but, more than Adenauer and De Gasperi, Schuman can be considered the real father of a unified western Europe. However, without Monnet, the mastermind and inspirer, there would have been no Schuman Plan. But without Schuman the Monnet Plan would have remained a draft. It was Schuman who took the political initiative to establish the Coal and Steel Union and pushed it through politically. Without him the EU of today would be unthinkable. The unique successes of the 1950s in western European's history of unification have led to their initiators and co-creators being honoured, revered and appreciated as 'founding fathers'. This approach also stands up to critical scrutiny, although venerating these actors as 'saints' does not seem advisable. However, the public recognition of these protagonists found justified expression in the naming of public squares and streets and in monuments, honours, commemorative publications and awards.

Recommended Reading

Böttcher, W. (ed.). *Europas vergessene Visionäre: Rückbesinnung in Zeiten akuter Krisen* (Baden-Baden, Nomos, 2019).

Böttcher, W. (ed.). *Klassiker des europäischen Denkens: Friedens- und Europavorstellungen aus 700 Jahren europäischer Kulturgeschichte* (Baden-Baden, Nomos, 2014).

---

109 A. Ziegerhofer-Prettenthaler, 'Altiero Spinelli', in Böttcher (ed.), *Klassiker des europäischen Denkens*, pp. 661–8.
110 Schirmann (ed.), *Robert Schuman et les Pères de l'Europe*.   111 See 'Pères de l'Europe'.

D'Auria, M. and J. Vermeiren (eds.). *Visions and Ideas of Europe during the First World War* (London and New York, NY, Routledge, 2020).

Duchêne, F. *Jean Monnet: The First Statesman of Interdependence* (New York, NY, Norton and Co., 1994).

Griffiths, R. T. 'The Founding Fathers', in E. Jones, A. Menon and S. Weatherill (eds.), *The Oxford Handbook of the European Union* (Oxford, Oxford University Press, 2012), pp. 181–92.

Große Hüttmann, M. 'Prägende Persönlichkeiten in der Geschichte der EU-Integration', in P. Becker and B. Lippert (eds.), *Handbuch Europäische Union*, vol. 1 (Wiesbaden, Springer Verlag, 2002), pp. 43–69.

Knipping, F. and M. Schönwald (eds.). *Aufbruch zum Europa der zweiten Generation* (Trier, Wissenschaftlicher Verlag, 2004).

Schirmann, S. (ed.). *Robert Schuman et les Pères de l'Europe* (Brussels, Peter Lang, 2008).

Schmidt, V. A. 'The Role of Ideas and Discourse in European Integration', in H. Heinelt and S. Münch (eds.), *Handbook of European Policies: Interpretive Approaches to the EU* (Cheltenham and Northampton, MA, Edward Elgar, 2018), pp. 35–54.

Varsori, A. 'A Historical Interpretation of the Process of European Integration', in J. M. Magone (ed.), *Routledge Handbook of European Politics* (London and New York, NY, Routledge, 2014), pp. 97–115.

Ziegerhofer-Prettenthaler, A. *Botschafter Europas: Richard Nikolaus Coudenhove-Kalergi und die Paneuropa-Bewegung in den zwanziger und dreißiger Jahren* (Vienna, Cologne and Weimar, Böhlau, 2004).

19

The EU and the Narrative of Prosperity

CLAUDIA HIEPEL

Introduction

Since its very beginnings, a central narrative of European integration has been that only a form of profound cooperation between the European states will allow the promotion of prosperity and social security. The narrative of prosperity is one of the oldest and most constant meta-arguments of regional European integration. The Schuman Declaration of 9 May 1950 already stated that the European Coal and Steel Community (ECSC) would contribute to 'raising living standards'.[1] In the European Union's (EU's) self-portrayal, prosperity, growth and employment are still among its hardly questioned and fundamental goals, as former President of the Commission Emanuel Barroso put it: 'Today the *raison d'être* of our Union is also the same that was there sixty years ago: peace, democracy, to be freed from fears, mistrust and divisions, to share security, stability and prosperity.'[2] In the public debate, the EU is perceived as a *Wohlstandsmaschine* (prosperity machine)[3] despite all the criticism of its policies in detail. Furthermore, the EU is seen as the best long-term answer to the challenges of globalisation. The data speak for themselves: 7 per cent of the global population generate a quarter of the world's gross domestic product (GDP). Half of the world's social expenditure is spent

---

1 'The Schuman Declaration (Paris, 9 May 1950)', in *Selection of Texts Concerning Institutional Matters of the Community from 1950 to 1982* (Luxembourg, European Parliament, 1982), pp. 47–8.
2 'Speech by President Barroso: "Tearing Down Walls – Building Bridges"' (2014), https://ec.europa.eu/commission/presscorner/detail/en/SPEECH_14_168.
3 A. Hagelüken, 'Europa, die Wohlstandsmaschine', *Süddeutsche Zeitung*, 13 July 2019, www.sueddeutsche.de/politik/ungleichheiten-wirtschaftswachstum-europaeischer-binnenmarkt-1.4522086.

within the EU.[4] For the EU's citizens, prosperity can be measured by the fact that most people are better off than previous generations in the central areas of life – housing, food, income, consumption and leisure behaviour.

In that sense, Europe can be considered a success story in terms of prosperity – despite every crisis, most recently the financial crisis of 2008. But, according to objections, the old narrative has run its course and a new, fresh narrative is needed to weatherproof the EU for its future in a globalised world. Narratives cannot be 'invented' that easily; they are meaningful and identifiable only if they are nourished by historical experience. Thus, the oldest European narrative, the narrative of peace, is – or was – so self-evident that it did not need any further explication. Narratives have to be spontaneously plausible and should describe a positive future.[5] The narratives' aim is to create identity and justify political projects.[6]

For some time now, however, there have been doubts about the identity-establishing function of the narrative of prosperity and the greater narratives in general. Europe has long since 'ceased to be in the visionary phase'.[7] The argument concerning peace seems to have been decommissioned and the advantages of prosperity no longer suffice to inspire European citizens. According to Timothy Garton Ash, the EU now needs not an 'old-fashioned grand narrative', but 'a new account of itself'.[8] Upon closer inspection, however, this proposed new narrative is a combination of separate narratives, among which the familiar narratives of peace and freedom as well as the narrative of prosperity can be found.

Clearly, ordinary Europeans are nowadays in search of a new narrative which is meaningful and inspirational in the present. This might be the main reason why the narrative of prosperity appears to be very resilient overall, despite the crisis it is experiencing. This can probably be ascribed to the fact that it is rarely found in isolation, but always mentioned in combination with other narratives. The conceptual pair of peace and

4 European Commission, *The EU in the World – 2020 Edition* (Luxembourg, Publications of the European Union, 2020), https://ec.europa.eu/eurostat/documents/3217494/10934 584/KS-EX-20-001-EN-N.pdf/8ac3b640-0c7e-65e2-9f79-d03f00169e17.

5 B. Franke, 'Größe macht dumm', *Die Zeit* no. 2, 2 January 2014, www.zeit.de/2014/02/ europa-krise-neue-leitmotive.

6 See, for example, C. Sternberg, 'Culture and the EU's Struggle for Legitimacy', in M. Segers and Y. Albrecht (eds.), *Re: Thinking Europe: Thoughts on Europe: Past, Present and Future* (Amsterdam, Amsterdam University Press, 2014), pp. 155–67.

7 E. König, 'Europäische Großbaustellen – Essay', *Aus Politik und Zeitgeschichte* no. 14 (2014), www.bpb.de/shop/zeitschriften/apuz/180368/europaeische-grossbaustellen-essay.

8 T. Garton Ash, 'Europe's True Stories', *Prospect Magazine*, 25 February 2007, www .prospectmagazine.co.uk/magazine/europestruestories.

prosperity is central to this. The narrative of peace as the oldest and central narrative of European integration gained its legitimacy and plausibility through the two world wars as well as the Cold War. The narrative of prosperity can hardly be separated from it, since prosperity was a guarantor of peace, and economic cooperation was the means to preserve peace. The argument had its strongest legitimacy during the Cold War, when the Western European Union staged itself as a rampart against and a counter-model to the 'Eastern bloc' and received its legitimacy through the economic-political comparison, even though European integration was not a 'direct product of the Cold War'.[9]

This chapter is not about deconstructing that narrative. It aims instead at a diachronic reconstruction of this narrative, which has been of importance for the process of European integration ever since its inception. The chapter starts in the inter-war period, during which economic arguments for the unification of the European continent played a prominent role for the first time in modern European history. Subsequently, the chapter examines the development of the idea of prosperity as a motor of integration over time, as well as the historical context of its occurrence and its discussion within political discourse. In addition, the meanings of the term prosperity are analysed in detail, as the question of how to measure prosperity, and according to which parameters prosperity should be determined, is far from having been answered conclusively in the existing research. Should growth be measured in terms of material goods and the GDP, or do parameters such as quality of life and prosperity play a part as well? The concept of prosperity encapsulates many different ideas of prosperity, but is generally used without any reflection on the deeper meaning.

The State of the Art

Would the development have been the same without the economic integration of western Europe, or do we owe regional integration of Europe to prosperity and social security? There is no consensus at all in the literature. Apart from the well-established unquestioned continuation of the narrative of success,[10] some

9 N. P. Ludlow, 'The History of the EC and the Cold War: Influenced and Influential, but Rarely Center Stage', in U. Krotz, K. K. Patel and F. Romero (eds.), *Europe's Cold War Relations: The EC Towards a Global Role* (London, Bloomsbury Academic, 2020), pp. 15–29, 18.

10 H. Kaelble, *A Social History of Europe, 1945–2000: Recovery and Transformation after Two World Wars* (New York, NY and Oxford, Berghahn, 2013). On European integration, see, for example, P. Gerbet, *La construction de l'Europe* (Paris, Imprimerie Nationale, 1999).

scholars question the success story and even aim at establishing a correlation between weak economic growth and integration.[11] Undoubtedly, the European continent is one of the most prosperous regions in the world with – in the long run – steady growth rates in such countries as France, Germany and Great Britain since the beginning of the twentieth century, interrupted only by the slumps during the two world wars.[12]

What Are the Reasons for Europe's Economic Growth?

Whilst the fact of growth is undisputed, the reasons for it are subject to debate about whether the famous *Trente Glorieuses*, the period of growth after 1945 up to the oil-price crisis,[13] are the result of European integration at all. It is, moreover, very difficult to exactly measure the effects of the continent's economic unification on Europe's prosperity in material terms. According to Kiran Klaus Patel, the effect amounted to less than 0.5 per cent additional GDP growth per year.[14] Generally, the counterfactual question of the effects of non-integration is difficult to answer. In addition, a forthright narrative of success always represents only half the truth, for it does not take into account the great social differences within the individual states, on the one hand, and between European states themselves, on the other. Last but not least, the economic success narrative is currently dissolving because the promise to future generations that they will be better off than their parents is losing credibility. The days of unstoppable growth and creation of wealth seem to be behind Europe already and the EU is confronted with faster-growing parts of the world such as China.

There is no doubt, however, that Europe initially experienced an unparalleled boom after the Second World War, which lasted until 1973. This postwar economic boom was referred to as the '*Wirtschaftswunder*', the '*Trente Glorieuses*' or the 'golden age'. In the following years, growth rates declined again. It is disputed whether this was a critical downward trend or a 'normalisation' after an unnatural period of growth and boom.[15]

---

11 W. Plumpe and A. Steiner, 'Dimensionen wirtschaftlicher Integrationsprozesse in West- und Osteuropa nach dem Zweiten Weltkrieg', *Jahrbuch für Wirtschaftsgeschichte* 2 (2008): 21–38. On the competing narratives of the EU's history in general, see M. Gilbert, 'Narrating the Process: Questioning the Progressive Story of European Integration', *Journal of Common Market Studies* 46, no. 3 (2008): 641–62.

12 H. James, *Europe Reborn: A History 1914–2000*, 2nd ed. (London, Routledge, 2019 [2003]).

13 J. Fourastié, *Les Trente Glorieuses ou la révolution invisible* (Paris, Pluriel, 2011).

14 K. K. Patel, *Project Europe: A History* (Cambridge, Cambridge University Press, 2020), p. 112.

15 See Patel, *Project Europe*, pp. 85ff.

The high and continuous growth rates until the beginning of the 1970s are not synonymous with an equally continuous improvement of people's living conditions. Improvements in living conditions tended to occur only after some delay and varied greatly from region to region within the EU. The gap between rich and poor decreased, as did the social disparities within as well as between societies. After the end of the war, the European economies faced considerable difficulties in financing food and capital goods. This was a central motif of the Marshall Plan, the European Recovery Programme, which was supposed to get the western European economy going again. At the same time, the recipient countries united in the Organisation for European Economic Co-operation (OEEC) were to commit themselves to the basic principles of the free market.[16] Scholars such as Barry Eichengreen argue that the Marshall Plan made an important contribution to the economic upswing in western Europe. Opinions differ regarding its scope. The German historian Werner Abelshauser holds a contradictory view by saying that the Marshall Plan had no decisive impact on growth for West Germany and was of only marginal importance for the rest of western Europe.[17] Western European countries also became part of a worldwide liberalisation of trade with the dismantling of tariff and non-tariff trade barriers through the Bretton Woods system, of which the General Agreement on Tariffs and Trade (GATT) was a part. The general mood of optimism after the war, the reconstruction and the intensification of the international division of labour combined with a surplus of labour, technical progress and structural change created the framework conditions for high growth rates and generated prosperity. If the beginning of European integration can be dated to the founding of the ECSC, it may be concluded that the boom began before the process of European integration took off in the form of the ECSC. The narrative of prosperity having arisen from integration would then accordingly have no basis.

Long-Term Economic Trends in Europe

Moreover, not only was the Europe of the six countries in the ECSC and European Economic Community (EEC) experiencing high growth rates, but so were other European states. It is also often argued that the boom existed

16 B. Eichengreen, *The European Economy since 1945: Coordinated Capitalism and Beyond* (Princeton, NJ, Princeton University Press, 2007), p. 105.
17 W. Abelshauser, 'Wiederaufbau vor dem Marshallplan', *Vierteljahrshefte für Zeitgeschichte* 29, no. 4 (1981): 545–78; H. van Buren Cleveland, 'If There Had Been No Marshall Plan . . .', in S. Hoffmann and C. Maier (eds.), *The Marshall Plan: A Retrospective* (London, Westview Press, 1984), pp. 59–64.

before the ECSC and began with the Marshall Plan and the OEEC. Accordingly, the EEC was not the trigger and starting point for an economically integrated western Europe, but rather the amplifier of a process in progress.[18] Politics, therefore, merely caught up with what market processes had already initiated. The ECSC and the European Common Market were part of a global economic order that the United States had already established during the war and in the immediate post-war period. The European institutions of economic integration continued this development and were part of a Pax Americana in which welfare, stability and prosperity played a decisive role in securing an economically liberal capitalist order and democracy.[19] European integration as part of a transnational process would thus actually be more of an Americanisation and less the result of European nation-state action.[20]

In contrast to that, other scholars describe a genuinely European character, a sort of 'European core' of integration that goes back to substantial interdependences that already existed during the nineteenth century. Between 1860 and 1914, there was a period of free trade in Europe combined with a high degree of interdependence of the markets for goods, capital and labour. The new start after 1945 allowed European states to restore traditional structures and patterns. Nevertheless, what happened was more than a mere institutionalisation of already existing trade. In fact, the EEC effectuated an intensification of the exchange of goods within the community, which developed into an engine of prosperity.[21] Trade between the Six grew faster than it would have done without the Common Market, with high growth rates and increases in income.[22] This argument also fits the view that not only the German economic miracle, but also the boom after 1945 in general, was not so much the result of US aid and transfers from outside, but rather

---

18 B. Eichengreen and A. Boltho, 'The Economic Impact of European Integration', in S. Broadberry and K. H. O'Rourke (eds.), *The Cambridge Economic History of Modern Europe*, vol. II: *1870 to the Present* (Cambridge, Cambridge University Press, 2010), pp. 267–95.
19 P. Ther, *Das andere Ende der Geschichte: Über die Große Transformation* (Berlin, Suhrkamp, 2019); Q. Slobodian, *Globalists: The End of Empire and the Birth of Neoliberalism* (Cambridge, MA, Harvard University Press, 2018); C. S. Maier, 'The Politics of Productivity: Foundations of American International Economic Policy after World War II', *International Organization* 31, no. 4 (1977): 607–33.
20 A. Milward, *The European Rescue of the Nation State*, 2nd ed. (London, Routledge, 2000 [1993]).
21 G. Thiemeyer, *Europäische Integration: Motive – Prozesse – Strukturen* (Cologne, Weimar and Vienna, Böhlau, 2010), p. 151.
22 Eichengreen, *The European Economy since 1945*, p. 17.

a return to a 'normal' path of growth that had only been interrupted by the world wars in the first half of the twentieth century.

The economic growth of the Six was not merely the result of liberalisation, but also depended on a specifically European tradition of organising labour relations. Neo-corporatism, partly based on Christian socialism, led to agreements between employers, workers and governments in various European countries.[23] Elements of economic planning played quite a significant role and were by no means frowned upon. Examples here would be the French model of *planification*, which combined elements of a planned economy with the principles of a free market economy, or the government industrial policy in Italy. Unlike socialist planned economy, those models included the development of key industrial sectors, which was then applied at a supranational level within the framework of the ECSC.

Was Europe a Social Market Economy?

The process of European integration as a whole cannot be assigned to a specific economic model. Depending on the respective phase and policy field, elements of trade liberalisation, competition and the free market or protectionism, regulation and centralised planning predominated. European integration can neither be fully attributed to neoliberalism nor attributed to French neo-corporatism or to German 'ordoliberalism'.

In general terms, the concept of a social market economy, defined in essence as the link between a free market and social balance, is the underlying model for the EU today. Prosperity for all – the leitmotif of the German economic miracle – has also enjoyed great popularity in the recent past. In a speech to the European Parliament on the occasion of his election as President of the European Commission, in 2014 Jean-Claude Juncker stated: 'I am an enthusiastic supporter of the social market economy. "Prosperity for all" is what Ludwig Erhard said. Not "prosperity for just a few".'[24] Leaving such catch-phrases aside, one should ask to what extent the idea of a European social market economy was realised within the European Community (EC) and the treaties. The social market economy was a child of the German Christian Democratic idea of 'ordoliberalism'. In the early days of integration, however, it was precisely the adherents of

---

23 P. Misner, *Catholic Labor Movements in Europe: Social Thought and Action 1914–1965* (Washington, DC, The Catholic University of America Press, 2015).

24 J.-C. Juncker, 'A New Start for Europe: My Agenda for Jobs, Growth, Fairness, and Democratic Change' (2014), https://ec.europa.eu/commission/presscorner/detail/en/SPEECH_14_546.

'ordoliberalism' who were very sceptical about the ECSC and the EEC. They were convinced that the state should do no more than provide a framework for a free enterprise economy to ensure fair and open competition. For them, the ECSC and its High Authority were an expression of *dirigisme*. This *dirigisme* was embodied by Jean Monnet, who not only brought the principle of supranational cooperation into European politics, but, as the first head of the Commissariat général du plan (French Planning Office), also designed modernisation programmes for the French economy that were closely linked to the idea of a western European Coal and Steel Community, which was ultimately a variant of the American planning founded in the New Deal.[25] The tension between the French model of neomercantilism and German 'ordoliberalism' shaped the negotiations on the ECSC and the EEC.[26]

French *dirigisme* fitted quite well into the period after 1945, in which a policy of *laissez-faire* was discredited. Indeed, the 1950s were not a heyday of *laissez-faire* capitalism; Milton Friedman, for instance, also spoke in favour of market regulation and laws against cartels and monopolies.[27] In post-war Germany, the social market economy as a 'third form' alongside the free market economy and the planned economy was designed as a counterweight to socialism/social democracy. The social market economy completely rejected active redistribution and control, but at the same time refrained from a free market economy in the sense of *laissez-faire*. In the founding phase of European integration, 'ordoliberalism' was in the unique position of being able to exert influence via the German federal government. Strong expansion of economic interventionism with simultaneous liberalisation towards the outside world accurately describes economic activities after 1945.

The competition policy of the EC Commission was strongly influenced by 'ordoliberalism'. It was then under social democratic influence in the 1970s that Keynesian elements became increasingly important. The state's demand-oriented policy included state-supported economic stimulus programmes and, in the boom years, the expansion of social welfare systems. The rise in public debt hit the economies hard in the 1970s, coupled with the oil-price crisis of 1973–4 and the end of the Bretton Woods system. With Milton Friedman's concept of monetarism, an alternative economic policy gained

25 K. K. Patel, *The New Deal: A Global History* (Princeton, NJ, Princeton University Press, 2016); F. Duchêne, *Jean Monnet: The First Statesman of Interdependence* (New York, NY, W. W. Norton, 1994).
26 L. Warlouzet, 'The EEC/EU as an Evolving Compromise between French Dirigism and German Ordoliberalism (1957–1995)', *Journal of Common Market Studies*, 57 (2019): 77–93.
27 Ther, *Das andere Ende der Geschichte*, p. 15.

importance in these years. The state was supposed to curb inflation and otherwise withdraw itself and leave the field to the market and the free play of forces.[28]

There was no return to the conditions of the boom phase anywhere in western Europe in the long term, although for individual countries, such as Ireland in the 1970s and Spain in the 1980s, accession to the EU was certainly associated with increases in prosperity. At the beginning of the 1980s, the pendulum clearly swung back in the direction of liberalisation. With the Single European Act (SEA), the focus was increasingly on the dismantling of trade barriers and deregulation. At the same time, however, the Common Agricultural Policy (CAP) remained a highly regulated policy area with quotas and market-regulating intervention mechanisms.[29] Neoliberalism played a greater role, but without being able to fully assert itself. To summarise, the economic policy was ambivalent and Janus-faced. The European integration process could not be attributed to a particular model.[30]

The Narrative

After the Second World War, there were several motives and driving forces underlying the European integration process. Among these were securing peace and resolving the German question as well as economic driving forces in the sense of modern markets becoming 'too small for rational production methods' to ensure prosperity.[31]

The Origins before 1945

The link between European unification and prosperity had been made as early as during the inter-war period. In 1929, French Foreign Minister Aristide Briand gave a speech to the League of Nations, in which he proposed creating a 'federative bond' that aimed at cooperation mechanisms which planned on the dismantling of trade barriers and the creation of connecting infrastructures.[32] As is well known, nothing ever came of it. Nevertheless,

28 L. Warlouzet, *Governing Europe in a Globalizing World: Neoliberalism and Its Alternatives Following the 1973 Oil Crisis* (London, Routledge, 2018).
29 For an overview of the history of the integration process, see W. Loth, *Building Europe: A History of European Unification* (Berlin and Boston, MA, De Gruyter, 2015).
30 Patel, *Project Europe*.
31 W. Loth, 'Explaining European Integration: The Contribution from Historians', *Journal of European Integration History* 14, no. 1 (2008): 9–26.
32 F. Kießling, 'Der Briand-Plan von 1929/30. Europa als Ordnungsvorstellung in den internationalen Beziehungen im 19. und frühen 20. Jahrhundert', Themenportal Europäische Geschichte (2008), www.europa.clio-online.de/essay/id/fdae-1457.

we can recognise a first occurrence of patterns of argumentation and ideas that could have been taken up after the Second World War.

When French Foreign Minister Robert Schuman presented the plan for a merger of German and French coal and steel production on 9 May 1950, he referred to the European ideas and European initiatives of the inter-war period right at the beginning. For more than 20 years, according to Schuman, France had been striving for a united Europe. Exactly 20 years earlier, Briand had presented his 'Memorandum', to which Schuman was obviously alluding here. Count Coudenhove-Kalergi's idea of a Pan-European Union in the 1920s also focused on the economy. He deplored the economic fragmentation that would destabilise the continent and which had to be overcome by creating a large interdependent economic region.[33] Further approaches to the idea of European unification by economic means can also be found in the political resistance movements against fascism and National Socialism and the German occupiers in the Second World War. Concepts for a post-war order were developed, which could certainly be taken up after 1945. In his paper 'For a European Economic Federation', Luigi Einaudi, an economics professor from Turin and member of the Italian resistance who later went on to become Italian president, outlined very detailed ideas about a European economic union.[34] In the French *résistance* and exile, Francis Gérard, who was later to play a role in the European Federalist Movement, considered it indispensable to create a unified economic area with freedom of movement for people, goods and capital, a common currency and exploitation of mineral resources in order to remove the basis for future conflicts and install a lasting order of peace.[35] Numerous other examples of these and similar ideas could be given that experienced a revival in the post-war European Movement.[36] A very influential document was that of Jean Monnet, who in his exile in Algiers in 1943 wrote a memorandum on the rebuilding of Europe after the war, the content of which anticipated the institutional integration of the 1950s and the formulations of which were to become part of the standard rhetorical repertoire of Europe's advocates:

> The countries of Europe are too small to guarantee their peoples the prosperity that modern conditions make possible and consequently

33 R. N. Coudenhove-Kalergi, *Paneuropa* (Vienna and Leipzig, Paneuropa-Verlag, 1926).

34 L. Einaudi, 'For an Economic Federation of Europe, 1 September 1943', in W. Lipgens (ed.), *Documents on the History of European Integration*, vol. 1: *Continental Plans for European Union 1939–1945* (Berlin and New York, NY, Walter de Gruyter, 1985), pp. 520–25.

35 F. Gérard, 'What Is to Be Done with Germany?', in Lipgens (ed.), *Documents*, vol. 1, pp. 322–4.

36 Ibid.

necessary. They need larger markets. It is also important that they do not devote a substantial share of their resources to maintaining supposedly 'key' industries to meet the requirements of national defence, industries which are rendered obligatory by the form that States take, with their 'national sovereignty' and protectionist reflexes, such as we saw before 1939. Prosperity for the States of Europe and the social developments that must go with it will only be possible if they form a federation or a 'European entity' that makes them into a common economic unit.[37]

Not only does the term prosperity appear for the first time explicitly in connection with European unification, but also this statement can be seen as the 'birth' of the influential narrative of the European states being too small, so that each of them individually is not in a position to guarantee the prosperity of its citizens. The egoism of nation-states is seen as an obstacle that has to be overcome through the creation of a (partly) supranational or federal order. Although supranationality is not yet explicitly mentioned here, all the principles of European integration are already hinted at in a nutshell.

With the end of the Second World War, however, the situation initially became confusing, as different actors now came into focus. At first, the European Movement, which was also staffed by actors from the resistance and the inter-war period, took up these ideas. Although there was no united European Movement, but rather groups and individual actors with very different ideological and political orientations, the narrative of prosperity was present in all concepts of the years between the end of the Second World War and the important Hague Congress in May 1948.

Winston Churchill set the high tone of the rhetoric of unification in his famous speech to students at the University of Zurich as early as September 1946, linking a bright future for the continent to economic prosperity: 'If Europe were once united in the sharing of its common inheritance there would be no limit to the happiness, prosperity and glory which its 300 million or 400 million people would enjoy.'[38] Prosperity did not just promise a materially better future, but was also seen as a linchpin for peace in Europe and the world. This argument was taken up by Churchill's son-in-law Duncan Sandys, who was one of the leading figures of the

37 J. Monnet, 'Thoughts on the Future', in Segers and Albrecht (eds.), *Re: Thinking Europe*, pp. 171–6.
38 'Address Given by Winston Churchill (Zurich, 19 September 1946)', www.cvce.eu/o bj/address_given_by_winston_churchill_zurich_19_september_1946-en-7dc5a4cc-4453 -4c2a-b130-b534b7d76ebd.html.

European Movement. Since Europe was regarded as 'the world's greatest fire risk' – to quote John Foster Dulles – and at the same time as one of the main starting points for economic depression, it was hence clear for him to draw the following conclusion: 'Establish prosperity and peace in Europe and you will have gone a very long way towards establishing them throughout the world.'[39]

Certainly, opinions on the form and institutional framework in which peace and prosperity should be secured differed widely within the European Movement. Should peace and prosperity be achieved through intergovernmental cooperation or in the framework of supranational organisations?

For some, the creation of a comprehensive European federation was the only conceivable institutional framework: 'This also means that in order to achieve these goals on which peace, the prosperity of nations and the happiness of peoples depend, we trust in federalist solutions alone: federalism everywhere, federalism at all levels and at all ranks of human society, from the bottom to the top.'[40] At the Congress of the Union of European Federalists in Montreux, Switzerland, in August 1947, activists considered the economic benefits of establishing a European Federation: 'Europe has a card to play which is the last, but also the most beautiful. It can immediately escape the economic annihilation or subjugation that awaits it and enter a period of prosperity that will leave the prodigious rise of the 19th century far behind. This unhoped-for opportunity is federalism.'[41]

The idea of federation was overloaded with hardly commensurable expectations of salvation that, ultimately, were not based on a specific economic concept. Federation was rather perceived as a necessity, which was linked to the expectation that only national economies that are closely interconnected do not go to war against each other. In this early phase of integration, the narrative of prosperity was always self-evidently linked to the narrative of peace and freedom. The triad of peace, prosperity and liberty not only shaped the European concepts of this phase, but also had a lasting effect

---

39 'Address Given by Duncan Sandys (Montreux, 27–31 August 1947)', in Union européenne des fédéralistes (ed.), *Rapport du premier congrès annuel de l'UEF 27–31 août 1947 Montreux (Suisse)* (Geneva, Union européenne des fédéralistes, 1947), www.cvce.eu /en/obj/address_given_by_duncan_sandys_montreux_27_31_august_1947-en-7243675 d-c365-4a09-8df4-aebbab2d2231.html.

40 'Resolution on General Policy (Montreux, 27–31 August 1947)', in Union européenne des fédéralistes (ed.), *Rapport du premier congrès annuel de l'UEF*.

41 'Economic Prospects of European Federalism (Montreux, 27–31 August 1947)', in Union européenne des fédéralistes (ed.), *Rapport du premier congrès annuel de l'UEF*.

on the discourses of the coming decades, which were often impregnated with this spirit of morality.

The United States was expected to supply the concrete economic ideas and decisions for which European federalism was to provide the political framework. The economic recovery of the devastated Europe should be accomplished by the creation of a European market that would enable production to be increased and the population's standard of living to be raised. Count Coudenhove-Kalergi articulated very concrete ideas, calling for a 'currency of a European character' that would create the 'necessary confidence for the establishment of a stable and prosperous economic system'.

This, however, could not be achieved within the framework of intergovernmental compromises by governments pursuing their own national interests. Europe needed a

> Federal authority, capable of removing by stages the economic barriers between European States, despite all particularistic opposition and obstruction. Moreover, even the operations of the OEEC, the productiveness of present relations between free Europe and the United States of America within the frame of the Marshall Plan and also the future of such relations, when implementation of the Marshall Plan has been concluded, will be facilitated and guaranteed when the United States will be able to deal with one European Federation whose objectives are united.[42]

The idea of an international distribution of tasks, in which Europe would organise itself federally and thus create the framework conditions for the development of the market economy order set in motion by the Marshall Plan and the OEEC, was not shared by all supporters of the European Movement. Even at the Hague Conference in May 1948, it proved difficult to bring the different ideas down to a common denominator. Some parties and political groupings were sceptical about this event, such as the British Labour Party and, in its wake, the Scandinavian and German Social Democratic Parties. Overall, however, the spectrum was very wide, ranging from conservative to Christian social and liberal ideas on the economic order of the continent. For this reason alone, the demands were very vague and general.[43]

---

42 R. Coudenhove-Kalergi, 'Memorandum by the EPU on the Structure of Europe (Gstaad, 17 October 1949), www.cvce.eu/obj/memorandum_by_the_epu_on_the_s tructure_of_europe_gstaad_17_october_1949-en-bbea2f29-2ea1-403d-8cbc-143f71e3e667 .html.

43 Loth, *Building Europe*, p. 23.

The Hague Conference's Economic and Social Resolution referred to the 'generous assistance of the United States of America'. With its help, 'there is a unique opportunity to build a new and better Europe if Europeans work together under a common plan to develop the economic strength of the Continent'. Rebuilding the national economy should not be done 'by old methods'. Progress could be achieved only if the rebuilding were 'accompanied at every step by a parallel policy of ever-closer political union. Europe must unite if it is to regain and surpass its former prosperity and re-assert its economic independence.'[44]

The post-1945 European Movement did not see itself as competing with the economic initiatives launched by the United States. It also regarded political and security integration initiatives as being interconnected with economic integration. The different levels of integration were logically inseparable, with economic integration regarded as being closely linked to European political and security integration. Similarly, the signatory states of the Treaty of Brussels of 17 March 1948, namely Belgium, France, Luxembourg, the Netherlands and the United Kingdom, committed themselves to economic, social and cultural collaboration and collective self-defence, to coordinate their economic activities and 'to promote the attainment of a higher standard of living by their peoples' (Article II).[45] And conversely, the Marshall Plan aimed not only at the improvement of the standard of living, but also at the creation of (political) European unity. In the words of the OEEC Statutes of 16 April 1948: 'Believing that only by close and lasting co-operation between the Contracting Parties can the prosperity of Europe be restored and maintained, and the ravages of war made good.'[46] And here, too, the triad of 'prosperous economy', 'individual liberty' and 'maintenance of peace' was used to justify European cooperation.

The Schuman Plan and the Creation of the ECSC

Ultimately, this narrative was also the basis of the speech by the French Foreign Minister Robert Schuman on 9 May 1950, which can be seen as the prelude to the founding of the ECSC as the first in a series of concrete steps of

---

44 'The Hague Congress: Economic and Social Resolution, 10 May 1948', in W. Lipgens and W. Loth (eds.), *Documents on the History of European Integration*, vol. IV: *Transnational Organizations of Political Parties and Pressure Groups in the Struggle for European Union, 1945–1950* (Berlin and New York, NY, Walter de Gruyter, 1991), pp. 347–50.

45 'The Brussels Treaty (17 March 1948)', www.cvce.eu/obj/the_brussels_treaty_17_march_1948-en-3467de5e-9802-4b65-8076-778bc7d164d3.html.

46 'Convention for European Economic Cooperation (Paris, 16 April 1948)', www.cvce.eu/obj/convention_for_european_economic_cooperation_paris_16_april_1948-en-769de8b7-fe5a-452c-b418-09b068bd748d.html.

institutional integration. The speech itself was the result of several developments: the urge of the allied partners to come to an arrangement with the
recently founded Federal Republic of Germany, the fear of an economic
strengthening of the Germans and the steel crisis.[47] These fears were now
constructively transformed into a positive vision of integration aiming to
secure prosperity and promising that (supranational) integration by economic means could produce the political unification of Europe some time
in the future. This path of integration, also called the functionalist '*méthode
Monnet*', after the originator of the Schuman Declaration speech, Jean
Monnet, served to secure peace between Germany and France as well as in
(western) Europe as a whole: 'By pooling basic production and by instituting
a new higher authority, whose decisions will bind France, Germany, and
other member countries, this proposal will lead to the realisation of the first
concrete foundation of a European federation indispensable to the preservation of peace.'[48]

This implicitly referred to growing prosperity and wealth creation, which
could no longer be guaranteed by the respective nation-states and therefore
necessitated the creation of larger economic units. 'There is no sustainable
national prosperity without the existence of a large market and membership
in a large economic group. [. . .] Experience has shown that prosperity within
the national framework is fragile,' said Pierre Uri, a close collaborator of Jean
Monnet, who was involved in the drafting of the ECSC Treaties and later the
Treaties of Rome.[49]

The Schuman Declaration and the ECSC were perceived as a decisive
point in the development of Europe, on which the success of all further
development would depend. In an address to the Consultative Assembly of
the Council of Europe, Belgian Foreign Minister Paul van Zeeland said:

> How many times during the past thirty or forty years have we not had the
> impression – terrifying or stimulating – that we were at the edge of the abyss,
> or else on the threshold of a magnificent period with unlimited possibilities.
> I think we are in this position today, and the next two months will decide our

47 J. Gillingham, *Coal, Steel, and the Rebirth of Europe, 1945–1955: The Germans and the French from Ruhr Conflict to Economic Community* (Cambridge, Cambridge University Press, 1991); W. I. Hitchcock, 'France, the Western Alliance, and the Origins of the Schuman Plan, 1948–50', *Diplomatic History* 21, no. 4 (1997): 603–30.
48 'Robert Schuman, Declaration of 9th May 1950', Fondation Robert Schuman, European Issue no. 204, 10 May 2011.
49 'Note de Pierre Uri sur les formes de l'intégration européenne (5 avril 1955)', www.cvce.eu/obj/note_de_pierre_uri_sur_les_formes_de_l_integration_europeenne_5_avril_1955-fr-1f39e94e-d121-4bf1-bdf2-0f252ec5b9a7.html.

fate. Let us within that space of time see the ratification of the European Community for Coal and Steel; let us jointly lay the foundations of the European Defence Community. If we do this, the new year will open under favourable auspices. Perhaps at last we may be able to read on the tablets of fate the three words so long awaited: United Europe, Peace, Prosperity.[50]

The Road to the EEC

European unification was not automatic, and the narrative of prosperity obviously was not convincing enough to be applied to other realms. The spillover to military integration failed. After years of negotiations, the plan for a European Defence Community proved to be a failure in 1954 because of the French National Assembly's rejection. In the end, the crisis of the European unification project led to a return to the economy as the motor of integration.

The Messina Conference of Foreign Ministers in June 1955 showed once again that willingness for integration was most likely to be found in the economic sphere. Subsequently, an intergovernmental conference led by Belgian Foreign Minister Paul-Henri Spaak drew up the treaties for the EEC and the European Atomic Energy Community, which were signed in Rome on 25 March 1957. Perhaps even more than in the early days of European unification, fundamental conflicts over the best economic path for Europe were under way. Each of the European nation-states had its own economic policy concepts, which reflected national traditions and interests. Although the narrative of prosperity itself was not called into question and the agreement on prosperity being the goal of unification was undisputed, there was a 'dispute over methods' and how to achieve this.

German 'ordoliberalism' and French neomercantilism were at the centre of the dispute. The Treaties of Rome therefore presented a mixture of different economic philosophies, whose reading was a matter of interpretation due to the general wording. The Common Market was to be built by a progressive approximation of the respective national economic policies and a harmonisation of economic activities with the aim of an accelerated raising of the standard of living (Article 2). The treaty did contain provisions with clearly liberal market features: the elimination of customs duties and of restrictions regarding the importation and exportation of goods, and the abolition of obstacles to the free movement of people, services and capital as well as to competition. On the other hand, there were elements of

50 Speech by Paul van Zeeland at the Council of Europe (Strasbourg, 10 December 1951) Council of Europe – Consultative Assembly. Reports. Third session. 26 November– 11 December 1951, Part VII (Strasbourg, Council of Europe, 1951), pp. 991–1000.

interventionism, such as the inauguration of a common agricultural policy, coordination of the economic policies of member states and also the creation of a European Social Fund 'in order to improve the possibilities of employment for workers and to contribute to the raising of their standard of living' (Article 3). However, the Rome Treaties did not tend to infringe on the rights of the member states to shape their own economic policy: 'This Treaty shall in no way prejudice the system existing in Member States in respect of property.' (Article 222). The EEC Treaty provided for the opening of capital markets only 'to the extent necessary for the functioning of the common market'. This did not necessarily imply complete liberalisation at that time.

Nevertheless, economic liberalisation was at the core of the EEC in the following years. It was due to the influence of German 'ordoliberalism', in particular the head of the Policy Principles Directorate of the Federal Ministry of Economics, Alfred Müller-Armack, and to Minister Ludwig Erhard, that competition policy and the 'Four Freedoms' were enshrined in the EEC.[51] Whether this was a triumph of neoliberalism is doubtful, especially since there were initially no mechanisms to enforce these concerns.

The Treaties of Rome can more accurately be described as a 'hybrid form',[52] which not only resulted from the different economic policy philosophies it had to accommodate, but was also rooted in the different ideas of the purpose and final end of the EEC. For German Chancellor Konrad Adenauer, as well as the Federal Foreign Office, the political goals were paramount.[53] Accordingly, the desired closer political union of the six member states could thus be achieved only with the creation of a customs union and a common market, not with the model of a free trade area.[54] Adenauer was thus following the line of the Spaak Report, whose objections to the creation of a free trade zone were also economic. Maintaining the national trade and customs policies towards third countries would – according to the argumentation – 'hinder the establishment of the conditions which are to lead to stability and prosperity in this internal market'.[55]

---

51 Slobodian, *Globalists*, pp. 289–300; D. J. Gerber, 'Constitutionalising the Economy: German Neoliberalism, Competition Law and the "New Europe"', *The American Journal of Comparative Law* 42 (1994): 25–84.

52 Slobodian, *Globalists*, p. 274.

53 U. Enders, 'Integration oder Kooperation? Ludwig Erhard und Franz Etzel im Streit über die Politik der europäischen Zusammenarbeit 1954–1956', *Vierteljahrshefte für Zeitgeschichte* 45, no. 1 (1997): 143–71.

54 'Stellungnahme des Auswärtigen Amts zu den Fragen der Freihandelszone (Bonn, 8. Juli 1957)', www.cvce.eu/de/obj/stellungnahme_des_auswartigen_amts_zu_den_fragen_der_freihandelszone_bonn_8_juli_1957-de-1bcee3a9-48fb-4fd4-9931-c99f64a098c8.html.

55 Comité intergouvernemental créé par la conférence de Messine, 'Rapport des chefs de délégation aux ministres des Affaires étrangères, Bruxelles: Secrétariat, 21 avril 1956',

Within this logic, the EEC was the model that guaranteed prosperity. The trade unions also supported this perspective. They expected the Common Market to raise living standards and enable full employment and social progress through harmonisation of social conditions.[56] This view was held by the (socialist) Free Trade Unions as well as by the Christian Trade Union movement:

> We note that economic integration is the most effective means of securing the development of the European economy and of ensuring real social progress through the steady improvement of the workers' standard of living. The prosperity of the working masses also constitutes an important contribution to the achievement of social peace and the consolidation of peace among nations.[57]

Alternatives beyond the EEC?

However, alternatives to the Common Market model existed. Parallel to the negotiations of the Six on the Common Market, the Council of the OEEC had installed a working group on British initiative with the aim of studying forms of association between the envisaged customs union of the Six and the member countries that would not participate in it. The British government presented a so-called 'Plan G' as a part of a broader project named Great Design: Co-operation with Western Europe. Plan G proposed the idea of a wider free trade area as a sort of trade bloc without customs duties, in accordance with the GATT.[58] This proposal was very much in the spirit of Ludwig Erhard, but did not correspond to the ideas of Italy and France, which were instead striving for a socially acceptable modernisation with the help of the EEC.

From the point of view of the 'ordoliberals' in the German Ministry of Economics, the creation of the EEC was redundant; they relied on the OEEC model. The claim to exclusivity regarding the narrative of prosperity made by

pp. 9–135. For a summary in English, see 'The Spaak Report', www.cvce.eu/en/obj/the_spaak_report-en-4b911a0a-6bd0-4e88-bff9-4c87690aa4e8.html.

56 'Déclaration de la Confédération internationale des syndicats libres (Bruxelles, 25–27 août 1955)', www.cvce.eu/obj/declaration_de_la_cisl_sur_la_relance_europeenne_bruxelles_25_27_aout_1955-fr-99477e0c-5546-48ce-bc8c-dfaec6495cd9.html.

57 'Note concernant les décisions de la Conférence de Messine et le programme de "reliance" européenne, 14 septembre 1955', www.cvce.eu/obj/note_de_la_confederation_internationale_des_syndicats_chretiens_14_septembre_1955-fr-228ae94f-5b8f-4c90-bd5a-93f8961ba2f9.html.

58 J. Ellison, *Threating Europe: Britain and the Creation of the European Community, 1955–58* (London, Macmillan, 2000), p. 97; M. Schaad, 'Plan G. A "Counterblast"? British Policy towards the Messina Countries 1956', *Contemporary European History* 7, no. 1 (1998): 39–60.

the EEC's advocates was denied vehemently. Accordingly, the OEEC by its very nature aimed towards 'raising the standard of living of its peoples' as well, and to this end, however, not integrating the economy, but solely modernising it, ensuring financial stability and guaranteeing the balance of payments.

Consequently, the results proved the OEEC right. The gross national product (GNP) of the OEEC states had an annual increase of 5 per cent. At the same time, crude steel production was increased by 10 million tonnes to 65 million tonnes. The Ministry of Economics calculated an annual increase of 7 per cent in energy demand.[59] The development of prosperity in Europe was considered 'generally satisfactory'.[60] More than anything, German representatives of 'ordoliberalism' were bothered by the linking of political goals with economic means. In their view, European integration required primarily political institutions, and any attempt to intertwine political goals with economic means was considered a serious mistake. Political and military problems – an allusion to the Suez Crisis – could easily have economic consequences, shake confidence in the Common Market and thus implicitly jeopardise the safeguarding of prosperity. In the Bundestag debate on the Treaties of Rome, Ludwig Erhard put it succinctly:

> If I had to examine the Common Market Treaty only from an economic point of view, I would first have to ask whether previous efforts to bring the countries of Europe together had not already produced such great successes that it might have been possible to refrain from a special construction.[61]

From Rome to Maastricht and Beyond

After the foundation of the EEC, however, a positive reading quickly became established, according to which liberalisation and growth in prosperity proceeded at the planned pace or even faster. Intra-European trade grew at an above average rate during these years, as did trade with the rest of the world. For Robert Marjolin, who was head of the French delegation in negotiations on the formation of the EEC and Commissioner for Economy and Finance in the first Hallstein Commission, this meant that the EEC was a factor for

---

59 K. Albrecht, 'Integration auf vielen Wegen', *Wirtschaftsdienst* 35 (1955): 499–505.
60 A. Müller-Armack, 'Fragen der europäischen Integration', E. Beckerath, F. Meyer and A. Müller-Armack (eds.), *Wirtschaftsfragen der freien Welt* (Frankfurt am Main, Fritz Knapp Verlag, 1957).
61 L. Erhard, 'Rede von Ludwig Erhard', in *Verhandlungen des deutschen Bundestages. 2. Deutscher Bundestag – 200. Sitzung vom 21. März 1957. Stenographische Berichte* (Bonn, Deutscher Bundestag und Bundesrat, 1957), pp. 11342–5.

prosperity for the entire world.[62] The narrative of prosperity was now also used to justify the communitarisation of further policies. Given the targeted growth rates, the question was, for instance, to what extent farmers should share in this growth.[63] Thus, the narrative of prosperity was also used to implement the CAP:

> The history of the last ten years has proved beyond doubt that the techno-logical and industrial revolution is bringing in its wake a great increase in prosperity. But it has also shown that, in the absence of a new approach, there is no chance of making sure that the agricultural population will share in the new prosperity to the same extent as other groups.[64]

In this context, the CAP must be evaluated ambivalently. On the one hand, it was extremely expensive for the EEC's consumers and taxpayers, and potentially reduced prosperity. On the other hand, it had a positive impact on farmers as producers, for whom it contributed to an increase in prosperity.[65]

The general economic situation in the 1950s and 1960s had favoured the development of economic integration. It was evident that the high growth rates during the boom phase could be attributed to the EEC/EC, which provided plausibility for the narrative of prosperity. The decades of uninter-rupted growth came to an end during the crisis-ridden developments of the 1970s. Monetary turmoil, oil-price shocks, inflation and unemployment put the EC under new pressure to justify itself. The crisis had an impact on Community policy and the narrative of prosperity. First of all, the crisis challenged the Community in economic and political terms. It reacted by establishing monetary cooperation, which in turn had the potential to pro-voke conflict between stability-oriented countries such as Germany and the

---

62 R. Marjolin, *Le travail d'une vie: Mémoires (1911–1986)* (Paris, Robert Laffont, 1986).

63 'Note de Sicco Mansholt relative à l'organisation européenne de l'agriculture (La Haye, 6 novembre 1950)', www.cvce.eu/obj/note_de_sicco_mansholt_relative_a_l_organi sation_europeenne_de_l_agriculture_la_haye_6_novembre_1950-fr-113bee94-d234-421 b-84bd-2c3917faf412.html.

64 'Memorandum on Agricultural Reform in the European Economic Community (21 December 1968)', in *Bulletin of the European Communities* (Brussels, Office for Official Publications of the European Communities, 1969), www.cvce.eu/en/obj/m emorandum_on_agricultural_reform_in_the_european_economic_community_21_ december_1968-en-aeeba4d9-1971-4e34-ae1c-ae90fc32c6ee.html.

65 A.-C. L. Knudsen, *Farmers on Welfare: The Making of Europe's Common Agricultural Policy* (Ithaca, NY, Cornell University Press, 2009); G. Thiemeyer, *Vom 'Pool Vert' zur Europäischen Wirtschaftsgemeinschaft: Europäische Integration, Kalter Krieg und die Anfänge der Gemeinsamen Europäischen Agrarpolitik 1950–1957* (Munich, Oldenbourg, 1999).

Netherlands and countries that accepted high inflation rates like France, Italy and Belgium.[66]

Here, the argument of prosperity was again the lowest common denominator supporting an initiative such as the Economic and Monetary Union (EMU) that should – as the interim report of the Werner Plan put it – 'improve on a lasting basis the prosperity of the Community and strengthen the Community's contribution to international, economic and monetary equilibrium'.[67] In the crisis of the 1970s, the EMU could not be realised. Instead, an exchange rate system was established in the form of the European Monetary System. Beyond such initiatives, the EC was able to unfold positive effects, especially during the crisis. According to recent research, the slump would have been more severe without the EC.[68]

The crisis was a reason to take corrective action, and it promoted the transition from the negative integration of the first decades to the positive integration of the 1980s, which led to the establishment of new policy fields and institutions at the EU level, such as the SEA of 1987 with the implementation of the European Single Market economically and the European Political Cooperation politically. The terms 'Eurosclerosis' and 'dark ages' have already been questioned,[69] since the 'Europe of the second generation'[70] built the necessary bridge for a renewed *relance* (revival) in the 1980s. The 'shock of the global'[71] led to the realisation that Europe could play a role in a globalising world only as an economic actor, not on the basis of political or military strength. The European *relance* was driven by the concern to preserve Europe's prosperity:

> If Europe cannot increase its cohesion and recover its dynamism, the difficult economic battle in which our countries are engaged will be lost. Not only Europe's prosperity but also its freedom would then ultimately be at risk.

66 Warlouzet, 'The EEC/EU as an Evolving Compromise', p. 88.
67 'Interim Report to the Council and the Commission on the Establishment by Stages of Economic and Monetary Union (23 July 1970) – Final Version', www.cvce.eu/obj/int erim_report_to_the_council_and_the_commission_on_the_establishment_by_stage s_of_economic_and_monetary_union_23_july_1970_final_version-en-0a3c4c2d-6242-49df-bc03-3ec72e28621a.html.
68 I. Berend, 'A Restructured Economy: From the Oil Crisis to the Financial Crisis, 1973–2009', in D. Stone (ed.), *The Oxford Handbook of Postwar European History* (Oxford, Oxford University Press, 2012), pp. 406–22.
69 C. Hiepel (ed.), *Europe in a Gobalising World: Global Challenges and European Responses in the 'Long' 1970s* (Baden-Baden, Nomos, 2014).
70 F. Knipping and M. Schönwald (eds.), *Aufbruch zum Europa der zweiten Generation: Die europäische Einigung 1969–1984* (Trier, Wissenschaftlicher Verlag Trier, 2004).
71 N. Ferguson, C. S. Maier, E. Manela and D. J. Sargent (eds.), *The Shock of the Global: The 1970s in Perspective* (Cambridge, MA, Belknap Press, 2010).

This would mean the loss of an important factor in maintaining world equilibrium.[72]

As has so often been the case, the crisis proved to be a driving force. The Single Market project and the SEA provided both the economy and the narrative with a fresh impetus. Among the priority objectives was now a homogeneous internal economic area, which should link the fully integrated internal market envisaged in the Treaty of Rome with the objective of an EMU that had been called for ever since the Werner Plan of 1972. This should give positive stimulation to create 'more jobs, more prosperity and faster growth'.[73]

The EC Commission was well aware of the fact that the creation of an integrated Community economy would demand some adjustments from the member countries. But the goal of greater progress, prosperity and a higher level of employment was considered too important for the difficulties involved to slow down the project: 'The Commission is firmly convinced that the completion of the Internal Market will provide an indispensable base for increasing the prosperity of the Community as a whole.' The wealth gap was to be moderated by structural funds.[74]

The narrative of prosperity experienced a renaissance in anticipation of an unprecedented upswing. The scientific study on the 'costs of non-Europe' commissioned by Commission President Jacques Delors, the so-called Cecchini Report, calculated that the completion of the Single Market would release considerable economic growth forces in Europe, which would be reflected in an increase in the GNP of the EC by 5 per cent. Unemployment was to fall considerably and public budgets were to record significant additional revenues.[75] The Single Market, it

72 'French Government Memorandum on Revitalization of the Community (13 October 1981)', in *Bulletin of the European Communities. November 1981, No. 11* (Luxembourg, Office for Official Publications of the European Communities, 1981), www.cvce.eu/content/publication/2002/10/16/a8377c45-380f-4679-8d17-62d42f4734 d5/publishable_en.pdf.

73 'Report from the ad hoc Committee on Institutional Affairs (Brussels, 29–30 March 1985)', in *Bulletin of the European Communities. March 1985, No. 3* (Luxembourg, Office for Official Publications of the European Communities, 1985), www.cvce.eu/en/obj/report_from_the_ad_hoc_committee_on_institutional_affairs_brussels_29_30_march_1985-en-17c22a e3-480a-4637-ad28-e152d86105b7.html, pp. 102–10.

74 'Completing the Internal Market: White Paper from the Commission to the European Council (Milan 28–29 June 1985)', https://op.europa.eu/de/publication-detail/-/publi cation/4ff490f3-dbb6-4331-a2ea-a3ca59f974a8/language-en.

75 P. Cecchini, *The European Challenge: 1992: The Benefits of a Single Market* (Aldershot, Wildwood House, 1989).

was hoped in the Commission, would give a 'permanent boost to prosperity'.[76]

However, the Commission also picked up on opposing trends, and from the 1990s onwards efforts were made to overcome the traditional narrowing of the concept of prosperity to economic growth. The White Paper on 'Growth, Competitiveness, and Employment', approved by the European Council on 11 December 1993, for the first time brought the environment and quality of life into play. It noted 'an "over-use" of environmental and natural resources [as] a burden for future generations and a reduced capacity for long term economic prosperity'. Clean technology was regarded as a key and major element of the new development model, which would make it necessary to 'uncouple future economic prosperity from environmental pollution and even to make the ecolo-economic relationship a positive instead of a negative one'.[77] Then the Lisbon European Council in 2000 established the narrative of science and knowledge as an engine of economic growth and equaliser of social contrasts: 'The new knowledge-based society offers tremendous potential for reducing social exclusion, both by creating the economic conditions for greater prosperity through higher levels of growth and employment, and by opening up new ways of participating in society.'[78] This strategy also marked a move towards a more active interventionist policies: measures to combat social exclusion were to be based on coordination which combined national action plans and Commission initiatives for cooperation in this field, which had to be presented by June 2000.[79]

Another area that was linked to the narrative of prosperity was, of course, the enlargement of the Community. Difficult as it was to predict and measure the short- and medium-term impact of enlargement on the prosperity of the regions, both positive and negative effects could be possible. It was estimated that enlargement would be 'an investment in peace, stability and prosperity for the people of Europe. The overall economic gains from enlargement will be beneficial to Community policies.'[80] Similarly, the neighbourhood policy of the EC/EU should serve 'to establish an area of prosperity and good

76 European Commission, 'Europe 1992: The Overall Challenge' (1988), http://aei .pitt.edu/3813.
77 European Commission, 'Growth, Competitiveness, and Employment. The Challenges and Ways Forward into the 21st Century', COM (93) 700 final, Brussels (1993).
78 Council of the European Union, 'Lisbon European Council 23 and 24 March 2000: Presidency Conclusions' (2005), www.europarl.europa.eu/summits/lis1_en.htm.
79 Ibid.
80 'Agenda 2000. The Challenge of Enlargement', COM (97) 2000 final, vol. 11 (Brussels, Commission of the European Communities, 1997).

neighbourliness, founded on the values of the Union and characterised by close and peaceful relations based on cooperation' in the EU's neighbouring states.[81]

Conclusion

The narrative of prosperity has consistently played a central role in the internal perspective of the EC. The term prosperity appears in a wide variety of contexts to justify the respective agenda. The narrative of prosperity has never been questioned at all. Normally, the concept of prosperity has been linked to economic growth. The narrative in terms of economic growth and the apparent limitlessness of resources is more than just a purely post-war narrative. It first appeared even before the actual integration process and it did not become blunted for decades. The quantitative concept of growth was largely adhered to, even at a time when the Club of Rome's report on the limits to growth subjected this concept to criticism in a broad public debate. Only in the more recent past of the EC/EU have environmental protection, social cohesion or knowledge been included as parameters of prosperity.

In this respect, the use of the concept of prosperity is always a mirror of the times. As a shifting concept that can be loaded with different meanings, it has proved to be astonishingly persistent. In this context, the Maastricht Treaty does not mark a real turning point. The narrative of prosperity, although questioned and recently having to assert itself more strongly alongside other narratives, will nevertheless repeatedly be mentioned in official statements of the EU and constitutes an accepted source of legitimacy in surveys of citizens.[82]

European integration has always been a liberalisation project at its core, although not without ambivalences, since it was also about channelling and cushioning the effects of market structures. The strategy of seeking compromises and the instrument of package solutions were therefore constitutive features of European integration, while the ultimate goal of the entire process of European integration was not abandoned. Prosperity was thus a buzzword of the greatest openness possible and an expression of a lowest common denominator at the same time. Just as peace was a self-evident motive of European unification, prosperity was a desirable goal of EC/EU policy that

---

81 'Treaty on European Union (Maastricht, 7 February 1992) – Consolidated Version 2007', www.cvce.eu/obj/treaty_on_european_union_maastricht_7_february_1992_consolidated_version_2007-en-e92737d6-7557-4ea1-9ca5-123368a7fb88.html.

82 H. Kaelble, *Der verkannte Bürger: Eine andere Geschichte der europäischen Integration seit 1950* (Frankfurt am Main and New York, NY, Campus, 2019).

could hardly be questioned. This made the use of the term possible despite partly conflicting objectives being embodied in it.

The narrative of prosperity cannot be assigned to one field in terms of the theory of integration either. It was used by representatives of federalism, especially in the early phase of European integration, but also by apologists of functionalism such as Jean Monnet. Last but not least, prosperity as a motif for unification is also central for nation-state actors and governments, and the narrative of prosperity is also in the repertoire of intergovernmentalism. Increasing prosperity was an end in itself of European unification, but also instrumental in regard to securing peace on the European continent. The concept of free trade played a role throughout European integration, as did the idea that growth would also generate social justice. Nevertheless, it was also clear that distributive justice had to be established, as expressed in institutions such as the European Regional Development Fund. The EC/ EU is thus a hybrid entity which generates cohesion and legitimacy through meaningful grand narratives such as the narrative of prosperity.

Recommended Reading

Berend, I. T. *An Economic History of Twentieth-Century Europe: Economic Regimes from Laissez-Faire to Globalization* (Cambridge, Cambridge University Press, 2016).

Eichengreen, B. *The European Economy since 1945: Coordinated Capitalism and Beyond* (Princeton, NJ, Princeton University Press, 2007).

Eichengreen, B. and A. Boltho. 'The Economic Impact of European Integration', in S. Broadberry and K. H. O'Rourke (eds.), *The Cambridge Economic History of Modern Europe*, vol. II: *1870 to the Present* (Cambridge, Cambridge University Press, 2010), pp. 267–95.

Kaelble, H. *A Social History of Europe, 1945–2000: Recovery and Transformation after Two World Wars* (New York, NY and Oxford, Berghahn, 2013).

Patel, K. K. *Project Europe: A History* (Cambridge, Cambridge University Press, 2020).

Warlouzet, L. *Governing Europe in a Globalizing World: Neoliberalism and Its Alternatives Following the 1973 Oil Crisis* (London, Routledge, 2018).

2 0

Changing Europe's Economic History

IVAN T. BEREND

The European Economy before Integration

From the late eighteenth century, Europe started rising to the top of the world. The first industrial revolution in Britain gradually spread over the continent and the first important steps of a second industrial revolution, partly by Germany, were made after the middle of the nineteenth century. By 1870, Europe produced 45 per cent of the world's total income. Around the turn of the century, however, Europe lost its leading position, and produced only 27 per cent of the world's total income by 1913. The combined per capita gross domestic product (GDP) of the overseas West (the United States, Canada, Australia and New Zealand) was already more than 70 per cent higher than that of western Europe. The United States took over the leading role and neared one-and-a-half times (143 per cent) the income level of western Europe. The gap narrowed somewhat in the inter-war decades, but remained huge.[1]

Before the Second World War in 1938, nevertheless, the leading western European countries' per capita GDPs were under half (47 per cent) of the United States' level. Income differences within Europe also increased, and the south and east of the continent produced less than half what the west produced (Table 20.1).[2]

---

1 In this chapter I draw on my previous books connected to this topic: *Europe in Crisis: Bolt from the Blue?* (London, Routledge, 2013); *An Economic History of Twentieth-Century Europe: Economic Regimes from Laissez-Faire to Globalization*, 2nd ed. (Cambridge, Cambridge University Press, 2016); *The History of European Integration: A New Perspective* (London, Routledge, 2016); *Economic History of a Divided Europe: Four Diverse Regions in an Integrating Continent* (London, Routledge, 2020); *The Economics and Politics of European Integration: Populism, Nationalism and the History of the EU* (London, Routledge, 2021).
2 A. Maddison, *Monitoring the World Economy, 1820–1992* (Paris, Organisation for Economic Co-operation and Development, 1995), p. 212.

Table 20.1 Economic growth – per capita GDP, 1870–1938 (in 1990 US$)

	Western Europe		Southern Europe		Eastern Europe	
Year	Per capita GDP	Percentage	Per capita GDP	Percentage	Per capita GDP	Percentage
1870	2,110	57%	1,111	63%	1,030	66%
1913	3,704	100%	1,753	100%	1,557	100%
1938	4,719	127%	1,931	110%	2,083	142%

War Devastation

The most devastating war in history, afflicting the continent between 1939 and 1945, left Europe in ruins and its population decimated.[3] An estimated 70–85 million people, about 4 per cent of the world's population, were killed, and Europe's share was an overwhelming 40 million deaths, roughly 10 per cent of the continent's population, but in some countries, such as the Soviet Union, Poland and Yugoslavia, about 15 per cent.

A significant part of the land remained uncultivated in 1944–5. Millions suffered from starvation. In the winter of 1944–5, 20,000 Dutch people died because of the severe hunger crisis. In the spring of 1945, the media reported about widespread famine and a 'critical situation' in Germany, Austria, Italy, Spain, Poland and Portugal. Hunger still hit the continent in 1945–6. By 1945, the high death toll and sharply declined birth rate had caused a population deficit of about 110–120 million in Europe.

The physical destruction was also unbelievable. In the Soviet Union, 1,700 towns and 70,000 villages were devastated. Germany lost about 70 per cent of its housing. In the forty-nine largest cities, most of the downtown centres were eliminated and nearly 40 per cent of the dwelling units were destroyed or seriously damaged. Britain lost 30 per cent, while France, Belgium and the Netherlands lost 20 per cent of the countries' dwellings. Transportation was totally paralysed, half of the European railroad capacity was eliminated. Half of Europe's entire industrial infrastructure had also gone. The destruction

3 See T. Judt, *A History of Europe since 1945* (London, Penguin, 2005); T. Judt (with T. Snyder), *Thinking the Twentieth Century* (London, Penguin, 2012); M. Mazower, *Dark Continent: Europe's Twentieth Century* (London, Allen Lane, 1995), p. 8; K. Lowe, *Savage Continent: Europe in the Aftermath of World War II* (New York, NY, St Martin's Press, 2012); T. Zahra, *The Lost Children: Reconstructing Europe's Families after World War II* (Cambridge, MA, Harvard University Press, 2011).

Table 20.2 Per capita GDP (in 1990 US$): post-war years compared with 1938

Year	Austria	Denmark	France	Germany	Italy	Nether-lands	Great Britain	United States
1938	3,583	5,544	4,424	5,129	3,244	5,122	5,938	6,134
1945	1,736	4,874	2,549	4,326	1,880	2,621	6,737	11,722
1946	1,969	5,577	3,818	2,503	2,448	4,348	6,440	9,207
1947	2,181	5,806	4,099	2,763	2,856	4,357	6,306	8,896

was catastrophic in Poland, Yugoslavia and Hungary. High inflation hit several countries.

Austria's and Germany's per capita national income (Table 20.2) dropped to less than half the pre-war level; for France, Italy and the Netherlands per capita GDP was somewhat more than half of the pre-war level at the end of the Second World War.[4] Devastated Europe's economy in 1945 had dropped back sharply to 35 per cent of the American level. That was the starting point before European integration began.

Europe's tragedy was completed by the sharp division and mutual isolation of the western and eastern halves of the continent. The territory east of the River Elbe, including a part of Germany, was cut off and reorganised as part of the Stalinist Soviet Bloc. This situation lasted until almost half a century later, when the communist regimes of eastern Europe collapsed in 1989–91, after which Europe, or at least a large part of it, could overcome the division.

Post-war Reconstruction in Integrating Europe

Most of the countries in Europe had re-reached their pre-war (1938) economic levels between 1948 and 1950. Traditionally, scholars have conceived of the post-war reconstruction period as marking the years until countries' outputs and GDPs reached the levels of the last pre-war year (1938). This concept, however, has been convincingly challenged by the Hungarian economist Ferenc Jánossy, who has redefined the concept of the post-war reconstruction period, arguing that this period should be measured not by the time it took countries to reach the economic level of the last pre-war year, but instead by the time it took countries to reach the GDP they would probably have attained if the wartime devastation had not happened, and if economic

4 Maddison, *Monitoring the World Economy*, pp. 195, 197.

growth had continued in accordance with the average long-term growth trend of the previous 50–70 years.[5] Measuring in this way means the reconstruction period actually ended in Europe – meaning that the production output reached the levels it should have attained if there had been no war – only in the late 1960s. This puts the unique post-war growth rate, the 'economic miracle' of the 1950s and 1960s, in a different light and suggests that the very fast post-war growth until the oil-price crisis of 1973 was characterised basically by a *special reconstruction growth*.

Besides fast reconstruction growth, another decisive factor of the post-war economy was the extensive *economic development model* Europe adopted, which was based on technology imports from the United States and using local labour input. America was the monopolist of the new technology, represented by the rising atomic age (electricity was generated from nuclear energy for the first time in 1951); transistors, the key elements of the electronic revolution (from 1947); and the inception of the computer and electronics revolution (the Electronic Numerical Integrator and Computer appeared in 1946). The United States, being involved in the Cold War confrontation with the Soviet Bloc and having started to build a Western Bloc, including by military alliance in 1949, was willing to share some of the technological novelties with its European allies.

A third major factor, *European integration*, also contributed to the post-war reconstruction. The first important steps of integration of the Western economies came about as an effect of the American Marshall Plan (1948–51) that made cooperation and tariff decreases compulsory among recipient countries. The European Payment Union was also established, and this introduced the multinational payment system among the sixteen Marshall Plan recipient countries that all joined the Organisation for European Economic Co-operation. 'Without question', concluded John Provan, 'the Marshall Plan laid the foundation of European integration, easing trade between member nations, setting up the institutions that coordinated the economies of Europe into a single efficient unit. It served as a prelude to the creation of the United Europe that we have today.'[6]

From the Marshall Plan years (1948 and 1952), European integration gained momentum, which led to the establishment of the European Coal and Steel Community (1952) and then the European Economic Community (1958) that

---

5 F. Jánossy, *The End of the Economic Miracle: Appearance and Reality in Economic Development* (London, Routledge, 1971).
6 J. Provan, 'The Marshall Plan and Its Consequences', www.george-marshall-society.org /george-c-marshall/the-marshall-plan-and-its-consequences.

became the European Union (EU, 1993). The process of integration thus accompanied the post-war reconstruction decades, and has continued in an even more effective way up to now. Integration played an important part in European recovery and the economic boom that characterised the peaceful last three-quarters of a century in western Europe.

The post-war European economy, quite to the contrary of dark forecasts made by excellent economists such as Paul Samuelson and Gunnar Myrdal,[7] experienced high prosperity. As early as during the two-decade-long post-war reconstruction period, integration became one of the important factors of post-war economic developments. The first steps towards the common market were taken, and the trade of goods among the member countries dramatically increased in volume by a facor of 6.5 during the 1950s and 1960s. This expansion of trade was much bigger than had happened at any time before in the history of Europe. By 1973, some of the member countries had increased their exports by a factor of ten to fifteen compared with the pre-war years. The volume of exports of Italy, for example, which was only 127 per cent of the 1913 value in 1950, increased to 1,619 per cent of the 1913 value by 1973. In the case of the Netherlands, the equivalent figures were 171 and 1,632 per cent. Because of the elimination of economic nationalism, tariffs and other restrictions, trade of goods significantly increased, and both exports and imports among the member countries intensified significantly.

The *structure* of trade also started to undergo a radical transformation. Until the middle of the twentieth century, the traditional division of labour between industrial and agricultural countries still dominated. This started to change: imports of food and raw materials of the industrialised countries of western Europe declined from 33 to 18 per cent of their total trade by 1970. Industrial exports to non-industrialised, partly non-European countries dropped from 30 to 17 per cent. *The new, emerging trade structure was characterised by trade between industrial countries when they traded industrial products and parts of products among themselves.* Several industrial products were produced in cooperation by several of the member countries: different countries produced various parts from which industrial products were assembled. Two of the most well-known instances of cooperation that reflectcd the importance of integration were the French–British Concord airplane programme, which was started in the late 1960s and led to commercial use in 1976, and the French–German Agreement in 1969 about the Airbus

---

7 P. Samuelson, 'Full Employment after the War', in S. E. Harris (ed.), *Postwar Economic Problems* (New York, NY, McGraw-Hill, 1943); G. Myrdal, *Warnung vor Friedensoptimismus* (Zurich, Europa Verlag, 1945).

Programme that soon included four other European countries too and produced airplanes in sixteen places. This new type of division of labour created the possibility of production at scale that helped to increase productivity and strongly contributed to the economic boom. The Geneva Declaration of 1950 led to the building of a connected western European network of roads. By 1975, more than one-third of the 64,000-kilometre-long system that connected the entire continent consisted of such roads.[8]

The western European energy systems were also revolutionised. In France, while energy consumption increased by 250 per cent between 1950 and 1970, the share of coal in this dropped from 74 to 17 per cent. Germany became the real engine of modernisation. The modern industrial sectors – chemical, electrical and electronic, precision-engineering, car and business machinery – increased their contribution to industrial value added from 26 to 42 per cent.

The citizens' living standards reached new heights. In 1950, a German or French citizen spent 43–45 per cent of their income on food and basics; by 1971, this share had dropped to 27 per cent. In 1950, only 20 per cent of French households owned a car; by 1972, already 60 per cent did. In the early 1970s, people spent 44 per cent of their income on health, entertainment or culture and for their home, nearly twice as much as in 1950.

A level of *consumerism* that had hitherto never existed flooded western Europe. Private consumption increased by 4–5 per cent per year in the 1970s. A new, modern consumption infrastructure, the supermarkets and retail chains, emerged.[9] Post-war German journalism characterised the rising living standards by speaking of five waves of elevated consumption: first the *Fressewelle* (gobbling wave), followed by the *Kleidungswelle* (clothing wave), *Einrichtungswelle* (wave of household rearrangement) and *Autowelle* (car wave), culminating in the *Reisewelle* (wave of travel). Optimism filled the air.

The member countries of the European Community increased their economic growth by a factor of three or four compared with the inter-war decades. Several of the western European countries experienced a great economic and consumption boom, and the decades until the late 1960s became the years of 'economic miracles', the German *Wirtschaftswunder*, the French *Trente Glorieuses* and the Italian *miracolo economico*.

---

8 'International E Road Network', www.roadtraffic-technology.com/projects/inter national-e-road-network.
9 V. De Grazia, 'Changing Consumption Regimes in Europe, 1930–1970', in S. Strasser, C. McGovern and M. Judt (eds.), *Getting and Spending: European and American Consumer Societies in the Twentieth Century* (Cambridge, Cambridge University Press, 1998), pp. 59–84, 59, 74, 79.

Globalisation and the European Economy

At the time when European reconstruction had been accomplished in the late 1960s, the world economy started changing in a significant way. The globalisation that gradually started after the war with a return to the free trade regime gradually progressed, with western European participation, from the late 1960s onwards. After three decades of dominant economic nationalism throughout the world, the capitalist world economic system, led by post-war America, gradually changed.

Multinational companies dominated the world market during the last third of the twentieth century.[10] In 1970, there were about 7,000 multinationals in the world; by 2006, there were 80,000. During this third of a century, about 900,000 subsidiaries and affiliates were established abroad, and the number of their employees increased by a factor of 3.5. In the early twenty-first century, they traded three-quarters of the world's manufactured products.

Globalisation was strongly assisted by the *technological-communication revolution* around the turn of the millennium. Revolutionised technology made global business possible partly by virtue of sharply decreased transportation and communication costs and partly by the invention of container transportation that made global production possible.[11] Commercial networks and enterprises were connected and documents, huge amounts of data, production plans and exact operational commands could be transmitted at an ever-increasing speed using the widely available modern Internet.[12]

Globalisation was combined with *neoliberal policy*, which had been prophesied by Friedrich Hayek and Milton Friedman, an ideology and practice of deregulation and uncontrolled market when society was subordinated to the market.[13] The American Presidents Richard Nixon and Ronald Reagan and the British Prime Minister Margaret Thatcher pioneered its practice. The United States closed the fixed exchange rate era of Bretton Woods in 1971, then, 3 years later abolished capital controls. Britain eliminated the 40-year-old capital control system in 1979. The New York Stock Exchange was deregulated in 1975 and a competitive deregulation race followed. By 1988,

10 K. Ohmae, *Beyond National Borders: Reflections to Japan and the World* (Homewood, Dow Jones-Irwin, 1987), pp. 35–9.
11 J. Levine, 'The History of the Shipping Container' (2016), www.freightos.com/the-history-of-the-shipping-container.
12 A. Wolinsky, *The History of the Internet and the World Wide Web* (Berkeley Heights, NJ, Enslow, 2000).
13 K. Polanyi, *The Great Transformation: The Political and Economic Origins of Our Time* (Boston, MA, Beacon Press, 2001 [1944]).

virtually the entire European Community had copied this move. The Western world turned to a self-regulated market system and the so-called Washington consensus made this system mandatory as a condition for International Monetary Fund (IMF) assistance.[14]

Some scholars, among them Quinn Slobodian, argue that the EU is following suit by implementing neoliberal policy,[15] and Perry Anderson goes as far as maintaining that

> The EU is now so path-dependent as a neoliberal construction that reform of it is no longer seriously conceivable. It would have to be undone before anything better could be built, either by breaking out of the current EU, or by reconstructing Europe on another foundation, committing Maastricht to the flames.[16]

This argumentation was basically wrong, since the EU applied neoliberal globalisation policy in a moderate way. Europe followed market economics, but not social deregulation. A Brookings Institution analysis of the topic in 2016 rightly stated: 'Deregulation of major industries in the United States began in the 1970s and spread to the United Kingdom and, to a *lesser* extent, to the European continent.'[17] Moreover, the EU very soon turned to *regionalisation* against globalisation, and after the end of the 2008 economic crisis, especially after 2016, when America returned to deregulation policy and in December 2017, President Trump announced the withdrawal of 1,579 regulations[18] – the EU did not follow suit.

A certain amount of distancing from de-regulated global capitalism, although Europe to a certain extent participated in it, characterised the EU, because globalisation also created an existential danger for Europe. Post-war reconstruction with American assistance and technology, although it helped to bring about a fast recovery, made Europe a follower of the United States. Western Europe remained behind the technological leaders. From the 1970s

---

14 See E. Helleiner, *States and the Reemergence of Global Finance: From Bretton Woods to the 1990s* (Ithaca, NY, Cornell University Press, 1994), pp. 168–70; J. Stiglitz, *Globalization and Its Discontents* (New York, NY, W. W. Norton, 2002), pp. 16, 17, 34, 53, 65.

15 Q. Slobodian, *Globalists: The End of Empire and the Birth of Neoliberalism* (Cambridge, MA, Harvard University Press, 2018).

16 P. Anderson, 'Why the System Will Still Win', *Le Monde Diplomatique*, 1 March 2017, https://mondediplo.com/2017/03/02brexit.

17 R. W. Crandall, 'Extending Deregulation: Make the U.S. Economy More Efficient', www.brookings.edu/wp-content/uploads/2016/06/pb_deregulation_crandall.pdf.

18 C. McNicholas, H Shierholz and M. von Wilpert, 'Workers' Health, Safety, and Pay Are among the Casualties of Trump's War on Regulations: A Deregulation Year in Review', Economic Policy Institute (2018), www.epi.org/publication/deregulation-year-in-review.

onwards, Europe had to face increasing competition partly from the United States and Japan, but also from the rising low-wage 'Small Asian Tigers'. The American International Business Machines Corporation established subsidiaries in Britain, Germany and France, and installed 75 per cent of the computers in the entire West. American companies had a 64 per cent share in the western European memory chip and microprocessor market, thereby dominating in the determinant parts of the most modern high-tech sector, the data-processing, telecoms, automation and consumer electronics industries. Western Europe's share of high-tech production declined from 16 to 10 per cent.[19] Japanese companies also opened subsidiaries in Britain, France, Germany and Portugal. In the mid 1980s the European Community's share in the European semiconductor market was only 9 per cent, compared with 56 per cent for American companies and 33 per cent for Japanese companies.

The labour-intensive textile, clothing and leather production markets of Europe were invaded by the 'Small Asian Tigers' and somewhat later China. A European Commission Working Document revealed that, while workers in these sectors employed within the Community earned on average $12,000 - per year, those in China were paid only $600. It was hard to compete with this kind of competition. The situation was similar in the European steel industry, which dismissed 100,000 employees in the Community. The European Commission reported in 1986 that the newly industrialising countries endanger 'the future of industry in the Community [because] these newly industrialized countries had been specializing in branches of industry similar to the Community'.[20]

The European business community 'found itself inadequately equipped to cope with the high technology threat from the US and Japan and the low-end technology threat from the Newly Industrializing Countries'.[21] After its miraculous post-war reconstruction and modernisation, western Europe suddenly found itself far behind. Europe lost ground to international competition in technology-intensive products. European companies held only a 9 per cent share of the world market in computer and data-processing

---

19 W. Sandholtz, *High-Tech Europe: The Politics of International Cooperation* (Berkeley, CA, University of California Press, 1992), p. 115.

20 Archive of European Integration, 'Improving Competitiveness and Industrial Structure in the Community', Commission Communication to the Council, COM (86) 40 final, 25 February 1986, p. 7.

21 W. Hulsink, 'From State Monopolies to Euro-Nationals and Global Alliances: The Case of the European Telecommunications Sector', in J. J. J. Dijk and J. P. M. Groenewegen (eds.), *Changing Business Systems in Europe: An Institutional Approach* (Brussels: VUB Press, 1994), p. 464.

products, 10 per cent in software, 13 per cent in satellites and launchers, and 29 per cent in data-transmission services.[22]

Between 1965 and 1984, the United States and Japan increased their combined share of world trade in the products of research and development (R&D)-intensive branches of industry from more than 30 per cent to more than 45 per cent, while the share of France, Germany and Britain combined decreased from 36 to 31 per cent.[23] Europe lost ground in the production of high-tech products, and the European Community's share dropped from 88 to 75 per cent of the average output of the Organisation for Economic Cooperation and Development (OECD) countries between 1970 and 1985.[24]

The European Community was shocked. In 1973, the Commission accepted an Action Programme that stated: 'The worsening positions of the European economy vis-à-vis Japan and the United States and the Third World subsequently saw a widespread acceptance by the European government agencies of the need to promote a more effectual restructuring of European industry.'[25] These dangers became the central topic of Jean-Jacques Servan-Schreiber's influential 1967 book Le défi américain (The American Challenge), followed by his Le défi mondial (The World-Wide Challenge) in 1980. He described the huge American subsidiary network in Europe as the second-largest industrial force of the world, second only to American industry in America, and spoke about European 'inferiority'. That was a dramatic warning and an influential cry for action.[26]

After the reconstruction period, economic success could no longer be built on the extensive development model, based on importation of American technology that tremendously helped reconstruction, but subordinated Europe to follower status. Further development had to be based on a change of strategy, to the intensive development model from the 1970s and 1980s onwards, in which, instead of American technology imports, Europe's own competitive research and inventions were employed to increase productivity.

22 OECD, Structural Adjustment and Economic Performance (Paris, OECD, 1987), p. 213.
23 F. Duchêne and G. Shepherd (eds.), Managing Industrial Change in Western Europe (London, Pinter, 1987), p. 36.
24 OECD, Structural Adjustment, pp. 214, 254.
25 L. Krieger Mytelka and M. Delapierre, 'The Alliance Strategies of European Firms in the Information Technology Industry and the Role of ESPIRIT', in J. H. Dunning and P. Robson (eds.), Multinationals and European Community (Oxford, Basil Blackwell, 1988), pp. 7, 113.
26 J.-J. Servan-Schreiber, Le défi américain (Paris, Denoël, 1967); J.-J. Servan-Schreiber, Le Défi mondial (Paris, Fayard, 1980). See also V. Schneider, 'Organized Interests in the European Telecommunication Sector', in J. Greenwood, J. R. Grote and K. Ronit (eds.), Organized Interest and the European Community (London, Sage, 1992), p. 50.

Regionalisation: Europe's Answer to Globalisation

European corporations pushed for further integration after the stagnation of the 1960s to the mid 1980s. The chief executives of twelve top European multinationals sent a letter to Étienne Davignon, Vice-President of the European Commission, stating that Europe's market position was miserable and its national programmes were hopeless, and 'unless a cooperative industrial programme of sufficient magnitude can be mounted, more if not all of the current Information Technology industry could disappear in a few years' time'.[27] Furthermore, 'A dissatisfaction with the national route of European policy-making provided incentives for European big business to organize politically at the European level.'[28]

In late 1981, at the invitation of Davignon, the directors of the twelve largest information technology companies met and formed the European Roundtable of Industrialists to help the Commission work out a programme.[29] In the 1980s, Wisse Dekker of Philips and Jacques Solvay of the Belgian Solvay Corporation 'were vigorously arguing for unification of the European Community's fragmented markets'. Philips published a booklet, stating in it: 'The only option left for the Community is to achieve the goals laid down in the Treaty of Rome. Only in this way can industry compete globally, by the exploiting of economies of scale, for what will then be the biggest home market in the world.'[30]

In October 1983, the Union des confédérations de l'industrie et des employeurs d'Europe (Union of Industrial and Employers' Confederations of Europe), the overarching organisation of European industry, made a declaration urging a 'fresh start for Europe'. In 1989, outlining a scenario for 1992, European multinationals 'have taken up the banner [. . .] collaborating with the Commission and exerting substantial influence [. . .] bypassed national governmental processes and shaped the agenda [for further integration] that compelled attention and action'.[31]

Furthermore, 'In 1983 [. . .] the European Roundtable of Industrialists drew up a list of proposals that became the basis for the Single European

27 Sandholtz, *High-Tech Europe*, p. 174.
28 M. Green Cowles, 'The Changing Architecture of Big Business', in J. Greenwood and M. Aspinwall (eds.), *Collective Action in the European Union: Interests and the New Politics of Associability* (London, Routledge, 1998), p. 112.
29 Ibid., pp. 163–4, 166.
30 Philips S.A. (Brussels), 'Europe 1990', quoted in W. Sandholtz and J. Zysman, '1992: Recasting the European Bargain', *World Politics* 42, no. 1 (1989): 95–128, 117.
31 Sandholtz and Zysman, '1992: Recasting the European Bargain', 116.

Act.'[32] Big corporations urged and even prepared major further steps of integration, to create a really borderless, integrated single market for European business. The newly appointed president of the Commission, Jacques Delors, after only 1 year in office, using all the information and suggestions, presented a plan of the required further integration in the form of the Single European Act in February 1986. The plan was to complete the internal market of the Community by eliminating borders and making possible the free movement of goods, services, capital and persons by the end of 1992.

European multinational corporations had largely pulled their business out from the endangered and uncertain global market. Newly independent countries, fighting for economic independence, turned against foreign companies, and even nationalised some of them. The return from investment in Third World countries dropped from more than 30 to 2.5 per cent during the 1980s.[33] The Dutch–British Unilever, one of the first multinationals in the world, sold more than seventy of its factories and subsidiaries outside Europe and turned towards the European market. Germany drastically decreased its investments outside Europe (from 40 to 17 per cent) and redirected them to European countries.[34] From the 1970s onwards, 'there was a general exodus from developing countries'[35] and the focus turned to Europe. The European economy gradually became 'Europeanised'. Via a thoroughly integrated European market with a streamlined standard of products and legal and regulatory system, the EU gradually regained its competitiveness and defended itself against competition from outside.

The realisation of this goal required tremendous preparations. A common market has to have common standards in order for the products to be saleable in all member countries of the Community. This was not only a tremendous amount of work for tens of thousands of products, but also required specialist knowledge in each of the manufacturing branches. The Commission had to work 'in close conjunction with [. . .]

32 A. Harmes, *The Return of the State: Protestors, Power-Brokers and the New Global Compromise* (Vancouver, Douglas and McIntyre, 2004), p. 126.
33 D. C. Thomas, *Theory and Practice of Third World Solidarity* (Westport, CT, Praeger, 2001), p. 147.
34 G. Jones and H. G. Schröter, *The Rise of Multinationals in Continental Europe* (Aldershot, Edward Elgar, 1993), p. 135.
35 G. Jones, 'Multinational Strategies and Developing Countries in Historical Perspective', Working Paper 10-076, Harvard Business School (2010), https://hbswk.hbs.edu/item/multinational-strategies-and-developing-countries-in-historical-perspective, pp. 16–17.

industry'.[36] 'We cannot do our work without information from interest groups [. . .] Sometimes it is very tempting to copy and paste their amendments.'[37] The Single Market laws on financial services were worked out in close cooperation with 'the European Banking Federation, the European Stock Exchange Federation [and] various insurance federations'.[38] The all-European automobile standards were defined in close collaboration with the Committee of Common Market Automobile Constructors. A several-year-long legal and regulatory effort concluded in 1992 with the creation of a set of unified rules, standards and a harmonised legal system, in order to eliminate obstacles to the creation of a Single Market with free movement of capital, goods, services and people.

Restrictions of capital movements among countries ended. The goal was 'the establishment of a Community-wide integrated financial system' with standardised rules and laws.[39] As part of this important change, the European Community introduced the Single Banking Licence or Single Passport in 1989. If a bank was licensed in one member country of the Community, it had the right to do business, including establishing branches and subsidiaries, in all other member countries. This principle became law in the Community by means of the creation of a single financial legislation and unified regulation. The First and Second Banking Directives were definitive steps towards a unified European financial market. Cross-border mergers rapidly progressed. By 2010, 166 French banks were operating under the European Passport. The merger process has advanced rapidly, with several cross-border acquisitions since the late 1980s. A few western European countries, namely France, Germany, Britain, Switzerland and the Netherlands, owned about half of all European banking assets. The leading European banking groups also became all-European by ownership. A huge part of their assets was owned by other countries' investors: more than half of the assets of Deutsche Bank were in foreign hands; the corresponding proportions were 64 per cent for the Spanish Santander, 62 per cent for the Italian

---

36 Archive of European Integration, 'Communication' (1996), p. 3; Archive of European Integration, 'The Single Market' (1996), p. 10.
37 Archive of European Integration, M. Kluger Rasmussen, 'Lobbying the European Parliament: A Necessary Evil', CEPS Policy Brief No. 242, May 2011.
38 R. Hull, 'Lobbying Brussels. A View from Within', in S. Mazey and J. Richardson, (eds.), *Lobbying in the European Community* (Oxford, Oxford University Press, 1993).
39 Archive of European Integration, Communication from the Commission to the Coucil, 'Programme for the Liberalization of Capital Movements in the Community', COM (86) 292 final 23 May 1986, pp. 8, 11.

UniCredito, 41 per cent for BNP Paribas and 29 per cent for Société Générale. Each of these banks also has at least 100 majority-owned subsidiaries and more than half have over 500 subsidiaries. Sixteen major banks held at least 25 per cent of their assets in other EU countries. Deutsche Bank, in 2012, had €2 trillion assets and 3,000 branches throughout Europe, with 100,000 employees, and gained 67 per cent of its revenue from the 'European home market'.[40] The French BNP Paribas bank with its almost €2 trillion assets and 200,000 employees (145,000 in Europe) also became a pan-European bank, with 31 per cent of its business concentrated in France, but 46 per cent in other European countries.[41]

Similarly to the Europeanised banking industry, manufacturing also became more all-European. The member countries of the Community invested in each other. In 1970, their stock of foreign direct investment was $5,128, but by 2007 it had increased to $857,118. Between 1998 and 2006 more than 43,000 mergers, two-thirds of the world's company mergers, happened in the European Community. Around the end of the first decade of the twenty-first century it was registered that 'the largest European corporations, have made most of their investments in the past twenty years within Europe'.[42]

European industry did indeed start to be 'Europeanised'. As the EU's Statistical Office (Eurostat) reported in 2012, 72 per cent of total inward foreign direct investments during the 1990s were intra-EU flows.[43] Joint production became widespread with the building up of all-European *value chains*. As a study of the European Central Bank stated in 2001, foreign value added in corporate output 'was to a major extent sourced from other euro area countries'. In intra-EU trade, more than a third (36 per cent) of imports was parts and components 'imported' from the value chain of other member countries in 1997.

In 2010, Volkswagen Group had sixty-one production plants and factories in fifteen European countries. The Italian FIAT company had fifty units in France, twenty-six in Britain, thirty in Germany, seventeen in Spain and ten in Poland. Of the company's seventy-seven research centres, fifty-two were operating in Europe. The Airbus programme has roughly 180 locations and 12,000 direct

---

40 A. M. Rugman and S. Collinson, 'Multinational Empires in the New Europe: Are They Really Global?' (2005), https://ideas.repec.org/p/iuk/wpaper/2005-12.html.
41 BNP Paribas, https://group.bnpparibas/uploads/file/ddr2017_bnp_paribas_gb.pdf, p. 4.
42 N. Fligstein, *Euroclash: The EU, European Identity, and the Future of Europe* (Oxford, Oxford University Press, 2008), p. 62.
43 See https://ec.europa.eu/eurostat/web/lucas/data/primary-data/2012.

suppliers from more than 20 countries.[44] The European Central Bank's study concluded:

> Internationalization of production and, more specifically, a higher degree of vertical integration into global value chains provided in recent years critical stimulus to the European economy. First, it fostered an industrial restructuring both across the European economies [. . .] which allowed European firms to vertically specialize in those activities in which they have a comparative advantage.[45]

'Europeanisation' also characterised the retail trade. Giant French, German, Dutch and other retail companies built huge networks within the EU. Between 1990 and 2000s, the French Carrefour supermarket chain covered Greece, Italy, Poland, Portugal, Belgium, Romania, Slovakia, Spain and the Czech Republic. Today, it has 6,132 stores in 29 countries. It is number one in Spain, Portugal and Greece and the second-largest chain in Italy. The German Metro Group also established a huge all-European network, employing 250,000 people in 32 countries. All in all, three-quarters of food retailing in the EU is controlled by three countries' giant retailers.[46]

The Bruegel Policy Brief noted that the 100 largest European companies' market became 'increasingly Europe as a whole rather than any particular country within it', with 65 per cent of their revenue coming from Europe.'[47]

The European Community also contributed to EU-wide inventions and innovations by assisting R&D, the crucial base for the intensive development model. The European Strategic Programme for Research and Development (ESPRIT) was launched in 1985 with 750 million European Currency Units (ECUs; the forerunner of, and basically equivalent to, the euro that was introduced a few years later). Further programmes such as the Research and

---

44 D. Slotnick, 'Airbus Is One of the Most Powerful Companies in Aviation. Here's a Closer Look at Its Rise from Upstart to Industry Titan' (2020), www.businessinsider.in/slide shows/miscellaneous/airbus-is-one-of-the-most-powerful-companies-in-aviation-heres-a-closer-look-at-its-rise-from-upstart-to-industry-titan-/slidelist/69588909.cms. See also https://www.airbus.com/company/history.html.

45 F. di Mauro, H. Plumper and R. Stehrer, 'Global Value Chains: A Case for Europe to Cheer Up' (2013), www.ecb.europa.eu/home/pdf/research/compnet/policy_brief_3_global_value_chains.pdf?fcccc5651bee912e1698e1019c8b3969; Groningen Growth and Development Centre, World Input Output Database, www.rug.nl/ggdc/value chain/wiod, July 1996, pp. 2, 5, 7, 16, 93.

46 Rugman and Collinson, 'Multinational Empires', p. 6; Metro Group, www .companieshistory.com/metro-group; Archive of European Integration, 'Green Paper on Vertical Restraints in EC Competition Policy', COM (96) 721 final, 22 January 1997.

47 Archive of European Integration, Bruegel Policy Brief, 'Farewell National Champion', 2006/04.4.

Technology Development Programme followed in 1987. From 1987 to 1991, 5.4 billion ECUs were invested in this programme, but the investment was increased to 12.3 billion ECUs by 1994–8. The EU initiative under ESPRIT, as a new development, established close cooperation among leading corporations such as Siemens, Allgemeine Elektricitäts-Gesellschaft, Bull, Thomson, Olivetti, Philips and six other companies, which received 70 per cent of the financing in the first stage of the programme. Several European 'showpieces' such as the Airbus programme also profited from it, and the R&D activity gained momentum.[48] In one-and-a-half decades, employment in the R&D sector in Europe increased by 34 per cent.

The free movement of people made possible by the Schengen Agreement led to the gradual abolition of checks at common borders. Its implementation started in 1995, initially involving seven EU states, but gradually nearly all member countries and even a few non-EU states joined. Any person from these countries may cross internal borders without any border checks, has the right to live and work permanently in other member countries and has an equal right to take jobs. About 20 million people from less developed member countries in the eastern half of the Union are working in western member countries, thereby helping to solve the labour shortage there.

The introduction of the single currency was also realised in three steps at the turn of the millennium. In 2002 the euro currency was physically introduced in the eleven countries which joined the monetary union. The European Central Bank, a federal monetary institute, was also established, and the member countries' national banks became parts of it. The Central Bank became a note-issuing institution. It also carries out operations on the open market, supports operations in the foreign exchange market, buys bonds of crisis-hit member countries and pumps money into the EU economy in critical crisis situations, creates a reserve, supervises banks and participates in policy-making. The introduction of the euro eliminated currency risks and provided a further push for integration and mergers in the European banking sector. Cross-border financial activities increased by 40 per cent in the eurozone. In 2008 the Single European Payment Area was also introduced, which established uniformity of conditions for

48 R. Béteille, 'Airbus or the Reconstruction of European Civil Aeronautics', in W. M. Leary (ed.), *From Airships to Airbus: The History of Civil and Commercial Aviation*, vol. 1: *Infrastructure and Environment* (Washington, DC, Smithsonian Institute Press, 1995); M. Kipping, 'European Industrial Policy in a Competitive Global Economy', in S. Stravridis, E. Mossialos, R. Morgan and H. Machin (eds.), *New Challenges to the European Union: Policies and Policy-Making* (Aldershot, Dartmouth, 1997), pp. 492–5, 497.

payments.[49] The common currency and the European Central Bank became the most important supranational institutions, and the eurozone of nineteen countries is the most integrated part of the EU.

The Economic Community as the 'Europeanisation' of banking, manufacturing and the service sectors reflected the turn towards *regionalisation* of the Community's economy, an efficient defence against globalisation. The market of nearly half-a-billion people offered a safe haven against global competition: 'Regionalism [...] in terms of political order constitutes a voluntary evolution of a group of formerly sovereign national, political units into a supranational security community, where sovereignty is pooled for the best of all.'[50] The member countries signed the Treaty on the European Union, as the culmination of European economic integration, on 7 February 1992.[51]

Modernised Structure, 'Europeanised' Industry and Services

The European economy, consequently, rose to a higher level. A radical structural modernisation started. Part of it was a dramatic change in *agriculture*. Agricultural employment declined in western Europe from 20–25 per cent in 1950 to 10 per cent by the 1970s. Parallel with it, virtually the entirety of farm production was mechanised. Another factor in the 'industrialising' of agriculture was a breakthrough in using much more artificial fertiliser after the war: by the mid 1970s, its usage was already 270–300 kg per hectare, and in some key countries 400–500 kg. Agricultural productivity increased by 2.5 per cent per year in western Europe and by 3 per cent per year in the Mediterranean countries. The EU became self-sufficient in food. Meanwhile, the share of the agricultural sector in the total economy dramatically decreased from 25–30 to 1–3 per cent in the various countries, and on average 1.5 per cent.

49 N. B. Murphy, E. P. M. Gardener, P. Molyneux and J. Williams, 'European Union Financial Developments: The Single Market, the Single Currency and Banking', www .researchgate.net/publication/265200020_European_Union_Financial_Development s_European_Union_Financial_Developments_The_Single_Market_the_Single_Curr ency_and_Banking; E. Grossman, 'Europeanization as an Interactive Process: German Public Banks Meet EU State Aid Policy', *Journal of Common Market Studies* 44, no. 2 (2006): 325–48.

50 B. Hettne, 'Globalism, the New Regionalism and East Asia', in T. Tanaka and T. Inoguchi (eds.), *Globalism and Regionalism* (United Nations University Press, 1996), https://archive.unu.edu/unupress/globalism.html#Globalization.

51 'Treaty on European Union', https://eur-lex.europa.eu/legal-content/EN/TXT/PD F/?uri=OJ:C:1992:191:FULL&from=EN; European Central Bank, 'Five Things You Need to Know about the Maastricht Treaty', www.ecb.europa.eu/ecb/educational/ explainers/tell-me-more/html/25_years_maastricht.en.html.

De-industrialisation and the service revolution radically changed the share of the *industrial sector* in the total economy as well. Manufacturing's share in some countries dropped from more than 40 to 11–12 per cent, but in others it fell only to 28–30 per cent, altogether on average a 23.8 per cent share in producing the EU's GDP. Meanwhile, the EU's industrial production dramatically increased. In 1950, the capital stock of Germany, France, Britain and the Netherlands combined amounted to only 40 per cent of the American level. By 1991, it surpassed the US level – which had itself increased nearly fourfold – by 8 per cent.[52] European industry became a major international player.

This happened partly because of a 'cross-merger mania'. Several major companies merged with competitors from other member countries. Between 1990 and 2011, nearly 5,000 mergers and acquisition happened, which built up a Europe-wide network of value chains.[53]

Some industries were especially 'Europeanised'. The defence and car industries played pioneering roles in joint production with factories in other member countries. 'European collaboration in space technology began after purely national space programs proved untenable. The sheer scale of national investments required to join the space race led national policy-makers to return to cooperation.'[54]

The car industry employs nearly 14 million people,[55] and the EU became the world's leading automotive manufacturing region, producing 34 per cent of the world's car production. The Volkswagen empire is an outstanding example of 'Europeanisation'. It bought the Spanish SEAT (in 1986), the Czech Škoda (in 1991 and 1995) and the Italian Lamborghini and Bugatti (in 1998). After the collapse of communism, Volkswagen built several major factories in Slovakia, which acquired the nickname of 'Volkswagen land', Hungary, Poland, Bosnia, Ukraine and Russia. In 2010, it had sixty-one production plants and factories in fifteen European countries. The group employs nearly 370,000 people and produces over 26,600 cars daily. Meanwhile, the ownership of the company – 53 per cent of the shares – has also become internationalised.[56]

---

52 A. Maddison, *Explaining the Economic Performance of Nations: Essays in Time and Space* (Aldershot, Edward Elgar, 1995), pp. 144–9, 154–5, 185–6.
53 'The EU Merger Regulation', https://my.slaughterandmay.com/insights/client-publications/the-eu-merger-regulation, p. 38.
54 Sandholtz, *High-Tech Europe*, pp.104–5.
55 G. Verheugen, 'CARS 21 High Level Group for a Competitive EU Car Industry' (2005), https://ec.europa.eu/commission/presscorner/detail/en/SPEECH_05_11.
56 *Automotive Manufacturing Solution* 15, no. 3 (2014): 11; *Automotive News Europe* 10, no. 5 (2005): 24; E. Grunow-Oswald, *Die Internationalisierung eines Konzerns: Daimler-Benz 1890–1997* (Vaihingen an der Enz, Nieman und Feldenkirchen, 2006), pp. 178, 284, 286, 346, 358–9, 365–7, 373, 376.

The aerospace industry employs over 4 million people; the greatest success was achieved by the Airbus programme, a cooperation between France and Germany that started in 1969, but which soon involved Britain, Spain and other countries. The company has roughly 180 sites and 12,000 direct suppliers from more than 20 countries. About 55,000 people work for Airbus in 16 places in 4 EU countries. Airbus conquered the first place in the world in the aerospace industry, with a market share of 52 per cent in 1998, in competition with the previously dominant American firm Boeing.[57] The European car, aerospace and defence industries, as well as the chemical industry – amounting to 27 per cent of the world's total production – became major players in the world economy.

As in modern economies in general, *banking and services* became dominant in the EU's economy, with a share in the production of the EU's GDP of 74.7 per cent, but in several countries 78 or 79 per cent.[58] The EU's economic structure became equal to that of the best developed economies.[59] As reported by the Bruegel Institute, 'There has been remarkable advance in financial integration in the EU [...] European financial markets today are more integrated than product markets.'[60] 'Europeanisation' also characterised other branches of the service industries, including the retail trade.[61]

Catching Up and Better Life of the Less Developed

During the great boom period, Europe became more than five times richer. Meanwhile, the less developed southern and eastern member countries made progress in catching up with the most developed western part of the EU. In 1950, the average per capita GDP of the Mediterranean countries and Ireland was only 51.2 per cent of the average GDP level of the northwestern European countries, but, after joining the EU, they had already achieved 75 per cent of that level by 2019. The central European and Baltic countries, when communism collapsed, had an average per capita GDP level only 23 per cent of that of the northwestern countries, but, after joining the EU

---

57 Slotnick, 'Airbus Is One of the Most Powerful Companies in Aviation'.
58 *The Economist, Pocket World in Figures 2017* (London, Profile Books, 2016).
59 G. Ballor, 'Enterprise and Integration: Big Business and the Making of the Single European Market' (Ph.D. dissertation, UCLA, 2018); G. Ballor, *Enterprise and Integration: Big Business and the Making of the Single European Market* (Cambridge, Cambridge University Press, 2024).
60 Archive of European Integration, J. Pisani-Ferry, 'Financial Integration and European Priorities', Bruegel Third Party Papers (2006), pp. 1–2.
61 Rugman and Collinson, 'Multinational Empires', p. 6; Metro Group, www .metrogroup.de/en/company/history; Archive of European Integration, 'Green Paper on Vertical Restraints'.

in the 2000s, they had already attained 36.4 per cent of that level in 2019. The catching-up process was initiated by investments from the more developed member countries, which established the previously lacking modern high- and semi-high-tech branches, and the EU provided significant financial assistance for less developed areas, amounting to 3–4 per cent of the less developed region's GDP.

This catching-up trend of the central and eastern European region is brand new in history, since, during the previous one-and-a-half centuries, the countries of the region had always declined economically compared with western Europe (see Table 20.3). This trend changed for the first time after the turn of the millennium, and catching up with the more advanced parts of the continent started as an outcome of integration.

Between 1973 and 2014, northwestern Europe increased its income level by nearly a factor of two (189 per cent), while the Mediterranean countries together with Ireland increased their average GDP by a factor of four (395 per cent), but Ireland taken alone increased its income level by almost a factor of eight (781 per cent).[62]

Table 20.3 Central Europe per capita GDP (pecentage) of northwestern Europe

Year	Central Europe GDP as percentage of that of northwestern Europe
1870	54
1913	50
1950	48
1990	37
2000	23
2019	36

The calculations up to 1990 are based on Maddison, *Monitoring the World Economy*. The 2000 and 2014 figures are calculated from The Economist, *Pocket World in Figures 2004* and The Economist, *Pocket World in Figures 2017*; the 2016 figure is based on https://web.archive.org/web/20171114110758/https:/statisticstimes.com/economy/countries-by-projected-gdp-capita.php for 2017.

62 The calculations up to 1990 are based on Maddison, *Monitoring the World Economy*. The 2000 and 2014 figures are calculated from The Economist, *Pocket World in Figures 2004* (London, Profile Books, 2004) and The Economist, *Pocket World in Figures 2017*; the 2016 figure is based on https://web.archive.org/web/20171114110758/https:/statisticstimes.com/economy/countries-by-projected-gdp-capita.php for 2017.

Table 20.4   Increase of per capita GDP in four European regions, 1913–2013

Year	Northwestern Europe	Mediterranean Europe and Ireland	Central Europe and the Baltics	Russia, Turkey and the Balkans
1913	100	100	100	100
1950	138	115	156	142
2013	12,163	16,413	8,471	3,667

Based on Maddison, *Monitoring the World Economy* for the 1913 and 1950 figures; and The Economist, *Pocket World in Figures 2017* for the 2013 figures.

The tremendous development within the EU is well documented if we compare the advancement during roughly the first half (1913–1950) of the twentieth century against that during roughly the second half (1950–2013) (see Table 20.4). If we compare the economic development of four European regions, three of which contain member countries of the EU and the fourth is the non-EU region of Russia, Turkey and the Balkans, the picture is similar (see Table 20.4).

Table 20.4 indicates that all of the European regions had made very slow progress between 1913 and 1950, whereas we witnessed a dramatic break-through and advancement between 1950 and 2013. The non-EU countries in the Russian–Turkish–Balkan region, however, made only rather moderate progress compared with the EU regions: only half of the progress of the central European–Baltic region, and one-third or one-quarter that of the southern and northwestern regions.

European Revival

Post-war European economic development started to reverse the trend of the previous three-quarters of a century, and the EU, with its twenty-seven integrated countries (EU-27), became an economic superpower. The combined area of the EU is only 12 per cent that of the combined territory of the other three great powers, the United States, China and Russia; and the EU's 446 million population is also only one-quarter that of the three other great powers' inhabitants combined. In 2019, the EU with its $18,292 trillion GDP represented 22 per cent of the global economy. The GDP per capita – in purchasing power parity – was $43,188 in 2018, compared with $62,869 in the United States, $44,246 in Japan and $18,116 in China. The EU, together with the non-EU-member, but connected, Norway, Switzerland and Iceland – members of the common market – accounted for 25.4 per cent of world output, compared with the American share of 22.5 per cent.

One of the great economic successes of the EU is its common currency, introduced at the turn of the millennium and used by nineteen countries of the eurozone and six non-member countries, altogether twenty-five European countries. Its value at its introduction was equal to the US dollar, but within a few years its value rose to become 50 per cent higher than that of the dollar. Nowadays, in April 2023, despite the crisis, its value is still 9 per cent higher. It is the second-largest reserve currency in the world after the American dollar.

The huge gap that existed between Europe and the United States in the middle of the twentieth century was closing. In the late 2010s, the nineteen eurozone countries reached 73 per cent of the American level.[63] In 2018, the average per capita GDP of the EU-27 countries, that is, including all the less developed central European and Balkan member countries, in purchasing power parity was 67 per cent that of the United States, virtually equal to the Japanese and more than double (238 per cent) the Chinese income level. However, even in the late 2010s the gap between the EU and the United States was still between one-quarter and one-third, with the advantage for America.

On looking into matters more closely, however, the gap is not big at all. The difference is influenced mainly by two main factors. The first one is the great income disparity among the member countries of the EU. The EU's income level is the average of highly developed and less developed member countries. The new, former communist member countries, when they joined in the twenty-first century, had only one-tenth to one-third of the northwestern European members' GDP. The low GDP levels of the new, less developed member countries lower the EU average significantly.

The second main reason for the difference in income level is that Europe has a more advanced social system and Europeans are working much less than Americans. By EU law, every member country of the EU must have at least four work weeks of paid vacation. The average number of paid working days of vacation is between 25 and 35 days per year in EU member states, while the average private sector US worker receives only 16 days of paid vacation per year. One in four Americans does not have a single paid day off,

---

63 From Maddison, *Monitoring the World Economy*; The Economist, *Pocket World in Figures 2020* (London, Profile Books, 2020).

because the United States is the only developed country without legally required paid vacation days.[64]

If we examine income per hour in France, Germany, Ireland, the Netherlands, Norway, Belgium and Luxembourg, all of them have surpassed the United States, although in some of them the average per capita income level is still somewhat behind because fewer hours of work are done. This means that the value produced in 1 hour in western Europe is basically the same as in America; thus the productivity level is quite similar, though the United States is stronger in knowledge-based sectors. Per capita productivity increases around the turn of the millennium, nevertheless, were pretty similar, 2.1 per cent in Europe and 2.2 per cent in the United States.[65]

All in all, the northwest European countries come very close to the American level. Moreover, three or four European countries are already richer than the United States, among them Ireland, which hardly attained 42 per cent of the US level when it joined the EU in 1973, but had surpassed it by 20 per cent by 2018. As Barry Eichengreen rightly concluded in his 2007 book, the dramatic transatlantic difference in quality of life that existed 50 years ago is effectively gone, because, in the second half of the twentieth century, the average European's buying power tripled, while working hours fell by a third.[66]

The European Single Market is one of the most attractive areas for investors. As the Commission reported in April 2020, 'The EU is the world's main provider and the top global destination of foreign investment. Foreign direct investment stocks held in the rest of the world by investors resident in the EU amounted to €8,750 billion, meanwhile, foreign direct investment stocks held by third country investors in the EU amounted to €7,197 billion at the end of 2018.'[67] In the less developed peripheries of the EU in southern and central Europe, 69 per cent of investments originated from the most

64 European Data Portal, 'Which Country in the EU Has the Most Annual Holidays?' (2016), https://data.europa.eu/en/publications/datastories/which-country-eu-has-most-annual-holidays; A. E. M. Hess, 'On Holiday: Countries with the Most Vacation Days', *USA Today*, 8 June 2013, https://eu.usatoday.com/story/money/business/2013/06/08/countries-most-vacation-days/2400193.

65 G. Cette, J. Fernald and B. Mojon, 'The Pre-Great Recession Slowdown in Productivity', Federal Reserve Bank of San Francisco (2016), www.frbsf.org/wp-content/uploads/sites/4/wp2016-08.pdf.

66 B. Eichengreen, *The European Economy since 1945: Coordinated Capitalism and Beyond* (Princeton, NJ, Princeton University Press, 2007).

67 European Commission, 'Investment' (2020), https://ec.europa.eu/trade/policy/accessing-markets/investment.

advanced EU countries. This share was 91 or 92 per cent in the Czech Republic and Poland between 1998 and 2010.[68]

Similarly, the EU is among the top traders in the world. While member countries' trade with each other is 64 per cent of their total trade, the EU has about 100 trade agreements with non-EU countries and the member states acquire the strongest possible negotiating position by making trade agreements together. In 2018, the EU's exports represented 15.2 per cent of global exports and its imports 15.1 per cent of global imports, making it the world's biggest trade player, while the United States' share of trade was 8.5 per cent.

The Impact of Integration

At this point there is an evident question to ask: what was the impact of integration on post-war European development? The answer to this question is not easy, partly because member countries joined at different times, some in the early 1950s, others in 1973 and the 1980s, and in 1995, and seventeen between 2004 and 2013. Furthermore, the 70-year-old integration process has itself had several stages. From the beginning until the 1960s, it took about one-and-a-half decades to eliminate tariffs among member countries. Integration became much deeper after the introduction of the Single Market in 1992, which eliminated most of the other restrictions, and again after the introduction of the common currency at the turn of the millennium. The character of integration somewhat changed again when several economically less developed countries joined the Union during the 1980s and the 2000s, which made it possible to include a cheap labour force in the value chains.[69]

A great number of economists, using various methods, analysed the impact and advantage of integration for economic development. It is seemingly unquestionable that integration has promoted capital accumulation, productivity and economic growth via an acceleration of intra-European trade and enlarged national markets to provide an all-European domestic market, macroeconomic and institutional stability, all-European financial integration, better resource allocation, a huge increase of foreign direct investment and, for the eurozone countries, a reduction of exchange rate volatility.

---

68 D. Filipović, N. Podrug and J. Prester, 'Cross-Border Mergers and Acquisitions in Southeast Europe. Cases from Croatia, Romania and Bulgaria', *International Journal of Management Cases* 14, no. 3 (2020): 32–40, 35.

69 S. Vass, 'EU Membership Has Many Benefits, but Economic Growth Is Not One of Them – New Findings', *The Conversation*, 7 February 2019, https://theconversation .com/eu-membership-has-many-benefits-but-economic-growth-is-not-one-of-them-new-findings-111206.

The EU member countries' economies thus became significantly 'Europeanised'. Leading industrial corporations established subsidiaries in several countries, built Europe-wide value chains, and now each producer of parts of the product is producing much bigger quantities that give the advantage of production at scale.

Leading banks, taking advantage of the EU's 'European passport', created huge networks of all-European branches and dominated the less developed countries' financial institutions; in the formerly communist countries more than 80 per cent of the entire banking system was established by them and supplied loans in countries with limited financial resources for the economic actors and the population. That improved the housing situation. All these developments had especially positive economic outcomes both for the advanced and for the less developed member countries.

When the Single Market and common currency were in place for the Union's common market of nearly 500 million people in mostly high-income communities, internal European trade of goods among member countries more than doubled (215 per cent) between 2002 and 2018. The less developed new member countries of central Europe increased their trade the most. While Germany and Belgium more than doubled their exports of goods to other EU member countries, Poland and Slovakia increased their exports by a factor of more than four.[70] Altogether, the member countries' trade of goods with each other reached 64 per cent of their total trade.[71] Europe became the most interconnected part of the entire world. In 2006, intra-Americas trade was almost 60 per cent and intra-Asia-Pacific trade was only 50 per cent of their total, while intra-European trade had risen to nearly 77 per cent of total trade in Europe.[72]

Some calculations concluded that the benefits from membership were about 0.6–0.8 per cent additional growth per year.[73] Some calculations on the economic impact of further steps of integration, accomplishing the Single

---

70 Eurostat, 'Intra-EU Trade in Goods – Main Features' (2019), https://web.archive.org /web/20200729234106/https:/ec.europa.eu/eurostat/statistics-explained/index.php?ti tle=Intra-EU_trade_in_goods_-_main_features.

71 M. Galar, 'Has the EU's Leading Position in Global Trade Changed since the Crisis?', ECFIN, *Economic Brief* no. 39 (2015), https://ec.europa.eu/economy_finance/publica tions/economic_briefs/2015/pdf/eb39_en.pdf; Eurostat, 'Intra-EU Trade in Goods'.

72 S. A. Altman and C. R. Bastian, 'DHL Global Connectedness Index' (2019), https:// www.dhl.com/content/dam/dhl/global/core/documents/pdf/go-en-gci-2019- update-complete-study.pdf.

73 N. F. Campos, F. Coricelli and L. Moretti, 'Deep Integration and Economic Growth: Counterfactual Evidence from Europe', 22nd Dubrovnik Economic Conference (2016), www.hnb.hr/documents/20182/783865/dec-22-campos-coricelli-moretti-growth-and- EU-Integr.pdf/e375a8b2-1cc2-4b5f-8b29-ada6454f2e1f; N. F. Campos, F. Coricelli and

Market, are also convincing. Rand Europe did calculations about the not yet exploited potential of the Single Market and concluded that an additional income of between $197 and $290 billion per year could be obtained if this potential were realised. Completing the EU digital single market could contribute $480 billion per year to Europe's economy. Coordinating armed forces across the member states could save between $3.23 and $9.7 billion a year on wages alone.[74] Integration has innumerable advantages that contribute to a better life for citizens of the Union. Strong evidence proves unquestionably that EU membership has highly positive net benefits, albeit with considerable heterogeneity across countries.

Summing up, calculations show that, for the EU as a whole, the outcome of integration increased per capita income in a range from a minimum gain of 5 per cent to a maximum gain of 20 per cent in various member countries. The EU assistance for less developed regions and countries alone generated 2–5 per cent of the increase of GDP in the central European and Balkans areas. Another kind of proof of the advantage of integration is the extraordinary growth of the founding countries of the European Community. Between 1950 and 1992, until the introduction of the Single Market, they increased their average per capita GDP by 363 per cent, while western Europe as a whole, including non-member countries, increased its average per capita GDP by only 295 per cent, the world average was 240 per cent, and the United States, Canada, Australia and New Zealand together increased their average per capita GDP by 225 per cent.[75] In the second half of the twentieth century and in the early twenty-first century integrated Europe experienced its best ever economic prosperity.

The Social Dimension of Economic Development

The capitalist economic regime required a major renewal in difficult times of exceptionally deep economic crisis and during the war years that required maximum national efforts and thus national solidarity. The first steps

L. Moretti, 'Economic Growth and Political Integration: Estimating the Benefits from Membership in the European Union Using the Synthetic Counterfactuals Method' (2014), https://docs.iza.org/dp8162.pdf; A. Boltho and B. Eichengreen, 'The Economic Impact of European Integration', CEPR Discussion Paper no. DP6820 (2008), https://papers.ssrn.com/sol3/papers.cfm?abstract_id=1143183#.

74 S. Hoorens, 'A Closer Europe Is a Better Europe', US News, 24 March 2017, www.usnews.com/opinion/world-report/articles/2017-03-24/sixty-years-later-european-integration-has-benefited-eu-countries.
75 Based on Maddison, Monitoring the World Economy.

towards a European welfare state were taken in Sweden in the middle of the Great Depression when the Social Democratic Party gained power in 1932. Winston Churchill's wartime coalition government in Britain appointed a committee, led by William Beveridge, to analyse the existing social services and make recommendations. The committee presented its report in 1942 and proposed the introduction of a comprehensive welfare system.[76] This became the basis for post-war reforms. The idea spread like wildfire throughout Europe. Austria initiated the *Sozialpartnerschaft* (social partnership), a pact among the trade unions, entrepreneurs and government in 1947, followed by second, third, fourth and fifth agreements. Price and wage control was introduced. Scandinavian socialists, conservative French Gaullists and German and Italian Christian democrats followed the same policy.[77] West Germany introduced the *soziale Marktwirtschaft* (social capitalism), a combination of free market capitalist economy and widespread social policies of the welfare state. They also enacted the Wohnungsbaugesetz (Housing Construction Law) in 1950 to build 1.8 million new apartments in 6 years in order to provide affordable housing.[78]

The new post-war European welfare capitalism, with some country-by-country differences, offered free social and health services, provided free schooling at all levels and targeted full employment, stable prices and increasing income. On that post-war basis, the EU also combined economic growth with better social well-being and better and cheaper, in several areas free of charge, health and educational services. In several countries – Austria, Sweden, Denmark and Germany – even higher education is available without tuition fees at public universities for students from all EU countries. In some other countries, students have to pay, but mostly very low amounts (in France between €170 and €650, in the Netherlands between €700 and €2,100 per year). European education is becoming more 'Europeanised', and students are rendered more all-European by spending time in other EU member countries.

Post-war economic development within the EU was closely combined with social welfare. The progress of the economy and social welfare together is measured by the Human Development Index (HDI), an index that

---

76 W. Beverage, *Social Insurance and Allied Services, a Government Report* (London, His Majesty's Stationery Office, 1942).
77 W. C. Baum, *The French Economy and the State* (Princeton, NJ, Princeton University Press, 1958), pp. 181–2, 274–5.
78 R. G. Wertheimer, 'The Miracle of German Housing in the Postwar Period', *Land Economics* 34, no. 4 (1958): 338–45.

Table 20.5   World HDI (maximum level is 1,000) in 2016

Region	HDI
World average	717
United States	920
Northwestern European average	915
Mediterranean–Irish average	881
Central European and Baltic average	856
Russian–Balkans–Turkish average	771
Latin American average	751
Developing countries average	670
Sub-Saharan African average	523

combines three factors, namely the economic development level, measured by average per capita income; the health level of the country, measured in an indirect way as the average lifespan; and the educational level, measured by the average number of years spent in school.

Table 20.5 reflects the fact that the countries and regions of the EU, together with the United States, are far ahead of the world average and among the top countries of the world.[79] Of the best ten countries regarding the world's HDI, seven are northwestern European countries, all of which are at a better development level than the United States, which is only in thirteenth place in the world. Taking the EU as a whole, however, the United States is somewhat ahead with its 920 points, although this advantage comes from the higher GDP, while the life expectancy, which is 79.5 years in America, is lower than the EU average of 81 years. The same is true in education: an average EU citizen spends 17.6 years in school over their lifetime, whereas in the United States the corresponding duration is 16.5 years.

The EU is combining the free market system with a welfare economy. In the 2010s, Japan spent 21.9 per cent of its GDP, the United States 18.7 percent, Australia 17.8 per cent, Iceland and Switzerland 16 per cent, Turkey 12.5 per cent, Chile 11 per cent and Mexico 7.5 per cent on social expenditures. The EU is far ahead in social spending. The rough average of the EU member

79 United Nations, *Human Development Report 2016: Human Development for Everyone* (New York City, NY, United Nations Development Programme, 2016), https://hdr.undp.org/system/files/documents/2016humandevelopmentreportpdfipdf.pdf.

countries' social spending is about 25–27 per cent of their aggregate GDP, although differences among member countries are significant, with this expenditure varying in the range 14–17 per cent, 18–25 per cent and, in some countries, 26–28 per cent. France is at the top, ahead of Denmark and Finland, spending 31–32 per cent of its GDP on social expenditures. In the eurozone countries, the numbers of medical doctors and hospital beds per 1,000 citizens are 3.9 (in the United States 2.6) and 6.2 (in the United States 2.9), respectively. Social expenditures are financed from state revenues, mostly taxation. Between 2006 and 2018, direct and indirect tax incomes in France, Finland and Belgium were equal at 43–44 per cent of GDP, but as an average in the EU about 33–40 per cent of GDP. This is significantly higher than the United States' 24.3 per cent, since social expenditure in the United States is lower and comprehensive welfare institutions do not exist.

Besides the social spending of the member states, the EU also supports social programmes from its central budget that represent roughly 1 per cent of the EU's aggregate GDP (in 2019 this amounted to €165.8 billion.) The EU's long-term budget for 2014–20 was €1,082.5 billion. Roughly one-third of it was spent on supporting the agricultural population, and even some-what more for creating growth and jobs and reducing economic gaps between the EU's various regions and countries. The so-called cohesion fund's budget for 2014–20 was €74,822,264,412, and the majority of it went to support fifteen countries, namely Bulgaria, Croatia, Cyprus, the Czech Republic, Estonia, Greece, Hungary, Latvia, Lithuania, Malta, Poland, Portugal, Romania, Slovakia and Slovenia, assisting their catching-up process.

In the mid 2010s, in spite of the 37 per cent difference between the European and American GDP per capita, to the advantage of America, the average gross annual income per household in the EU was actually the same as that in the USA: in the EU it was €35,000 (compared with the American €35,000–36,000). The average net annual family income was €24,000 in the EU (compared with the American €24,610).

A More Balanced Income Distribution

Another major social achievement of the EU is that economic growth was accompanied by the acievement of a relatively more balanced income distribution. Inequality is measured by the Gini coefficient on a scale between 0 and 1. These numbers represent extreme cases: 0 hypothetically means that every citizen has the same income, while 1 means that one person gets the entire income of a country. Thus, the lower the index, the more equal the income distribution; and vice versa, higher numbers reflect higher inequality.

Thomas Piketty, in his famous book *Capital in the Twenty-First Century*, proved that the generally accepted theory of the American Simon Kuznetz, that inequality is decreasing with the development and maturity of capitalism is nothing other than an ideological 'cold war theory' and is not true. Capitalism has the inherent tendency to increase profit and inequality and only outside, non-economic, mostly political factors can generate opposite trends. Piketty documented that the values of the Gini coefficient measuring differences within and among countries steadily increased from the late eighteenth century to the middle of the twentieth century. In 1820, the world average Gini coefficient within countries was 0.43, but in 1913 it was already 0.61; inequality among countries as measured by the Gini coefficient was 0.16 in 1820, but 0.55 in 1950.

During the Cold War decades, between 1950 and the 1980s, because of the welfare race between the rival systems, one can speak about an 'egalitarian revolution'. In the mid 1980s, most of the European countries had a relatively well-balanced income distribution, and the Gini index was mostly around the low numbers of 0.20–0.25. After the collapse of communism and the Soviet Bloc, inequality started increasing world-wide, including in Europe again.

Social differences started broadening and the income of the top 1 per cent of the population sharply increased after the end of the Cold War. The world index of incomes shows that the income of the top 1 per cent on the income ladder increased by 6.8 per cent per annum while the average income of wage earner adults increased only by 2.1 per cent. Since the 1960s, managers' income has jumped to 10–17 times that of a factory worker even in 1992, but 13–25 times by 2000.

In the contemporary world 746 million people still suffer from extreme poverty (they live on no more – in 2019 prices – than $2.16 per day). They are mostly living in Africa and some parts of Asia. Their number in Europe is only 0.7 million, but in North America it is still 13 million. Nevertheless, according to Eurostat's figures from 2019, 5.6 per cent of EU citizens still live in very poor conditions, with the risk of poverty and social exclusion. The situation is at its worst in Bulgaria (with a poverty level of almost 20 per cent), Greece (almost 16 per cent) and Romania (more than 12 per cent), followed by Lithuania, Cyprus, Hungary and Slovakia (more than or about 8 per cent), Poland (almost 4 per cent) and the Czech Republic (nearly 3 per cent), while in Sweden, the Netherlands and Finland this layer of the society is minimal (1.5–2.5 per cent).[80]

The EU, especially the advanced northwestern European EU member countries, represents a more socially oriented system. The growing discrepancy between top earners and average wage earners in Germany and Sweden is roughly half that in several other countries.

Income inequality has increased significantly in the world and has returned to the level of early capitalism. The global Gini index in 2000 was already 0.66, which is higher than it was in 1820. Inequality increased within the EU as well. Already during the one-and-a-half decades between 1985 and 2000, the western European Gini index increased from 0.27 to 0.35. In spite of growing inequality in the world, income disparities in the EU remained much lower than the world or the American average disparities. In Greece, Italy, France, Germany and Britain by the 2010s, the Gini index became between 0.30 and 0.34. In some of the formerly egalitarian communist countries, inequality also increased: in Bulgaria, Croatia, Poland and Bosnia it rose to 0.30–0.37. On the other hand, Sweden, Denmark and Finland preserved their more egalitarian system, with index values of 0.25–0.28.

The entire EU has a more balanced income distribution than the United States, whose Gini index is 0.41, surprisingly the same as that of Russia, a country which went from being very egalitarian to becoming extremely unequal. The latter countries moved nearer to the extremely unequal Latin American and Third World countries with Gini index levels in the range 0.57–0.63 than to northwestern Europe.[81] Growing inequality after the half-a-century decrease has become one of the main factors of peoples' dissatisfaction throughout the world.

2020: The Impact of Brexit

At the end of January 2020, Great Britain became the first and only member country to have left the EU. This is a definitive weakening of the Community. What is the economic impact of Brexit on the EU? On the one hand, it is evidently harmful. One well-developed western European country, second-biggest economically in the EU after Germany and representing 12 per cent of the EU's GDP, left the Union, no longer contributed to its budget (a net loss of more than $11 billion), certainly did not remain in its

---

80 Eurostat, 'Can You Afford the Basics of Life?' (2020), https://ec.europa.eu/eurostat/web/products-eurostat-news/-/DDN-20200429-1.
81 OECD, 'Understanding the Socio-economic Divide in Europe' (2017), www.oecd.org/els/soc/cope-divide-europe-2017-background-report.pdf.

common market and weakened the all-European value-chain networks. Europe consequently became less 'Europeanised'.

Several calculations tried to measure the possible losses for the EU-27. All agreed that the potential losses are not substantial and real output – according an IMF analysis – would be lower by just 0.2 per cent, but some countries may lose more, such as Ireland, which may lose about 2.5 per cent growth, followed by the Netherlands, Denmark, Belgium and the Czech Republic. In the case of a so-called 'hard landing', thus without a trade agreement with the EU, which is becoming more plausible, European output loss might be somewhat bigger, 0.5 per cent for the EU-27, but 4 per cent for Ireland, given the substantial increase in both tariff and non-tariff barriers.[82] However, some regions and sectors will be hit harder on the continent. Transport vehicles, machinery, electronics, textiles and furniture, foodstuffs, wood, chemicals and plastics may lose markets. Britain had been buying industrial products from the EU. This may decrease after Brexit, and that will hurt certain continental regions in France (Midi-Pyrénées), Germany (Stuttgart and Tübingen) and Italy (Emilia Romagna and Tuscany) and also in the Czech Republic, Romania and Bulgaria.[83]

While the economic loss because of Brexit for the EU during the 2020s could be relatively insignificant, the Rand Corporation's experts calculated that, in the case of a 'hard landing', which is more than possible in the autumn of 2020, Britain's GDP would decline by 5 per cent in the 10 years after Brexit, or lose $140 billion, compared with the case in which Britain's membership of the EU would have been maintained.[84] The situation became much gloomier after the Covid-19 pandemic hit Britain hard. The effects of those two factors combined, Brexit-generated and coronavirus-generated economic recessions, might have disastrous consequences for Britain. According to the Bank of England's projections in April 2020, Britain is heading for its worst crash in more than 300 years and will suffer the most tragic economic slump since 1706. The British economy could shrink by about 30 per cent compared with the end of 2019. Several other forecasts mostly agree that the decline might be between 13 and 15 per cent.[85]

82 J. Chen, C. Ebeke, L. Lin, H. Qu and J. Siminitz, 'The Long-Term Impact of Brexit on the European Union', IMF Blog (2018), https://blogs.imf.org/2018/08/10/the-long-term-impact-of-brexit-on-the-european-union.

83 European Committee of the Regions, 'Assessing the Impact of the UK's Withdrawal from the EU on Regions and Cities in EU27' (2018), https://cor.europa.eu/Documents/Migrated/news/impact-brexit.pdf.

84 Rand Corporation, 'Economic Inplications of Brexit', www.rand.org/randeurope/research/projects/brexit-economic-implications.html.

85 BBC News, 2 April 2020, 'Record Fall in UK Economy Forecast', www.bbc.com/news/business-52232639.

All in all, Brexit will cause tremendous trouble for Britain, but, except for some companies and smaller regions, would not harm the EU very much. On the other hand, Britain, during its four decades of membership in the EU, always consistently opposed any step of further integration. Now that Britain has left the Union, a major barrier to further integration has thus been eliminated, which could have a positive impact on economic growth.

2020: The Impact of the Covid-19 Crisis

The coronavirus pandemic hit the world, including Europe, very hard in 2020. The unavoidable introduction of social distancing virtually closed down the European economy. The economic decline caused by the pandemic ended a promising period between 2013 and 2019, the most recent post-crisis years in Europe, when economic growth had returned to normal: the EU as a whole averaged about 2 per cent per year, while some countries reached about 3–4 per cent and Ireland experienced almost 9 per cent annual growth. Investments in 2019 as an average over the EU countries again reached 22 per cent of the GDP.

This promising trend came to an end, and about one-third of the economic activity of the EU, as the Commission's economy chief Paolo Gentiloni calculated, stopped 'practically overnight'. The Union, he continued, 'will experience a recession of historic proportions this year [...] Europe is experiencing an economic shock without precedent since the Great Depression.'[86] This report predicted a 7.5 per cent decline of the EU's economy in 2020 (in contrast to the worst crisis year of the Great Recession in 2009, when the decline was 4.5 per cent).

The analyses also clearly clarified that the Covid recession hit the member countries very unevenly. Some countries, such as France, but especially the southern members such as Italy, Spain, Portugal and Greece, were hit harder.

The worst part of the economic recession is the consequences arising from the increase of the debt burden of the member countries by about 20 per cent of the GDP that might push the already heavily indebted member countries to the brink. The ratio of debt to GDP is likely to exceed 200 per cent in Greece, 150 per cent in Italy and 100 per cent in Spain and Portugal, but also in Belgium and France.

---

86 J. Parrock and N. Huet, 'EU Forecasts "Recession of Historic Proportions" This Year', Euronews (2020), www.euronews.com/my-europe/2020/05/06/eu-forecasts-recession-of-historic-proportions-this-year.

The European Central Bank recommended to the eurozone finance ministers that they should decide upon a stimulus package of about €1.5 trillion ($1.6 trillion) and itself – similarly to what it did during the financial crisis after 2008 – launched a $750 billion emergency debt-buying programme to keep borrowing costs low. Christine Lagarde, the new president of the Bank, following in the footsteps of her predecessor, also announced, on 30 April 2020, that 'These purchases will continue to be conducted in a flexible manner over time.'[87]

In the spring of 2020, the eurozone ministers discussed the possibility of easing the burden of the most endangered mostly southern countries and decided on a rescue deal of about €540 billion ($590 billion) to help the bloc's coronavirus-stricken economies. The optimal solution would be to transfer the additional debt to the all-European level. This solution would, indeed, mobilise about €1.4–2.1 trillion, 10–15 per cent of the EU's GDP, in the form of joint bonds. Jürgen Hardt, a German Christlich Demokratische Union politician emphasised that this crisis was threatening the European idea. He said that Germany, the Netherlands and other countries with economic and financial power would have to repeat what the United States did after the Second World War: 'Germany benefited very much from the European recovery program (the Marshall Plan) [. . . that] helped us back on our feet after the Second World War. I think we need something like that now from the economically stronger European countries. It would be a strong signal to those countries who doubt the EU right now.'[88]

The radical steps of solidarity would become the symbol of the EU's emergence from the pandemic crisis stronger and more unified.

Conclusion

The EU, besides its impressive economic modernisation and growth, achieved in large part by the 'Europeanisation' of industry, banking and services, besides closing the gap on the other highly developed countries and reaching the most advanced economic level of the world, combined its good economic performance with a marked social orientation and a social market system. The EU's social, health and educational achievements and

---

87 P. Bofinger, 'The "Frugal Four" Should Save the European Project', Social Europe (2020), www.socialeurope.eu/the-frugal-four-should-save-the-european-project.
88 H. J. Mai, 'The Coronavirus Could Tear the EU Apart', VOX (2020), www.vox.com /world/2020/4/21/21228578/coronavirus-europe-eu-economic-crisis-eurozone-debt.

more balanced income distribution are major historical achievements. The EU has changed the economic history of Europe and made it again one of the best regions of the world.

Recommended Reading

Berend, I. T. *An Economic History of Twentieth-Century Europe: Economic Regimes from Laissez-Faire to Globalization* (Cambridge, Cambridge University Press, 2016).

Eichengreen, B. *The European Economy since 1945: Coordinated Capitalism and Beyond* (Princeton, NJ, Princeton University Press, 2007).

Judt, T. (with T. Snyder). *Thinking the Twentieth Century* (London, Penguin, 2012).

Lowe, K. *Savage Continent: Europe in the Aftermath of World War II* (New York, NY, St Martin's Press, 2012).

Mazower, M. *Dark Continent: Europe's Twentieth Century* (London, Allen Lane, 1995).

Polanyi, K. *The Great Transformation: The Political and Economic Origins of Our Time* (Boston, MA, Beacon Press, 2001 [1944]).

Sandholtz, W. *High-Tech Europe: The Politics of International Cooperation* (Berkeley, CA, University of California Press, 1992).

Servan-Schreiber, J.-J. *Le défi américain* (Paris, Denoël, 1967).

21

The EU and the Narrative of Solidarity

MALCOLM ROSS

Introduction

Solidarity is a contested and elusive concept. Nevertheless, it has made a considerable contribution to the shape and character of European Union (EU) integration from pre-European Economic Community (EEC) days to ongoing debates in the Conference on the Future of Europe. Indeed, solidarity has been characterised as 'both the *raison d'être* and the objective of the European project'.[1] Yet that impact has been achieved despite a less than obvious 'fit' between classical notions of solidarity and the complex system that constitutes the EU. Without adopting any essentialist approach to the meaning of solidarity, orthodox expositions emphasise close ties between individuals that involve sharing or redistributing resources, usually carrying connotations of political action and often situated in the social sphere. Put another way, solidarity is frequently understood as an affective condition defending particular values and usually most effective at local levels. In this sense, solidarity operates as a moral and political force rather than a justiciable legal norm or rule. This is not to downplay the weight or rigour of solidarity; as a source of moral authority, solidarity can provide legitimacy for political change.

Promoting solidarity in the multilevel governance framework of the EU is clearly challenging. Core aspects of integration, such as the single market, free movement, competition and EU citizenship, are built on legal rights for individuals and businesses that are enforceable in the courts. Policy actions at EU level are always limited by the competences provided in the treaties. As a result, opportunities for social interventions are notably more restricted than in other fields, leading to a tension between the preservation of national welfare states and EU free movement rules. EU institutional governance has

---

[1] AG Bot, Opinion, Cases C-643/15 and C-647/15 *Slovak Republic and Hungary v. Council of the European Union*, EU:C:2017:618.

yet to yield a sustainable transnational political space, leaving the balance of power still tilted towards member states despite the directly elected European Parliament's co-legislator role with the Council across significant swathes of policy. Thus, there is a mismatch between solidarity's centre of gravity in social values, reciprocity and political expression and the EU's foundations of markets, legal rules and cooperation. However, it is too simplistic to represent solidarity as a binary choice of values over economic efficiency or a political force divorced from law. Rather, the full significance of solidarity emerges only when seen against the distinctive but evolving character of the EU. This relationship is a dynamic interconnective process affecting macro, meso and micro levels of governance.

Solidarity's strong purchase on the EU's own narrative reflects both the ongoing contestation of the EU's objectives and priorities and the resilience of solidarity as a practical force. Recurring questions about the EU – for example, whether it is a coming together of states or individuals, whether it mainly aspires to be an economic union, social project or global political actor – invite recourse to solidarity both in framing those problems and in suggesting solutions or directions of travel. Successive crises this century, especially the financial crash, rows over migration and asylum seekers, Brexit, the Covid-19 pandemic and 'rule of law' controversies, have all tested not just solidarity but the existential core of the EU itself. At a time when the need for some sort of 'reboot' of the EU is widely accepted, solidarity's capacity to provide the momentum for a paradigm shift could be a determining factor in the battle of ideas to ensure the sustainability of the EU. Put at its strongest, solidarity offers an alternative vision of the EU as a transnational citizen space rather than a vehicle for the pursuit of national interests.

Accordingly, this chapter takes a non-linear approach to assess solidarity as a game-changer. After a brief literature review, the first section identifies how solidarity is firmly anchored in successive treaties and institutionalised through key EU agencies, mechanisms and policies. This is not just to establish the persistent presence of solidarity as a value but to confirm its embedded centrality in political and legal discourse and its capacity for further, constitutional, development. Despite the more frequent references to solidarity among member states in these founding measures, it is striking that solidarity among citizens is also plainly contemplated. In other words, the EU is foreseen as both a 'transfer Union' for allocating resources between member states and a 'citizens' Europe' engaging reciprocal rights and obligations. The second section then demonstrates solidarity's critical role in any 'social' turn in the trajectory of the EU. It explores how the social orientation of solidarity acted as a brake on the ordoliberal and neoliberal ideas that originally underpinned the single market and competition core of the Union. In doing so, solidarity has been central to developing what the EU's 'social market economy' actually means. The Court of Justice, in particular, has used solidarity to steer a path between markets and welfare and to patrol the inroads of integration into national solidarities. The impact of EU citizenship rights has intensified those debates and the extent to which host states must provide 'solidarity with strangers'. Finally, the third section analyses key battlegrounds in ideas that will shape the solidarity narrative and its contribution to the paradigm shift. It contrasts the limitations of member-state-level solidarity exposed by successive EU crises with strong research evidence of grassroots, citizen-based solidarity attitudes and actions. It also highlights the critical role of EU institutions in supporting or frustrating solidarity trajectories. To various degrees, all dimensions of solidarity exhibit limitations of contractual bargaining, deservingness and other forms of conditionality. But there is still a substantial well of solidarity to be drawn upon. The chapter concludes that solidarity has been ever-present in the EU; the key juncture today is whether the shaping and articulation of solidarity is shifting from states to citizens. This narrative, especially the signs of a putative and particular form of transnational solidarity, culminates (for now) in alliance with ideas of resilience and social justice as the basis to contest the fundamental (re)orientation of the EU.

Literature Review

Solidarity as a scholarly topic pre-dates European integration,[2] attracting theoretical and empirical investigation across numerous disciplines. This century has seen much more specific research into solidarity in its EU context and the question of how any European solidarity relates to other concepts such as cosmopolitanism or universal humanity.[3]

Classical expositions of solidarity focus on its historical manifestations in family and religious bonds, the conditions for its creation and normative power.[4] Theorising solidarity in a European context has attracted

---

2 É. Durkheim, *The Division of Labour in Society* (New York, NY, Free Press; London, Macmillan, 1984 [1893]).

3 N. Stevenson, 'European Cosmopolitan Solidarity', *European Journal of Social Theory* 9, no. 4 (2006): 485–500; G. Delanty, *The European Heritage: A Critical Re-interpretation* (Abingdon, Routledge, 2018).

4 K. Bayertz (ed.), *Solidarity* (Dordrecht, Kluwer, 1999); S. Stjernø, *Solidarity in Europe: The History of an Idea* (Cambridge, Cambridge University Press, 2009).

interdisciplinary collections.[5] Specific disciplines include political science,[6] philosophy,[7] law[8] and sociology.[9] Frameworks for the construction of solidarity include discourse analysis,[10] political joint action[11] and external relations.[12] The scope for transnational solidarity in the EU is an increasing focus, especially horizontal solidarities between citizens.[13]

A number of EU-funded research projects have provided substantial empirical insights into solidarities in Europe[14] and allied concepts such as EU citizenship.[15] Using varying conceptualisations of solidarity, these studies explore attitudes and behaviours across a number of European countries and

5 N. Karagiannis (ed.), *European Solidarity* (Liverpool, Liverpool University Press, 2007); M. Ross and Y. Borgmann-Prebil (eds.), *Promoting Solidarity in the European Union* (Oxford, Oxford University Press, 2010); A. Grimmel and S. M. Giang (eds.), *Solidarity in the EU: A Fundamental Value in Crisis* (Cham, Springer, 2017).

6 S. Verhaegen, 'What to Expect from European Identity? Explaining Support for Solidarity in Times of Crisis', *Comparative European Politics* 16 (2018): 871–904; S. Koos, 'Crises and the Reconfiguration of Solidarities in Europe – Origins, Scope, Variations', *European Societies* 21, no. 5 (2019): 629–48.

7 J. Habermas, 'Democracy, Solidarity and the European Crisis' (2013), www.pro-europa.eu /europe/jurgen-habermas-democracy-solidarity-and-the-european-crisis; A. Sangiovanni, 'Solidarity as Joint Action', *Journal of Applied Philosophy* 32, no. 4 (2015): 340–59; A. Kolers, *A Moral Theory of Solidarity* (Oxford, Oxford University Press, 2016); B. Wolthuis, 'The European Union between Solidarity and Justice', *Acta Politica* 56 (2021): 261–75.

8 A. Sangiovanni, 'Solidarity in the European Union', *Oxford Journal of Legal Studies* 33, no. 2 (2013): 213–41; A. Biondi, E. Dagilytė and E. Küçük (eds.), *Solidarity in EU Law: Legal Principle in the Making* (Cheltenham, Edward Elgar, 2018).

9 Delanty, *The European Heritage*.

10 S. Wallaschek, 'Contested Solidarity in the Euro Crisis and Europe's Migration Crisis: A Discourse Network Analysis', *Journal of European Public Policy* 27, no. 7 (2020): 1034–53.

11 Sangiovanni, 'Solidarity as Joint Action'.

12 S. Schieder, R. Folz and S. Musekamp, 'The Social Construction of European Solidarity: Germany and France in the EU Policy towards the States of Africa, the Caribbean, and the Pacific (ACP) and Central and Eastern European Countries (CEEC)', *Journal of International Relations and Development* 14 (2011): 469–505.

13 F. De Witte, *Justice in the EU: The Emergence of Transnational Solidarity* (Oxford, Oxford University Press, 2015); F. Kommer, 'The Clash of Solidarities in the European Union: Rethinking Jürgen Habermas' Conception of Solidarity in the Transnational Context', *Fudan Journal of the Humanities and Social Sciences* 11, no. 2 (2018): 175–90; C. Lahusen and M. Theiss, 'European Transnational Solidarity: Citizenship in Action?', *American Behavioural Scientist* 63, no. 4 (2019): 444–58; M. Ross, 'Transnational Solidarity: A Transformative Narrative for the EU and its Citizens?', *Acta Politica* 56 (2021): 220–41.

14 EUCROSS, 'The Europeanisation of Everyday Life: Cross-Border Practices and Transnational Identities among EU and Third-Country Citizens', https://cordis .europa.eu/project/rcn/98871/reporting/en;REScEU, 'Reconciling Economic and Social Europe: Values, Ideas and Politics', https://cordis.europa.eu/pro ject/id/340534; SOLIDUS, 'Solidarity in European Societies: Empowerment, Social Justice and Citizenship', https://cordis.europa.eu/project/rcn/194587_en .html; TransSOL, 'European Paths to Transnational Solidarity at Times of Crisis: Conditions, Forms, Role-Models and Policy Responses', https://cordis .europa.eu/project/rcn/194579_en.html.

15 BEUCITIZEN, 'All Rights Reserved? Barriers towards EUropean CITIZENship', https://cordis.europa.eu/project/rcn/108458/reporting.

address specific groups or sectors, including fiscal, territorial, welfare and refugee solidarities.[16] Particular questions relate to individual transnational practices,[17] different policy fields,[18] the impact of civil society organisations[19] and attitudes to EU social solidarity actions.[20] Data indicating strength of support for EU-level measures can be seen in relation to policy-differentiated solidarities.[21] Other studies map constitutional and jurisprudential embodiments of solidarity, both nationally and at EU level.[22] Many of these projects have been independently reviewed in policy papers for the European Commission.[23]

Analysis of solidarity in successive EU crises can be seen regarding sovereignty,[24] refugees and asylum seekers[25] and the Covid-19 pandemic.[26]

16 J. Gerhards, H. Lengfeld, Z. Ignácz, F. Kley and M. Priem, *European Solidarity in Times of Crisis: Insights from a Thirteen-Country Survey* (London and New York, NY, Routledge, 2019).

17 EUCROSS, 'The Europeanisation of Everyday Life'; I. Ciornei and E. Recchi, 'At the Source of European Solidarity: Assessing the Effects of Cross-Border Practices and Political Attitudes', *Journal of Common Market Studies* 55, no. 3 (2017): 468–85; C. Lahusen and M. Grasso (eds.), *Solidarity in Europe: Citizens' Responses in Times of Crisis* (London, Palgrave Macmillan, 2018); J. Díez Medrano, I. Ciornei and F. Apaydin, 'Explaining Supranational Solidarity', in E. Recchi, A. Favell, F. Apaydin et al., *Everyday Europe: Social Transnationalism in an Unsettled Continent* (Bristol, Policy Press, 2019), pp. 121–45.

18 SOLIDUS, 'Solidarity in European Societies'; TransSOL, 'European Paths to Transnational Solidarity'.

19 C. Lahusen and M. Grasso, *Solidarity in Europe*; L. Durán Mogollón, O. Eisele and M. Paschou, 'Applied Solidarity in Times of Crisis: Exploring the Contexts of Civil Society Activities in Greece and Germany', *Acta Politica* 56 (2021): 308–29.

20 Gerhards et al. *European Solidarity in Times of Crisis*; H. Lengfeld and F. K. Kley, 'Conditioned Solidarity: EU Citizens' Attitudes towards Economic and Social Austerities for Crisis Countries Receiving Financial Aid', *Acta Politica* 21 (2020): 330–50.

21 Verhaegen, 'What to Expect from European Identity?'; S. Baute, K. Abts and B. Meuleman, 'Public Support for European Solidarity: Between Euroscepticism and EU Agenda Preferences?', *Journal of Common Market Studies* 57, no. 3 (2019): 533–50; M. Ferrera and C. Burelli, 'Cross-National Solidarity and Political Sustainability in the EU after the Crisis', *Journal of Common Market Studies* 57, no. 1 (2019): 94–110; S. Weko, 'Communitarians, Cosmopolitans, and Climate Change: Why Identity Matters for EU Climate and Energy Policy', *Journal of European Public Policy* 29, no. 7 (2021): 1072–91.

22 V. Federico and C. Lahusen (eds.), *Solidarity as a Public Virtue?* (Baden-Baden, Nomos, 2018).

23 European Commission, 'Solidarity in Europe: Alive and Active' (2018), https://op.europa.eu/en/publication-detail/-/publication/9adba623-d66f-11e8-9424-01aa75ed71a1/language-en/format-PDF/source-128300143; European Commission, 'Transformations of European Citizenship: Beyond Free Movement' (2019), https://op.europa.eu/en/publication-detail/-/publication/c83d6aa4-3d1f-11ea-ba6e-01aa75ed71a1.

24 A. Grimmel, '"Le Grand absent Européen": Solidarity in the Politics of European Integration', *Acta Politica* 56 (2021): 242–60.

25 A. Grimmel and S. M Giang, *Solidarity in the EU*.

26 Y. Bertoncini, 'European Solidarity in Times of Crisis: A Legacy to Develop in the Face of COVID-19', *European Issues* no. 555 (2020), www.robert-schuman.eu/en/doc/questions-d-europe/qe-555-en.pdf; G. Bouckaert, D. Galli, S. Kuhlmann, R. Reiter and

Broader positioning of solidarity places it in the context of the EU as a social union[27] amid competing visions of what the future EU could look like.[28]

The Solidarity Narrative

The EU's Solidarity Heritage

Solidarity has a long European pedigree, especially in the vocabularies of politics and law. It can be seen not just in the EU's own antecedents, but also in the constitutional traditions of many member states. Indeed, solidarity can be traced back to Roman law (*solidum*) and legal contractual responsibilities. The communities established by medieval guilds can be understood as examples of Durkheimian organic solidarity. More of solidarity's political connotations can be seen in the Napoleonic Code of 1804 (*fraternité*) and the discourse of mid-nineteenth-century revolutions across Europe. The end of the Second World War saw a burgeoning of rights-based constitutions and allusions to solidarity. The 1948 Italian Constitution, for example, referred to 'the performance of the unalterable duty to political, economic and social solidarity'. Heralding the first of the pre-EU structures, the European Coal and Steel Community, the 1950 Schuman Declaration stated: 'Europe will not be made all at once, or according to a single plan. It will be built through concrete achievements which first create a *de facto* solidarity.' The original EEC Treaty listed solidarity among states as a 'task' of the Community. Although solidarity is rarely defined or elaborated in these examples, the concept occupies central importance in the political *and* legal framework. Indeed, in some national constitutions – such as that of Italy – solidarity is a foundational (or meta) principle, permeating all relations in the constitution.

In the light of this heritage, it is not surprising that the EU Treaties make widespread reference to solidarity. Equally unremarkably, they only cite 'solidarity' and do not trumpet any new 'European' solidarity as

S. Van Hecke, 'European Coronationalism? A Hot Spot Governing a Pandemic Crisis', *Public Administration Review* 80, no. 5 (2020): 765–73; L. Cicchi, P. Genschel, A. Hemerijck and M. Nasr, 'EU Solidarity in Times of Covid-19', EUI Policy Brief 2020/34 (2020), https://op.europa.eu/en/publication-detail/-/publication/74f1faa2-35 16-11eb-b27b-01aa75ed71a1/language-en.

27 F. Vandenbroucke, C. Barnard and G. De Baere (eds.), *A European Social Union after the Crisis* (Cambridge, Cambridge University Press, 2017).

28 European Commission, 'Reflection Paper on the Social Dimension of Europe', COM (2017) 206 final; Delanty, *The European Heritage*; EUSOCIALCIT, 'The Future of European Social Citizenship', https://cordis.europa.eu/project/id/870978.

a particular concept to transcend or replace national versions. However, more than 60 years of developments suggest that such an evolution is well under way. As a starting point, the EU's three primary treaties in place since the Lisbon settlement adopt solidarity explicitly across a number of policy fields and relationships. At the broadest conceptual and constitutional level, the Treaty on the European Union (TEU) includes solidarity, but surprisingly not in its list of values. Yet solidarity satisfies archetypal characteristics of values: they cannot be directly observed, they engage moral considerations and they are conceptions of the desirable.

Importantly, however, Article 2 TEU instead refers to 'a society in which pluralism, non-discrimination, tolerance, justice, solidarity and equality between women and men prevail'. This formulation recognises solidarity as a stable and enduring phenomenon. Moreover, solidarity is significantly presented as a *means* of creating a European *society*. This notion can be seen in earlier reform drafts under the auspices of the Future of Europe Convention which had presented the EU's aim as 'a society at peace, through the *practice* of tolerance, justice and solidarity' (emphasis added).[29] However, the Draft Constitutional Treaty which emerged from that Convention failed to obtain ratification in 2005. Although the intergovernmental conference mandate for the subsequent Lisbon Treaty purported to reject the 'constitutional' route, the introduction of Article 2 is inescapably a constitutional provision. The link it envisages between values and a specific society is of a different character from the 'mere' coordination or harmonisation of particular policies. Putting solidarity forward as an essential force for achieving that society has significant consequences – not just for legitimising a social 'turn' for the EU but also the potential meta-status and justiciability of solidarity as a principle in managing future integration.

As for solidarity's meaning and policy application, the Union's objectives in Article 3 TEU refer to solidarity 'between generations', 'among Member States' and also contributing to 'solidarity and mutual respect among peoples' in regard to the EU's relations with the wider world. More concretely, the Treaty on the Functioning of the European Union (TFEU), which sets out the operational rules for EU policies, refers to immigration and asylum being based on the principle of solidarity and fair sharing of responsibility, including its financial implications, between member states. Energy policy under Article 194 TFEU also expressly provides for EU legislative decisions 'in a spirit of solidarity' between member states. In extreme circumstances,

29 CONV 528/03 6 February 2003.

Article 222 TFEU (named the 'Solidarity Clause') can trigger joint action by the Union and member states 'in a spirit of solidarity' if a member state is the victim of a natural or man-made disaster. A similar clause in Article 196 TFEU is the basis of the EU's Civil Protection Mechanism to improve the effectiveness of systems protecting against such disasters – which has recently been relevant for the Covid pandemic. Finally, the Preamble to the EU's Charter of Fundamental Rights – of equal legal value to the two other principal treaties – states that, 'Conscious of its spiritual and moral heritage, the Union is founded on the indivisible, universal values of human dignity, freedom, equality and solidarity.' The Charter's substance adopts solidarity as the title to Chapter IV for rights in areas that include the workplace, family life, welfare provision and health. Although the Charter somewhat confusingly veers between rights and principles and purports to attach only to the EU, member states and public bodies, its fields of application clearly cover the social sphere.

The commitment to solidarity permeates beyond treaty goals and rights to the macro-restructuring devices that support integration. Importantly, the original EEC was never a purely economic project, despite the name. Foundational policies such as those concerning agriculture were understood in solidarity terms. Similarly, later developments in regional and structural policy following the 1973 enlargement and the Single European Act 1986 were deliberately positioned as redistributive solidarity measures. Today's Structural and Cohesion Funds constitute a significant institutionalisation of solidarity as essentially preventative tools, providing resources aimed at reducing inequalities of various kinds across regions. These structural elements of solidarity are thus connected to wider EU resilience – for example, cohesion measures adopted in response to the Covid-19 pandemic aim to address shocks to employment markets and impacts on vulnerable groups.

A different kind of institutionalisation of solidarity is evident in construction of the EU's external relations and development policies. The dynamic here stems from the histories of individual member states. On the one hand, French colonial involvement in Africa dominated the initial (largely non-reciprocal) EU arrangements with the (then) African, Caribbean and Pacific (ACP) states from the 1970s until more World Trade Organization-compatible rules were adopted under the Cotonou Partnership Agreement of 2000. On the other, Germany's push for central and eastern European enlargement in the 1990s – and a shift away from ACP priorities – can be understood as part of 'special' ties with candidate countries among its Visegrád Group neighbours (the Czech Republic, Hungary, Poland and

Slovakia). In other words, in this period external relations were constructed in part from competing national solidarity narratives. However, subsequent prioritisation of strengthening the EU as an international actor has arguably seen a different approach in negotiating the EU's post-Cotonou arrangements with the ACP's successor group of states, the Organisation of African, Caribbean and Pacific States. The new agreement,[30] based on reciprocal interests, is significantly different from the original ACP package. Evolving development policy faces a dilemma between a paradigm of solidarity that addresses poverty in other countries and a more instrumentalist approach that ties aid to other discourses, involving conditions such as cooperation over migration and security.

Finally, as regards heritage, solidarity's entrenched importance can also be seen in jurisprudence stretching back to the 1970s, when the Court said that 'failure in the duty of solidarity accepted by Member States by the fact of their adherence to the Community strikes at the fundamental basis of the Community legal order'.[31] However, there has been equally long-running uncertainty as to the precise legal status and scope of solidarity. As recently as 2019, even the Commission was trying to categorise the concept as 'a political notion' incapable of justiciability. This stance was forcefully dismissed in the context of Article 194 TFEU and energy by the Grand Chamber of the Court of Justice.[32] Notably, it described solidarity as 'one of the fundamental principles of EU law' which 'underpins the entire legal system of the European Union'. Likening solidarity to other established general principles of EU law, the Court ruled that solidarity is a criterion for judicial review of measures adopted by EU institutions. This definitively settles the argument as to whether (lack of) solidarity can ever be invoked to challenge institutional decision-making. Moreover, the formulation as a general principle means that the idea is transferable to other policy areas. Opening up review in this way further enshrines solidarity in the constitutional framework, a conclusion expressly adopted by the Advocate General.[33] In his view, 'even though the principle of solidarity is multifaceted and deployed at different levels, its importance in primary law as a value and an objective in

---

30 'Post-Cotonou: Negotiators Reach a Political Deal on a New EU/Africa–Caribbean–Pacific Partnership Agreement' (2020), https://ec.europa.eu/commission/presscor ner/detail/en/ip_20_2291.

31 Case 39/72 *Premiums for Slaughtering Cows*, ECLI:EU:C:1973:13.

32 Case C-848/19P *Germany v. Poland and European Commission*, ECLI:EU:C:2021:598.

33 AG Campos Sánchez-Bordana, Opinion, Case C-848/19P, paras. 60–1.

the process of European integration is such that it may be regarded as significant enough to create legal consequences'.[34]

However, the untested step for the constitutional significance of solidarity is how far it goes beyond binding EU/member state levels of *political* solidarity to embrace more tangible forms of *social* solidarity affecting citizens in their ordinary lives. Momentum is undoubtedly building in that direction. A forthright example is AG Sharpston's Opinion in relation to EU policies of asylum and protection. In her view, 'Solidarity is the lifeblood of the European project [. . .] Member States *and their nationals* have obligations as well as benefits, duties as well as rights. Sharing in the European 'demos' is not a matter of [. . .] what one can claim. It also requires one to shoulder collective responsibilities and (yes) *burdens to further the common good.*' (emphasis added).[35] Whether this idea of solidarity as a public good which states and citizens must actively protect has taken root in the EU narrative – with concomitant social policy applications – is the subject of the remaining sections.

Solidarity and Integration: Steering a 'Social' Turn

Although the Preamble to the founding Rome Treaty declared the intention of the EEC to 'ensure through common action the economic and social progress of their countries', the treaties have always been asymmetrically weighted towards economic policies. To that extent, solidarity has always faced an uphill struggle as a driver of the EU narrative. On the one hand, its lack of clear, detailed exposition puts it at the easy-to-dismiss end of the spectrum when compared with more fleshed-out operational provisions. On the other, its strong presence at national level invites invocations of solidarity to resist EU actions on grounds of subsidiarity or outright nationalism. In that sense a discourse can flourish that pitches the EU *against* solidarity, at least in emotional terms, where the EU is portrayed as an intellectualised, rights-based, economic elite contrasted with 'felt' togetherness within nation-states. This difficulty recalls Commission President Delors' line that 'you cannot fall in love with a single market'.[36] Yet, it should be added, national solidarities have long since extended beyond family or religious ties, so that to deny the

---

34 Ibid., para. 70.
35 Cases C-715, 718, 719/17 *Commission v. Poland, Hungary and Czech Republic*, ECLI:EU: C:2019:917.
36 'Address Given by Jacques Delors to the European Parliament (17 January 1989)', www .cvce.eu/en/obj/address_given_by_jacques_delors_to_the_european_parlia ment_17_january_1989-en-b9c06b95-db97-4774-a700-e8aea5172233.html.

scope for any constructed EU solidarity on the basis of a lack of 'we'-ness may be based on a false premise. Nonetheless, building policies beyond the market from which popular bonding or support can be forged provides a real challenge for the EU. Exploring the capacity of the EU to adopt a greater social 'turn' – and solidarity's role within it – is central to shaping that narrative.

Solidarity's relationship with market integration is a microcosm of the wider question of the social–economic tension at EU level generally. In particular, solidarity has been closely involved in the interpretation of the free movement and competition core of the single market. A key theoretical conflict played out particularly in competition regulation was the early dominance of (largely German-inspired) ordoliberal thinking in which social effects and benefits were the trickle-down consequences of free competition rather than an end in themselves. This approach morphed into neoliberalism, a wider political position dominant from the 1980s to the early 2000s, whereby markets were seen as the solution to welfare issues and, in particular, it was believed that public services could be delivered more effectively in this way. However, the process of delimiting the boundaries to this adherence to competition and market solutions also provided a forum for the debate on solidarity and the inroads of EU law into national welfare settings. In this way, the narrative of the EU opened a pathway for solidarity as a governing interpretative principle.

This opportunity crystallised around changes introduced by the Lisbon Treaty. At the conceptual level, Article 3 TEU explicitly formulated the EU for the first time as a 'highly competitive social market economy', albeit without further elaboration as to its meaning. But it should be noted that the much older German concept of a *Soziale Marktwirtschaft* (social market economy) was part of the ordoliberal tradition in which social progress is ensured by market performance. The qualifying 'highly competitive' phrase in Artcle 3 may not seem miles away from that stance. However, as an EU concept, the scope of 'social market economy' must be understood against the treaty as a whole – including therefore its social goals and provisions. Thus, attention must be paid to the myriad references to 'combating social exclusion', promoting 'social justice', the aims of 'social cohesion' and 'social progress' and the 'guarantee of social protection'. More specifically, Artcle 14 TFEU amended provisions first established by the 1997 Treaty of Amsterdam regarding the place of 'services of general economic interest' in the 'shared values of the Union and their role in promoting social and territorial cohesion'. In other words, the treaty framework firmly allied solidarity with the kind of society that the EU should be. Article 14 also provided fertile territory for using solidarity as a means to interpret the trajectory of the EU's integrative enterprise and the interface between it and national systems of public services and welfare provision.

The controversial approach to public services reflects significant theoretical and political cleavages. On the one hand, the compromises between member states that led to the rather open-ended wording of Article 14 TFEU reflected their fears about ceding control over nationally organised, funded or managed public services. By making it clear that it did not affect national competences, member states may have thought they were entrenching national solidarities. Yet, on the other hand, the fact that Article 14 was not only inserted at all, but highlighted the societal and cohesive value of public services, introduced a legal springboard to launch a greater 'EU' component later. In fact, it only took the short time between the Amsterdam and Lisbon Treaties to introduce a limited legislative competence for the EU to act in relation to the *principles* by which services of general economic interest should operate. At the same time, member states secured – in their view – an additional defensive bridgehead in the form of an express protocol that 'The provisions of the Treaties do not affect in any way the competence of Member States to provide, commission and organise *non-economic* services of general interest' (emphasis added). This attempt at a new line in the sand between national solidarity arrangements and EU supervisory powers was quickly washed away by heated debates over what was 'economic' and, especially, how to categorise *social* services of general interest, such as social security schemes or social housing arrangements for vulnerable citizens. In effect, member states found it harder to categorise national solidarity systems as beyond the reach of EU law. The question instead was how EU law might treat them – as undertakings subject to 'ordinary' market rules or whether some special regime of privilege or exemption should apply. Hence the scope for normal EU competition rules to recognise – or even be trumped by – welfare and other social concerns was expanded.

This evolution marks a major contribution to developing a specific EU understanding of the 'social market economy'. The overarching point is that solidarity's role in linking public services to the values of the Union in Article 14 TFEU underlines a society-building process that transcends 'mere' market opening and neoliberal values. By 2008 the European Commission was using solidarity in this broad sense: 'Solidarity is part of how European society works [. . .] Solidarity means fostering social inclusion and integration,

participation and dialogue and combating poverty.'[37] This theme has continued through to expression of the Commission's own work programme
priorities for 2019–24 in terms of 'promoting our European way of life'. As the
third section below suggests, the Commission's uptake of solidarity in driving
effective social interventions will signify how far it has really departed from
neoliberal convictions.

It should be stressed that solidarity has not done all the conceptual heavy
lifting when it comes to ensuring that integration has transcended any purely
economic paradigm. In particular, the advent of EU citizenship as a result of
the Maastricht Treaty offered a significant institution in which to frame
individual rights and to elevate the constitutional relevance of citizens.
Unlike competition policy's focus on the relations between commercial
undertakings, the free movement rules were always likely to generate
more direct conflict with solidarity values because of the need – from an
integrationist perspective – to ensure that mobile Europeans could move
freely with their families and participate in the everyday life of a host state.
The citizenship rules of the treaties and the language of rights thus became
the armoury for challenging national obstacles to that enjoyment. But, as
with competition developments mentioned above, the free movement rules
have been interpreted in ways that use solidarity in different senses. In early
cases in areas such as healthcare or social insurance, the Court of Justice used
national solidarity concerns (especially relating to the funding/benefits basis
of different welfare regimes) to trump the free movement rules of the EU. At
the same time, giving primacy to EU citizenship mobility rights meant that
member states were forced to defend their rules against EU norms rather
than having an inalienable right to pursue them. Member states accordingly
owed a degree of a different kind of solidarity to non-national incomers
seeking access to benefits or social entitlements available to nationals.
Decades of jurisprudence have since refined that solidarity obligation –
extending and then retrenching on its scope. In brief, it should be noted
that the Court of Justice introduced tests that in effect made solidarity
conditional. For example, the greater the degree of integration of an individual into the host state society, the more likely it is that an entitlement to
associated benefits would be found. Furthermore, the creativity of the Court
was to some extent reined in by the member states in the form of the

---

37 European Commission, 'Renewed Social Agenda: Opportunities, Access and Solidarity
in 21st Century Europe' (2008), https://eur-lex.europa.eu/LexUriServ/LexUriServ.do?
uri=COM:2008:0412:FIN:EN:PDF.

Citizens' Directive,[38] which also set up categories of entitlements for citizens in relation to residence and access to benefits.

The relationship between citizenship and solidarity is complex. The obvious similarities are that both concepts are bounded and engage rights *and* duties. Yet there is a potential dissonance between protecting EU citizenship's thrust towards individual rights and solidarity's pursuit of collective obligations, togetherness and sharing of resources. EU citizenship discourse has been primarily conducted in the context of host state/non-national relations in regard to individual rights to mobility, residence and freedom from discrimination. In effect, EU citizenship confers the right to be treated as if one were a national of the host state. The result has been that the most controversial examples of citizenship focus upon challenges to national solidarities and the extent to which 'solidarity with strangers' is perceived as affordable or fair by host state nationals or their governments. In a sense, therefore, EU citizenship could almost be said to have been built without recourse to EU solidarity; instead, citizenship rights claims make significant but limited inroads into national (welfare) solidarity. This orientation, of course, also makes EU citizenship unusual if set against more classical versions that focus on active political membership of a community.

The singularity of EU citizenship flows in part from member states' insistence that it should be additional to, and not replace, national citizenship. The narrow, legal version of citizenship constructed in the EU does not yet depend upon – or require – any transnational solidarity between citizens. In other words, there remains a critical gap between the integrative effects of mobility that require a breaking up of national solidarities and any pan-EU solidarity mechanisms operating horizontally between citizens. Solidarity has not yet culminated in widespread EU-level social support measures, whilst citizenship struggles to present a coherent pan-EU political face or force. This remains so, despite it being 20 years since the seminal ruling of the Court of Justice that EU citizenship was destined to be the 'fundamental status' of nationals of the member states.[39] The conceptual tension between solidarity and individualism thus remains a major issue in how a 'social turn' may play out in the EU. On one view, greater social rights are the necessary precursor to 'full' EU citizenship. A different discourse might argue that greater solidarity – in the sense of inclusively addressing social deprivations and inequalities, whether concerning 'movers' or 'stayers' – can effectively bypass arguments around citizenship and directly improve lives. Securing either trajectory

---

38 Directive 2004/38 *OJ* 2004, L158/77.   39 Case C-184/99 *Grzelczyk*, EU:C:2001:458.

represents a key challenge when contemplating the appropriate paths for developing enhanced legitimacy for the EU in the eyes of its citizens and the evolution of any transnational political culture.

The focus of EU steps towards a 'social turn' has been increasingly rights-oriented, notably by giving enhanced legal status to the EU's Charter of Fundamental Rights in 2007 and the proclamation of a Pillar of Social Rights in 2017, followed by a detailed Action Plan in 2021 that strives for a new 'social rulebook' to implement the twenty principles of the Pillar.[40] From a theoretical perspective, however, these developments do not dismantle the asymmetrical construction of the social market economy that provides for only limited EU social interventions to complement member states' activities. On the one hand, the EU is cast as the guarantor of social rights; but on the other, the EU's function is largely to support member states in their social policies, rather than the EU itself being the direct provider of rights. Delivery of the Action Plan is reliant upon member states, social partners and civil society, albeit with a major role for the Commission in identifying strategies.

However, 'solidarity as a connection between citizens may not flourish automatically from claims-making and (additional) rights entitlements'.[41] A more plausible projection for deepening any putative European solidarity may therefore be in terms of its enhanced profile or visibility in delivering citizen welfare, all the way from ideas conception to everyday operability. Crucially, this approach shifts the focus to how and where solidarity is derived or created, especially in relation to citizens' involvement and empowerment. In turn, it emphasises the political aspect of active solidarity and invites consideration of what institutional factors could underpin any specifically EU type of solidarity. The following section accordingly addresses these questions that could fundamentally affect the narrative not only of solidarity, but of the EU itself.

The Battle of Ideas: Political Solidarity of States or Social Solidarity between Citizens?

The discussion so far has stressed the pervasiveness and embeddedness of solidarity and its influence on the evolving, but specifically EU, conceptualisation of the 'social market economy'. This section is more forward-looking

40 European Commission, 'The European Pillar of Social Rights Action Plan' (2021), https://op.europa.eu/webpub/empl/european-pillar-of-social-rights/en; 'Porto Social Commitment' (2021), www.2021portugal.eu/en/porto-social-summit/porto-social-commitment.

41 European Commission, 'Transformations of European Citizenship: Beyond Free Movement' (2020), https://op.europa.eu/en/publication-detail/-/publication/c83d6a a4-3d1f-11ea-ba6e-01aa75ed71a1, p. 49.

and assesses key obstacles and threats to fulfilment of solidarity's capacity as a game-changer. In particular, the ongoing narrative of solidarity throws into sharper contrast the different trajectories of inter-state solidarity and citizens' solidarity, as well as the role of EU institutions in mediating those relationships. Solidarity forms the specific context for revisiting the most basic question of all: what is the EU actually *for*? Or, perhaps more accurately, the playing out of solidarity's narrative will reflect the type of EU that evolves post-Brexit and post-Covid. In other words, the form and extent of solidarity provide a proxy for the character and values of the EU. As a relative and contextualised concept, solidarity is increasingly acquiring a particular EU imprint. Exploring this requires greater elaboration of how solidarity is mutating in meaning and application.

To begin, there is no necessary contradiction between solidarity of member states and solidarity between citizens. However, how solidarities are constructed, intersect and – especially – politicised is of fundamental concern and impact in relation to the development of complex, transnational governance. This in turn implies a reasonable expectation that EU institutions would be more proactively involved in facilitating the durability and resilience of solidarities at all levels – micro, meso or macro. Or, to put it more strongly, establishing the public and political space for solidarities to flourish is a responsibility incumbent upon EU institutions. Indeed, arguably this is both a political and a legal duty – one which consists of securing that the EU acts in accordance with its treaty *values*, not just its operational rules.

The recent history of solidarity between member states is routinely portrayed as a succession of crises, with any solidarity the (usually diluted) outcome of lengthy bargaining around economic and political costs or threats. Pinch-points are well-documented across financial, migration and Covid-19 examples. These include the original 'no bail-out' position adopted towards Greece and other states in the sovereign debt crisis, the inability to come up with a workable plan to spread the impact of large numbers of asylum seekers across member states in 2015 and the fact that, when Covid-19 struck, Italy's call to invoke the EU's Civil Protection Mechanism met with initial silence from other member states. Indeed, the European Commission even had to remind member states that forbidding exports of medical equipment to Italy was a flagrant breach of single market rules. Assistance during the early stages of the pandemic was often the product of bilateral arrangements between member states or between member states and third countries. At the same time, the Commission's insistence on collective solidarity delayed the roll-out of vaccines in the EU. The long-term impact of this strategy on ordinary citizens' perception of the value of EU solidarity remains to be seen.

Closer scrutiny, however, suggests a more nuanced understanding of member state solidarity. First, it is indeed clear that solidarity is limited by negotiation, whether driven by the different interests of net contributor and net beneficiary states or by other cleavages. This is unsurprising, given that solidarity between states is not likely primarily to be an emotional or 'felt' experience. The price for benefiting from solidarity – typically financial support or relief from exposure – often entails a burden of responsibility. This may impose restrictions upon a member state's policy autonomy, spending discipline or even a requirement for supervision. Moreover, the impact on the 'beneficiary' state's citizens may be loss of wages, jobs, pensions and public services – political solidarities can inflict significant social damage. Nevertheless, even if bargaining is an essential part of the EU's ongoing internal political viability, it does not make solidarity an entirely empty vessel. Rather, it represents an improvised force to find innovative and practicable responses which may then push the boundaries of the treaties, or at least stretch their interpretation. The protracted and contested steps in tackling the sovereign debt issue eventually produced a solution that left the eurozone intact and did not invoke the full strictness of its previous operational rules. As examples, the pre-financial crisis Economic and Monetary Union (EMU) rule limiting debt to below 3 per cent of gross domestic product (GDP) was suspended after the eurozone crisis. The Stability Pact was then generally suspended in response to Covid-19. State aid, which had been ruled out in the EMU context via the 'no bail outs' condition, became possible under subsequent financial mechanisms (the European Financial Stabilisation Mechanism) and then unconditional in the Covid-19 context if applied for health expenses.

Solidarity in these extreme situations can be construed as the embodiment of a meta-obligation among member states to secure the future of the EU, even at the expense of hitherto 'sacred cows' under financial rules. This has been achieved despite heated disagreements, including the ugly stereotyping and blame game conducted by some states towards Greece and Portugal in the eurozone crisis. Moral hazard, the fear that lack of strict rules for 'giving' solidarity would disincentivise national recovery measures, was certainly well to the fore. Indeed, similar ructions initially dogged negotiations to tackle Covid-19 that led to the NextGenerationEU package, including an EU Recovery and Resilience Facility (RRF). However, the 'Frugal Four' (the Netherlands, Austria, Denmark and Sweden) were ultimately overridden once Germany had changed its position. Other decisions in the wake of Covid-19, such as the European Central Bank's indication that it could repurchase national debt without following requirements of proportionality, have nevertheless offended some national sensitivities. Whilst the dial may be shifting away from solidarity as a straitjacket, there remains pressure for solidarity to be conditional to achieve member state resource-sharing.

A second, allied, aspect of twenty-first-century developments is that member states' solidarity is at risk of being overlain – even ousted – by other discourses. Certainly, the need for crisis management has been at the forefront of the EU's reaction to financial, migration and pandemic threats. To that extent the presence of other factors (e.g., eurozone or budgetary stability, external relations, domestic politics, upcoming elections) may overshadow solidarity as a concept in national or EU negotiations. Even where solidarity seemingly prevails, as in the sovereign debt crisis, it may be at the expense of social justice values. Moreover, displacing solidarity can lead to very different outcomes. It was notable, for example, that the narrative surrounding asylum and migration very swiftly moved from a humanitarian or solidarity agenda ('Wir schaffen das' ('We'll do it'), as Chancellor Merkel put it)[42] to one of security and the need to limit incoming numbers. Instead of a solidarity-led resolution based on shared EU-wide relocation of individuals and reform of the 'Dublin' regulations, the agreed arrangements were based on enhanced border controls and surveillance, plus an outsourcing of the problem to Turkey.

Solidarity between member states therefore sits in a volatile position – impelling creative pooling of ideas and conflict resolution to avoid systemic catastrophe, on the one hand, but also vulnerable to hijack by other priorities and discourses. Yet it is notable that only one member state so far has seen fit to leave the Union. Brexit, on this interpretation, stands as a repudiation of what it actually means to be a member state, namely rejecting the first-order importance of solidarity values and obligations. Brexit might also be understood as the promotion of an alternative discourse – identity and 'Britishness' – to secure the 2016 referendum outcome; in other words, privileging a national form of solidarity, however mythical or misrepresented, over a more abstractly constructed transnational one. Alternatively, and with crucial lessons for the remaining twenty-seven EU member states, Brexit highlights a solidarity gap in the EU – the need to embrace a *different* type of solidarity, a social one that looks after the disadvantaged or excluded and connects with all citizens.

42 'Sommerpressekonferenz von Bundeskanzlerin Merkel' (2015), www.cvce.eu/en/obj/ the_spaak_report-en-4b911a0a-6bd0-4e88-bff9-4c87690aa4e8.html.

Of course, it is unrealistic to discuss member state solidarity without reference to EU institutions and their inputs into bargaining and goal-setting. The Commission holds critical guardianship and policy initiation roles, but its endorsement of solidarity has been inconsistent. Certainly, particularly with regard to the eurozone crisis, its thinking has been especially criticised for being too preoccupied (still) with neoliberal values and, where budgets and finance are concerned, too loyal to the de facto hegemony of German-inspired doctrines, discipline and sanctions. The 2008 rejection of the creation of an EU joint stabilisation fund in favour of cooperation between states typified the preeminence of Chancellor Merkel's stance on bailouts, namely that she would not use German taxpayers to fund other states' problems. Yet, in the later Covid-19 crisis, the Commission relied more explicitly on solidarity as an overarching consideration to drive EU and member state actions: 'We need solidarity between countries, regions, cities and citizens [. . .] Close cooperation among all relevant actors is key.'[43] In regard to the single market and securing supplies of protective equipment, medicines, vaccines and so on, the Commission urged that 'It is crucial that national measures pursue the primary objective of health protection in a spirit of European solidarity and cooperation.'

One interpretation of this forceful advocacy of European solidarity is that the Commission feared a 'free-for-all' among member states seeking to outdo each other in the chase for emergency supplies and imposition of unilateral restrictions. However, as the pandemic unfolded, there was movement away from reliance upon member state cooperation towards the establishment of EU-level interventions. Two developments already seem significant. First, although EU action was late getting going, setting up the RRF appears to have made a major financial contribution to a solidarity approach without the most rigorous or burdensome features of the responses to the earlier eurozone crisis. Indeed, the EU's Economic and Social Committee welcomed the wider NextGenerationEU package as an 'unprecedented exercise in solidarity'.[44] Nevertheless, one should not overlook the prolonged wrangling that preceded it. Secondly, Covid-19 is provoking more ambitious and creative thinking among EU institutions. In particular, the call for a European

43 European Commission, 'Communication on Coordinated Economic Response to the Covid-19 Outbreak' (2020), https://eur-lex.europa.eu/legal-content/EN/TXT/HTML/?uri=CELEX:52020DC0112&rid=6.
44 'Next Generation EU Recovery Plan – An Unprecedented Exercise in Solidarity' (2020), www.eesc.europa.eu/en/news-media/press-releases/next-generation-eu-recovery-plan-unprecedented-exercise-solidarity.

Health Union, if enacted, could produce a more effective set of permanent institutional solidarity tools to deal with future health emergencies. Moreover, it would add weight to the idea of nurturing a European society where health is clearly a service of general interest. The Health Union has been strongly backed by the Commission, expressly citing solidarity in its proposals.[45]

Nevertheless, whether the latest developments herald a real shift in inter-state solidarity is subject to caveats. At present, health is a shared competence with member states, with the EU having only a supportive role – though the measures under the Civil Protection Mechanism demonstrate the worth of the latter. There is accordingly a significant question about whether member states will provide new competences for a future Health Union. As regards the RRF, it should be remembered that the (eventual) strength of solidarity in relation to the pandemic is possibly linked to Covid-19 being an exogenous threat to the EU. The eurozone crisis, on the other hand, was essentially an endogenous problem. As such, arguably, moral hazard concerns are likelier to flourish in the latter case, so it may not be surprising that state solidarity was more evidently present in the pandemic context. The negative aspects for solidarity in the two crises perhaps boil down to lack of trust about other member states' behaviours (in the eurozone crisis) and acute immediate self-preservation (with Covid-19). Nevertheless, the implication is that significant financial exposure need not be automatically fatal to solidarity between member states. Who wins or loses financially in arriving at pan-EU solutions seems less significant for exogenous threats such as Covid-19 – possibly suggesting a stronger green light for more ambitious solidarity arguments to be invoked in shaping European strategies for handling the other global emergency of the 2020s, climate change.

Any response to climate change must engage with its complex and asymmetrical impacts across regions, populations and policy sectors. Echoing earlier crises, mitigating measures are likely to trigger alternative discourses to solidarity. Displaced communities, for example, may attract the lens of security first rather than accommodation through solidarity. Decarbonisation choices may be harder for particular member states, exacerbating political cleavages and creating special pleading for resources. Institutionally, the 'coronationalism' evident in the pandemic does not augur well for durable intra-EU solidarity. Nevertheless, the Commission has identified solidarity,

---

45 European Commission, 'Building a European Health Union: Reinforcing the EU's Resilience for Cross-Border Health Threats', COM(2020) 724.

especially inter-generational and international, as a 'defining principle' for delivering the range of measures comprising the EU's Green Deal.[46] Critically, the Commission acknowledges the need for a socially fair transition, recognising the opportunity to address existing systemic inequalities likely to be exacerbated by climate change. Connecting with, and nurturing support from, citizens is accordingly integral to viable solidarity – and consistent with a more embedded 'social turn'.

A narrative involving solidarity of citizens is essential for obvious reasons. The EU, after all, is formally conceived as an 'ever closer union among peoples'. The evolution from EEC to EU contains a substantial thread of people-oriented rhetoric, policies and actions. For example, by 1985 the Adonnino Report was emphasising the need for a 'clearer perception of the dimension and existence of the [EEC]' for individual citizens. The introduction of EU citizenship in the Maastricht Treaty marked a particular turning point, conferring both significant rights against discrimination and limited political rights for nationals and their families moving to other member states. Yet, by the turn of the century, the EU was under considerable fire for its lack of connection to the lived experiences of ordinary citizens. EU citizenship had become, in effect, little more than the fifth freedom of movement alongside goods, services, capital and workers – tantamount to a 'market citizenship' only. Resolving the gap between citizenship as a top-down legal construct and addressing grassroots social inequalities has accordingly opened up renewed interest in solidarity's capacity to provide bottom-up strategies. As Commission President Juncker observed, solidarity 'must come from the heart, it cannot be forced'.[47] The key question thus becomes how to create and nurture such an affective phenomenon.

Rich empirical evidence now exists about solidarity practices and the social welfare interventions (local, national or EU-level) that citizens would support. In effect, there is a solidarity infrastructure waiting to be tapped, together with a receptiveness for further development. As the findings from the TransSol and SOLIDUS projects show, solidarity practices are not only widespread, but engaged in by groups irrespective of gender, age, education or class. Typical actions include food banks, debt support, migrant advice, employment campaigns and housing projects – involvement inspired by social-justice-led values

46 European Commission, '"Fit for 55": Delivering the EU's 2030 Climate Target on the Way to Climate Neutrality', COM(2021) 550 final.
47 J.-C. Juncker, 'State of the Union Address 2016: Towards a Better Europe – a Europe That Protects, Empowers and Defends' (2016), http://europa.eu/rapid/press-release_SPEECH-16-3043_en.htm.

that seek to combat social exclusion and alleviate poverty. Civil society organisations, often reliant on volunteers, are key conduits of solidarity and can provide swifter, more flexible and better targeted action than more institutionalised levels of support. Significantly, solidarity is a meaningful experience for providers and receivers alike, but of particular impact for the 'precariat', who are not helped by the mobility-based rights notion of EU citizenship. For groups disproportionately hit by austerity and recession, the promotion of solidarity rather than citizenship appears more relevant.

Attitudinal surveys, with the usual caveat that attitudes are snapshots and not necessarily converted into actions, indicate receptiveness for EU-level welfare interventions. Unsurprisingly, citizens expect help from their own state in the first instance. But the Transnational European Solidarity Survey (TESS) findings[48] showed support for European responsibilities in relation to the sick, elderly and unemployed that lagged only marginally behind the primary duties of states. Moreover, TESS found majority support (57 per cent) for a European welfare system, although respondents in the richer states were less keen. The REScEU project in six member states similarly found that an overwhelming majority (89 per cent) believed that the EU should ensure that no citizen remains without means of subsistence. Indeed, more than three in four respondents favoured a specific EU-funded scheme to support people in severe poverty, and 77 per cent supported an increase in the EU budget to support the jobless in a crisis. This suggests that a greater institutionalisation of solidarity could be a significant addition to the EU's contribution to welfare.

More widely, a recent YouGov survey at the start of the Covid-19 pandemic[49] confirmed public support for fiscal solidarity to other European states, although this was likely to be stronger in respect of near-neighbours and also in relation to exogenous rather than endogenous threats. The same survey also found that the drivers of solidarity varied, with 40 per cent choosing reciprocity, 24 per cent saying it was the right moral thing to do and 13 per cent believing that solidarity was based on shared identity. Again, attitudes to fiscal solidarity preferred EU-level institutional responses to ad hoc or bilateral measures. This position tallies with the kind of Europe that citizens would most like to live in according to the same respondents. A market Europe ranked bottom (15 per cent) and a global Europe that acts as a leader on climate, human rights and global

---

48 Gerhards et al., *European Solidarity in Times of Crisis*.
49 Cicchi et al., 'EU Solidarity in Times of Crisis.'

peace came second (33 per cent), with the top preference (37 per cent) being a protective Europe that defends the European way of life and welfare against internal and external threats. The latter finding suggests the potential narrative power of associating European solidarity with social justice in public mindsets.

Harnessing this widespread positivity about solidarity nevertheless encounters clear limitations and obstacles. Solidarity is policy-dependent, support being much more likely to be shown, for example, towards the elderly and the disabled rather than the unemployed, immigrants and refugees. Conditionality is also a clear feature of citizens' attitudes, with significant variations as to the point, for example, at which migrants should be able to access social benefits in a receiving state (e.g., immediately, after living and/or working for a year or only after becoming citizens of the host country). Deservingness, conflated with – or even instead of – need, appears to be a significant criterion for solidarity. But conditionality is not itself a block to solidarity; after all, solidarity is not charity.

However, greater obstacles to a transnational, European form stem from difficulties in scaling up local or national activities and establishing enduring mechanisms or structures. For example, although civil society organisations (CSOs) are prominent nationally and locally, making them transnational runs into funding, organisational or legal difficulties. In addition, activating solidarity in a pan-EU political arena is problematic. The combined impact of national welfare discourses and provision, local needs and ad hoc solidarity practices makes recourse to EU-level support less practicable. An EU political space, in the sense of an imagined community where EU solidarity is shaped and interrogated, is largely missing. This is the area that could be occupied by fresh or renewed political processes and institutionalised arrangements – maybe including permanent measures such as an EU minimum wage. Without a path to create transnational communication, there seems little likelihood that European solidarity will emerge on an enduring and resilient basis.

This is not to overlook other strategies besides political engagement to create, capture or sustain citizen solidarity. Education, culture and emblematic developments are also involved in embedding solidarity as an EU public good, value and experience for the long-term. Although not the principal focus of this chapter, initiatives such as Erasmus exchanges, youth competitions and the European Solidarity Corps all offer opportunities to connect the EU and solidarity to popular mindsets and to expand and deepen the solidarity infrastructure. The same is true for media activity and claims-making in the public sphere, where a solidarity narrative could be conducted through, for example, CSOs. At present, in the worst-case view, citizens' solidarity is widespread, visible and genuine yet also ad hoc, conditional and fragile. But, if solidarity really is the distinctive heart of the Union, then strengthening it is a proxy for ensuring the EU's own resilience to withstand existential threats.

Concluding Remarks

Solidarity as generally understood has myriad guises: moral value, principle, ideal, norm, emotion or rhetorical call to arms. In the context of the EU, it is equally multidimensional and challenging to pin down. The bargained solidarity of member states is a different species from that displayed by and towards citizens. Although political and social solidarities could be conceptualised as commonly grounded in providing resources to combat adversity, there is clearly an asymmetry between them. In part this is because of the structural imbalance in the EU Treaties between economic and social competences. However, the narrative of solidarity is not a zero-sum game: national and EU solidarities can coexist, as can political and social ones, without being inevitably in conflict with, or displacing, each other. Rather, the question is how the orbits of political (member state) and social (citizens) solidarity can fruitfully be aligned or connected in ways that improve the quality of life for citizens and foster solidaristic relations. However simplistic or idealistic the latter might appear as a goal, it represents the heritage of the Union and the basic tenet of the treaties as a community of values built around solidarity, justice and equalities. This is why solidarity's status as a foundational organisational principle, capable of interpreting powers and actions across the treaties, is so critical. Having a social justice-based solidarity 'baked into' the way the EU operates provides the authority for a significant departure from 'market Europe' by realigning the conceptualisation of the 'social market economy'.

Delivering this implies a rebalancing of the EU away from national interests towards citizen protection and empowerment; in other words, advancing the narrative of solidarity being less about states engaged in crisis management and more engaged with progressing social cohesion. Evidence already supports a nascent 'European' form of solidarity, social in character and distinctive from other incarnations such as cosmopolitan or humanitarian solidarity. In particular, this chapter has suggested a trajectory for solidarity that consists of recalibrating the values, discourse and lived experience of the Union and its citizens. This could be viewed as an evolving social citizenship, but not of the imposed, formal kind currently constituted by EU citizenship. Empirical research increasingly suggests that, even though their support is not unconditional, citizens are probably more enthusiastic about European solidarities than previously imagined. Moreover, the Europe that citizens value most seems to be socially protective rather than a market regulator.

Solidarity is no chimera; it is alive and active. But its de facto existence does not automatically guarantee success in building the EU as a community of values where citizens feel protected. This is the challenge for solidarity: to succeed in that function where the formal institution of EU citizenship has so far fallen short. Accordingly, solidarity has to continue to be created, nurtured and sustained towards a trajectory of meaningful, genuinely transnational pan-EU effectiveness. The Green Deal and NextGenerationEU recovery initiatives from member states and EU institutions are potentially consistent with that direction. But, crucially, political processes are needed that emphasise bottom-up approaches, constructing legitimacy through a public sphere and encouraging citizens' faith in political methods. In other words, sustaining and developing solidarity is intimately connected to the political renewal and resilience of the EU as well as delivery of social justice. At the same time, a stronger, bolder Commission leadership and facilitative role is also clearly justifiable from survey evidence, marking a clearer break with its neoliberal stance of the past. Accordingly, the Conference on the Future of Europe has the opportunity – even responsibility – to debate how to translate solidarity support into durable political mechanisms, participation and social interventions. The EU's sustainability may well depend on a genuine and transformative paradigm shift in its existential core narrative from markets to solidarity.

Recommended Reading

Beutler, B. 'Solidarity in the EU: A Critique of Solidarity and of the EU', in A. Grimmel and S. M. Giang (eds.), *Solidarity in the European Union* (Cham, Springer, 2017), pp. 21–35.

Delanty, G. 'What Unites Europe and What Divides It? Solidarity and the European Heritage Reconsidered', *Asian Journal of German and European Studies* 3 (2018), https://ajges.springeropen.com/articles/10.1186/s40856-018-0025-x.

Furness, M., L. A. Ghica, S. Lightfoot and B. Szent-Iványi. 'EU Development Policy: Evolving as an Instrument of Foreign Policy and as an Expression of Solidarity', *Journal of Contemporary European Research* 16, no. 2 (2020): 89–100.

Lahusen, C. 'European Solidarity: An Introduction to a Multifaceted Phenomenon', in C. Lahusen (ed.), *Citizens' Solidarity in Europe: Civic Engagement and Public Discourse in Times of Crises* (Cheltenham, Edward Elgar, 2020), pp. 1–28.

Pornschlegel. S. ' Solidarity in the EU: More Hype Than Substance?', EPC Issue Paper 21, Charlemagne Prize Academy (2021), https://epc.eu/content/PDF/2021/EU_solidarity_IP.pdf.

Reinl, A. K. 'Transnational Solidarity within the EU: Public Support for Risk-Sharing and Redistribution', *Social Indicators Research* 163 (2022): 1373–97.

Wallaschek, S. 'The Discursive Construction of Solidarity: Analysing Public Claims in Europe's Migration Crisis', *Political Studies* 68, no. 1 (2019): 74–92.

22

European Solidarity: The Difficult Art of Managing Interdependence

AMANDINE CRESPY AND NICOLAS VERSCHUEREN

Solidarity has been consistently the cornerstone of prevailing narratives about the continent's unification. From Schuman's *solidarité de fait* (de facto solidarity) until today's Commission President von der Leyen, who made solidarity the buzzword underpinning the measures taken by the European Union (EU) to tackle the ongoing Covid-19 pandemic, European elites have repeatedly legitimised further steps on the path of integration through the notion that centralisation was generating more prosperity for all instead of war, disunion and socio-economic stagnation. The idea that supranational institutions and policies were unilaterally vectors of pan-European solidarity has nevertheless proved contentious.[1] This is especially true when considering solidarity in terms of social justice and welfare shared equally among all Europeans regardless of their country of origin. This contribution focuses on the internal dimension of solidarity in terms of socio-economic welfare (including aspects relating to agriculture, health and the environment). It will not look at the international dimension of solidarity in the EU's actions (as in development policy) or at burden-sharing issues, such as in the area of migration.

As a matter of fact, the ambition to foster the upward convergence of welfare and working conditions was a key ambition at the outset of European integration in the immediate post-war period, something which has not changed in the era of twenty-first-century globalisation. At the same time, the reference to a 'highly competitive social market economy' in Article 3.3 of the Treaty on the EU reflects how the longstanding doctrine of continental social market economies has been infused with the neoliberal approach to economics in the era of financial capitalism.

---

1 A. Crespy, *The European Social Question: Tackling Key Controversies* (Newcastle, Agenda, 2022).

As early as 1953, Paul Finet, a Belgian socialist trade union leader and future President of the High Authority of the European Coal and Steel Community (ECSC), stressed that the newly created supranational institution had extensive and detailed powers in economic and financial matters, whereas mechanisms for the progressive harmonisation of working and living conditions turned out to be unclear and imprecise.[2] Five years later, union leaders from the coal and steel industries gathered in the so-called Committee 21 expressed their bitter disappointment regarding European social ambitions. From the outset, the social dimension of the unification process led to misunderstandings and illusions about the very nature of the newly created supranational institutions.[3] In that respect, André Renard, a prominent figure of Belgian socialist unionism, proved a relentless advocate of European social harmonisation while consistently calling for European strikes as the greatest expression of solidarity among Europeans. After 20 years of expectation, gestation and resignation, the European social agenda was still weak, but showed some signs of life. The Court of Justice of the EU (CJEU) championed anti-discrimination and gender equality, thus recalling that the member states' commitment to social progress was embedded in the European Economic Community (EEC) Treaty. With the Delors Commission and the inception of an embryonic supranational neo-corporatism (labelled European social dialogue), the perspective from which to see the European Community as a space of solidarity found its culmination. Soon after, in the course of the 1990s, though, such beliefs were superseded by the idea that the EU was above all a place for market extension and competition. As various forms of social dumping emerged and proliferated, the EU appeared rather as a threat to national solidarity. Debates about the neoliberal nature of the EU Treaties, surrounding notably ratification of the Constitutional Treaty in 2004–5, the EU's austeritarian response and the social hardship imposed upon southern Europe after the 2008 financial crisis, or even the debates about social insecurity during the campaign leading to Brexit all account for citizens' mistrust in the notion that the EU ever was a place of solidarity.

---

2 André Renard Foundation, Archives André Renard, 1, Workers and the ECSC, Paul Finet's speech in Liège during the 6th Congress of the Socialist Movement for the United States of Europe, 1953, p. 23.
3 P. Pasture, 'Adieu aux illusions. La CISC devant la CEE. 1958–1974', in E. Bussière and M. Dumoulin (eds.), *Milieux économiques et intégration européenne* (Artois, Artois Presse Université, 1998), pp. 371–86.

This contribution is an attempt to provide an overview of what the EEC – and later the EU – has delivered in terms of solidarity over the last 70 years. With obvious historical shortcuts and imprecisions, it aims to highlight a 'back and forth process' rather than an eschatological path leading to ever greater solidarity among Europeans. The meaning of solidarity has changed over time, moving from a 'Europe of workers' in the 1950s and 1960s, to the blurry and feeble expression of 'Social Europe' and then finally solidarity between citizens, generations, genders or countries. The quest for EU solidarity in practice is therefore a moving target depending on historical contexts and approaches. Two peculiarities of European integration nevertheless provide key threads. First, solidarity cannot be understood in isolation from market integration through the Single Market, which has been the baseline of regional integration in Europe. This has meant, secondly, that EU integration has been as much about generating new forms of interdependence (Monnet's vision) as about managing them and tackling the problematic aspects of market competition (Delors' vision), with the aim of ensuring the sustainability of an alliance made of diverse societies and states.

Against this background, this chapter seeks to show how European integration has generated mechanisms to enhance solidarity beyond market competition; at the same time, the emerging new forms of socio-economic interdependence have contributed to distend, disrupt and reconfigure those older forms of interdependence that had been blended in with post-war welfare states and neo-corporatism. From a scholarly viewpoint, understanding the link between broad historical developments in Europe's economies and societies and supranational social policy, including jurisprudence, is a tricky endeavour in which causes and effects are far from being obvious.[4] Has the ECSC played a role in the decline of the coal and steel industry in Europe? Did the Common Agricultural Policy (CAP) contribute to the impoverishment of European farmers? Were there any clear relations between the setting up of the Common Market and the 'Golden Sixties'? In an attempt to capture the multiple facets of European solidarity, three areas of thought and practice will be considered. First, we will explore how European institutions contributed to the emergence of a *transnational solidarity* among Europeans by fostering the implementation of common rules beyond national boundaries. Secondly, we will consider *national solidarity* to understand how the EU turned out to have an important – if contested – role in promoting and sometimes undermining solidarity

---

4 See, for instance, H. Kaelble, *Sozialgeschichte Europas: 1945 bis zur Gegenwart* (Munich, Beck, 2007).

within member states. Finally, we will focus on mechanisms of *international solidarity* among member states through the means of redistribution of fiscal resources from the EU budget. While we use them as heuristic devices to address empirical complexity in an analytical fashion, those three forms of solidarity are in no way silos isolated from each other. On the contrary, they are closely intertwined and exist in tension with one another.

Transnational Solidarity among Europeans: Between Competition and Social Convergence

Pointing out the discrepancy between the social ambitions enshrined in the ECSC or EEC Treaty and tangible achievements is now a truism in European studies. However, the socio-economic model on which European policy making was developed is still being discussed. The historian René Leboutte emphasises how the first European institutions were mainly inspired by economic planning and Keynesianism, with social justice and solidarity as the foundation of European peace, prosperity and perhaps unity.[5] Conversely, John Gillingham straightforwardly asserted that the market economy and neoliberal dynamic have driven the European integration project.[6] Straightforward social harmonisation soon appeared to be an unrealistic – or undesirable – objective. With supranational institutions deprived of substantive prerogatives in the social domain, a small body of limited social provisions built up over time. In an ever-enlarging union, which has become extremely diverse culturally and socially, the contradiction between economic freedom and social solidarity has become the European never-ending 'Rumble in the Jungle'.

The Creation of the Single Market and Elusive Social Harmonisation

From the outset, the fledgling High Authority was depicted as the first supranational institution with notable competences in social matters in order to preclude any criticism from working-class organisations or left-wing political parties.[7] Therefore, numerous social measures and ambitious

5 R. Leboutte, *Histoire économique et sociale de la construction européenne* (Brussels, Peter Lang, 2008).
6 J. Gillingham, *European Integration 1950–2003: Superstate or New Market Economy?* (Cambridge, Cambridge University Press, 2003).
7 B. Vayssière, 'Le spectre communiste, un fantôme dans la maison européenne', *Les Cahiers de Framespa. Nouveaux champs de l'histoire sociale* 36 (2021), https://journals.openedition.org/framespa/10299.

social policies were initiated or supported by European institutions, mainly by the High Authority and the Common Assembly. Among these initiatives and dispositions, various mechanisms of solidarity were unfolded to guarantee economic growth, stability and social harmonisation. The prevailing view held that workers, and subsequently farmers, had to be protected from the opening of the Common Market, its potential effects on employment (Conventions on the Transitional Provisions, Section 23) or from technological innovations which would lead to job losses (ECSC Treaty, Article 56). Initially, these measures of 'workers' re-adaptation' were intended to ease the impact of labour market competition and to bring assistance to workers made redundant after the opening of the Common Market.[8] The re-adaptation scheme included allowance for redundant workers between jobs, resettlement grants (accommodation and transfer), financial support for professional training or payment of temporary allowances in a situation where a worker had to do a less well-paid job than the previous one.[9] The application and effectiveness of these European financial aids remains difficult to assess, but would represent 115,000 workers being financially supported by the European re-adaptation programme in the 1950s.[10] What lay behind these labour market policies was the commitment to preserve full employment despite plant closures and, from a more general perspective, that workers should not be negatively affected by the Common Market.

The living and working conditions should, furthermore, not be lowered by the evolution of the coal and steel industries or by economic recession. Indeed, the range of these social policies was initially limited in time and was dedicated to marginal companies that were unable to be competitive. The rapid decline of the coal industry in the late 1950s confirmed the need of European solidarity for redundant workers. According to Alan Milward, the extension and strengthening of these re-adaptation policies could be seen as the preservation of the post-war social and political consensus at the European level.[11] These social dispositions found, to some extent, a continuity in the European Social Fund (ESF) proposed in the Spaak Report and set up by the Treaty of Rome (Article 123). However, along

8 D. Collins, *The European Communities: The Social Policies of the First Phase*, vol. 1: *The European Coal and Steel Community 1951–1970* (London, Martin Robertson, 1975).

9 N. Verschueren, *Fermer les mines en construisant l'Europe: Une histoire sociale de l'intégration européenne* (Brussels, Peter Lang, 2013).

10 EEC, Ninth General Report (1961), p. 291.

11 A. S. Milward, *The European Rescue of the Nation State* (London, Routledge, 1992).

with the development of the Common Market, free movement of labour and European workforce competition became subjects of growing concern.

Since the Schuman Declaration, the European unification process has been steered towards integration through the market, awakening fears of social dumping. In a political cartoon in *L'Humanité* on 29 March 1957, Pierre Donga portrayed how capitalism through the Common Market will degrade French working and living conditions.[12] Although this cartoon was produced by a Communist Party newspaper, it revealed some relentless worries about upward or downward harmonisation inside the European Community. The possible deconstruction of labour law and social benefits generated by the opening of the Common Market gave rise to acrimonious debates before the ratification of the Treaty of Rome and even after. Yet, Guy Mollet's demand for social harmonisation as a precondition for the integration of national economies in a common market reflected these concerns.[13] In his 1956 book, Albert Delpérée, a Belgian official in charge of social security, underlined that tensions and conflicts about social harmonisation and solidarity were bound to increase in a market grounded in free movement of goods and workers. Should European institutions have strong competences to implement upward social harmonisation? Should the European Commission be able to develop redistributive policies or would the Common Market foster upward social harmonisation by itself? In 1955, the International Labour Organization (ILO) mandated an expert group chaired by Bertil Ohlin to answer these questions. The former Swedish Minister of Commerce was a longstanding advocate of lowering customs barriers as a means to bring about automatically an increase in living conditions.[14] Therefore, the report unsurprisingly concluded that social harmonisation was not required as a precondition for the opening of the Common Market. In addition, the conclusion underlined that European social harmonisation would be achieved without specific policies and advanced the idea of

---

12 'Cartoon by Donga on the Social Implications of the EEC Treaty (29 March 1957)', www.cvce.eu/en/obj/cartoon_by_donga_on_the_social_implications_of_the_eec_treaty_29_march_1957-en-2756beeb-30fb-4368-ac13-289ef599c9c7.html.

13 F. Scharpf, 'The European social model', *Journal of Common Market Studies* 40, no. 4 (2002): 645–70; L. Rye, 'The Rise and Fall of the French Demand for Social Harmonization in the EEC, 1955–1966', in K. Rücker (ed.), *Quelle(s) Europe(s)? Nouvelles approches en histoire de l'intégration européenne* (Brussels, Peter Lang, 2006), pp. 155–68.

14 L. Mechi, 'Managing the Labour Market in an Open Economy: From the International Labour Organisation to the European Communities', *Contemporary European History* 27, no. 2 (2018): 221–38.

a minimalist view of social policy requirements.[15] This solution also stemmed from the growing weight of German ordoliberalism in the shape of an emerging European economic model which was still being nurtured by various post-war economic legacies.[16] To some extent, this twofold approach based on social harmonisation through the market, on the one hand, and the ordoliberalism which was spreading in European institutions during the 1950s and 1960s, on the other, paved the way to the future European single market.

From early on, the prevalent paradigm was therefore that an improvement of living conditions would result from the proper functioning of the Common Market as it is clearly stipulated in the EEC Treaty in its Article 117. In 1957, the liberal turn of the European integration project became obvious for many federalists and trade union leaders, and the dream of a European redistributive model was buried, while welfare states served to institutionalise solidarity at the national level. As Patel points out, 'the fear that "more Europe" would mean "less welfare state" was always strong. Here the price of European solidarity appeared too high to most governments.'[17] However, the European Community, later the EU, remained a field of struggle generating demands for more solidarity and transnational redistribution.

This is illustrated by a defining episode from the early days of integration. On 8 August 1956, the Belgian industrial town of Marcinelle was hit by a mine disaster killing 262 mineworkers, half of whom were Italians. In the aftermath of the emotional trauma, a project emerged from socialist trade union leaders who wanted to harmonise progressively the working conditions of all mineworkers in the ECSC. Soon, this ambitious project received support from the High Authority and the Common Assembly. In July 1964, the first European demonstration gathering 25,000 miners was organised in Dortmund by socialist trade unions demanding the setting up of a European status of mineworkers and advocating for a 'Social Europe'.[18] Three years later, after numerous debates, much resistance, amendments and counter-proposals, the project of social harmonisation at the European level was torn apart by the

---

15 C. Hoskyns, *Integrating Gender: Women, Law and Politics in the European Union* (London, Verso, 1996), p. 49.

16 M. Segers, 'Eclipsing Atlantis: Trans-Atlantic Multilateralism in Trade and Monetary Affairs as a Pre-history to the Genesis of Social Market Europe (1942–1950)', *Journal of Common Market Studes* 51, no. 1 (2019): 159–74; L. Warlouzet, 'The EEC/EU as an Evolving Compromise between French Dirigism and German Ordoliberalism (1957–1995)', *Journal of Common Market Studies* 51, no. 1 (2019): 77–93.

17 K. K. Patel, *Project Europa: A History* (Cambridge, Cambridge University Press, 2020), p. 106.

18 *La Tribune socialiste*, 11 July 1964.

Council, and the proposal was dropped. Besides the originality and ambition of this demand for a European status, it was also the first attempt to overcome Common Market rules under which a national social benefit could be seen as a distortion of competition. As a matter of fact, the Court of Justice of the European Communities (CJEU) considered in February 1961 that the German allowance for mineworkers was a state aid prohibited under Article 4(c) of the ECSC Treaty. Therefore, German trade union leaders tried to straddle the fence through the Europeanisation of this social benefit by its incorporation in the European status of mineworkers, aiming to achieve in this way the harmonisation of progress asserted by the treaty. This specific example epitomises the limits to the envisaged social harmonisation at the European level. As we will see below, the path chosen was therefore that of minimum coordination of social security instead of harmonisation. This, however, did not preclude the emergence of new forms of solidarity in the form of transnational rights, often pioneered by the CJEU.

The Limited and Increasingly Contentious Regulation of a Pan-European Labour Market

The European history of combating discrimination initially focused on equality between men and women in the workplace. In 1966, the workers of the national armaments factory in Herstal, near Liège, in Belgium, went on strike to demand that the principle of equal pay for men and women enshrined in Article 119 of the Treaty of Rome be implemented. This episode resulted in a wave of feminist mobilisation and a series of cases brought before the CJEU in favour of women. The 8 April 1976 decision C-43/75, *Defrenne v. Sabena*, marks the beginning of the EU's policy on equality between men and women. The judges in Luxembourg boldly ruled that Article 119 of the Treaty of Rome on the equal treatment of men and women (Article 157 of the Treaty on the Functioning of the European Union (TFEU)) should apply directly in the member states and that pension rights were an integral part of remuneration. In 1984, in its decision on the Raj and Beydoun case (C-75/82), the Court recognised equality between men and women as a fundamental right. Protection of pension rights was subsequently extended by jurisprudence to part-time workers (in 1984) and transsexuals (in 1996). The principles set out by the Court were then codified in an important legislative body of fifteen directives and regulations adopted between 1975 and 2010.[19] The first

---

19 S. Jacquot, *Transformations in EU Gender Equality Policy: From Emergence to Dismantling* (Basingstoke and New York, NY, Palgrave, 2015), p. 208.

texts focused on equal pay, broadly understood, and access to social security and pension rights. In 1992, Directive 92/85/EEC established a minimum duration of maternity leave of fourteen continuous weeks.

With the new regulatory competence introduced by the Treaty of Amsterdam (Article 13), the EU's field of action extended beyond gender equality. On the one hand, Directive 2000/78/EC on equal treatment in the field of employment (dubbed 'the employment equality directive') covers discrimination based on religion, disability, age or sexual orientation. On the other hand, Directive 2000/43/EC on equality irrespective of race or ethnic origin (dubbed the 'racial equality directive') applies not only to employment and training, but also to access to social protection or to goods and services in general. Yet, progress soon stalled. In 2008, the European Commission submitted a proposal to extend the fight against discrimination based on religion, disability, age or sexual orientation beyond the field of employment to social protection, education and access to goods and services that are commercially available to the public. Despite the fact that a majority of Members of the European Parliament (EP) voted in favour of the text in 2009, the issue has now been blocked in the Council for over a decade. As in other areas, EU regulation on discrimination has become more divisive over time.

In many ways, most competences and actions of the EU to regulate a pan-European labour market date back to the Protocol on Social Policy appended to the Treaty of Maastricht. The protocol gave a significant impetus to the EU's social action in two ways. First, it formalised the legislative competence of the EU in a number of issues relating to labour law and industrial relations: according to Article 2 of the Protocol, 'the improvement in particular of the working environment to protect workers' health and safety; working conditions; the information and consultation of workers; equality between men and women with regard to labour market opportunities and treatment at work; the integration of persons excluded from the labour market'. Secondly, it marked the inception of the European social dialogue promoting negotiations among the social partners at EU level. The European social dialogue foresees especially two procedures whereby (a) consultation of the social partners by the European Commission is mandatory when it comes to legislation in the area of social affairs and (b) framework agreements negotiated by the social partners can be turned into binding legislation by the social partners. The European social dialogue has produced only meagre outcomes over a period of 30 years. Three cross-sectoral and nine sectoral binding agreements have been concluded since 1993. A further six cross-sectoral and four sectoral agreements which are autonomously implemented by the social partners at the national level have been concluded. However, the Commission has made strategic use of the legal basis provided by the Social Protocol on 'health and safety at work' – which was then expanded into the Chapter on Social Policy in the Amsterdam Treaty and subsequent treaties. This led it to, for instance, put forward regulation on the protection of fixed-term or temporary contract workers (91/383/EEC), pregnant workers (92/85/EEC) and young people (94/33/EEC) or, more recently, minimum wages.

Two political and legal 'sagas' are highly illustrative of the battles that have taken place in the field of health and safety. Those related to working time, on the one hand, and maternity leave, on the other. The regulation of working time through an EU directive dates back to 1993 and was contested from the outset by the government of the United Kingdom (UK). The UK obtained not only the exemption of many sectors from the directive, but also a general opt-out from the key provision, namely the 48-hours working time weekly limit. Following suit, most member states adopted sectoral or total opt-outs from the rule. While the CJEU adopted a pro-regulation stance, two attempts in 2004 and 2010 to revise the directive and suppress the possibility of an opt-out failed due to disagreements among member states and the social partners.

The maternity leave directive, a key piece of legislation in the EU's body of social law, finds itself at the intersection of labour law and family policy, an area where the EU has enjoyed weak legitimacy to act and which has long been divisive 'along ideological lines both within and between countries'.[20] In 2008, the European Commission proposed revising the 1992 Directive on maternity leave. But this triggered an intractable conflict between the EP, where a left-wing coalition sought to introduce major innovations such as mandatory paid paternity leave, and the Council, which adopted a more conservative stance. After the Council had blocked the text for 4 years, it was withdrawn by the Commission in 2015. These two examples show that, after the adoption of initial, embryonic regulations in the 1990s, the modernisation of the social *acquis* has proved contentious and difficult in recent decades.

In 2016–17 the European Commission under Jean-Claude Juncker attempted to relaunch the social agenda of the EU by promoting the so-called European Pillar of Social Rights, a catalogue of twenty political objectives for addressing problems of social inclusion, fair working conditions and the struggle against all forms of discrimination. The Pillar was criticised for its vague legal nature insofar as it guarantees no new rights for people in

---

20 L. Hantrais, *Social Policy in the European Union* (Basingstoke, Macmillan, 1995), p. 79.

the judicial sense, nor does it create new competences for the EU, and its implementation occurs through both hard and soft law.[21]

The von der Leyen Commission, which took office in October 2019, nevertheless confirmed the commitment to achieving the goals set in the Pillar. It put forward a number of legislative initiatives aiming to re-regulate labour markets and improve working conditions, including remuneration. A directive on adequate minimum wages (adopted in 2022) promotes a standard above 60 per cent of respective national median wages. Furthermore, the negotiations on a directive proposal on working conditions in platform work (ongoing at the time of writing) target the exploitative use of the status of independent workers (as opposed to employees) in platform-based services. Thus, after a long decade of austerity during which EU policy-making has contributed to the deregulation of labour markets and wage stagnation, the EU has engaged with a revival of its social regulation agenda in order to tackle poverty and indecent working conditions in times of labour shortages and high inflation.

Today, the body of social law, protecting both mobile and non-mobile workers throughout the EU, amounts to over 160 legally binding acts, according to the criteria used by the database of the European Trade Union Institute. Although it is not insignificant, the EU's regulatory action is restricted by the specific competences granted in Article 153 TFEU on social policy. Strikingly, two paramount issues regarding solidarity among workers, namely the right to strike and the negotiation of pay, are explicitly excluded from the EU's field of action. Furthermore, the tensions surrounding solidarity and competition among workers have only been exacerbated as the EEC and then the EU enlarged to incorporate countries with very contrasted levels of labour costs and socio-economic protection.

National Solidarity and the EU: Between Competition and Coordination

Early on, the European integration project was seen as partly undermining national solidarity. In media coverage of the Marcinelle disaster in 1956, the High Authority was pictured as a cold technocratic body with no consideration for the fate of thousands of Italian workers who had been sacrificed in the name of productivity and economic growth. After the commotion, it

---

21 S. Garben, 'The European Pillar of Social Rights: Effectively Addressing Displacement?', *European Constitutional Law Review* 14, no. 1 (2018): 210–30.

became obvious that European institutions had hardly any authority to improve living and working conditions in the Community. Until today, the idea that there is a division of labour whereby the EU is responsible for making the economy and the market work while national states should care for social policy has remained deeply anchored among European elites. Over time, the EEC and the EU have asserted a highly ambivalent role vis-à-vis national welfare states. On the one hand, free movement has contributed to disruption of the national 'boundaries of welfare' in ways that have fuelled welfare chauvinism.[22] On the other, there has been an ambition to offset the negative effects of market competition on national societies by regulating free movement to protect social solidarity. At the same time, though, minimal coordination and the fragmentary opening between national welfare states hindered the development of a substantive social dimension for European citizenship, which has remained at best very thin and ruled by marketisation and the commodification of labour.[23]

Free Movement as a Thorn in the Side of National Solidarity

Ironically, when Article 119 on equal pay between men and women was included in the Treaty of Rome, the underpinning concern was that of social dumping and the suspicion that women would constitute a cheaper reserve of labour. Later on, starting from the relaunch of the Single Market and the enlargements to the south in the 1980s, differences in remuneration and social protection between EEC member states raised fears of social dumping by countries sending workers to wealthier countries. Social dumping refers to 'the practice of undermining or evading existing social regulations with the aim of gaining a competitive advantage',[24] including not only wages but also social protection (leave, social security, safety, etc.). In the European context, social dumping is made possible by the significant differences in living standards between European countries, a phenomenon which has been exacerbated by the EU's continuous enlargement.

The posting of workers in particular is at the centre of one of the greatest political and regulatory sagas in the history of the single market and offers a striking illustration of the tension between the freedom to move in

---

22 M. Ferrera, *The Boundaries of Welfare: European Integration and the New Spatial Politics of Social Protection* (Oxford and New York, NY, Oxford University Press, 2005).
23 L. Magnusson and B. Strath (eds.), *A European Social Citizenship? Preconditions for Future Policies from a Historical Perspective* (Brussels, Peter Lang, 2004).
24 M. Bernaciak, 'Social Dumping and the EU Integration Process' (2014), www.etui.org /publications/working-papers/social-dumping-and-the-eu-integration-process.

a common labour market – consecrated by the EU as a fundamental right – and the social protection of workers stemming from national social struggles and institution building. A posted worker is sent by their company to another country to work for a limited period of time. There are over 2 million posted workers in the EU, with a 69 per cent increase between 2010 and 2016, and they are mainly concentrated in the building sector, followed by industry and the social services and healthcare sectors. Germany, France and Belgium receive about 50 per cent of all posted workers, while Germany and Slovenia are the main sending countries.[25]

In its *Rush Portuguesa* decision from 1990, the CJEU ruled that governments could apply their own labour laws to posted workers. This position was, however, challenged by the Commission, who considered it to be an obstacle to the freedom to provide services for foreign companies. A compromise was found in 1996 with the adoption of Directive 96/71/EC, which establishes the law of the country of origin as a rule, except for a core of critical rights (pay and leave). This was believed to facilitate the mobility of workers while ensuring the protection of workers' rights. Quickly, however, the directive was deemed insufficient by receiving states in western Europe and by trade unions, which deplored social dumping. The situation was exacerbated by the enlargements into central and eastern Europe in 2004 and 2007 as various forms of abuse (tax evasion, non-enforcement of workers' rights, letterbox companies, etc.) could be documented.

The European Commission and the CJEU further led a pro-market offensive in the mid 2000s. The Commission submitted the Services Directive (also known as the 'Bolkestein Directive') in 2004 to impose the primacy of the law of the country of origin throughout the entire services sector. It was nevertheless watered down after a broad campaign of opposition led by left-wing civil society organisations and trade unions.[26] At the same time, far-right claims about 'Polish plumbers' stealing French jobs contributed a great deal to the failure of the European Constitutional Treaty ratification in May 2005. As for the Court, it issued, in 2007–8, four decisions known as *Viking, Laval, Rüffert* and *Luxembourg*,[27] which dramatically reversed its earlier jurisprudence in *Rush Portuguesa* to subject national labour law (especially collective

---

25 EP, 'Posted Workers: The Facts on the Reform (Infographic)' (2019), www.europarl
.europa.eu/news/en/headlines/society/20171012STO85930/posted-workers-the-facts-
on-the-reform-infographic.
26 A. Crespy, *Qui a peur de Bolkestein? Conflit, résistances et démocratie dans l'Union
européenne* (Paris, Economica, 2012).
27 *Viking*, C-438/05; *Laval*, C-341/05; *Rüffert*, C-346/06; *Luxembourg*, C-319/06.

agreements and procurement law) to the freedom to provide services in the EU. This jurisprudence hammered national traditions of collective bargaining and provided leverage for employers to take advantage of wage competition. In Sweden, for instance, large companies have been happy to ignore national collective agreements when hiring an increasing number of foreign workers.[28]

When he took office as the President of the European Commission in 2014, Jean-Claude Juncker made the re-regulation of posting one of his priorities. After 5 years of economic recession and accusations of austeritarian policy, the new president of the Commission claimed he wanted to make the EU worthy of a 'social triple A'. In March 2016, the Commission proposed revising the 1996 directive on posting along three main lines. (a) Posted workers should get equal pay for equal work in the same workplace. Contrary to the prevailing situation so far, this means that, on the one hand, collective agreements negotiated among social partners should apply to posted workers and, on the other hand, (b) the duration of posting should be limited to 2 years. (c) Equal treatment will also apply to workers hired via temporary work agencies. In the preceding 2015 public consultation, a joint letter from Germany, France, Austria, the Benelux countries and Sweden demanded the introduction of the principle of 'equal pay for equal work in the same place' and the adoption of clearer maximum posting duration. The Visegrád Group, as well as Bulgaria, Romania and the Baltic states, opposed the revision.[29] The negotiations were arduous, both in the Council and in the EP, and climaxed when Emmanuel Macron was elected to the French Presidency in May 2017. In line with his campaign pledge to tackle the ills of Europe, he called for even stricter regulation and travelled to central Europe to put pressure on reluctant leaders in the region. As the revised directive came into force in July 2020, the European Trade Union Confederation (ETUC) issued a positive statement claiming that 'two million posted workers finally receive equal pay'.[30]

However, most national trade unions, as well as political parties criticising the EU from a social angle, deplore the fact that social dumping is still

28 D. Seikel, 'Class Struggle in the Shadow of Luxembourg. The Domestic Impact of the European Court of Justice's Case Law on the Regulation of Working Conditions', *Journal of European Public Policy* 22, no. 8 (2015): 1166–85.

29 A. Lubow and S. K. Schmidt, 'A Hidden Champion? The European Court of Justice as an Agenda-Setter in the Case of Posted Workers', *Public Administration* 99 (2021), 321–34.

30 ETUC, 'Two Million Posted Workers Finally Receive Equal Pay' (2020), www.etuc.org /en/pressrelease/two-million-posted-workers-finally-receive-equal-pay.

occurring due to legal gaps in implementation, transposition or enforcement and to the loosely coordinated (rather than harmonised) social security of workers.[31] Indeed, social security coverage and the related employers' contributions still depend on the workers' country of origin. This means that posted workers coming from countries with lower social standards still remain significantly cheaper than local workers in main recipient countries such as Belgium, France and Germany.

A major omission from the directive on posted workers was the regulation of the road transport sector, which has seen a rise in abusive practices of social dumping. As documented by the Belgian journalist Bryan Carter in his prize-winning documentary *EUtopia*, western European companies in the logistics sector have increasingly established subsidiaries in eastern countries with low pay and social protection to exploit truck drivers, who work and live on the road for months in deplorable conditions, leading notably to the deaths of two Polish drivers in a Belgian warehouse in 2012.[32] In July 2020, a set of three regulations dubbed the 'mobility package' was further adopted to address this longstanding issue. Among other provisions, the package contains reinforced rules on access to the profession, maximum work and minimum rest times for drivers (controlled by means of a tachometer), and it lays down rules on the posting of drivers; it also includes provisions concerning enforcement and control.

In the latter regard, a European labour authority (located in Bratislava) was set up in 2019 in order to coordinate member states' action to guarantee the effectiveness of EU social regulation in practice. The deliberations leading to the decision to establish the authority proved contentious from the point of view of subsidiarity. The main task of the authority is to assist member states and the Commission in their effective application and enforcement of Union law related to labour mobility across the Union and the coordination of social security systems within the Union.[33]

---

31 See, for example, B. Fox, 'We Want Positive Action to Combat Exploitative Labour in EU Construction', interview with Tom Deleu, General Secretary of the European Federation of Building and Woodworkers, Euractiv (2021), www.euractiv.com/sec tion/economy-jobs/interview/we-want-positive-action-to-combat-exploitative-labour -in-eu-construction.

32 B. Carter, *EUtopia* (Pokitin Productions, 2020). The extended English version is available at https://vimeo.com/462096862.

33 Regulation (EU) 2019/1149 of the European Parliament and of the Council of 20 June 2019 Establishing a European Labour Authority.

In the post-2004 enlarged Union, competition rather than solidarity has often opposed workers (and often unions) from the west, seeking to preserve decent levels of pay and social protection, on the one hand, and those from the east, who regard mobility as a main opportunity for seeking work, on the other hand. In the face of such disparities, the EU has provided only a limited level of coordination and conditional opening of national welfare states.

Minimal Coordination and Conditional Opening of National Welfare States

As explained above, in spite of repeated social demands from the unions, social harmonisation was initially deemed neither realistic nor desirable by European elites cheering the virtues of market integration (read competition) and subsidiarity (read sovereignty) in social matters. Yet, a minimal level of social security coordination proved necessary to facilitate the mobility of workers. The Europeanisation of social security found its first application in two regulations dating from 1958 (3/58 and 4/58) aiming at promoting mobility and regulating the rights of migrant workers throughout the EEC. To ensure the continuity of rights and avoid social dumping, non-national workers were to be covered by the social security system of the country in which they work. These regulations were revised in 1971 (1408/71) and again in 2004 (883/2004). The rights related to free movement were consolidated in the 1960s and 1970s by a series of regulations that guaranteed mobility and the right to family reunification.[34] These texts are based on four principles: equal treatment of nationals and non-nationals; the aggregation of benefits accrued in different countries; the portability of these rights; and the non-overlap of protection regimes and contributions in different member states.[35] Instead of harmonisation, these provisions amount to a complex regime which often makes it difficult for workers – whether migrant or suffering from occupational injury or diseases – and retirees to enforce their social rights.

Nevertheless, the European social policy took shape in the European agenda that was ushered in during the 1970s by the Hague Summit, the 1972 Paris Summit and the 1974–6 Social Action Programme.[36] This new impetus given to European solidarity flowed from the increasing economic

---

34 Regulation of 16 August 1961; Regulation 38/1964; Regulation 1612/68; Directive 68/360; Regulation 1251/70; Regulation 1408/71.
35 K. Anderson, *Social Policy in the European Union* (Basingstoke, Palgrave Macmillan, 2015), p. 91.
36 R. Geyer, 'The State of the European Union Social Policy', *Policy Studies* 21, no. 3 (2000): 245–61.

instability, but also from the resurgence of class conflicts in Europe.[37] The accomplishment of this ambitious social programme was still largely incomplete and remained shrouded in obscurity at the dawn of the neoliberal turn due to the unanimity rule in the Council as well as the resistance to the Europeanisation of social security mechanisms. Furthermore, these rights concern only a small minority of mobile Europeans, but one whose numbers are growing steadily. Currently, approximately 17 million Europeans live or work in a member state other than their country of origin, which is twice as many as in 2010.[38]

In the 1990s and 2000s, these provisions were consolidated and extended in two directions: the rights of mobile workers to social benefits increased (early retirement, unemployment, etc.), on the one hand, and access to these rights has been extended to other categories of non-nationals (students, unemployed people, pensioners), on the other. The so-called Citizenship Directive of 2004 (2004/38/EC) established the right for all EU citizens to access social benefits. If no harmonisation was to occur, the principle of non-discrimination implied the mutual opening of national welfare states, thus creating an embryo of pan-European social citizenship. The 2004 directive was based essentially on the case law of the Court, which, in 1998 and 2001, had established the right of residency as a cornerstone of European citizenship. However, in the 2010s, the CJEU gave in to the prevailing mood of welfare chauvinism whereby large portions of national publics regard non-nationals (especially Europeans coming from the east) as practising 'welfare tourism'.[39] The underpinning idea is that of the need for a tangible link between the non-national resident and the host country to justify access to social benefits. In the Brey case from 2013 (C-140/12), the CJEU set out a list of criteria allowing national authorities to justify denial of access to benefits for inactive non-nationals. In further decisions from 2014 and 2015 opposing unemployed people from eastern Europe against German regional authorities, the Court considered that jobseekers no longer enjoy a right to social benefits beyond a period of 6 months of inactivity. Rendered a week before the referendum on Brexit in June 2016, the Court's decision in the *Commission v. United Kingdom*, which recognises a legitimate right for governments to

---

37 C. Crouch and A. Pizzorno (eds.), *The Resurgence of Class Conflict in Western Europe since 1968* (London, Macmillan, 1978).
38 According to the European Labour Authority, www.ela.europa.eu/en.
39 M. Blauberger, A. Heindlmaier, D. Kramer et al., 'ECJ Judges Read the Morning Papers. Explaining the Turnaround of European Citizenship Jurisprudence', *Journal of European Public Policy* 25, no. 10 (2018): 1422–41.

safeguard their public finance by not granting social benefits to non-permanent residents, offers a textbook example of the permeability of EU law to political concerns. In that sense, it is fair to say that the absence of pan-European social re-regulation (or social harmonisation) was never offset by a complete opening of national welfare states. The extension of national solidarity to non-national European citizens occurred in a progressive and piecemeal fashion in the 1990s, only to have been put into question more recently.

Solidarity among Member States: The Long and Winding Road to Fiscal Sharing

In order to alleviate the tensions and disruptions caused by the competition of economic agents in the Single Market, the EEC and the EU have developed over time a set of financial instruments grounded in the EU budget. The purpose is to foster a general upward convergence of welfare levels implying that poorer regions should be able to catch up in terms of socio-economic development. In this perspective, the funds appear mainly as a practical means for managing interdependence stemming from market and monetary integration in order to safeguard Europe's economic and political stability. Whether this is done in a way which sets national autonomy, equality among member states and (social) justice as the normative underpinnings of such solidarity has been discussed by political scientists and theorists.[40] The way in which the EU institutions managed the Eurocrisis in 2010–15 through the actions of the Troika in over-indebted countries has certainly spurred criticism and depictions of the EU as a regime of domination and asymmetrical sovereignty.[41] The lack of fiscal solidarity to underpin the Monetary Union has been at the heart of many debates. From 2020, though, the major economic downturn caused by the Covid-19 pandemic and the ensuing adoption of a recovery agenda dubbed NextGenerationEU have opened an era of de facto fiscal solidarity.

The European Funds

In many ways, the CAP elaborated after the 1958 Stresa Conference could be seen as the main redistributive policy carried out at the European level. After

---

40 A. Sangiovani, 'Solidarity in the European Union', *Oxford Journal of Legal Studies* 33, no. 2 (2013): 213–41.
41 S. Fabbrini, 'From Consensus to Domination: The Intergovernmental Union in a Crisis Situation', *Journal of European Integration* 38, no. 5 (2016): 587–99.

the Second World War, one of the main goals of the CAP was to guarantee a satisfactory level of income for farmers despite the evolution of global prices, overproduction or adverse weather conditions.[42] By protecting farmers' revenues through the European Guidance and Guarantee Fund, the expensive cost of the CAP (approximately 70 per cent of the European budget in the 1970s) would turn out to be an outstanding act of solidarity between European citizens or between consumers and European farmers. Although it is unusual to consider the CAP as a social policy, this revealed how the European Communities and policies were designed to ensure social stability both in the working class as well as in rural communities. For instance French Minister for Overseas Territories Pierre Pflimlin gave a speech during an agriculture conference in 1952 in which he associated the agricultural pool with economic growth, peace, European stability and improvement of living conditions.[43] This commitment to European solidarity and to the steadiness of the first European institutions is, for instance, exemplified by the position of Italy accepting for a long time a CAP which was scarcely adequate for Italian farmers' needs.[44] Rapidly, however, the CAP turned out to support mainly the largest and wealthier farmers as it accompanied the intensification of agriculture.

In many studies on European social policies, the period from 1957 to the Single European Act is often a blank page or an historical leap with minor adjustments. In practical terms, member states barely applied for re-adaptation financial support or to the European social funds during the 1960s,[45] but the need for European solidarity flared up again at the end of the decade with the rapid rise of collective lay-offs and the beginning of industrial relocation in Europe and overseas. From the outset, it was not foreseeable that European institutions would have to organise an economic rebalancing among European countries. Yet, a twofold regional process hampered economic growth in all areas of the Community. On the one hand, as mentioned above, the rapid decline of the coal industry was somewhat unexpected, and the High Authority, which was supposed to increase

42 A.-C. Knudsen, *Farmers on Welfare: The Making of Europe's Common Agricultural Policy* (Ithaca, NY, Cornell University Press, 2008).

43 'Speech by Pierre Pflimlin (Paris, 25 March 1952)', www.cvce.eu/obj/speech_by_pier re_pflimlin_paris_25_march_1952-en-19b8f280-e2ff-4ad5-b426-6319fea131fd.html.

44 P. Ludlow, *The European Community and the Crises of the 1960s: Negotiating the Gaullist Challenge* (London, Routledge, 2006).

45 L. Mechi, 'Managing the Labour Market in an Open Economy: From the International Labour Organisation to the European Communities', *Contemporary European History* 27, no. 2 (2006): 221–38.

industrial productivity, played a new role in regenerating derelict industrial areas such as the Borinage in Belgium and Carbonia in Sardinia. On the other hand, the question of underdeveloped areas such as the Mezzogiorno in Italy laid the basis for a regional solidarity among the member states. The regional development issue was quite new on the political agenda in the 1950s. For a long time, the main principle resided in the idea that workers and their families should follow the geographical flow of industrial activities. After the Hague Summit in 1969, the ESF, which had been set up in 1962, was reshaped to follow Community criteria rather than national ones. Over time, though, it appeared that the working class was much more reluctant to engage in collective migration than had been expected; every organised workforce migration had echoes of deportation or forced labour, especially after the Second World War.[46] Furthermore, the purpose of the Common Market was not to create economic deserts, but rather to foster industrial relocation in underdeveloped areas and therefore try to spread economic growth fairly inside the Community.[47] After some empirical steps and attempts to define the best practice to regenerate declining industrial areas and to promote economic activities,[48] the ECSC and the EEC soon became laboratories for economists and geographers looking for appropriate good practice in the realm of economic relocations.[49] In that respect, the creation of the European Investment Bank (Treaty of Rome, Article 129) aims to fulfil the demand for balanced economic growth across the Community and not only in its most prosperous areas.

Against this background, the EEC's first enlargement to the north led to the setting up of the European Regional and Development Fund (ERDF) aimed at supporting de-industrialized regions. The two oil-price shocks of the 1970s, which reinforced the crisis of the manufacturing sector, also further widened the scope of the ESF's action. Back then, the ESF was anchored both in the logic of state intervention and in the redistributive logic of convergence between European territories. In the 1980s, the southern enlargement to Greece (in 1981), Spain and Portugal (both in 1986) significantly increased

---

46 S. Moscovici, 'La résistance à la mobilité géographique dans les expériences de reconversion', *Sociologie du Travail* 1, no. 4 (1959): 24–36.

47 Economic Commission for Europe, étude sur la situation économique de l'Europe après la guerre, 1953; N. Verschueren, 'Crises et intégration européenne. Experts et pratiques de la restructuration industrielle durant les années 1960', *20 & 21. Revue d'histoire* no. 144 (2019): 52–64.

48 For an account of these hesitating beginnings, see 'Interview with Bonnemaison, Michel' (2004), https://archives.eui.eu/en/oral_history/INT704.

49 Verschueren, 'Crises et intégration européenne'.

the demand for such policies. The accession of regions with much lower levels of development meant increased flows of workers from the south to the north of Europe. Alongside other structural funds, the ESF then had to help offset the negative effects of increased competition within the common market on the poorer regions. The Cohesion Fund was created to allow the renewal of infrastructure and networks, notably in southern Europe. The budget devoted to structural funds was increased several times, especially after the entry into force of the Single Act in 1987 and after the southern enlargement. The EU budget devoted €875 billion (at 2011 prices) to the ERDF and the Cohesion Fund between 1989 and 2020, with a tremendous increase after the Maastricht Treaty.[50]

Starting at the end of the 1980s, the ESF entered a new era amid the effects of globalisation coupled with the launch of the Economic and Monetary Union (EMU). French socialist President François Mitterrand, relinquishing a radically Keynesian policy, and the Margaret Thatcher era in the UK (along with Ronald Reagan in the United States) paved the way for Europe's gradual conversion to neoliberalism. The Single European Act of 1986 and then the Maastricht Treaty accelerated the deepening of the single market, based on a far-reaching liberalisation not only of trade in goods but also of capital and financial services. In the 1990s, all European countries faced the relocation of productive and industrial activities to regions with cheap labour, mainly outside Europe, and the mass unemployment that came with it. Among other regions, the new eastern German *Länder*, formerly East German territories which joined the EEC following German reunification, received massive aid to cope with the necessary conversion of their industry and high unemployment rate.[51] The move towards the single currency increased pressure on certain member states, especially those in the south, to reform their welfare state in order to meet the convergence criteria on debt and public deficit for membership of the EMU. In this respect, transfers via the ESF were aimed at alleviating the effects of convergence on public finances rather than facilitating socio-economic convergence as such.

Increasingly, the various EU funds – recently relabelled European Strategic and Investment Funds – have been used as financial support for reaching

50 European Commission, *Investments for Jobs and Growth: Promoting Development and Good Governance in EU Regions and Cities. Sixth Report on Economic, Social and Territorial Cohesion* (Luxembourg, Publications Office of the European Union, 2014), p. 188.
51 Bundesministerium für Arbeit und Soziales, '60 Jahre europäischer Sozialfonds – Investitionen in Menschen/Le Fonds social européen a 60 ans – Des investissements dans le capital humain', www.bmas.de/SharedDocs/Downloads/DE/Publikationen/37850-le-fonds-social-europeen-a-60-ans.pdf?__blob=publicationFile&v=3.

policy objectives set out in broad agendas, or strategies, supposed to serve as a compass for all socio-economic reforms undertaken by national governments in a therefore coordinated – if voluntary – fashion. In 2000, the Lisbon Strategy endorsed by all of the heads of state and governments and leaders of EU institutions put forward the ambition of making the EU 'the most competitive and dynamic knowledge-based economy in the world, capable of sustainable economic growth with more and better jobs and greater social cohesion' within 10 years. When the latest financial crisis hit Europe in 2009 and 2010, though, Europe was struggling with slow growth, high unemployment and persistent social inequalities.

In many respects, the various EU funds materialise solidarity between member states as well as an attempt to correct the social inequalities and economic disparities induced by the Single Market. In spite of the EU structural funds amounting to over 1.5 per cent of southern and eastern member states' gross domestic product (GDP), they 'have not reached their objectives of reducing the gap between poorer and richer regions. This is due in part because the funds are not targeted at the least developed regions in the peripheries.'[52] On a different note, some political economists, including Thomas Piketty, question the redistributive nature of the east–west relationship by pointing to the fact that amounts of capital flowing out of central and eastern Europe due to profit-making by foreign (read 'western European') companies were exceeding by far the benefits of the cohesion policy.[53] The question as to *who* is really enjoying the benefits of European integration therefore remains debated.

From the Eurocrisis to the Recovery Agenda: The Coming of Age of Fiscal Solidarity?

The Eurozone crisis in 2010–15 reignited the controversy – which had already surrounded the Treaty of Maastricht – about whether the institutional architecture and principles underpinning the EMU were well-grounded or misconceived.[54] From a solidarity point of view, the response to the 2008 financial crisis (and the ensuing debt crisis) by internal devaluation and the imposition of social hardship in the south in particular brought about debates

52 K. Makszin, G. Medve-Bálint and D. Bohle, 'North and South, East and West: Is It Possible to Bridge the Gap?', in R. Coman, A. Crespy and V. A. Schmidt (eds.), *Governance and Politics in the Post-crisis European Union* (Cambridge, Cambridge University Press, 2020), pp. 335–57, 343.
53 Ibid., p. 350.
54 E. Mourlon-Druol, 'Don't Blame the Euro: Historical Reflections on the Roots of the Eurozone Crisis', *West European Politics* 37, no. 6 (2014): 1282–96.

about the need for more solidarity, for instance in the form of stabilisation instruments which could be activated in times of economic downturn. More specifically, the idea of a European unemployment benefit scheme was much discussed among researchers and policy-makers, climaxing in a high-level conference in Brussels in July 2016 under the auspices of the Centre for European Policy Studies. High-ranking politicians and economists, including Marianne Thyssen, Pierre Moscovici, Pier Carlo Padoan, Sebastian Dullien and Paul De Grauwe, promoted the idea of setting up a fund and discussed the various designs put forward in a number of studies.[55] The most realistic options do not involve direct transfers from the EU to unemployed individuals. Rather, the prevailing design promoted is a sort of insurance fund which would flow into national schemes. The funds could be activated by those countries most affected by external shocks, thus tackling the problems of collective coordination and reduced national budgets in times of crisis. Although the idea has been much discussed and on the public agenda since 2013 at least, no political support for such a mechanism could be found among European and national decision-makers. Especially among the richer, creditor countries, there are concerns that such a European unemployment insurance fund would act as a de facto mechanism for organising permanent financial transfers towards the more vulnerable EU members with high unemployment figures. There is a belief that unemployment issues should instead be solved through boosting GDP and deregulating labour markets.

In the decade 2010–20, European debates about fiscal solidarity seemed to have stalled and crystallised on the dichotomy 'responsibility' versus 'solidarity'. On the one hand, a coalition of creditors, the so-called 'new Hanseatic League' (gathering the Netherlands, Finland, Denmark and the Baltic states), joined by Austria and Germany, expressed fears that the EU would become a Union of transfers because of the 'moral hazard' implied by more fiscal sharing. On the other hand, southern states, headed by France and Italy, called for more common instruments to sustain a better-functioning EMU. Instead of a genuine budget of the Eurozone, long wanted by the French, the talks resulted in the adoption of an undersized 'budgetary instrument for convergence and competitiveness' in December 2018.[56]

---

55 See, for example, F. Vandenbroucke, C. Luigjes, D. J. Wood and K. Lievens, "Institutional Moral Hazard in the Multi-tiered Regulation of Unemployment and Social Assistance Benefits' (2016), https://papers.ssrn.com/sol3/papers.cfm?abstract_id=2782375.

56 General Secretariat of the Council, Statement agreed at the Euro summit, EURO 503/18, 14 December 2018.

Within just a few months, the outbreak of the Covid-19 pandemic in 2020 upset this political configuration. Talks about how to manage the historic economic recession ensuing from the pandemic intersected with the already controversial adoption of the EU budget for 2021–7. After months of heated negotiations, the EU budget was adopted with an add-on of €750 billion under the motto of 'recovery and resilience'. This was largely the result of a Franco-German plan orchestrated by the European Commission, whereby Chancellor Merkel carried out a historic about turn overcoming Germany's reticence against the setting up of a 'Transfer Union'.[57] Besides its unprecedented level of fiscal pooling at EU level, this package exhibits two outstanding features. First, €312.5 million will be distributed as grants to member states through the RRF from 2022 onwards. After drafting and submitting their national recovery and resilience plans, member states will therefore receive money from the EU budget which they will not need to reimburse. With the three main recipients being Italy, France and Spain, the purpose of the facility is clearly to dampen the effects of the pandemic-induced recession on already fragile economies and prevent the southern periphery from drifting further from the wealthier northern core of the continent. Secondly, the package is to be financed through common EU debt, a first in the history in the EU. This led the German Finance Minister Olaf Scholz to call the outcome of the negotiations Europe's 'Hamiltonian moment',[58] in a reference to the federal leap through common debt in the history of the United States. Overall, the von der Leyen Commission proved proactive in increasing its supervision, crisis management and executive powers in shaping the response to the crisis. A good illustration is provided by the setting up of the Support to Mitigate Unemployment Risks in an Emergency (SURE), an EU loan facility aiming at supporting national short-time work schemes tackling the pandemic-induced skyrocketing unemployment. In many ways, SURE can be regarded as a prefiguration of the long-promoted unemployment insurance scheme discussed above. Furthermore, an Action Plan adopted in 2021 is serving to pursue the tangible implementation of the European Pillar of Social Rights, involving not only new leglisation at EU level, but also about 100 measures that member states should adopt at the national level.

---

57 A. Crespy and L. Schramm, 'Breaking the Budgetary Taboo: German Preference Formation in the EU's Response to the Covid-19 Crisis', *German Politics*, (2021), www .tandfonline.com/doi/full/10.1080/09644008.2021.2020253.

58 B. Hall, S. Fleming and G. Chazan, 'Is the Franco-German Plan Europe's "Hamiltonian" Moment?', *Financial Times*, 21 May 2020, www.ft.com/content/2735a3 f1-bc58-477c-9315-c98129d12852.

A final important aspect concerns the convergence between the recovery agenda and the EU's environmental agenda. The December 2020 political agreement in the European Council foresees that 40 per cent of all spending from EU funds should be earmarked as green. After years of inertia, the European Commission made an historic move to spearhead the fight against climate change both internally and globally as it issued its communication for the European Green Deal in December 2019, with key goals ranging from clean energy to the protection of ecosystems and the decarbonisation of transport and housing.[59] Furthermore, the European Commission has largely embraced the notion of a 'just transition', as its Vice-President in charge of the Green Deal, Frans Timmermans, repeatedly insisted that the ecological transition should 'leave no one behind'. In this perspective, two key new financial instruments have been set up. The first is a Just Transition Fund serving to distribute over €17 billion to regions with the most carbon-dependent economies (mostly in central and eastern Europe). The second is a Social Climate Fund endowed with €86 billion for governments to invest in clean infrastructure and support financially the households most affected by the taxing of CO_2 emissions in transport and housing. Overall, though, a close examination of the EU's strategy reveals that it is very unlikely to tackle the exacerbation of social inequality by the green transition.[60]

Conclusion

As Jacques Delors reminded his readers in a recent text, solidarity in the EU should be regarded less as generosity than as 'enlightened self-interest'.[61] As the unification of the continent has moved forward over the past 70 years, the level of interdependence between people, economic agents and states has continuously increased. This begs the question of how to manage such interdependence in a just and effective manner. Although it is of existential importance, this endeavour has mainly met political resistance due to diverging views among decision-makers about how much solidarity was necessary,

---

59 European Commission, Communication on 'The European Green Deal', COM(2019) 640, 11 December 2019.

60 A. Crespy and M. Munta, 'Lost in Transition? Social Justice and the Politics of the EU Green Transition', *Transfer: European Review of Labour and Research* (2023), https://journals.sagepub.com/doi/10.1177/10242589231173072.

61 J. Delors, 'Foreword', in S. Fernandes and E. Rubio, 'Solidarity within the Eurozone: How Much, What for, for How Long?' (2011), unpaginated, https://institutdelors.eu/wp-content/uploads/2020/04/solidarityemus.fernandes-e.rubionefeb2012-gliss%C3%A9es.pdf.

on the one hand, and whether the EU or states should be in charge of dealing with solidarity, on the other. Early on, the homogenisation of living standards appeared to be neither feasible, nor desirable. With economic competition as the key driver of integration, a piecemeal set of rules, policies and rights led to the emergence of a minimal level of *transnational solidarity* mainly anchored in the legal principle of non-discrimination. Competition and anti-discrimination nevertheless often entered into conflict with entrenched forms of solidarity through collective bargaining and welfare states. Minimal coordination and mutual recognition were the paths chosen to curtail – with limited success – the impact of free movement of capital, money and workers on national solidarities. Eventually, the tentative de-nationalisation of solidarity provoked a backlash in terms of forms of welfare chauvinism, preventing the full opening of welfare states in the absence of a genuine pan-European social citizenship. Finally, the EU has a long history of redistributing money through funds in an attempt to spur upward convergence. More than an altruistic conception of solidarity, forms of *international solidarity* among member states relying on a common budget account for an existential need to ensure the coherence of the Union and its capacity to address increasingly transnational challenges in economic, social and environmental terms. The rapid adoption of an historic €750 billion recovery package in the heat of the Covid-19 pandemic is highly illustrative of how a higher degree of interdependence necessarily brings about more financial solidarity and common policy instruments in spite of all political divisions.

Recommended Reading

Crespy, A. *The European Social Question: Tackling Key Controversies* (Newcastle, Agenda, 2022).

Ferrera, M. *The Boundaries of Welfare: European Integration and the New Spatial Politics of Social Protection* (Oxford and New York, NY, Oxford University Press, 2005).

Mechi, L. 'Managing the Labour Market in an Open Economy: From the International Labour Organisation to the European Communities', *Contemporary European History* 27, no. 2 (2018): 221–38.

Patel, K. K. *Project Europa: A History* (Cambridge, Cambridge University Press, 2020).

Verschueren, N. *Fermer les mines en construisant l'Europe: Une histoire sociale de l'intégration européenne* (Brussels, Peter Lang, 2012).

Warlouzet, L. 'The EEC/EU as an Evolving Compromise between French Dirigism and German Ordoliberalism (1957–1995)', *Journal of Common Market Studies* 51, no. 1 (2019): 77–93.

23

Ideologies of EU Democracy since 1950

CLAUDIA STERNBERG

Introduction

How democratic were the European Communities, and later the European Union (EU), how democratic did they *need* to be, and what would this *mean* in the first place? Throughout the course of European integration, none of the answers was self-evident, and all were the stuff of continuous discursive construction, reconstruction and contestation. In this chapter I trace shifts and clashes in collective imaginations of EU democracy since 1950, exploring how what it made sense to say about EU democracy changed over time. I analyse discourses, or ensembles of ideas, concepts, narratives or categories, through which meaning was given to 'democracy', for the case of the EU and its institutional predecessors (for the sake of better readability, I sometimes use the label 'EU' to refer both to the EU as such and to its institutional predecessors in this chapter).

Discourses around EU democracy shaped what was politically possible in designing and adapting the EU's institutional set-up, and in making it come to life through policies and politics. Conversely, what was politically possible, or desired, for example in negotiating the founding treaties, influenced which discourses gained dominance over others.[1] Either way, competing understandings around EU democracy functioned as ideologies; benchmarks to which different actors committed themselves and others, supporting endeavours to change and uphold, criticise and justify the emerging institutional, political and social arrangements.

---

1 See L. Rye, 'The Legitimacy of the EU in Historical Perspective: History of a Never-Ending Quest', *European Papers* 5 (2020): 191–207; A. Boerger-De Smedt, 'Negotiating the Foundations of European Law, 1950–57: The Legal History of the Treaties of Paris and Rome', *Contemporary European History* 21, no. 3 (2012): 339–56; A. S. Milward, *The Reconstruction of Western Europe 1945–51* (London, Routledge, 1984); S. Goetze and B. Rittberger, 'A Matter of Habit: The Sociological Foundations of Empowering the European Parliament', *Comparative European Politics* 8, no. 1 (2010): 37–54.

Like political philosophies, ideologies are configurations of concepts but, unlike them, they are not reducible to specific authors but rather are characteristic of certain forms of group thinking.[2] In this chapter, I tell a story of shifts and clashes in EU-official 'group thinking' around EU democracy.

More specifically, I tell the story of how the European institutions and their representatives spoke about EU democracy, what they said, what they took for granted, what they deemed generally plausible – and how this related to changes in embedding social imaginaries and understandings of the role of modern democracy at large, in the member state societies and beyond. The sources I analyse range eclectically from treaty preambles, official declarations and political speeches, via reports, strategy and policy papers, to newspaper articles. While my focus in this chapter is on the official discourses reflected in this corpus, I contextualise them in embedding debates and paradigm shifts in the wider public and academic public spheres, developing analyses presented elsewhere.[3] Importantly, I concentrate on overarching long-term collective patterns and developments rather than differences between the various EU institutions.

My aim is to analyse broad trends in official rhetoric and discourses in their interplay with broader, embedding evolutions in understandings of the role of democracy in European integration and beyond. To this end, I use interpretive non-quantitative textual analysis, by which I mean analysis concerned empirically with meaning, which works through the close reading of texts identified, in an iterative circle, as illustrating broader discursive patterns. In other words, rather than quantifying just how dominant which discursive patterns were compared with others at what point in time, I scrutinise their narrative and argumentative content; what they said and *how* they said it, on what grounds, and what they took for granted – and what sort of understandings of the EU and its democratic qualities this made emerge.

The chapter opens by briefly situating my analysis in the academic literature. This is followed by the chapter's core – a potted history of narratives

---

2 M. Freeden, *Ideologies and Political Theory: A Conceptual Approach* (Oxford, Oxford University Press, 1998), p. 8; K. Nicolaidis, 'Kant's Mantle: Cosmopolitanism, Federalism and Constitutionalism as European Ideologies', *Journal of European Public Policy* 27, no. 9 (2020): 1307–28; J. Komárek (ed.), *European Constitutional Imaginaries: Between Ideology and Utopia* (Oxford, Oxford University Press, 2023).

3 C. Sternberg. *The Struggle for EU Legitimacy: Public Contestation, 1950s–2005* (Basingstoke, Palgrave Macmillan, 2013).

around EU democracy over time. Each subsection turns to a major shift in how EU democracy was understood: early apparent silences on the matter of democracy; a turn to the citizens from the late 1970s and the 1980s; the EU's 'crusade for democracy' following the Maastricht ratification crisis; and various assertions of sovereignty since then. The final fourth section concludes the chapter.

The State of the Art and Points of Reference

A common reading is that the democratic character of the European Coal and Steel Community (ECSC) and of the European Communities was not an issue of concern on their agenda for the early decades of integration. In this reading, democracy became an issue only as the Communities gained more and more competences, which brought questions of democratic representation, control and accountability to the fore, and eventually led the EU to entrench more democracy in its institutions, practices and rhetoric, mainly from Maastricht to Lisbon.[4]

With this chapter I join a historiography giving nuance to this narrative. On the one hand, there were voices that did indeed have something to say about EU democracy early on. On the other, if democracy did initially stay relatively out of the limelight only to then move right into the centre of attention, this raises the question of how this discursive dynamic *came into being*, of its genealogy.[5] What were the understandings of the nature of the integration project and of political life which underpinned both the early lack of concern and the subsequent 'democratic turn'?

What is more, early discourses may not have been silent on the matter of democracy but rather have worked on the basis of *different notions* of democracy – this 'essentially contested concept' if there is one; a concept for which there is no generally accepted standard use or

4 See, for example, Rye, 'The Legitimacy of the EU', 191; S. Smismans, 'Democracy and Legitimacy in the European Union', in M. Cini and N. Pérez-Solórzano Borragán (eds.), *European Union Politics*, 6th ed. (Oxford, Oxford University Press, 2019), pp. 127–40, 128–30; H. Schulz-Forberg and B. Stråth, *The Political History of European Integration: The Hypocrisy of Democracy-Through-Market* (London, Taylor & Francis, 2010).
5 See M. Bevir and R. Phillips, 'EU Democracy and the Treaty of Lisbon', *Comparative European Politics* 15, no. 5 (2016): 705–28. For further studies sensitive to the genealogy of European integration, see P. L. Lindseth, *Power and Legitimacy: Reconciling Europe and the Nation-State* (Oxford, Oxford University Press, 2010); C. Parsons, *A Certain Idea of Europe* (Ithaca, NY, Cornell University Press, 2003); Goetze and Rittberger, 'A Matter of Habit'; M. Burgess, *Federalism and European Union: The Building of Europe, 1950–2000* (London, Routledge, 2000); Sternberg, *The Struggle for EU Legitimacy*.

meaning.[6] 'Democracy' everywhere is subject to never-ending processes of social construction and contestation, collective meaning-making and knowledge production, in adaptation to changing circumstances. If we take into account these processes and how, over time, rival projections of the EU and the role of democracy in legitimating it played out against each other, emerged out of each other and became dominant or faded into the background, we discern much greater continuity than is implied by the simpler narrative that democracy was at first a non-issue and then became an issue.

Finally, the collective imagination and re-imagination of EU democracy did not occur in isolation. This chapter puts them in dialogue with embedding broader understandings of political life, history, the state, its place in the world and the legitimacy of modern democracy, in the member states and beyond.[7] Academic debates on EU democracy too provided not only critical analysis, but also inspiration to EU-official imaginations of what democracy could or should mean in the case of the EU.[8]

A rich and vibrant scholarship has not only analysed the extent to which the EU suffers from a 'democratic deficit', and the nature of this defict, but also de- and re-constructed the normative standards for EU democracy, for which many of the nation-centric yardsticks were arguably unsuitable.[9] Unlike most of this literature, what follows offers neither an assessment of the EU's evolving democratic credentials, nor a discussion of what the standards for such an assessment should be. Instead, I trace *how what it made sense to say about EU democracy* changed over time. I chart the long-term production and contestation

---

6 W. B. Gallie, 'Essentially Contested Concepts', *Proceedings of the Aristotelian Society* 56 (1956): 167–98, 168. See also Y. Mény, 'De La Démocratie en Europe: Old Concepts and New Challenges', *Journal of Common Market Studies* 41, no. 1 (2003): 1–13, 8.

7 See J.-W. Müller, *Contesting Democracy: Political Ideas in Twentieth-Century Europe* (New Haven, CT, Yale University Press, 2013); M. Conway, *Western Europe's Democratic Age: 1945–1968* (Princeton, NJ, Princeton University Press, 2020); P. Rosanvallon, *Democratic Legitimacy: Impartiality, Reflexivity, Proximity* (Princeton, NJ, Princeton University Press, 2011).

8 See Chapter 24 by Wouter Wolfs in this volume. For excellent overviews of this debate, see, for example, H. Bang, M. D. Jensen and P. Nedergaard, '"We the People" versus "We the Heads of States": The Debate on the Democratic Deficit of the European Union', *Policy Studies* 36, no. 2 (2015): 196–216; T. Jensen, 'The Democratic Deficit of the European Union', *Living Reviews in Democracy* 1, no. 2 (2009): 1–8. For edited volumes representing the state of the art, see B. Kohler-Koch and B. Rittberger (eds.), *Debating the Democratic Legitimacy of the European Union* (Lanham, MD, Rowman & Littlefield, 2007); S. Piattoni (ed.), *The European Union: Democratic Principles and Institutional Architectures in Times of Crisis* (Oxford, Oxford University Press, 2015).

9 See, for example, Mény, 'De La Démocratie en Europe'; C. Lord and D. Beetham, 'Legitimizing the EU: Is There a "Post-parliamentary Basis" for Its Legitimation?', *Journal of Common Market Studies* 39, no. 3 (2001): 443–62.

of collective meaning – of the 'necessary fictions' that people rely on in making sense of their experience of collective life and the 'imagined democracies' that make political rule possible in the face of the inescapable contradictions, clashes and compromises involved wherever ideals are pursued.[10]

The Historical Narrative

Early Silences?

At face value, early official discourse was indeed strikingly silent on the matter of democracy. Neither the 1950 Schuman Declaration nor the Paris or Rome Treaties even contained the word 'democracy' or 'democratic'.[11] Many of those shaping the European Communities considered democracy not especially suited for legitimating the nascent European construct.[12] Jean Monnet, for one, felt that allowing too much popular input risked obstructing the integration process.[13]

And yet, the project of European integration was very much *about* democracy. It was about safeguarding democracy at the national, not the European, level; about making the *member states* 'safe for democracy', invoking Woodrow Wilson's phrase in asking the US Congress to support a declaration of war on Germany in 1917 on the grounds that 'The world must be made safe for democracy.'[14] Against the background of recent history and the ongoing communist threat, European integration was to lock in the liberal-democratic arrangements of the member states and prevent them from back-sliding into authoritarianism.[15] Integration, according to this foundational storyline, would keep totalitarianism at bay at home as well as abroad, containing old demons and keeping the 'Eastern powers' from striving for 'the control of Europe and the continuation of the world revolution'.[16]

10 Y. Ezrahi, *Imagined Democracies: Necessary Political Fictions* (Cambridge, Cambridge University Press, 2012). See also C. Sternberg, 'Ideologies and Imaginaries of Legitimacy from the 1950s to Today: Trajectories of EU-Official Discourses Read against Rosanvallon's Democratic Legitimacy', in J. Komárek (ed.), *European Constitutional Imaginaries: Between Ideology and Utopia* (Oxford, Oxford University Press, 2023), pp. 92–116.
11 R. Schuman, (1950), 'Schuman Declaration May 1950', https://europa.eu/european-union/about-eu/symbols/europe-day/schuman-declaration_en.
12 Burgess, *Federalism and European Union*, pp. 31–6; Milward, *The Reconstruction of Western Europe*, p. 409.
13 J. Monnet, *Memoirs* (London, Collins, 1978), p. 93.
14 Schulz-Forberg and Stråth, *The Political History of European Integration*, pp. 4, 12.
15 Lindseth, *Power and Legitimacy*, p. 104; J.-W. Müller, *Contesting Democracy: Political Ideas in Twentieth-Century Europe* (New Haven, CT, Yale University Press, 2013), p. 149. See also Milward, *The Reconstruction of Western Europe*.
16 W. Hallstein, 'Auf dem Weg zur europäischen Einheit. German radio broadcast on the decisions taken at Messina in June 1955', *Bulletin des Presse- und Informationsamtes der*

European integration was part and parcel of western Europe's post-war 'constitutionalist settlement'.[17] A deep distrust of popular sovereignty, mass democracy and unchecked majority rule underlay not just the beginnings of European integration but also the political reconstruction of western Europe after 1945, leading to an insulation of the emerging political systems from popular pressures. Constitutional courts were created and eventually accepted, and parliaments deliberately weakened to the benefit of strong national executives (Britain becoming an outlier in continuing to see parliamentary supremacy as legitimate).[18]

Democracy emerged as a key source of political legitimacy only over the course of the next decade-and-a-half.[19] The decades after the war further saw the building of strong welfare and regulatory states, and many of their functions were delegated to administrative agencies subject to robust judicial and administrative oversight and the 'plebiscitary leadership' of national chief executives over the administrative-technocratic sphere.[20]

Quite in tune with this expansion of administrative government across modern democracies, the member states delegated powers not only to unelected domestic institutions, but also to supranational bodies under the close supervision of national governments (rather than parliaments, again). Democratic legitimacy here rested centrally on the transfer of normative power to the European level through successive 'outline treaties', which fixed the general principles and objectives of common policies and the 'normative frameworks' and rules within which they would subsequently be worked out.[21] Insofar as the national context was concerned, it was the parliaments which effected such delegation in the first instance, but once legislative enactment was complete, the focus of legitimation shifted away from them.

Bundesregierung no. 228, 6 December 1955. See similarly Schuman, 'Schuman Declaration May 1950'; EEC Treaty, Preamble.

17 Lindseth, *Power and Legitimacy*, pp. 130, 264; Müller, *Contesting Democracy*.

18 Müller, *Contesting Democracy*, pp. 146–50.

19 See M. Conway, *Western Europe's Democratic Age*.

20 Lindseth, *Power and Legitimacy*, pp. 130, 264; Müller, *Contesting Democracy*.

21 W. Hallstein, 'Address Given at the British Institute of International and Comparative Law', London 25 March 1965, Commission (1965) 3574/X/65-E. See also, for example, European Commission, 'Third General Report on the Activities of the Community (2 March 1959–15 May 1960)' (1960); European Commission, 'Report of the Working Party Examining the Problem of the Enlargement of the Powers of the European Parliament. "Vedel Report"', BEC Supplement 4/72 (1972); European Commission, 'First General Report on the Activities of the Community (1/01/1958–17/09/1958)'. On the treaties' affinities to a *loi-cadre* or *traité-cadre* on the national level, see Lindseth, *Power and Legitimacy*, pp. 2, 12, 51, 104; G. Majone *Dilemmas of European Integration: The Ambiguities and Pitfalls of Integration by Stealth* (Oxford, Oxford University Press, 2009), p. 7.

There were competing blueprints of where the delegated legitimate authority was to go. Jean Monnet's vision was to establish supranational technocratic autonomy: 'Once the institution is in place and the breakthrough consolidated, the moment of the technicians arrives.'[22] Counter to this ran what has been referred to as 'the establishment of national-executive leadership over the integration process', through the Council of Ministers and a dense bureaucracy of nationally dominated committees staffed by national civil servants to oversee the Commission's implementation of delegated acts, as well as through the crises of the 1960s, which further 'marginalised the Commission as an autonomous technocratic policy maker' (even if they resulted more in national executive oversight than in the kind of control Charles de Gaulle would have wanted).[23] All these steps and developments were embedded in discourses justifying them as well as criticising them, which constructed blueprints of democratic solutions for Europe.

In general, the democratic legitimacy of the European system of administrative governance was to an important degree borrowed from *national* mechanisms of legitimation, including legislative enactment and executive, administrative and judicial oversight.[24] A competing discourse, to be sure, aimed to establish that there was, and needed to be, a distinct and new democratic legitimacy specific to the nascent Community system. Commission President Hallstein, for example, referred to the Rome Treaty as reminiscent of 'the constitution of a modern State', constituting its very own 'separation of powers', with the Commission and the Council in charge of 'creating a European system of law and of bringing it into force', while the European Parliament and the Court of Justice undertook 'the task of control'.[25]

On the whole, as for this last quote, claims to the early Communities' legitimacy, even those that did not turn on the European Parliament and its role (on which more in the section after the next), played on a whole range of registers of democratic legitimacy: the electoral legitimacy of national parliaments and executives, the legitimacy arising from lawfulness and accordance with democratic and administrative processes, and constitutional commitments to collective democratic structures and individual rights. And yet, these registers arguably mainly only framed and complemented a largely overpowering different theme, that of the *bureaucratic legitimacy* of the European Communities.

---

22 Monnet, *Memoirs*, p. 321.   23 Lindseth, *Power and Legitimacy*, pp. 91, 100.
24 Ibid., pp. 86–90.
25 Hallstein, 'Address Given at the British Institute of International and Comparative Law'.

Bureaucratic Legitimacy and the European Common Good

Bureaucratic legitimacy claims had their heyday across Europe, and else-where, in the 30 years or so after the Second World War, when civil servants dedicated to an agenda of modernisation portrayed themselves as the representatives of a new type of legitimacy based on efficiency and compe-tence, rationality and disinterestedness.[26] Good government in this imagin-ary was government that was effective in solving concrete problems, and did so in a professional, impartial and predictable manner, following clear procedures.[27]

This mode of legitimation, rooted in a cultural background of early-twentieth-century theories of scientific management and mystiques of rationality, was welcomed as a way to overcome the discontents of electoral and party democracy.[28] In contrast to the latter, public power was legitimated not so much by its origin but rather by the 'services' it rendered in furthering the general interest – and it is this orientation towards generality that arguably makes it a type of *democratic* legitimacy.[29]

The Communities' bureaucratic legitimacy was firmly implanted in a wider belief in progress, and in government intervention and an active, 'caring state', at the time widely considered the 'most suitable means for the promotion of "the good" of both the individual and the collective'.[30] Early Community-official rhetoric invoked hope, agency and the determination to bring about a better future through political action, hailing European inte-gration as the 'greatest voluntary and purposeful transformation in the history of Europe'.[31] Integration featured as the apex and 'natural extension

26 Rosanvallon, *Democratic Legitimacy*, pp. 50–3. See also C. Sternberg, 'Ideologies and Imaginaries of Legitimacy from the 1950s to Today'.
27 W. Walters and J. H. Haahr, *Governing Europe: Discourse, Governmentality and European Integration* (London and New York, NY, Routledge, 2005), pp. 21–41; Conway, *Western Europe's Democratic Age.*
28 Rosanvallon, *Democratic Legitimacy.*
29 Rosanvallon, *Democratic Legitimacy*, pp. 39, 45. See also Walters and Haahr, *Governing Europe*. On the theoretical concepts of 'input' and 'output legitimacy', and their roles in the discursive history of EU legitimation, see C. Sternberg, 'Political Legitimacy between Democracy and Effectiveness: Trade-offs, Interdependencies, and Discursive Constructions by the EU institutions', *European Political Science Review* 7, no. 4 (2015): 615–38.
30 D. Held, *Models of Democracy* (Stanford, CA, Stanford University Press, 2006), p. 186.
31 P. H. Spaak, 'Discours à l'occasion de la signature des Traités instituant la Communauté Economique Européenne et la Communauté Européenne de l'Energie Atomique (25/03/1957)', Archives historiques des Communautés européennes, Florence, Villa Il Poggiolo CM/3/NEGO/091.

of the processes of social and political rationalization already well advanced in the historical evolution of modern states'.[32]

Substantively, the central promises of integration, throughout the 1950s and 1960s and beyond, were, of course, peace and prosperity.[33] The declared motivation for European integration was to make war 'not only unthinkable, but materially impossible'.[34] Closely connected to this – and often with the subtext that one was not to be had without the other – was the other emblematic promise of integration, that of better living conditions and a 'higher standard of living', of 'economic and social progress'.[35]

A common pro-integration discursive technique framed European integration against the supposed alternative of war and economic destitution, as indispensable to achieving both peace and prosperity, and, given the absolute necessity of both, as simply indispensable. In this indispensability discourse, integration was a matter of 'no alternative' and even of survival. This discourse was used to give urgency both to the project as a whole and to specific measures and approaches. It was often grounded on the member states' increasing, inescapable *interdependence*, given international relations in the Cold War era as well as the inexorable evolution of modern technology and mass production – not to forget that the Europeans had sealed their already inevitably interconnected fate as a 'community of destiny' with the deliberate, functionalist 'fusion of their essential interests' in the integration project.[36]

Together, these patterns worked towards entrenching the notion that there was such a thing as a European 'common good' or 'common interest'

32 L. Hansen and M. C. Williams, 'The Myths of Europe: Legitimacy, Community and the "Crisis" of the EU', *Journal of Common Market Studies* 37 (1999): 233–49, 243. See also Walters and Haahr, *Governing Europe*; Rosanvallon, *Democratic Legitimacy*.

33 See Claudia Hiepel's Chapter 19 in this volume.

34 Schuman, 'Schuman Declaration May 1950'.

35 The governments, 'Resolution Adopted by the Ministers of Foreign Affairs of the Member States of the E.C.S.C. at Their Meeting at Messina (June 1 to 3, 1955)', www .cvce.eu/en/education/unit-content/-/unit/1c8aa583-8ec5-41c4-9ad8-73674ea7f4a7/41e c71a6-2eb5-43c7-97e2-75ca55472r7e/Resources#d1086bae-0c13-4a00-8608-73c75ce54fad_ en&overlay; European Commission, 'First General Report' (1958), p. 9; W. Hallstein, 'Address Given by Walter Hallstein on the Schuman Plan (28 April 1958)' www.cvce.eu /en/obj/address_given_by_walter_hallstein_on_the_schuman_plan_28_april_1951-en-81868a56-1b45-446e-a572-f14085701773.html, p. 3; Spaak, 'Discours à l'occasion de la signature des Traités'; ECSC Treaty, Preamble. See also Ivan T. Berend's Chapter 20 in this volume.

36 J. Monnet, 'L'Europe unie sera démocratique', BEEC 03/1963(3); ECSC Treaty, Preamble. See similarly E. B. Haas, 'Technocracy, Pluralism and the New Europe. International Regionalism', in J. S. Nye (ed.), *International Regionalism* (Boston, MA, Little Brown, 1968), pp. 149–76, 456; European Commission, 'European Union. Report by Mr. Leo Tindemans, Prime Minister of Belgium, to the European Council, 27 December 1975', *Bulletin of the European Communities* Suppl. 1/76 (1976): 11–35.

(often used interchangeably); that this was furthered by integration in its emerging form; and that there was a broad consensus on this. A sort of Rousseauean 'general will' oriented towards the common good, in this discourse, arose not only from insight into integration's existential necessity, but also from moral rectitude and the willingness to leave behind the divisive passions, impulses and 'excited demands' associated with 'politics', in order to achieve social and economic progress, and peace for all.[37]

The notion of there being a readily identifiable and reasonably consensual common good was crucial to grounding claims to the bureaucratic legitimacy of the Communities. It allowed the framing of the emerging 'grand design for Europe' as a win–win enterprise, 'not a game in which one side wins and the other loses'.[38] This, in turn, justified the Communities' technocratic mode of operation on the grounds of the principle that 'government action follows the advice of experts' who furthered this European common good.[39]

The Commission, as the Communities' professional and merit-based civil service, had a particular interest in fashioning itself as the Communities' 'champion of generality', their 'initiator, planner and mediator for the common good', providing independent, impartial and technically sound proposals. It defined its role as giving concrete meaning to the supposed European general will and interpreting the general interest.[40]

The crucial weakness both of the technocratic modus operandi and of the underlying topos of a European common good was that they rested on depoliticisation. They glossed over the inescapably divisive and contested nature not only of the ends and goals of (any) governance, but also of how these should be pursued, not to speak of how the costs and benefits of common actions should be divided. They tried to move innately and undeniably political institutional and policy choices *out* of the realms of politicised

---

37 Haas, 'Technocracy, Pluralism and the New Europe', p. 159. See also European Commission, 'European Union. Report by Mr. Leo Tindemans', 11; Assemblée parlementaire européenne, 'Rapport fait au nom de la commission des affairs politiques et des questions institutionnelles sur l'élection de l'Assemblée parlementaire européenne au suffrage universel direct. Rapporteurs Emilio Battista, Fernand Dehousse, Maurice Faure, W. J. Schuijt, and Ludwig Metzger', *EP Session Documents 1960–61*, 30 April 1960, Document 22 (henceforth 'Dehousse Report'), particularly pp. 16–17.
38 'Une Europe empirique', *Le Monde*, 26 March 1957, 1.
39 K. Featherstone, 'Jean Monnet and the "Democratic Deficit" in the European Union', *Journal of Common Market Studies* 32, no. 2 (1994): 149–70, 150, 154.
40 European Commission, 'Vedel Report', pp. 17, 73.

political will formation through the electoral process and wider public debate.[41]

For a while, in common with the climate in the member states, the ubiquitous anti-totalitarian imperative, and indeed the presence of a totalitarian alternative in central and eastern Europe, helped to downplay the existence of economic ideological choices, and even the possibility of a different political system and ideology of legitimacy. By the 1970s, however, this initial period of grace was over.[42]

European Electoral Democracy and Early Politicisation
Strategies

Moreover, deliberate politicisation strategies had already been at work at least from the 1960s onwards. They had marked much of Community discourse and practice and met with important critical counter-efforts, aimed at politicising what the European Communities should be doing and how.

Advocates of a strong and directly elected European Parliament (EP), in particular, took the 'eminently political' nature of integration as the starting point for their demands. Not everyone, the argument went – fuelled forcefully by the crises of the 1960 – agreed on what the new political structure should be doing, how and why. The 'fundamental choices' that needed to be made both about the 'guiding goals' of integration and about its specific policies as well as the 'ways and means' of pursuing them were too 'far-reaching' and too existential a 'gamble on the future' of 'the whole economic life of our six countries' to be left to 'a handful of good experts' who would 'settle all problems to general satisfaction'.[43]

The only conclusion from this could be the need to give the Community 'its own democratic legitimation beyond that which can be transmitted to it by the governments responsible' or the national parliaments.[44] The campaign for European elections here revived and leaned on older federalist visions for Europe (overruled in the treaty negotiations), which had envisioned

---

41 Sternberg, *The Struggle for EU Legitimacy*, pp. 14–44. See also L. van Middelaar, *Alarums and Excursions: Improvising Politics on the European Stage* (Newcastle-upon-Tyne, Agenda, 2019), p. 228.
42 Müller, *Contesting Democracy*. See also Sternberg, *The Struggle for EU Legitimacy*, pp. 210–24.
43 Assemblée parlementaire européenne, 'Dehousse Report', p. 17.
44 European Commission, 'Vedel Report', pp. 12, 32. See further, for example, EP, 'Résolution du Parlement européen, du 27 juin 1963, sur les compétences et les pouvoirs du Parlement européen', *Journal Officiel de la Communauté Européenne* 106 (1963): 1916–63; EP, 'Résolution relative à l'élection des membres du Parlement européen au suffrage universel direct (12 mars 1969)', *Journal Officiel de la Communauté Européenne* 41 (1969): 12; European Commission, 'Third General Report on the Activities of the Community' (1960), http://aei.pitt.edu/30806/1/67367_EEC_3rd.pdf, p. 19.

European unity as resulting from the impetus of a directly elected European parliament – and which one may have expected to carry greater weight given their prevalence in the pre-Second World War period.[45]

Arguments for strengthening European electoral democracy notably rested *both* on claims about the feasibility or sustainability of integration *and* on normative claims about ideal conditions of democratic legitimacy. Its proponents canvassed for a strong, elected EP on the grounds that this would help to improve political representation in Europe in a whole range of the ideal-typical ways defined by Hannah Pitkin.[46] One such type of argument was that it would strengthen *formal* representation, 'free elections' being the only known means of 'expressing the will of the people' and doing them justice as 'not objects but subjects of the law'.[47] Another frequent case made was that such a parliament would promote what Pitkin termed *substantive* representation as in the Communities' responsiveness to citizen needs and preferences; a strong and elected EP would keep them 'in close and permanent touch with political and human realities'.[48]

Probably the most powerful and prevalent argument advanced in favour of European elections, however, appealed to what would become *symbolic* representation, whereby a political order or its elites are representative because the people believe in them and trust them to represent their interests. Pro-election advocacy rested prominently on the claim that elections were the way 'to associate the peoples with the building of Europe'.[49] European elections and electoral symbolism were argued to have the

---

45 See, for example, R. N. Coudenhove-Kalergi, *Pan-Europa* (Vienna and Leipzig, Pan-Europa-Verlag, 1924); A. Spinelli, *The Eurocrats: Conflict and Crisis in the European Community* (Baltimore, MA, Johns Hopkins Press, 1966); M. Steed, 'The European Parliament: The Significance of Direct Election', *Government and Opposition* 6, no. 4 (1971): 462–76, 462; Burgess, *Federalism and European Union*, pp. 31–6; Rye, 'The Legitimacy of the EU'; Milward, *The Reconstruction of Western Europe*, p. 409. On this ideal underlying the preferences of particularly the German delegation in negotiations around the Schuman Plan and the eventual founding treaties, see Goetze and Rittberger, 'A Matter of Habit', 44–7.

46 See H. F. Pitkin, *The Concept of Representation* (Berkeley, CA and Los Angeles, CA, University of California Press, 1967).

47 Assemblée parlementaire européenne, 'General Report by Fernand Dehousse, Member of the European Parliamentary Assembly (20 April 1960)' (henceforth 'Dehousse Report'), www.cvce.eu/en/obj/general_report_by_fernand_dehousse_member_of_the_european_parliamentary_assembly_30_april_1960-en-89c2a74e-fb16-4b7f-b796-d3759876ddfe.html, pp. 16–17.

48 European Commission, 'Fourth General Report on the Activities of the Community' (1961)', http://aei.pitt.edu/30807/1/67557_EEC_4th.pdf.

49 Assemblée parlementaire européenne, 'Textes relatifs à l'élection de l'Assemblée parlementaire européenne au suffrage universel direct', *Journal Officiel de la Communauté Européenne* 60, no. 2 (1960): 834. See also Assemblée parlementaire européenne, 'Dehousse Report', p. 16.

potential to help make 'triumph the European idea in public opinion'[50] and to forge a 'European consciousness' in people.[51] A strong and elected EP, so the argument went, would lead directly to public endorsement and make further steps of integration feasible and sustainable.

Of course, by the time the first European elections were held in 1979, with disappointing turnouts, the Communities were facing serious difficulties in delivering on their prosperity and peace promises, given the financial and economic crises of the 1970s and early 1980s combined with renewed international tensions. With the 'cake' no longer growing, narratives of integration furthering an uncontroversial or even indivisible common European good were crumbling. The fiction of the Community bureaucracy and its policies being apolitical or politically neutral was unravelling.[52]

The member states too experienced fierce social critiques and disagreements over economic ideology, and debates raged on the 'legitimation crisis' of the capitalist welfare state, with 'overloaded' government and administrative systems failing to cope with economic pressures.[53] All this manifested itself not least in a loss of confidence in the impartiality and rationality of the bureaucracy.[54] In depictions of European integration, 'Eurocracy' became a dominant emblem. Integration ground to a halt, with a real threat of disintegration of the Community looming.

The Turn to the Citizens and the People's Europe: 1976–1980s

Proposals regarding how to revitalise integration, and subsequently legitimate the ensuing revitalisation, with the 1986 Single European Act and the project of completing the Single Market by 1992, reflected a sea change in the discourses of the European institutions around EU democracy and legitimacy. They henceforth centred on the viewpoint of the European citizens, on 'what the citizens wanted': 'We must listen to our people. What do the Europeans want? What do they expect from a united Europe?'[55]

50 EP, 'Rapport fait au nom de la commission politique sur les compétences et les pouvoirs du Parlement européen. Rapporteur Hans Furler. Documents de séance 31, 14 juin 1983', EP Session Documents 1963–64 no. 31, 14 June 1963, pp. 1–37, 25.
51 Assemblée parlementaire européenne, 'Dehousse Report', pp. 1, 16.
52 See M. Tsakatika, 'Claims to Legitimacy: The European Commission between Continuity and Change', Journal of Common Market Studies 43, no. 1 (2005): 193–220; Featherstone, 'Jean Monnet and the "Democratic Deficit"'; Sternberg, The Struggle for EU Legitimacy, pp. 69–71.
53 J. Habermas, Legitimation Crisis (Boston, MA, Beacon, 1973). See also Held, Models of Democracy, pp. 190–6; Müller, Contesting Democracy.
54 Rosanvallon, Democratic Legitimacy, pp. 67–8.
55 European Commission, 'Report on European Union (29 December 1975)', www.cvce.eu/en/education/unit-content/-/unit/02bb76df-d066-4c08-a58a-d4686a3e68ff/63f5fc

This discursive shift, making its first appearances in the mid to late 1970s, became policy in the European institutions' joint campaign of the 1980s to transform Community Europe into a 'People's Europe'. The aim of this campaign was to 'bring Europe closer to its citizens'[56] and to make it 'respond to the expectations of the people of Europe'.[57] This was to be achieved by appealing to people not just as 'market citizens' and consumers of security or energy, but as culturally embedded human beings, and as political citizens – 'Union citizens', who held rights *specific* to the European Community. The idea was to make Europe present and tangible in their everyday lives through symbols, material benefits and specific entitlements, and to actively forge a European identity through solemn declaration as well as, not least, by multiplying budgets for the communication and cultural policies, aimed at making people associate Europe with culture, and this culture with themselves.[58]

To be sure, the fact that the citizens and 'what they wanted' were now at the centre of official EU discourse did not necessarily mean that these people got more of an actual say. They remained objects, spectators and addressees, rather than authors, of EU action. The will of the citizens, with its echoes of the trope of the 'will of the people', had a double status; it was referred to *both* as an independent source of legitimacy *and*, at the same time, as an object of manipulation, through cultural and identity-building policies, as well as through professionalised communication and information policies guided by the Eurobarometer.[59]

Moreover, giving the citizens what they wanted remained a matter of efficient policy-making – only now this was framed in terms of citizens'

a7-54ec-4792-8723-1e626324f9e3 / Resources#284c9784-9bd2-472b-b704-ba4bb1f3122d_
en&overlay, p. 11

56 European Commission, 'Reports from the Ad Hoc Committee on a People's Europe, Brussels, chaired by Pietro Adonnino, 25 and 26 June 1985, and 29 and 30 March 1985', *Bulletin of the European Economic Community* Supplement 7/85 (1985): 2–33 (henceforth 'Adonnino Reports').

57 European Council, 'Conclusions of the Sessions of the European Council, Fontainebleau, 25 and 26 June', *Bulletin of the European Communities* no. 6 (1984): 10–11. See also European Commission, 'Tindemans Report', p. 13; European Commission, 'Adonnino Reports', p. 5.

58 See European Commission, 'Document on the European Identity Published by the Nine Foreign Ministers in Copenhagen on 14 December 1973, "Declaration on European Identity"', BEC 1973(12): 118–22 (henceforth 'Document on the European Identity'); C. Shore, *Building Europe: The Cultural Politics of European Integration* (London, Routledge, 2000); Sternberg, *The Struggle for EU Legitimacy*, pp. 76–102.

59 See European Commission, 'Adonnino Reports', pp. 10–11, 20; C. Sternberg, 'Public Opinion in the EU Institutions' Discourses on EU Legitimacy from the Beginnings of Integration to Today', *Politique européenne* 54, no. 4 (2016): 24–56, especially 37–9; Sternberg, *The Struggle for EU Legitimacy*, pp. 67–102, in particular pp. 80–2, 100–2.

expectations.[60] It was a matter of greater sophistication in mapping as well as tweaking these expectations: in other words, of bringing the citizens closer to the EU, rather than bringing the EU closer to them.

The Post-Maastricht Crusade for Democracy

The Maastricht Treaty's thorny ratification, combined with plummeting support rates, once again changed the landscape of what could plausibly be said about the EU's legitimacy. It became difficult to maintain that the EU reflected what the Europeans wanted. Political actors could no longer act on the assumption that the citizens would not interfere with the deepening and widening of integration. The 'permissive consensus' was dead.[61]

In discursively managing this crisis, the European institutions framed the EU's 'all of a sudden very visible and audible, real and evident' legitimacy gap almost exclusively in term of its 'democratic deficit'. In this, they responded to critiques in the intense member state debates on Maastricht, including to the 'no demos' critique, that resounded far beyond the German legal community, and 'national republican' discourses that limited the practice of democracy and 'politics' to the community of the French and other nations. But they also relegated at least as pressing public concerns with monetary union, or with the power balance in post-Cold War Europe, to the background.[62] EU democracy was now firmly on the agenda. The next chapter in this volume explores how EU initiatives to tackle this democratic deficit have evolved since Maastricht. Here, I shall single out three ways in which the EU institutions effectively stretched and redefined the meaning of 'democracy' in managing the Maastricht ratification crisis and the ensuing (arguably ongoing) crisis of the EU's legitimacy.

First, during and immediately after the ratification crisis, the 'crusade for democracy' declared by the Commission 'in close cooperation' with the EP

---

60 See, for example, European Commission, 'Document on the European Identity', Section 1; J. Santer, 'Déclaration de Monsieur Jacques Santer, Président du Gouvernement, Président en exercise du Conseil Européen sur la Session du Conseil Européen de Milan les 28 et 29 juin 1985', *Bulletin de documentation* 4 (1985): 14–18; European Council, 'Conclusions of the Sessions of the European Council, Fontainebleau, 25 and 26 June', BEC, 1984(6), 10–11.

61 See, for example, European Council, 'European Council in Edinburgh (11/12 December 1992). Conclusions of the Presidency and Annexes. The Ratification of the Maastricht Treaty' (henceforth 'Edinburgh Conclusions'), in F. Laursen and S. Vanhoonacker (eds.), *The Ratification of the Maastricht Treaty: Issues, Debates and Future Implications* (Maastricht, European Institute of Public Administration and Martinus Nijhof, 1994), pp. 411–41, 411; EP, 'Reflection Group's Report' (1995), http://aei.pitt.edu/49155/1/B0015.pdf, p. 2.

62 Eurobarometer 38 (December 1992), p. vi.

centred on the openness and transparency of EU decision-making, as well as the principle of subsidiarity.[63]

Augmenting openness and transparency was hailed as a way to increase citizens' influence in that it would bring the EU's actions to greater scrutiny by the public as well as by the national parliaments, also 'ensur[ing] a better informed public debate on its activities'.[64] In effect, of course, the people's role in the logic of this transparency/openness discourse was limited to *observing* rather than sanctioning or actually deciding.

Subsidiarity in turn was presented in part as an apolitical instrument of better law-making.[65] In addition, it was presented as the answer to a common political discourse, according to which the votes of individual citizens counted less the greater the overall number of voters. The suggestion was that decisions taken at the lowest possible level of decision-making (representing smaller pools of voters) would be taken under the citizens' critical gaze, scrutiny and control. The subsidiarity discourse implied a natural link between subsidiarity and transparency.[66] Often, moreover, it simply equated subsidiarity with 'nearness' or 'closeness' to the citizens.[67]

Both the openness/transparency discourse and the subsidiarity discourse evoked a strengthening of democratic accountability, but equally a transformational effect in mobilising lost popular support.[68] They neglected the fact that citizens' being able to better 'see' European decision-making and observe it from closer up did not necessarily give them influence over it.[69]

Secondly, in the medium term the paradigm of *governance* proposed nothing less than a full re-imagination of democracy: a superior, more genuine, 'complete and thoroughgoing' alternative to traditional

---

63 See, for example, J. Delors, 'Address to the European Parliament, 10 February 1993, on the Occasion of the Investiture Debate Following Appointment of the New Commission' (1993), https://op.europa.eu/en/publication-detail/-/publication/76643950-0a1d-4692-a384-3e97bf559309.

64 European Council, 'Edinburgh Conclusions', pp. 409, 412–13; R. Prodi, 'Speech by Romano Prodi, President-Designate of the European Commission to the European Parliament, Strasbourg 14 September' (1999), https://ec.europa.eu/commission/presscorner/detail/en/SPEECH_99_114.

65 S. Van Hecke, 'The Principle of Subsidiarity: Ten Years of Application in the European Union', *Regional and Federal Studies* 13, no. 1 (2003): 55–80.

66 European Commission, 'Report on the Operation of the Treaty on European Union (presented by the Commission)', SEC (95) 731 final, 10 May 1995, p. 5.

67 See European Council, 'Edinburgh Conclusions', p. 410; EP, 'Reflection Group's Report', p. 2.

68 For example, European Council, 'Edinburgh Conclusions', p. 410; EP, 'Reflection Group's Report', p. 4 and Section I.

69 P. Magnette, 'European Governance and Civic Participation: Beyond Elitist Citizenship?', *Political Studies* 51, no. 1 (2003): 144–60.

representation – with which citizens across liberal democracies were becoming disenchanted.[70] Governance was 'the kind of democracy our fellow-citizens want'.[71] There is an abundant political science literature on EU governance.[72]

How was this supposed to work? 'Governance' focused attention on the top-down consultation of civil society organisations, as opposed to individual citizens or the people as a whole. As did the technocratic–bureaucratic mode of operation and legitimation, governance thus prioritised *responsiveness* to citizens' expectations over democratic control, representation or accountability.[73] It gave a voice to, and structurally favoured, organised and highly informed interest groups, explicitly pledging, incidentally, to raise popular 'confidence in expert advice'.[74] On these grounds, many critics regarded it 'as a restatement of the Technocratic Europe's *raison d'être* – "leave it to the experts"'.[75]

Another commonality with bureaucratic legitimacy, as well as with the turn to the citizens of the 1970s and 1980s, was that '[e]ffective action by European institutions' continued to be framed as 'the greatest source of their legitimacy', of higher priority than arguments about accountability or formal representation.[76] What had changed was that civil society consultation offered a new means of *identifying* citizens' preferences that could then be catered for. 'Participation is not about institutionalising protest. It is about more effective policy shaping.'[77] The governance discourse assumed that European citizens ultimately preferred entrusting civic participation in political decision-making and policy-making to civil society organisations over parliamentary representation.

Thirdly and finally, institutional discourses and policies projected Union citizenship and identity-building as solutions to the EU's democratic deficit. If there wasn't a European demos, the challenge was to forge one, complete

---

70 European Commission, 'European Governance. A White Paper' (2001) (henceforth 'Governance White Paper'), www.ab.gov.tr/files/ardb/evt/1_avrupa_birligi/1_6_ra porlar/1_1_white_papers/com2001_white_paper_european_governance.pdf, p. 32.
71 R. Prodi, 'The European Union and Its Citizens: a Matter of Democracy' (2001), https://ec.europa.eu/commission/presscorner/detail/en/SPEECH_01_365.
72 See, for example, B. Kohler-Koch, *The Transformation of Governance in the European Union* (London, Routledge, 2002) and the references in what follows.
73 P. Magnette, 'European Governance'; J. Mather, *Legitimating the European Union: Aspirations, Inputs and Performance* (Basingstoke, Palgrave Macmillan, 2006).
74 European Commission, 'Governance White Paper', p. 19.
75 Mather, *Legitimating the European Union*, p. 85; Tsakatika, 'Claims to Legitimacy'. See also B. Kohler-Koch, 'Framing: The Bottleneck of Constructing Legitimate Institutions', *Journal of European Public Policy* 7, no. 4 (2000): 513–31, 522.
76 R. Prodi, '2000–2005: Shaping the New Europe' (2000), https://ec.europa.eu/commis sion/presscorner/detail/en/SPEECH_00_41. See also European Commission, 'Governance White Paper', pp. 2, 5.
77 European Commission, 'Governance White Paper', p. 15.

with constitutional patriotism. This was in continuity with earlier identity-building efforts touched upon above, and with efforts to naturalise European governance by positively affecting people's everyday experiences through symbols as well as policies.[78] These approaches culminated in the project of an 'EU constitution', which was designed to bring the EU 'closer to its citizens', in order to give birth to a constitutive constitutional moment, European constitutional patriotism and, indeed, a European people.[79]

Assertions of Popular Sovereignty and Redoubled Politicisation

Of course, the constitutional treaty's public reception in the member states, and later on the Brexit debate and campaign, may suggest that the official emphasis on EU democracy of the 1990s and early 2000s either backfired, or else failed to turn the tide of wider public understandings of integration and democracy at large. Democracy did play a key role in these debates, but *not* in the re-imagined senses advanced by official rhetoric in the 1990s and early 2000s.

The referendums on the Constitutional Treaty and on Brexit can be read as assertions of popular sovereignty and the voters' will to shape their countries' economic and social future – insisting on the means of electoral and competitive party democracy, as opposed to either outsourcing participation to organised professionals or reinforcing a technocratic and constitutionalising dynamics.[80] An important discourse in the 2005 French 'no' campaign cast the rejection of the constitutional treaty as a reclaiming of 'the political' – against these de-politicising tendencies. Democracy and 'the political' in this discourse were not only confined essentially to the nation, but also re-cast as being essentially about enabling and channelling contestation.[81] 'No' voters were asserting their right to fight and have a say over what the EU should be doing and how, and where it should stop.

---

78 See K. McNamara, *The Politics of Everyday Europe: Constructing Authority in the European Union* (Oxford, Oxford University Press, 2017).

79 European Council, 'Laeken Declaration on the Future of the European Union (15 December 2001), Presidency Conclusions of the Laeken European Council', *Bulletin of the European Union* no. 12 (2001): 19–23.

80 C. Sternberg, 'The French and Dutch Block the Constitutional Treaty', in J. E. Smith (ed.), *The Palgrave Handbook of European Referendums* (London, Palgrave Macmillan, 2021), pp. 583–600; Sternberg, *The Struggle for EU Legitimacy*, pp. 145–86. See also C. Sternberg, 'What Were the French Telling Us by Voting Down the "EU Constitution"? A Case for Interpretive Research on Referendum Debates', *Comparative European Politics* 16 (2018): 145–70.

81 See Sternberg, *The Struggle for EU Legitimacy*, pp. 145–86.

If the 2005 referendums were resounding statements against the 'unwillingness' on the part of Europe's political and administrative elites 'to subject the question of integration to meaningful political contestation in domestic politics',[82] then the later critiques of the EU's handling of the euro crisis as well as the Euroscepticism rising in many member states[83] drove this message home with even greater force. The euro crisis at the latest made it undeniable that the stakes of EU politics were inescapably conflictual and controversial, the challenge being how to democratically negotiate, channel and mutually recognise clashing interests, needs and concerns.[84] Brexit campaigners, in turn, took this one step further, to questioning, or politicising, the legitimacy of supranational integration as such, under the banners of 'taking back control' and reclaiming 'sovereignty'.[85] Only the British people, through Parliament, could legitimately decide over Britain's social and economic future and its boundaries. A new type of British Euroscepticism was centred on the claim that, given shared interests, the benefits of supranational cooperation could be had without compromising sovereignty.[86]

Concluding Remarks

Where does this run-through of major shifts in official imaginations of EU democracy leave us? On a first level, playing different imaginations against each other defamiliarises us from any teleological understanding that may underpin the term 'democratic deficit', of the 'EU as a project of progress towards a predetermined goal, as a self-propelling engine towards a European democracy'.[87]

Just as the EU has many democratic deficits, it has also had a range of possible democratic futures over time. Maastricht was indeed a turning point in the evolution of discourses on EU democracy over time but, as we have seen, democracy was not a non-issue before. Rather, it was imagined in a variety of ways.

82 A. Glencross, 'The Difficulty of Justifying European Integration as a Consequence of Depoliticization: Evidence from the 2005 French Referendum', *Government and Opposition* 44, no. 3 (2009): 243–61.
83 See Chapter 24 by Wouter Wolfs in this volume.
84 C. Sternberg, K. Gartzou-Katsouyanni and K. Nicolaïdis, *The Greco-German Affair in the Euro Crisis: Mutual Recognition Lost?* (London, Palgrave Macmillan, 2018).
85 See B. Martill and U. Staiger (eds.), *Brexit and Beyond: Rethinking the Futures of Europe* (London, University College London Press, 2018).
86 S. Usherwood, 'The Third Era of British Euroscepticism: Brexit as a Paradigm Shift', *The Political Quarterly* 89, no. 4 (2018): 553–9. On the rise of Euroscepticism more broadly, see Chapter 24 by Wouter Wolfs in this volume.
87 Schulz-Forberg and Stråth, *The Political History of European Integration*, p. 4.

The changing imaginaries of EU democracy, moreover, communicated closely with broader shifts in the social imaginaries of modern democracy. European integration was part and parcel of Europe's post-war constitutional ethos, and the Communities' nature as a top-down enterprise in social engineering lent itself to the bureaucratic mode of legitimation characterising the 1950s and 1960s more broadly, all the while being framed by embedding discourses on delegation and the need for a strong and elected EP. The turn to the citizens, the 'People's Europe' discourse and the redefinition of EU democracy in the EU institutions post-Maastricht underline how constructions of EU democracy provided a 'laboratory' for experimenting with alternative modes of legitimation emerging also at the national level, while simultaneously feeding on them for their own rationalisations, directive utopias and pragmatic critiques of the EU's legitimacy.[88]

Particularly the search for more 'genuine' alternatives to electoral democracy underlying the governance discourse was in sync with a general disillusionment with democracy starting in the 1980s; with what Pierre Rosanvallon has called the 'de-sacralisation' of elections and 'collapse of democratic legitimacy'. The discourses on closeness to the citizens, openness and transparency, likewise, read almost as if taken from the playbook of the 'revolution in the conception of legitimacy' and 'decentering of democracy' that he describes (and proscribes), whereby democracy became 'something more than merely electing representatives'.[89] And yet, the debates and votes on the Constitutional Treaty and on Brexit can be read as an assertion of the will to exercise popular sovereignty through the classic means of electoral competitive democracy.

Finally, in common with modern democracy at large, the discursive history of ideas around EU democracy can be told as a history of progressive politicisation, of how it became increasingly implausible to take for granted any consensus on the guiding goals of integration and policy, or on how to pursue them. It is a story not least of how it increasingly became undeniable that virtually any choice in integration politics creates winners and losers, of how any discourses glossing over this and instead emphasising harmony effectively became counter-productive. The challenge for democracy in the EU is to provide mechanisms, and norms, for collective and representative decision-making under conditions of essential disagreement and difference.

---

88 Rosanvallon, *Democratic Legitimacy*, pp. 232–4; Sternberg, 'Ideologies and Imaginaries of Legitimacy'.
89 Rosanvallon, *Democratic Legitimacy*, pp. 69–79. See also Sternberg, 'Ideologies and Imaginaries of Legitimacy'.

Any exercise by the EU institutions to strengthen the democracy narrative in any reforms to its policies and institutions, including most recently the Conference on the Future of Europe, must take this into account.

Recommended Reading

Bang, H., M. D. Jensen and P. Nedergaard. '"We the People" versus "We the Heads of States": The Debate on the Democratic Deficit of the European Union', *Policy Studies* 36, no. 2 (2015): 196–216.

Kohler-Koch, B. and B. Rittberger (eds.). *Debating the Democratic Legitimacy of the European Union* (Lanham, MD, Rowman & Littlefield, 2007).

Piattoni, S. (ed.). *The European Union: Democratic Principles and Institutional Architectures in Times of Crisis* (Oxford, Oxford University Press, 2015).

Sternberg, C. S. *The Struggle for EU Legitimacy: Public Contestation, 1950–2005* (Basingstoke, Palgrave Macmillan, 2013).

24

Democratic Challenges since Maastricht

WOUTER WOLFS

Introduction

The Treaty of Maastricht signified an end to the permissive consensus that had characterised the first decades of the European integration project: the European Union (EU) as a political issue not only became more salient, but also aroused more public discontent. From the perspective of the political elite, the 1990s were a decade of optimism focused on deepening and widening the European project, with, for example, the imminent introduction of the euro and the EU enlargement with central and eastern European countries. At the level of the general public, European integration became increasingly contested, and claims about a 'democratic deficit' of the EU became ubiquitous. Although the Maastricht Treaty was not the starting point,[1] it substantially amplified the democratic debates about the EU.

After the treaty revisions of Amsterdam (1997) and Nice (2001), European leaders wanted to tackle this challenge and called during the European Council meeting in Laeken in December 2001 for 'more democracy, transparency and efficiency in the European Union'. This 'Laeken Declaration' was the starting point of the Convention on the Future of Europe that culminated in the drafting of a European Constitution in 2004. However, the enthusiasm surrounding the new Constitution soon faded when it was rejected by the French and Dutch populations in referendums in the spring of 2005. The heads of state and government announced a period of reflection to 'enable a broad debate to take place in each of our countries, involving citizens, civil society, social partners, national parliaments and political

The author wishes to acknowledge the financial support of the Postgraduate Research Grant on Christian Democracy and European Integration (EPP Group and the European University Institute).
1 See, for example, Chapter 23 by Claudia Sternberg in this volume.

parties'.[2] As its main contribution to this debate, the European Commission launched a Plan D for Democracy, Dialogue and Debate in October 2005.[3]

In 2007, most provisions of the failed Constitutional Treaty were revived by the Treaty of Lisbon, which eventually entered into force in December 2009. This treaty, however, did not put an end to the democratic debate at European level. The most recent era of the 'polycrisis' (sovereign debt and economic crisis, refugee crisis, Covid-19 pandemic) has only intensified the EU's democratic challenges. The debate on the democratic deficit has come to encompass many different aspects.

This chapter provides an overview of the main democratic debates at the European level since the Treaty of Maastricht. The focus is on the actions, positions and proposals of the EU institutions themselves, mainly through an analysis of primary documents. Existing scholarly work is used instrumentally to provide context and background to the main findings. Yet an exhaustive overview of the academic debates on the topic of the democratic deficit cannot be grasped in the framework of a single chapter and thus goes beyond the scope of this study. The chapter concentrates on four main dimensions of the democracy debate: (1) the inter-institutional dimension, which focuses on the discussions on the balance of power between the EU institutions, with particular attention to the position of the European Parliament (EP); (2) the partisan dimension, which is related to initiatives that have been proposed and introduced to strengthen (party) political competition at the EU level; (3) the public dimension, which entails those efforts to strengthen the input of citizens into European decision-making, both directly and indirectly, and proactive as well as reactive; and (4) the national dimension, focusing on the debate on the interaction of democracy at the European level with that at the national level.

The Inter-Institutional Dimension: Empowering the EP

This first dimension focuses on those debates that are related to the inter-institutional relations. Several initiatives have been put forward over the years to alter the balance of power between the EU institutions. In practice,

---

2 European Council, 'Declaration by the Heads of State or Government of the Member States of the EU on the Ratification of the Treaty Establishing a Constitution for Europe, Brussels, 18 June 2005', www.consilium.europa.eu/uedocs/cms_Data/docs/pressdata/en/ec/85325.pdf.

3 European Commission, 'The Commission's Contribution to the Period of Reflection and Beyond: Plan-D for Democracy, Dialogue and Debate', COM(2005) 494 final, Brussels, 13 October 2005.

this has mainly resulted in attributing more powers to the EP, a position fiercely defended by many Members of the EP (MEPs) themselves.

Since the beginning of the European integration project in the 1950s, the balance of power between the institutions has been the object of a significant evolution. The main beneficiary of this process has been the EP, that gradually evolved from a consultative body composed of delegations from national parliaments to a directly elected institution with wide-ranging powers in most EU policy fields. This has been neither an easy nor a straightforward process, as can be illustrated by the Dehousse Report of 1960. In the report – which was aimed at developing proposals for the direct universal election of the parliamentary assembly – the MEPs were unable to agree on a uniform electoral procedure for the (mere) six member states at that time, or even on whether all members of the assembly should be directly elected.[4] The Treaty of Maastricht certainly signified an important turning point with the introduction of the co-decision procedure, bringing the Parliament on an equal footing with the Council of Ministers in the legislative decision-making process in several policy areas. In the decades after the Maastricht Treaty, the power balance has continued to shift. By making full use of – or even overextending – its competences and by continuously pushing for more influence in a context of often 'incomplete' treaty provisions, the Parliament has been relatively successful in broadening its powers in terms of legislation, treaty provisions and scrutiny of the Commission as well as the EU budget. This was done by relying on a discourse of 'democratisation through parliamentarisation': the EU's democratic deficit could be tackled by strengthening the powers of the EP.[5]

The Growing Legislative Role of the EP

In terms of legislation, the EP collided with the Council on the interpretation of the co-decision provisions soon after the entry into force of the Maastricht Treaty. The Council considered the Parliament's position as primarily consultative – as a continuation of the pre-Maastricht situation – and refused to engage in substantive negotiations. The EP's interpretation was that the two institutions were on equal footing and both had to approve

---

4 'Rapport général de Fernand Dehousse, président du groupe de travail pour les élections européennes, relatif au Projet de convention sur l'élection de l'Assemblée parlementaire européenne au suffrage universel direct, soumis à l'Assemblée le 30 avril 1960', www .cvce.eu/content/publication/1997/10/13/89c2a74e-fb16-4b7f-b796-d3759876ddfe/pub lishable_fr.pdf.

5 See, for example, European Parliament, 'Report on the Information Policy of the European Community' (A3-0238/93), 14 July 1993, pp. 11–12.

a common text. The disagreement led to an open conflict in 1994, when the Parliament voted down the Open Network Provision on Voice Telephony when the Council had reintroduced its common position after the conciliation negotiations failed to produce a compromise.[6] Formally, the Council could reintroduce its common position after failed conciliation negotiations, but the EP refused in principle to accept this, and the Council never made a new attempt afterwards.

One of the main consequences of this evolution was the development of informal meetings between delegations of the EP, the Council and the Commission – called *trilogues* – in order to find a compromise. Initially, these meetings were held during the second reading phase of some legislative files, after both institutions had formally determined their position in the first reading phase. Yet, increasingly, these trilogues have become common practice and have been held in the first reading phase before a formal vote of the Parliament and Council. Since the seventh parliamentary term, the great majority of legislation is agreed through trilogues in first reading.[7] However, this use of trilogues has been increasingly criticised and labelled undemocratic, because the negotiations take place behind closed doors and because the legislative texts are decided by a small group of people.[8]

The EP and Treaty Revision

Although the EP did not have any formal role in the revision of the treaties, it nonetheless made strong attempts to put its mark on the negotiations. In the run-up to the Treaty of Amsterdam, the Parliament invested heavily in discussing its position with national ministers and members of the Commission.[9] The increased powers that were subsequently entrusted to the Parliament in the treaty text were the result of

---

6 European Parliament, 'Activity Report 1 November 1993–30 April 1999: From Entry into Force of the Treaty of Maastricht to Entry into Force of the Treaty of Amsterdam, Brussels, 6 May 1999', www.europarl.europa.eu/cmsdata/198147/activity_repor t_1993_99_en.pdf, pp. 5–6.

7 European Parliamentary Research Service, 'European Parliament: Facts and Figures' (2019), www.europarl.europa.eu/RegData/etudes/BRIE/2019/635515/EPRS_BRI(2019) 635515_EN.pdf, p. 10.

8 See, for example, European Economic and Social Committee, 'Investigation of Informal Trilogue Negotiations since the Lisbon Treaty – Added Value, Lack of Transparency and Possible Democratic Deficit' (2017), www.eesc.europa.eu/en/our-work/publications-other-work/publications/investigation-informal-trilogue-negotiations-lisbon-treaty-added-value-lack-transparency-and-possible-democratic-deficit, pp. 68–75.

9 See, for example, European Parliament, 'Resolution on the Scope of Codecision Procedure', OJ C 362, 2 December 1996, p. 267.

a process of codification of existing practices and a response from the governments to increased public calls to reduce the EU's democratic deficit.[10] Yet, despite similarly strong attempts by the Parliament to acquire more powers in the run-up to the Treaty of Nice,[11] the resulting treaty change included few additional powers for the EP. The Parliament was more successful with the EU Constitutional Treaty. Capitalising on the Laeken Declaration that was aimed at 'tackling the democratic challenge facing Europe' and setting up a 'representative' European Convention, the EP gained a seat at the table. In contrast to the previous treaty reforms, in which the EP merely had observer status, the delegation of MEPs at the Convention would now have the opportunity to influence the text of the Constitutional Treaty. Despite authors arguing that the Convention was overshadowed by the subsequent intergovernmental conference (IGC), that the Convention President Valéry Giscard d'Estaing was especially sensitive to the interests of the bigger member states and that the logic of intergovernmental bargains characterised the proceedings,[12] the Parliament managed to secure – with the support of the Commission in an attempt to strengthen its own democratic legitimacy – some successes, such as the extension of the co-decision procedure or the acquisition of more power in the EU budget and trade policy.[13] Although the Constitutional Treaty failed, most of these provisions were upheld in the Lisbon Treaty. While the Parliament has itself always been on a quest for a stronger position in the EU's political system, the member state governments' response to a perceived lack of democratic legitimacy of the EU has also been an important driver for the granting of increased powers to the EP in the subsequent treaty revisions.[14]

10 S. Hix, 'Constitutional Agenda-Setting through Discretion in Rule Interpretation: Why the European Parliament Won at Amsterdam', *British Journal of Political Science* 32, no. 2 (2002): 259–80.

11 European Parliament, 'Resolution of the European Parliament on the Convening of the IGC (3 February 2000)', www.cvce.eu/content/publication/2013/10/9/fa327a8e-13b2-4813-a196-eaf1cab955ff/publishable_en.pdf.

12 P. Magnette and K. Nicolaïdis, 'The European Convention: Bargaining in the Shadow of Rhetoric', *West European Politics* 27, no. 3 (2004): 381–404.

13 G. Rosen, 'A Match Made in Heaven? Explaining Patterns of Cooperation between the Commission and the European Parliament', *Journal of European Integration* 38, no. 4 (2016): 409–24; D. Beach, 'The European Parliament in the 2000 IGC and the Constitutional Treaty Negotiations: From Loser to Winner', *Journal of European Public Policy* 14, no. 8 (2007): 1271–92.

14 See, for example, S. Goetz and B. Rittberger, 'A Matter of Habit? The Sociological Foundations of Empowering the European Parliament', *Comparative European Politics* 8, no. 1 (2010): 37–54.

Controlling the Executive

Regarding its relations with the European Commission, the Parliament has been able to use the 'incomplete contract' in the treaty provisions on the Commission investiture to strengthen its control. The Maastricht Treaty stipulated that the member states had to agree on a candidate for Commission President after consulting the Parliament, after which the Commission as a whole had to be approved through a vote of confidence in the EP.[15] The EP used the vagueness of the provisions – it was not stated *how* it should be consulted – to maximise its influence. It made its approval of the whole Commission dependent on a preceding vote on the candidate for Commission president proposed by the Council, giving it a de facto veto on the nomination of this position. For example, in 1994, the Parliament threatened to vote down the entire Commission if the candidate proposed by the Council did not receive a majority.[16] This new practice was subsequently codified in the Treaty of Amsterdam, despite initial opposition from several member states. More specifically, the United Kingdom (UK), Finland and Ireland objected to the formalisation of this practice.[17]

In addition, the required approval of the whole European Commission was also used by the Parliament to assert its influence on the nomination of individual Commissioners. The EP created an internal rule stating that the Commission could be approved only after confirmation hearings with the persons nominated by the member states for the posts of European Commissioner.[18] The candidates had to appear before the applicable parliamentary committee(s) and would be questioned intensively on their knowledge of the policy field and regarding political sensitivities. Despite initial opposition from the European Commission,[19] the procedure has become standard, and several candidates have been rejected over the years or forced

---

15 European Parliament, 'Role and Election of the President of the European Commission' (2014), www.europarl.europa.eu/EPRS/140829REV1-Role-of-the-President-of-the-European-Commission-FINAL.pdf.

16 European Parliament, 'Resolution on the Investiture of the Commission', *Journal officiel des Communautés européennes* no. C 128 (1994): 358. See also A. Heritier, *Explaining Institutional Change in Europe* (Oxford, Oxford University Press, 2007), pp. 139–59; Hix, 'Constitutional Agenda-Setting'.

17 See É. Guigou and E. Brok, 'Non-legislative Powers of the European Parliament', Conférence des représentants des gouvernements des États Membres (letter, 29 January 1997) (CONF/3810/97).

18 Rule 29a of the Rules of Procedure, 'Minutes of Proceedings of the Sitting of Wednesday, 15 September 1993' (93/C 268/03) (OJ C 268/58).

19 European Parliament Directorate-General for Internal Policies, 'The European Parliament as a Driving Force of Constitutionalisation' (2015), https://cadmus.eui.eu/bitstream/handle/1814/43425/2015-09-RR_eudo.pdf?sequence=1, p. 41.

to take on a different policy portfolio, for example Rocco Buttiglione in 2004, Rumiana Jeleva in 2009, Alenka Bratušek in 2014 and Sylvie Goulard in 2019. Although this procedure is not explicitly stipulated in the treaty text, the Parliament thus gained a de facto veto over individual designate-Commissioners. This also requires the Commission President to allocate the portfolios among the candidates before the entire Commission is approved by the Parliament. Consequently, these developments have turned the EU's political system into a hybrid mix of elements common to presidential and parliamentary systems.

The EP and the EU Budget

Finally, the EP has also been able to strengthen its position with regard to the EU budget. The relation between the different EU institutions in budgetary matters has mostly been regulated through inter-institutional agreements (in 1993, 1996, 1999, 2006, 2013 and 2020). These agreements have been used by the Parliament to increase its influence. In 1993, the EP refused to give its consent to the inter-institutional agreement until it received guarantees that more cooperation would be forthcoming from the Council. This resulted in more informal trilogues and conciliation meetings during the budgetary procedure. In addition, the EP has also consistently insisted on abolishing the distinction between compulsory and non-compulsory expenditure, because the Council had the final say over the former category,[20] which was eventually realised in the Treaty of Lisbon. Finally, the EP was able to overcome the Council's reluctance to introduce more flexibility on the ceilings determined by the Multi-annual Financial Framework. For example, in the run-up to the Inter-institutional Agreement of 1999, the EP was able to accomplish the setting up of a new flexibility reserve to fund new expenses.[21] Consequently, although the revenue of the EU budget is still largely determined by the member states, the EP has been able to gain more influence over the EU's expenditure.

Despite the fact that the evolution of the EU's balance of power has clearly shifted in favour of the EP during the first two decades after the Treaty of Maastricht, the measures taken to tackle the European debt crisis have put the

20 For an early example, see European Parliament, 'Report of the Temporary Committee "From the Single Act to Maastricht and Beyond" on the Commission Communication "From the Single Act to Maastricht and Beyond – the Means to Match Our Ambitions"', COM(92)2000 – C3-0061/92 (A3-0209/Part C), 27 May 1992, p. 18.
21 See European Parliament, 'Working Document No. 3 on Structure and Flexibility in Future Financial Perspectives' (1998), www.europarl.europa.eu/doceo/document/A-4-1999-0230_EN.html. For more information, see J. Lindner, *Conflict and Change in EU Budgetary Politics* (London and New York, NY, Routledge, 2006), pp. 188–99.

member states back in the driving seat. In the framework of the new economic governance, the Parliament has the right to be informed and consulted, and can invite members of the European Commission, Council and President of the European Council and of the Eurogroup, but does not have a formal say in the decision-making process.[22] The economic governance of the EU – including, among other things, the European Stability Mechanism, the Single Resolution Fund and the important role of the Eurogroup – is fundamentally intergovernmental in nature, although the European Commission has also received substantial new powers. Together with the loss of influence of national parliaments in this realm, the EP's lack of power has been often categorised as a new 'democratic deficit' in the EU's decision-making.[23]

A similar 'deficit' that has been intensively discussed is the lack of legislative initiative of the EP. The Parliament itself has frequently called for the introduction of such a right,[24] and has developed several mechanisms to maximise its impact on the legislative agenda. It can request the Commission to come forward with any appropriate legislative proposal (Article 225 of the Treaty on the Functioning of the European Union (TFEU)). A similar right has been granted to the Council of Ministers (Article 241 TFEU). In addition, the 2016 Interinstitutional Agreement on Better Law-Making includes provisions (Articles 4–11) that compel the Commission to provide prompt and detailed consideration of these requests from the Parliament or the Council and ensure the involvement of both institutions in the Commission's annual and multi-annual legislative planning.

The Partisan Dimension: The Quest for EU Party Politics

A second cluster of debates has revolved around the role of party politics in EU democracy. In line with the premise shared by academics that a more pronounced ideological and partisan competition at EU level would create

---

22 European Parliament, 'Resolution on Future Legislative Proposals on EMU: In Response to the Commission Communications (2013/2609(RSP))' (2013), www .europarl.europa.eu/doceo/document/TA-7-2013-0222_EN.html, para. 7.

23 See P. Kratochvil and Z. Sychra, 'The End of Democracy in the EU? The Eurozone Crisis and the EU's Democratic Deficit', *Journal of European Integration* 41, no. 2 (2019): 169–85; C. Fasone, 'European Economic Governance and Parliamentary Representation: What Place for the European Parliament?', *European Law Journal* 20, no. 2 (2014): 164–85, 184.

24 See, for example, European Parliament, 'Resolution on the State of the Debate on the Future of Europe' (2019), www.europarl.europa.eu/doceo/document/TA-8-2019-009 8_EN.html.

democratic benefits,[25] several proposals have been put forward to increase the role of European political parties in EU politics and in the European elections. These proposals focused on the introduction of public funding and a legal statute for European political parties, the system of lead candidates (*Spitzenkandidaten*) and the introduction of transnational lists for the European elections.

A Legal Statute and Public Funding for European Political Parties

The first step for the introduction of subsidies for European political parties was made in the Treaty of Maastricht, which included a new article stating that 'political parties at European level are important as a factor for integration within the Union. They contribute to forming a European awareness and to expressing the political will of the citizens of the Union.' (Article 138A). This 'constitutional mission' entrusted to the Europarties was endorsed by the EP in a 1996 resolution stipulating that, 'without a functioning party system, a strong and robust democracy in which the citizen participates actively is inconceivable'.[26] The resolution also called for a European legislative initiative to establish an EU legal status and public funding for the Europarties. However, it was not until the article was amended in the Treaty of Nice – following pressure from the main EP political groups and Europarties – that a sufficient legal basis was provided for the introduction of Europarty subsidies. This happened eventually in 2003.

In 2007, EU public funding was expanded to European political foundations, the think tanks affiliated to the Europarties. This had been encouraged by advocates in the EP who wanted to strengthen the partisan dimension of EU politics,[27] and was welcomed by the European Commission. In particular, Commissioner Wallström stressed that, in this respect, Europarties and their affiliated political foundations are 'part and parcel of building this real European public sphere, where different opinions can challenge each other'.[28] Consequently, the main role attributed to these Eurofoundations was to

---

25 See, for example, S. Hix, *What's Wrong with the European Union and How to Fix It* (Cambridge, MA, Polity Press, 2008).

26 European Parliament, 'Report on the Constitutional Status of the European Political Parties' (1996), www.europarl.europa.eu/doceo/document/A-4-1996-0342_EN.html.

27 European Parliament, 'Resolution on European Political Parties' (2006), www.europarl.europa.eu/doceo/document/TA-6-2006-03-23_EN.html#sdocta13.

28 European Parliament, Debate in the European Parliament, 13 November 2007, www.europarl.europa.eu/doceo/document/CRE-6-2007-11-13_EN.html#creitem31.

invigorate the ideological debate at European level.[29] After difficult negotiations between the EP and the Council of Ministers, the regulatory framework for European political parties was again changed in 2014. The European parties and foundations now received a European legal status, although in practice this did not substantially change their day-to-day functioning.[30]

While the funding of European political parties has been championed by the main pro-European groups in the EP and the European Commission, the Eurosceptic forces have traditionally been opposed to the Europarty funding system. They have quite systematically voted against the establishment of the system, and several Eurosceptic national parties have – unsuccessfully – challenged the EU regulation before the EU Court of Justice.[31] Over time, however, most Eurosceptics have taken a more pragmatic attitude and established European political parties of their own. Even a number of extreme-right parties – such as the British National Party and Golden Dawn from Greece – were able to secure EU funding. Attempts by the EP to refuse these groups European subsidies proved unsuccessful. For example, the EP attempted to reclaim the EU subsidies from the Alliance for Peace and Freedom, because the European party did not respect the fundamental values of the EU.[32] Around the same time, several scandals were exposed: some Eurosceptic parties had used their EU funding for national party purposes, in direct violation of the rules. These events – together with increased budgetary pressures experienced by the main European political parties – led to additional changes in the regulatory framework for Europarties, raising the thresholds for European parties to gain access to funding and at the same time lowering the requirements for party groups to receive the entire EU subsidy. Despite the substantial funding that the European political parties have received over time – more than €500 million from 2004 to 2020 – their involvement in and impact on EU decision-making remains limited.[33]

29 W. Gagatek and S. Van Hecke, 'Towards Policy-Seeking Europarties? The Development of European Political Foundations', EUDO – European Union Democracy Observatory (2011), https://cadmus.eui.eu/bitstream/handle/1814/19156/RSCAS_2011_58.pdf?sequence=1&isAllowed=y.

30 See, for example, W. Wolfs, *European Political Parties and Party Finance Reform: Funding Democracy?* (London, Palgrave Macmillan, 2022).

31 *Bonde and Others v. European Parliament and Council* (Case T-13/04) of 14 January 2004; *Front National and Others v. European Parliament and Council* (Case T-17/04) of 13 January 2003.

32 See European Parliament, 'Activity Report of the Committee on Constitutional Affairs: 8th Parliamentary Term (July 2014–June 2019)' (2019), www.europarl.europa.eu/cms data/185548/1184322EN.pdf, p. 49; A. Eriksson, 'MEPs Look for Ways to Defund Far-Right Party' (2017), https://euobserver.com/news/136858.

33 W. Wolfs, *European Political Parties and Party Finance Reform*; L. Norman and W. Wolfs, 'Is the Governance of Europe's Transnational Party System Contributing to EU Democracy?', *Journal of Common Market Studies* 60, no. 2 (2022): 463–79.

The Spitzenkandidaten Process: Choosing the Commission President

A key aspect that has strengthened the position of the European political parties in EU politics has been the Spitzenkandidaten system. This entails that all Europarties put forward their candidate for the presidency of the European Commission in the run-up to the European elections. The candidate who is able to secure the support of a majority in the EP should subsequently become the new Commission President. Consequently, the system contributes to the parliamentarisation of EU decision-making, with stronger (partisan) links between the Parliament and Commission.

The necessary foundations were laid in the Treaty of Maastricht, which extended the Commission's term of office to 5 years and brought it in line with the legislative term of the Parliament. Following the European People's Party's (EPP's) disappointment with the 1999 elections – in which they became the largest force in the EP for the first time since 1979, but failed to secure the Commission's presidency – the Europarty emphasised in the run-up to the 2004 European elections that the next President of the European Commission should be one of its members if it remained the largest group in the EP. This was realised with the nomination of Portuguese Prime Minister José Manuel Barroso. In 2009, he was put forward by the EPP for a second term, which made him the first Spitzenkandidat. Disagreements within the socialist family impeded the presentation of an alternative candidate by the Party of European Socialists (PES).[34] Since the EPP again became the strongest force in the EP, Barroso's second term could be secured.

These actions of the Europarties coincided with related developments in the EP. Following the Treaty of Amsterdam – in which it was stipulated that the Commission President had to be approved by the EP – the Parliament changed its internal rules of procedure and included the provision that the outcome of the European elections should be taken into account to determine who should hold the office of President of the Commission.[35] The issue was taken up in the context of the European Convention, which deliberated on changing the treaty article on the nomination of the Commission President. The Presidium of the Convention proposed a text that was close

---

34 S. Van Hecke, W. Wolfs and V. De Groof, '25 Years of Spitzenkandidaten: What does the Future Hold?', Wilfried Martens Centre of European Studies (2018), www .martenscentre.eu/wp-content/uploads/2020/06/ces_policybrief_spitzenkandidaten-web.pdf, pp. 2–4.

35 A. Héritier, K. L. Meissner, C. Moury and M. G. Schoeller, *European Parliament Ascendant: Parliamentary Strategies of Self-Empowerment in the EU* (New York, NY, Springer International, 2019), p. 71.

to the EP's interpretation in its internal rules: 'taking into account the elections to the European Parliament, the European Council, deciding by [qualified majority voting], shall put forward to the European Parliament its proposed candidate for the Presidency of the Commission. The European Parliament by a majority of its members shall elect this candidate.' This appeared as a compromise between the EPP, which was advocating the 'election of a candidate named by the Council', and the PES, which wanted a direct election by the EP from a list of several potential candidates, and between the member states that advocated for a direct election by the Parliament on the basis of one or more proposed candidates by the Council – including Belgium, the Netherlands, Luxembourg, Greece and Portugal – and member states that wanted to maintain the status quo – such as Finland, Ireland, Sweden and the UK.[36] The proposal was included in the final text of the European Constitution, and only slightly adjusted in the Treaty of Lisbon.

In particular, the first part of the treaty article – 'taking into account the elections to the European Parliament' – was used by the Commission and the EP to further develop the Spitzenkandidaten system. Disappointed with the second Barroso term as Commission President and its own incapability to put forward an alternative candidate in 2009, the PES decided already in December 2010 to nominate a common candidate for the Commission presidency in the run-up to the 2014 elections. The Commission explicitly supported this approach, as President Barroso stated in his 2012 State of the Union address that 'an important means to deepen the pan-European political debate would be the presentation by European political parties of their candidate for the post of Commission President at the European Parliament elections already in 2014'.[37] In its recommendation on the European elections from March 2013, the Commission repeated that the selection of lead candidates by the Europarties 'would make concrete and visible the link between the individual vote of a citizen of the Union for a political party in the European elections and the candidate for President of the Commission supported by that party',[38] thereby increasing the democratic legitimacy of EU policy-making in general and of the European Commission in particular.

---

36 Ibid., p. 38.

37 European Commission, 'State of the Union 2012 Address' (2012), https://ec.europa.eu/commission/presscorner/detail/en/SPEECH_12_596.

38 European Commission, 'Recommendation Enhancing the Democratic and Efficient Conduct of the Elections to the European Parliament' (2013), https://eur-lex.europa.eu/legal-content/EN/TXT/?uri=CELEX%3A32013H0142.

Similarly, the EP urged 'the European political parties to nominate candidates for the Presidency of the Commission and expect those candidates to play a leading role in the parliamentary electoral campaign' in a resolution of 22 November 2012.[39] One year before the 2014 elections, in July 2013, the EP repeated its support for the Spitzenkandidaten process, and called upon the European Council to first consider that candidate who was put forward by the European party that wins the most seats in the European elections.[40]

In the run-up to the 2014 European elections, five European political parties selected their lead candidates.[41] The EPP emerged from the elections as the largest political force, and the main political groups in the EP decided to support the nomination of its lead candidate, Jean-Claude Juncker, for the presidency of the European Commission.[42] The European Council, however, was much more reluctant,[43] and maintained that it was its prerogative to propose a name for the top Commission post. The EP was on the winning side of the inter-institutional struggle, as Jean-Claude Juncker was eventually nominated by the European Council and elected by the EP.

In the preparation of the 2019 elections, the Commission and Parliament strongly supported a continuation of the Spitzenkandidaten system.[44] This time, seven European political parties selected a lead candidate.[45] The EPP again constituted the largest political group in the EP, but its lead candidate, Manfred Weber, did not enjoy sufficient support among the heads of state and government. The lead candidates of the other main Europarties were

39 European Parliament, 'Elections to the European Parliament in 2014' (2012), https://eur-lex.europa.eu/legal-content/EN/TXT/PDF/?uri=CELEX:52012IP0462&from=EN.

40 European Parliament, 'Resolution on Improving the Practical Arrangements for the Holding of the European Elections in 2014' (2013), www.europarl.europa.eu/doceo/document/TA-7-2013-0323_EN.html, Article 15.

41 G.-J. Put, S. Van Hecke, C. Cunningham and W. Wolfs, 'The Choice of Spitzenkandidaten: A Comparative Analysis of the Europarties' Selection Procedures', *Politics and Governance* 4, no. 1 (2016): 9–22.

42 European Parliament, 'Conference of Presidents Statement on Commission President Election' (2014), www.europarl.europa.eu/news/en/press-room/20140527IPR48501/conference-of-presidents-statement-on-commission-president-election.

43 European Council, 'Remarks by President Herman Van Rompuy Following the Informal Dinner of Heads of State or Government' (2014), www.consilium.europa.eu/media/25752/142862.pdf.

44 European Commission, 'A Europe That Delivers: Commission Presents Ideas for a More Efficient European Union' (2018), https://ec.europa.eu/commission/presscorner/detail/en/IP_18_743; European Parliament, 'Decision of 7 February 2018 on the Revision of the Framework Agreement on Relations between the European Parliament and the European Commission' (2018), https://eur-lex.europa.eu/legal-content/EN/TXT/?uri=CELEX%3A52018DP0030.

45 W. Wolfs, G.-J. Put and S. Van Hecke, 'Explaining the Reform of the Europarties' Selection Procedures for Spitzenkandidaten', *Journal of European Integration* 43, no. 7 (2021): 891–914.

also considered during several meetings, but eventually the European Council nominated Ursula von der Leyen (Germany, EPP),[46] who had not been a (lead) candidate in the European elections. The EP reluctantly approved von der Leyen, after she had agreed a policy programme for her term with the main political groups. Consequently, in contrast to 2014, the Spitzenkandidaten system failed in the 2019 elections.

Transnational Lists: A Pan-European Electoral District

The system is closely related to another proposal to give European political parties a stronger role in European elections: the introduction of transnational lists on which these Europarties can present candidates to all voters across the EU. This idea of a pan-European constituency had been supported by the EP in the 1990s,[47] and was included in the Laeken Declaration. Several practical proposals were put forward during the Constitutional Convention, but none made it into the final text. The topic of transnational lists was again intensively debated in the EP on several occasions from 2011 onwards.[48] However, no consensus could be found because of disagreements between and within the political groups on the added value and practical implementation of the concept.

Proponents of transnational lists have argued that it would strengthen the European dimension of the (campaigns and debates in the) elections to the EP. Other advantages that have been put forward include that it would provide MEPs with a stronger democratic mandate from all EU citizens and improve their accountability, and would strengthen the role of European political parties and the ideological debate on EU-related issues. The main arguments against such a pan-European district are that it would give rise to first- and second-order MEPs (the former elected on transnational

---

46 European Council, 'European Council Conclusions, 30 June–2 July' (2019), www .consilium.europa.eu/en/press/press-releases/2019/07/02/european-council-conclusions-30-june-2-july-2019.

47 European Parliament, 'Resolution on a Draft Electoral Procedure Incorporating Common Principles (15 July 1998)', www.cvce.eu/content/publication/1999/1/1/d3 e39c10-733a-4f6e-9dbd-046ef8d76d45/publishable_en.pdf.

48 See, for example, A. Duff, 'Report on a Proposal for a Modification of the Act Concerning the Election of the Members of the European Parliament by Direct Universal Suffrage of 20 September 1976' (2011), www.europarl.europa.eu/doceo/document/A-7-2011-0176_EN .html; A. Duff, 'Second Report on a Proposal for a Modification of the Act Concerning the Election of the Members of the European Parliament by Direct Universal Suffrage of 20 September 1976' (2012), www.europarl.europa.eu/doceo/document/A-7-2012-0027_E N.html; Hübner–Leinen Report, 'European Parliament Resolution of 11 November 2015 on the Reform of the Electoral Law of the European Union' (2015), www.europarl.europa .eu/doceo/document/TA-8-2015-0395_EN.html?redirect.

lists and the latter on national lists), it would widen – and not reduce – the distance between citizens and MEPs, and it would favour candidates from larger member states to the disadvantage of smaller and medium-sized EU countries.[49] In addition, even if transnational lists were introduced, genuine EU-wide electoral campaigns would be hampered by language barriers and a plethora of electoral and campaign (finance) rules in the different member states. Despite more recent support from heads of state such as Emmanuel Macron and Commission President Ursula von der Leyen,[50] and from citizens during the Conference on the Future of Europe, the idea of a pan-European electoral district has not (yet) materialised.

The Popular Dimension: (Re)connecting with EU Citizens

As the Treaty of Maastricht awakened the 'sleeping giant' of popular discontent with European integration, the involvement of citizens in the EU's decision-making process has become an important point of attention at European level. However, in the first decade after the Maastricht Treaty, public involvement was predominantly seen as a top-down exercise. Although it is also acknowledged that citizens should be able to provide input in the policy-making process, the dominant interpretation was that this should be done through (elections for) the EP.[51] The main focus was on improving communication to the European public in order to 'increase awareness of the achievements and advantages of the Union and foster public support for the forthcoming stages of the integration process'.[52] This had to be achieved through better coordination in terms of communication between the main EU institutions, a professionalisation of the EU's

---

49 For a recent overview of the debates, see M. Diaz Crego, 'Transnational Electoral Lists: Ways to Europeanize Elections to the European Parliament', European Parliamentary Research Service (2021), www.europarl.europa.eu/RegData/etudes/S TUD/2021/679084/EPRS_STU(2021)679084_EN.pdf.

50 E. Macron, 'Initiative pour l'Europe' (2017), www.elysee.fr/emmanuel-macron/2017/09/ 26/initiative-pour-l-europe-discours-d-emmanuel-macron-pour-une-europe-souveraine-unie-democratique; U. von der Leyen, 'Opening Statement in the European Parliament Plenary Session' (2019), https://ec.europa.eu/commission/presscorner/detail/en/ SPEECH_19_4230.

51 See, for example, European Parliament, 'Report on the Information Policy of the European Community' (1993), http://aei.pitt.edu/13426, p. 13.

52 European Parliament, 'Report on the Information and Communication Policy in the European Union' (1998), www.europarl.europa.eu/doceo/document/A-4-1998-0115_ EN.html, p. 4.

communication policy (including more funding) and a process of decentral-isation of communication.[53]

Deliberative Initiatives: Discussing Europe with Its Citizens

Only after the failed referendums on the Constitutional Treaty did the com-munication paradigm from the EU institutions fundamentally change. As a response, the European Commission launched in 2005 Plan D for Democracy, Dialogue and Debate, the aim of which was to 'reinvigorate European democracy and help the emergence of a European public sphere, where citizens are given the information and the tools to actively participate [...] and gain ownership of the European project'.[54] The main aim was to organise national debates in the member states as a deliberative effort to discuss the future of Europe. This resulted in the Commission's Citizen's Agenda in 2006: a set of twelve policy initiatives to strengthen prosperity, solidarity and security in the EU.[55] The participatory effort was continued with the Debate Europe Programme in 2008, which focused on the formulation of proposals to policy-makers following citizen consultations.[56]

As part of these efforts to strengthen participative and deliberative democ-racy, European Citizens' Consultations (ECCs) were organised. The first ECCs were organised in the framework of Plan D in 2007 and were experi-mental in nature: 28 national consultations with a representative (and rather limited) sample of 1,800 citizens that formulated a set of policy proposals. In 2009, further ECCs were a combination of online forums that involved up to 30,000 citizens and in-person consultations in the member states. Despite high ambitions, the actual policy impact was rather low.[57]

The second Barroso Commission (2009–14) applied a more traditional one-way communication approach. For example, in 2013 the 'New Narrative for Europe' was launched, which ran until 2018. Instead of directly involving citizens, the approach was focused on communicating the importance of the

---

53 Ibid.
54 European Commission, 'The Commission's Contribution to the Period of Reflection and Beyond: Plan-D for Democracy, Dialogue and Debate' (2005), https://eur-lex.europa.eu/LexUriServ/LexUriServ.do?uri=COM:2005:0494:FIN:en:PDF.
55 European Commission, 'A Citizens' Agenda: Delivering Results for Europe' (2006), www.astrid-online.it/static/upload/protected/EUCo/EUComm_CitizenAgenda_10 mayo6.pdf .
56 European Commission, 'Debate Europe – Building on the Experience of Plan D for Democracy, Dialogue and Debate' (2008), https://eur-lex.europa.eu/legal-content/E N/ALL/?uri=CELEX:52008DC0158.
57 M. Karlsson, 'Digital Democracy and the European Union', in A. Bakardjieva Engelbrekt, K. Leijon, A. Michalski and L. Oxelheim (eds.), *The European Union and the Technology Shift* (Basingstoke, Palgrave Macmillan, 2021), pp. 237–61, 248–9.

EU.[58] The Juncker Commission revived the participatory effort, and organised more than 1,500 Citizen Dialogues in 'town hall type meetings' in which European Commissioners debated the future of Europe – as set out in the Commission's white paper on the subject – with close to 200,000 citizens. The first Citizen Dialogue was organised in 2013 in the context of the European Year of the Citizens.[59] Following an initiative from French President Emmanuel Macron in his 2017 Sorbonne speech, a new series of ECCs were organised. However, compared with the 2007 and 2009 editions, there were substantial differences regarding the topics discussed and the practical design of the national consultations.[60]

The most recent and ambitious attempt to include citizens in European policy-making has been the Conference on the Future of Europe. Inspired by an idea put forward by French President Macron in the run-up to the 2019 European elections,[61] the Conference was an important commitment for the 'new push for European democracy' of Ursula von der Leyen before her election as Commission President in July 2019.[62] Despite substantial support in the EP and among some member states,[63] the organisation of the Conference was delayed due to the Covid-19 crisis and strong disagreements between the institutions on the governance and purpose of the Conference. Particular points of discussion were who should lead the Conference and whether or not the suggestions expressed could give rise to a change of the European treaties. Eventually, in April 2021, the Conference was initiated with the launch of a multilingual digital platform. An important part was formed by the European Citizens Panels: four groups of 200 randomly selected citizens from all member states balanced in terms of gender, age, socio-economic background and level of education, that discussed the various EU-related topics and provided a set of recommendations to the Conference plenary. The final

---

58 W. Kaiser, 'One Narrative or Several? Politics, Cultural Elites, and Citizens in Constructing a "New Narrative for Europe"', *National Identities* 19, no. 2 (2017): 215–30.

59 European Commission, 'Citizens' Dialogues and Citizens' Consultations: Key Conclusions' (2019), https://op.europa.eu/en/publication-detail/-/publication/5a54 a0f2-80f1-11e9-9f05-01aa75ed71a1; European Commission, 'White Paper on the Future of Europe: Avenues for Unity for the EU at 27' (2017), https://ec.europa.eu/commis sion/presscorner/detail/en/IP_17_385.

60 Karlsson, 'Digital Democracy', p. 250.

61 E. Macron, 'For European Renewal' (2019), www.elysee.fr/en/emmanuel-macron/2 019/03/04/for-european-renewal.

62 U. von der Leyen, 'Opening Statement in the European Parliament Plenary Session by Ursula von der Leyen, Candidate for President of the European Commission' (2019), https://ec.europa.eu/dorie/fileDownload.do?docId=6198158&cardId=6198157.

63 See, for example, 'Franco-German Non-paper on Key Questions and Guidelines' (2019), www.politico.eu/wp-content/uploads/2019/11/Conference-on-the-Future-of-Europe.pdf.

conclusions of the Conference on the Future of Europe were presented on 9 May 2022, with forty-nine specific proposals clustered in nine main policy themes.[64]

Direct Democratic Efforts

Aside from these deliberative efforts, the introduction of mechanisms to give citizens a direct impact in EU decision-making has been an important point of attention since the beginning of the 1990s. The Treaty of Maastricht already provided European citizens with the possibility of petitioning the EP. Every EU citizen – and natural or legal person residing in the EU – can address a complaint or request for action to the EP's Committee on Petitions (Article 227 TFEU).

In addition, several new proposals were put forward to introduce instruments of direct democracy into the EU's institutional set-up, in particular popular referendums. As early as 1988, the EP in a resolution called for 'a parallel strategy to allow the popular will to express itself [. . .] by popular initiative referendum' and for the introduction of popular consultations.[65] The possibility of a European legislative referendum and citizens' ballots on 'Community decisions' was discussed in the Public Liberty and Domestic Affairs Commission of the EP in December 1993,[66] but was not pursued afterwards.[67] During the negotiations on the Treaty of Amsterdam, the Foreign Minister of Austria Wolfgang Schüssel and his Italian counterpart, Lamberto Dini, proposed the inclusion of a Citizens Initiative in the text of the treaty, but were unable to find substantial support. Their proposal stipulated that 10 per cent of the EU's population could present a legislative proposal to the EP, which would be obliged to consider it.[68]

It was only during the Constitutional Convention in 2003 that an agreement was reached on the introduction of a direct democracy instrument: the European Citizens' Initiative (ECI). In its section on the 'democratic life of the Union', the draft constitution stipulated that the functioning of the Union

64 European Parliament, 'Conference on the Future of Europe: Report on the Final Outcome' (2022), www.europarl.europa.eu/resources/library/media/20220509RE S29121/20220509RES29121.pdf.

65 European Parliament, 'Resolution on Ways of Consulting European Citizens about the EU' (OJ C 187/231), 1988.

66 See B. Kaufmann, 'Transnational "Babystep": The European Citizens' Initiative', in M. Setälä and T. Schiller (eds.), Citizens' Initiatives in Europe: Procedures and Consequences of Agenda-Setting by Citizens (Basingstoke, Palgrave Macmillan, 2012), pp. 228–42, 230.

67 European Parliament, 'Resolution on the Constitution of the European Union of 10 February 1994' (A3-0064/94), Official Journal of the European Communities no. C 61 (1994): 155–70.

68 See Kaufmann, 'Transnational "Babystep"', p. 231.

was founded on the principles of representative democracy (Article I-46), but also distinguished a number of principles of participatory democracy (Article I-47). While the first drafts of the latter section referred only to participation by means of a civil dialogue and consultation – in practice mainly reserved for collective actors such as the umbrella organisations of trade unions or small to medium-sized enterprises – the final version also foresaw the direct participation of citizens.[69] Some authors have even argued against the participatory nature of these mechanisms.[70]

Despite the failure of the Constitutional Treaty, the provisions on the ECI were included without fundamental alterations in the Lisbon Treaty (Articles 9–12 of the Treaty on the European Union (TEU)). It allows 1 million European citizens from at least a quarter of the member states to directly call upon the European Commission to come forward with a legislative proposal. The conditions and procedure of the ECI are stipulated in Artcle 24(1) TFEU. Consequently, it is a form of indirect popular initiative (also called an *agenda initiative*) and differs from a direct popular initiative (or *referendum initiative*) in that a political demand put forward by a predetermined number of citizens does not lead to a popular referendum, but merely entails a non-binding proposal for an EU legislative measure.[71] The European Commission can still change the proposal or choose not to act.

Interestingly, the ECI was not a result of proposals put forward by the EU institutions or member states, but was the consequence of a targeted campaign by activists who had been calling for direct democracy instruments for over a decade.[72] The 'agenda initiative' was only one of the many proposals on participatory democracy that was discussed in the context of the Convention, with others including a citizen referendum initiative, or the possibility to hold continent-wide referendums on EU legislation or treaty changes. For example, MEP Alain Lamassoure introduced an amendment stating that the European Council, after assent of the EP, could decide to submit a bill or treaty for ratification by a popular referendum.[73] Austrian

69 H. Heinlet, 'Participatory Governance and European Democracy', in B. Kohler-Koch and B. Rittberger (eds.), *Debating the Democratic Legitimacy of the European Union* (Lanham, MD, Rowman & Littlefield, 2007), pp. 217–32, 225.

70 See M. Greven, 'Some Considerations on Participation in Participatory Governance', in Kohler-Koch and Rittberger (eds.), *Debating the Democratic Legitimacy of the European Union*, pp. 233–48.

71 V. Cuesta-López, 'A Comparative Approach to the Regulation on the European Citizens' Initiative', *Perspectives on European Politics and Society* 13 (2012): 257–69, 257–8.

72 For a more general overview, see Kaufmann, 'Transnational "Babystep"', pp. 228–42.

73 European Convention, 'Proposition d'amendement à l'Article 34 (bis) déposée par Monsieur Alain Lamassoure', https://ec.europa.eu/dorie/fileDownload.do;jsessionid=

MEPs Caspar Einem and Maria Berger proposed that 1.5 per cent of the European citizens could demand a EU-wide referendum on their proposed topic.[74] The proposal for an ECI was included in the treaty text only during the last stages of the Convention by Member of the German Bundestag Jürgen Meyer. According to Meyer, the initiative aimed 'to bring Europe closer to the people, as Laeken recommended. It represents a large step in the democratisation of the Union.'[75]

In the first decade of its existence, more than seventy initiatives have been registered with the Commission, but the numbers clearly show a declining trend over time. The administrative process has been characterised as too demanding, which has hindered citizens attempting to successfully complete an ECI. In addition, the European Commission has refused more than one-third of the proposals, because they allegedly fell outside the scope of the European treaties.[76] There have been wide calls – including from the EP and the European Ombudsman – to reform the ECI. In response, the ECI Regulation has been revised with the aim of making the procedure more efficient and practical. The new rules have been in force since January 2020.

The National Dimension: Bringing in the Member States

More recently, the national level has become more prominent in the debate about democracy in the EU, regarding both the bottom-up and the top-down aspect.

The Role of National Parliaments

The debate on the bottom-up aspects has mainly focused on the principle of subsidiarity and the role of national parliaments in EU decision-making. Historically, the national governments have been intensively involved – and

WNaih-wErfWkrENKXEnkrOcLHMsVkyOKwtk703DSpCeZjKJ9bgvJ!2052287358? docId=252181&cardId=252181.

74 M. C. Einem and M. Berger, 'Suggestion for Amendment of Article 34a: Suggestion for Part III', https://ec.europa.eu/dorie/fileDownload.do;jsessionid=idZ2HQZ32y6opett5r qB_WthwX_34NiWBU_ixqxZa36fuKifxqVm!2134958119?docId=295133&cardId=295133.

75 European Convention, 'Suggestion for Amendment of Article I-46, Part I, Title VI' (2003), https://data.consilium.europa.eu/doc/document/CV%20724%202003%20RE V%201/EN/pdf; European Convention, 'Cover Note: Revised Texts', Brussels, 12 June 2003, p. 5.

76 European Parliamentary Research Service, 'Revising the European Citizens' Initiative' (2019), www.europarl.europa.eu/RegData/etudes/ATAG/2019/635550/EPRS_ATA(2019)635550_EN.pdf, p. 3.

even decisive – in EU decision-making, while the participation of national parliaments did not receive much attention for a long time. In the early decades of European integration, the involvement of national parliaments was ensured through the dual mandate of Members of the Parliamentary Assembly. Ever since the direct election of MEPs in 1979, the role of parliamentarians in the member states has been largely limited to scrutinising the position of their government in the Council of Ministers. In the Maastricht Treaty, two (non-binding) declarations were included that called for increased exchange of information and contacts between the EP and national parliaments (Declaration 13), and the possibility of organising a joint 'Conference of the Parliaments' that should be consulted on the main features of the EU (Declaration 14). In the Treaty of Amsterdam, this was strengthened through an attached protocol (Protocol no. 9 on the role of national parliaments in the EU) that ensured that all (consultation and legislative) documents would be promptly forwarded to national parliaments, and stipulated that the Conference of European Affairs Committees could provide any contribution on EU legislative proposals.

The role of national parliaments in EU decision-making was institutionalised in the Constitutional Treaty – taken over by the Treaty of Lisbon – which stated that national parliaments had to 'contribute actively to the good functioning of the Union' (Article 12 TEU). The treaty also established the so-called Early Warning System (EWS), which provided national parliaments with the ability to monitor respect for the principle of subsidiarity. When the European Commission comes forward with a legislative proposal, national parliaments have 8 weeks to scrutinise the text and send a 'reasoned opinion' to the Commission if they consider that it breaches the principle of subsidiarity. If one-third of the parliaments issue a reasoned opinion, a 'yellow card' is triggered. The Commission must then reconsider its proposal and can withdraw, amend or maintain it (but with a justification). If half of the parliaments submit a reasoned opinion, an 'orange card' is drawn. Similarly, the Commission must reconsider the draft legislation, but it also becomes easier for the Parliament and the Council to dismiss the proposal.

Although the EWS provides national parliaments with a formal role in EU decision-making, the instrument's performance has been contested. Since it was introduced in the Lisbon Treaty, a yellow card has been issued only three times (in 2012 on a proposal for a regulation on the exercise of the right to take collective action (the 'Monti II Regulation'); in 2013 on the proposal for a regulation establishing the European Public Prosecutor's Office; in 2016 on the review of the posting of workers directive),[77] and an orange card has never been triggered. Only in one of these three cases did the Commission withdraw its proposal, mainly as a result of opposition in the EP and the Council, and not because it followed the view of the national parliaments that it would breach the principle of subsidiarity.[78] Consequently, the scope and effectiveness of the EWS have been intensively debated.

Three main discussions can be distinguished. The first discussion focuses on the scope of the EWS: should national parliaments exclusively assess a proposal with regard to subsidiarity, or can they also raise objections in terms of the proportionality of the draft legislation. Broadening the scope of the mechanism has indeed been advocated by several national parliaments.[79] Secondly, several parliamentary assemblies have called for a more 'constructive' mechanism in EU decision-making by establishing a 'green card': suggest a legislative initiative to the European Commission. This proposal was initially put forward by the UK House of Lords EU Select Committee in 2014, and has received increasing support from many additional national parliaments. In 2015, a first informal green card was issued on the problem of food waste. In 2017, the EP voiced its support for the idea and proposed 'complementing and enhancing the powers of national parliaments by introducing a "green card" procedure whereby national parliaments could submit legislative proposals to the Council for its consideration'.[80]

Thirdly, some authors have argued for the possibility of a 'red card', providing national parliaments with a real veto on legislative proposals in the case of a breach of subsidiarity.[81] In November 2015, UK Prime Minister David Cameron suggested giving national parliaments the ability to stop EU laws through a 'red card'. A weaker proposal was included in the 2016 deal between the UK and the EU,[82] but never materialised.

77 See European Commission, 'Subsidiarity Control Mechanism', https://commission .europa.eu/law/law-making-process/adopting-eu-law/relations-national-parliaments /subsidiarity-control-mechanism_en.
78 Ibid.
79 See House of Lords European Union Committee, *The Role of National Parliaments in the European Union* (London, House of Lords European Union Committee, 2014), p. 26.
80 European Parliament, 'Resolution on Possible Evolutions of and Adjustments to the Current Institutional Set-up of the European Union' (2017), https://eur-lex.europa.eu/ legal-content/EN/TXT/?uri=CELEX%3A52017IP0048.
81 See, for example several of the chapters in A. Cornell and M. Goldoni (eds.), *National and Regional Parliaments in the EU-Legislative Procedure Post-Lisbon* (Portland, OR, Hart, 2017).
82 V. Kreilinger, 'Strengthening Parliamentary Voices in the EU's Multi-level System', Jacques Delors Institute (2018), https://institutdelors.eu/wp-content/uploads/2018/06/ ParliamentaryVoicesintheEUMultilevelSystem-Kreilinger-June2018.pdf, p. 12; European Council, 'Draft Decision of the Heads of State or Government, Meeting within the

Guarding the Rule of Law at National Level

Since the 2010s, the European democracy debate has increasingly been characterised by a top-down perspective: an appeal for a more far-reaching EU oversight and even intervention in cases of democratic relapse in the member states. However, whereas the EU has substantial leverage and mechanisms to set democratic conditions in its foreign policy and for candidate countries, its instruments to steer its member states in this respect are much more limited. Although there have been discussions on the state of democracy at the national level before – in particular with regard to media freedom,[83] the main debate arose after the Fidesz party came to power in Hungary after the 2010 elections and changed the constitution and the country's media laws. The calls for EU action intensified when the Law and Justice government in Poland initiated its controversial reforms of the judiciary in 2015.

In response to these democratic challenges, the EP has been most vocal in urging that the EU should take strong action. Following constant political pressure from the Parliament and several member states, the European Commission has undertaken several initiatives. In this respect, it has made strong efforts to prevent the perception that its actions were politically motivated to target specific member states and often opted for a holistic, EU-wide approach, with a particular focus on the assessment of the rule of law situation. The result is an extensive policy 'toolbox', ranging from soft law initiatives to legally binding mechanisms, aimed at both preventing and responding to democratic challenges at national level. However, despite this plethora of policy instruments, the EU has been unable to successfully mitigate the situation of democratic backsliding in the member states that had provoked this debate.

The most far-reaching instrument is enshrined in Article 7 TEU, which was introduced in the Treaty of Amsterdam. The article includes a sanctioning mechanism in cases in which the fundamental values of the EU – as described in Article 2 TEU – are seriously breached in a member state. The mechanism

---

European Council, Concerning a New Settlement for the United Kingdom within the European Union' (2016), https://eur-lex.europa.eu/legal-content/EN/TXT/?uri=CELEX%3A52017IP0048.

83 See, for example, European Parliament, 'Resolution on the Risks of Violation, in the EU and Especially in Italy, of Freedom of Expression and Information' (2004), https://eur-lex.europa.eu/legal-content/EN/TXT/?uri=CELEX%3A52017IP0048, p. 1026; European Parliament, 'Resolution on Concentration and Pluralism in the Media in the European Union' (2010), https://eur-lex.europa.eu/legal-content/HR/TXT/?uri=CELEX:52008IP0459, p. 85.

contains multiple stages that can eventually lead to the suspension of the voting rights in the Council of Ministers of the country concerned. However, there has been substantial hesitation at the European level to use this mechanism, for two main reasons. First, it was considered the 'nuclear option', which should be used only as an instrument of last resort.[84] Secondly, and seemingly contradictorily, many doubts have been expressed about the effectiveness of the mechanism. In order to suspend a member state's voting rights, unanimity in the Council is required, which means that one of the two main countries subject to criticism, Hungary or Poland, could block any attempt to impose such a sanction on the other country.

The European Commission – and to a lesser extent the Council – have therefore initially resorted to the creation and use of soft law instruments, aimed at finding a common solution through dialogue. Since 2013, the European Commission has been publishing its annual EU Justice Scoreboard, an overview of the independence, quality and efficiency of the justice systems of all EU member states.[85] It is largely an informative tool, although it can give rise to country-specific recommendations in the context of the European Semester. In order to complement this comparative over-view, the von der Leyen Commission decided in 2019 to launch an annual rule of law review cycle.[86] This results in an annual EU Rule of Law Report, which consists of detailed assessments of the situation of the rule of law in each EU member state. However, also this 'preventive' instrument depends on the voluntary collaboration of the countries, as it 'should help all Member States examine how challenges can be addressed, how they can learn from each other's experiences'. The first EU Rule of Law Report was published in September 2020.[87]

Calls for the establishment of a stronger mechanism to effectively sanction non-compliance were increasingly expressed by the EP and some member states. As early as in 2013, the foreign ministers of Denmark, Finland,

---

84 See, for example, European Commission, 'European Commission Presents a Framework to Safeguard the Rule of Law in the European Union' (2014), https://ec .europa.eu/commission/presscorner/detail/en/IP_14_237; Frans Timmermans, 'The European Union and the Rule of Law' (2015), https://web.archive.org/web/20151026 225827/http:/ec.europa.eu/commission/2014-2019/timmermans/announcements/eu ropean-union-and-rule-law-keynote-speech-conference-rule-law-tilburg-university-31-august-2015_en.

85 European Commission, 'EU Justice Scoreboard', https://ec.europa.eu/info/policies/ justice-and-fundamental-rights/upholding-rule-law/eu-justice-scoreboard_en.

86 European Commission, 'Strengthening the Rule of Law within the Union: A Blueprint for Action' (COM(2019)343 final), Brussels, 17 July 2019.

87 European Commission, '2020 Rule of Law Report: The Rule of Law Situation in the European Union' (COM(2020)580 final), Brussels, 30 September 2020.

Germany and the Netherlands sent a letter to Commission President Barroso, calling for an effective mechanism 'to address deficits in a given country at an early stage and – if sufficiently supported by Member States – require the country in question to remedy the situation'.[88] In 2014, the Council decided to hold an annual 'dialogue' in the General Affairs Council on the situation of the rule of law in the different member states.[89] During the same year, the European Commission launched its Rule of Law Framework,[90] a non-binding mechanism that can be launched whenever a systematic threat to the rule of law is identified in an EU member state. The framework foresees a Commission assessment of the situation and specific recommendations to address the rule of law issue followed by a monitoring of the follow-up of the Commission's recommendation by the member state concerned. The Rule of Law Framework has been used only in the case of Poland, with the European Commission starting a structured dialogue and issuing three detailed recommendations in 2016–17,[91] but without any tangible improvement having been achieved.

Because of this lack of results, and following continuous pressure from the EP (which has issued multiple resolutions criticising the rule of law situation in Poland in 2016–18),[92] the European Commission eventually started the

---

88 G. Westerwelle, F. Timmermans, V. Sovndal and E. Tuomioja, Letter to Mr. José Manuel Barroso, President of the European Commission, 6 March 2013, https://ecer .minbuza.nl/documents/20142/1067958/Rechtsstatelijkheid.pdf/a4b3bae5-c4ee-b103-3 72f-c51dbd0fb604?t=1545242467773.

89 Council of the European Union, 'Conclusions of the Council of the European Union and the Member States Meeting within the Council on Ensuring Respect for the Rule of Law', Brussels, 16 December 2014, www.consilium.europa.eu/en/meetings/gac/2 014/12/16.

90 European Commission, 'A New EU Framework to Strengthen the Rule of Law' (COM (2014)158 final), Brussels, 11 March 2014.

91 See Commission Recommendation (EU) 2016/1374 of 27 July 2016 regarding the rule of law in Poland (*OJ* L 2017, 12 August 2016, pp. 53–68), Commission Recommendation (EU) 2017/146 of 21 December 2016 regarding the rule of law in Poland complementary to Recommendation (EU) 2016/1374 (*OJ* L 22, 27 January 2017, pp. 65–81); Commission Recommendation (EU) 2017/1520 of 26 July 2017 regarding the rule of law in Poland complementary to Recommendations (EU) 2016/1374 and (EU) 2017/146 (*OJ* L 228, 22 September 2017, pp. 19–32).

92 European Parliament, 'Resolution of 13 April 2016 on the Situation in Poland', www .europarl.europa.eu/doceo/document/TA-8-2016-0123_EN.html; European Parliament, 'Resolution of 14 September 2016 on the Recent Developments in Poland and Their Impact on Fundamental Rights as Laid Down in the Charter of Fundamental Rights of the European Union', www.europarl.europa.eu/doceo/document/TA-8-2016-0344_EN.html ; European Parliament, 'Resolution of 15 November 2017 on the Situation of the Rule of law and democracy in Poland', www.europarl.europa.eu/doceo/document/TA-8-2017-0 442_EN.html; European Parliament, 'Resolution of 1 March 2018 on the Commission's Decision to Activate Article 7(1) TEU as Regards the Situation in Poland', www.europarl .europa.eu/doceo/document/TA-8-2018-0055_EN.html.

Article 7 procedure against Poland in December 2017.[93] In the course of 2018, three hearings were held in the General Affairs framework of the Article 7 procedure, but the procedure stalled afterwards. The EP strongly supported the Commission's decision regarding Poland,[94] and triggered the Article 7 procedure with regard to Hungary in September 2018.[95] This multiple-stage procedure is aimed at tackling a breach of the EU's fundamental values (as stipulated in Article 2 TEU, which states that the EU 'is founded on the values of respect for human dignity, freedom, democracy, equality, the rule of law and respect for human rights, including the rights of persons belonging to minorities. These values are common to the Member States.'), and could eventually result in the suspension of voting rights in the Council of Ministers. However, as already mentioned, in order to take such a decision, unanimity is required in the Council, and Hungary has announced several times that it would block any efforts to take such action against Poland.

In February 2017, Justice Commissioner Věra Jourová proposed to introduce a rule of law conditionality for the use of EU funds.[96] The initiative built on various other conditionality mechanisms that were linked to EU spending, and became part of the Commission's legislative package for the multi-annual financial framework for 2021–27. The principle was maintained in the NextGenerationEU/Recovery Instrument proposal to tackle the implications of the Covid-19 pandemic in Europe. During the European Council Meeting in December 2020, the heads of state and government reached an agreement on the issue: they endorsed the Multi-annual Financial Framework and the NextGenerationEU fund, but allowed for a possible delay of the rule of law conditionality if it were brought before the EU Court of Justice.[97]

---

93 European Commission, 'Proposal for a Council Decision on the Determination of a Clear Risk of a Serious Breach by the Republic of Poland of the Rule of Law' (2017), https://eur-lex.europa.eu/legal-content/EN/TXT/?uri=CELEX%3A52017PC0835.

94 European Parliament, 'Resolution on the Commission's Decision to Activate Article 7(1) TEU as Regards the Situation in Poland' (P8_TA(2018)0055), Strasbourg, 1 March 2018.

95 European Parliament, 'Resolution on a Proposal Calling on the Council to Determine, Pursuant to Article 7(1) of the Treaty on European Union, the Existence of a Clear Risk of a Serious Breach by Hungary of the Values on which the Union Is Founded' (P8_TA (2018)0340), Strasbourg, 12 September 2018.

96 V. Jourová, '10 Years of the EU Fundamental Rights Agency: A Call to Action in Defence of Fundamental Rights, Democracy and the Rule of Law' (2017), www.europa-nu.nl/id/vkc4r6kq4ttm/nieuws/speech_by_commissioner_jourova_10_years?ctx=vjmx9ghlouy9&tab=0.

97 European Council, 'European Council Meeting (10 and 11 December 2020) – Conclusions', (2020), www.consilium.europa.eu/media/47296/1011-12-20-euco-conclusions-en.pdf, pp. 1–2.

Conclusions

The overview of the debates in this chapter shows the substantial variety and complexity of democracy at the European level. The term 'democratic deficit' is often associated with the EU, but this deficit can be understood in many different ways and comprises multiple dimensions. With regard to inter-institutional relations, strengthening the position of the Community institutions – the European Commission and in particular the EP – is often hailed as a tool for democratisation. An alternative appeal for more democracy has emphasised the need for more (party) politicisation of European decision-making by improving the role of European political parties. A third perspective has criticised the distance between the EU institutions and European citizens, and has focused on initiatives to 'close this gap' and increase public involvement in European decision-making. Finally and more recently, a fourth perspective has emerged that has stressed the importance of the member states for EU democracy, both with regard to the input from the national level – and in particular the parliamentary assemblies – at the European level and regarding the need for monitoring by the EU and even enforcement against breaches of the rule of law and democratic standards in the EU countries.

The findings in this chapter also show that the normative debates on EU democracy are inherently connected to (perceived) interests and power. The EP has eagerly instrumentalised rhetoric about a democratic deficit to improve its own position in European decision-making, emphasising its legitimacy as the only directly elected EU institution. Similarly, initiatives to improve the importance of European political parties, European citizens or national parliaments are often only half-heartedly welcomed by the EU actors, because they might result in a loss of influence. The position that democratic backsliding in some member states constitutes a threat to the EU itself and requires stronger oversight by the EU institutions also touches upon fundamental questions of sovereignty. Consequently, the overview of this chapter shows the need for a broad and multifaceted approach towards democratic challenges in Europe, and demonstrates why democracy will remain part of the main debates on the future direction of the EU.

Recommended Reading

Cornell, A. J. and M. Goldoni (eds.). *National and Regional Parliaments in the EU-Legislative Procedure Post-Lisbon: The Impact of the Early Warning Mechanism* (London, Bloomsbury, 2017).

Greenwood, J. 'The European Citizens' Initiative: Bringing the EU Closer to Its Citizens?', *Comparative European Politics* 17, no. 6 (2019): 940–56.

Héritier, A., K. L. Meissner, C. Moury and M. G. Schoeller. *European Parliament Ascendant: Parliamentary Strategies of Self-Empowerment in the EU* (New York, NY, Springer International, 2019).

Hix, S. *What's Wrong with the European Union and How to Fix It* (Cambridge, MA, Polity Press, 2013).

Müller, J.-W. 'Should the EU Protect Democracy and the Rule of Law inside Member States?', *European Law Journal* 21, no. 2 (2015): 141–60.

Van Hecke, S. (lead author). 'Reconnecting European Political Parties with European Union Citizens', International IDEA Discussion Paper (2018), www.idea.int/sites/default/files/publications/reconnecting-european-political-parties-with-european-union-citizens.pdf.

Wolfs, W. *European Political Parties and Party Finance Reform: Funding Democracy?* (London, Palgrave Macmillan, 2022).

Index